PLAYS FOR
THE THEATRE

SEVENTH EDITION

PLAYS FOR THE THEATRE

Seventh Edition

Oscar G. Brockett

University of Texas at Austin

with

Robert J. Ball

Vanderbilt University

HARCOURT BRACE COLLEGE PUBLISHERS

Fort Worth Philadelphia San Diego New York Orlando Austin San Antonio
Toronto Montreal London Sydney Tokyo

Publisher:	Earl McPeek
Executive Editor:	David C. Tatom
Acquisitions Editor:	Terry Johnson
Market Strategist:	Laura Brennan
Project Editor:	Travis Tyre
Art Director:	Chris Morrow
Production Manager:	Serena Barnett
Cover Photo:	Richard Feldman (*A Midsummer Night's Dream* performed at The American Repertory Theatre)

ISBN: 0-15-507230-7
Library of Congress Catalog Card Number: 98-75702

Copyright © 2000 by Harcourt Brace & Company

Portions of this work were published in previous editions.

Literary credits appear
on page 623 and constitute a continuation of the copyright page.

Address for orders:
Harcourt Brace & Company
6277 Sea Harbor Drive
Orlando, FL 32887-6777
1-800-782-4479

Address for editorial correspondence:
Harcourt Brace College Publishers
301 Commerce Street, Suite 3700
Fort Worth, TX 76102

Web site address:
http://www.hbcollege.com

Printed in the United States of America

9 0 1 2 3 4 5 6 7 8   039   9 8 7 6 5 4 3

Preface

This Seventh Edition of *Plays for the Theatre* is a substantial revision of its predecessor. Although it contains fourteen plays, as did the sixth edition, three of the plays are new to this collection.

Selecting plays for an anthology is always risky business. For each play chosen, many others, perhaps equally worthy, must be rejected. In choosing plays for inclusion in the present edition, the goal has been to provide a selection both of representative plays from the past and of recent culturally diverse plays.

The works included in this anthology are drawn from many periods, ranging from ancient Greece, the Middle Ages, the seventeenth century, the eighteenth century, the late nineteenth century, and the twentieth century. The plays are by major playwrights—Sophocles, Shakespeare, Molière, Goldoni, Ibsen, O'Neill, Brecht, Williams, and Beckett—as well as an anonymous author of a medieval mystery play. The recent plays—one each by an African American, an Asian American, a Latina, and an American female—have been chosen both for their cultural diversity and their dramatic power. Additional diversity is achieved through the inclusion of some plays that touch on gay subjects, although none is specifically a gay or lesbian play.

Each of these plays is discussed at some length in a companion book, *The Essential Theatre*, Seventh Edition, also published by Harcourt Brace College Publishers. This companion volume places each of the plays within its historical and cultural context. Although each book can stand alone, together they provide a greater understanding of the plays than when used separately.

We would like to thank the reviewers who took the time to provide insight and guidance on this project: Sam Abel, University of Vermont; Lawrence Leach, Monroe Community College; Susan Kattwinker, College of Charleston; Rebecca Rubo, University of Connecticut; and Steve Woods, Louisiana State University.

We would also like to thank the editorial and production teams at Harcourt Brace College Publishers: Terry Johnson, acquisitions editor; Cathy Richard, developmental editor; Laura Brennan, market strategist; Travis Tyre, project editor; Serena Barnett, production manager; and Chris Morrow, art director.

Contents

Sophocles (495–406 B.C.)

Oedipus Rex (c. 430 B.C.)

Oedipus Rex was first performed in Athens at the City Dionysia (a major religious and civic festival held annually in honor of Dionysus, the god of wine and fertility) in competition with works by two other playwrights. Each dramatist presented three tragedies and one satyr play each time they competed before the audience of approximately fifteen thousand spectators. Sophocles was awarded first prize for the group of plays that included *Oedipus Rex*, considered by the Greek philosopher Aristotle an ideal example of tragic form.

The most striking feature of Greek tragedy is the alternation of dramatic episodes with choral passages. In Sophocles' day, the tragic chorus included fifteen performers who sang (or recited) and danced the choral passages to musical accompaniment. Other typical features of Greek tragedy are the small number of individualized characters, the restriction of the action to a single place, the tightly unified plot, the serious and philosophic tone, and the poetic language.

The action of *Oedipus Rex* is extremely concentrated: A complete reversal of the protagonist's fortune takes place in a single day. The story follows Oedipus, king of Thebes, as he attempts to discover the murderer of Laïos, the former king, after an oracle declares that the plague now destroying the city will not be lifted until the guilty one is cast out. Oedipus' search gradually uncovers terrible truths about the past and his own origins. The initial suspicion that Oedipus himself may be the slayer of Laïos is rapidly followed by other electrifying moments (among them Iocaste's recognition that she is not only Oedipus' wife but also his mother), and the ultimate outcome: blindness, exile, and anguish for the once-powerful king.

Sophocles is admired particularly for his skillful management of extensive plot materials: He accomplishes the gradual unveiling of mystery after mystery and a steady increase in dramatic tension with the utmost economy of means. Although, like most great plays, *Oedipus Rex* is open to many interpretations, most critics have agreed that a central concern is the uncertainty of fate and humanity's helplessness in the face of destiny.

Sophocles

Oedipus Rex

English Version by Dudley Fitts and Robert Fitzgerald

PERSONS REPRESENTED

OEDIPUS
A PRIEST
CREON
TEIRESIAS
IOCASTE [JOCASTA]
MESSENGER
SHEPHERD OF LAÏOS
SECOND MESSENGER
CHORUS OF THEBAN ELDERS

THE SCENE————*Before the palace of* OEDIPUS, *King of Thebes. A central door and two lateral doors open onto a platform which runs the length of the façade. On the platform, right and left, are altars; and three steps lead down into the "orchestra," or chorusground. At the beginning of the action these steps are crowded by suppliants who have brought branches and chaplets of olive leaves and who lie in various attitudes of despair.* OEDIPUS *enters.*

PROLOGUE

OEDIPUS: My children, generations of the living
In the line of Kadmos, nursed at his ancient hearth:
Why have you strewn yourselves before these altars
In supplication, with your boughs and garlands?
The breath of incense rises from the city
With a sound of prayer and lamentation.
                              Children,
I would not have you speak through messengers,
And therefore I have come myself to hear you—
I, Oedipus, who bear the famous name.
    [*To a* PRIEST.]
You, there, since you are eldest in the company,
Speak for them all, tell me what preys upon you,
Whether you come in dread, or crave some blessing:

Tell me, and never doubt that I will help you
In every way I can; I should be heartless
Were I not moved to find you suppliant here.
PRIEST: Great Oedipus, O powerful King of Thebes!
You see how all the ages of our people
Cling to your altar steps: here are boys
Who can barely stand alone, and here are priests
By weight of age, as I am a priest of God,
And young men chosen from those yet unmarried;
As for the others, all that multitude,
They wait with olive chaplets in the squares,
At the two shrines of Pallas, and where Apollo
Speaks in the glowing embers.

                      Your own eyes
Must tell you: Thebes is tossed on a murdering sea
And can not lift her head from the death surge.
A rust consumes the buds and fruits of the earth;
The herds are sick; children die unborn,
And labor is vain. The god of plague and pyre
Raids like detestable lightning through the city,
And all the house of Kadmos is laid waste,
All emptied, and all darkened; Death alone
Battens upon the misery of Thebes.

You are not one of the immortal gods, we know;
Yet we have come to you to make our prayer
As to the man surest in mortal ways
And wisest in the ways of God. You saved us
From the Sphinx, that flinty singer, and the tribute
We paid to her so long; yet you were never
Better informed than we, nor could we teach you:
It was some god breathed in you to set us free.

Therefore, O mighty King, we turn to you:
Find us our safety, find us a remedy,
Whether by counsel of the gods or men.
A king of wisdom tested in the past
Can act in a time of troubles, and act well.
Noblest of men, restore
Life to your city! Think how all men call you
Liberator for your triumph long ago;
Ah, when your years of kingship are remembered,
Let them not say *We rose, but later fell*—
Keep the State from going down in the storm!
Once, years ago, with a happy augury,
You brought us fortune; be the same again!
No man questions your power to rule the land:
But rule over men, not over a dead city!

Ships are only hulls, citadels are nothing,
When no life moves in the empty passageways.
OEDIPUS: Poor children! You may be sure I know
All that you longed for in your coming here.
I know that you are deathly sick; and yet,
Sick as you are, not one is as sick as I.
Each of you suffers in himself alone
His anguish, not another's; but my spirit
Groans for the city, for myself, for you.

I was not sleeping, you are not waking me.
No, I have been in tears for a long while
And in my restless thought walked many ways.
In all my search, I found one helpful course,
And that I have taken: I have sent Creon,
Son of Menoikeus, brother of the Queen,
To Delphi, Apollo's place of revelation,
To learn there, if he can,
What act or pledge of mine may save the city.
I have counted the days, and now, this very day,
I am troubled, for he has overstayed his time.
What is he doing? He has been gone too long.
Yet whenever he comes back, I should do ill
To scant whatever duty God reveals.
PRIEST: It is a timely promise. At this instant
They tell me Creon is here.
OEDIPUS: O Lord Apollo!
May his news be fair as his face is radiant!
PRIEST: It could not be otherwise: he is crowned with bay,
The chaplet is thick with berries.
OEDIPUS: We shall soon know;
He is near enough to hear us now.
          [*Enter* CREON.]
                                              O Prince:
Brother: son of Menoikeus:
What answer do you bring us from the god?
CREON: A strong one. I can tell you, great afflictions
Will turn out well, if they are taken well.
OEDIPUS: What was the oracle? These vague words
Leave me still hanging between hope and fear.
CREON: Is it your pleasure to hear me with all these
Gathered around us? I am prepared to speak,
But should we not go in?
OEDIPUS: Let them all hear it.
It is for them I suffer, more than for myself.
CREON: Then I will tell you what I heard at Delphi.
In plain words
The god commands us to expel from the land of Thebes

An old defilement we are sheltering.
It is a deathly thing, beyond cure;
We must not let it feed upon us longer.
OEDIPUS: What defilement? How shall we rid ourselves of it?
CREON: By exile or death, blood for blood. It was
    Murder that brought the plague-wind on the city.
OEDIPUS: Murder of whom? Surely the god has named him?
CREON: My lord: long ago Laïos was our king,
    Before you came to govern us.
OEDIPUS: I know;
    I learned of him from others; I never saw him.
CREON: He was murdered; and Apollo commands us now
    To take revenge upon whoever killed him.
OEDIPUS: Upon whom? Where are they? Where shall we find a clue
    To solve that crime, after so many years?
CREON: Here in this land, he said
                                    If we make enquiry,
    We may touch things that otherwise escape us.
OEDIPUS: Tell me: Was Laïos murdered in his house,
    Or in the fields, or in some foreign country?
CREON: He said he planned to make a pilgrimage.
    He did not come home again.
OEDIPUS: And was there no one,
    No witness, no companion, to tell what happened?
CREON: They were all killed but one, and he got away
    So frightened that he could remember one thing only.
OEDIPUS: What was that one thing? One may be the key
    To everything, if we resolve to use it.
CREON: He said that a band of highwaymen attacked them,
    Outnumbered them, and overwhelmed the King.
OEDIPUS: Strange, that a highwayman should be so daring—
    Unless some faction here bribed him to do it.
CREON: We thought of that. But after Laïos' death
    New troubles arose and he had no avenger.
OEDIPUS: What troubles could prevent your hunting down the killers?
CREON: The riddling Sphinx's song
    Made us deaf to all mysteries but her own.
OEDIPUS: Then once more I must bring what is dark to light.
    It is most fitting that Apollo shows,
    As you do, this compunction for the dead.
    You shall see how I stand by you, as I should,
    To avenge the city and the city's god,
    And not as though it were for some distant friend,
    But for my own sake, to be rid of evil.
    Whoever killed King Laïos might—who knows?—
    Decide at any moment to kill me as well.
    By avenging the murdered king I protect myself.
    Come, then, my children: leave the altar steps,

Lift up your olive boughs!
                            One of you go
And summon the people of Kadmos to gather here.
I will do all that I can; you may tell them that.
        [*Exit a* PAGE.]
So, with the help of God,
We shall be saved—or else indeed we are lost.
PRIEST: Let us rise, children. It was for this we came,
And now the King has promised it himself.
Phoibos has sent us an oracle; may he descend
Himself to save us and drive out the plague.
        [*Exeunt* OEDIPUS *and* CREON *into the palace by the central door. The*
        PRIEST *and the* SUPPLIANTS *disperse R and L. After a short pause the*
        CHORUS *enters the orchestra.*]

                        PARODOS

CHORUS: What is God singing in his profound   [STROPHE 1]
        Delphi of gold and shadow?
        What oracle for Thebes, the sunwhipped city?

        Fear unjoints me, the roots of my heart tremble.

        Now I remember, O Healer, your power, and wonder:
        Will you send doom like a sudden cloud, or weave it
        Like nightfall of the past?

        Speak, speak to us, issue a holy sound:
        Dearest to our expectancy: be tender!

        Let me pray to Athenê, the immortal daughter of Zeus, [ANTISTROPHE 1]
        And to Artemis her sister
        Who keeps her famous throne in the market ring,
        And to Apollo, bowman at the far butts of heaven—

        O gods, descend! Like three streams leap against
        The fires of our grief, the fires of darkness;
        Be swift to bring us rest!

        As in the old time from the brilliant house
        Of air you stepped to save us, come again!

        Now our afflictions have no end,   [STROPHE 2]
        Now all our stricken host lies down
        And no man fights off death with his mind;
        The noble plowland bears no grain,
        And groaning mothers can not bear—

See, how our lives like birds take wing,
Like sparks that fly when a fire soars,
To the shore of the god of evening.

The plague burns on; it is pitiless,   [ANTISTROPHE 2]
Though pallid children laden with death
Lie unwept in the stony ways,

And old gray women by every path
Flock to the strand about the altars

There to strike their breasts and cry
Worship of Phoibos in wailing prayers:
Be kind, God's golden child!

There are no swords in this attack by fire,   [STROPHE 3]
No shields, but we are ringed with cries.
Send the besieger plunging from our homes
Into the vast sea-room of the Atlantic
Or into the waves that foam eastward of Thrace—

For the day ravages what the night spares—

Destroy our enemy, lord of the thunder!
Let him be riven by lightning from heaven!

Phoibos Apollo, stretch the sun's bowstring,   [ANTISTROPHE 3]
That golden cord, until it sings for us,
Flashing arrows in heaven!
                         Artemis, Huntress,
Race with flaring lights upon our mountains!

O scarlet god, O golden-banded brow,
O Theban Bacchos in a storm of Maenads,
        [*Enter* OEDIPUS, *C.*]
Whirl upon Death, that all the Undying hate.
Come with blinding torches, come in joy!

SCENE I

OEDIPUS: Is this your prayer? It may be answered. Come,
        Listen to me, act as the crisis demands,
        And you shall have relief from all these evils.

        Until now I was a stranger to this tale,
        As I had been a stranger to the crime.
        Could I track down the murderer without a clue?

But now, friends,
As one who became a citizen after the murder,
I make this proclamation to all Thebans:
If any man knows by whose hand Laïos, son of Labdakos,
Met his death, I direct that man to tell me everything,
No matter what he fears for having so long withheld it.
Let it stand as promised that no further trouble
Will come to him, but he may leave the land in safety.

Moreover: If anyone knows the murderer to be foreign,
Let him not keep silent: he shall have his reward from me.
However, if he does conceal it; if any man
Fearing for his friend or for himself disobeys this edict,
Hear what I propose to do:

I solemnly forbid the people of this country,
Where power and throne are mine, ever to receive that man
Or speak to him, no matter who he is, or let him
Join in sacrifice, lustration, or in prayer.
I decree that he be driven from every house,
Being, as he is, corruption itself to us: the Delphic
Voice of Zeus has pronounced this revelation.
Thus I associate myself with the oracle
And take the side of the murdered king.

As for the criminal, I pray to God—
Whether it be a lurking thief, or one of a number—
I pray that that man's life be consumed in evil and wretchedness.
And as for me, this curse applies no less
If it should turn out that the culprit is my guest here,
Sharing my hearth.
                    You have heard the penalty.
I lay it on you now to attend to this
For my sake, for Apollo's, for the sick
Sterile city that heaven has abandoned.
Suppose the oracle had given you no command:
Should this defilement go uncleansed for ever?
You should have found the murderer: your king,
A noble king, had been destroyed!
                              Now I,
Having the power that he held for me,
Having his bed, begetting children there
Upon his wife, as he would have, had he lived—
Their son would have been my children's brother,
If Laïos had had luck in fatherhood!
(But surely ill luck rushed upon his reign)—
I say I take the son's part, just as though
I were his son, to press the fight for him

And see it won! I'll find the hand that brought
Death to Labdakos' and Polydoros' child,
Heir to Kadmos' and Agenor's line.
And as for those who fail me,
May the gods deny them the fruit of the earth,
Fruit of the womb, and may they rot utterly!
Let them be wretched as we are wretched, and worse!

For you, for loyal Thebans, and for all
who find my actions right, I pray the favor
Of justice, and of all the immortal gods.
CHORAGOS: Since I am under oath, my lord, I swear
I did not do the murder, I can not name
The murderer. Might not the oracle
That has ordained the search tell where to find him?
OEDIPUS: An honest question. But no man in the world
Can make the gods do more than the gods will.
CHORAGOS: There is one last expedient—
OEDIPUS: Tell me what it is.
Though it seem slight, you must not hold it back.
CHORAGOS: A lord clairvoyant to the lord Apollo,
As we all know, is the skilled Teiresias.
One might learn much about this from him, Oedipus.
OEDIPUS: I am not wasting time:
Creon spoke of this, and I have sent for him—
Twice, in fact; it is strange that he is not here.
CHORAGOS: The other matter—that old report—seems useless.
OEDIPUS: Tell me. I am interested in all reports.
CHORAGOS: The King was said to have been killed by highwaymen.
OEDIPUS: I know. But we have no witnesses to that.
CHORAGOS: If the killer can feel a particle of dread,
Your curse will bring him out of hiding!
OEDIPUS: No.
The man who dared that act will fear no curse.
    [*Enter the blind seer* TEIRESIAS, *led by a* PAGE.]
CHORAGOS: But there is one man who may detect the criminal.
This is Teiresias, this is the holy prophet
In whom, alone of all men, truth was born.
OEDIPUS: Teiresias: seer: student of mysteries,
Of all that's taught and all that no man tells,
Secrets of Heaven and secrets of the earth:
Blind though you are, you know the city lies
Slick with plague; and from this plague, my lord,
We find that you alone can guard or save us.

Possibly you did not hear the messengers?
Apollo, when we sent to him,
Sent us back word that this great pestilence

Would lift, but only if we established clearly
The identity of those who murdered Laïos.
They must be killed or exiled.
                                        Can you use
Birdflight or any art of divination
To purify yourself, and Thebes, and me
From this contagion? We are in your hands.
There is no fairer duty
Than that of helping others in distress.
TEIRESIAS: How dreadful knowledge of the truth can be
    When there's no help in truth! I knew this well,
    But made myself forget. I should not have come.
OEDIPUS: What is troubling you? Why are your eyes so cold?
TEIRESIAS: Let me go home. Bear your own fate, and I'll
    Bear mine. It is better so: trust what I say.
OEDIPUS: What you say is ungracious and unhelpful
    To your native country. Do not refuse to speak.
TEIRESIAS: When it comes to speech, your own is neither temperate
    Nor opportune. I wish to be more prudent.
OEDIPUS: In God's name, we all beg you—
TEIRESIAS: You are all ignorant.
    No; I will never tell you what I know.
    Now it is my misery; then, it would be yours.
OEDIPUS: What! You do know something, and will not tell us?
    You would betray us all and wreck the State?
TEIRESIAS: I do not intend to torture myself, or you.
    Why persist in asking? You will not persuade me.
OEDIPUS: What a wicked old man you are! You'd try a stone's
    Patience! Out with it! Have you no feeling at all?
TEIRESIAS: You call me unfeeling. If you could only see
    The nature of your own feelings . . .
OEDIPUS: Why,
    Who would not feel as I do? Who could endure
    Your arrogance toward the city?
TEIRESIAS: What does it matter!
    Whether I speak or not, it is bound to come.
OEDIPUS: Then, if "it" is bound to come, you are bound to tell me.
TEIRESIAS: No, I will not go on. Rage as you please.
OEDIPUS: Rage? Why not!
                            And I'll tell you what I think:
    You planned it, you had it done, you all but
    Killed him with your own hands: if you had eyes,
    I'd say the crime was yours, and yours alone.
TEIRESIAS: So? I charge you, then,
    Abide by the proclamation you have made:
    From this day forth
    Never speak again to these men or to me;
    You yourself are the pollution of this country.

OEDIPUS: You dare say that! Can you possibly think you have
      Some way of going free, after such insolence?
TEIRESIAS: I have gone free. It is the truth sustains me.
OEDIPUS: Who taught you shamelessness? It was not your craft.
TEIRESIAS: You did. You made me speak. I did not want to.
OEDIPUS: Speak what? Let me hear it again more clearly.
TEIRESIAS: Was it not clear before? Are you tempting me?
OEDIPUS: I did not understand it. Say it again.
TEIRESIAS: I say that you are the murderer whom you seek.
OEDIPUS: Now twice you have spat out infamy. You'll pay for it!
TEIRESIAS: Would you care for more? Do you wish to be really angry?
OEDIPUS: Say what you will. Whatever you say is worthless.
TEIRESIAS: I say you live in hideous shame with those
      Most dear to you. You can not see the evil.
OEDIPUS: It seems you can go on mouthing like this for ever.
TEIRESIAS: I can, if there is power in truth.
OEDIPUS: There is:
      But not for you, not for you,
      You sightless, witless, senseless, mad old man!
TEIRESIAS: You are the madman. There is no one here
      Who will not curse you soon, as you curse me.
OEDIPUS: You child of endless night! You can not hurt me
      Or any other man who sees the sun.
TEIRESIAS: True: it is not from me your fate will come.
      That lies within Apollo's competence.
      As it is his concern.
OEDIPUS: Tell me.
      Are you speaking for Creon, or for yourself?
TEIRESIAS: Creon is no threat. You weave your own doom.
OEDIPUS: Wealth, power, craft of statesmanship!
      Kingly position, everywhere admired!
      What savage envy is stored up against these,
      If Creon, whom I trusted, Creon my friend,
      For this great office which the city once
      Put in my hands unsought—if for this power
      Creon desires in secret to destroy me!

      He has bought this decrepit fortune-teller, this
      Collector of dirty pennies, this prophet fraud—
      Why, he is no more clairvoyant than I am!
                                                    Tell us.
      Has your mystic mummery ever approached the truth?
      When that hellcat the Sphinx was performing here,
      What help were you to these people?
      Her magic was not for the first man who came along:
      It demanded a real exorcist. Your birds—
      What good were they? or the gods, for the matter of that?
      But I came by,

Oedipus, the simple man, who knows nothing—
I thought it out for myself, no birds helped me!
And this is the man you think you can destroy,
That you may be close to Creon when he's king!
Well, you and your friend Creon, it seems to me,
Will suffer most. If you were not an old man,
You would have paid already for your plot.

CHORAGOS: We can not see that his words or yours
　　　　Have been spoken except in anger, Oedipus,
　　　　And of anger we have no need. How can God's will
　　　　Be accomplished best? That is what most concerns us.

TEIRESIAS: You are a king. But where argument's concerned
　　　　I am your man, as much a king as you.
　　　　I am not your servant, but Apollo's.
　　　　I have no need of Creon to speak for me.

　　　　Listen to me. You mock my blindness, do you?
　　　　But I say that you, with both your eyes, are blind:
　　　　You can not see the wretchedness of your life,
　　　　Nor in whose house you live, no, nor with whom.
　　　　Who are your father and mother? Can you tell me?
　　　　You do not even know the blind wrongs
　　　　That you have done them, on earth and in the world below.
　　　　But the double lash of your parents' curse will whip you
　　　　Out of this land some day, with only night
　　　　Upon your precious eyes.
　　　　Your cries then—where will they not be heard?
　　　　What fastness of Kithairon will not echo them?
　　　　And that bridal-descant of yours—you'll know it then,
　　　　The song they sang when you came here to Thebes
　　　　And found your misguided berthing.
　　　　All this, and more, that you can not guess at now,
　　　　Will bring you to yourself among your children.

　　　　Be angry, then. Curse Creon. Curse my words.
　　　　I tell you, no man that walks upon the earth
　　　　Shall be rooted out more horribly than you.

OEDIPUS: Am I to bear this from him?—Damnation
　　　　Take you! Out of this place! Out of my sight!

TEIRESIAS: I would not have come at all if you had not asked me.

OEDIPUS: Could I have told that you'd talk nonsense, that
　　　　You'd come here to make a fool of yourself, and of me?

TEIRESIAS: A fool? Your parents thought me sane enough.

OEDIPUS: My parents again!—Wait: who were my parents?

TEIRESIAS: This day will give you a father, and break your heart.

OEDIPUS: Your infantile riddles! Your damned abracadabra!

TEIRESIAS: You were a great man once at solving riddles.

OEDIPUS: Mock me with that if you like; you will find it true.
TEIRESIAS: It was true enough. It brought about your ruin.
OEDIPUS: But if it saved this town?
TEIRESIAS: [*to the* PAGE] Boy, give me your hand.
OEDIPUS: Yes, boy; lead him away.
                              —While you are here
    We can do nothing. Go; leave us in peace.
TEIRESIAS: I will go when I have said what I have to say.
    How can you hurt me? And I tell you again:
    The man you have been looking for all this time,
    The damned man, the murderer of Laïos,
    That man is in Thebes. To your mind he is foreign-born,
    But it will soon be shown that he is Theban,
    A revelation that will fail to please.
                         A blind man,
    Who has his eyes now; a penniless man, who is rich now;
    And he will go tapping the strange earth with his staff
    To the children with whom he lives now he will be
    Brother and father—the very same; to her
    Who bore him, son and husband—the very same
    Who came to his father's bed, wet with his father's blood.

    Enough. Go think that over.
    If later you find error in what I have said,
    You may say that I have no skill in prophecy.
        [*Exit* TEIRESIAS, *led by his* PAGE. OEDIPUS *goes into the palace.*]

ODE I

CHORUS: The Delphic stone of prophecies   [STROPHE 1]
    Remembers ancient regicide
    And a still bloody hand.
    That killer's hour of flight has come.
    He must be stronger than riderless
    Coursers of untiring wind,
    For the son of Zeus armed with his father's thunder
    Leaps in lightning after him;
    And the Furies follow him, the sad Furies.

    Holy Parnassos' peak of snow   [ANTISTROPHE 1]
    Flashes and blinds that secret man,
    That all shall hunt him down:
    Though he may roam the forest shade
    Like a bull wild from pasture
    To rage through glooms of stone.
    Doom comes down on him; flight will not avail him;
    For the world's heart calls him desolate,
    And the immortal Furies follow, forever follow.

But now a wilder thing is heard   [STROPHE 2]
From the old man skilled at hearing Fate in the wingbeat of a bird.
Bewildered as a blown bird, my soul hovers and can not find
Foothold in this debate, or any reason or rest of mind.
But no man ever brought—none can bring
Proof of strife between Thebes' royal house,
Labdakos' line, and the son of Polybos;
And never until now has any man brought word
Of Laïos' dark death staining Oedipus the King.

Divine Zeus and Apollo hold   [ANTISTROPHE 2]
Perfect intelligence alone of all tales ever told;
And well though this diviner works, he works in his own night;
No man can judge that rough unknown or trust in second sight,
For wisdom changes hands among the wise.
Shall I believe my great lord criminal
At a raging word that a blind old man let fall?
I saw him, when the carrion woman faced him of old,
Prove his heroic mind! These evil words are lies.

SCENE II

CREON: Men of Thebes:
    I am told that heavy accusations
    Have been brought against me by King Oedipus.

    I am not the kind of man to bear this tamely.

    If in these present difficulties
    He holds me accountable for any harm to him
    Through anything I have said or done—why, then,
    I do not value life in this dishonor.
    It is not as though this rumor touched upon
    Some private indiscretion. The matter is grave.
    The fact is that I am being called disloyal
    To the State, to my fellow citizens, to my friends.
CHORAGOS: He may have spoken in anger, not from his mind.
CREON: But did you not hear him say I was the one
    Who seduced the old prophet into lying?
CHORAGOS: The thing was said; I do not know how seriously.
CREON: But you were watching him! Were his eyes steady?
    Did he look like a man in his right mind?
CHORAGOS: I do not know.
    I can not judge the behavior of great men.
    But here is the King himself.
            [*Enter* OEDIPUS.]
OEDIPUS: So you dared come back.
    Why? How brazen of you to come to my house,
    You murderer!

Do you think I do not know
That you plotted to kill me, plotted to steal my throne?
Tell me, in God's name: am I coward, a fool,
That you should dream you could accomplish this?
A fool who could not see your slippery game?
A coward, not to fight back when I saw it?
You are the fool, Creon, are you not? hoping
Without support or friends to get a throne?
Thrones may be won or bought: you could do neither.

CREON: Now listen to me. You have talked; let me talk, too.
    You can not judge unless you know the facts.

OEDIPUS: You speak well: there is one fact; but I find it hard
    To learn from the deadliest enemy I have.

CREON: That above all I must dispute with you.

OEDIPUS: That above all I will not hear you deny.

CREON: If you think there is anything good in being stubborn
    Against all reason, then I say you are wrong.

OEDIPUS: If you think a man can sin against his own kind
    And not be punished for it, I say you are mad.

CREON: I agree. But tell me: what have I done to you?

OEDIPUS: You advised me to send for that wizard, did you not?

CREON: I did. I should do it again.

OEDIPUS: Very well. Now tell me:
    How long has it been since Laïos—

CREON: What of Laïos?

OEDIPUS: Since he vanished in that onset by the road?

CREON: It was long ago, a long time.

OEDIPUS: And this prophet,
    Was he practicing here then?

CREON: He was; and with honor, as now.

OEDIPUS: Did he speak of me at that time?

CREON: He never did:
    At least, not when I was present.

OEDIPUS: But . . . the enquiry?
    I suppose you held one?

CREON: We did, but we learned nothing.

OEDIPUS: Why did the prophet not speak against me then?

CREON: I do not know; and I am the kind of man
    Who holds his tongue when he has no facts to go on.

OEDIPUS: There's one fact that you know, and you could tell it.

CREON: What fact is that? If I know it, you shall have it.

OEDIPUS: If he were not involved with you, he could not say
    That it was I who murdered Laïos.

CREON: If he says that, you are the one that knows it!—
    But now it is my turn to question you.

OEDIPUS: Put your questions. I am no murderer.

CREON: First, then: You married my sister?

OEDIPUS: I married your sister.

CREON: And you rule the kingdom equally with her?
OEDIPUS: Everything that she wants she has from me.
CREON: And I am the third, equal to both of you?
OEDIPUS: That is why I call you a bad friend.
CREON: No. Reason it out, as I have done.
　　　　Think of this first: Would any sane man prefer
　　　　Power, with all a king's anxieties,
　　　　To that same power and the grace of sleep?
　　　　Certainly not I.
　　　　I have never longed for the king's power—only his rights.
　　　　Would any wise man differ from me in this?
　　　　As matters stand, I have my way in everything
　　　　With your consent, and no responsibilities.
　　　　If I were king, I should be a slave to policy.

　　　　How could I desire a scepter more
　　　　Than what is now mine—untroubled influence?
　　　　No, I have not gone mad; I need no honors,
　　　　Except those with the perquisites I have now.
　　　　I am welcome everywhere; every man salutes me,
　　　　And those who want your favor seek my ear,
　　　　Since I know how to manage what they ask.
　　　　Should I exchange this case for that anxiety?
　　　　Besides, no sober mind is treasonable.
　　　　I hate anarchy
　　　　And never would deal with any man who likes it.

　　　　Test what I have said. Go to the priestess
　　　　At Delphi; ask if I quoted her correctly.
　　　　And as for this other thing: if I am found
　　　　Guilty of treason with Teiresias,
　　　　Then sentence me to death! You have my word
　　　　It is a sentence I should cast my vote for—
　　　　But not without evidence!
　　　　　　　　　　　　You do wrong
　　　　When you take good men for bad, bad men for good.
　　　　A true friend thrown aside—why, life itself
　　　　Is not more precious!
　　　　　　　　　　　　In time you will know this well:
　　　　For time, and time alone, will show the just man,
　　　　Though scoundrels are discovered in a day.
CHORAGOS: This is well said, and a prudent man would ponder it.
　　　　Judgments too quickly formed are dangerous.
OEDIPUS: But is he not quick in his duplicity?
　　　　And shall I not be quick to parry him?
　　　　Would you have me stand still, hold my peace, and let
　　　　This man win everything, through my inaction?
CREON: And you want—what is it, then? To banish me?

OEDIPUS: No, not exile. It is your death I want,
     So that all the world may see what treason means.
CREON: You will persist, then? You will not believe me?
OEDIPUS: How can I believe you?
CREON: Then you are a fool.
OEDIPUS: To save myself?
CREON: In justice, think of me.
OEDIPUS: You are evil incarnate.
CREON: But suppose that you are wrong?
OEDIPUS: Still I must rule.
CREON: But not if you rule badly.
OEDIPUS: O city, city!
CREON: It is my city, too!
CHORAGOS: Now, my lords, be still, I see the Queen,
     Iocastê, coming from her palace chambers;
     And it is time she came, for the sake of you both.
     This dreadful quarrel can be resolved through her.
          [*Enter* IOCASTE.]
IOCASTE: Poor foolish men, what wicked din is this?
     With Thebes sick to death, is it not shameful
     That you should rake some private quarrel up?
          [*To* OEDIPUS:]
     Come into the house.

                              —And you, Creon, go now:
     Let us have no more of this tumult over nothing.
CREON: Nothing? No, sister: what your husband plans for me
     Is one of two great evils: exile or death.
OEDIPUS: He is right.
                         Why, woman, I have caught him squarely
     Plotting against my life.
CREON: No! let me die
     Accurst if ever I have wished you harm!
IOCASTE: Ah, believe it, Oedipus!
     In the name of the gods, respect this oath of his
     For my sake, for the sake of these people here!   [STROPHE 1]

CHORAGOS: Open your mind to her, my lord, Be ruled by her, I beg you!
OEDIPUS: What would you have me do?
CHORAGOS: Respect Creon's word. He has never spoken like a fool,
     And now he has sworn an oath.
OEDIPUS: You know what you ask?
CHORAGOS: I do.
OEDIPUS: Speak on, then.
CHORAGOS: A friend so sworn should not be baited so,
     In blind malice, and without final proof.
OEDIPUS: You are aware, I hope, that what you say
     Means death for me, or exile at the least.

CHORAGOS: No, I swear by Helios, first in Heaven!
 May I die friendless and accurst,
 The worst of deaths, if ever I meant that!
  It is the withering fields
   That hurt my sick heart:
  Must we bear all these ills,
   And now your bad blood as well?
OEDIPUS: Then let him go. And let me die, if I must,
 Or be driven by him in shame from the land of Thebes.
 It is your unhappiness, and not his talk,
 That touches me.
     As for him—
 Wherever he goes, hatred will follow him.
CREON: Ugly in yielding, as you were ugly in rage!
 Natures like yours chiefly torment themselves.
OEDIPUS: Can you not go? Can you not leave me?
CREON: I can.
 You do not know me; but the city knows me,
 And in its eyes, I am just, if not in yours.
   [*Exit* CREON.]

                [ANTISTROPHE 1]
CHORAGOS: Lady Iocastê, did you not ask the King to go to his chambers?
IOCASTE: First tell me what has happened.
CHORAGOS: There was suspicion without evidence: yet it rankled
 As even false charges will.
IOCASTE: On both sides?
CHORAGOS: On both.
IOCASTE: But what was said?
CHORAGOS: Oh let it rest, let it be done with!
 Have we not suffered enough?
OEDIPUS: You see to what your decency has brought you:
 You have made difficulties where my heart saw none.
CHORAGOS: Oedipus, it is not once only I have told you— [ANTISTROPHE 2]
  You must know I should count myself unwise
 To the point of madness, should I now forsake you—
  You, under whose hand,
   In the storm of another time,
  Our dear land sailed out free.
   But now stand fast at the helm!
IOCASTE: In God's name, Oedipus, inform your wife as well:
 Why are you so set in this hard anger?
OEDIPUS: I will tell you, for none of these men deserves
 My confidence as you do. It is Creon's work,
 His treachery, his plotting against me.
IOCASTE: Go on, if you can make this clear to me.
OEDIPUS: He charges me with the murder of Laïos.
IOCASTE: Has he some knowledge? Or does he speak from hearsay?

OEDIPUS: He would not commit himself to such a charge,
　　　But he has brought in that damnable soothsayer
　　　To tell his story.

IOCASTE:　　　　　　　Set your mind at rest.
　　　If it is a question of soothsayers, I tell you
　　　That you will find no man whose craft gives knowledge
　　　Of the unknowable.

　　　　　　　　Here is my proof.

　　　An oracle was reported to Laïos once
　　　(I will not say from Phoibos himself, but from
　　　His appointed ministers, at any rate)
　　　That his doom would be death at the hands of his own son—
　　　His son, born of his flesh and of mine!

　　　Now, you remember the story: Laïos was killed
　　　By marauding strangers where three highways meet.
　　　But his child had not been three days in this world
　　　Before the King had pierced the baby's ankles
　　　And left him to die on a lonely mountainside.

　　　Thus, Apollo never caused that child
　　　To kill his father, and it was not Laïos' fate
　　　To die at the hands of his son, as he had feared.
　　　This is what prophets and prophecies are worth!
　　　Have no dread of them.
　　　　　　　　　　It is God himself
　　　Who can show us what he wills, in his own way.

OEDIPUS: How strange a shadowy memory crossed my mind,
　　　Just now while you were speaking; it chilled my heart.

IOCASTE: What do you mean? What memory do you speak of?

OEDIPUS: If I understand you, Laïos was killed
　　　At a place where three roads meet.

IOCASTE:　　　　　　　　　　So it was said;
　　　We have no later story.

OEDIPUS:　　　　　　　Where did it happen?

IOCASTE: Phokis, it is called: at a place where the Theban Way
　　　Divides into the roads toward Delphi and Daulia.

OEDIPUS: When?

IOCASTE: We had the news not long before you came
　　　And proved the right to your succession here.

OEDIPUS: Ah, what net has God been weaving for me?

IOCASTE: Oedipus! Why does this trouble you?

OEDIPUS:　　　　　　　　　　Do not ask me yet.
　　　First, tell me how Laïos looked, and tell me
　　　How old he was.

IOCASTE: He was tall, his hair just touched
    With white; his form was not unlike your own.
OEDIPUS: I think that I myself may be accurst
    By my own ignorant edict.
IOCASTE: You speak strangely.
    It makes me tremble to look at you, my King.
OEDIPUS: I am not sure that the blind man can not see.
    But I should know better if you were to tell me—
IOCASTE: Anything—though I dread to hear you ask it.
OEDIPUS: Was the King lightly escorted, or did he ride
    With a large company, as a ruler should?
IOCASTE: There were five men with him in all: one was a herald,
    And a single chariot, which he was driving.
OEDIPUS: Alas, that makes it plain enough!

                                        But who—
    Who told you how it happened?
IOCASTE: A household servant,
    The only one to escape.
OEDIPUS: And is he still
    A servant of ours?
IOCASTE: No; for when he came back at last
    And found you enthroned in the place of the dead king,
    He came to me, touched my hand with his, and begged
    That I would send him away to the frontier district
    Where only the shepherds go—
    As far away from the city as I could send him.
    I granted his prayer; for although the man was a slave,
    He had earned more than this favor at my hands.
OEDIPUS: Can he be called back quickly?
IOCASTE: Easily.
    But why?
OEDIPUS: I have taken too much upon myself
    Without enquiry; therefore I wish to consult him.
IOCASTE: Then he shall come.
                            But am I not one also
    To whom you might confide these fears of yours?
OEDIPUS: That is your right; it will not be denied you,
    Now least of all; for I have reached a pitch
    Of wild foreboding. Is there anyone
    To whom I should sooner speak?

    Polybos of Corinth is my father.
    My mother is a Dorian: Meropê.
    I grew up chief among the men of Corinth
    Until a strange thing happened—
    Not worth my passion, it may be, but strange.

At a feast, a drunken man maundering in his cups
Cries out that I am not my father's son!

I contained myself that night, though I felt anger
And a sinking heart. The next day I visited
My father and mother, and questioned them. They stormed,
Calling it all the slanderous rant of a fool;
And this relieved me. Yet the suspicion
Remained always aching in my mind;
I know there was talk; I could not rest;
And finally, saying nothing to my parents,
I went to the shrine at Delphi.
The god dismissed my question without reply;
He spoke of other things.
                              Some were clear,
Full of wretchedness, dreadful, unbearable:
As, that I should lie with my own mother, breed
Children from whom all men would turn their eyes;
And that I should be my father's murderer.

I heard all this, and fled. And from that day
Corinth to me was only in the stars
Descending in that quarter of the sky,
As I wandered farther and farther on my way
To a land where I should never see the evil
Sung by the oracle. And I came to this country
Where, so you say, King Laïos was killed.

I will tell you all that happened there, my lady.
There were three highways
Coming together at a place I passed;
And there a herald came towards me, and a chariot
Drawn by horses, with a man such as you describe
Seated in it. The groom leading the horses
Forced me off the road at his lord's command;
But as this charioteer lurched over towards me
I struck him in my rage. The old man saw me
And brought his double goad down upon my head
As I came abreast.
                              He was paid back, and more!
Swinging my club in this right hand I knocked him
Out of his car, and he rolled on the ground.
                              I killed him.
I killed them all.
Now if that stranger and Laïos were—kin,
Where is a man more miserable than I?

More hated by the gods? Citizen and alien alike
Must never shelter me or speak to me—
I must be shunned by all.
                              And I myself
Pronounced this malediction upon myself!
Think of it: I have touched you with these hands,
These hands that killed your husband. What defilement!
Am I all evil, then? It must be so,
Since I must flee from Thebes, yet never again
See my own countrymen, my own country,
For fear of joining my mother in marriage
And killing Polybos, my father.
                              Ah,
If I was created so, born to this fate,
Who could deny the savagery of God?

O holy majesty of heavenly powers!
May I never see that day! Never!
Rather let me vanish from the race of men
Than know the abomination destined me!

CHORAGOS: We, too, my lord, have felt dismay at this.
       But there is hope: you have yet to hear the shepherd.

OEDIPUS: Indeed, I fear no other hope is left me.

IOCASTE: What do you hope from him when he comes?

OEDIPUS: This much:
       If his account of the murder tallies with yours,
       Then I am cleared.

IOCASTE: What was it that I said
       Of such importance?

OEDIPUS: Why, "marauders," you said,
       Killed the King, according to this man's story.
       If he maintains that still, if there were several,
       Clearly the guilt is not mine: I was alone.
       But if he says one man, singlehanded, did it,
       Then the evidence all points to me.

IOCASTE: You may be sure that he said there were several;
       And can he call back that story now? He can not.
       The whole city heard it as plainly as I.
       But suppose he alters some detail of it:
       He can not ever show that Laïos' death
       Fulfilled the oracle: for Apollo said
       My child was doomed to kill him; and my child—
       Poor baby!—it was my child that died first.
       No. From now on, where oracles are concerned,
       I would not waste a second thought on any.

OEDIPUS: You might be right.
                              But come: let someone go
       For the shepherd at once. This matter must be settled.

IOCASTE: I will send for him.
>   I would not wish to cross you in anything,
>   And surely not in this.—Let us go in.
>   [*Exeunt into the palace.*]

ODE II

CHORUS: Let me be reverent in the ways of right,   [STROPHE 1]
>   Lowly the paths I journey on;
>   Let all my words and actions keep
>   The laws of the pure universe
>   From highest Heaven handed down.
>   For Heaven is their bright nurse,
>   Those generations of the realms of light;
>   Ah, never of mortal kind were they begot,
>   Nor are they slaves of memory, lost in sleep;
>   Their Father is greater than Time, and ages not.

>   The tyrant is a child of Pride   [ANTISTROPHE 1]
>   Who drinks from his great sickening cup
>   Recklessness and vanity,
>   Until from his high crest headlong
>   He plummets to the dust of hope.
>   That strong man is not strong.
>   But let no fair ambition be denied;
>   May God protect the wrestler for the State
>   In government, in comely policy,
>   Who will fear God, and on His ordinance wait.

>   Haughtiness and the high hand of disdain   [STROPHE 2]
>   Tempt and outrage God's holy law;
>   And any mortal who dares hold
>   No immortal Power in awe
>   Will be caught up in a net of pain:
>   The price for which his levity is sold.
>   Let each man take due earnings, then,
>   And keep his hands from holy things,
>   And from blasphemy stand apart—
>   Else the crackling blast of heaven
>   Blows on his head, and on his desperate heart;
>   Though fools will honor impious men,
>   In their cities no tragic poet sings.
>   Shall we lose faith in Delphi's obscurities,   [ANTISTROPHE 2]
>   We who have heard the world's core
>   Discredited, and the sacred wood
>   Of Zeus at Elis praised no more?
>   The deeds and the strange prophecies
>   Must make a pattern yet to be understood.

Zeus, if indeed you are lord of all,
Throned in light over night and day,
Mirror this in your endless mind:
Our masters call the oracle
Words on the wind, and the Delphic vision blind!
Their hearts no longer know Apollo,
And reverence for the gods has died away.

SCENE III

[*Enter* IOCASTE.]

IOCASTE: Princes of Thebes, it has occurred to me
To visit the altars of the gods, bearing
These branches as a suppliant, and this incense.
Our King is not himself: his noble soul
Is overwrought with fantasies of dread,
Else he would consider
The new prophecies in the light of the old.
He will listen to any voice that speaks disaster,
And my advice goes for nothing.
[*She approaches the altar, R.*]
To you, then, Apollo,
Lycean lord, since you are nearest, I turn in prayer.
Receive these offerings, and grant us deliverance
From defilement. Our hearts are heavy with fear
When we see our leader distracted, as helpless sailors
Are terrified by the confusion of their helmsman.
[*Enter* MESSENGER.]

MESSENGER: Friends, no doubt you can direct me:
Where shall I find the house of Oedipus,
Or, better still, where is the King himself?

CHORAGOS: It is this very place, stranger; he is inside.
This is his wife and mother of his children.

MESSENGER: I wish her happiness in a happy house,
Blest in all the fulfillment of her marriage.

IOCASTE: I wish as much for you: your courtesy
Deserves a like good fortune. But now, tell me:
Why have you come? What have you to say to us?

MESSENGER: Good news, my lady, for your house and your husband.

IOCASTE: What news? Who sent you here?

MESSENGER: I am from Corinth.
The news I bring ought to mean joy for you,
Though it may be you will find some grief in it.

IOCASTE: What is it? How can it touch us in both ways?

MESSENGER: The word is that the people of the Isthmus
Intend to call Oedipus to be their king.

IOCASTE: But old King Polybos—is he not reigning still?

MESSENGER: No. Death holds him in his sepulchre.

IOCASTE: What are you saying? Polybos is dead?

MESSENGER: If I am not telling the truth, may I die myself.

IOCASTE: [*to a* MAIDSERVANT:] Go in, go quickly; tell this to your master.
    O riddlers of God's will, where are you now!
    This was the man whom Oedipus, long ago,
    Feared so, fled so, in dread of destroying him—
    But it was another fate by which he died.
        [*Enter* OEDIPUS, *C.*]

OEDIPUS: Dearest Iocastê, why have you sent for me?

IOCASTE: Listen to what this man says, and then tell me
    What has become of the solemn prophecies.

OEDIPUS: Who is this man? What is his news for me?

IOCASTE: He has come from Corinth to announce your father's death!

OEDIPUS: Is it true, stranger? Tell me in your own words.

MESSENGER: I can not say it more clearly: the King is dead.

OEDIPUS: Was it by treason? Or by an attack of illness?

MESSENGER: A little thing brings old men to their rest.

OEDIPUS: It was sickness, then?

MESSENGER: Yes, and his many years.

OEDIPUS: Ah!
    Why should a man respect the Pythian hearth, or
    Give heed to the birds that jangle above his head?
    They prophesied that I should kill Polybos,
    Kill my own father; but he is dead and buried,
    And I am here—I never touched him, never,
    Unless he died of grief for my departure,
    And thus, in a sense, through me. No. Polybos
    Has packed the oracles off with him underground.
    They are empty words.

IOCASTE: Had I not told you so?

OEDIPUS: You had; it was my faint heart that betrayed me.

IOCASTE: From now on never think of those things again.

OEDIPUS: And yet—must I not fear my mother's bed?

IOCASTE: Why should anyone in this world be afraid,
    Since Fate rules us and nothing can be foreseen?
    A man should live only for the present day.

    Have no more fear of sleeping with your mother:
    How many men, in dreams, have lain with their mothers!
    No reasonable man is troubled by such things.

OEDIPUS: That is true; only—
    If only my mother were not still alive!
    But she is alive. I can not help my dread.

IOCASTE: Yet this news of your father's death is wonderful.

OEDIPUS: Wonderful. But I fear the living woman.

MESSENGER: Tell me, who is this woman that you fear?

OEDIPUS: It is Meropê, man; the wife of King Polybos.

MESSENGER: Meropê? Why should you be afraid of her?

OEDIPUS: An oracle of the gods, a dreadful saying.

MESSENGER: Can you tell me about it or are you sworn to silence?

OEDIPUS: I can tell you, and I will.

> Apollo said through his prophet that I was the man
> Who should marry his own mother, shed his father's blood
> With his own hands. And so, for all these years
> I have kept clear of Corinth, and no harm has come—
> Though it would have been sweet to see my parents again.

MESSENGER: And is this the fear that drove you out of Corinth?

OEDIPUS: Would you have me kill my father?

MESSENGER: As for that
> You must be reassured by the news I gave you.

OEDIPUS: If you could reassure me, I would reward you.

MESSENGER: I had that in mind, I will confess: I thought
> I could count on you when you returned to Corinth.

OEDIPUS: No: I will never go near my parents again.

MESSENGER: Ah, son, you still do not know what you are doing—

OEDIPUS: What do you mean? In the name of God tell me!

MESSENGER: —If these are your reasons for not going home.

OEDIPUS: I tell you, I fear the oracle may come true.

MESSENGER: And guilt may come upon you through your parents?

OEDIPUS: That is the dread that is always in my heart.

MESSENGER: Can you not see that all your fears are groundless?

OEDIPUS: How can you say that? They are my parents, surely?

MESSENGER: Polybos was not your father.

OEDIPUS: Not my father?

MESSENGER: No more your father than the man speaking to you.

OEDIPUS: But you are nothing to me!

MESSENGER: Neither was he.

OEDIPUS: Then why did he call me son?

MESSENGER: I will tell you:
> Long ago he had you from my hands, as a gift.

OEDIPUS: Then how could he love me so, if I was not his?

MESSENGER: He had no children, and his heart turned to you.

OEDIPUS: What of you? Did you buy me? Did you find me by chance?

MESSENGER: I came upon you in the crooked pass of Kithairon.

OEDIPUS: And what were you doing there?

MESSENGER: Tending my flocks.

OEDIPUS: A wandering shepherd?

MESSENGER: But your savior, son, that day.

OEDIPUS: From what did you save me?

MESSENGER: Your ankles should tell you that.

OEDIPUS: Ah, stranger, why do you speak of that childhood pain?

MESSENGER: I cut the bonds that tied your ankles together.

OEDIPUS: I have had the mark as long as I can remember.

MESSENGER: That was why you were given the name you bear.

OEDIPUS: God! Was it my father or my mother who did it?
> Tell me!

MESSENGER: I do not know. The man who gave you to me
    Can tell you better than I.
OEDIPUS: It was not you that found me, but another?
MESSENGER: It was another shepherd gave you to me.
OEDIPUS: Who was he? Can you tell me who he was?
MESSENGER: I think he was said to be one of Laïos' people.
OEDIPUS: You mean the Laïos who was king here years ago?
MESSENGER: Yes; King Laïos; and the man was one of his herdsmen.
OEDIPUS: Is he still alive? Can I see him?
MESSENGER: These men here
    Know best about such things.
OEDIPUS: Does anyone here
    Know this shepherd that he is talking about?
    Have you seen him in the fields, or in the town?
    If you have, tell me. It is time things were made plain.
CHORAGOS: I think the man he means is that same shepherd
    You have already asked to see. Iocastê perhaps
    Could tell you something.
OEDIPUS: Do you know anything
    About him, Lady? Is he the man we have summoned?
    Is that the man this shepherd means?
IOCASTE: Why think of him?
    Forget this herdsman. Forget it all.
    This talk is a waste of time.
OEDIPUS: How can you say that?
    When the clues to my true birth are in my hands?
IOCASTE: For God's love, let us have no more questioning!
    Is your life nothing to you?
    My own is pain enough for me to bear.
OEDIPUS: You need not worry. Suppose my mother a slave,
    And born of slaves: no baseness can touch you.
IOCASTE: Listen to me, I beg you: do not do this thing!
OEDIPUS: I will not listen; the truth must be made known.
IOCASTE: Everything that I say is for your own good!
OEDIPUS: My own good
    Snaps my patience, then; I want none of it.
IOCASTE: You are fatally wrong! May you never learn who you are!
OEDIPUS: Go, one of you, and bring the shepherd here.
    Let us leave this woman to brag of her royal name.
IOCASTE: Ah, miserable!
    That is the only word I have for you now.
    That is the only word I can ever have.
        [*Exit into the palace.*]
CHORAGOS: Why has she left us, Oedipus? Why has she gone
    In such a passion of sorrow? I fear this silence:
    Something dreadful may come of it.
OEDIPUS: Let it come!
    However base my birth, I must know about it.

The Queen, like a woman, is perhaps ashamed
To think of my low origin. But I
Am a child of Luck; I can not be dishonored.
Luck is my mother; the passing months, my brothers,
Have seen me rich and poor.
                              If this is so,
How could I wish that I were someone else?
How could I not be glad to know my birth?

ODE III

CHORUS: If ever the coming time were known   [STROPHE]
        To my heart's pondering,
        Kithairon, now by Heaven I see the torches
        At the festival of the next full moon,
        And see the dance, and hear the choir sing
        A grace to your gentle shade:
        Mountain where Oedipus was found,
        O mountain guard of a noble race!
        May the god who heals us lend his aid,
        And let that glory come to pass
        For our king's cradling-ground.

        Of the nymphs that flower beyond the years,   [ANTISTROPHE]
        Who bore you, royal child,
        To Pan of the hills or the timberline, Apollo,
        Cold in delight where the upland clears,
        Or Hermês for whom Kyllenê's heights are piled?
        Or flushed as evening cloud,
        Great Dionysos, roamer of mountains,
        He—was it he who found you there,
        And caught you up in his own proud
        Arms from the sweet god-ravisher
        Who laughed by the Muses' fountains?

SCENE IV

OEDIPUS: Sirs: though I do not know the man,
        I think I see him coming, this shepherd we want:
        He is old, like our friend here, and the men
        Bringing him seem to be servants of my house.
        But you can tell, if you have ever seen him.
            [*Enter* SHEPHERD *escorted by servants.*]
CHORAGOS: I know him, he was Laïos' man. You can trust him.
OEDIPUS: Tell me first, you from Corinth: is this the shepherd
        We were discussing?
MESSENGER: This is the very man.

OEDIPUS: [*to* SHEPHERD] Come here. No, look at me. You must answer
    Everything I ask.—You belonged to Laïos?
SHEPHERD: Yes: born his slave, brought up in his house.
OEDIPUS: Tell me: what kind of work did you do for him?
SHEPHERD: I was a shepherd of his, most of my life.
OEDIPUS: Where mainly did you go for pasturage?
SHEPHERD: Sometimes Kithairon, sometimes the hills nearby.
OEDIPUS: Do you remember ever seeing this man out there?
SHEPHERD: What would he be doing there? This man?
OEDIPUS: This man standing here. Have you ever seen him before?
SHEPHERD: No. At least, not to my recollection.
MESSENGER: And that is not strange, my lord. But I'll refresh
    His memory: he must remember when we two
    Spent three whole seasons together, March to September,
    On Kithairon or thereabouts. He had two flocks;
    I had one. Each autumn I'd drive mine home
    And he would go back with his to Laïos' sheepfold.—
    Is this not true, just as I have described it?
SHEPHERD: True, yes; but it was all so long ago.
MESSENGER: Well, then: do you remember, back in those days,
    That you gave me a baby boy to bring up as my own?
SHEPHERD: What if I did? What are you trying to say?
MESSENGER: King Oedipus was once that little child.
SHEPHERD: Damn you, hold your tongue!
OEDIPUS: No more of that!
    It is your tongue needs watching, not this man's.
SHEPHERD: My King, my Master, what is it I have done wrong?
OEDIPUS: You have not answered his question about the boy.
SHEPHERD: He does not know . . . He is only making trouble . . .
OEDIPUS: Come, speak plainly, or it will go hard with you.
SHEPHERD: In God's name, do not torture an old man!
OEDIPUS: Come here, one of you; bind his arms behind him.
SHEPHERD: Unhappy king! What more do you wish to learn?
OEDIPUS: Did you give this man the child he speaks of?
SHEPHERD: I did.
    And I would to God I had died that very day.
OEDIPUS: You will die now unless you speak the truth.
SHEPHERD: Yet if I speak the truth, I am worse than dead.
OEDIPUS: Very well; since you insist upon delaying—
SHEPHERD: No! I have told you already that I gave him the boy.
OEDIPUS: Where did you get him? From your house? From somewhere else?
SHEPHERD: Not from mine, no. A man gave him to me.
OEDIPUS: Is that man here? Do you know whose slave he was?
SHEPHERD: For God's love, my King, do not ask me any more!
OEDIPUS: You are a dead man if I have to ask you again.
SHEPHERD: Then . . . Then the child was from the palace of Laïos.
OEDIPUS: A slave child? or a child of his own line?

SHEPHERD: Ah, I am on the brink of dreadful speech!

OEDIPUS: And I of dreadful hearing. Yet I must hear.

SHEPHERD: If you must be told, then . . .

                                They said it was Laïos' child;

    But it is your wife who can tell you about that.

OEDIPUS: My wife!—Did she give it to you?

SHEPHERD: My lord, she did.

OEDIPUS: Do you know why?

SHEPHERD: I was told to get rid of it.

OEDIPUS: An unspeakable mother!

SHEPHERD: There had been prophecies . . .

OEDIPUS: Tell me.

SHEPHERD: It was said that the boy would kill his own father.

OEDIPUS: Then why did you give him over to this old man?

SHEPHERD: I pitied the baby, my King.

    And I thought that this man would take him far away

    To his own country.

                  He saved him—but for what a fate!

    For if you are what this man says you are,

    No man living is more wretched than Oedipus.

OEDIPUS: Ah God!

    It was true!

        All the prophecies!

               —Now,

    O, Light, may I look on you for the last time!

    I, Oedipus,

    Oedipus, damned in his birth, in his marriage damned,

    Damned in the blood he shed with his own hand!

    [*He rushes into the palace.*]

ODE IV

CHORUS: Alas for the seed of men.   [STROPHE 1]

    What measure shall I give these generations
    That breathe on the void and are void
    And exist and do not exist?

    Who bears more weight of joy
    Than mass of sunlight shifting in images,
    Or who shall make his thought stay on
    That down time drifts away?

    Your splendor is all fallen.

    O naked brow of wrath and tears,
    O change of Oedipus!
    I who saw your days call no man blest—

Your great days like ghósts góne.
That mind was a strong bow. [ANTISTROPHE 1]

Deep, how deep you drew it then, hard archer,
At a dim fearful range,
And brought dear glory down!

You overcame the stranger—
The virgin with her hooking lion claws—
And though death sang, stood like a tower
To make pale Thebes take heart.

Fortress against our sorrow!

True king, giver of laws,
Majestic Oedipus!
No prince in Thebes had ever such renown,
No prince won such grace of power.

And now of all men ever known [STROPHE 2]
Most pitiful is this man's story:
His fortunes are most changed, his state
Fallen to a low slave's
Ground under bitter fate.

O Oedipus, most royal one!
The great door that expelled you to the light
Gave at night—ah, gave night to your glory:
As to the father, to the fathering son.

All understood too late.

How could that queen whom Laïos won,
The garden that he harrowed at his height,
Be silent when that act was done?

But all eyes fail before time's eye, [ANTISTROPHE 2]
All actions come to justice there.
Though never willed, though far down the deep past,
Your bed, your dread sirings,
Are brought to book at last.
Child by Laïos doomed to die,
Then doomed to lose that fortunate little death,
Would God you never took breath in this air
That with my wailing lips I take to cry:
For I weep the world's outcast.

I was blind, and now I can tell why:
Asleep, for you had given ease of breath
To Thebes, while the false years went by.

ÉXODUS

[*Enter, from the palace,* SECOND MESSENGER.]
SECOND MESSENGER: Elders of Thebes, most honored in this land,
     What horrors are yours to see and hear, what weight
     Of sorrow to be endured, if, true to your birth,
     You venerate the line of Labdakos!
     I think neither Istros nor Phasis, those great rivers,
     Could purify this place of the corruption
     It shelters now, or soon must bring to light—
     Evil not done unconsciously, but willed.

     The greatest griefs are those we cause ourselves.
CHORAGOS: Surely, friend, we have grief enough already;
     What new sorrow do you mean?
SECOND MESSENGER: The Queen is dead.
CHORAGOS: Iocastê? Dead? But at whose hand?
SECOND MESSENGER: Her own.
     The full horror of what happened you can not know,
     For you did not see it; but I, who did, will tell you
     As clearly as I can how she met her death.

     When she had left us,
     In passionate silence, passing through the court,
     She ran to her apartment in the house,
     Her hair clutched by the fingers of both hands.
     She closed the doors behind her; then, by that bed
     Where long ago the fatal son was conceived—
     That son who should bring about his father's death—
     We hear her call upon Laïos, dead so many years,
     And heard her wail for the double fruit of her marriage,
     A husband by her husband, children by her child.

     Exactly how she died I do not know:
     For Oedipus burst in moaning and would not let us
     Keep vigil to the end: it was by him
     As he stormed about the room that our eyes were caught.
     From one to another of us he went, begging a sword,
     Cursing the wife who was not his wife, the mother
     Whose womb had carried his own children and himself.
     I do not know: it was none of us aided him,
     But surely one of the gods was in control!
     For with a dreadful cry
     He hurled his weight, as though wrenched out of himself,
     At the twin doors: the bolts gave, and he rushed in.
     And there we saw her hanging, her body swaying
     From the cruel cord she had noosed about her neck.
     A great sob broke from him, heartbreaking to hear,

As he loosed the rope and lowered her to the ground.
I would blot out from my mind what happened next!
For the King ripped from her gown the golden brooches
That were her ornament, and raised them, and lunged them down
Straight into his own eyeballs, crying, "No more,
No more shall you look on the misery about me,
The horrors of my own doing! Too long you have known
The faces of those whom I should never have seen,
Too long been blind to those for whom I was searching!
From this hour, go in darkness!" And as he spoke,
He struck at his eyes—not once, but many times;
And the blood spattered his beard,
Bursting from his ruined sockets like red hail.

So from the unhappiness of two this evil has sprung,
A curse on the man and woman alike. The old
Happiness of the house of Labdakos
Was happiness enough: where is it today?
It is all wailing and ruin, disgrace, death—all
The misery of mankind that has a name—
And it is wholly and for ever theirs.

CHORAGOS: Is he in agony still? Is there no rest for him?

SECOND MESSENGER: He is calling for someone to lead him to the gates
So that all the children of Kadmos may look upon
His father's murderer, his mother's—no,
I can not say it!
              And then he will leave Thebes,
Self-exiled, in order that the curse
Which he himself pronounced may depart from the house.
He is weak, and there is none to lead him,
So terrible is his suffering.
              But you will see:
Look, the doors are opening; in a moment
You will see a thing that would crush a heart of stone.

[*The central door is opened;* OEDIPUS, *blinded, is led in.*]

CHORAGOS: Dreadful indeed for men to see.
Never have my own eyes
Looked on a sight so full of fear.

Oedipus!
What madness came upon you, what daemon
Leaped on your life with heavier
Punishment than a mortal man can bear?
No: I can not even
Look at you, poor ruined one.
And I would speak, question, ponder,
If I were able. No.
You make me shudder.

OEDIPUS: God.   God.
> Is there a sorrow greater?
> Where shall I find harbor in this world?
> My voice is hurled far on a dark wind.
> What has God done to me?

CHORAGOS: Too terrible to think of, or to see.

OEDIPUS: O cloud of night,   [STROPHE 1]
> Never to be turned away: night coming on,
> I can not tell how: night like a shroud!

> My fair winds brought me here.
>   O God. Again
> The pain of the spikes where I had sight,
> The flooding pain
> Of memory, never to be gouged out.

CHORAGOS: This is not strange.
> You suffer it all twice over, remorse in pain,
> Pain in remorse.

OEDIPUS: Ah dear friend   [ANTISTROPHE 1]
> Are you faithful even yet, you alone?
> Are you still standing near me, will you stay here,
> Patient, to care for the blind?
>   The blind man!
> Yet even blind I know who it is attends me,
> By the voice's tone—
> Though my new darkness hide the comforter.

CHORAGOS: Oh fearful act!
> What god was it drove you to rake black
> Night across your eyes?

OEDIPUS: Apollo. Apollo. Dear   [STROPHE 2]
> Children, the god was Apollo.
> He brought my sick, sick fate upon me.
> But the blinding hand was my own!
> How could I bear to see
> When all my sight was horror everywhere?

CHORAGOS: Everywhere; that is true.

OEDIPUS: And now what is left?
> Images? Love? A greeting even,
> Sweet to the senses? Is there anything?
> Ah, no, friends: lead me away.
> Lead me away from Thebes.
>   Lead the great wreck
> And hell of Oedipus, whom the gods hate.

CHORAGOS: Your fate is clear, you are not blind to that.
> Would God you had never found it out!

OEDIPUS: Death take the man who unbound   [ANTISTROPHE 2]
> My feet on that hillside
> And delivered me from death to life! What life?

If only I had died,
This weight of monstrous doom
Could not have dragged me and my darlings down.
CHORAGOS: I would have wished the same.
OEDIPUS: Oh never to have come here
       With my father's blood upon me! Never
       To have been the man they call his mother's husband!
       Oh accurst! Oh child of evil,
       To have entered that wretched bed—
                                   the selfsame one!
       More primal than sin itself, this fell to me.

CHORAGOS: I do not know how I can answer you.
       You were better dead than alive and blind.
OEDIPUS: Do not counsel me any more. This punishment
       That I have laid upon myself is just.
       If I had eyes,
       I do not know how I could bear the sight
       Of my father, when I came to the house of Death,
       Or my mother: for I have sinned against them both
       So vilely that I could not make my peace
       By strangling my own life.
                           Or do you think my children,
       Born as they were born, would be sweet to my eyes?
       Ah never, never! Nor this town with its high walls,
       Nor the holy images of the gods.
                           For I,
       Thrice miserable!—Oedipus, noblest of all the line
       Of Kadmos, have condemned myself to enjoy
       These things no more, by my own malediction
       Expelling that man whom the gods declared
       To be a defilement in the house of Laïos.
       After exposing the rankness of my own guilt,
       How could I look men frankly in the eyes?
       No, I swear it,
       If I could have stifled my hearing at its source,
       I would have done it and made all this body
       A tight cell of misery, blank to light and sound:
       So I should have been safe in a dark agony
       Beyond all recollection.
                           Ah Kithairon!
       Why did you shelter me? When I was cast upon you,
       Why did I not die? Then I should never
       Have shown the world my execrable birth.

       Ah Polybos! Corinth, city that I believed
       The ancient seat of my ancestors: how fair
       I seemed, your child! And all the while this evil

Was cancerous within me!
                                   For I am sick
In my daily life, sick in my origin.

O three roads, dark ravine, woodland and way
Where three roads met: you, drinking my father's blood,
My own blood, spilled by my own hand: can you remember
The unspeakable things I did there, and the things
I went on from there to do?
                                   O marriage, marriage!
The act that engendered me, and again the act
Performed by the son in the same bed—
                                                   Ah, the net
Of incest, mingling fathers, brothers, sons,
With brides, wives, mothers: the last evil
That can be known by men: no tongue can say
How evil!
            No. For the love of God, conceal me
Somewhere far from Thebes; or kill me; or hurl me
Into the sea, away from men's eyes for ever.

Come, lead me. You need not fear to touch me.
Of all men, I alone can bear this guilt.
            [*Enter* CREON.]
CHORAGOS: We are not the ones to decide; but Creon here
      May fitly judge of what you ask. He only
      Is left to protect the city in your place.
OEDIPUS: Alas, how can I speak to him? What right have I
      To beg his courtesy whom I have deeply wronged?
CREON: I have not come to mock you, Oedipus,
      Or to reproach you either.
            [*To* ATTENDANTS:]—You, standing there:
      If you have lost all respect for man's dignity,
      At least respect the flame of Lord Helios:
      Do not allow this pollution to show itself
      Openly here, an affront to the earth
      And Heaven's rain and the light of day. No, take him
      Into the house as quickly as you can.
      For it is proper
      That only the close kindred see his grief.
OEDIPUS: I pray you in God's name, since your courtesy
      Ignores my dark expectation, visiting
      With mercy this man of all men most execrable:
      Give me what I ask—for your good, not for mine.
CREON: And what is it that you would have me do?
OEDIPUS: Drive me out of this country as quickly as may be
      To a place where no human voice can ever greet me.

CREON: I should have done that before now—only,
    God's will had not been wholly revealed to me.
OEDIPUS: But his command is plain: the parricide
    Must be destroyed. I am that evil man.
CREON: That is the sense of it, yes; but as things are,
    We had best discover clearly what is to be done.
OEDIPUS: You would learn more about a man like me?
CREON: You are ready now to listen to the god.
OEDIPUS: I will listen. But it is to you
    That I must turn for help. I beg you, hear me.
    The woman in there—
    Give her whatever funeral you think proper:
    She is your sister.
                —But let me go, Creon!
    Let me purge my father's Thebes of the pollution
    Of my living here, and go out to the wild hills,
    To Kithairon, that has won such fame with me,
    The tomb my mother and father appointed for me,
    And let me die there, as they willed I should.
    And yet I know
    Death will not ever come to me through sickness
    Or in any natural way: I have been preserved
    For some unthinkable fate. But let that be.

    As for my sons, you need not care for them.
    They are men, they will find some way to live.
    But my poor daughters, who have shared my table,
    Who never before have been parted from their father—
    Take care of them. Creon; do this for me.
    And will you let me touch them with my hands
    A last time, and let us weep together?
    Be kind, my lord.
    Great prince, be kind!
                Could I but touch them,
    They would be mine again, as when I had my eyes.
    [*Enter* ANTIGONE *and* ISMENE, *attended.*]
    Ah, God!
    Is it my dearest children I hear weeping?
    Has Creon pitied me and sent my daughters?
CREON: Yes, Oedipus: I knew that they were dear to you
    In the old days, and know you must love them still.
OEDIPUS: May God bless you for this—and be a friendlier
    Guardian to you than he has been to me!
    Children, where are you?
    Come quickly to my hands: they are your brother's—
    Hands that have brought your father's once clear eyes
    To this way of seeing—

Ah dearest ones,
I had neither sight nor knowledge then, your father
By the woman who was the source of his own life!
And I weep for you—having no strength to see you—,
I weep for you when I think of the bitterness
That men will visit upon you all your lives.
What homes, what festivals can you attend
Without being forced to depart again in tears?
And when you come to marriageable age,
Where is the man, my daughters, who would dare
Risk the bane that lies on all my children?
Is there any evil wanting? Your father killed
His father; sowed the womb of her who bore him;
Engendered you at the fount of his own existence!
That is what they will say of you

                              Then, whom
Can you ever marry? There are no bridegrooms for you,
And your lives must wither away in sterile dreaming.

O Creon, son of Menoikeus!
You are the only father my daughters have,
Since we, their parents, are both of us gone for ever.
They are your own blood: you will not let them
Fall into beggary and loneliness;
You will keep them from the miseries that are mine!
Take pity on them; see, they are only children,
Friendless except for you. Promise me this,
Great Prince, and give me your hand in token of it.
     [CREON *clasps his right hand.*]
Children:
I could say much, if you could understand me,
But as it is, I have only this prayer for you:
Live where you can, be as happy as you can—
Happier, please God, than God has made your father!

CREON: Enough. You have wept enough. Now go within.
OEDIPUS: I must; but it is hard.
CREON: Time eases all things.
OEDIPUS: But you must promise—
CREON: Say what you desire.
OEDIPUS: Send me from Thebes!
CREON: God grant that I may!
OEDIPUS: But since God hates me . . .
CREON: No, he will grant your wish.
OEDIPUS: You promise?
CREON: I can not speak beyond my knowledge.
OEDIPUS: Then lead me in.
CREON: Come now, and leave your children.
OEDIPUS: No! Do not take them from me!

CREON: Think no longer
    That you are in command here, but rather think
    How, when you were, you served your own destruction.
        [*Exeunt into the house all but the* CHORUS; *the* CHORAGOS *chants directly*
        to the audience:]
CHORAGOS: Men of Thebes: look upon Oedipus.

    This is the king who solved the famous riddle
    And towered up, most powerful of men.
    No mortal eyes but looked on him with envy,
    Yet in the end ruin swept over him.

    Let every man in mankind's frailty
    Consider his last day; and let none
    Presume on his good fortune until he find
    Life, at his death, a memory without pain.

Anonymous

Noah and His Sons
(A.D. 1425–1450)

Noah and His Sons was presented at Wakefield (England), the third of the thirty-two short plays that together dramatized the biblical account of human existence from Creation to the Last Judgment. The entire cycle was presented out of doors during the Corpus Christi festival, a religious celebration of the sacrament of bread and wine (the body and blood of Christ), the union of the human and divine in the person of Christ, and the promise of redemption through His sacrifice.

The central feature of the Corpus Christi festival was a procession (which included representatives from every rank and profession) through the town with the consecrated bread and wine. This procession may have been the inspiration for the staging of the cycle: mounting plays on wagons and performing them at various stops along a processional route. Each play was assigned to a different trade guild that was then responsible for mounting and financing its play. The overall cycle was under the supervision of the town council, and the scripts had to be approved by the church.

Noah and His Sons is one of five plays identified as the work of the "Wakefield Master," works considered far superior to the other plays in the same cycle. *Noah* is noted in part for the variety achieved through the comic bickering of the title character and his wife, an element that locates the action in a world familiar to the medieval audience. The play is short (558 lines), made up of sixty-two nine-line stanzas. The structure of the stanzas suggests a formalized delivery by the performers.

The play is divided into three parts of approximately equal length: the opening expository scene with God and Noah establishing justification for the flood; two scenes of bickering between Noah and his wife; and the scenes showing first the building of the ark and then the time on board. It is clear, entertaining, and didactic.

Wakefield Cycle—Anonymous

Noah and His Sons

Edited by Oscar G. Brockett

CHARACTERS

NOAH
GOD
NOAH'S WIFE
FIRST SON
SECOND SON
THIRD SON
FIRST WIFE
SECOND WIFE
THIRD WIFE

Note: Many obsolete words have been retained so as not to alter unduly the rhyme scheme. The first four lines of each nine-line stanza use both end and mid-line rhymes; the fifth and ninth lines rhyme, as do lines six through eight. To clarify obsolete words, modern equivalents have been placed in brackets immediately following the words they clarify.

NOAH: Mightful god veray [truly], Maker of all that is,
 Three persons, none say nay, one god in endless bliss,
 Thou made both night and day, beast, fowl, and fish,
 All creatures that live may, wrought thou at thy wish,
  As thou well might;
 The sun, the moon, verament [truly],
 Thou made; the firmament,
 The stars also, full fervent,
  To shine thou made full bright.

 Angels thou made full even, all orders that is,
 To have the bliss in heaven. This did thou more and less,
 Full marvelous to neven [tell]; yet was there unkindness,
 More by folds seven than I can well express;
  For why?
 Of all angels in brightness
 God gave Lucifer most lightness,
 Yet proudly he fled his dais,
  And set him even Him by.

He thought himself as worthy as Him that him made;
In brightness, in beauty, therefore God did him degrade;
Put him in a low degree soon after, in a brade [minute],
Him and all his menye [minions], where he may be unglad
     For ever.
Shall they never win away,
Hence unto doomsday,
But burn in hell for aye,
     Shall they depart never.

Soon after, that gracious lord in His likeness made man,
That place to be restored, even as he began,
Of the Trinity by accord, Adam and Eve, that woman,
To multiply without discord, in paradise put He them,
     And sayeth to both
Gave in commandment,
On the tree of life to lay no hand;
But yet the false fiend
     Made Him with man wroth,

Enticed man to gluttony, stirred him to sin in pride;
But in paradise securely might no sin abide,
And therefore man full hastily was put out, in that tide [time],
In woe and wretchedness for to be, in pains full cried,
     To know,
First on earth, and then in hell
With fiends for to dwell,
But He his mercy mell [dispenses]
     To those that will Him trow [swear allegiance].

Oil of mercy He has hight [promised], as I have heard said,
To every living wight that would love Him and dread;
But now before His sight every living leyde [person],
Most party day and night, sin in word and deed
     Full bold;
Some in pride, ire, and envy,
Some in covetousness and gluttony,
Some in sloth and lechery,
     And otherwise manifold.

Therefore I dread lest God on us will take vengeance
For sin is now allowed without any repentance;
Six hundred years and odd have I, without distance [dispute],
On earth, as any sod, lived with great grievance
     Always;
And now I wax old,
Sick, sorry, and cold,
As muck upon mold

I wither away;
But yet will I cry for mercy and call;
Noah thy servant, am I, Lord over all!
Lest me and my fry shall also fall;
Save from villainy and bring to Thy hall
    In heaven;
And keep me from sin,
This world within;
Comely king of mankind,
    I pray Thee, hear my stevyn [voice]!

      [GOD *appears above.*]

GOD: Since I have made all thing that is liffand [living],
    Duke, emperor, and king, with mine own hand,
    For to have their liking by sea and by sand,
    Every man to my bidding should be bound
        Full fervent;
    That made man such a creature,
    Fairest of favor,
    Man must love me par-amour,
        By reason, and repent.

    Methought I showed man love when I made him to be
    All angels above, like to the Trinity;
    And now in great reproof full low lies he,
    On earth himself to stuff with sin that displeases me
        Most of all;
    Vengeance will I take,
    In earth for sin's sake,
    My anger thus will I wake,
        Both of great and small.

    I repent full sore that ever I made man,
    By me he sets no store, and I am his sovereign;
    I will destroy, therefore, both beast, man and woman,
    All shall perish, less and more; that bargain may they ban [regret],
        That ill has done.
    In earth I see right naught
    But sin that is unsought [unrepented];
    Of those that well has wrought
        Find I almost none.

    Therefore shall I undo [destroy] all this middle erd [earth]
    With floods that shall flow and run with hideous rerd [noise];
    I have good cause thereto: of me no man is afeard,
    As I say, shall I do: of vengeance draw my sword,
        And make end
    Of all that bears life,

Save Noah and his wife,
For they would never strive
   With me nor me offend.

To him to great win [joy] hastily will I go,
To Noah my servant, ere I blyn [stop] to warn him of his woe.
In earth I see but sin running to and fro,
Among both more and min [less], each the other's foe;
   With all their intent;
They shall I forego [destroy]
With floods that shall flow,
I shall work them woe,
   That will not repent.

     [GOD *descends and comes to* NOAH.]
GOD: Noah, my friend, I thee command, from cares thee dispel,
A ship I do demand of nail and board full well.
Thou was e'er a trusty man, to me true as steel,
To my bidding obedient; friendship shall thou feel
   To mede [in reward].
Of length thy ship be
Three hundred cubits, warn I thee,
Of height even thirty,
   Of fifty also in brede [breadth].

Anoint thy ship with pitch and tar without and also within,
The water out to spar [keep] this is a helpful gyn [means];
Look no man thee mar. Three tiers of chambers begin,
Thou must spend many a spar, this work ere thou win
   To end fully.
Make in thy ship also,
Parlors one or two,
And other houses mo [more],
   For beasts that there must be.

One cubit in height a window shall thou make;
On the side a doore with slyght [skill] beneath shall thou take;
With thee shall no man fight, nor do thee any kind of hate.
When all is done thus right, thy wife, that is thy mate,
   Take in to thee;
Thy sons of good fame,
Shem, Japhet, and Ham,
Take in also them,
   Their wives also three.

For all shall be undone [destroyed] that live on land but ye,
With floods that from above shall fall, and that plentily;

It shall begin full soon to rain incessantly,
After seven days 'twill come, and endure days forty,
   Without fail.
Take to thy ship also
Of each kind, beasts two,
Male and female, but no more,
   Ere thou pull up thy sail.

For they may thee avail when all this thing is wrought;
Stuff thy ship with victual, for hunger that ye perish nought;
Of beasts, fowl, and cattle, for them have thou in thought,
For them in my counsel, that some succor be sought,
   In haste;
They must have corn and hay,
And other meat alway;
Do now as I thee say,
   In the name of the Holy Ghost.

NOAH: Ah! Benedicite! What art thou that thus
   Tells afore that shall be? Thou art full marvelous!
   Tell me, for charity, thy name so gracious.
GOD: My name is of dignity and also full glorious
   To know.
   I am God most mighty,
   One God in Trinity,
   Made thee and each man to be;
   To love me well thou owe.

NOAH: I thank thee, lord so dear, that would vouch safe
   Thus low to appear to a simple knave;
   Bless us, lord, here, for charity I it crave,
   The better may we steer the ship that we shall have,
   Certain.
GOD: Noah, to thee and thy fry
   My blessing grant I;
   Ye shall wax and multiply,
   And fill the earth again,

When all these floods are past and fully gone away.
NOAH: Lord, homeward will I haste as fast as that I may;
   My wife will I frast [ask] what she will say, [*Exit* GOD]
   And I am aghast that we get some fray
   Betwixt us both;
   For she is full testy,
   For little oft angry,
   If anything wrong be,
   Soon is she wroth. [*He goes to his wife.*]

God speed, dear wife, how fare ye?
WIFE: Now, as ever I might thrive, the worst is I see thee;
  Do tell me belife [quickly] where has thou thus long be?
  To death may we drive, or live for thee [for all you care],
   For want indeed.
  When we sweat or swink [labor],
  Thou does what thou think,
  Yet of meat and of drink
   Have we great need.

NOAH: Wife, we are hard stead with tidings new.
WIFE: But thou were worthy be clad in Stafford blue [be beaten blue];
  For thou art always afraid, be it false or true;
  But God knows I am led, and that may I rue,
   For ill;
  For I dare be thy borrow [pledge],
  From even unto morrow,
  Thou speaks ever of sorrow;
   God send thee once thy fill!

  We women may wary [curse] all ill husbands;
  I have one, by Mary, that loosed me of my bands;
  If he be troubled I must tarry, how so ever it stands,
  With semblance full sorry, wringing both my hands
   For dread.
  But yet other while,
  With pleasure and with guile,
  I shall smite and smile,
   And quit him his mede [give him what he deserves].

NOAH: Well! hold thy tongue ram-skyt, or I shall thee still!
WIFE: By my thrift, if thou smite, I shall turn thee until!
NOAH: We shall assay as tight! Have at thee, Gill!
  Upon the bone shall it bite!
WIFE: Ah, so, marry! thou smitest ill!
   But I suppose
  I shall not in thy debt,
  Flee from this flett [floor]!
  Take thee there a langett [thong]
   To tie up thy hose!

NOAH: A! wilt thou so? Marry, that is mine.
WIFE: Thou shall three for two, I swear by God's pain!
NOAH: And I shall return them though, in faith, ere syne [long].
WIFE: Out upon thee, ho!
NOAH: Thou can both bite and whine,
   with a rerd [noise];
  For all if she strike,

Yet fast will she shriek,
In faith I hold none like
    In all middle-earth;

But I will keep charity, for I have work to do.
WIFE: Here shall no man tarry thee. I pray thee go to!
    Full well may we miss thee as ever have I ro [peace];
    To spin will I dress me.
NOAH: Well, farewell, lo!
        But wife,
    Pray for me busily,
    Till again I come unto thee.
WIFE: Even as thou prays for me,
        As ever might I thrive. [*Exit* WIFE.]

NOAH: I tarry full long from my work, I trow;
    Now my gear will I fang [take] and thitherward draw;
    I may full ill gang [go], the truth for to know,
    But if God help not among, I may sit down daw [melancholy]
        To ken;
    Now assay will I
    How I can of wrightry [workmanship],
    In nomine patris et filii, et spiritus sancti,
        Amen.

To begin of this tree, my bones will I bend,
I trust from the Trinity succor will be sent;
It fares full fair, think me, this work to my hand;
Now blessed be he that this can amend.
    Lo, here the length,
Three hundred cubits evenly,
Of breadth, lo, is it fifty,
The height is even thirty
    Cubits full strength.

Now my gown will I cast, and work in my coat,
Make will I the mast ere I shift one foot,
A! my back, I trow, will burst! This is a sorry note!
It is wonder that I last, such an old dote
    All dulled,
To begin such a work!
My bones are so stark [stiff],
No wonder if they wark [ache],
    For I am full old.

The top and the sail both will I make,
The helm and the castle also will I take;
To drive each single nail will I not forsake;

This gear may never fail, that dare I undertake
    At once.
This is a noble gin [device]
These nails so they run,
Through more and min [less],
    These boards each one;

Window and door, even as he said,
Three chief chambers, they are well made;
Pitch and tar full sure thereupon laid,
This will ever endure, thereof am I paid;
    for why?
It is better wrought
Than I could have thought;
Him that made all of nought
    I thank only.

Now will I hie me and nothing be lither [slow],
My wife and my meneye [family], to bring even hither.
Attend hither tidily wife, and consider,
Hence must us flee, all of us together,
    In haste.
WIFE: Why, sir, what ails you?
    Who is't that assails you?
    To flee it avails you,
        And ye be aghast [afraid].

NOAH: [*seeing his wife spinning*] There is yarn on the reel other, my dame.
WIFE: Tell me that each deal, else get ye blame.
NOAH: He that cares may keill [cool] blessed be his name!
    He has for our seyll [happiness] to shield us from shame,
        And said,
    All this world about
    With floods so stout,
    That shall run on a route,
        Shall be overlaid.

He said all shall be slain but only we,
Our sons that are bayn [obedient] and their wives three;
A ship he bade me ordain, to save us and our fee [property],
Therefore with all our main, thank we that free
    Healer of bayll [sorrow];
Hie us fast, go we thither.
WIFE: I know never whither,
    I am dazed and I dither
        For fear of that tale.

NOAH: Be not afeard, have done. Pack up our gear,
    That we be there ere noon without more dere [hindrance].

FIRST SON: It shall be done full soon. Brothers, help to bear.
SECOND SON: Full long shall I not hoyne [delay] to do my share,
      Brother Shem.
THIRD SON: Without any yelp,
    With my might shall I help.
WIFE: Yet for dread of a skelp [blow]
    Help well thy dam.

NOAH: Now are we there as we should be;
    To get in our gear, our cattle and fee,
    In this vessel here, my children free.
WIFE: I was never shut up ere, as now might I be,
      In such an hostel as this,
    In faith I can not find
    Which is before, which is behind.
    But shall we here be confined,
      Noah, as have thou bliss?

NOAH: Dame, as it is skill [reason], here must us abide grace;
    Therefore, wife, with good will come into this place.
WIFE: Sir, for Jack nor for Jill will I turn my face
    Till I have on this hill spun a space
      on my rok [distaff];
    Well were he, might get me,
    Now will I down set me,
    Yet reede [warn] I no man let me [stop me],
      For dread of a knock.

NOAH: Behold from the heaven the cararacts all,
    That are open full even, great and small,
    And the planets seven gone from their stall,
    These thunders and levyn [lightning] down make fall
      Full stout,
    Both halls and bowers,
    Castles and towers;
    Full sharp are these showers,
      That rain about;

    Therefore, wife, have done. Come into ship fast.
WIFE: Yea, Noah, go patch thy shone [shoes] the better will they last.
FIRST WIFE: Good mother, come in soon, for all is overcast,
    Both the sun and the moon.
SECOND WIFE: And many winds blast
      Full sharp.
    These floods so thay run,
    Therefore, mother, come in.
WIFE: In faith, yet will I spin;
    All in vain ye carp.

THIRD WIFE: If ye like ye may spin, Mother, in the ship.
NOAH: Now is this twice. Come in, dame, on my friendship.
WIFE: Whether I lose or I win, in faith, for thy fellowship
    Care I not a pin. This spindle will I slip
       Upon this hill,
    Ere I stir one foot.
NOAH: Peter! I trow we dote;
    Without any more note
       Come in if ye will.

WIFE: Yea, water nighs so near that I sit not dry;
    Into the ship with a byr [rush] therefore will I hie
    For dread that I drown here.
NOAH: Dame, securely,
    It be bought full dear, ye abode so long by
       Out of the ship.
WIFE: I will not, for thy bidding,
    Go from door to midding [dunghill; do whatever you demand].
NOAH: In faith, and for your long tarrying
       Ye shall taste of the whip.

WIFE: Spare me not, I pray thee, but even as thou think,
    These great words shall not flay me.
NOAH: Abide, dame, and drink,
    For beaten shall thou be, with this staff till thou stink;
    Are the strokes good? say me.
WIFE: What say ye, Wat Wynk?
NOAH: Speak!
    Cry me mercy, I say!
WIFE: Thereto say I nay.
NOAH: Unless thou do, by this day,
       Thy head shall I break.

        [to women in the audience]
WIFE: Lord, I were at rest and heartily full whole,
    Might I once have a mess of widow's coyll [fare];
    For thy soul, without jest, should I deal penny doyll [alms],
    So would more, no frese [fear], that I see in this sole [place]
       Of wives that are here
    For the life they have led
    Would their husbands were dead
    For, as ever ate I bread,
       So would I our sire were.

[to men in the audience]
NOAH: Ye men who have wives whilst they are young,
    If you love your lives, chastise their tongue:

Methinks my heart rives, both liver and lung,
To see such strifes, wedmen among;
    But I,
As have I bliss,
Shall chastise this.
WIFE: Yet may you miss,
    Nicholl Neddy!

NOAH: I shall make thee still as stone, beginner of blunder!
    I shall beat thee back and bone and break all asunder.
        [*They fight.*]
WIFE: Oh, alas, I am gone! Out upon thee, man's wonder!
NOAH: See how she can groan, and I lie under!
        But, wife,
    In this haste let us ho [stop],
    For my back is near in two.
WIFE: And I am beat so blue
        That I may not thrive.
        [*They enter the ark.*]

FIRST SON: Ah! why fare ye thus? Father and mother both!
SECOND SON: Ye should not be so spitus [spiteful] standing in such a
    woth [danger].
THIRD SON: These weathers are so hidus [hideous] with many a cold
    coth [disease].
NOAH: We will do as ye bid us. We will no more be wroth,
        Dear bairns!
    Now to the helm will I hent [go],
    And to my ship tend.
WIFE: I see on the firmament,
        Methinks, the seven stars.

NOAH: This is a great flood, wife, take heed.
WIFE: So me thought, as I stood. We are in great dread;
        These waves are so wode [wild].
NOAH: Help, God, in this need!
    As thou art steerman good and best, as I rede [counsel],
        Of all;
    Thou rule us in this race,
    As thou me promised has.
WIFE: This is a perilous case:
        Help, God, when we call!

NOAH: Wife, attend the steer-tree, and I shall assay
    The deepness of the sea that we bear, if I may.
WIFE: That shall I do full wisely. Now go thy way,
        For upon this flood have we floated many a day,
            With pain.

NOAH: Now the water will I sound
        Ah! it is far to the ground;
        This travail I expound
            Had I to tyne [lose].

        Above all hills bedeyn [completely] the water is risen late
        Cubits fifteen, but in a higher state
        It may not be, I ween, for this well I wate [know],
        This forty days has rain been. It will therefore abate
            Full lele [loyal].
        This water in haste,
        Eft will I test;
        Now am I aghast,
            It is waned a great deal.

        Now are the weathers ceased and cataracts quit,
        Both the most and the least.
WIFE: Methink, by my wit,
        The sun shines in the east. Lo, is not yond it?
        We should have a good feast were these floods flit
            So spytus [malicious].
NOAH: We have been here, all we,
        Three hundred days and fifty.
WIFE: Yea, now wanes the sea;
            Lord, well is us!

NOAH: The third time will I prove [test] what deepness we bear.
WIFE: How long shall thou heave. Lay in thy line there.
NOAH: I may touch with my lufe [hand] the ground even here.
WIFE: Then begins to grufe [grow] to us merry cheer;
            But, husband,
        What ground may this be?
NOAH: The hills of Armenia.
WIFE: Now blessed be he
            That thus for us ordained!

NOAH: I see tops of hills he [high] many at a sight,
        Nothing to hinder me, the weather is so bright.
WIFE: These are of mercy, tokens full right.
NOAH: Dame, thou counsel me what fowl best might
            And cowth [could],
        With flight of wing
        Bring, without tarrying,
        Of mercy some tokening
            Either by north or south.
        For this is the first day of the tenth moon.
WIFE: The raven, dare I lay, will come again soon;
        As fast as thou may cast him forth, have done,

He may happen to day come again ere noon
  Without delay.
NOAH: I will cast out also
  Doves one or two:
  Go your way, go,
   God send you some prey!

Now are these fowls flown into separate country;
Pray we fast each one, kneeling on our knee,
To him that is alone worthiest of degree,
That he would send anon our fowls some fee
  To glad us.
WIFE: They may not fail of land,
  The water is so wanand [waning].
NOAH: Thank we God all weldand [wielding],
   That lord that made us.

It is a wondrous thing, me thinks soothly,
They are so long tarrying, the fowls that we
Cast out in the morning.
WIFE: Sir, it may be
  They tarry till they bring.
NOAH: The raven is a-hungry
  Alway;
  He is without any reason,
  If he find any carrion,
  As peradventure may befon [befall],
   He will not away;

The dove is more gentle, her trust I unto,
Like unto the turtle, for she is ay true.
WIFE: Hence but a little. She comes, lew, lew!
  She brings in her bill some novels [signs] new;
   Behold!
  It is of an olive tree
  A branch, thinkest me.
NOAH: It is so, perde [par dieu; by our God],
   Right so is it called.

Dove, bird full blest, fair might thee befall!
Thou art true for to trust as stone in the wall;
Full well I it wist [knew] thou would come to thy hall.
WIFE: A true token is't we shall be saved all;
   For why?
  The water, since she come,
  Of deepness plumb,
  Is fallen a fathom,
   And more hardily [certainly].

FIRST SON: These floods are gone. Father, behold!
SECOND SON: There is left right none, and that be ye bold.
THIRD SON: As still as a stone, our ship is stalled.
NOAH: Upon land here anon that we were, fain I would;
    My childer dear,
  Shem, Japhet, and Ham,
  With glee and with gam [sport],
  Come we all sam [together],
    We will no longer abide here.

WIFE: Here have we been, Noah, long enough,
  With trouble and with teyn [grief], and endured much woe.
NOAH: Behold on this green neither cart nor plough
  Is left, as I ween, neither tree nor bough,
    Nor other thing,
  But all is away;
  Many castles, I say,
  Great towns of array,
    Flit [destroyed] has this flowyng [flood].

WIFE: These floods, not afright, all this world so wide
  Has moved with might, on sea and by side.
NOAH: To death are they dyght [gone], proudest of pride,
  Every wight that ever was spied,
    With sin,
  All are they slain,
  And put unto pain.
WIFE: From thence again
    May they never win.

NOAH: Win? no, I-wis, but He that might has
  Would remember their mys [misery] and admit them to
    grace;
  As He in misfortune is bliss, I pray Him in this space,
  In heaven high with His, to secure us a place,
    That we,
  With His saints in sight,
  And His angels bright,
  May come to His light:
    Amen, for charity.

William Shakespeare (1564–1616)

Hamlet, Prince of Denmark (c. 1600)

During the sixteenth century, after religious drama was forbidden, the groups that had financed and staged the cycle plays ceased their support of theatre, disapproving of the professional and commercial role that theatre had been forced to adopt in order to survive. The necessity of attracting a paying audience motivated acting companies to offer a different play each day (though the same play might be repeated at intervals during a season) and thus they created an ongoing demand for new plays. Partially for this reason, the years between 1585 and 1610 produced an exceptional number of outstanding English playwrights. William Shakespeare is universally acknowledged the greatest, and possibly the greatest playwright the world has known.

In addition to being a playwright, Shakespeare was an actor, a shareholder (part owner) both in his acting company and in the theatre in which the company performed. As the company's principal playwright, he wrote an average of two plays each season. Among his thirty-eight surviving plays, *Hamlet* is one of the most admired.

Hamlet, like *Oedipus Rex,* has as its protagonist a man who is charged with punishing the murderer of a king. But Shakespeare uses a much broader canvas than Sophocles does and includes within his drama more facets of his story, more characters, and a wider sweep of time and place. Shakespeare's play develops chronologically and places all important incidents on stage. The only important events that precede the play's opening (Claudius' seduction of his brother's wife and his murder of his brother) are replicated in the play-within-the-play. The rapid shifts in time and place are made possible by theatrical conventions that establish locale and other significant conditions through spoken passages ("spoken decor") that localize as needed the fixed facade against which the action occurred.

Hamlet is thematically rich: the pervasiveness of betrayal (brother of brother, wife of husband, parent of child, friend of friend): the opposing demands made on Hamlet (that he revenge his father's murder and that he adhere to Christian doctrine against murder): the nature of kingship and the need to rule oneself before ruling others: and several other themes. Shakespeare's dramatic poetry is generally conceded to be the finest in the English language. The basic medium is blank verse, which allows the flexibility of ordinary speech while elevating it through imagery and rhythm.

Because of its compelling story, powerful characters, and great poetry, *Hamlet* is one of the world's finest achievements in drama. Although it embodies many ideas typical of its time, it transcends the limitations of a particular era. It continues to move spectators in the theatre as it has since its first presentation around 1600.

William Shakespeare

Hamlet, Prince
of Denmark

DRAMATIS PERSONAE

CLAUDIUS, *king of Denmark*
HAMLET, *son to the former and nephew to the present king*
POLONIUS, *Lord Chamberlain*
HORATIO, *friend to Hamlet*
LAERTES, *son to Polonius*
VOLTEMAND ⎫
CORNELIUS ⎪
ROSENCRANTZ ⎬ *courtiers*
GUILDENSTERN ⎪
OSRIC ⎪
A GENTLEMAN ⎭
A PRIEST
MARCELLUS ⎫ *officers*
BERNARDO ⎭
FRANCISCO, *a soldier*
REYNALDO, *servant to Polonius*
PLAYERS
TWO CLOWNS, *grave diggers*
FORTINBRAS, *prince of Norway*
A NORWEGIAN CAPTAIN
ENGLISH AMBASSADORS
GERTRUDE, *queen of Denmark, and mother of Hamlet*
OPHELIA, *daughter to Polonius*
GHOST *of Hamlet's father*
LORDS, LADIES, OFFICERS, SOLDIERS, SAILORS, MESSENGERS,
   AND ATTENDANTS

SCENE———*Denmark.*

ACT I

SCENE I———*Elsinore. The guard-platform of the Castle.*

[FRANCISCO *at his post. Enter to him* BERNARDO.]
BERNARDO: Who's there?

FRANCISCO: Nay, answer me. Stand and unfold* yourself.
BERNARDO: Long live the king!
FRANCISCO: Bernardo?
BERNARDO: He.   5
FRANCISCO: You come most carefully upon your hour.
BERNARDO: 'Tis now struck twelve; get thee to bed, Francisco.
FRANCISCO: For this relief much thanks. 'Tis bitter cold,
    And I am sick at heart.
BERNARDO: Have you had quiet guard?   10
FRANCISCO: Not a mouse stirring.
BERNARDO: Well; good night.
    If you do meet Horatio and Marcellus,
    The rivals* of my watch, bid them make haste.
        [*Enter* HORATIO *and* MARCELLUS.]
FRANCISCO: I think I hear them. Stand, ho! Who is there?   15
HORATIO: Friends to this ground.
MARCELLUS: And liegemen to the Dane.*
FRANCISCO: Give you good night.
MARCELLUS: O, farewell, honest soldier!
    Who hath reliev'd you?   20
FRANCISCO: Bernardo hath my place.
    Give you good night.   [*Exit.*]
MARCELLUS: Holla, Bernardo!
BERNARDO: Say—
    What, is Horatio there?   25
HORATIO: A piece of him.
BERNARDO: Welcome, Horatio; welcome, good Marcellus.
HORATIO: What, has this thing appear'd again to-night?
BERNARDO: I have seen nothing.
MARCELLUS: Horatio says 'tis but our fantasy,   30
    And will not let belief take hold of him
    Touching this dreaded sight, twice seen of us;
    Therefore I have entreated him along
    With us to watch the minutes of this night,
    That, if again this apparition come,   35
    He may approve* our eyes and speak to it.
HORATIO: Tush, tush, 'twill not appear.
BERNARDO: Sit down awhile,
    And let us once again assail your ears,
    That are so fortified against our story,   40
    What we have two nights seen.

---

*indicates a note identified by line number. The textual reference is given in bold type, its clarification in roman type.
[1.i.2] **unfold** identify
[14] **rivals** companions
[17] **liegemen to the Dane** loyal subjects to the king of Denmark
[36] **approve** confirm

HORATIO: Well, sit we down,
        And let us hear Bernardo speak of this.
BERNARDO: Last night of all,
        When yond same star that's westward from the pole   45
        Had made his course t' illume that part of heaven
        Where now it burns, Marcellus and myself,
        The bell then beating one—
                [*Enter* GHOST.]
MARCELLUS: Peace, break thee off; look where it comes again.
BERNARDO: In the same figure, like the King that's dead.   50
MARCELLUS: Thou art a scholar; speak to it, Horatio.
BERNARDO: Looks 'a not like the King? Mark it, Horatio.
HORATIO: Most like. It harrows me with fear and wonder.
BERNARDO: It would be spoke to.
MARCELLUS: Question it, Horatio.   55
HORATIO: What art thou that usurp'st this time of night
        Together with that fair and warlike form
        In which the majesty of buried Denmark*
        Did sometimes march? By heaven I charge thee, speak!
MARCELLUS: It is offended.   60
BERNARDO: See, it stalks away.
HORATIO: Stay! speak, speak! I charge thee, speak!
                [*Exit* GHOST.]
MARCELLUS: 'Tis gone, and will not answer.
BERNARDO: How now, Horatio! You tremble and look pale.
        Is not this something more than fantasy?   65
        What think you on't?
HORATIO: Before my God, I might not this believe
        Without the sensible and true avouch*
        Of mine own eyes.
MARCELLUS: Is it not like the King?   70
HORATIO: As thou art to thyself:
        Such was the very armour he had on
        When he the ambitious Norway* combated;
        So frown'd he once when, in an angry parle,*
        He smote the sledded Polacks* on the ice.   75
        'Tis strange.
MARCELLUS: Thus twice before, and jump* at this dead hour,
        With martial stalk hath he gone by our watch.
HORATIO: In what particular thought to work I know not;
        But, in the gross and scope* of mine opinion,   80

---

[58] **buried Denmark** buried king of Denmark
[68] **avouch** proof
[73] **Norway** king of Norway
[74] **parle** parley
[75] **sledded Polacks** Poles on sleds
[77] **jump** just
[80] **gross and scope** general drift

This bodes some strange eruption to our state.
MARCELLUS: Good now, sit down, and tell me, he that knows,
    Why this same strict and most observant watch
    So nightly toils the subject* of the land;
    And why such daily cast of brazen cannon, 85
    And foreign mart* for implements of war;
    Why such impress* of shipwrights, whose sore task
    Does not divide the Sunday from the week;
    What might be toward,* that this sweaty haste
    Doth make the night joint-labourer with the day: 90
    Who is't that can inform me?
HORATIO: That can I;
    At least, the whisper goes so. Our last King,
    Whose image even but now appear'd to us,
    Was, as you know, by Fortinbras of Norway, 95
    Thereto prick'd on by a most emulate pride,
    Dar'd to the combat; in which our valiant Hamlet—
    For so this side of our known world esteem'd him—
    Did slay this Fortinbras; who, by a seal'd compact,
    Well ratified by law and heraldry,* 100
    Did forfeit, with his life, all those his lands
    Which he stood seiz'd of,* to the conqueror;
    Against the which a moiety competent*
    Was gaged* by our King; which had return'd
    To the inheritance of Fortinbras, 105
    Had he been vanquisher; as, by the same comart*
    And carriage of the article design'd,*
    His fell to Hamlet. Now, sir, young Fortinbras,
    Of unimproved* mettle hot and full,
    Hath in the skirts* of Norway, here and there, 110
    Shark'd up a list of lawless resolutes,*
    For food and diet, to some enterprise
    That hath a stomach in't,* which is no other,
    As it doth well appear unto our state,
    But to recover of us, by strong hand 115

[84] **nightly toils the subject** citizens work by night (as well as by day)
[86] **mart** trade
[87] **impress** forced service
[89] **toward** in preparation
[100] **law and heraldry** heraldic law
[102] **seiz'd of** in possession of
[103] **moiety competent** like portion
[104] **gaged** pledged
[106] **comart** agreement
[107] **carriage of the article design'd** provisions of the pact
[109] **unimproved** unproved
[110] **skirts** borders, outskirts
[111] **Shark'd up a list of lawless resolutes** enlisted a force of desperate men
[113] **hath a stomach in't** requires courage

And terms compulsatory, those foresaid lands
So by his father lost; and this, I take it,
Is the main motive of our preparations,
The source of this our watch, and the chief head*
Of this post-haste and romage* in the land.   120
BERNARDO: I think it be no other but e'en so.
    Well may it sort,* that this portentous figure
Comes armed through our watch; so like the King
That was and is the question of these wars.
HORATIO: A mote it is to trouble the mind's eye.   125
    In the most high and palmy state of Rome,
A little ere the mightiest Julius fell,
The graves stood tenantless, and the sheeted dead
Did squeak and gibber in the Roman streets;
As, stars with trains of fire, and dews of blood,   130
Disasters* in the sun; and the moist star*
Upon whose influence Neptune's empire* stands
Was sick almost to doomsday with eclipse;
And even the like precurse* of fear'd events,
As harbingers preceding still the fates   135
And prologue to the omen coming on,
Have heaven and earth together demonstrated
Unto our climatures* and countrymen.
      [*Reenter* GHOST.]
But, soft, behold! Lo, where it comes again!
I'll cross it,* though it blast me. Stay, illusion.   140
      [GHOST *spreads its arms.*]
If thou hast any sound or use of voice,
Speak to me.
If there be any good thing to be done,
That may to thee do ease and grace to me,
Speak to me.   145
If thou art privy to thy country's fate,
Which happily* foreknowing may avoid,
O, speak!
Or if thou hast uphoarded in thy life
Extorted treasure in the womb of earth,   150

---

119 **chief head** principal reason
120 **romage** bustling activity
122 **sort** turn out
131 **Disasters** threatening signs
131 **moist star** the moon
132 **Neptune's empire** the ocean (the Roman god Neptune's domain)
134 **precurse** foreshadowing
138 **climatures** regions
140 **cross it** cross its path
147 **happily** haply, perhaps

For which, they say, you spirits oft walk in death,
   [*The cock crows.*]
Speak of it. Stay, and speak. Stop it, Marcellus.
MARCELLUS: Shall I strike at it with my partisan?*
HORATIO: Do, if it will not stand.
BERNARDO: 'Tis here!   155
HORATIO: 'Tis here!
MARCELLUS: 'Tis gone!   [*Exit* GHOST.]
We do it wrong, being so majestical,
To offer it the show of violence;
For it is, as the air, invulnerable,   160
And our vain blows malicious mockery.
BERNARDO: It was about to speak, when the cock crew.
HORATIO: And then it started like a guilty thing
Upon a fearful summons. I have heard
The cock, that is the trumpet to the morn,   165
Doth with his lofty and shrill-sounding throat
Awake the god of day; and at his warning,
Whether in sea or fire, in earth or air,
Th' extravagant and erring* spirit hies
To his confine; and of the truth herein   170
This present object made probation.*
MARCELLUS: It faded on the crowing of the cock.
Some say that ever 'gainst* that season comes
Wherein our Saviour's birth is celebrated,
This bird of dawning singeth all night long;   175
And then, they say, no spirit dare stir abroad,
The nights are wholesome, then no planets strike,*
No fairy takes, nor witch hath power to charm,
So hallowed and so gracious is that time.
HORATIO: So have I heard, and do in part believe it.   180
But look, the morn, in russet mantle clad,
Walks o'er the dew of yon high eastward hill.
Break we our watch up; and, by my advice,
Let us impart what we have seen to-night
Unto young Hamlet; for, upon my life,   185
This spirit, dumb to us, will speak to him.
Do you consent we shall acquaint him with it,
As needful in our loves, fitting our duty?
MARCELLUS: Let's do't, I pray; and I this morning know
Where we shall find him most convenient.   190
    [*Exeunt.*]

---

[153] **partisan** pike (weapon)
[169] **extravagant and erring** wandering outside its proper realm
[171] **made probation** gives proof
[173] **ever 'gainst** just before
[177] **strike** exert evil influence

SCENE II————*Elsinore. The Castle.*

[*Flourish.* Enter* CLAUDIUS KING OF DENMARK, GERTRUDE THE
QUEEN, *and* COUNCILLORS, *including* POLONIUS, *his son* LAERTES,
VOLTEMAND, CORNELIUS, *and* HAMLET.]

KING: Though yet of Hamlet our dear brother's death
    The memory be green; and that it us befitted
    To bear our hearts in grief, and our whole kingdom
    To be contracted in one brow of woe;
    Yet so far hath discretion fought with nature   5
    That we with wisest sorrow think on him,
    Together with remembrance of ourselves.
    Therefore our sometime sister,* now our queen,
    Th' imperial jointress* to this warlike state,
    Have we, as 'twere with a defeated joy,   10
    With an auspicious and a dropping eye,
    With mirth in funeral, and with dirge in marriage,
    In equal scale weighing delight and dole,
    Taken to wife; nor have we herein barr'd
    Your better wisdoms, which have freely gone   15
    With this affair along. For all, our thanks.
    Now follows that you know: young Fortinbras,
    Holding a weak supposal of our worth,
    Or thinking by our late dear brother's death
    Our state to be disjoint and out of frame,*   20
    Co-leagued with this dream of his advantage*—
    He hath not fail'd to pester us with message
    Importing the surrender of those lands
    Lost by his father, with all bands of law,
    To our most valiant brother. So much for him.   25
    Now for ourself, and for this time of meeting,
    Thus much the business is: we have here writ
    To Norway, uncle of young Fortinbras—
    Who, impotent and bed-rid, scarcely hears
    Of this his nephew's purpose—to suppress   30
    His further gait* herein, in that the levies,
    The lists, and full proportions,* are all made
    Out of his subject;* and we here dispatch
    You, good Cornelius, and you, Voltemand,
    For bearers of this greeting to old Norway;   35

[I,ii] (stage direction) **Flourish** trumpet fanfare
[8] **our sometime sister** my former sister-in-law
[9] **jointress** joint ruler
[20] **frame** order
[21] **advantage** superior power
[31] **gait** proceeding
[32] **proportions** war supplies
[33] **Out of his subject** out of the Norwegian king's subjects

Giving to you no further personal power
To business with the King more than the scope
Of these dilated articles* allow.
Farewell; and let your haste commend your duty.

CORNELIUS: ⎱
VOLTEMAND: ⎰ In that and all things will we show our duty. 40

KING: We doubt it nothing; heartily farewell.
        [*Exeunt* VOLTEMAND *and* CORNELIUS.]
And now, Laertes, what's the news with you?
You told us of some suit; what is't, Laertes?
You cannot speak of reason to the Dane
And lose your voice.* What wouldst thou beg, Laertes, 45
That shall not be my offer, not thy asking?
The head is not more native* to the heart,
The hand more instrumental to the mouth,
Than is the throne of Denmark to thy father.
What wouldst thou have, Laertes? 50
LAERTES: My dread lord,
Your leave and favour to return to France;
From whence though willingly I came to Denmark
To show my duty in your coronation,
Yet now, I must confess, that duty done, 55
My thoughts and wishes bend again toward France,
And bow them to your gracious leave and pardon.
KING: Have you your father's leave? What says Polonius?
POLONIUS: 'A hath, my lord, wrung from me my slow leave
By laboursome petition; and at last 60
Upon his will I seal'd my hard consent.*
I do beseech you, give him leave to go.
KING: Take thy fair hour, Laertes; time be thine,
And thy best graces spend it at thy will!
But now, my cousin* Hamlet, and my son— 65
HAMLET: [*aside*] A little more than kin, and less than kind.
KING: How is it that the clouds* still hang on you?
HAMLET: Not so, my Lord; I am too much in the sun.
QUEEN: Good Hamlet, cast thy nighted colour off,
And let thine eye look like a friend on Denmark. 70
Do not for ever with thy vailed lids*
Seek for thy noble father in the dust.
Thou know'st 'tis common—all that lives must die,
Passing through nature to eternity.

---

38 **dilated articles** detailed documents
45 **lose your voice** waste your breath
47 **native** related
61 **hard consent** reluctantly gave consent
65 **cousin** kinsman
67 **clouds** grief; mourning dress
71 **vailed lids** lowered eyes

HAMLET: Ay, madam, it is common.   75
QUEEN: If it be,
    Why seems it so particular with thee?
HAMLET: Seems, madam! Nay, it is; I know not seems.
    'Tis not alone my inky cloak, good mother,
    Nor customary suits of solemn black,   80
    Nor windy suspiration* of forc'd breath,
    No, nor the fruitful river in the eye,
    Nor the dejected haviour of the visage,
    Together with all forms, moods, shapes of grief,
    That can denote me truly. These, indeed, seem;   85
    For they are actions that a man might play;
    But I have that within which passes show—
    These but the trappings and the suits of woe.
KING: 'Tis sweet and commendable in your nature, Hamlet,
    To give these mourning duties to your father;   90
    But you must know your father lost a father;
    That father lost, lost his; and the survivor bound,
    In filial obligation, for some term
    To do obsequious* sorrow. But to persever
    In obstinate condolement* is a course   95
    Of impious stubbornness; 'tis unmanly grief;
    It shows a will most incorrect to heaven,
    A heart unfortified, a mind impatient,
    An understanding simple and unschool'd;
    For what we know must be, and is as common   100
    As any the most vulgar thing to sense,
    Why should we in our peevish opposition
    Take it to heart? Fie! 'tis a fault to heaven,
    A fault against the dead, a fault to nature,
    To reason most absurd; whose common theme   105
    Is death of fathers, and who still hath cried,
    From the first corse* till he that died to-day,
    'This must be so.' We pray you throw to earth
    This unprevailing* woe, and think of us
    As of a father; for let the world take note   110
    You are the most immediate to our throne;
    And with no less nobility of love
    Than that which dearest father bears his son
    Do I impart toward you. For your intent
    In going back to school in Wittenberg,   115
    It is most retrograde* to our desire;

[81] **windy suspiration** heavy sighs
[94] **obsequious** funereal
[95] **condolement** mourning
[107] **corse** corpse
[109] **unprevailing** unavailing
[116] **retrograde** contrary

And we beseech you bend you* to remain
Here, in the cheer and comfort of our eye,
Our chiefest courtier, cousin, and our son.
QUEEN: Let not thy mother lose her prayers, Hamlet: 120
  I pray thee stay with us; go not to Wittenberg.
HAMLET: I shall in all my best obey you, madam.
KING: Why, 'tis a loving and a fair reply.
  Be as ourself in Denmark. Madam, come;
  This gentle and unforc'd accord of Hamlet   125
  Sits smiling to my heart; in grace whereof,
  No jocund health that Denmark drinks to-day
  But the great cannon to the clouds shall tell
  And the King's rouse* the heaven shall bruit* again,
  Re-speaking earthly thunder. Come away.   130
    [*Flourish. Exeunt all but* HAMLET.]
HAMLET: O, that this too too solid flesh would melt,
  Thaw, and resolve itself into a dew!
  Or that the Everlasting had not fix'd
  His canon* 'gainst self-slaughter! O God! God!
  How weary, stale, flat, and unprofitable,   135
  Seem to me all the uses of this world!
  Fie on't! Ah, fie! 'tis an unweeded garden,
  That grows to seed; things rank and gross in nature
  Possess it merely.* That it should come to this!
  But two months dead! Nay, not so much, not two.   140
  So excellent a king that was to this
  Hyperion* to a satyr, so loving to my mother,
  That he might not beteem* the winds of heaven
  Visit her face too roughly. Heaven and earth!
  Must I remember? Why, she would hang on him   145
  As if increase of appetite had grown
  By what it fed on; and yet, within a month—
  Let me not think on't. Frailty, thy name is woman!—
  A little month, or ere those shoes were old
  With which she followed my poor father's body,   150
  Like Niobe,* all tears—why she, even she—
  O God! a beast that wants discourse of reason*
  Would have mourn'd longer—married with my uncle,
  My father's brother; but no more like my father
  Than I to Hercules. Within a month,   155

[117] **bend you** agree
[129] **rouse** drinking, carousing
[129] **bruit** noisily announce
[134] **canon** law
[139] **merely** completely
[142] **Hyperion** the sun god noted for beauty
[143] **beteem** permit
[151] **Niobe** mother in Greek mythology who wept without stopping for the death of her children
[152] **wants discourse of reason** lacks reasoning power

Ere yet the salt of most unrighteous tears
Had left the flushing in her galled eyes,
She married. O, most wicked speed, to post*
With such dexterity to incestuous* sheets!
It is not, nor it cannot come to good.   160
But break, my heart, for I must hold my tongue.
          [*Enter* HORATIO, MARCELLUS, *and* BERNARDO.]
HORATIO: Hail to your lordship!
HAMLET: I am glad to see you well.
          Horatio—or I do forget myself.
HORATIO: The same, my lord, and your poor servant ever.   165
HAMLET: Sir, my good friend. I'll change* that name with you.
          And what make you from Wittenberg, Horatio?
          Marcellus?
MARCELLUS: My good lord!
HAMLET: I am very glad to see you. [*to* BERNARDO] Good even, sir.—   170
          But what, in faith, make you from Wittenberg?
HORATIO: A truant disposition, good my lord.
HAMLET: I would not hear your enemy say so;
          Nor shall you do my ear that violence,
          To make it truster* of your own report.   175
          Against yourself. I know you are no truant.
          But what is your affair in Elsinore?
          We'll teach you to drink deep ere you depart.
HORATIO: My lord, I came to see your father's funeral.
HAMLET: I prithee do not mock me, fellow-student;   180
          I think it was to see my mother's wedding.
HORATIO: Indeed, my lord, it followed hard upon.
HAMLET: Thrift, thrift, Horatio! The funeral bak'd-meats
          Did coldly furnish forth the marriage tables.
          Would I had met my dearest* foe in heaven   185
          Or ever I had seen that day, Horatio!
          My father—methinks I see my father.
HORATIO: Where, my lord?
HAMLET: In my mind's eye, Horatio.
HORATIO: I saw him once; 'a was a goodly king.   190
HAMLET: 'A* was a man, take him for all in all,
          I shall not look upon his like again.
HORATIO: My lord, I think I saw him yesternight.
HAMLET: Saw who?
HORATIO: My lord, the King your father.   195
HAMLET: The King my father!

---

158 **post** hasten
159 **incestuous** incestuous because the church considered a sister-in-law equivalent to being a sister
166 **change** exchange
175 **truster** believer
185 **dearest** most hated
191 **'A** he

HORATIO: Season your admiration* for a while
    With an attent ear, till I may deliver,
    Upon the witness of these gentlemen,
    This marvel to you. 200
HAMLET: For God's love, let me hear.
HORATIO: Two nights together had these gentlemen,
    Marcellus and Bernardo, on their watch,
    In the dead waste and middle of the night,
    Been thus encount'red. A figure like your father, 205
    Armed at point exactly, cap-a-pe,*
    Appears before them, and with solemn march
    Goes slow and stately by them; thrice he walk'd
    By their oppress'd and fear-surprised eyes,
    Within his truncheon's length,* whilst they, distill'd* 210
    Almost to jelly with the act of fear,
    Stand dumb and speak not to him. This to me
    In dreadful* secrecy impart they did;
    And I with them the third night kept the watch;
    Where, as they had delivered, both in time, 215
    Form of the thing, each word made true and good,
    The apparition comes. I knew your father;
    These hands are not more like.
HAMLET: But where was this?
MARCELLUS: My lord, upon the platform where we watch. 220
HAMLET: Did you not speak to it?
HORATIO: My lord, I did;
    But answer made it none; yet once methought
    It lifted up its head and did address
    Itself to motion, like as it would speak; 225
    But even then the morning cock crew loud,
    And at the sound it shrunk in haste away
    And vanish'd from our sight.
HAMLET: 'Tis very strange.
HORATIO: As I do live, my honour'd lord, 'tis true; 230
    And we did think it writ down in our duty
    To let you know of it.
HAMLET: Indeed, indeed, sirs, but this troubles me.
    Hold you the watch to-night?
ALL: We do, my lord. 235
HAMLET: Arm'd, say you?
ALL: Arm'd, my lord.
HAMLET: From top to toe?
ALL: My lord, from head to foot.

---

[197] **Season your admiration** control your wonder
[206] **cap-a-pe** head to foot
[210] **truncheon's length** space of a short club
[210] **distill'd** reduced
[213] **dreadful** terrified

HAMLET: Then saw you not his face?   240
HORATIO: O yes, my lord; he wore his beaver* up.
HAMLET: What, look'd he frowningly?
HORATIO: A countenance more in sorrow than in anger.
HAMLET: Pale or red?
HORATIO: Nay, very pale.   245
HAMLET: And fix'd his eyes upon you?
HORATIO: Most constantly.
HAMLET: I would I had been there.
HORATIO: It would have much amaz'd you.
HAMLET: Very like, very like. Stay'd it long?
HORATIO: While one with moderate haste might tell* a hundred.   250
BOTH: Longer, longer.
HORATIO: Not when I saw't.
HAMLET: His beard was grizzl'd*—no?
HORATIO: It was, as I have seen it in his life,
          A sable silver'd.*   255
HAMLET: I will watch to-night;
          Perchance 'twill walk again.
HORATIO: I warr'nt it will.
HAMLET: If it assume my noble father's person.   260
          I'll speak to it, though hell itself should gape
          And bid me hold my peace, I pray you all,
          If you have hitherto conceal'd this sight,
          Let it be tenable* in your silence still;
          And whatsoever else shall hap to-night,   265
          Give it an understanding, but no tongue;
          I will requite your loves. So, fare you well—
          Upon the platform, 'twixt eleven and twelve,
          I'll visit you.
ALL: Our duty to your honour.   270
HAMLET: Your loves, as mine to you; farewell.
                  [*Exeunt all but* HAMLET.]
          My father's spirit in arms! All is not well.
          I doubt* some foul play. Would the night were come!
          Till then sit still, my soul. Foul deeds will rise,
          Though all the earth o'erwhelm them, to men's eyes.   [*Exit.*] 275

          SCENE III————*Elsinore. The house of* POLONIUS.

          [*Enter* LAERTES *and* OPHELIA *his sister.*]
LAERTES: My necessaries are embark'd. Farewell.
          And, sister, as the winds give benefit

241 **beaver** visor, face guard
251 **tell** count
253 **grizzl'd** gray
255 **sable silver'd** black mixed with gray
264 **tenable** held
273 **doubt** suspect

And convoy* is assistant, do not sleep,
But let me hear from you.
OPHELIA: Do you doubt that? 5
LAERTES: For Hamlet, and the trifling of his favour,
    Hold it a fashion and a toy* in blood,
    A violet in the youth of primy* nature,
    Forward* not permanent, sweet not lasting,
    The perfume and suppliance* of a minute; 10
    No more.
OPHELIA: No more but so?
LAERTES: Think it no more;
    For nature crescent* does not grow alone
    In thews* and bulk, but as this temple* waxes, 15
    The inward service of the mind and soul
    Grows wide withal. Perhaps he loves you now,
    And now no soil nor cautel* doth besmirch
    The virtue of his will; but you must fear,
    His greatness weigh'd,* his will is not his own; 20
    For he himself is subject to his birth:
    He may not, as unvalued* persons do,
    Carve for himself; for on his choice depends
    The sanity and health of this whole state;
    And therefore must his choice be circumscrib'd 25
    Unto the voice and yielding of that body
    Whereof he is the head. Then if he says he loves you,
    It fits your wisdom so far to believe it
    As he in his particular act and place
    May give his saying deed; which is no further 30
    Than the main voice of Denmark goes withal.
    Then weigh what loss your honour may sustain,
    If with too credent* ear you list his songs,
    Or lose your heart, or your chaste treasure open
    To his unmast'red importunity. 35
    Fear it, Ophelia, fear it, my dear sister;
    And keep you in the rear of your affection,
    Out of the shot and danger of desire.
    The chariest maid is prodigal enough

I,iii,3 **convoy** conveyance
[7] **toy** idle fancy
[8] **primy** youthful, springlike
[9] **Forward** premature
[10] **suppliance** diversion
[14] **crescent** increasing
[15] **thews** sinews
[15] **temple** the body
[18] **cautel** deceit
[20] **greatness weigh'd** high rank considered
[22] **unvalued** of low rank
[33] **credent** credulous

If she unmask her beauty to the moon.   40
Virtue itself scapes not calumnious strokes;
The canker* galls the infants of the spring
Too oft before their buttons* be disclos'd;
And in the morn and liquid dew of youth
Contagious blastments are most imminent.   45
Be wary, then; best safety lies in fear:
Youth to itself rebels, though none else near.
OPHELIA: I shall the effect of this good lesson keep
As watchman to my heart. But, good my brother,
Do not, as some ungracious* pastors do,   50
Show me the steep and thorny way to heaven,
Whiles, like a puff'd and reckless libertine,
Himself the primrose path of dalliance treads
And recks not his own rede.*
LAERTES: O, fear me not!   55
          [*Enter* POLONIUS.]
I stay too long. But here my father comes.
A double blessing is a double grace;
Occasion smiles upon a second leave.
POLONIUS: Yet here, Laertes! Aboard, aboard, for shame!
The wind sits in the shoulder of your sail,   60
And you are stay'd for. There—my blessing with thee!
And these few precepts in thy memory
Look thou character.* Give thy thoughts no tongue,
Nor any unproportion'd* thought his act.
Be thou familiar, but by no means vulgar.   65
Those friends thou hast, and their adoption tried,
Grapple them to thy soul with hoops of steel;
But do not dull thy palm with entertainment
Of each new-hatch'd, unfledg'd comrade. Beware
Of entrance to a quarrel; but, being in,   70
Bear't that th' opposed may beware of thee.
Give every man thy ear, but few thy voice;
Take each man's censure, but reserve thy judgment.
Costly thy habit as thy purse can buy,
But not express'd in fancy; rich, not gaudy;   75
For the apparel oft proclaims the man;
And they in France of the best rank and station
Are of a most select and generous choice in that.
Neither a borrower nor a lender be;

---

[42] **canker** worm
[43] **buttons** buds
[50] **ungracious** without themselves being in God's grace
[54] **recks not his own rede** doesn't heed his own advice
[63] **character** inscribe
[64] **unproportion'd** unconsidered

For loan oft loses both itself and friend,   80
And borrowing dulls the edge of husbandry.*
This above all—to thine own self be true,
And it must follow, as the night the day,
Thou canst not then be false to any man.
Farewell; my blessing season* this in thee!   85
LAERTES: Most humbly do I take my leave, my lord.
POLONIUS: The time invites you; go, your servants tend.*
LAERTES: Farewell, Ophelia; and remember well
    What I have said to you.
OPHELIA: 'Tis in my memory lock'd,   90
    And you yourself shall keep the key of it.
LAERTES: Farewell.
POLONIUS: What is't, Ophelia, he hath said to you?
OPHELIA: So please you, something touching the Lord Hamlet.
POLONIUS: Marry,* well bethought!   95
    'Tis told me he hath very oft of late
    Given private time to you; and you yourself
    Have of your audience been most free and bounteous.
    If it be so—as so 'tis put on me,
    And that in way of caution—I must tell you   100
    You do not understand yourself so clearly
    As it behooves my daughter and your honour.
    What is between you? Give me up the truth.
OPHELIA: He hath, my lord, of late made many tenders
    Of his affection to me.   105
POLONIUS: Affection! Pooh! You speak like a green girl,
    Unsifted* in such perilous circumstance.
    Do you believe his tenders, as you call them?
OPHELIA: I do not know, my lord, what I should think.
POLONIUS: Marry, I will teach you: think yourself a baby   110
    That you have ta'en these tenders for true pay
    Which are not sterling. Tender yourself more dearly;
    Or—not to crack the wind of the poor phrase,
    Running it thus—you'll tender me a fool.*
OPHELIA: My lord, he hath importun'd me with love   115
    In honourable fashion.
POLONIUS: Ay, fashion you may call it; go to, go to.
OPHELIA: And hath given countenance to his speech, my lord,
    With almost all the holy vows of heaven.

---

⁸¹ **husbandry** thrift
⁸⁵ **season** make fruitful
⁸⁷ **tend** await
⁹⁵ **Marry** By the Virgin Mary
¹⁰⁷ **Unsifted** untried
¹¹⁴ **tender me a fool** present me with a baby

POLONIUS: Ay, springes to catch woodcocks!* I do know,   120
    When the blood burns, how prodigal the soul
    Lends the tongue vows. These blazes, daughter,
    Giving more light than heat—extinct in both,
    Even in their promise, as it is a-making—
    You must not take for fire. From this time   125
    Be something scanter of your maiden presence;
    Set your entreatments* at a higher rate
    Than a command to parle. For Lord Hamlet,
    Believe so much in him, that he is young,
    And with a larger tether may he walk   130
    Than may be given you. In few, Ophelia,
    Do not believe his vows; for they are brokers,*
    Not of that dye* which their investments* show,
    But mere implorators* of unholy suits,
    Breathing like sanctified and pious bonds,*   135
    The better to beguile. This is for all—
    I would not, in plain terms, from this time forth
    Have you so slander* any moment leisure
    As to give words or walk with the Lord Hamlet.
    Look to't, I charge you. Come your ways.   140
OPHELIA: I shall obey, my lord.   *[Exeunt.]*

SCENE IV————*Elsinore. The guard-platform of the Castle.*

[*Enter* HAMLET, HORATIO, *and* MARCELLUS.]
HAMLET: The air bites shrewdly;* it is very cold.
HORATIO: It is a nipping and an eager* air.
HAMLET: What hour now?
HORATIO: I think it lacks of twelve.
MARCELLUS: No, it is struck.   5
HORATIO: Indeed? I heard it not. It then draws near the season
    Wherein the spirit held his wont to walk.
        [*A flourish of trumpets, and two pieces go off.*]
    What does this mean, my lord?
HAMLET: The King doth wake* to-night and takes his rouse,*
    Keeps wassail, and the swagg'ring up-spring* reels,   10

120 **springes to catch woodcocks** snares to catch unwary birds
127 **entreatments** conversations
132 **brokers** procurers
133 **dye** kind
133 **investments** outer garments
134 **implorators** solicitors
135 **bonds** pledges
138 **slander** disgrace
I,iv,1 **shrewdly** bitterly
2 **eager** sharp
9 **wake** revel
9 **rouse** carouses
10 **up-spring** dance

And, as he drains his draughts of Rhenish* down,
The kettledrum and trumpet thus bray out
The triumph of his pledge.*
HORATIO: Is it a custom?
HAMLET: Ay, marry, is't;   15
But to my mind, though I am native here
And to the manner born, it is a custom
More honour'd in the breach than the observance.
This heavy-headed revel east and west
Makes us traduc'd and tax'd of* other nations;   20
They clepe* us drunkards, and with swinish phrase
Soil our addition,* and, indeed, it takes
From our achievements, though perform'd at height,
The pith and marrow of our attribute.*
So, oft it chances in particular men   25
That, for some vicious mole* of nature in them,
As in their birth, wherein they are not guilty,
Since nature cannot choose his origin;
By the o'ergrowth of some complexion,*
Oft breaking down the pales* and forts of reason;   30
Or by some habit that too much o'er-leavens*
The form of plausive* manners—that these men,
Carrying, I say, the stamp of one defect,
Being nature's livery or fortune's star,*
His virtues else, be they as pure as grace,   35
As infinite as man may undergo,
Shall in the general censure* take corruption
From that particular fault. The dram of eale
Doth all the noble substance of a doubt
To his own scandal.   40
          [*Enter* GHOST.]
HORATIO: Look, my lord, it comes.
HAMLET: Angels and ministers of grace defend us!
Be thou a spirit of health* or goblin damn'd,
Bring with thee airs from heaven or blasts from hell,

---

[11] **Rhenish** Rhine wine
[13] **The triumph of his pledge** drinking a glass of wine in one draught
[20] **tax'd of** accused by
[21] **clepe** call
[22] **addition** honor
[24] **attribute** reputation
[26] **mole** blemish
[29] **complexion** natural disposition
[30] **pales** walls
[31] **o'er-leavens** overdoes, corrupts
[32] **plausive** pleasing
[34] **nature's livery or fortune's star** determined by nature or by the stars
[37] **general censure** popular judgment
[43] **spirit of health** good spirit

Be thy intents wicked or charitable,   45
Thou com'st in such a questionable* shape
That I will speak to thee. I'll call thee Hamlet,
King, father, royal Dane. O, answer me!
Let me not burst in ignorance, but tell
Why thy canoniz'd* bones, hearsed in death,   50
Have burst their cerements;* why the sepulchre
Wherein we saw thee quietly enurn'd
Have op'd his ponderous and marble jaws
To cast thee up again. What may this mean
That thou, dead corse, again in complete steel   55
Revisits thus the glimpses of the moon,
Making night hideous, and we fools of nature
So horridly to shake our disposition*
With thoughts beyond the reaches of our souls?
Say, why is this? wherefore? What should we do?   60
              [GHOST *beckons* HAMLET.]
HORATIO: It beckons you to go away with it,
       As if some impartment* did desire
       To you alone.
MARCELLUS: Look with what courteous action
       It waves you to a more removed ground.   65
       But do not go with it.
HORATIO: No, by no means.
HAMLET: It will not speak; then I will follow it.
HORATIO: Do not, my lord.
HAMLET: Why, what should be the fear?   70
       I do not set my life at a pin's fee;
       And for my soul, what can it do to that,
       Being a thing immortal as itself?
       It waves me forth again; I'll follow it.
HORATIO: What if it tempt you toward the flood, my lord,   75
       Or to the dreadful summit of the cliff
       That beetles* o'er his base into the sea,
       And there assume some other horrible form,
       Which might deprive your sovereignty of reason
       And draw you into madness? Think of it: 80
       The very place puts toys* of desperation,
       Without more motive, into every brain
       That looks so many fathoms to the sea

---

⁴⁶ **questionable** of dubious identity
⁵⁰ **canoniz'd** buried according to church rules
⁵¹ **cerements** burial garments
⁵⁸ **shake our disposition** unsettle our minds
⁶² **impartment** message to impart
⁷⁷ **beetles** juts out
⁸¹ **toys** notions

And hears it roar beneath.
HAMLET: It waves me still. 85
    Go on; I'll follow thee.
MARCELLUS: You shall not go, my lord.
HAMLET: Hold off your hands.
HORATIO: Be rul'd; you shall not go.
HAMLET: My fate cries out, 90
    And makes each petty arture* in this body
    As hardy as the Nemean lion's nerve.*   [GHOST *beckons.*]
    Still am I call'd. Unhand me, gentlemen.
    By heaven, I'll make a ghost of him that lets* me.
    I say, away! Go on; I'll follow thee. 95
    [*Exeunt* GHOST *and* HAMLET.]
HORATIO: He waxes desperate with imagination.
MARCELLUS: Let's follow; 'tis not fit thus to obey him.
HORATIO: Have after. To what issue will this come?
MARCELLUS: Something is rotten in the state of Denmark.
HORATIO: Heaven will direct it. 100
MARCELLUS: Nay, let's follow him.   [*Exeunt.*]

      SCENE V————*Elsinore. The battlements of the Castle.*

    [*Enter* GHOST *and* HAMLET.]
HAMLET: Whither wilt thou lead me? Speak. I'll go no further.
GHOST: Mark me.
HAMLET: I will.
GHOST: My hour is almost come,
    When I to sulph'rous and tormenting flames 5
    Must render up myself.
HAMLET: Alas, poor ghost!
GHOST: Pity me not, but lend thy serious hearing
    To what I shall unfold.
HAMLET: Speak; I am bound to hear. 10
GHOST: So art thou to revenge, when thou shalt hear.
HAMLET: What?
GHOST: I am thy father's spirit,
    Doom'd for a certain term to walk the night,
    And for the day confin'd to fast in fires, 15
    Till the foul crimes done in my days of nature
    Are burnt and purg'd away. But that I am forbid
    To tell the secrets of my prison-house,
    I could a tale unfold whose lightest word
    Would harrow up thy soul, freeze thy young blood, 20
    Make thy two eyes, like stars, start from their spheres,

---

[91] **arture** artery
[92] **Nemean lion's nerve** sinews of the mythical lion slain by Heracles
[94] **lets** hinders

Thy knotted and combined locks to part,
And each particular hair to stand an end,
Like quills upon the fretful porpentine.*
But this eternal blazon* must not be   25
To ears of flesh and blood. List, list, O, list!
If thou didst ever thy dear father love—
HAMLET: O God!
GHOST: Revenge his foul and most unnatural murder.
HAMLET: Murder!   30
GHOST: Murder most foul, as in the best it is;
    But this most foul, strange, and unnatural.
HAMLET: Haste me to know't, that I, with wings as swift
    As meditation or the thoughts of love,
    May sweep to my revenge.   35
GHOST: I find thee apt;
    And duller shouldst thou be than the fat weed
    That roots itself in ease on Lethe wharf,*
    Wouldst thou not stir in this. Now, Hamlet, hear:
    'Tis given out that, sleeping in my orchard,   40
    A serpent stung me; so the whole ear of Denmark
    Is by a forged process* of my death
    Rankly abus'd; but know, thou noble youth,
    The serpent that did sting thy father's life
    Now wears his crown.   45
HAMLET: O my prophetic soul!
    My uncle!
GHOST: Ay, that incestuous, that adulterate* beast,
    With witchcraft of his wits, with traitorous gifts—
    O wicked wit and gifts that have the power   50
    So to seduce—won to his shameful lust
    The will of my most seeming virtuous queen.
    O Hamlet, what a falling off was there,
    From me, whose love was of that dignity
    That it went hand in hand even with the vow   55
    I made to her in marriage; and to decline
    Upon a wretch whose natural gifts were poor
    To those of mine!
    But virtue, as it never will be moved,
    Though lewdness court it in a shape of heaven,   60
    So lust, though to a radiant angel link'd,
    Will sate itself in a celestial bed
    And prey on garbage.
    But soft! methinks I scent the morning air.

---

[24] **fretful porpentine** fearful porcupine
[25] **eternal blazon** revelation about eternity
[38] **Lethe wharf** bank of the river of forgetfulness in Hades
[42] **forged process** false account
[48] **adulterate** adulterous

Brief let me be. Sleeping within my orchard,   65
My custom always of the afternoon,
Upon my secure* hour thy uncle stole,
With juice of cursed hebona* in a vial,
And in the porches of my ears did pour
The leperous distilment; whose effect   70
Holds such an enmity with blood of man
That swift as quicksilver it courses through
The natural gates and alleys of the body;
And with a sudden vigour it doth posset*   .
And curd, like eager* droppings into milk,   75
The thin and wholesome blood. So did it mine;
And a most instant tetter* bark'd about,
Most lazar-like,* with vile and loathsome crust,
All my smooth body.
Thus was I, sleeping, by a brother's hand   80
Of life, of crown, of queen, at once dispatch'd;
Cut off even in the blossoms of my sin,
Unhous'led, disappointed, unanel'd;*
No reck'ning made, but sent to my account
With all my imperfections on my head.   85
O, horrible! O, horrible! most horrible!
If thou hast nature in thee, bear it not;
Let not the royal bed of Denmark be
A couch for luxury* and damned incest.
But howsoever thou pursuest this act,   90
Taint not thy mind, nor let thy soul contrive
Against thy mother aught; leave her to heaven,
And to those thorns that in her bosom lodge
To prick and sting her. Fare thee well at once.
The glowworm shows the matin* to be near,   95
And gins to pale his uneffectual fire.
Adieu, adieu, adieu! Remember me.   [*Exit.*]
HAMLET: O all you host of heaven! O earth! What else?
And shall I couple hell? O, fie! Hold, hold, my heart;
And you, my sinews, grow not instant old,   100
But bear me stiffly up. Remember thee!
Ay, thou poor ghost, whiles memory holds a seat

---

⁶⁷ **secure** unsuspecting
⁶⁸ **hebona** poisonous plant
⁷⁴ **posset** curdle
⁷⁵ **eager** acid
⁷⁷ **tetter** inflammation of the skin
⁷⁸ **lazar-like** leperlike
⁸³ **Unhous'led, disappointed, unanel'd** without the sacrament of communion, unabsolved of sin, without extreme unction
⁸⁹ **luxury** lust
⁹⁵ **matin** morning

In this distracted globe.* Remember thee!
Yea, from the table* of my memory
I'll wipe away all trivial fond* records,   105
All saws* of books, all forms, all pressures* past,
That youth and observation copied there,
And thy commandment all alone shall live
Within the book and volume of my brain,
Unmix'd with baser matter. Yes, by heaven!   110
O most pernicious woman!
O villain, villain, smiling, damned villain!
My tables—meet it is I set it down
That one may smile, and smile, and be a villain;
At least I am sure it may be so in Denmark. [*writing*]   115
So, uncle, there you are. Now to my word:
It is 'Adieu, adieu! Remember me.'
I have sworn't.
HORATIO: [*within*] My lord, my lord!
            [*Enter* HORATIO *and* MARCELLUS.]
MARCELLUS: Lord Hamlet!   120
HORATIO: Heavens secure him!
HAMLET: So be it!
MARCELLUS: Illo, ho, ho,* my lord!
HAMLET: Hillo, ho, ho, boy! Come, bird, come.
MARCELLUS: How is't, my noble lord?   125
HORATIO: What news, my lord?
HAMLET: O, wonderful!
HORATIO: Good my lord, tell it.
HAMLET: No; you will reveal it.
HORATIO: Not I, my lord, by heaven!   130
MARCELLUS: Nor I, my lord.
HAMLET: How say you, then; would heart of man once think it?
    But you'll be secret?
BOTH: Ay, by heaven, my lord!
HAMLET: There's never a villain dwelling in all Denmark   135
    But he's an arrant knave.
HORATIO: There needs no ghost, my lord, come from the grave
    To tell us this.
HAMLET: Why, right; you are in the right;
    And so, without more circumstance* at all,   140
    I hold it fit that we shake hands and part;
    You, as your business and desire shall point you—

---

[103] **globe** head
[104] **table** tablet
[105] **fond** foolish
[106] **saws** maxims
[106] **pressures** impressions
[123] **Illo, ho, ho** falconer's call to his hawk
[140] **circumstance** details

For every man hath business and desire,
Such as it is; and for my own poor part,
Look you, I will go pray. 145
HORATIO: These are but wild and whirling words, my lord.
HAMLET: I am sorry they offend you, heartily;
Yes, faith, heartily.
HORATIO: There's no offence, my lord.
HAMLET: Yes, by Saint Patrick, but there is, Horatio, 150
And much offence, too. Touching this vision here—
It is an honest ghost,* that let me tell you.
For your desire to know what is between us,
O'ermaster't as you may. And now, good friends,
As you are friends, scholars, and soldiers, 155
Give me one poor request.
HORATIO: What is't, my lord? We will.
HAMLET: Never make known what you have seen to-night.
BOTH: My lord, we will not.
HAMLET: Nay, but swear't. 160
HORATIO: In faith,
My lord, not I.
MARCELLUS: Nor I, my lord, in faith.
HAMLET: Upon my sword.
MARCELLUS: We have sworn, my lord, already. 165
HAMLET: Indeed, upon my sword, indeed.
GHOST: [*cries under the stage*] Swear.
HAMLET: Ha, ha, boy! say'st thou so? Art thou there, true-penny?*
Come on. You hear this fellow in the cellarage:
Consent to swear. 170
HORATIO: Propose the oath, my lord.
HAMLET: Never to speak of this that you have seen,
Swear by my sword.
GHOST: [*beneath*] Swear.
HAMLET: Hic et ubique?* Then we'll shift our ground. 175
Come hither, gentlemen,
And lay your hands again upon my sword.
Swear by my sword
Never to speak of this that you have heard.
GHOST: [*beneath*] Swear, by his sword. 180
HAMLET: Well said, old mole! Canst work i' th' earth so fast?
A worthy pioneer!* Once more remove, good friends.
HORATIO: O day and night, but this is wondrous strange!
HAMLET: And therefore as a stranger give it welcome.
There are more things in heaven and earth, Horatio, 185
Than are dreamt of in your philosophy.

[152] **honest ghost** true ghost of his father rather than a demon
[168] **true-penny** honest fellow
[175] **Hic et ubique** here and everywhere
[182] **pioneer** miner

But come.
Here, as before, never, so help you mercy,
How strange or odd soe'er I bear myself—
As I perchance hereafter shall think meet   190
To put an antic disposition* on—
That you, at such times, seeing me, never shall,
With arms encumb'red* thus, or this head-shake,
Or by pronouncing of some doubtful phrase,
As 'Well, well, we know' or 'We could, an if we would'   195
Or, 'If we list to speak' or 'There be, an if they might'
Or such ambiguous giving out, to note
That you know aught of me—this do swear,
So grace and mercy at your most need help you.
GHOST: [*beneath*] Swear.   200
HAMLET: Rest, rest, perturbed spirit! So, gentlemen,
    With all my love I do commend me* to you;
    And what so poor a man as Hamlet is
    May do t'express his love and friending to you,
    God willing, shall not lack. Let us go in together;   205
    And still your fingers on your lips, I pray.
    The time is out of joint. O cursed spite,
    That ever I was born to set it right!
    Nay, come, let's go together.   [*Exeunt.*]

ACT II

SCENE I———*Elsinore. The house of* POLONIUS.

[*Enter* POLONIUS *and* REYNALDO.]
POLONIUS: Give him this money and these notes, Reynaldo.
REYNALDO: I will, my lord.
POLONIUS: You shall do marvellous wisely, good Reynaldo,
    Before you visit him, to make inquire
    Of his behaviour.   5
REYNALDO: My lord, I did intend it.
POLONIUS: Marry, well said; very well said. Look you, sir,
    Enquire me first what Danskers* are in Paris;
    And how, and who, what means, and where they keep,*
    What company, at what expense; and finding   10
    By this encompassment and drift of question
    That they do know my son, come you more nearer
    Than your particular demands will touch it.
    Take you, as 'twere, some distant knowledge of him;

---

¹⁹¹ **antic disposition** strange behavior
¹⁹³ **encumb'red** folded
²⁰² **commend me** entrust myself
^{II,i,8} **Danskers** Danes
⁹ **keep** dwell

As thus: 'I know his father and his friends, 15
And in part him.' Do you mark this, Reynaldo?
REYNALDO: Ay, very well, my lord.
POLONIUS: 'And in part him—but' you may say 'not well;
But if't be he I mean, he's very wild;
Addicted so and so'; and there put on him 20
What forgeries you please; marry, none so rank
As may dishonour him; take heed of that;
But, sir, such wanton, wild, and usual slips
As are companions noted and most known
To youth and liberty. 25
REYNALDO: As gaming, my lord.
POLONIUS: Ay, or drinking, fencing, swearing, quarrelling.
Drabbing*—you may go so far.
REYNALDO: My lord, that would dishonour him.
POLONIUS: Faith, no; as you may season it in the charge. 30
You must not put another scandal on him,
That he is open to incontinency;
That's not my meaning. But breathe his faults so quaintly*
That they may seem the taints of liberty;
The flash and outbreak of a fiery mind, 35
A savageness in unreclaimed blood,
Of general assault.*
REYNALDO: But, my good lord—
POLONIUS: Wherefore should you do this?
REYNALDO: Ay, my lord, 40
I would know that.
POLONIUS: Marry, sir, here's my drift,
And I believe it is a fetch of warrant:*
You laying these slight sullies on my son,
As 'twere a thing a little soil'd wi' th' working, 45
Mark you,
Your party in converse, him you would sound,
Having ever seen in the prenominate crimes*
The youth you breathe of guilty, be assur'd
He closes with you in this consequence—* 50
'Good sir' or so, or 'friend' or 'gentleman'
According to the phrase or the addition*
Of man and country.
REYNALDO: Very good, my lord.

---

28 **Drabbing** womanizing
33 **quaintly** ingeniously
37 **Of general assault** common to all men
43 **fetch of warrant** justifiable device
48 **Having ... crimes** if he has ever seen the aforementioned crimes
50 **He closes ... this consequence** agrees with you
52 **addition** title

POLONIUS: And then, sir, does 'a* this—'a does—What was   55
    I about to say? By the mass, I was about to say something;
    Where did I leave?
REYNALDO: At 'closes in the consequence,' at 'friend or so' and 'gentleman.'
POLONIUS: At 'closes in the consequence'—ay, marry,
    He closes thus: 'I know the gentleman;   60
    I saw him yesterday, or t'other day,
    Or then, or then; with such, or such; and, as you say,
    There was 'a gaming; there o'ertook in's rouse;
    There falling out at tennis'; or perchance
    'I saw him enter such a house of sale,'   65
    Videlicet,* a brothel, or so forth. See you now
    Your bait of falsehood take this carp of truth;
    And thus do we of wisdom and of reach,
    With windlasses and with assays of bias,*
    By indirections find directions out;   70
    So, by my former lecture and advice,
    Shall you my son. You have me, have you not?
REYNALDO: My lord, I have.
POLONIUS: God buy ye; fare ye well.
REYNALDO: Good my lord!   75
POLONIUS: Observe his inclination in yourself.*
REYNALDO: I shall, my lord.
POLONIUS: And let him ply his music.
REYNALDO: Well, my lord.
POLONIUS: Farewell!   [*Exit* REYNALDO.] 80
      [*Enter* OPHELIA.]
    How now, Ophelia! What's the matter?
OPHELIA: O my lord, my lord, I have been so affrighted!
POLONIUS: With what, i' th' name of God?
OPHELIA: My lord, as I was sewing in my closet,*
    Lord Hamlet, with his doublet all unbrac'd,*   85
    No hat upon his head, his stockings fouled,
    Ungart'red and down-gyved* to his ankle;
    Pale as his shirt, his knees knocking each other,
    And with a look so piteous in purport
    As if he had been loosed out of hell   90
    To speak of horrors—he comes before me.
POLONIUS: Mad for thy love?
OPHELIA: My lord, I do not know,
    But truly I do fear it.

---

[55] **'a** he
[66] **Videlicet** namely
[69] **windlasses . . . bias** indirect means
[76] **in yourself** for yourself
[84] **closet** private room
[85] **doublet all unbrac'd** jacket entirely unlaced/open
[87] **down-gyved** hanging down

POLONIUS: What said he? 95
OPHELIA: He took me by the wrist, and held me hard;
    Then goes he to the length of all his arm,
    And, with his other hand thus o'er his brow,
    He falls to such a perusal of my face
    As 'a would draw it. Long stay'd he so. 100
    At last, a little shaking of mine arm,
    And thrice his head thus waving up and down,
    He rais'd a sigh so piteous and profound
    As it did seem to shatter all his bulk
    And end his being. That done, he lets me go, 105
    And, with his head over his shoulder turn'd,
    He seem'd to find his way without his eyes;
    For out adoors he went without their help
    And to the last bended their light on me.
POLONIUS: Come, go with me. I will go seek the King. 110
    This is the very ecstasy* of love,
    Whose violent property fordoes* itself,
    And leads the will to desperate undertakings
    As oft as any passion under heaven
    That does afflict our natures. I am sorry— 115
    What, have you given him any hard words of late?
OPHELIA: No, my good lord; but, as you did command,
    I did repel his letters, and denied
    His access to me.
POLONIUS: That hath made him mad. 120
    I am sorry that with better heed and judgment
    I had not quoted* him. I fear'd he did but trifle,
    And meant to wreck thee; but beshrew my jealousy!*
    By heaven, it is as proper to our age
    To cast beyond ourselves in our opinions 125
    As it is common for the younger sort
    To lack discretion. Come, go we to the King.
    This must be known; which, being kept close, might move
    More grief to hide than hate to utter love.*
    Come. [*Exeunt.*] 130

SCENE II————*Elsinore. The Castle.*

[*Flourish. Enter* KING, QUEEN, ROSENCRANTZ, GUILDENSTERN, *and attendants.*]
KING: Welcome, dear Rosencrantz and Guildenstern!
    Moreover that we much did long to see you,

---

[111] **ecstasy** madness
[112] **property fordoes** quality destroys
[122] **quoted** noted
[123] **beshrew my jealousy** curse on my suspicions
[127–29] **Come, go ... utter love** telling the king may anger him, but not telling him might anger him more

The need we have to use you did provoke
Our hasty sending. Something have you heard
Of Hamlet's transformation; so I call it,   5
Sith* nor th' exterior nor the inward man
Resembles that it was. What it should be,
More than his father's death, that thus hath put him
So much from th' understanding of himself,
I cannot deem of. I entreat you both   10
That, being of so* young days brought up with him,
And sith so neighboured to his youth and haviour,
That you vouchsafe your rest* here in our court
Some little time; so by your companies
To draw him on to pleasures, and to gather,   15
So much as from occasion you may glean,
Whether aught to us unknown afflicts him thus
That, open'd,* lies within our remedy.
QUEEN: Good gentlemen, he hath much talk'd of you;
    And sure I am two men there is not living   20
    To whom he more adheres. If it will please you
    To show us so much gentry* and good will
    As to expend your time with us awhile
    For the supply and profit of our hope,
    Your visitation shall receive such thanks   25
    As fits a king's remembrance.
ROSENCRANTZ: Both your Majesties
    Might, by the sovereign power you have of us,
    Put your dread pleasures more into command
    Than to entreaty.   30
GUILDENSTERN: But we both obey,
    And here give up ourselves, in the full bent,*
    To lay our service freely at your feet,
    To be commanded.
KING: Thanks, Rosencrantz and gentle Guildenstern.   35
QUEEN: Thanks, Guildenstern and gentle Rosencrantz.
    And I beseech you instantly to visit
    My too much changed son. Go, some of you,
    And bring these gentlemen where Hamlet is.
GUILDENSTERN: Heavens make our presence and our practices   40
    Pleasant and helpful to him!
QUEEN: Aye amen! [*Exeunt* ROSENCRANTZ, GUILDENSTERN, *and some attendants.*]
    [*Enter* POLONIUS.]

II,i,6 **Sith** since
11 **of so** from such
13 **vouchsafe your rest** consent to remain
18 **open'd** revealed
22 **gentry** courtesy
32 **in the full bent** entirely

POLONIUS: Th' ambassadors from Norway, my good lord,
    Are joyfully return'd.
KING: Thou still hast been the father of good news.   45
POLONIUS: Have I, my lord? I assure you, my good liege,
    I hold my duty, as I hold my soul,
    Both to my God and to my gracious King;
    And I do think—or else this brain of mine
    Hunts not the trail of policy so sure   50
    As it hath us'd to do—that I have found
    The very cause of Hamlet's lunacy.
KING: O, speak of that; that do I long to hear.
POLONIUS: Give first admittance to th' ambassadors;
    My news shall be the fruit to that great feast.   55
KING: Thyself do grace to them, and bring them in.
        [*Exit* POLONIUS.]
    He tells me, my dear Gertrude, he hath found
    The head and source of all your son's distemper.
QUEEN: I doubt it is no other but the main,
    His father's death and our o'erhasty marriage.   60
KING: Well, we shall sift him.
        [*Reenter* POLONIUS, *with* VOLTEMAND *and* CORNELIUS.]
    Welcome, my good friends!
    Say, Voltemand, what from our brother Norway?
VOLTEMAND: Most fair return of greetings and desires.
    Upon our first,* he sent out to suppress   65
    His nephew's levies; which to him appear'd
    To be a preparation 'gainst the Polack;
    But, better look'd into, he truly found
    It was against your Highness. Whereat griev'd,
    That so his sickness, age, and impotence,   70
    Was falsely borne in hand,* sends out arrests
    On Fortinbras; which he, in brief, obeys;
    Receives rebuke from Norway; and, in fine,
    Makes vow before his uncle never more
    To give th' assay of arms against your Majesty.   75
    Whereon old Norway, overcome with joy,
    Gives him threescore thousand crowns in annual fee,
    And his commission to employ those soldiers,
    So levied as before, against the Polack;
    With an entreaty, herein further shown, [*gives a paper*]   80
    That it might please you to give quiet pass
    Through your dominions for this enterprise,
    On such regards of safety and allowance
    As therein are set down.
KING: It likes us well;   85
    And at our more considered time we'll read,

---

⁶⁵ **first** first meeting
⁷¹ **borne in hand** deceived

Answer, and think upon this business.
Meantime we thank you for your well-took labour.
Go to your rest; at night we'll feast together.
Most welcome home!   [*Exeunt* AMBASSADORS *and attendants.*] 90
POLONIUS: This business is well ended.
My liege, and madam, to expostulate
What majesty should be, what duty is,
Why day is day, night night, and time is time,
Were nothing, but to waste night, day, and time.   95
Therefore, since brevity is the soul of wit,
And tediousness the limbs and outward flourishes,
I will be brief. Your noble son is mad.
Mad call I it; for, to define true madness,
What is't but to be nothing else but mad?   100
But let that go.
QUEEN: More matter with less art.
POLONIUS: Madam, I swear I use no art at all.
That he's mad, 'tis true: 'tis true 'tis pity;
And pity 'tis 'tis true. A foolish figure!   105
But farewell it, for I will use no art.
Mad let us grant him, then; and now remains
That we find out the cause of this effect;
Or rather say the cause of this defect,
For this effect defective comes by cause.   110
Thus it remains, and the remainder thus.
Perpend.*
I have a daughter—have while she is mine—
Who in her duty and obedience, mark,
Hath given me this. Now gather, and surmise. [*reads*]   115
'*To the celestial, and my soul's idol, the most beautified Ophelia.*' That's an ill
        phrase, a vile phrase; 'beautified' is a vile phrase. But you shall hear.
        Thus: [*reads*]
'*In her excellent white bosom, these, &c.*'
QUEEN: Came this from Hamlet to her?   120
POLONIUS: Good madam, stay awhile; I will be faithful. [*reads*]
'*Doubt thou the stars are fire;*
        Doubt that the sun doth move;
Doubt* truth to be a liar;
        But never doubt I love.   125
'*O dear Ophelia, I am ill at these numbers.* I have not art to reckon my groans;*
        but that I love thee best, O most best, believe it. Adieu.
                                '*Thine evermore, most dear lady, whilst*
                                        this machine is to him,
                                                        Hamlet.' 130

---

¹¹² **Perpend** consider carefully
¹²⁴ **Doubt** suspect
¹²⁶ **ill at these numbers** unskilled at versifying

This, in obedience, hath my daughter shown me;
And more above,* hath his solicitings,
As they fell out by time, by means, and place,
All given to mine ear.
KING: But how hath she   135
   Receiv'd his love?
POLONIUS: What do you think of me?
KING: As of a man faithful and honourable.
POLONIUS: I would fain prove so. But what might you think,
   When I had seen this hot love on the wing,   140
   As I perceiv'd it, I must tell you that,
   Before my daughter told me—what might you,
   Or my dear Majesty your Queen here think,
   If I had play'd the desk or table-book;*
   Or given my heart a winking,* mute and dumb;   145
   Or look'd upon this love with idle sight—
   What might you think? No, I went round to work,
   And my young mistress thus I did bespeak:
   'Lord Hamlet is a prince out of thy star;
   This must not be.' And then I prescripts gave her,   150
   That she should lock herself from his resort,
   Admit no messengers, receive no tokens.
   Which done, she took the fruits of my advice;
   And he repelled, a short tale to make,
   Fell into a sadness, then into a fast,   155
   Thence to a watch,* thence into a weakness,
   Thence to a lightness,* and, by this declension,
   Into the madness wherein now he raves
   And all we mourn for.
KING: Do you think 'tis this?   160
QUEEN: It may be, very like.
POLONIUS: Hath there been such a time—I would fain know that—
   That I have positively said ''Tis so,'
   When it prov'd otherwise?
KING: Not that I know.   165
POLONIUS: Take this from this,* if this be otherwise.
   If circumstances lead me, I will find
   Where truth is hid, though it were hid indeed
   Within the centre.*
KING: How may we try it further?   170

---

¹³² **above** besides
¹⁴⁴ **play'd the desk or table-book** been a passive receiver of secrets
¹⁴⁵ **winking** closed my eyes
¹⁵⁶ **watch** wakefulness
¹⁵⁷ **lightness** mental derangement
¹⁶⁶ **this from this** (indicating by pointing) head from body
¹⁶⁹ **centre** center of the earth

POLONIUS: You may know sometimes he walks four hours together,
    Here in the lobby.
QUEEN: So he does, indeed.
POLONIUS: At such a time I'll loose my daughter to him.
    Be you and I behind an arras* then;   175
    Mark the encounter: if he love her not,
    And be not from his reason fall'n thereon,
    Let me be no assistant for a state,
    But keep a farm and carters.
KING: We will try it.   180
    [*Enter* HAMLET, *reading on a book.*]
QUEEN: But look where sadly the poor wretch comes reading.
POLONIUS: Away, I do beseech you, both away:
    I'll board him presently.* O, give me leave.
    [*Exeunt* KING *and* QUEEN.]
    How does my good Lord Hamlet?
HAMLET: Well, God-a-mercy.   185
POLONIUS: Do you know me, my lord?
HAMLET: Excellent well; you are a fishmonger.*
POLONIUS: Not I, my lord.
HAMLET: Then I would you were so honest a man.
POLONIUS: Honest, my lord!   190
HAMLET: Ay, sir; to be honest, as this world goes, is to be one man pick'd out of
    ten thousand.
POLONIUS: That's very true, my lord.
HAMLET: For if the sun breed maggots in a dead dog, being a good kissing
    carrion—Have you a daughter?   195
POLONIUS: I have, my lord.
HAMLET: Let her not walk i' th' sun. Conception* is a blessing. But as your
    daughter may conceive—friend, look to't.
POLONIUS: How say you by that? [*aside*] Still harping on my daughter. Yet he
    knew me not at first; 'a said I was a fishmonger. 'A is far gone, far gone. And 200
    truly in my youth I suff'red much extremity for love. Very near this. I'll
    speak to him again.—What do you read, my lord?
HAMLET: Words, words, words.
POLONIUS: What is the matter, my lord?
HAMLET: Between who?   205
POLONIUS: I mean, the matter that you read, my lord.
HAMLET: Slanders, sir; for the satirical rogue says here that old men have grey
    beards; that their faces are wrinkled; their eyes purging thick amber and
    plum-tree gum; and that they have a plentiful lack of wit, together with
    most weak hams—all which, sir, though I most powerfully and potently be- 210
    lieve, yet I hold it not honesty to have it thus set down; for you yourself, sir,
    shall grow old as I am, if, like a crab, you could go backward.

---

[175] **arras** tapestry
[183] **board him presently** accost him at once
[187] **fishmonger** dealer in fish (slang for procurer)
[197] **Conception** understanding; becoming pregnant

POLONIUS: [*aside*] Though this be madness, yet there is method in't.—Will you
walk out of the air, my lord?

HAMLET: Into my grave? 215

POLONIUS: Indeed, that's out of the air. [*aside*] How pregnant sometimes his
replies are! a happiness that often madness hits on, which reason and san-
ity could not so prosperously be delivered of. I will leave him, and suddenly
contrive the means of meeting between him and my daughter.—My lord. I
will take my leave of you. 220

HAMLET: You cannot, sir, take from me anything that I will more willingly part
withal—except my life, except my life, except my life.
[*Enter* ROSENCRANTZ *and* GUILDENSTERN.]

POLONIUS: Fare you well, my lord.

HAMLET: These tedious old fools!

POLONIUS: You go to seek the Lord Hamlet; there he is. 225

ROSENCRANTZ: [*to* POLONIUS] God save you, sir!
[*Exit* POLONIUS.]

GUILDENSTERN: My honour'd lord!

ROSENCRANTZ: My most dear lord!

HAMLET: My excellent good friends! How dost thou, Guildenstern? Ah, Rosencrantz! Good lads, how do you both? 230

ROSENCRANTZ: As the indifferent* children of the earth.

GUILDENSTERN: Happy in that we are not over-happy;
On fortune's cap we are not the very button.

HAMLET: Nor the soles of her shoe?

ROSENCRANTZ: Neither, my lord. 235

HAMLET: Then you live about her waist, or in the middle of her favours?

GUILDENSTERN: Faith, her privates we.

HAMLET: In the secret parts of Fortune? O, most true; she is a strumpet. What
news?

ROSENCRANTZ: None, my lord, but that the world's grown honest. 240

HAMLET: Then is doomsday near. But your news is not true. Let me question
more in particular. What have you, my good friends, deserved at the hands
of Fortune, that she sends you to prison hither?

GUILDENSTERN: Prison, my lord!

HAMLET: Denmark's a prison. 245

ROSENCRANTZ: Then is the world one.

HAMLET: A goodly one; in which there are many confines, wards, and dungeons,
Denmark being one o' th' worst.

ROSENCRANTZ: We think not so, my lord.

HAMLET: Why, then, 'tis none to you; for there is nothing either good or bad, but 250
thinking makes it so. To me it is a prison.

ROSENCRANTZ: Why, then your ambition makes it one; 'tis too narrow for your
mind.

HAMLET: O God, I could be bounded in a nutshell and count myself a king of
infinite space, were it not that I have bad dreams. 255

---

²³¹ **indifferent** ordinary

GUILDENSTERN: Which dreams indeed are ambition; for the very substance of
    the ambitious is merely the shadow of a dream.

HAMLET: A dream itself is but a shadow.

ROSENCRANTZ: Truly, and I hold ambition of so airy and light a quality that it is
    but a shadow's shadow.   260

HAMLET: Then are our beggars bodies, and our monarchs and oustretch'd heroes
    the beggars' shadows. Shall we to th' court? for, by my fay,* I cannot reason.

BOTH: We'll wait upon you.

HAMLET: No such matter. I will not sort you with the rest of my servants; for, to
    speak to you like an honest man, I am most dreadfully attended. But, in the 265
    beaten way of friendship, what make you at Elsinore?

ROSENCRANTZ: To visit you, my lord; no other occasion.

HAMLET: Beggar that I am, I am even poor in thanks; but I thank you; and sure,
    dear friends, my thanks are too dear a half-penny.* Were you not sent for?
    Is it your own inclining? It is a free visitation? Come, come, deal justly with 270
    me. Come, come; nay, speak.

GUILDENSTERN: What should we say, my lord?

HAMLET: Why, any thing. But to th' purpose: you were sent for; and there is a
    kind of confession in your looks, which your modesties have not craft
    enough to colour; I know the good King and Queen have sent for you.   275

ROSENCRANTZ: To what end, my lord?

HAMLET: That you must teach me. But let me conjure you by the rights of our
    fellowship, by the consonancy of our youth, by the obligation of our ever-
    preserved love, and by what more dear a better proposer can charge you
    withal, be even and direct with me, whether you were sent for or no?   280

ROSENCRANTZ: [*aside to* GUILDENSTERN] What say you?

HAMLET: [*aside*] Nay, then, I have an eye of you.—If you love me, hold not off.

GUILDENSTERN: My lord, we were sent for.

HAMLET: I will tell you why; so shall my anticipation prevent your discovery,*
    and your secrecy to the King and Queen moult no feather. I have of late— 285
    but wherefore I know not—lost all my mirth, forgone all custom of exer-
    cises; and indeed it goes so heavily with my disposition that this goodly
    frame, the earth, seems to me a sterile promontory; this most excellent
    canopy the air, look you, this brave o'er-hanging firmament, this majestical
    roof fretted* with golden fire—why, it appeareth no other thing to me than 290
    a foul and pestilent congregation of vapours. What a piece of work is man!
    How noble in reason! how infinite in faculties! in form and moving, how
    express* and admirable! in action, how like an angel! in apprehension, how
    like a god! the beauty of the world! the paragon of animals! And yet, to me,
    what is this quintessence of dust? Man delights not me—no, nor woman 295
    neither, though by your smiling you seem to say so.

ROSENCRANTZ: My lord, there was no such stuff in my thoughts.

HAMLET: Why did ye laugh, then, when I said 'Man delights not me'?

---

[262] **fay** faith

[269] **too dear a half-penny** not worth a half-penny

[284] **prevent your discovery** forestall your disclosure

[289] **fretted** adorned

[292] **express** exact

ROSENCRANTZ: To think, my lord, if you delight not in man, what lenten enter- tainment the players shall receive from you. We coted* them on the way; 300 and hither are they coming to offer you service.

HAMLET: He that plays the king shall be welcome—his Majesty shall have trib- ute on me; the adventurous knight shall use his foil and target;* the lover shall not sigh gratis; the humorous man shall end his part in peace; the clown shall make those laugh whose lungs are tickle o' th' sere;* and the lady 305 shall say her mind freely, or the blank verse shall halt* for't. What players are they?

ROSENCRANTZ: Even those you were wont to take such delight in—the tragedi- ans of the city.

HAMLET: How chances it they travel? Their residence, both in reputation and 310 profit, was better both ways.

ROSENCRANTZ: I think their inhibition* comes by the means of the late innova- tion.*

HAMLET: Do they hold the same estimation they did when I was in the city? Are they so followed? 315

ROSENCRANTZ: No, indeed, are they not.

HAMLET: How comes it? Do they grow rusty?

ROSENCRANTZ: Nay, their endeavour keeps in the wonted pace; but there is, sir, an eyrie* of children, little eyases that cry out on the top of question,* and are most tyrannically clapp'd* for't. These are now the fashion, and so be- 320 rattle the common stages*—so they call them—that many wearing rapiers are afraid of goose quills* and dare scarce come thither.

HAMLET: What, are they children? Who maintains 'em? How are they escoted?* Will they pursue the quality* no longer than they can sing? Will they not say afterwards, if they should grow themselves to common players—as it is 325 most like, if their means are no better—their writers do them wrong to make them exclaim against their own succession?*

ROSENCRANTZ: Faith, there has been much to-do on both sides; and the nation holds it no sin to tarre* them to controversy. There was for a while no money bid for argument,* unless the poet and the player went to cuffs in 330 the question.

---

[300] **coted** overtook
[303] **target** shield
[305] **tickle o' th' sere** on a hair trigger
[306] **halt** limp
[312] **inhibition** hindrance
[312] **innovation** probably a reference to the boys' theatre companies that were at this time offering se- rious competition to the adult companies
[319] **eyrie** nest
[319] **little eyases . . . question** young hawks that cry shrilly above others in a debate
[320] **tyrannically clapp'd** violently applauded
[320-21] **berattle the common stages** put down the public theatres
[322] **goose quills** pens (of those who satirize the public theatres and their audiences)
[323] **escoted** financially supported
[324] **quality** profession of acting
[327] **succession** future profession
[329] **tarre** incite
[330] **argument** for a playscript

HAMLET: Is't possible?

GUILDENSTERN: O, there has been much throwing about of brains.

HAMLET: Do the boys carry it away?

ROSENCRANTZ: Ay, that they do, my lord—Hercules and his load,* too.   335

HAMLET: It is not very strange; for my uncle is King of Denmark, and those that
would make mows at him while my father lived give twenty, forty, fifty, a
hundred ducats apiece for his picture in little. 'Sblood, there is something
in this more than natural, if philosophy could find it out.
        [*a flourish*]

GUILDENSTERN: There are the players.   340

HAMLET: Gentlemen, you are welcome to Elsinore. Your hands, come then; th'
appurtenance of welcome is fashion and ceremony. Let me comply* with
you in this garb;* lest my extent* to the players, which, I tell you, must show
fairly outwards, should more appear like entertainments than yours. You are
welcome. But my uncle-father and aunt-mother are deceived.   345

GUILDENSTERN: In what, my dear lord?

HAMLET: I am but mad north-north-west; when the wind is southerly I know a
hawk from a handsaw.
        [*Reenter* POLONIUS.]

POLONIUS: Well be with you, gentlemen!

HAMLET: Hark you, Guildenstern, and you, too—at each ear a hearer: that great 350
baby you see there is not yet out of his swaddling clouts.

ROSENCRANTZ: Happily* he is the second time come to them; for they say an old
man is twice a child.

HAMLET: I will prophesy he comes to tell me of the players; mark it. You say
right, sir: a Monday morning; 'twas then indeed.   355

POLONIUS: My lord, I have news to tell you.

HAMLET: My lord, I have news to tell you. When Roscius was an actor in
Rome—

POLONIUS: The actors are come hither, my lord.

HAMLET: Buzz, buzz!   360

POLONIUS: Upon my honour—

HAMLET: They came each actor on his ass—

POLONIUS: The best actors in the world, either for tragedy, comedy, history,
pastoral, pastoral-comical, historical-pastoral, tragical-historical, tragical-
comical-historical-pastoral, scene individable, or poem unlimited. Seneca 365
cannot be too heavy nor Plautus too light. For the law of writ and the liberty,* these are the only men.

HAMLET: O Jephthah, judge of Israel, what a treasure hadst thou!

POLONIUS: What a treasure had he, my lord?

---

335 **Hercules and his load** reference to the Globe Theatre, whose sign showed Hercules carrying the
globe on his shoulders
342 **comply** be courteous
343 **garb** outward show
343 **extent** behavior
352 **Happily** perhaps
366–67 **law of writ and the liberty** sticking to the text and improvising

HAMLET: Why— 370

> '*One fair daughter, and no more,*
> *The which he loved passing well.*'

POLONIUS: [*aside*] Still on my daughter.

HAMLET: Am I not i' th' right, old Jephthah?

POLONIUS: If you call me Jephthah, my lord, I have a daughter that I love pass- 375
ing well.

HAMLET: Nay, that follows not.

POLONIUS: What follows then, my lord?

HAMLET: Why—

> '*As by lot, God wot*' 380

and then, you know,

> '*It came to pass, as most like it was.*'

The first row of the pious chanson* will show you more; for look where my
abridgement* comes.

[*Enter the* PLAYERS.]

You are welcome, masters; welcome all.—I am glad to see thee well.— 385
Welcome, good friends.—O, my old friend! Why thy face is valanc'd* since
I saw thee last; com'st thou to beard me in Denmark?—What, my young
lady* and mistress! By'r lady, your ladyship is nearer to heaven than when I
saw you last by the altitude of a chopine.* Pray God, your voice, like a piece
of uncurrent gold, be not crack'd within the ring.*—Masters, you are all 390
welcome. We'll e'en to't like French falconers, fly at anything we see. We'll
have a speech straight. Come, give us a taste of your quality; come, a passionate speech.

FIRST PLAYER: What speech, my good lord?

HAMLET: I heard thee speak me a speech once, but it was never acted; or, if it was, 395
not above once; for the play, I remember, pleas'd not the million; 'twas
caviary to the general.* But it was—as I received it, and others whose judgments in such matters cried in the top of mine*—an excellent play, well di-
gested in the scenes, set down with as much modesty as cunning.* I remember one said there were no sallets* in the lines to make the matter 400
savoury, nor no matter in the phrase that might indict the author of affectation; but call'd it an honest method, as wholesome as sweet, and by very
much more handsome than fine.* One speech in it I chiefly lov'd; 'twas
Aeneas' tale to Dido; and thereabout of it especially where he speaks of
Priam's slaughter. If it live in your memory, begin at this line—let me see: 405

---

383 **first row of the pious chanson** first stanza of a religious song
384 **abridgement** interruption
386 **valanc'd** furnished with a beard
387-88 **young lady** boy who played female roles
389 **chopine** thick-soled shoe
390 **crack'd within the ring** comparing a boy's breaking voice with a cracked coin (which it was illegal
to use)
397 **caviary to the general** too rich for the common audience
398 **top of mine** agreed with or exceeded mine
399 **modesty as cunning** restraint as cleverness
400 **sallets** salads (spicy jests)
403 **more handsome than fine** well proportioned rather than ornamented

         'The rugged Pyrrhus, like th' Hyrcanian beast,'*
'Tis not so; it begins with Pyrrhus.
         'The rugged Pyrrhus, he whose sable* arms,
         Black as his purpose, did the night resemble
         When he lay couched in the ominous horse,*   410
         Hath now this dread and black complexion smear'd
         With heraldry more dismal; head to foot
         Now is he total gules, horridly trick'd*
         With blood of fathers, mothers, daughters, sons,
         Bak'd and impasted* with the parching streets,   415
         That lend a tyrannous and damned light
         To their lord's murder. Roasted in wrath and fire,
         And thus o'er-sized* with coagulate gore,
         With eyes like carbuncles, the hellish Pyrrhus
         Old grandsire Priam seeks.'   420
    So proceed you.
POLONIUS: Fore God, my lord, well spoken, with good accent and good discretion.
FIRST PLAYER: *'Anon he finds him*
         Striking too short at Greeks; his antique sword,
         Rebellious to his arm, lies where it falls,   425
         Repugnant to command. Unequal match'd,
         Pyrrhus at Priam drives, in rage strikes wide;
         But with the whiff and wind of his fell sword
         Th' unnerved father falls. Then senseless Ilium,*
         Seeming to feel this blow, with flaming top   430
         Stoops to his base,* and with a hideous crash
         Takes prisoner Pyrrhus' ear. For, lo! his sword,
         Which was declining on the milky head
         Of reverend Priam, seem'd i' th' air to stick.
         So, as a painted tyrant, Pyrrhus stood   435
         And, like a neutral to his will and matter,
         Did nothing.
         But as we often see, against* some storm,
         A silence in the heavens, the rack* stand still,
         The bold winds speechless, and the orb below   440
         As hush as death, anon the dreadful thunder
         Doth rend the region; so, after Pyrrhus' pause,
         A roused vengeance sets him new a-work;

[406] **Hyrcanian beast** tiger
[408] **sable** black
[410] **ominous horse** the wooden horse used in taking Troy
[413] **total gules, horridly trick'd** entirely red, horridly adorned
[415] **impasted** encrusted
[418] **o'er-sized** smeared over
[429] **Ilium** Troy
[431] **Stoops to his base** collapses
[438] **against** before
[439] **rack** clouds

> *And never did the Cyclops' hammers fall*
> *On Mars' armour, forg'd for proof eterne,** 445
> *With less remorse than Pyrrhus' bleeding sword*
> *Now falls on Priam.*
> *Out, out, thou strumpet, Fortune! All you gods,*
> *In general synod,* take away her power;*
> *Break all the spokes and fellies* from her wheel,* 450
> *And bowl the round nave* down the hill of heaven,*
> *As low as to the fiends.'*

POLONIUS: This is too long.

HAMLET: It shall to the barber's, with your beard. Prithee say on. He's for a jig, or a tale of bawdry, or he sleeps. Say on; come to Hecuba. 455

FIRST PLAYER: *'But who, ah, who had seen the mobled* queen—'*

HAMLET: 'The mobled queen'?

POLONIUS: That's good; 'mobled queen' is good.

FIRST PLAYER: *'Run barefoot up and down, threat'ning the flames*
> *With bisson rheum,* a clout* upon that head* 460
> *Where late the diadem stood, and for a robe,*
> *About her lank and all o'er-teemed loins,**
> *A blanket, in the alarm of fear caught up—*
> *Who this had seen, with tongue in venom steep'd,*
> *'Gainst Fortune's state would treason have pronounc'd.* 465
> *But if the gods themselves did see her then,*
> *When she saw Pyrrhus make malicious sport*
> *In mincing with his sword her husband's limbs,*
> *The instant burst of clamour that she made—*
> *Unless things mortal move them not at all—* 470
> *Would have made milch* the burning eyes of heaven,*
> *And passion in the gods.'*

POLONIUS: Look whe'er* he has not turn'd his colour, and has tears in 's eyes. Prithee no more.

HAMLET: 'Tis well; I'll have thee speak out the rest of this soon.—Good my lord, 475 will you see the players well bestowed? Do you hear: let them be well used; for they are the abstract and brief chronicles of the time; after your death you were better have a bad epitaph than their ill report while you live.

POLONIUS: My lord, I will use them according to their desert.

HAMLET: God's bodykins, man, much better. Use every man after his desert, and 480 who shall 'scape whipping? Use them after your own honour and dignity; the less they deserve, the more merit is in your bounty. Take them in.

---

[445] **proof eterne** to last forever
[449] **synod** council
[450] **fellies** rims
[451] **nave** hub
[456] **mobled** muffled
[460] **bisson rheum** blinding tears
[460] **clout** rag
[462] **o'er-teemed loins** exhausted with childbearing
[471] **milch** moist
[473] **whe'er** whether

POLONIUS: Come, sirs.

HAMLET: Follow him, friends. We'll hear a play to-morrow. Dost thou hear me,
    old friend; can you play 'The Murder of Gonzago'?   485

FIRST PLAYER: Ay, my lord.

HAMLET: We'll ha't to-morrow night. You could, for a need, study a speech of
    some dozen or sixteen lines which I would set down and insert in't, could
    you not?

FIRST PLAYER: Ay, my lord.   490

HAMLET: Very well. Follow that lord; and look you mock him not. [*Exeunt*
    POLONIUS *and* PLAYERS.] My good friends, I'll leave you till night. You are
    welcome to Elsinore.

ROSENCRANTZ: Good my lord!
       [*Exeunt* ROSENCRANTZ *and* GUILDENSTERN.]

HAMLET: Ay, so God buy to you! Now I am alone.   495
    O, what a rogue and peasant slave am I!
    Is it not monstrous that this player here,
    But in a fiction, in a dream of passion,
    Could force his soul so to his own conceit*
    That from her working all his visage wann'd;   500
    Tears in his eyes, distraction in's aspect,
    A broken voice, and his whole function* suiting
    With forms* to his conceit? And all for nothing!
    For Hecuba!
    What's Hecuba to him or he to Hecuba,   505
    That he should weep for her? What would he do,
    Had he the motive and the cue for passion
    That I have? He would drown the stage with tears,
    And cleave the general ear with horrid speech;
    Make mad the guilty, and appal the free,*   510
    Confound the ignorant, and amaze indeed
    The very faculties of eyes and ears.
    Yet I,
    A dull and muddy-mettl'd* rascal, peak,
    Like John-a-dreams,* unpregnant of* my cause,   515
    And can say nothing; no, not for a king
    Upon whose property and most dear life
    A damn'd defeat was made. Am I a coward?
    Who calls me villain, breaks my pate across,
    Plucks off my beard and blows it in my face,   520
    Tweaks me by the nose, gives me the lie i' th' throat
    As deep as to the lungs? Who does me this?
    Ha!

499 **conceit** imagination
502 **function** action
503 **forms** bodily expressions
510 **appal the free** terrify the guiltless
514 **muddy-mettl'd** weak spirited
514–15 **peak, Like John-a-dreams** mope like a dreamer
515 **unpregnant of** unmoved by

'Swounds, I should take it; for it cannot be
But I am pigeon-liver'd* and lack gall   525
To make oppression bitter, or ere this
I should 'a fatted all the region kites*
With this slave's offal. Bloody, bawdy villain!
Remorseless, treacherous, lecherous, kindless* villain!
O, vengeance!   530
Why, what an ass am I! This is most brave,
That I, the son of a dear father murder'd,
Prompted to my revenge by heaven and hell,
Must, like a whore, unpack my heart with words,
And fall a-cursing like a very drab,*   535
A scullion!* Fie upon't! foh!
About,* my brains. Hum—I have heard
That guilty creatures, sitting at a play,
Have by the very cunning of the scene
Been struck so to the soul that presently*   540
They have proclaim'd their malefactions;
For murder, though it have no tongue, will speak
With most miraculous organ. I'll have these players
Play something like the murder of my father
Before mine uncle. I'll observe his looks;   545
I'll tent* him to the quick. If 'a do blench,*
I know my course. The spirit that I have seen
May be a devil; and the devil hath power
T'assume a pleasing shape; yea and perhaps
Out of my weakness and my melancholy,   550
As he is very potent with such spirits,
Abuses me to damn me. I'll have grounds
More relative* than this. The play's the thing
Wherein I'll catch the conscience of the King.   [*Exit.*]

ACT III

SCENE I————*Elsinore. The Castle.*

[*Enter* KING, QUEEN, POLONIUS, OPHELIA, ROSENCRANTZ, *and* GUILD-
ENSTERN.]
KING: And can you by no drift of conference*

---

525 **pigeon-liver'd** a coward
527 **kites** scavenger birds
529 **kindless** unnatural
535 **drab** prostitute
536 **scullion** kitchen servant
537 **About** to work
540 **presently** immediately
546 **tent** probe
546 **blench** blanch
553 **relative** certain
III,i,1 **conference** conversation

Get from him why he puts on this confusion,
Grating so harshly all his days of quiet
With turbulent and dangerous lunacy?
ROSENCRANTZ: He does confess he feels himself distracted,   5
But from what cause 'a will by no means speak.
GUILDENSTERN: Nor do we find him forward to be sounded;*
But, with a crafty madness, keeps aloof
When we would bring him on to some confession
Of his true state.   10
QUEEN: Did he receive you well?
ROSENCRANTZ: Most like a gentleman.
GUILDENSTERN: But with much forcing of his disposition.*
ROSENCRANTZ: Niggard of question; but of our demands
Most free in his reply.   15
QUEEN: Did you assay* him
To any pastime?
ROSENCRANTZ: Madam, it so fell out that certain players
We o'er-raught* on the way. Of these we told him;
And there did seem in him a kind of joy   20
To hear of it. They are here about the court,
And, as I think, they have already order
This night to play before him.
POLONIUS: 'Tis most true;
And he beseech'd me to entreat your Majesties   25
To hear and see the matter.
KING: With all my heart; and it doth much content me
To hear him so inclin'd.
Good gentlemen, give him a further edge,
And drive his purpose into these delights.   30
ROSENCRANTZ: We shall, my lord.
          [*Exeunt* ROSENCRANTZ *and* GUILDENSTERN.]
KING: Sweet Gertrude, leave us, too;
For we have closely* sent for Hamlet hither,
That he, as 'twere by accident, may here
Affront* Ophelia.   35
Her father and myself—lawful espials*—
Will so bestow ourselves that, seeing unseen,
We may of their encounter frankly judge,
And gather by him, as he is behav'd,
If 't be th' affliction of his love or no   40
That thus he suffers for.

---

[7] **forward to be sounded** willing to be questioned
[13] **forcing of his disposition** effort
[16] **assay** tempt
[19] **o'er-raught** overtook
[33] **closely** secretly
[35] **Affront** meet face to face
[36] **espials** observers

QUEEN: I shall obey you;
     And for your part, Ophelia, I do wish
     That your good beauties be the happy cause
     Of Hamlet's wildness; so shall I hope your virtues   45
     Will bring him to his wonted way again,
     To both your honours.
OPHELIA: Madam, I wish it may.   [*Exit* QUEEN.]
POLONIUS: Ophelia, walk you here.—Gracious, so please you,
     We will bestow ourselves.—Read on this book;   50
     That show of such an exercise may colour*
     Your loneliness.—We are oft to blame in this:
     'Tis too much prov'd, that with devotion's visage
     And pious action we do sugar o'er
     The devil himself.   55
KING: [*aside*] O, 'tis too true!
     How smart a lash that speech doth give my conscience!
     The harlot's cheek, beautied with plast'ring art,
     Is not more ugly to the thing that helps it
     Than is my deed to my most painted word.   60
     O heavy burden!
POLONIUS: I hear him coming; let's withdraw, my lord.
     [*Exeunt* KING *and* POLONIUS.]
     [*Enter* HAMLET.]
HAMLET: To be, or not to be—that is the question;
     Whether 'tis nobler in the mind to suffer
     The slings and arrows of outrageous fortune,   65
     Or to take arms against a sea of troubles,
     And by opposing end them? To die, to sleep—
     No more; and by a sleep to say we end
     The heart-ache and the thousand natural shocks
     That flesh is heir to. 'Tis a consummation   70
     Devoutly to be wish'd. To die, to sleep;
     To sleep, perchance to dream. Ay, there's the rub;*
     For in that sleep of death what dreams may come,
     When we have shuffled off this mortal coil,*
     Must give us pause. There's the respect*   75
     That makes calamity of so long life;
     For who would bear the whips and scorns of time,
     Th' oppressor's wrong, the proud man's contumely,
     The pangs of despis'd love, the law's delay,
     The insolence of office, and the spurns   80
     That patient merit of th' unworthy takes,
     When he himself might his quietus* make

---

[51] **colour** give an excuse for
[72] **rub** impediment
[74] **shuffled off this mortal coil** separated body from soul
[75] **respect** consideration
[82] **quietus** end

With a bare bodkin?* Who would these fardels* bear,
To grunt and sweat under a weary life,
But that the dread of something after death—   85
The undiscover'd country, from whose bourn*
No traveller returns—puzzles the will,
And makes us rather bear those ills we have
Than fly to others that we know not of?
Thus conscience does make cowards of us all;   90
And thus the native hue of resolution
Is sicklied o'er with the pale cast* of thought,
And enterprises of great pitch and moment,
With this regard, their currents turn awry
And lose the name of action.—Soft you now!   95
The fair Ophelia.—Nymph, in thy orisons*
Be all my sins rememb'red.

OPHELIA: Good my lord,
   How does your honour for this many a day?
HAMLET: I humbly thank you; well, well, well.   100
OPHELIA: My lord, I have remembrance of yours
   That I have longed to re-deliver.
   I pray you now receive them.
HAMLET: No, not I;
   I never gave you aught.   105
OPHELIA: My honour'd lord, you know right well you did,
   And with them words of so sweet breath compos'd
   As made the things more rich; their perfume lost,
   Take these again; for to the noble mind
   Rich gifts wax poor when givers prove unkind.   110
   There, my lord.
HAMLET: Ha, Ha! Are you honest?*
OPHELIA: My lord?
HAMLET: Are you fair?
OPHELIA: What means your lordship?   115
HAMLET: That if you be honest and fair, your honesty should admit no discourse
   to your beauty.
OPHELIA: Could beauty, my lord, have better commerce than with honesty?
HAMLET: Ay, truly; for the power of beauty will sooner transform honesty from
   what it is to a bawd* than the force of honesty can translate beauty into his 120
   likeness. This was sometime a paradox, but now the time gives it proof. I
   did love you once.
OPHELIA: Indeed, my lord, you made me believe so.

---

83 **bodkin** dagger
83 **fardels** burdens
86 **bourn** region
92 **cast** color
96 **orisons** prayers
112 **Are you honest?** are you modest; chaste; truthful
120 **bawd** procurer

HAMLET: You should not have believ'd me; for virtue cannot so inoculate our old
    stock but we shall relish of it.* I loved you not.   125
OPHELIA: I was the more deceived.
HAMLET: Get thee to a nunnery. Why wouldst thou be a breeder of sinners? I am
    myself indifferent honest,* but yet I could accuse me of such things that it
    were better my mother had not borne me: I am very proud, revengeful, am-
    bitious; with more offences at my beck than I have thoughts to put them in,   130
    imagination to give them shape, or time to act them in. What should such
    fellows as I do crawling between earth and heaven? We are arrant knaves, all;
    believe none of us. Go thy ways to a nunnery. Where's your father?
OPHELIA: At home, my lord.
HAMLET: Let the doors be shut upon him, that he may play the fool nowhere but   135
    in's own house. Farewell.
OPHELIA: O, help him, you sweet heavens!
HAMLET: If thou dost marry, I'll give thee this plague for thy dowry: be thou as
    chaste as ice, as pure as snow, thou shalt not escape calumny. Get thee to a
    nunnery, go, farewell. Or, if thou wilt needs marry, marry a fool; for wise   140
    men know well enough what monsters* you make of them. To a nunnery
    go; and quickly, too. Farewell.
OPHELIA: O heavenly powers, restore him!
HAMLET: I have heard of your paintings, too, well enough; God hath given you
    one face, and you make yourselves another. You jig and amble, and you lisp,   145
    and nickname God's creatures, and make your wantonness your ignorance.*
    Go to, I'll no more on't; it hath made me mad. I say we will have no more
    marriage: those that are married already, all but one, shall live; the rest shall
    keep as they are. To a nunnery, go.
      [*Exit.*]
OPHELIA: O, what a noble mind is here o'erthrown!   150
    The courtier's, soldier's, scholar's, eye, tongue, sword;
    Th' expectancy and rose* of the fair state,
    The glass of fashion and the mould of form,*
    Th' observ'd of all observers—quite, quite down!
    And I, of ladies most deject and wretched,   155
    That suck'd the honey of his music vows,
    Now see that noble and most sovereign reason,
    Like sweet bells jangled, out of time and harsh;
    That unmatch'd form and feature of blown* youth
    Blasted with ecstasy.* O, woe is me   160
    T' have seen what I have seen, see what I see!
      [*Reenter* KING *and* POLONIUS.]

[124-25] **virtue cannot . . . relish of it** virtue cannot shield us from still desiring sinful pleasures
[128] **indifferent honest** modestly virtuous
[141] **monsters** cuckolds
[146] **make your wantonness your ignorance** excuse your wantonness by pretending ignorance
[152] **expectancy and rose** hope
[153] **mould of form** pattern of excellent behavior
[159] **blown** blooming
[160] **ecstasy** madness

KING: Love! His affections do not that way tend;
    Nor what he spake, though it lack'd form a little,
    Was not like madness. There's something in his soul
    O'er which his melancholy sits on brood;   165
    And I do doubt* the hatch and the disclose
    Will be some danger; which to prevent
    I have in quick determination
    Thus set it down: he shall with speed to England
    For the demand of our neglected tribute.   170
    Haply the seas and countries different,
    With variable objects, shall expel
    This something-settled matter in his heart
    Whereon his brains still beating puts him thus
    From fashion of himself. What think you on't?   175
POLONIUS: It shall do well. But yet do I believe
    The origin and commencement of his grief
    Sprung from neglected love. How now, Ophelia!
    You need not tell us what Lord Hamlet said;
    We heard it all. My lord, do as you please;   180
    But if you hold it fit, after the play
    Let his queen mother all alone entreat him
    To show his grief. Let her be round* with him;
    And I'll be placed, so please you, in the ear
    Of all their conference. If she find him not,*   185
    To England send him; or confine him where
    Your wisdom best shall think.
KING: It shall be so:
    Madness in great ones must not unwatch'd go.
      [*Exeunt.*]

SCENE II————Elsinore. The Castle.

[*Enter* HAMLET *and three of the* PLAYERS.]

HAMLET: Speak the speech, I pray you, as I pronounc'd it to you, trippingly on
the tongue; but if you mouth it, as many of our players do, I had as lief the
towncrier spoke my lines. Nor do not saw the air too much with your hand,
thus, but use all gently; for in the very torrent, tempest, and, as I may say,
whirlwind of your passion, you must acquire and beget a temperance that 5
may give it smoothness. O, it offends me to the soul to hear a robustious
periwig-pated* fellow tear a passion to tatters, to very rags, to split the ears
of the groundlings,* who, for the most part, are capable of nothing* but

---

[166] **doubt** fear
[183] **round** blunt
[185] **find him not** doesn't find out what is bothering him
[III,ii,7] **periwig-pated** wig-wearing
[8] **groundlings** spectators who stood in the space surrounding the stage; presumably the poorest and
least-educated spectators
[8] **are capable of nothing** understand nothing

inexplicable dumb shows* and noise. I would have such a fellow whipp'd for
o'erdoing Termagant; it out-herods Herod.* Pray you avoid it. 10
FIRST PLAYER: I warrant your honour.
HAMLET: Be not too tame neither, but let your own discretion be your tutor. Suit
the action to the word, the word to the action; with this special observance,
that you o'erstep not the modesty of nature; for anything so o'erdone is
from* the purpose of playing, whose end, both at the first and now, was and 15
is to hold, as 'twere, the mirror up to nature; to show virtue her own feature,
scorn her own image, and the very age and body of the time his form and
pressure.* Now, this overdone or come tardy off, though it makes the un-
skilful laugh, cannot but make the judicious grieve; the censure of the which
one must, in your allowance, o'erweigh a whole theatre of others. O, there 20
be players that I have seen play—and heard others praise, and that highly—
not to speak it profanely, that, neither having th' accent of Christians, nor
the gait of Christian, pagan, nor man, have so strutted and bellowed that I
have thought some of Nature's journeymen* had made men, and not made
them well, they imitated humanity so abominably. 25
FIRST PLAYER: I hope we have reform'd that indifferently* with us, sir.
HAMLET: O, reform it altogether. And let those that play your clowns speak no
more than is set down for them; for there be of them that will themselves
laugh, to set on some quantity of barren spectators to laugh, too, though in
the meantime some necessary question of the play be then to be considered. 30
That's villainous, and shows a most pitiful ambition in the fool that uses it.
Go, make you ready.
[*Exeunt* PLAYERS.]
[*Enter* POLONIUS, ROSENCRANTZ, *and* GUILDENSTERN.]
How now, my lord! Will the King hear this piece of work?
POLONIUS: And the Queen, too, and that presently.
HAMLET: Bid the players make haste. [*Exit* POLONIUS.] 35
Will you two help to hasten them?
ROSENCRANTZ: Ay, my lord. [*Exeunt they two.*]
HAMLET: What, ho, Horatio!
[*Enter* HORATIO.]
HORATIO: Here, sweet lord, at your service.
HAMLET: Horatio, thou art e'en as just a man 40
As e'er my conversation cop'd withal.*
HORATIO: O my dear lord!
HAMLET: Nay, do not think I flatter;
For what advancement may I hope from thee,
That no revenue hast but thy good spirits 45
To feed and clothe thee? Why should the poor be flatter'd?

---

[9] **dumb shows** silent miming (used, as later in this scene, as prologues to plays)
[10] **Termagant . . . Herod** exaggeratedly overacted roles in medieval mystery plays
[15] **from** contrary to
[18] **pressure** image
[24] **journeymen** workers not yet masters of their craft
[26] **indifferently** mostly
[41] **cop'd withal** met with

No, let the candied* tongue lick absurd pomp,
And crook the pregnant hinges of the knee*
Where thrift* may follow fawning. Dost thou hear?
Since my dear soul was mistress of her choice   50
And could of men distinguish her election,
S'hath seal'd thee* for herself; for thou hast been
As one, in suff'ring all, that suffers nothing;
A man that Fortune's buffets and rewards
Hast ta'en with equal thanks; and blest are those   55
Whose blood* and judgment are so well commingled
That they are not a pipe for Fortune's finger
To sound what stop she please. Give me that man
That is not passion's slave, and I will wear him
In my heart's core, ay, in my heart of heart,   60
As I do thee. Something too much of this.
There is a play to-night before the King;
One scene of it comes near the circumstance
Which I have told thee of my father's death.
I prithee, when thou seest that act afoot,   65
Even with the very comment* of thy soul
Observe my uncle. If his occulted* guilt
Do not itself unkennel in one speech,
It is a damned ghost that we have seen,
And my imaginations are as foul   70
As Vulcan's stithy.* Give him heedful note;
For I mine eyes will rivet to his face;
And, after, we will both our judgments join
In censure of his seeming.*
HORATIO: Well, my lord.   75
If 'a steal aught the whilst this play is playing,
And 'scape detecting, I will pay the theft.
        [*Enter trumpets and kettledrums. Danish march. Sound a flourish. Enter*
        KING, QUEEN, POLONIUS, OPHELIA, ROSENCRANTZ, GUILDENSTERN,
        and other LORDS *attendant, with the guard carrying torches.*]
HAMLET: They are coming to the play; I must be idle.*
        Get you a place.
KING: How fares our cousin Hamlet?   80

---

47 **candied** sugared, flattering
48 **pregnant hinges of the knee** quick to curtsy and kneel
49 **thrift** profit
52 **S'hath seal'd thee** my soul has chosen you
56 **blood** feelings
66 **very comment** deepest wisdom
67 **occulted** hidden
71 **Vulcan's stithy** forge of the Greek god
74 **censure of his seeming** judgment on his response
78 **be idle** play the fool

HAMLET: Excellent, i' faith; of the chameleon's dish.* I eat the air promise-
cramm'd; you cannot feed capons so.

KING: I have nothing with this answer, Hamlet; these words are not mine.

HAMLET: No, nor mine now. [*to* POLONIUS] My lord, you play'd once in th' university, you say? 85

POLONIUS: That did I, my lord, and was accounted a good actor.

HAMLET: What did you enact?

POLONIUS: I did enact Julius Caesar; I was kill'd i' th' Capitol; Brutus kill'd me.

HAMLET: It was a brute part of him to kill so capital a calf there. Be the players
ready? 90

ROSENCRANTZ: Ay, my lord; they stay upon your patience.

QUEEN: Come hither, my dear Hamlet, sit by me.

HAMLET: No, good mother; here's metal more attractive.*

POLONIUS: [*to the* KING] O, ho! do you mark that?

HAMLET: Lady, shall I lie in your lap? [*lying down at* OPHELIA'S *feet*] 95

OPHELIA: No, my lord.

HAMLET: I mean, my head upon your lap?

OPHELIA: Ay, my lord.

HAMLET: Do you think I meant country matters?*

OPHELIA: I think nothing, my lord. 100

HAMLET: That's a fair thought to lie between maids' legs.

OPHELIA: What is, my lord?

HAMLET: Nothing.

OPHELIA: You are merry, my lord.

HAMLET: Who, I? 105

OPHELIA: Ay, my lord.

HAMLET: O God, your only jig-maker!* What should a man do but be merry?
For look you how cheerfully my mother looks, and my father died within's
two hours.

OPHELIA: Nay, 'tis twice two months, my lord. 110

HAMLET: So long? Nay then, let the devil wear black, for I'll have a suit of sables.
O heavens! die two months ago, and not forgotten yet? Then there's hope
a great man's memory may outlive his life half a year; but, by'r lady, 'a must
build churches, then; or else shall 'a suffer not thinking on, with the hobby-
horse,* whose epitaph is 'For O, for O, the hobby-horse is forgot!' 115

[*The trumpet sounds. Hautboys play. The Dumb Show enters.*]

[*Enter a* KING *and a* QUEEN, *very lovingly; the* QUEEN *embracing him and
he her. She kneels, and makes a show of protestation unto him. He takes her
up, and declines his head upon her neck. He lies him down upon a bank of
flowers; she, seeing him asleep, leaves him. Anon comes in a* FELLOW, *takes
off his crown, kisses it, pours poison in the sleeper's ears, and leaves him. The*

---

[81] **chameleon's dish** air on which chameleons were thought to live
[93] **attractive** magnetic
[99] **country matters** a sexual innuendo
[107] **jig-maker** composer of songs and dances (jigs were often performed as afterpieces in the theatre,
and often by the fool)
[114] **hobby-horse** mock horse worn by a performer in mummers plays

QUEEN *returns; finds the* KING *dead, and makes passionate action. The* POI-
SONER, *with some two or three* MUTES, *comes in again, seeming to condole
with her. The dead body is carried away. The* POISONER *woos the* QUEEN
with gifts: she seems harsh awhile, but in the end accepts his love. Exeunt.]

OPHELIA: What means this, my lord?

HAMLET: Marry, this is miching mallecho;* it means mischief.

OPHELIA: Belike this show imports the argument* of the play.
    [*Enter* PROLOGUE.]

HAMLET: We shall know by this fellow: the players cannot keep counsel; they'll
    tell all.   120

OPHELIA: Will 'a tell us what this show meant?

HAMLET: Ay, or any show that you show him. Be not you asham'd to show, he'll
    not shame to tell you what it means.

OPHELIA: You are naught, you are naught.* I'll mark the play.

PROLOGUE: *For us, and for our tragedy,*   125
    Here stooping to your clemency,
    We beg your hearing patiently.
    [*Exit.*]

HAMLET: Is this a prologue, or the posy of a ring?*

OPHELIA: 'Tis brief, my lord.

HAMLET: As woman's love.   130
    [*Enter the* PLAYER KING *and* QUEEN.]

PLAYER KING: *Full thirty times hath Phoebus' cart* gone round*
    Neptune's salt wash and Tellus's* orbed ground,*
    And thirty dozen moons with borrowed sheen
    About the world have times twelve thirties been,
    Since love our hearts and Hymen did our hands*   135
    Unite comutual in most sacred bands.

PLAYER QUEEN: *So many journeys may the sun and moon*
    Make us again count o'er ere love be done!
    But, woe is me, you are so sick of late,
    So far from cheer and from your former state,   140
    That I distrust you. Yet, though I distrust,*
    Discomfort you, my lord, it nothing must;
    For women fear too much even as they love,
    And women's fear and love hold quantity,
    In neither aught, or in extremity.   145
    Now, what my love is, proof hath made you know;
    And as my love is siz'd, my fear is so.

---

[117] **miching mallecho** sneaky mischief
[118] **argument** plot
[124] **naught** naughty
[128] **posy of a ring** sentiment inscribed in a ring
[131] **Phoebus' cart** the sun god's chariot
[132] **Neptune's salt wash** the sea
[132] **Tellus** Roman goddess of the Earth
[135] **Hymen** god of marriage
[141] **distrust** am anxious about

    Where love is great, the littlest doubts are fear;
    Where little fears grow great, great love grows there.
PLAYER KING: *Faith, I must leave thee, love, and shortly, too:*   150
    My operant* powers their functions leave to do;
    And thou shalt live in this fair world behind,
    Honour'd, belov'd; and haply one as kind
    For husband shalt thou—
PLAYER QUEEN: *O, confound the rest!*   155
    Such love must needs be treason in my breast.
    In second husband let me be accurst!
    None wed the second but who kill'd the first.
HAMLET: That's wormwood, wormwood.*
PLAYER QUEEN: *The instances* that second marriage move**   160
    Are base respects of thrift,* but none of love.
    A second time I kill my husband dead,
    When second husband kisses me in bed.
PLAYER KING: *I do believe you think what now you speak;*
    But what we do determine oft we break.   165
    Purpose is but the slave to memory,
    Of violent birth, but poor validity;*
    Which now, the fruit unripe, sticks on the tree;
    But fall unshaken when they mellow be.
    Most necessary 'tis that we forget   170
    To pay ourselves what to ourselves is debt.
    What to ourselves in passion we propose,
    The passion ending, doth the purpose lose,
    The violence of either grief or joy
    Their own enactures* with themselves destroy.   175
    Where joy most revels grief doth most lament;
    Grief joys, joy grieves, on slender accident.
    This world is not for aye; nor 'tis not strange
    That even our loves should with our fortunes change;
    For 'tis a question left us yet to prove,   180
    Whether love lead fortune or else fortune love.
    The great man down, you mark his favourite flies;
    The poor advanc'd makes friends of enemies.
    And hitherto doth love on fortune tend;
    For who not needs shall never lack a friend,   185
    And who in want a hollow friend doth try,
    Directly seasons* him his enemy.

---

[151] **operant** active
[159] **wormwood** a bitter herb
[160] **instances** motives
[160] **move** induce
[161] **base respects of thrift** considerations of profit
[167] **validity** strength
[175] **enactures** acts
[187] **seasons** ripens him into

But, orderly to end where I begun,
Our wills and fates do so contrary run
That our devices still are overthrown;   190
Our thoughts are ours, their ends none of our own.
So think thou wilt no second husband wed;
But die thy thoughts when thy first lord is dead.

PLAYER QUEEN: *Nor earth to me give food, nor heaven light,*
Sport and repose lock from me day and night,   195
To desperation turn my trust and hope,
An anchor's cheer in prison be my scope,*
Each opposite that blanks the face of joy*
Meet what I would have well, and it destroy,
Both here and hence pursue my lasting strife,   200
If, once a widow, ever I be wife!

HAMLET: If she should break it now!

PLAYER KING: *'Tis deeply sworn. Sweet, leave me here awhile;*
My spirits grow dull, and fain I would beguile
The tedious day with sleep.   [Sleeps.] 205

PLAYER QUEEN: *Sleep rock thy brain,*
And never come mischance between us twain!

HAMLET: Madam, how like you this play?

QUEEN: The lady doth protest too much, methinks.

HAMLET: O, but she'll keep her word.   210

KING: Have you heard the argument?* Is there no offence in't?

HAMLET: No, no; they do but jest, poison in jest; no offence i' th' world.

KING: What do you call the play?

HAMLET: 'The Mouse-trap.' Marry, how? Tropically.* This play is the image of a
    murder done in Vienna: Gonzago is the duke's name; his wife, Baptista. 215
    You shall see anon. 'Tis a knavish piece of work; but what of that? Your
    Majesty, and we that have free* souls, it touches us not. Let the galled jade*
    wince, our withers are unwrung.
        [*Enter* LUCIANUS.]
    This is one Lucianus, nephew to the King.

OPHELIA: You are as good as a chorus, my lord.   220

HAMLET: I could interpret* between you and your love, if I could see the puppets
    dallying.

OPHELIA: You are keen, my lord, you are keen.

HAMLET: It would cost you a groaning to take off mine edge.*

OPHELIA: Still better, and worse.   225

---

¹⁹⁷ **anchor's** anchorite, hermit
¹⁹⁸ **opposite that blanks** adverse thing that makes the face blanch
²¹¹ **argument** plot
²¹⁴ **Tropically** figuratively
²¹⁷ **free** souls free of guilt
²¹⁷ **galled jade** chafed horse
²²¹ **interpret** explain like a puppet master if he could see the puppets playing wantonly
²²⁴ **cost . . . edge** a sexual reference

HAMLET: So you mis-take* your husbands.—Begin, murderer; pox, leave thy damnable faces and begin. Come; the croaking raven doth bellow for revenge.

LUCIANUS: *Thoughts black, hands apt, drugs fit, and time agreeing;*
    Confederate season, else no creature seeing;*   230
    Thou mixture rank, of midnight weeds collected,
    With Hecate's ban thrice blasted, thrice infected.*
    *Thy natural magic and dire property**
    On wholesome life usurps immediately.
    [*Pours the poison in his ears.*]

HAMLET: 'A poisons him i' th' garden for his estate. His name's Gonzago. The 235 story is extant, and written in very choice Italian. You shall see anon how the murderer gets the love of Gonzago's wife.

OPHELIA: The King rises.

HAMLET: What, frighted with false fire!*

QUEEN: How fares my lord?   240

POLONIUS: Give o'er the play.

KING: Give me some light. Away!

POLONIUS: Lights, lights, lights!
    [*Exeunt all but* HAMLET *and* HORATIO.]

HAMLET: Why, let the strucken deer go weep,
    The hart ungalled play;   245
For some must watch, while some must sleep;
    Thus runs the world away.
Would not this, sir, and a forest of feathers*—if the rest of my fortunes turn Turk* with me—with two Provincial roses on my raz'd shoes,* get me a fellowship in a cry of players,* sir?   250

HORATIO: Half a share.

HAMLET: A whole one, I.
For thou dost know, O Damon dear,
    This realm dismantled was
Of Jove himself; and now reigns here   255
    A very, very—peacock.

HORATIO: You might have rhym'd.

HAMLET: O good Horatio, I'll take the ghost's word for a thousand pound. Didst perceive?

HORATIO: Very well, my lord.   260

HAMLET: Upon the talk of the poisoning.

HORATIO: I did very well note him.

---

[226] **mis-take** err in taking
[230] **Confederate season** the opportunity offered me
[232] **Hecate's ban** the goddess of sorcery's curse
[233] **property** nature
[239] **false fire** blank firing of a gun
[248] **forest of feathers** costume with feathers
[248-49] **turn Turk** go badly
[249] **raz'd shoes** shoes ornamented with slashes
[250] **cry of players** company of actors

HAMLET: Ah, ha! Come, some music. Come, the recorders.
      For if the King like not the comedy,
        Why, then, belike he likes it not, perdy.*   265
    Come, some music.
        [*Reenter* ROSENCRANTZ *and* GUILDENSTERN.]
GUILDENSTERN: Good my lord, vouchsafe me a word with you.
HAMLET: Sir, a whole history.
GUILDENSTERN: The King, sir—
HAMLET: Ay, sir, what of him?   270
GUILDENSTERN: Is, in his retirement, marvellous distemp'red.
HAMLET: With drink, sir?
GUILDENSTERN: No, my lord, rather with choler.*
HAMLET: Your wisdom should show itself more richer to signify this to his doc-
    tor; for for me to put him to his purgation would perhaps plunge him into 275
    far more choler.
GUILDENSTERN: Good my lord, put your discourse into some frame,* and start
    not so wildly from my affair.
HAMLET: I am tame, sir. Pronounce.
GUILDENSTERN: The Queen, your mother, in most great affliction of spirit, hath 280
    sent me to you.
HAMLET: You are welcome.
GUILDENSTERN: Nay, good my lord, this courtesy is not of the right breed. If it
    shall please you to make me a wholesome answer, I will do your mother's
    commandment; if not, your pardon and my return shall be the end of my 285
    business.
HAMLET: Sir, I cannot.
ROSENCRANTZ: What, my lord?
HAMLET: Make you a wholesome* answer, my wit's diseas'd. But, sir, such answer
    as I can make, you shall command: or rather, as you say, my mother. There- 290
    fore no more, but to the matter: my mother, you say—
ROSENCRANTZ: Then thus she says: your behaviour hath struck her into amaze-
    ment and admiration.*
HAMLET: O wonderful son, that can so stonish a mother! But is there no sequel
    at the heels of this mother's admiration? Impart.   295
ROSENCRANTZ: She desires to speak with you in her closet ere you go to bed.
HAMLET: We shall obey, were she ten times our mother. Have you any further
    trade with us?
ROSENCRANTZ: My lord, you once did love me.
HAMLET: And do still, by these pickers and stealers.*   300
ROSENCRANTZ: Good my lord, what is your cause of distemper? You do surely
    bar the door upon your own liberty, if you deny your griefs to your friend.

---

265 **perdy** by God (par dieu)
273 **choler** anger
277 **frame** order, control
289 **wholesome** sane
293 **admiration** wonder
300 **pickers and stealers** hands

HAMLET: Sir, I lack advancement.*
ROSENCRANTZ: How can that be, when you have the voice of the King himself
    for your succession in Denmark?   305
HAMLET: Ay, sir, but 'While the grass grows'—the proverb* is something musty.
    [*Reenter the* PLAYERS, *with recorders.*]
    O, the recorders! Let me see one. To withdraw* with you—why do you go
    about to recover the wind of me,* as if you would drive me into a toil?*
GUILDENSTERN: O my lord, if my duty be too bold, my love is too unmannerly.*
HAMLET: I do not well understand that. Will you play upon this pipe?   310
GUILDENSTERN: My lord, I cannot.
HAMLET: I pray you.
GUILDENSTERN: Believe me, I cannot.
HAMLET: I do beseech you.
GUILDENSTERN: I know no touch of it, my lord.   315
HAMLET: It is as easy as lying: govern these ventages* with your fingers and
    thumb, give it breath with your mouth, and it will discourse most eloquent
    music. Look you, these are the stops.
GUILDENSTERN: But these cannot I command to any utterance of harmony; I
    have not the skill.   320
HAMLET: Why, look you now, how unworthy a thing you make of me! You would
    play upon me; you would seem to know my stops; you would pluck out the
    heart of my mystery; you would sound me from my lowest note to the top
    of my compass;* and there is much music, excellent voice, in this little or-
    gan,* yet cannot you make it speak. 'Sblood, do you think I am easier to be   325
    play'd on than a pipe? Call me what instrument you will, though you can
    fret me, yet you cannot play upon me.
    [*Reenter* POLONIUS.]
    God bless you, sir!
POLONIUS: My lord, the Queen would speak with you, and presently.
HAMLET: Do you see yonder cloud that's almost in shape of a camel?   330
POLONIUS: By th' mass, and 'tis like a camel indeed.
HAMLET: Methinks it is like a weasel.
POLONIUS: It is back'd like a weasel.
HAMLET: Or like a whale?
POLONIUS: Very like a whale.   335
HAMLET: Then I will come to my mother by and by. [*aside*] They fool me to the
    top of my bent.*—I will come by and by.

---

303 **advancement** promotion
306 **proverb** (the rest of the proverb is "the horse starveth")
307 **withdraw** speak privately
308 **recover the wind of me** get on the windward side of me
308 **toil** snare
309 **duty . . . unmannerly** if I have seemed rude it is because my love for you leads me beyond good
manners
316 **ventages** vents, stops on a musical instrument
324 **compass** range
324 **organ** the recorder
336–37 **fool me . . . my bent** they force me to play the fool to the fullest

POLONIUS: I will say so.   [*Exit* POLONIUS.]
HAMLET: 'By and by' is easily said. Leave me, friends.
    [*Exeunt all but* HAMLET.]
      'Tis now the very witching time of night,   340
      When churchyards yawn, and hell itself breathes out
      Contagion to this world. Now could I drink hot blood,
      And do such bitter business as the day
      Would quake to look on. Soft! now to my mother.
      O heart, lose not thy nature; let not ever   345
      The soul of Nero* enter this firm bosom.
      Let me be cruel, not unnatural:
      I will speak daggers to her, but use none.
      My tongue and soul in this be hypocrites—
      How in my words somever she be shent,*   350
      To give them seals* never, my soul, consent!
    [*Exit.*]

SCENE III————*Elsinore. The Castle.*

    [*Enter* KING, ROSENCRANTZ, *and* GUILDENSTERN.]
KING: I like him not; nor stands it safe with us
      To let his madness range. Therefore prepare you;
      I your commission will forthwith dispatch,
      And he to England shall along with you.
      The terms* of our estate may not endure   5
      Hazard so near's as doth hourly grow
      Out of his brows.
GUILDENSTERN: We will ourselves provide.
      Most holy and religious fear it is
      To keep those many many bodies safe   10
      That live and feed upon your Majesty.
ROSENCRANTZ: The single and peculiar* life is bound
      With all the strength and armour of the mind
      To keep itself from noyance;* but much more
      That spirit upon whose weal depends and rests   15
      The lives of many. The cease of majesty
      Dies not alone, but like a gulf* doth draw
      What's near it with it. It is a massy wheel,
      Fix'd on the summit of the highest mount,
      To whose huge spokes ten thousand lesser things   20
      Are mortis'd and adjoin'd; which when it falls,
      Each small annexment, petty consequence,

[346] **Nero** Roman emperor who killed his mother
[350] **shent** rebuked
[351] **give them seals** confirm them with deeds
III,iii,5 **terms** conditions
[12] **peculiar** private
[14] **noyance** injury
[17] **gulf** whirlpool

Attends the boist'rous ruin. Never alone
Did the king sigh, but with a general groan.
KING: Arm* you, I pray you, to this speedy voyage;   25
For we will fetters put about this fear,
Which now goes too free-footed.
ROSENCRANTZ: We will haste us.
        [*Exeunt* ROSENCRANTZ *and* GUILDENSTERN.]
        [*Enter* POLONIUS.]
POLONIUS: My lord, he's going to his mother's closet.
Behind the arras I'll convey myself   30
To hear the process.* I'll warrant she'll tax him home;*
And, as you said, and wisely was it said,
'Tis meet that some more audience than a mother,
Since nature makes them partial, should o'erhear
The speech, of vantage.* Fare you well, my liege.   35
I'll call upon you ere you go to bed,
And tell you what I know.
KING: Thanks, dear my lord.   [*Exit* POLONIUS.]
O, my offence is rank, it smells to heaven;
It hath the primal eldest curse* upon't—   40
A brother's murder! Pray can I not,
Though inclination be as sharp as will.
My stronger guilt defeats my strong intent,
And, like a man to double business bound,
I stand in pause where I shall first begin,   45
And both neglect. What if this cursed hand
Were thicker than itself with brother's blood,
Is there not rain enough in the sweet heavens
To wash it white as snow? Whereto serves mercy
But to confront the visage of offence?   50
And what's in prayer but this twofold force,
To be forestalled ere we come to fall,
Or pardon'd being down? Then I'll look up;
My fault is past. But, O, what form of prayer
Can serve my turn? 'Forgive me my foul murder'!   55
That cannot be; since I am still possess'd
Of those effects* for which I did the murder—
My crown, mine own ambition, and my queen.
May one be pardon'd and retain th' offence?
In the corrupted currents of this world   60
Offence's gilded hand may shove by justice;
And oft 'tis seen the wicked prize itself

---

²⁵ **Arm** prepare
³¹ **process** proceedings
³¹ **tax him home** rebuke him sharply
³⁵ **of vantage** from some advantageous place
⁴⁰ **primal eldest curse** oldest curse (Cain's murder of his brother Abel)
⁵⁷ **effects** things gained

Buys out the law. But 'tis not so above:
There is no shuffling;* there the action lies
In his true nature; and we ourselves compell'd,   65
Even to the teeth and forehead of our faults,
To give in evidence. What then? What rests?*
Try what repentance can. What can it not?
Yet what can it when one cannot repent?
O wretched state! O bosom black as death!   70
O limed* soul, that, struggling to be free,
Art more engag'd!* Help, angels. Make assay:
Bow, stubborn knees; and, heart, with strings of steel,
Be soft as sinews of the new-born babe.
All may be well.   [*He kneels.*] 75
      [*Enter* HAMLET.]
HAMLET: Now might I do it pat, now 'a is a-praying;
    And now I'll do't—and so 'a goes to heaven,
    And so am I reveng'd. That would be scann'd.*
    A villain kills my father; and for that,
    I, his sole son, do this same villain send   80
    To heaven.
    Why, this is hire and salary, not revenge.
    'A took my father grossly, full of bread,*
    With all his crimes broad blown, as flush* as May;
    And how his audit* stands who knows save heaven?   85
    But in our circumstance and course of thought
    'Tis heavy with him; and am I then reveng'd
    To take him in the purging of his soul,
    When he is fit and season'd for his passage?
    No.   90
    Up, sword, and know thou a more horrid hent.
    When he is drunk asleep, or in his rage;
    Or in th' incestuous pleasure of his bed;
    At game, a-swearing, or about some act
    That has no relish of salvation in't—   95
    Then trip him, that his heels my kick at heaven,
    And that his soul may be as damn'd and black
    As hell, whereto it goes. My mother stays.
    This physic* but prolongs thy sickly days.   [*Exit.*]
KING: [*rising*] My words fly up, my thoughts remain below.   100
    Words without thoughts never to heaven go.   [*Exit.*]

---

64 **shuffling** trickery
67 **rests** remains
71 **limed** trapped (birds were caught by liming tree limbs with a sticky substance)
72 **engag'd** entrapped
78 **would be scann'd** needs to be thought about
83 **full of bread** worldly gratifications
84 **crimes . . . flush** sins in full bloom as flowers in May
85 **audit** account
99 **physic** (to Claudius) this medicine (prayer)

SCENE IV————*The* QUEEN's *closet.*

[*Enter* QUEEN *and* POLONIUS.]
POLONIUS: 'A will come straight. Look you lay home* to him;
    Tell him his pranks have been too broad* to bear with,
    And that your Grace hath screen'd and stood between
    Much heat and him. I'll silence me even here.
    Pray you be round with him. 5
HAMLET: [*within*] Mother, mother, mother!
QUEEN: I'll warrant you. Fear me not.
    Withdraw, I hear him coming.
        [POLONIUS *goes behind the arras.*]
        [*Enter* HAMLET.]
HAMLET: Now, mother, what's the matter?
QUEEN: Hamlet, thou hast thy father much offended. 10
HAMLET: Mother, you have my father much offended.
QUEEN: Come, come, you answer with an idle* tongue.
HAMLET: Go, go, you question with a wicked tongue.
QUEEN: Why, how now, Hamlet!
HAMLET: What's the matter now? 15
QUEEN: Have you forgot me?
HAMLET: No, by the rood,* not so:
    You are the Queen, your husband's brother's wife;
    And—would it were not so!—you are my mother.
QUEEN: Nay then, I'll set those to you that can speak. 20
HAMLET: Come, come, and sit you down; you shall not budge.
    You go not till I set you up a glass*
    Where you may see the inmost part of you.
QUEEN: What wilt thou do? Thou wilt not murder me?
    Help, help, ho! 25
POLONIUS: [*behind*] What, ho! help, help, help!
HAMLET: [*draws*] How now! a rat?
    Dead, for a ducat, dead!
        [*kills* POLONIUS *with a pass through the arras*]
POLONIUS: [*behind*] O, I am slain!
QUEEN: O me, what hast thou done? 30
HAMLET: Nay, I know not:
    Is it the King?
QUEEN: O, what a rash and bloody deed is this!
HAMLET: A bloody deed!—almost as bad, good mother,
    As kill a king and marry with his brother. 35
QUEEN: As kill a king!
HAMLET: Ay, lady, it was my word. [*parting the arras*]
    Thou wretched, rash, intruding fool, farewell!

III,iv,1 **lay home** rebuke him sharply
2 **broad** unrestrained
12 **idle** foolish
17 **rood** cross
22 **glass** mirror

I took thee for thy better. Take thy fortune;
Thou find'st to be too busy is some danger.   40
Leave wringing of your hands. Peace; sit you down,
And let me wring your heart; for so I shall,
If it be made of penetrable stuff;
If damned custom have not braz'd* it so
That it be proof and bulwark against sense.*   45
QUEEN: What have I done that thou dar'st wag thy tongue
          In noise so rude against me?
HAMLET: Such an act
          That blurs the grace and blush of modesty;
          Calls virtue hypocrite; takes off the rose   50
          From the fair forehead of an innocent love,
          And sets a blister there,* makes marriage-vows
          As false as dicers' oaths. O, such a deed
          As from the body of contraction* plucks
          The very soul, and sweet religion makes   55
          A rhapsody* of words. Heaven's face does glow
          O'er this solidity and compound mass
          With heated visage, as against the doom—
          Is thought-sick at the act.
QUEEN: Ay me, what act,   60
          That roars so loud and thunders in the index?*
HAMLET: Look here upon this picture and on this,
          The counterfeit presentment* of two brothers.
          See what a grace was seated on this brow;
          Hyperion's curls; the front* of Jove himself;   65
          An eye like Mars, to threaten and command;
          A station* like the herald Mercury
          New lighted on a heaven-kissing hill—
          A combination and a form indeed
          Where every god did seem to set his seal,   70
          To give the world assurance of a man.
          This was your husband. Look you now what follows:
          Here is your husband, like a mildew'd ear
          Blasting his wholesome brother. Have you eyes?
          Could you on this fair mountain leave to feed,   75
          And batten* on this moor? Ha! have you eyes?
          You cannot call it love; for at your age

---

⁴⁴ **braz'd** hardened
⁴⁵ **proof . . . sense** armored against feeling
⁵² **sets a blister** brands (as a harlot)
⁵⁴ **contraction** marriage contract
⁵⁶ **rhapsody** senseless string
⁶¹ **index** prologue
⁶³ **counterfeit presentment** represented image
⁶⁵ **front** forehead
⁶⁷ **station** bearing
⁷⁶ **batten** feed gluttonously

The heyday in the blood is tame, it's humble,
And waits upon the judgment; and what judgment
Would step from this to this? Sense, sure, you have,   80
Else could you not have motion; but sure that sense
Is apoplex'd;* for madness would not err,
Nor sense to ecstasy* was ne'er so thrall'd
But it reserv'd some quantity of choice
To serve in such a difference. What devil was't   85
That thus hath cozen'd you at hoodman-blind?*
Eyes without feeling, feeling without sight.
Ears without hands or eyes, smelling sans* all,
Or but a sickly part of one true sense
Could not so mope.* O shame! where is thy blush?   90
Rebellious hell,
If thou canst mutine in a matron's bones,
To flaming youth let virtue be as wax
And melt in her own fire; proclaim no shame
When the compulsive ardour gives the charge,   95
Since frost itself as actively doth burn,
And reason panders will.*
QUEEN: O Hamlet, speak no more!
Thou turn'st my eyes into my very soul;
And there I see such black and grained spots   100
As will not leave their tinct.*
HAMLET: Nay, but to live
In the rank sweat of an enseamed* bed,
Stew'd in corruption, honeying and making love
Over the nasty sty!   105
QUEEN: O, speak to me no more!
These words like daggers enter in my ears;
No more, sweet Hamlet.
HAMLET: A murderer and a villain!
A slave that is not twentieth part the tithe*   110
Of your precedent lord; a vice* of kings;
A cutpurse of the empire and the rule,
That from a shelf the precious diadem stole
And put it in his pocket!
QUEEN: No more!   115

---

⁸² **apoplex'd** paralyzed
⁸³ **ecstasy** madness
⁸⁶ **hoodman-blind** cheated you at blindman's buff
⁸⁸ **sans** without
⁹⁰ **so mope** be so stupid
⁹⁷ **reason panders will** reason acts as a panderer for desire
¹⁰¹ **tinct** color
¹⁰³ **enseamed** rumpled
¹¹⁰ **tithe** tenth part
¹¹¹ **vice** wicked character in medieval plays

[*Enter* GHOST.]
HAMLET: A king of shreds and patches—
    Save me, and hover o'er me with your wings,
    You heavenly guards! What would your gracious figure?
QUEEN: Alas, he's mad!   120
HAMLET: Do you not come your tardy son to chide,
    That, laps'd in time and passion, lets go by
    Th' important acting of your dread command?
    O, say!
GHOST: Do not forget; this visitation
    Is but to whet thy almost blunted purpose.   125
    But look, amazement on thy mother sits.
    O, step between her and her fighting soul!
    Conceit* in weakest bodies strongest works.
    Speak to her, Hamlet.
HAMLET: How is it with you, lady?   130
QUEEN: Alas, how is't with you,
    That you do bend your eye on vacancy,
    And with th' incorporal* air do hold discourse?
    Forth at your eyes and spirits wildly peep;
    And, as the sleeping soldiers in th' alarm,   135
    Your bedded* hairs like life in excrements*
    Start up and stand an end. O gentle son,
    Upon the heat and flame of thy distemper
    Sprinkle cool patience! Whereon do you look?
HAMLET: On him, on him! Look you how pale he glares.   140
    His form and cause conjoin'd, preaching to stones,
    Would make them capable.*—Do not look upon me,
    Lest with this piteous action you convert
    My stern effects;* then what I have to do
    Will want true colour—tears perchance for blood.   145
QUEEN: To whom do you speak this?
HAMLET: Do you see nothing there?
QUEEN: Nothing at all; yet all that is I see.
HAMLET: Nor did you nothing hear?
QUEEN: No, nothing but ourselves.   150
HAMLET: Why, look you there. Look how it steals away.
    My father, in his habit* as he liv'd!
    Look where he goes even now out at the portal.
        [*Exit* GHOST.]

---

[128] **Conceit** imagination
[133] **incorporal** empty, bodiless
[136] **bedded** flat-lying
[136] **excrements** outgrowths
[142] **capable** receptive
[143–44] **convert my stern effects** divert my serious purpose
[152] **habit** garment

QUEEN: This is the very coinage of your brain.
    This bodiless creation ecstasy 155
    Is very cunning in.
HAMLET: Ecstasy!
    My pulse as yours doth temperately keep time.
    And makes as healthful music. It is not madness
    That I have utt'red. Bring me to the test, 160
    And I the matter will re-word which madness
    Would gambol* from. Mother, for love of grace,
    Lay not that flattering unction* to your soul,
    That not your trespass but my madness speaks:
    It will but skin and film the ulcerous place, 165
    Whiles rank corruption, mining* all within,
    Infects unseen. Confess yourself to heaven;
    Repent what's past; avoid what is to come;
    And do not spread the compost on the weeds,
    To make them ranker. Forgive me this my virtue; 170
    For in the fatness of these pursy* times
    Virtue itself of vice must pardon beg,
    Yea, curb* and woo for leave to do him good.
QUEEN: O Hamlet, thou hast cleft my heart in twain.
HAMLET: O, throw away the worser part of it, 175
    And live the purer with the other half.
    Good night—but go not to my uncle's bed;
    Assume a virtue, if you have it not.
    That monster custom, who all sense doth eat,
    Of habits devil, is angel yet in this, 180
    That to the use* of actions fair and good
    He likewise gives a frock or livery
    That aptly is put on. Refrain to-night;
    And that shall lend a kind of easiness
    To the next abstinence; the next more easy; 185
    For use almost can change the stamp of nature,
    And either curb the devil, or throw him out,
    With wondrous potency. Once more, good night;
    And when you are desirous to be blest,
    I'll blessing beg of you. For this same lord 190
    I do repent; but Heaven hath pleas'd it so,
    To punish me with this, and this with me,
    That I must be their scourge and minister.
    I will bestow him, and will answer well

[162] **gambol** start away
[163] **unction** ointment
[166] **mining** undermining
[171] **pursy** bloated
[173] **curb** bow low
[181] **use** practice

The death I gave him. So, again, good night.   195
I must be cruel only to be kind;
Thus bad begins and worse remains behind.
One word more, good lady.
QUEEN: What shall I do?
HAMLET: Not this, by no means, that I bid you do: 200
Let the bloat King tempt you again to bed;
Pinch wanton on your cheek; call you his mouse;
And let him, for a pair of reechy* kisses,
Or paddling in your neck with his damn'd fingers,
Make you to ravel all this matter out,   205
That I essentially am not in madness,
But mad in craft. 'Twere good you let him know;
For who that's but a queen, fair, sober, wise,
Would from a paddock,* from a bat, a gib,*
Such dear concernings hide? Who would do so?   210
No, in despite of sense and secrecy,
Unpeg the basket on the house's top,
Let the birds fly, and, like the famous ape,
To try conclusions,* in the basket creep
And break your own neck down.   215
QUEEN: Be thou assur'd, if words be made of breath
And breath of life, I have no life to breathe
What thou hast said to me.
HAMLET: I must to England; you know that?
QUEEN: Alack,   220
I had forgot. 'Tis so concluded on.
HAMLET: There's letters seal'd; and my two school-fellows,
Whom I will trust as I will adders fang'd—
They bear the mandate;* they must sweep my way
And marshal me to knavery. Let it work;   225
For 'tis the sport to have the engineer
Hoist with his own petar;* and't shall go hard
But I will delve one yard below their mines
And blow them at the moon, O, 'tis most sweet
When in one line two crafts* directly meet.   230
This man shall set me packing.
I'll lug the guts into the neighbour room.
Mother, good night. Indeed, this counsellor
Is now most still, most secret, and most grave,

---

203 **reechy** foul
209 **paddock** toad
209 **gib** tomcat
214 **try conclusions** make experiments
224 **mandate** command
227 **petar** bomb
230 **crafts** intrigues

Who was in life a foolish prating knave.   235
Come, sir, to draw toward an end with you.
Good night, mother.
            [*Exeunt severally;* HAMLET *tugging in* POLONIUS.]

ACT IV

SCENE I————*Elsinore. The Castle.*

[*Enter* KING, QUEEN, ROSENCRANTZ, *and* GUILDENSTERN.]
KING: There's matter in these sighs, these profound heaves,
    You must translate; 'tis fit we understand them.
    Where is your son?
QUEEN: Bestow this place on us a little while.
            [*Exeunt* ROSENCRANTZ *and* GUILDENSTERN.]
    Ah, mine own lord, what have I seen to-night!   5
KING: What, Gertrude? How does Hamlet?
QUEEN: Mad as the sea and wind, when both contend
    Which is the mightier. In his lawless fit,
    Behind the arras hearing something stir,
    Whips out his rapier, cries 'A rat, a rat!'   10
    And in this brainish apprehension* kills
    The unseen good old man.
KING: O heavy deed!
    It had been so with us had we been there.
    His liberty is full of threats to all—   15
    To you yourself, to us, to every one.
    Alas, how shall this bloody deed be answer'd?
    It will be laid to us, whose providence*
    Should have kept short, restrain'd, and out of haunt,*
    This mad young man. But so much was our love,   20
    We would not understand what was most fit;
    But, like the owner of a foul disease,
    To keep it from divulging, let it feed
    Even on the pith of life. Where is he gone?
QUEEN: To draw apart the body he hath kill'd;   25
    O'er whom his very madness, like some ore
    Among a mineral of metals base,*
    Shows itself pure: 'a weeps for what is done.
KING: O Gertrude, come away!
    The sun no sooner shall the mountains touch   30
    But we will ship him hence; and this vile deed
    We must with all our majesty and skill
    Both countenance and excuse. Ho Guildenstern!

IV,i,11 **brainish apprehension** mad imagination
18 **providence** foresight
19 **out of haunt** away from association with others
26-27 **ore . . . base** like gold among baser metals

[*Reenter* ROSENCRANTZ *and* GUILDENSTERN.]
Friends, both go join you with some further aid:
Hamlet in madness hath Polonius slain,   35
And from his mother's closet hath he dragg'd him;
Go seek him out; speak fair, and bring the body
Into the chapel. I pray you haste in this.
        [*Exeunt* ROSENCRANTZ *and* GUILDENSTERN.]
Come, Gertrude, we'll call up our wisest friends
And let them know both what we mean to do   40
And what's untimely done; so haply slander—
Whose whisper o'er the world's diameter,
As level as the cannon to his blank,*
Transports his pois'ned shot—may miss our name,
And hit the woundless* air. O, come away!   45
My soul is full of discord and dismay.   [*Exeunt.*]

SCENE II———*Elsinore. The Castle.*

[*Enter* HAMLET.]
HAMLET: Safely stow'd.
GENTLEMEN: [*within*] Hamlet! Lord Hamlet!
HAMLET: But soft! What noise? Who calls on Hamlet? O, here they come!
        [*Enter* ROSENCRANTZ *and* GUILDENSTERN.]
ROSENCRANTZ: What have you done, my lord, with the dead body?
HAMLET: Compounded it with dust, whereto 'tis kin.   5
ROSENCRANTZ: Tell us where 'tis, that we may take it thence. And bear it to the
    chapel.
HAMLET: Do not believe it.
ROSENCRANTZ: Believe what?
HAMLET: That I can keep your counsel, and not mine own. Besides, to be de-   10
    manded of* a sponge—what replication* should be made by the son of a
    king?
ROSENCRANTZ: Take you me for a sponge, my lord?
HAMLET: Ay, sir; that soaks up the King's countenance,* his rewards, his author-
    ities. But such officers do the King best service in the end: he keeps them   15
    like an ape an apple in the corner of his jaw; first mouth'd to be last swal-
    lowed; when he needs what you have glean'd, it is but squeezing you and,
    sponge, you shall be dry again.
ROSENCRANTZ: I understand you not, my lord.
HAMLET: I am glad of it; a knavish speech sleeps in a foolish ear.   20
ROSENCRANTZ: My lord, you must tell us where the body is, and go with us to
    the King.
HAMLET: The body is with the King, but the King is not with the body. The King
    is a thing—

---

43 **blank** white center of a target
45 **woundless** invulnerable
IV,ii,10-11 **demanded of** questioned by
11 **replication** reply
14 **countenance** favor

GUILDENSTERN: A thing, my lord!   25
HAMLET: Of nothing. Bring me to him. Hide fox, and all after.*   [*Exeunt.*]

SCENE III————*Elsinore. The Castle.*

[*Enter* KING, *attended.*]
KING: I have sent to seek him, and to find the body.
　　How dangerous is it that this man goes loose!
　　Yet must not we put the strong law on him:
　　He's lov'd of the distracted* multitude,
　　Who like not in their judgment but their eyes;   5
　　And where 'tis so, th' offender's scourge is weigh'd,
　　But never the offence. To bear* all smooth and even,
　　This sudden sending him away must seem
　　Deliberate pause.* Diseases desperate grown
　　By desperate appliance are reliev'd,   10
　　Or not at all.
　　　　[*Enter* ROSENCRANTZ.]
　　How now! what hath befall'n?
ROSENCRANTZ: Where the dead body is bestow'd, my lord,
　　We cannot get from him.
KING: But where is he?   15
ROSENCRANTZ: Without, my lord; guarded, to know your pleasure.
KING: Bring him before us.
ROSENCRANTZ: Ho, Guildenstern! bring in the lord.
　　　　[*Enter* HAMLET *and* GUILDENSTERN.]
KING: Now, Hamlet, where's Polonius?
HAMLET: At supper.   20
KING: At supper! Where?
HAMLET: Not where he eats, but where 'a is eaten; a certain convocation of
　　politic* worms are e'en at him. Your worm is your only emperor for diet: we
　　fat all creatures else to fat us, and we fat ourselves for maggots; your fat king
　　and your lean beggar is but variable service*—two dishes, but to one table. 25
　　That's the end.
KING: Alas, alas!
HAMLET: A man may fish with the worm that hath eat of a king, and eat of the
　　fish that hath fed of that worm.
KING: What dost thou mean by this?   30
HAMLET: Nothing but to show you how a king may go a progress through the
　　guts of a beggar.
KING: Where is Polonius?

---

[26] **Hide fox, and all after** call in game (as in hide-and-seek)
[IV,iii,4] **distracted** confused
[7] **bear** carry out
[9] **pause** planning
[23] **politic** statesmanlike
[25] **variable service** different courses

HAMLET: In heaven; send thither to see; if your messenger find him not there,
    seek him i' th' other place yourself. But if, indeed, you find him not within 35
    this month, you shall nose him as you go up the stairs into the lobby.

KING: [*to attendants*] Go seek him there.

HAMLET: 'A will stay till you come.   [*Exeunt attendants.*]

KING: Hamlet, this deed, for thine especial safety—
    Which we do tender,* as we dearly grieve   40
    For that which thou hast done—must send thee hence
    With fiery quickness. Therefore prepare thyself;
    The bark is ready, and the wind at help,
    Th' associates tend,* and everything is bent
    For England.   45

HAMLET: For England!

KING: Ay, Hamlet.

HAMLET: Good!

KING: So is it, if thou knew'st our purposes.

HAMLET: I see a cherub that sees them. But, come; for England! Farewell, dear 50
    mother.

KING: Thy loving father, Hamlet.

HAMLET: My mother: father and mother is man and wife; man and wife is one
    flesh; and so, my mother. Come, for England.   [*Exit.*]

KING: Follow him at foot;* tempt him with speed aboard;   55
    Delay it not; I'll have him hence to-night.
    Away! for everything is seal'd and done
    That else leans* on th' affair. Pray you make haste.
        [*Exeunt all but the* KING.]
    And, England, if my love thou hold'st at aught—
    As my great power thereof may give thee sense,   60
    Since yet thy cicatrice* looks raw and red
    After the Danish sword, and thy free awe*
    Pays homage to us—thou mayst not coldly set
    Our sovereign process;* which imports at full,
    By letters congruing to that effect,   65
    The present* death of Hamlet. Do it, England:
    For like the hectic* in my blood he rages,
    And thou must cure me. Till I know 'tis done,
    Howe'er my haps,* my joys were ne'er begun.   [*Exit.*]

---

[40] **tender** hold dear
[44] **tend** wait
[55] **at foot** closely
[58] **leans** depends
[61] **cicatrice** scar
[62] **free awe** uncompelled submission
[63–64] **coldly set our sovereign process** disregard our royal command
[66] **present** immediate
[67] **hectic** fever
[69] **haps** fortunes

SCENE IV————*A plain in Denmark.*

[*Enter* FORTINBRAS *with his army over the stage.*]

FORTINBRAS: Go, Captain, from me greet the Danish king.
　　Tell him that by his license Fortinbras
　　Craves the conveyance of a promis'd march
　　Over his kingdom. You know the rendezvous.
　　If that his Majesty would aught with us,　　　　　　　　5
　　We shall express our duty in his eye;*
　　And let him know so.

CAPTAIN: I will do't, my lord.

FORTINBRAS: Go softly* on.　　　　　　[*Exeunt all but the* CAPTAIN.]

[*Enter* HAMLET, ROSENCRANTZ, GUILDENSTERN, *and others.*]

HAMLET: Good sir, whose powers are these?　　　　　　　10

CAPTAIN: They are of Norway, sir.

HAMLET: How purpos'd, sir, I pray you?

CAPTAIN: Against some part of Poland.

HAMLET: Who commands them, sir?

CAPTAIN: The nephew to old Norway, Fortinbras.　　　　15

HAMLET: Goes it against the main* of Poland, sir,
　　Or for some frontier?

CAPTAIN: Truly to speak, and with no addition,
　　We go to gain a little patch of ground
　　That hath in it no profit but the name.　　　　　　　20
　　To pay five ducats, five, I would not farm it;
　　Nor will it yield to Norway or the Pole
　　A ranker* rate should it be sold in fee.*

HAMLET: Why, then the Polack never will defend it.

CAPTAIN: Yes, it is already garrison'd.　　　　　　　　25

HAMLET: Two thousand souls and twenty thousand ducats
　　Will not debate* the question of this straw.
　　This is th' imposthume* of much wealth and peace,
　　That inward breaks, and shows no cause without
　　Why the man dies. I humbly thank you, sir.　　　　30

CAPTAIN: God buy you, sir.

ROSENCRANTZ: Will't please you go, my lord?

HAMLET: I'll be with you straight. Go a little before.
　　　　[*Exeunt all but* HAMLET.]
　　How all occasions do inform against me,
　　And spur my dull revenge! What is a man,　　　　　35
　　If his chief good and market* of his time

IV,iv,6 **in his eye** in his presence
9 **softly** slowly
16 **main** main part
23 **ranker** higher
23 **in fee** outright
27 **debate** settle
28 **imposthume** ulcer
36 **market** profit

Be but to sleep and feed? A beast, no more!
Sure he that made us with such large discourse,*
Looking before and after, gave us not
That capability and godlike reason   40
To fust* in us unus'd. Now, whether it be
Bestial oblivion, or some craven scruple
Of thinking too precisely on th' event—
A thought which, quarter'd, hath but one part wisdom
And ever three parts coward—I do not know   45
Why yet I live to say 'This thing's to do,'
Sith I have cause, and will, and strength, and means,
To do't. Examples gross* as earth exhort me:
Witness this army, of such mass and charge,*
Led by a delicate and tender prince,   50
Whose spirit, with divine ambition puff'd,
Makes mouths at the invisible event,*
Exposing what is mortal and unsure
To all that fortune, death, and danger dare,
Even for an egg-shell. Rightly to be great   55
Is not to stir without great argument,*
But greatly* to find quarrel in a straw,
When honour's at the stake. How stand I, then,
That have a father kill'd, a mother stain'd,
Excitements* of my reason and my blood,   60
And let all sleep, while to my shame I see
The imminent death of twenty thousand men
That, for a fantasy and trick of fame,
Go to their graves like beds, fight for a plot
Whereon the numbers cannot try the cause,   65
Which is not tomb enough and continent*
To hide the slain? O, from this time forth,
My thoughts be bloody, or be nothing worth!   [*Exit.*]

SCENE V———*Elsinore. The Castle.*

[*Enter* QUEEN, HORATIO, *and a* GENTLEMAN.]
QUEEN: I will not speak with her.
GENTLEMAN: She is importunate, indeed distract.
    Her mood will needs be pitied.
QUEEN: What would she have?

³⁸ **discourse** understanding
⁴¹ **fust** grow moldy
⁴⁸ **gross** large
⁴⁹ **charge** expense
⁵² **Makes mouths . . . event** scorns the outcome
⁵⁶ **argument** reason
⁵⁷ **greatly** nobly
⁶⁰ **Excitements** incentives
⁶⁶ **continent** container

GENTLEMAN: She speaks much of her father; says she hears   5
    There's tricks i' th' world, and hems, and beats her heart;
    Spurns enviously at straws;* speaks things in doubt,*
    That carry but half sense. Her speech is nothing,
    Yet the unshaped use of it doth move
    The hearers to collection;* they yawn* at it,   10
    And botch the words up fit to their own thoughts;
    Which, as her winks and nods and gestures yield them,
    Indeed would make one think there might be thought,
    Though nothing sure, yet much unhappily.
HORATIO: 'Twere good she were spoken with; for she may strew   15
    Dangerous conjectures in ill-breeding minds.
QUEEN: Let her come in.   *[Exit* GENTLEMAN.]
    [aside] To my sick soul, as sin's true nature is,
    Each toy seems prologue to some great amiss.*
    So full of artless jealousy* is guilt,   20
    It spills* itself in fearing to be spilt.
    [Enter OPHELIA *distracted.]*
OPHELIA: Where is the beauteous Majesty of Denmark?
QUEEN: How now, Ophelia!
OPHELIA: *[sings]*

        How should I your true love know
          From another one?   25
        By his cockle hat and staff,
          *And his sandal shoon.**

QUEEN: Alas, sweet lady, what imports this song?
OPHELIA: Say you? Nay, pray you, mark.   *[sings]*

        He is dead and gone, lady,   30
          He is dead and gone;
        At his head a grass-green turf,
          At his heels a stone.

    O, ho!
QUEEN: Nay, but, Ophelia—   35
OPHELIA: Pray you, mark.   *[sings]*
        White his shroud as the mountain snow—
    [Enter KING.]
QUEEN: Alas, look here, my lord.
OPHELIA: *Larded* with sweet flowers;*
        Which bewept to the grave did not go   40
        With true-love showers.

IV,v,7 **Spurns . . . straws** objects to insignificant matters
7 **in doubt** uncertainly
10 **collection** gather and listen
10 **yawn** gape
19 **amiss** misfortune
20 **artless jealousy** crude suspicion
21 **spills** destroys
27 **shoon** shoes
39 **Larded** decorated

KING: How do you, pretty lady?

OPHELIA: Well, God dild* you! They say the owl was a baker's daughter. Lord,
we know that we are, but know not what we may be. God be at your table!

KING: Conceit* upon her father.   45

OPHELIA: Pray let's have no words of this; but when they ask you what it means,
say you this: [*sings*]

> *To-morrow is Saint Valentine's day,*
> *All in the morning betime,*
> *And I a maid at your window,*   50
> *To be your Valentine.*
> *Then up he rose, and donn'd his clothes,*
> *And dupp'd* the chamber-door;*
> *Let in the maid, that out a maid*
> *Never departed more.*   55

KING: Pretty Ophelia!

OPHELIA: Indeed, la, without an oath, I'll make an end on't.   [*sings*]

> *By Gis* and by Saint Charity,*
> *Alack, and fie for shame!*
> *Young men will do't, if they come to't;*   60
> *By Cock, they are to blame.*
> *Quoth she 'Before you tumbled me,*
> *You promis'd me to wed.'*

He answers:

> *'So would I 'a done, by yonder sun,*   65
> *An thou hadst not come to my bed.'*

KING: How long hath she been thus?

OPHELIA: I hope all will be well. We must be patient; but I cannot choose but
weep to think they would lay him i' th' cold ground. My brother shall know
of it; and so I thank you for your good counsel. Come, my coach! Good 70
night, ladies; good night, sweet ladies, good night, good night.
    [*Exit.*]

KING: Follow her close; give her good watch, I pray you.
    [*Exeunt* HORATIO *and* GENTLEMAN.]
O, this is the poison of deep grief; it springs
All from her father's death. And now behold—
O Gertrude, Gertrude!   75
When sorrows come, they come not single spies,
But in battalions! First, her father slain;
Next, your son gone, and he most violent author
Of his own just remove; the people muddied,*
Thick and unwholesome in their thoughts and whispers   80
For good Polonius' death; and we have done but greenly*

---

43 **dild** reward
45 **Conceit** brooding
53 **dupp'd** opened
58 **Gis** Jesus
79 **muddied** confused
81 **greenly** foolishly

In hugger-mugger* to inter him; poor Ophelia
Divided from herself and her fair judgment,
Without the which we are pictures, or mere beasts;
Last, and as much containing as all these,   85
Her brother is in secret come from France;
Feeds on his wonder,* keeps himself in clouds,
And wants not buzzers* to infect his ear
With pestilent speeches of his father's death;
Wherein necessity, of matter beggar'd,*   90
Will nothing stick* our person to arraign
In ear and ear. O my dear Gertrude, this,
Like to a murd'ring piece,* in many places
Gives me superfluous death.   [*a noise within*]
QUEEN: Alack, what noise is this?   95
KING: Attend!
        [*Enter a* GENTLEMAN.]
    Where are my Switzers!* Let them guard the door.
    What is the matter?
GENTLEMAN: Save yourself, my lord:
    The ocean, overpeering of his list,*   100
    Eats not the flats with more impetuous haste
    Than young Laertes, in a riotous head,*
    O'erbears your officers. The rabble call him lord;
    And, as the world were now but to begin,
    Antiquity forgot, custom not known,   105
    The ratifiers and props of every word,
    They cry 'Choose we; Laertes shall be king.'
    Caps, hands, and tongues, applaud it to the clouds,
    'Laertes shall be king, Laertes king.'
QUEEN: How cheerfully on the false trail they cry!   110
        [*noise within*]
    O, this is counter, you false Danish dogs!
KING: The doors are broke.
        [*Enter* LAERTES, *with others, in arms.*]
LAERTES: Where is this king?—Sirs, stand you all without.
ALL: No, let's come in.
LAERTES: I pray you give me leave.   115
ALL: We will, we will.
        [*Exeunt.*]

82 **hugger-mugger** secret haste
87 **wonder** suspicion
88 **buzzers** tale bearers
90 **beggar'd** lacking facts
91 **Will nothing stick** will not hesitate
93 **murd'ring piece** cannon
97 **Switzers** Swiss guards
100 **list** shore
102 **in a riotous head** with a rebellious mob

LAERTES: I thank you. Keep the door.—O thou vile king,
    Give me my father!
QUEEN: Calmly, good Laertes.
LAERTES: That drop of blood that's calm proclaims me bastard;   120
    Cries cuckold to my father; brands the harlot
    Even here, between the chaste unsmirched brow
    Of my true mother.
KING: What is the cause, Laertes,
    That thy rebellion looks so giant-like?   125
    Let him go, Gertrude; do not fear our person:
    There's such divinity doth hedge a king
    That treason can but peep to what it would,
    Acts little of his will. Tell me, Laertes,
    Why thou art thus incens'd. Let him go, Gertrude.   130
    Speak, man.
LAERTES: Where is my father?
KING: Dead.
QUEEN: But not by him.
KING: Let him demand his fill.   135
LAERTES: How came he dead? I'll not be juggled with.
    To hell, allegiance! Vows, to the blackest devil!
    Conscience and grace, to the profoundest pit!
    I dare damnation. To this point I stand,
    That both the worlds I give to negligence,*   140
    Let come what comes; only I'll be reveng'd
    Most thoroughly for my father.
KING: Who shall stay you?
LAERTES: My will, not all the world's.
    And for my means, I'll husband them* so well   145
    They shall go far with little.
KING: Good Laertes,
    If you desire to know the certainty
    Of your dear father, is't writ in your revenge
    That, swoopstake,* you will draw both friend and foe,   150
    Winner and loser?
LAERTES: None but his enemies.
KING: Will you know them, then?
LAERTES: To his good friends thus wide I'll ope my arms
    And, like the kind life-rend'ring pelican,   155
    Repast* them with my blood.
KING: Why, now you speak
    Like a good child and a true gentleman.
    That I am guiltless of your father's death,
    And am most sensibly in grief for it,   160

---

[140] **both the worlds . . . negligence** I care not what may happen to me in this world or the next
[145] **husband them** use them economically
[150] **swoopstake** in a full sweep
[155-56] **pelican, repast** (pelicans were thought to use their own blood to feed their young)

It shall as level to your judgment 'pear
As day does to your eye.   [*A noise within:* 'Let her come in.']
LAERTES: How now! What noise is that?
  [*Reenter* OPHELIA.]
O, heat dry up my brains! tears seven times salt
Burn out the sense and virtue* of mine eye!   165
By heaven, thy madness shall be paid with weight
Till our scale turn the beam.* O rose of May!
Dear maid, kind sister, sweet Ophelia!
O heavens! is't possible a young maid's wits
Should be as mortal as an old man's life?   170
Nature is fine* in love; and where 'tis fine
It sends some precious instance* of itself
After the thing it loves.
OPHELIA: [*sings*]
    They bore him barefac'd on the bier;
    Hey non nonny, nonny, hey nonny;   175
    And in his grave rain'd many a tear—
Fare you well, my dove!
LAERTES: Hadst thou thy wits, and didst persuade revenge,
  It could not move thus.
OPHELIA: You must sing 'A-down, a-down,' an you call him a-down-a. O, how the   180
  wheel becomes it! It is the false steward, that stole his master's daughter.
LAERTES: This nothing's more than matter.*
OPHELIA: There's rosemary, that's for remembrance; pray you, love, remember.
  And there is pansies, that's for thoughts.
LAERTES: A document* in madness—thoughts and remembrance fitted.   185
OPHELIA: There's fennel for you, and columbines. There's rue for you; and here's
  some for me. We may call it herb of grace a Sundays. O, you must wear your
  rue with a difference. There's a daisy. I would give you some violets, but they
  wither'd all when my father died. They say 'a made a good end.
  [*sings*] *For bonny sweet Robin is all my joy.*   190
LAERTES: Thought and affliction, passion, hell itself,
  She turns to favour* and to prettiness.
OPHELIA: [*sings*]
    And will 'a not come again?
    And will 'a not come again?
    No, no, he is dead,   195
    Go to thy death-bed,
    He never will come again.

---

[165] **virtue** power
[167] **scale down the beam** weigh down the balance of a scale
[171] **fine** refined
[172] **instance** sample
[182] **nothing's . . . matter** this nonsense contains more meaning than does a statement of great matter
[185] **document** lesson
[192] **favour** to beauty

> *His beard was as white as snow,*
> *All flaxen was his poll;**
> *He is gone, he is gone,*   200
> *And we cast away moan:*
> *God-a-mercy on his soul!*

And of all Christian souls, I pray God. God buy you.
  [*Exit.*]
LAERTES: Do you see this, O Gòd?
KING: Laertes, I must commune with your grief,   205
  Or you deny me right. Go but apart,
  Make choice of whom your wisest friends you will,
  And they shall hear and judge 'twixt you and me.
  If by direct or by collateral* hand
  They find us touch'd,* we will our kingdom give,   210
  Our crown, our life, and all that we call ours,
  To you in satisfaction; but if not,
  Be you content to lend your patience to us,
  And we shall jointly labour with your soul
  To give it due content.   215
LAERTES: Let this be so.
  His means of death, his obscure funeral—
  No trophy, sword, nor hatchment,* o'er his bones,
  No noble rite nor formal ostentation*—
  Cry to be heard, as 'twere from heaven to earth,   220
  That I must call't in question.
KING: So you shall;
  And where th' offence is, let the great axe fall.
  I pray you go with me.
    [*Exeunt.*]

SCENE VI————*Elsinore. The Castle.*

[*Enter* HORATIO *with an* ATTENDANT.]
HORATIO: What are they that would speak with me?
ATTENDANT: Sea-faring men, sir; they say they have letters for you.
HORATIO: Let them come in.   [*Exit* ATTENDANT.]
  I do not know from what part of the world
  I should be greeted, if not from Lord Hamlet.   5
    [*Enter* SAILORS.]
SAILOR: God bless you, sir.
HORATIO: Let Him bless thee, too.
SAILOR: 'A shall, sir, an't please Him. There's a letter for you, sir; it came from th'
  ambassador that was bound for England—if your name be Horatio, as I am
  let to know it is.   10

¹⁹⁹ **flaxen was his poll** his hair was white
²⁰⁹ **collateral** indirect
²¹⁰ **touch'd** implicated
²¹⁸ **hatchment** stone bearing coat of arms
²¹⁹ **ostentation** ceremony

HORATIO: [*reads*] 'Horatio, when thou shalt have overlook'd* this, give these fellows some means to the King: they have letters for him. Ere we were two
days old at sea, a pirate of very warlike appointment gave us chase. Finding
ourselves too slow of sail, we put on a compelled valour; and in the grapple
I boarded them. On the instant they got clear of our ship; so I alone became   15
their prisoner. They have dealt with me like thieves of mercy; but they knew
what they did; I am to do a good turn for them. Let the King have the letters I have sent; and repair thou to me with as much speed as thou wouldest
fly death. I have words to speak in thine ear will make thee dumb; yet are
they much too light for the bore of the matter. These good fellows will   20
bring thee where I am. Rosencrantz and Guildenstern hold their course for
England; of them I have much to tell thee. Farewell.

                          He that thou knowest thine, Hamlet.'

Come, I will give you way for these your letters,
And do't the speedier that you may direct me   25
To him from whom you brought them.   [*Exeunt.*]

SCENE VII————*Elsinore. The Castle.*

[*Enter* KING *and* LAERTES.]

KING: Now must your conscience my acquittance seal,
    And you must put me in your heart for friend,
    Sith you have heard, and with a knowing ear,
    That he which hath your noble father slain
    Pursu'd my life.   5
LAERTES: It well appears. But tell me
    Why you proceeded not against these feats,
    So crimeful and so capital* in nature,
    As by your safety, wisdom, all things else,
    You mainly were stirr'd up.   10
KING: O, for two special reasons,
    Which may to you, perhaps, seem much unsinew'd,*
    But yet to me th' are strong. The Queen his mother
    Lives almost by his looks; and for myself,
    My virtue or my plague, be it either which—   15
    She is so conjunctive* to my life and soul
    That, as the star moves not but in his sphere,
    I could not but by her. The other motive,
    Why to a public count I might not go,
    Is the great love the general gender* bear him;   20
    Who, dipping all his faults in their affection,
    Work like the spring that turneth wood to stone,
    Convert his gyves* to graces; so that my arrows,

IV,vi,11 **overlook'd** read
IV,vii,8 **capital** deserving death
12 **unsinew'd** weak
16 **conjunctive** closely united
20 **general gender** common people
23 **gyves** fetters

Too slightly timber'd* for so loud a wind,
Would have reverted to my bow again,   25
But not where I have aim'd them.
LAERTES: And so have I a noble father lost;
A sister driven into desp'rate terms,
Whose worth, if praises may go back again,
Stood challenger on mount of all the age   30
For her perfections. But my revenge will come.
KING: Break not your sleeps for that. You must not think
That we are made of stuff so flat and dull
That we can let our beard be shook with danger,
And think it pastime. You shortly shall hear more.   35
I lov'd your father, and we love our self;
And that, I hope, will teach you to imagine—
        [*Enter a* MESSENGER *with letters.*]
How now! What news?
MESSENGER: Letters, my lord, from Hamlet:
These to your Majesty; this to the Queen.   40
KING: From Hamlet! Who brought them?
MESSENGER: Sailors, my lord, they say; I saw them not.
They were given me by Claudio; he receiv'd them
Of him that brought them.
KING: Laertes, you shall hear them.   45
Leave us.   [*Exit* MESSENGER.]
[*reads*] 'High and Mighty. You shall know I am set naked* on your king-
dom. To-morrow shall I beg leave to see your kingly eyes; when I shall, first
asking your pardon thereunto, recount the occasion of my sudden and more
strange return.   50
                                                                  Hamlet.'

What should this mean? Are all the rest come back?
Or is it some abuse,* and no such thing?
LAERTES: Know you the hand?
KING: 'Tis Hamlet's character. 'Naked'!   55
And in a postscript here, he says 'alone.'
Can you devise* me?
LAERTES: I am lost in it, my lord. But let him come;
It warms the very sickness in my heart
That I shall live and tell him to his teeth   60
'Thus didest thou.'
KING: If it be so, Laertes—
As how should it be so, how otherwise?—
Will you be rul'd by me?
LAERTES: Ay, my lord;   65
So you will not o'errule me to a peace.

---

²⁴ **timber'd** shafted
⁴⁷ **naked** destitute
⁵³ **abuse** deception
⁵⁷ **devise** advise

KING: To thine own peace. If he be now return'd,
    As checking at* his voyage, and that he means
    No more to undertake it, I will work him
    To an exploit now ripe in my device,   70
    Under the which he shall not choose but fall;
    And for his death, no wind of blame shall breathe;
    But even his mother shall uncharge the practice
    And call it accident.
LAERTES: My lord, I will be rul'd   75
    The rather, if you could devise it so
    That I might be the organ.
KING: It falls right.
    You have been talk'd of since your travel much,
    And that in Hamlet's hearing, for a quality   80
    Wherein they say you shine. Your sum of parts
    Did not together pluck such envy from him
    As did that one; and that, in my regard,
    Of the unworthiest siege.*
LAERTES: What part is that, my lord?   85
KING: A very riband in the cap of youth,
    Yet needful, too; for youth no less becomes
    The light and careless livery that it wears
    Than settled age his sables and his weeds,*
    Importing health and graveness. Two months since   90
    Here was a gentleman of Normandy—
    I have seen myself, and serv'd against, the French,
    And they can well on horseback; but this gallant
    Had witchcraft in't; he grew into his seat,
    And to such wondrous doing brought his horse,   95
    As had he been incorps'd and demi-natur'd
    With the brave beast. So far he topp'd my thought,
    That I, in forgery* of shapes and tricks,
    Come short of what he did.
LAERTES: A Norman was't?   100
KING: A Norman.
LAERTES: Upon my life, Lamord.
KING: The very same.
LAERTES: I know him well. He is the brooch* indeed
    And gem of all the nation.   105
KING: He made confession* of you;
    And gave you such a masterly report
    For art and exercise in your defence,

---

68 **checking at** abandoning
84 **siege** rank
89 **weeds** sober attire
98 **forgery** invention
104 **brooch** ornament
106 **confession** report

And for your rapier most especial,
That he cried out 'twould be a sight indeed   110
If one could match you. The scrimers* of their nation
He swore had neither motion, guard, nor eye,
If you oppos'd them. Sir, this report of his
Did Hamlet so envenom with his envy
That he could nothing do but wish and beg   115
Your sudden coming o'er, to play with you.
Now out of this—
LAERTES: What out of this, my lord?
KING: Laertes, was your father dear to you?
    Or are you like the painting of a sorrow,   120
    A face without a heart?
LAERTES: Why ask you this?
KING: Not that I think you did not love your father;
    But that I know love is begun by time,
    And that I see, in passages of proof,*   125
    Time qualifies* the spark and fire of it.
    There lives within the very flame of love
    A kind of wick or snuff that will abate it;
    And nothing is at a like goodness still;
    For goodness, growing to a pleurisy,*   130
    Dies in his own too much. That we would do,
    We should do when we would; for this 'would' changes,
    And hath abatements and delays as many
    As there are tongues, are hands, are accidents;
    And then this 'should' is like a spendthrift's sigh   135
    That hurts by easing. But to the quick* of th' ulcer:
    Hamlet comes back; what would you undertake
    To show yourself in deed your father's son
    More than in words?
LAERTES: To cut his throat i' th' church.   140
KING: No place, indeed, should murder sanctuarize;*
    Revenge should have no bounds. But, good Laertes,
    Will you do this? Keep close within your chamber.
    Hamlet return'd shall know you are come home.
    We'll put on those shall praise your excellence,   145
    And set a double varnish on the fame
    The Frenchman gave you; bring you, in fine,* together,
    And wager on your heads. He, being remiss,
    Most generous, and free from all contriving,

---

[111] **scrimers** fencers
[125] **passages of proof** proved cases
[126] **qualifies** diminishes
[130] **pleurisy** excess
[136] **quick** sensitive part
[141] **sanctuarize** protect
[147] **in fine** finally

Will not peruse the foils; so that with ease   150
Or with a little shuffling, you may choose
A sword unbated,* and, in a pass of practice,*
Requite him for your father.
LAERTES: I will do't;
And for that purpose I'll anoint my sword.   155
I bought an unction of a mountebank,
So mortal that but dip a knife in it,
Where it draws blood no cataplasm* so rare,
Collected from all simples* that have virtue
Under the moon, can save the thing from death   160
That is but scratch'd withal. I'll touch my point
With this contagion, that, if I gall him slightly,
It may be death.
KING: Let's further think of this;
Weigh what convenience both of time and means   165
May fit us to our shape.* If this should fail,
And that our drift look through* our bad performance,
'Twere better not assay'd, therefore this project
Should have a back or second, that might hold
If this did blast in proof.* Soft! let me see.   170
We'll make a solemn wager on your cunnings—
I ha't.
When in your motion you are hot and dry—
As make your bouts more violent to that end—
And that he calls for drink, I'll have preferr'd him   175
A chalice for the nonce,* whereon but sipping,
If he by chance escape your venom'd stuck,*
Our purpose may hold there. But stay; what noise?
    [*Enter* QUEEN.]
QUEEN: One woe doth tread upon another's heel,
So fast they follow. Your sister's drown'd, Laertes.   180
LAERTES: Drown'd? O, where?
QUEEN: There is a willow grows aslant the brook
That shows his hoar* leaves in the glassy stream;
Therewith fantastic garlands did she make
Of crowflowers, nettles, daisies, and long purples   185
That liberal* shepherds give a grosser name,

---

152 **unbated** not blunted
152 **pass of practice** treacherous thrust
158 **cataplasm** poultice
159 **simples** medicinal herbs
166 **shape** role
167 **drift look through** purpose show through
170 **blast in proof** fail in performance
176 **nonce** occasion
177 **stuck** thrust
183 **hoar** silver gray
186 **liberal** coarse-mouthed

But our cold maids do dead men's fingers call them.
There, on the pendent boughs her coronet weeds
Clamb'ring to hang, an envious sliver broke;
When down her weedy trophies and herself   190
Feel in the weeping brook. Her clothes spread wide
And, mermaid-like, awhile they bore her up;
Which time she chanted snatches of old lauds,*
As one incapable* of her own distress,
Or like a creature native and indued*   195
Unto that element; but long it could not be
Till that her garments, heavy with their drink,
Pull'd the poor wretch from her melodious lay
To muddy death.
LAERTES: Alas, then she is drown'd!   200
QUEEN: Drown'd, drown'd.
LAERTES: Too much of water hast thou, poor Ophelia,
And therefore I forbid my tears; but yet
It is our trick,* nature her custom holds,
Let shame say what it will. When these are gone,   205
The woman* will be out. Adieu, my lord.
I have a speech o' fire that fain would blaze
But that this folly douts it.   [*Exit.*]
KING: Let's follow, Gertrude.
How much I had to do to calm his rage!   210
Now fear I this will give it start again;
Therefore let's follow.   [*Exeunt.*]

ACT V

SCENE I————*Elsinore. A churchyard.*

[*Enter two* CLOWNS *with spades and picks.*]
FIRST CLOWN: Is she to be buried in Christian burial when she wilfully seeks her
own salvation?
SECOND CLOWN: I tell thee she is; therefore make her grave straight.* The
crowner* hath sat on her, and finds it Christian burial.   5
FIRST CLOWN: How can that be, unless she drown'd herself in her own defence?
SECOND CLOWN: Why, 'tis found so.
FIRST CLOWN: It must be 'se offendendo';* it cannot be else. For here lies
the point: if I drown myself wittingly, it argues an act; and an act hath

---

¹⁹³ **lauds** hymns
¹⁹⁴ **incapable** unaware
¹⁹⁵ **indued** in harmony with
²⁰⁴ **trick** way
²⁰⁶ **woman** womanly part
ⱽ·¹·³ **straight** straight way
⁴ **crowner** coroner
⁷ **se offendendo** false Latin, instead of "se defendendo" meaning "in self-defense"

three branches—it is to act, to do, to perform; argal,* she drown'd herself
wittingly. 10

SECOND CLOWN: Nay, but hear you, Goodman Delver.

FIRST CLOWN: Give me leave. Here lies the water; good. Here stands the man;
good. If the man go to this water and drown himself, it is, will he, nill he,
he goes—mark you that; but if the water come to him and drown him, he
drowns not himself. Argal, he that is not guilty of his own death shortens 15
not his own life.

SECOND CLOWN: But is this law?

FIRST CLOWN: Ay, marry is't; crowner's quest* law.

SECOND CLOWN: Will you ha' the truth an't? If this had not been a gentlewoman,
she should have been buried out a Christian burial. 20

FIRST CLOWN: Why, there thou say'st; and the more pity that great folk should
have count'nance* in this world to drown or hang themselves more than
their even Christen.* Come, my spade. There is no ancient gentlemen but
gard'ners, ditchers, and grave-makers; they hold up* Adam's profession.

SECOND CLOWN: Was he a gentleman? 25

FIRST CLOWN: 'A was the first that ever bore arms.*

SECOND CLOWN: Why, he had none.

FIRST CLOWN: What, art a heathen? How dost thou understand the Scripture?
The Scripture says Adam digg'd. Could he dig without arms? I'll put another question to thee. If thou answerest me not to the purpose, confess 30
thyself—

SECOND CLOWN: Go to.

FIRST CLOWN: What is he that builds stronger than either the mason, the shipwright, or the carpenter?

SECOND CLOWN: The gallows-maker; for that frame outlives a thousand tenants. 35

FIRST CLOWN: I like thy wit well; in good faith the gallows does well; but how
does it well? It does well to those that do ill. Now thou dost ill to say the
gallows is built stronger than the church; argal, the gallows may do well to
thee. To't again, come.

SECOND CLOWN: Who builds stronger than a mason, a shipwright, or a carpenter? 40

FIRST CLOWN: Ay, tell me that, and unyoke.*

SECOND CLOWN: Marry, now I can tell.

FIRST CLOWN: To't.

SECOND CLOWN: Mass, I cannot tell.

[*Enter* HAMLET *and* HORATIO, *afar off.*]

FIRST CLOWN: Cudgel thy brains no more about it, for your dull ass will not 45
mend his pace with beating, and when you are ask'd this question next, say
'a grave-maker': the house he makes lasts till doomsday. Go, get thee to
Yaughan; fetch me a stoup* of liquor. [*Exit* SECOND CLOWN.]

---

⁹ **argal** false Latin for "ergo" ("therefore")
¹⁸ **crowner's quest** coroner's inquest
²² **count'nance** privilege
²³ **even Christen** fellow Christian
²⁴ **hold up** keep up
²⁶ **bore arms** had a coat of arms
⁴¹ **unyoke** quit work for the day
⁴⁸ **stoup** tankard

[digs and sings]
    In youth, when I did love, did love
     Methought it was very sweet,   50
    To contract-o-the time for-a my behove,*
    O, methought there-a-was nothing-a meet.

HAMLET: Has this fellow no feeling of his business, that 'a sings in grave-making?

HORATIO: Custom hath made it in him a property of easiness.*

HAMLET: 'Tis e'en so; the hand of little employment hath the daintier sense. 55

FIRST CLOWN: *[sings]*
    But age, with his stealing steps,
     Hath clawed me in his clutch,
    And hath shipped me intil the land,
     As if I had never been such.

[throws up a skull]

HAMLET: That skull had a tongue in it, and could sing once. How the knave 60
jowls* it to the ground, as if 'twere Cain's jawbone, that did the first murder! This might be the pate of a politician, which this ass now o'erreaches;
one that would circumvent God, might it not?

HORATIO: It might, my lord.

HAMLET: Or of a courtier; which could say 'Good morrow, sweet lord! How dost 65
thou, sweet lord?' This might be my Lord Such-a-one, that praised my
Lord Such-a-one's horse, when 'a meant to beg it—might it not?

HORATIO: Ay, my lord.

HAMLET: Why, e'en so; and now my Lady Worm's, chapless,* and knock'd about
the mazard* with a sexton's spade. Here's fine revolution, an we had the 70
trick to see't. Did these bones cost no more the breeding but to play at log-
gats* with them? Mine ache to think on't.

FIRST CLOWN: *[sings]*
    A pick-axe and a spade, a spade
     For and a shrouding sheet:
    O, a pit of clay for to be made   75
     For such a guest is meet.

[throws up another skull]

HAMLET: There's another. Why may not that be the skull of a lawyer? Where be
his quiddities* now, his quillets,* his cases, his tenures,* and his tricks? Why
does he suffer this rude knave now to knock him about the sconce* with a
dirty shovel, and will not tell him of his action of battery? Hum! This fel- 80
low might be in's time a great buyer of land, with his statutes, his recog-
nizances, his fines,* his double vouchers, his recoveries. Is this the fine* of
his fines, and the recovery of his recoveries, to have his fine pate full of fine

---

[51] **behove** advantage
[54] **Custom . . . easiness** constant practice has made it easy
[61] **jowls** hurls
[69] **chapless** missing the lower jaw
[70] **mazard** head
[71] **loggats** a game involving throwing at objects
[78] **quiddities, quillets, tenures** legal terms
[79] **sconce** head
[82-83] **fines, fine** play on words for documents, death, and so on

dirt? Will his vouchers vouch him no more of his purchases, and double
ones, too, than the length and breadth of a pair of indentures?* The very 85
conveyances of his lands will scarcely lie in this box; and must th' inheritor
himself have no more, ha?

HORATIO: Not a jot more, my lord.

HAMLET: Is not parchment made of sheep-skins?

HORATIO: Ay, my lord, and of calves' skins, too. 90

HAMLET: They are sheep and calves which seek out assurance in that. I will speak
to this fellow. Whose grave's this, sirrah?

FIRST CLOWN: Mine, sir. [*sings*]

> *O, a pit of clay for to be made*
> *For such a guest is meet.* 95

HAMLET: I think it be thine indeed, for thou liest in't.

FIRST CLOWN: You lie out on't, sir, and therefore 'tis not yours. For my part, I do
not lie in't, yet it is mine.

HAMLET: Thou dost lie in't, to be in't and say it is thine; 'tis for the dead, not for
the quick; therefore thou liest. 100

FIRST CLOWN: 'Tis a quick lie, sir; 'twill away again from me to you.

HAMLET: What man dost thou dig it for?

FIRST CLOWN: For no man, sir.

HAMLET: What woman, then?

FIRST CLOWN: For none neither. 105

HAMLET: Who is to be buried in't?

FIRST CLOWN: One that was a woman, sir; but, rest her soul, she's dead.

HAMLET: How absolute* the knave is! We must speak by the card,* or equivoca-
tion will undo us. By the Lord, Horatio, this three years I have took note of
it: the age is grown so picked* that the toe of the peasant comes so near the 110
heel of the courtier, he galls his kibe.* How long hast thou been a grave-
maker?

FIRST CLOWN: Of all the days i' th' year, I came to't that day that our last King
Hamlet overcame Fortinbras.

HAMLET: How long is that since? 115

FIRST CLOWN: Cannot you tell that? Every fool can tell that: it was that very day
that young Hamlet was born—he that is mad, and sent into England.

HAMLET: Ay, marry, why was he sent into England?

FIRST CLOWN: Why, because 'a was mad: 'a shall recover his wits there; or, if 'a do
not, 'tis no great matter there. 120

HAMLET: Why?

FIRST CLOWN: 'Twill not be seen in him there: there the men are as mad as he.

HAMLET: How came he mad?

FIRST CLOWN: Very strangely, they say.

HAMLET: How strangely? 125

---

[85] **indentures** contracts
[108] **absolute** positive, certain
[108] **card** exactly
[110] **picked** refined
[111] **kibe** sore on the heel

FIRST CLOWN: Faith, e'en with losing his wits.

HAMLET: Upon what ground?

FIRST CLOWN: Why, here in Denmark. I have been sexton here, man and boy, thirty years.

HAMLET: How long will a man lie i' th' earth ere he rot?   130

FIRST CLOWN: Faith, if 'a be not rotten before 'a die—as we have many pocky corses* now-a-days that will scarce hold the laying in—'a will last you some eight year or nine year. A tanner will last you nine year.

HAMLET: Why he more than another?

FIRST CLOWN: Why, sir, his hide is so tann'd with his trade that 'a will keep out 135 water a great while; and your water is a sore decayer of your whoreson dead body. Here's a skull now; this skull has lien you i' th' earth three and twenty years.

HAMLET: Whose was it?

FIRST CLOWN: A whoreson mad fellow's it was. Whose do you think it was?   140

HAMLET: Nay, I know not.

FIRST CLOWN: A pestilence on him for a mad rogue! 'A poured a flagon of Rhenish on my head once. This same skull, sir, was, sir, Yorick's skull, the King's jester.

HAMLET: This?   145

FIRST CLOWN: E'en that.

HAMLET: Let me see. [*takes the skull*] Alas, poor Yorick! I knew him, Horatio: a fellow of infinite jest, of most excellent fancy; he hath borne me on his back a thousand times. And now how abhorred in my imagination it is! My gorge rises at it. Here hung those lips that I have kiss'd I know not how oft. 150 Where be your gibes now, your gambols, your songs, your flashes of merriment that were wont to set the table on a roar? Not one now to mock your own grinning—quite chap-fall'n?* Now get you to my lady's chamber, and tell her, let her paint an inch thick, to this favour* she must come; make her laugh at that. Prithee, Horatio, tell me one thing.   155

HORATIO: What's that, my lord?

HAMLET: Dost thou think Alexander look'd o' this fashion i' th' earth?

HORATIO: E'en so.

HAMLET: And smelt so? Pah   [*throws down the skull*]

HORATIO: E'en so, my lord.   160

HAMLET: To what base uses we may return, Horatio! Why may not imagination trace the noble dust of Alexander till 'a find it stopping a bung-hole?

HORATIO: 'Twere to consider too curiously* to consider so.

HAMLET: No, faith, not a jot; but to follow him thither with modesty enough, and likelihood to lead it, as thus: Alexander died, Alexander was buried, Alexan- 165 der returneth to dust; the dust is earth; of earth we make loam, and why of that loam whereto he was converted might they not stop a beer-barrel?

---

131 **pocky corses** corpses of those with syphilis
153 **chap-fall'n** jawless (down in the mouth)
154 **favour** appearance, condition
163 **curiously** minutely

> Imperious Caesar, dead and turn'd to clay,
> Might stop a hole to keep the wind away.
> O, that that earth which kept the world in awe   170
> Should patch a wall t' expel the winter's flaw!*

But soft! but soft! awhile. Here comes the King.

[*Enter the* KING, QUEEN, LAERTES, *in funeral procession after the coffin, with* PRIEST *and* LORDS *attendant.*]

The Queen, the courtiers. Who is this they follow?
And with such maimed* rites? This doth betoken
The corse they follow did with desperate hand   175
Fordo it own life. 'Twas of some estate.*
Couch* we awhile and mark.   [*retiring with* HORATIO]

LAERTES: What ceremony else?
HAMLET: That is Laertes, a very noble youth. Mark.
LAERTES: What ceremony else?   180
PRIEST: Her obsequies have been so far enlarg'd
    As we have warrantise. Her death was doubtful;
    And, but that great command o'ersways the order,
    She should in ground unsanctified have lodg'd
    Till the last trumpet; for charitable prayers,   185
    Shards, flints, and pebbles, should be thrown on her;
    Yet here she is allow'd her virgin crants,*
    Her maiden strewments, and the bringing home
    Of bell and burial.
LAERTES: Must there no more be done?   190
PRIEST: No more be done.
    We should profane the service of the dead
    To sing sage requiem and such rest to her
    As to peace-parted souls.
LAERTES: Lay her i' th' earth;   195
    And from her fair and unpolluted flesh
    May violets spring! I tell thee, churlish priest,
    A minist'ring angel shall my sister be
    When thou liest howling.
HAMLET: What, the fair Ophelia!   200
QUEEN: Sweets to the sweet; farewell! [*scattering flowers*]
    I hop'd thou shouldst have been my Hamlet's wife;
    I thought thy bride-bed to have deck'd, sweet maid,
    And not have strew'd thy grave.
LAERTES: O, treble woe   205
    Fall ten times treble on that cursed head
    Whose wicked deed thy most ingenious sense*

---

[171] **flaw** gust
[174] **maimed** curtailed
[176] **estate** high rank
[177] **Couch** hide
[187] **crants** garlands
[207] **ingenious sense** finely endowed mind

Depriv'd thee of! Hold off the earth awhile,
Till I have caught her once more in mine arms.
        [*leaps into the grave*]
Now pile your dust upon the quick and dead,   210
Till of this flat a mountain you have made
T' o'er-top old Pelion or the skyish head
Of blue Olympus.
HAMLET: [*advancing*] What is he whose grief
        Bears such an emphasis, whose phrase of sorrow   215
        Conjures the wand'ring stars, and makes them stand
        Like wonder-wounded hearers? This is I,
        Hamlet, the Dane.   [*leaps into the grave*]
LAERTES: The devil take thy soul! [*grappling with him*]
HAMLET: Thou pray'st not well.   220
        I prithee take thy fingers from my throat;
        For, though I am not splenitive* and rash,
        Yet have I in me something dangerous,
        Which let thy wiseness fear. Hold off thy hand.
KING: Pluck them asunder.   225
QUEEN: Hamlet! Hamlet!
ALL: Gentlemen!
HORATIO: Good my lord, be quiet.
        [*The attendants part them, and they come out of the grave.*]
HAMLET: Why, I will fight with him upon this theme
        Until my eyelids will no longer wag.   230
QUEEN: O my son, what theme?
HAMLET: I lov'd Ophelia: forty thousand brothers
        Could not, with all their quantity of love
        Make up my sum. What wilt thou do for her?
KING: O, he is mad, Laertes.   235
QUEEN: For love of God, forbear him.
HAMLET: 'Swounds, show me what th'owt do:
        Woo't weep, woo't fight, woo't fast, woo't tear thyself,
        Woo't drink up eisel,* eat a crocodile?
        I'll do't. Dost come here to whine?   240
        To outface me with leaping in her grave?
        Be buried quick with her, and so will I;
        And, if thou prate of mountains, let them throw
        Millions of acres on us, till our ground,
        Singeing his pate against the burning zone,*   245
        Make Ossa like a wart! Nay, an thou'lt mouth,
        I'll rant as well as thou.
QUEEN: This is mere madness;
        And thus awhile the fit will work on him;
        Anon, as patient as the female dove   250

---

222 **splenitive** fiery spirited
239 **eisel** vinegar
245 **burning zone** the sun

When that her golden couplets are disclos'd*
His silence will sit drooping.
HAMLET: Hear you, sir:
What is the reason that you use me thus?
I lov'd you ever. But it is no matter.   255
Let Hercules himself do what he may,
The cat will mew, and dog will have his day.   [*Exit.*]
KING: I pray thee, good Horatio, wait upon him.
          [*Exit* HORATIO.]
[*to* LAERTES] Strengthen your patience in our last night's speech;
We'll put the matter to the present push.*—   260
Good Gertrude, set some watch over your son.—
This grave shall have a living* monument.
An hour of quiet shortly shall we see;
Till then in patience our proceeding be.   [*Exeunt.*]

SCENE II————*Elsinore. The Castle.*

[*Enter* HAMLET *and* HORATIO.]
HAMLET: So much for this, sir; now shall you see the other.
You do remember all the circumstance?
HORATIO: Remember it, my lord!
HAMLET: Sir, in my heart there was a kind of fighting
That would not let me sleep. Methought I lay   5
Worse than the mutines in the bilboes.* Rashly,
And prais'd be rashness for it—let us know,
Our indiscretion sometime serves us well,
When our deep plots do pall,* and that should learn us
There's a divinity that shapes our ends,   10
Rough-hew them how we will.
HORATIO: That is most certain.
HAMLET: Up from my cabin,
My sea-gown scarf'd about me, in the dark
Grop'd to find out them; had my desire;   15
Finger'd* their packet, and in fine withdrew
To mine own room again, making so bold,
My fears forgetting manners, to unseal
Their grand commission; where I found, Horatio,
Ah, royal knavery! an exact command,   20
Larded* with many several sorts of reasons,
Importing Denmark's health and England's, too,

With, ho! such bugs and goblins in my life*—
That, on the supervise,* no leisure bated,*
No, not to stay the grinding of the axe,   25
My head should be struck off.
HORATIO: Is't possible?
HAMLET: Here's the commission; read it at more leisure.
    But wilt thou hear now how I did proceed?
HORATIO: I beseech you.   30
HAMLET: Being thus benetted round with villainies—
    Ere I could make a prologue to my brains,
    They had begun the play—I sat me down;
    Devis'd a new commission; wrote it fair.
    I once did hold it, as our statists* do,   35
    A baseness to write fair,* and labour'd much
    How to forget that learning; but sir, now
    It did me yeoman's service. Wilt thou know
    Th' effect* of what I wrote?
HORATIO: Ay, good my lord.   40
HAMLET: An earnest conjuration from the King,
    As England was his faithful tributary,
    As love between them like the palm might flourish,
    As peace should still her wheaten garland wear
    And stand a comma* tween their amities,   45
    And many such like as's of great charge,
    That, on the view and knowing of these contents,
    Without debatement further more or less,
    He should those bearers put to sudden death,
    Not shriving-time* allow'd.   50
HORATIO: How was this seal'd?
HAMLET: Why, even in that was heaven ordinant.*
    I had my father's signet in my purse,
    Which was the model of that Danish seal;
    Folded the writ up in the form of th' other;   55
    Subscrib'd it, gave't th' impression, plac'd it safely,
    The changeling never known. Now, the next day
    Was our sea-fight; and what to this was sequent
    Thou knowest already.
HORATIO: So Guildenstern and Rosencrantz go to't.   60
HAMLET: Why, man, they did make love to this employment;
    They are not near my conscience; their defeat

---

23 **bugs . . . my life** imagined terrors if I were allowed to live
24 **supervise** reading
24 **leisure baited** delay allowed
35 **statists** statesmen
36 **fair** clearly
39 **effect** purport
45 **comma** link
50 **shriving-time** time to be absolved of sin
52 **ordinant** on my side

Does by their own insinuation* grow:
'Tis dangerous when the baser nature comes
Between the pass and fell* incensed points   65
Of mighty opposites.
HORATIO: Why, what a king is this!
HAMLET: Does it not, think thee, stand me now upon*—
He that hath kill'd my king and whor'd my mother,
Popp'd in between th' election* and my hopes;   70
Thrown out his angle for my proper life,*
And with such coz'nage*—is't not perfect conscience
To quit* him with this arm? And is't not to be damn'd
To let this canker of our nature come
In further evil?   75
HORATIO: It must be shortly known to him from England
What is the issue of the business there.
HAMLET: It will be short; the interim is mine.
And a man's life's no more than to say 'one.'
But I am very sorry, good Horatio,   80
That to Laertes I forgot myself;
For by the image of my cause I see
The portraiture of his. I'll court his favours.
But sure the bravery of his grief did put me
Into a tow'ring passion.   85
HORATIO: Peace; who comes here?
          [*Enter young* OSRIC.]
OSRIC: Your lordship is right welcome back to Denmark.
HAMLET: I humbly thank you, sir. [*aside to* HORATIO] Dost know this water-fly?
HORATIO: [*aside to* HAMLET] No, my good lord.
HAMLET: [*aside to* HORATIO] Thy state is the more gracious; for 'tis a vice to know 90
him. He hath much land, and fertile. Let a beast be lord of beasts, and his
crib shall stand at the king's mess!* 'Tis a chough,* but, as I say, spacious*
in the possession of dirt.
OSRIC: Sweet lord, if your lordship were at leisure, I should impart a thing to you
from his Majesty.   95
HAMLET: I will receive it, sir, with all diligence of spirit. Put your bonnet to his
right use, 'tis for the head.
OSRIC: I thank your lordship; it is very hot.
HAMLET: No, believe me, 'tis very cold; the wind is northerly.

---

[63] **insinuation** meddling
[65] **pass and fell** thrust and cruel
[68] **stand me now upon** became incumbent on me
[70] **election** selection to be king
[71] **angle for my proper life** tried to end my own life
[72] **coz'nage** trickery
[73] **quit** pay back
[92] **mess** table
[92] **chough** chatterer
[92] **spacious** well off

OSRIC: It is indifferent cold, my lord, indeed.   100

HAMLET: But yet methinks it is very sultry and hot for my complexion.*

OSRIC: Exceedingly, my lord; it is very sultry, as 'twere—I cannot tell how. But, my lord, his Majesty bade me signify to you that 'a has laid a great wager on your head. Sir, this is the matter—

HAMLET: I beseech you, remember.   105

[HAMLET *moves him to put on his hat.*]

OSRIC: Nay, good my lord; for my ease, in good faith. Sir, here is newly come to court Laertes; believe me, an absolute gentleman, full of most excellent differences,* of very soft society and great showing. Indeed, to speak feelingly of him, he is the card* or calendar of gentry, for you shall find in him the continent* of what part a gentleman would see.   110

HAMLET: Sir, his definement* suffers no perdition* in you; though, I know, to divide him inventorially would dozy* th' arithmetic of memory, and yet but yaw neither in respect of his quick sail. But, in the verity of extolment, I take him to be a soul of great article, and his infusion of such dearth and rareness, as to make true diction of him, his semblable is his mirror, and 115 who else would trace him, his umbrage, nothing more.

OSRIC: Your lordship speaks most infallibly of him.

HAMLET: The concernancy,* sir? Why do we wrap the gentleman in our more rawer breath?

OSRIC: Sir?   120

HORATIO: [*aside to* HAMLET] Is't not possible to understand in another tongue? You will to't, sir, really.

HAMLET: What imports the nomination of this gentleman?

OSRIC: Of Laertes?

HORATIO: [*aside*] His purse is empty already; all's golden words are spent.   125

HAMLET: Of him, sir.

OSRIC: I know you are not ignorant—

HAMLET: I would you did, sir; yet, in faith, if you did, it would not much approve* me. Well, sir.

OSRIC: You are not ignorant of what excellence Laertes is—   130

HAMLET: I dare not confess that, lest I should compare with him in excellence; but to know a man well were to know himself.

OSRIC: I mean, sir, for his weapon; but in the imputation* laid on him by them, in his meed* he's unfellowed.

HAMLET: What's his weapon?   135

OSRIC: Rapier and dagger.

---

[101] **complexion** temperament

[107] **differences** distinguishing characteristics

[109] **card** model

[110] **continent** summary

[111] **definement** description

[111] **perdition** loss (this entire speech mocks Osric's use of overblown language)

[112] **dozy** dizzy

[118] **concernancy** meaning

[128] **approve** commend

[133] **imputation** reputation

[134] **meed** merit

HAMLET: That's two of his weapons—but well.

OSRIC: The King, sir, hath wager'd him with six Barbary horses; against the which he has impon'd,* as I take it, six French rapiers and poniards, with their assigns,* as girdle, hangers, and so—three of the carriages, in faith, are 140 very dear to fancy, very responsive to the hilts, most delicate carriages, and of very liberal conceit.

HAMLET: What call you the carriages?

HORATIO: [*aside to* HAMLET] I knew you must be edified by the margent* ere you had done. 145

OSRIC: The carriages, sir, are the hangers.

HAMLET: The phrase would be more germane to the matter if we could carry a cannon by our sides. I would it might be hangers till then. But on: six Barbary horses against six French swords, their assigns, and three liberal conceited carriages; that's the French bet against the Danish. Why is this all 150 impon'd, as you call it?

OSRIC: The King, sir, hath laid, sir, that in a dozen passes between yourself and him he shall not exceed you three hits; he hath laid on twelve for nine, and it would come to immediate trial if your lordship would vouchsafe the answer.

HAMLET: How if I answer no? 155

OSRIC: I mean, my lord, the opposition of your person in trial.

HAMLET: Sir, I will walk here in the hall. If it please his Majesty, it is the breathing time of day* with me; let the foils be brought, the gentlemen willing, and the King hold his purpose, I will win for him an I can; if not, I will gain nothing but my shame and the odd hits. 160

OSRIC: Shall I redeliver you e'en so?

HAMLET: To this effect, sir, after what flourish your nature will.

OSRIC: I commend my duty to your lordship.

HAMLET: Yours, yours. [*Exit* OSRIC.] He does well to commend it himself; there are no tongues else for's turn. 165

HORATIO: This lapwing runs away with the shell on his head.

HAMLET: 'A did comply, sir, with his dug before 'a suck'd it.* Thus has he, and many more of the same bevy, that I know the drossy age dotes on, only got the tune of the time and outward habit of encounter*—a kind of yesty* collection, which carries them through and through the most fann'd and winnowed opinions; and do but blow them to their trial, the bubbles are out.* 170

[*Enter a* LORD.]

LORD: My lord, his Majesty commended him to you by young Osric, who brings back to him that you attend him in the hall. He sends to know if your pleasure hold to play with Laertes, or that you will take longer time.

---

139 **impon'd** wagered
140 **assigns** accompaniments
144 **margent** exaggerated terminology
157-58 **breathing time of day** time when I do my exercises
167 **'A did comply . . . suck'd it** He was ceremoniously polite to his mother's breast before he sucked it
169 **habit of encounter** superficial way of talking to people
169 **yesty** frothy
171 **blow them . . . bubbles are out** question them and they are at a loss

HAMLET: I am constant to my purposes; they follow the king's pleasure: if his fit- 175
    ness speaks, mine is ready now—or whensoever, provided I be so able as
    now.

LORD: The King and Queen and all are coming down.

HAMLET: In happy time.

LORD: The Queen desires you to use some gentle entertainment* to Laertes be- 180
    fore you fall to play.

HAMLET: She well instructs me.   [*Exit* LORD.]

HORATIO: You will lose this wager, my lord.

HAMLET: I do not think so; since he went into France I have been in continual
    practice. I shall win at the odds. But thou wouldst not think how ill all's 185
    here about my heart; but it is no matter.

HORATIO: Nay, good my lord—

HAMLET: It is but foolery; but it is such a kind of gaingiving* as would perhaps
    trouble a woman.

HORATIO: If your mind dislike anything, obey it. I will forestall their repair 190
    hither, and say you are not fit.

HAMLET: Not a whit, we defy augury: there is a special providence in the fall of
    a sparrow. If it be now, 'tis not to come; if it be not to come, it will be now;
    if it be not now, yet it will come—the readiness is all. Since no man owes
    of aught he leaves, what is't to leave betimes?* Let be.   195
        [*A table prepared. Trumpets, drums, and officers with cushions, foils, and*
        daggers. Enter KING, QUEEN, LAERTES, *and all the state.*]

KING: Come, Hamlet, come, and take this hand from me.
        [*The* KING *puts* LAERTES' *hand into* HAMLET'S.]

HAMLET: Give me your pardon, sir. I have done you wrong;
    But pardon't, as you are a gentleman.
    This presence* knows,
    And you must needs have heard how I am punish'd   200
    With a sore distraction. What I have done
    That might your nature, honour, and exception,*
    Roughly awake, I here proclaim was madness.
    Was't Hamlet wrong'd Laertes? Never Hamlet.
    If Hamlet from himself be ta'en away,   205
    And when he's not himself does wrong Laertes,
    Then Hamlet does it not, Hamlet denies it.
    Who does it, then? His madness. If't be so,
    Hamlet is of the faction* that is wrong'd;
    His madness is poor Hamlet's enemy.   210
    Sir, in this audience,
    Let my disclaiming from a purpos'd evil
    Free me so far in your most generous thoughts

---

[180] **gentle entertainment** be courteous
[188] **gaingiving** misgiving
[195] **betimes** early
[199] **presence** assembly
[202] **exception** disapproval
[209] **faction** group

   That I have shot my arrow o'er the house
   And hurt my brother.   215
LAERTES: I am satisfied in nature,
   Whose motive in this case should stir me most
   To my revenge; but in my terms of honour
   I stand aloof, and will no reconcilement
   Till by some elder masters of known honour   220
   I have a voice and precedent of peace
   To keep my name ungor'd—but till that time
   I do receive your offer'd love like love,
   And will not wrong it.
HAMLET: I embrace it freely;   225
   And will this brother's wager frankly play.
   Give us the foils. Come on.
LAERTES: Come, one for me.
HAMLET: I'll be your foil, Laertes; in mine ignorance
   Your skill shall, like a star i' th' darkest night,   230
   Stick fiery off* indeed.
LAERTES: You mock me, sir.
HAMLET: No, by this hand.
KING: Give them the foils, young Osric. Cousin Hamlet,
   You know the wager?   235
HAMLET: Very well, my lord;
   Your Grace has laid the odds a' th' weaker side.
KING: I do not fear it: I have seen you both;
   But since he's better'd,* we have therefore odds.
LAERTES: This is too heavy; let me see another.   240
HAMLET: This likes me well. These foils have all a length?
   [*They prepare to play.*]
OSRIC: Ay, my good lord.
KING: Set me the stoups of wine upon that table.
   If Hamlet give the first or second hit,
   Or quit in answer of the third exchange,   245
   Let all the battlements their ordnance fire;
   The King shall drink to Hamlet's better breath,
   And in the cup an union* shall he throw,
   Richer than that which four successive kings
   In Denmark's crown have worn. Give me the cups;   250
   And let the kettle* to the trumpet speak,
   The trumpet to the cannoneer without,
   The cannons to the heavens, the heaven to earth,
   'Now the King drinks to Hamlet.' Come, begin—
   And you, the judges, bear a wary eye.   255

[231] **stick fiery off** stand out brilliantly
[239] **better'd** improved
[248] **union** pearl
[251] **kettle** kettledrum

HAMLET: Come on, sir.
LAERTES: Come, my lord.   [*They play.*]
HAMLET: One.
LAERTES: No.
HAMLET: Judgment?   260
OSRIC: A hit, a very palpable hit.
LAERTES: Well, again.
KING: Stay, give me drink. Hamlet, this pearl is thine;
     Here's to thy health. [*drum, trumpets, and shot*] Give him the cup.
HAMLET: I'll play this bout first; set it by awhile.   265
     Come. [*They play.*] Another hit; what say you?
LAERTES: A touch, a touch, I do confess't.
KING: Our son shall win.
QUEEN: He's fat,* and scant of breath.
     Here, Hamlet, take my napkin, rub thy brows.   270
     The Queen carouses to thy fortune, Hamlet.
HAMLET: Good madam!
KING: Gertrude, do not drink.
QUEEN: I will, my lord; I pray you pardon me.
KING: [*aside*] It is the poison'd cup; it is too late.   275
HAMLET: I dare not drink yet, madam; by and by.
QUEEN: Come, let me wipe thy face.
LAERTES: My lord, I'll hit him now.
KING: I do not think't.
LAERTES: [*aside*] And yet it is almost against my conscience.   280
HAMLET: Come, for the third. Laertes, you do but dally;
     I pray you pass with your best violence;
     I am afeard you make a wanton* of me.
LAERTES: Say you so? Come on.   [*They play.*]
OSRIC: Nothing, neither way.   285
LAERTES: Have at you now!
          [LAERTES *wounds* HAMLET; *then, in scuffling, they change rapiers, and*
          HAMLET *wounds* LAERTES.]
KING: Part them; they are incens'd.
HAMLET: Nay, come again.   [*The* QUEEN *falls.*]
OSRIC: Look to the Queen there, ho!
HORATIO: They bleed on both sides. How is it, my lord?   290
OSRIC: How is't, Laertes?
LAERTES: Why, as a woodcock, to mine own springe,* Osric;
     I am justly kill'd with mine own treachery.
HAMLET: How does the Queen?
KING: She swoons to see them bleed.   295
QUEEN: No, no, the drink, the drink! O my dear Hamlet!
     The drink, the drink! I am poison'd.   [*dies*]

²⁶⁹ **fat** sweaty
²⁸³ **wanton** spoiled child
²⁹² **springe** snare

HAMLET: O, villainy! Ho! let the door be lock'd.
    Treachery! Seek it out.   [LAERTES *falls.*]
LAERTES: It is here, Hamlet. Hamlet, thou art slain;   300
    No med'cine in the world can do thee good;
    In thee there is not half an hour's life;
    The treacherous instrument is in thy hand,
    Unbated and envenom'd. The foul practice*
    Hath turn'd itself on me; lo, here I lie,   305
    Never to rise again. Thy mother's poison'd.
    I can no more. The King, the King's to blame.
HAMLET: The point envenom'd, too!
    Then, venom, to thy work.   [*stabs the* KING]
ALL: Treason! treason!   310
KING: O, yet defend me, friends; I am but hurt.
HAMLET: Here, thou incestuous, murd'rous, damned Dane,
    Drink off this potion. Is thy union here?
    Follow my mother.   [KING *dies.*]
LAERTES: He is justly serv'd: 315
    It is a poison temper'd* by himself.
    Exchange forgiveness with me, noble Hamlet.
    Mine and my father's death come not upon thee,
    Nor thine on me!   [*dies*]
HAMLET: Heaven make thee free of it! I follow thee.   320
    I am dead, Horatio. Wretched Queen, adieu!
    You that look pale and tremble at this chance,
    That are but mutes or audience to this act,
    Had I but time, as this fell sergeant Death
    Is strict in his arrest, O, I could tell you—   325
    But let it be. Horatio, I am dead:
    Thou livest; report me and my cause aright
    To the unsatisfied.
HORATIO: Never believe it.
    I am more an antique Roman* than a Dane;   330
    Here's yet some liquor left.
HAMLET: As th'art a man,
    Give me the cup. Let go. By heaven, I'll ha't.
    O good Horatio, what a wounded name,
    Things standing thus unknown, shall live behind me!   335
    If thou didst ever hold me in thy heart,
    Absent thee from felicity awhile,
    And in this harsh world draw thy breath in pain,
    To tell my story. [*march afar off, and shot within*] What warlike noise
        is this?

---

304 **foul practice** deception
316 **temper'd** mixed
330 **antique Roman** given to suicide

OSRIC: Young Fortinbras, with conquest come from Poland,   340
    To th'ambassadors of England gives
    This warlike volley.
HAMLET: O, I die, Horatio!
    The potent poison quite o'er-crows* my spirit.
    I cannot live to hear the news from England,   345
    But I do prophesy th' election lights
    On Fortinbras; he has my dying voice.
    So tell him, with th' occurrents,* more and less,
    Which have solicited*—the rest is silence.   [*dies*]
HORATIO: Now cracks a noble heart. Good night, sweet prince,   350
    And flights of angels sing thee to thy rest!   [*march within*]
    Why does the drum come hither?
      [*Enter* FORTINBRAS *and* ENGLISH AMBASSADORS, *with drum, colours,*
      and attendants.]
FORTINBRAS: Where is this sight?
HORATIO: What is it you would see?
    If aught of woe or wonder, cease your search.   355
FORTINBRAS: This quarry* cries on havoc.* O proud death,
    What feast is toward* in thine eternal cell
    That thou so many princes at a shot
    So bloodily hast struck?
FIRST AMBASSADOR: The sight is dismal;   360
    And our affairs from England come too late:
    The ears are senseless that should give us hearing
    To tell him his commandment is fulfill'd
    That Rosencrantz and Guildenstern are dead.
    Where should we have our thanks?   365
HORATIO: Not from his* mouth,
    Had it th' ability of life to thank you:
    He never gave commandment for their death.
    But since, so jump* upon this bloody question,
    You from the Polack wars, and you from England,   370
    And here arrived, give order that these bodies
    High on a stage* be placed to the view;
    And let me speak to th' yet unknowing world
    How these things came about. So shall you hear
    Of carnal, bloody, and unnatural acts;   375

---

[344] **o'er-crows** overpowers
[348] **occurrents** occurrences
[349] **solicited** incited
[356] **quarry** heap of slain bodies
[356] **cries on havoc** proclaims general slaughter
[357] **toward** in preparation
[366] **his** Claudius'
[369] **jump** precisely
[372] **stage** platform

Of accidental judgments, casual* slaughters;
Of deaths put on by cunning and forc'd cause;
And, in this upshot, purposes mistook
Fall'n on th' inventors' heads—all this can I
Truly deliver.   380
FORTINBRAS: Let us haste to hear it,
And call the noblest to the audience.
For me, with sorrow I embrace my fortune;
I have some rights of memory* in this kingdom,
Which now to claim my vantage doth invite me.   385
HORATIO: Of that I shall have also cause to speak,
And from his mouth whose voice will draw on more.*
But let this same be presently perform'd,
Even while men's minds are wild, lest more mischance
On* plots and errors happen.   390
FORTINBRAS: Let four captains
Bear Hamlet like a soldier to the stage;
For he was likely, had he been put on,
To have prov'd most royal; and for his passage*
The soldier's music and the rite of war   395
Speak loudly for him.
Take up the bodies. Such a sight as this
Becomes the field, but here shows much amiss.
Go, bid the soldiers shoot.
        [*Exeunt marching. A peal of ordnance shot off.*]

---

[376] **casual** unplanned
[384] **rights of memory** past claims
[387] **voice will draw on more** vote will influence others
[390] **On** on top of earlier
[394] **passage** death

The Servant of Two Masters (1745)

Carlo Goldoni (1707–1793)

English version by Edward J. Dent

Commedia dell'arte was one of the most popular of all theatrical forms between 1575 and 1775. Originally, a *commedia* script was merely a scenario that outlined the situation, complications, and outcome. In performance, the actors improvised the dialogue and fleshed out the action. The plots were most often comic, revolving around love affairs, comic misunderstandings, and deliberate deceptions. The actors also developed a number of surefire bits of comic business (*lazzi*) that could be brought in as the actors saw fit.

    Commedia scripts utilized a number of stock characters. There were usually two pairs of young lovers. Unlike the other roles, these did not make use of masks, and they dressed in the latest fashions. They were usually the children of other stock characters, most often Pantalone (a Venetian merchant) and Dottore (a doctor or lawyer who loved to show off his spurious learning). These latter characters had fixed costumes and masks. The most varied of the *commedia* types were the servants (*zanni*), of whom the most popular was Arlecchino (Harlequin), a character with a mixture of cunning and simplemindedness who was usually at the center of every intrigue and mix-up. His mask was black, and his costume was made of diamond-shaped red, green, and blue-patterned cloth. Sometimes the character was called by other names (in *The Servant of Two Masters* he is called Truffaldino). Among the other servants, a rather coarse, somewhat bawdy maid figured prominently. In *The Servant of Two Masters* she is called Smeraldina.

    By the 1730s, *commedia* had lost much of its vitality, in part because it had become repetitive and predictable. Carlo Goldoni, a Venetian playwright, sought to revive it by reforming some of its conventions. He convinced some companies to let him write out all the dialogue but to leave room for improvisation. *The Servant of Two Masters* is among the most successful plays of this type. Through it, we can recapture much of the flavor and spirit of *commedia*, even though the element of improvisation has been greatly reduced.

    The Servant of Two Masters incorporates the stock characters of *commedia*. There are two pairs of lovers (Clarice and Silvio; Beatrice and Florindo), two masters (Pantalone and Dottore), and three servants (Truffaldino, Smeraldina, and Brighella—although Brighella has been transformed into an innkeeper). By far the most important character is Truffaldino, for, though the story revolves around the lovers, it is Truffaldino's simplemindedness that creates most of the difficulties and his cleverness that resolves them. He is also offered several opportunities to improvise *lazzi*.

Goldoni is a master of plot development. Everything is set up carefully in the opening scenes, although much of the subsequent action is dependent on coincidence—especially that Beatrice (disguised as her brother) and Florindo (her lover) take up residence in the same inn and each hires Truffaldino as a servant.

In *The Servant of Two Masters*, Goldoni is concerned primarily with providing entertainment for a popular audience and with reworking the conventions of a long-familiar form. That he succeeded is indicated by the continuing popularity of the play.

Fantasticks

Carlo Goldoni

The Servant of Two Masters

English Version by Edward J. Dent

CHARACTERS

PANTALONE DEI BISOGNOSI, *a Venetian merchant*
CLARICE, *his daughter*
DR. LOMBARDI
SILVIO, *his son*
BEATRICE RASPONI, *a lady of Turin, disguised as her brother*
    FEDERICO RASPONI
FLORINDO ARETUSI, *of Turin, lover of* BEATRICE
BRIGHELLA, *an innkeeper*
SMERALDINA, *maidservant to* CLARICE
TRUFFALDINO, *servant first to* BEATRICE, *and afterward to* FLORINDO
FIRST WAITER
SECOND WAITER
FIRST PORTER
SECOND PORTER

The scene is laid in Venice. The action takes place within a single day.

ACT I

SCENE I———*A Room in the House of* PANTALONE.

SILVIO: [*offering his hand to* CLARICE] Here is my hand, and with it I give you my
    whole heart.
PANTALONE: [*to* CLARICE] Come, come, not so shy, give him your hand too. Then
    you will be betrothed, and very soon you will be married.
CLARICE: Dear Silvio, here is my hand. I promise to be your wife.
SILVIO: And I promise to be your husband.
    [*They take hands.*]
DR. LOMBARDI: Well done. Now that is settled, and there's no going back on it.
SMERALDINA: [*aside*] There's luck for you! And me just bursting to get married!
PANTALONE: [*to* BRIGHELLA *and* SMERALDINA] You two shall be witnesses of this
    betrothal of my daughter Clarice to Signor Silvio, the worthy son of our
    good Dr. Lombardi!

BRIGHELLA: [*to* PANTALONE] We will, sir, and I thank you for the honor.

PANTALONE: Look you, I was witness at your wedding, and now you are a witness to my daughter's. I have asked no great company of friends and relations, for the doctor too is a man of my sort. We will have dinner together; we will enjoy ourselves and nobody shall disturb us.

    [*to* CLARICE *and* SILVIO]

What say you, children, does that suit you?

SILVIO: I desire nothing better than to be near my beloved bride.

SMERALDINA: [*aside*] Yes, that's the best of all foods.

DR. LOMBARDI: My son is no lover of vanities. He is an honest lad; he loves your daughter and thinks of nothing else.

PANTALONE: Truly we may say that this marriage was made in Heaven, for had it not been for the death of Federigo Rasponi, my correspondent at Turin, you know, I had promised my daughter to him.

    [*to* SILVIO]

I could not then have given her to my dear son-in-law.

SILVIO: I can call myself fortunate indeed, sir; I know not if Signora Clarice will say the same.

CLARICE: You wrong me, dear Silvio. You should know if I love you. I should have married Signor Rasponi in obedience to my father; but my heart has always been yours.

DR. LOMBARDI: 'Tis true indeed, the will of Heaven is wrought in unexpected ways.

    [*to* PANTALONE]

Pray, sir, how did Federigo Rasponi come to die?

PANTALONE: Poor wretch, I hardly know. He was killed one night on account of some affair about his sister. Someone ran a sword through him and that was the end of him.

BRIGHELLA: Did that happen at Turin, sir?

PANTALONE: At Turin.

BRIGHELLA: Alas, poor gentleman! I am indeed sorry to hear it.

PANTALONE: [*to* BRIGHELLA] Did you know Signor Federigo Rasponi?

BRIGHELLA: Indeed and I did, sir. I was three years at Turin. I knew his sister too—a fine high-spirited young woman—dressed like a man and rode a-horseback; and he loved her more than anyone in the world. Lord! Who'd ha' thought it?

PANTALONE: Well, misfortune waits for all of us. But come, let us talk no more of sad things. Do you know what I have in mind, good master Brighella? I know you love to show your skill in the kitchen. Now, I would have you make us a few dishes of your best.

BRIGHELLA: 'Tis a pleasure to serve you, sir. Though I say it that shouldn't, customers are always well contented at my house. They say there's no place where they eat as they do there. You shall taste something fine, sir.

PANTALONE: Good, good. Let's have something with plenty of gravy that we can sop the bread in.

    [*a knock at the door*]

Oh! Someone is knocking. Smeraldina, see who it is.

SMERALDINA: Yes, sir.

[*goes to door*]

CLARICE: [*wishing to retire*] Sir, may I beg your leave?

PANTALONE: Wait; we are all coming. Let us hear who is there.

SMERALDINA: [*coming back*] Sir, there is a gentleman's servant below who desires to give you a message. He would tell me nothing. He says he would speak to the master.

PANTALONE: Tell him to come up. We'll hear what he has to say.

SMERALDINA: I'll fetch him, sir.

[*Exit.*]

CLARICE: May I not go, sir?

PANTALONE: Whither then, madam?

CLARICE: I know not—to my own room—

PANTALONE: No, madam, no; you stay here.

[*aside to* DR. LOMBARDI]

These lovebirds can't be left alone just yet for a while.

DR. LOMBARDI: [*aside to* PANTALONE] Prudence above all things!

[SMERALDINA *brings in* TRUFFALDINO.]

TRUFFALDINO: My most humble duty to the ladies and gentlemen. And a very fine company too, to be sure! Very fine, indeed!

PANTALONE: Who are you, my good friend? And what is your business?

TRUFFALDINO: [*to* PANTALONE, *pointing to* CLARICE] Who is this fair gentlewoman?

PANTALONE: That is my daughter.

TRUFFALDINO: Delighted to hear it.

SMERALDINA: [*to* TRUFFALDINO] What's more, she is going to be married.

TRUFFALDINO: I'm sorry to hear it. And who are you?

SMERALDINA: I am her maid, sir.

TRUFFALDINO: I congratulate her.

PANTALONE: Come, sir, have done with ceremony. What do you want with me? Who are you? Who sends you hither?

TRUFFALDINO: Patience, patience, my good sir, take it easy. Three questions at once is too much for a poor man.

PANTALONE: [*aside to* DR. LOMBARDI] I think the man's a fool.

DR. LOMBARDI: [*aside to* PANTALONE] I think he's playing the fool.

TRUFFALDINO: [*to* SMERALDINA] Is it you that are going to be married?

SMERALDINA: [*sighs*] No, sir.

PANTALONE: Will you tell me who you are, or will you go about your business?

TRUFFALDINO: If you only want to know who I am, I'll tell you in two words. I am the servant of my master.

[*turns to* SMERALDINA]

To go back to what I was saying—

PANTALONE: But who is your master?

TRUFFALDINO: [*to* PANTALONE] He is a gentleman who desires the honor of paying his respects to you.

[*to* SMERALDINA]

We must have a talk about this marriage.

PANTALONE: Who is this gentleman, I say? What is his name?

TRUFFALDINO: Oh, that's a long story. Si'or Federigo Rasponi of Turin, that's my
master, and he sends his compliments, and he has come to see you, and he's
down below, and he sends me to say that he would like to come up and he's
waiting for an answer. Anything else, or will that do?
[*All look surprised.*]
[*to* SMERALDINA, *as before*]
Let's begin again.

PANTALONE: Come here and talk to me. What the devil do you mean?

TRUFFALDINO: And if you want to know who I am, I am Truffaldin' Battocchio
from Bergamo.

PANTALONE: I don't care who *you* are. Tell me again, who is this master of yours?
I fear I did not understand you rightly.

TRUFFALDINO: Poor old gentleman! He must be hard of hearing. My master is
Si'or Federigo Rasponi of Turin.

PANTALONE: Away! You must be mad. Signor Federigo Rasponi of Turin is dead.

TRUFFALDINO: Dead?

PANTALONE: To be sure he's dead, worse luck for him.

TRUFFALDINO: [*aside*] The devil! My master dead? Why, I left him alive downstairs!
[*to* PANTALONE]
You really mean he is dead?

PANTALONE: I tell you for an absolute certainty, he is dead.

DR. LOMBARDI: 'Tis the honest truth; he is dead; we can have no doubt about it.

TRUFFALDINO: [*aside*] Alas, my poor master! He must have met with an accident.
[*to* PANTALONE *as if retiring*]
Your very humble servant, sir.

PANTALONE: Can I do nothing more for you?

TRUFFALDINO: If he's dead, there's nothing more to do.
[*aside*]
But I'm going to see if it's true or not.
[*Exit.*]

PANTALONE: What are we to make of this fellow? Is he knave or fool?

DR. LOMBARDI: I really don't know. Probably a little of both.

BRIGHELLA: I should say he was just a zany. He comes from Bergamo; I can't
think he is a knave.

SMERALDINA: He's not such a fool, neither.
[*aside*]
I like that little dark fellow.

PANTALONE: But what is this nightmare about Signor Federigo?

CLARICE: If 'tis true indeed that he is here, it would be the worst of news
for me.

PANTALONE: What nonsense! Did not you see the letters yourself?

SILVIO: If he *is* alive and here after all, he has come too late.
[*reenter* TRUFFALDINO.]

TRUFFALDINO: Gentlemen, I am surprised at you. Is that the way to treat a poor
man? Is that the way you deceive strangers? Is that the behavior of a gentleman? I shall insist upon satisfaction.

PANTALONE: [*to* DR. LOMBARDI] We must be careful, the man's mad.

[*to* TRUFFALDINO]

What's the matter? What have they done to you?

TRUFFALDINO: To go and tell me that Si'or Federigo Rasponi was dead!

PANTALONE: Well, what then?

TRUFFALDINO: What then? Well, he's here, safe and sound, in good health and spirits, and he desires to pay his respects to you, with your kind permission.

PANTALONE: Signor Federigo?

TRUFFALDINO: Si'or Federigo.

PANTALONE: Rasponi?

TRUFFALDINO: Rasponi.

PANTALONE: Of Turin?

TRUFFALDINO: Of Turin.

PANTALONE: Be off to Bedlam, my lad; that's the place for you.

TRUFFALDINO: The Devil take *you* there, sir! You'll make me swear like a Turk. I tell you he's here, in the house, in the next room, bad luck to you.

PANTALONE: If you say any more I'll break your head.

DR. LOMBARDI: No, no, Signor Pantalone; I tell you what to do. Tell him to bring in this person whom he thinks to be Federigo Rasponi.

PANTALONE: Well, bring in this man that is risen from the dead.

TRUFFALDINO: He may have been dead and risen from the dead, for all I know. That's no affair of mine. But he's alive now, sure enough, and you shall see him with your own eyes. I'll go and tell him to come.

[*angrily to* PANTALONE]

And 'tis time you learned how to behave properly to strangers, to gentlemen of my position, to honorable citizens of Bergamo.

[*to* SMERALDINA]

Young woman, we will have some talk together when you will.

[*Exit.*]

CLARICE: Silvio, I am all of a tremble.

SILVIO: Have no fear; whatever happens, you shall be mine.

DR. LOMBARDI: Now we shall discover the truth.

PANTALONE: Some rogue, I dare say, come to tell me a string of lies.

BRIGHELLA: Sir, as I told you just now, I knew Signor Federigo; we shall see if it be he.

SMERALDINA: [*aside*] That little dark fellow doesn't look like a liar. I wonder, now, if—

[*curtsy to* PANTALONE]

By your good leave, sir.

[*Exit.*]

[*Enter* BEATRICE, *dressed as a man.*]

BEATRICE: Signor Pantalone, that courtesy which I have so much admired in your correspondence is but ill matched in the treatment which I have received from you in person. I send my servant to pay you my respects, and you keep me standing in the street for half an hour before you condescend to allow me to enter.

PANTALONE: [*nervously*] I ask your pardon. But, sir, who are you?

BEATRICE: Your obedient servant, sir, Federigo Rasponi of Turin.

[*All look bewildered.*]

PANTALONE: Extraordinary!

BRIGHELLA: [*aside*] What does this mean? This is not Federigo, this is his sister Beatrice.

PANTALONE: I rejoice to see you, sir, alive and in health, after the bad news which we had received.
[*aside to* DR. LOMBARDI]
I tell you, I am not convinced yet.

BEATRICE: I know; 'twas reported that I was killed in a duel. Heaven be praised, I was but wounded; and no sooner was I restored to health than I set out for Venice, according to our previous arrangement.

PANTALONE: I don't know what to say. You have the appearance of an honest man, sir, but I have sure and certain evidence that Signor Federigo is dead, and you will understand that if you cannot give us proof of the contrary—

BEATRICE: Your doubt is most natural; I recognize that I must give you proof of my identify. Here are four letters from correspondents of yours whom you know personally; one of them is from the manager of our bank. You will recognize the signatures and you will satisfy yourself as to who I am.
[*gives four letters to* PANTALONE, *who reads them to himself*]

CLARICE: Ah, Silvio, we are lost.

SILVIO: I will lose my life before I lose you.

BEATRICE: [*noticing* BRIGHELLA, *aside*] Heavens! Brighella! How the devil does he come to be here? If he betrays me—
[*aloud to* BRIGHELLA]
Friend, I think I know you.

BRIGHELLA: Indeed yes, sir; do you not remember Brighella Cavicchio at Turin?

BEATRICE: Ah yes, now I recognize you.
[*goes up to him*]
And what are you doing in Venice, my good fellow?
[*aside to* BRIGHELLA]
For the love of heaven do not betray me.

BRIGHELLA: [*aside to* BEATRICE] Trust me.
[*aloud*]
I keep an inn, sir, at your service.

BEATRICE: The very thing for me; as I have the pleasure of your acquaintance, I shall come to lodge at your inn.

BRIGHELLA: You do me honor, sir.
[*aside*]
Running contraband, I'll be bound.

PANTALONE: I have read the letters. Certainly they present Signor Federigo Rasponi to me, and if you present them, I am bound to believe that you are—the person named therein.

BEATRICE: If you are still in doubt, here is Master Brighella; he knows me, he can assure you as to who I am.

BRIGHELLA: Of course, sir, I am happy to assure you.

PANTALONE: Well, if that be so, and my good friend Brighella confirms the testimony of the letters, then, dear Signor Federigo, I am delighted to see you and I ask your pardon for having doubted your word.

CLARICE: Then, sir, this gentleman is indeed Signor Federigo Rasponi?

PANTALONE: But of course he is.

CLARICE: [*aside to* SILVIO] Oh misery, what will happen to us?

SILVIO: [*aside to* CLARICE] Don't be frightened; you are mine and I will protect you.

PANTALONE: [*aside to* DR. LOMBARDI] What do you say to it, Doctor? He has come just in the nick of time.

DR. LOMBARDI: *Accidit in puncto, quod non contingit in anno.*

BEATRICE: [*pointing to* CLARICE] Signor Panatlone, who is that young lady?

PANTALONE: That is my daughter Clarice.

BEATRICE: The one who was promised in marriage to me?

PANTALONE: Precisely, sir; that is she.

> [*aside*]
> Now I am in a pretty mess.

BEATRICE: [*to* CLARICE] Madam, permit me to have the honor.

CLARICE: [*stiffly*] Your most humble servant, sir.

BEATRICE: [*to* PANTALONE] She receives me somewhat coldly.

PANTALONE: You must forgive her, she is shy by nature.

BEATRICE: [*to* PANTALONE, *pointing at* SILVIO] And this gentleman is a relative of yours?

PANTALONE: Yes, sir; he is a nephew of mine.

SILVIO: [*to* BEATRICE] No, sir, I am not his nephew at all; I am the promised husband of Signora Clarice.

DR. LOMBARDI: [*aside to* SILVIO] Well said, my boy! Don't lose your chance! Stand up for your rights, but do nothing rash.

BEATRICE: What? You the promised husband of Signora Clarice? Was she not promised to me?

PANTALONE: There, there, I'll explain the whole matter. My dear Signor Federigo, I fully believed that the story of your accident was true, that you were dead, in fact, and so I had promised my daughter to Signor Silvio; but there is not the least harm done. You have arrived at last, just in time. Clarice is yours, if you will have her, and I am here to keep my word. Signor Silvio, I don't know what to say; you can see the position yourself. You remember what I said to you; and you will have no cause to bear me ill-will.

SILVIO: But Signor Federigo will never consent to take a bride who has given her hand to another.

BEATRICE: Oh, I am not so fastidious. I will take her in spite of that.

> [*aside*]
> I mean to have some fun out of this.

DR. LOMBARDI: [*sarcastically*] There's a fine fashionable husband! I like him.

BEATRICE: I hope Signora Clarice will not refuse me her hand.

SILVIO: Sir, you have arrived too late. Signora Clarice is to be *my* wife, and you need have no hope that I will yield her to you. If Signor Pantalone does me wrong, I will be avenged upon him; and whoever presumes to desire Clarice will have to fight for her against this sword.

DR. LOMBARDI: [*aside*] That's a fine boy, by the Lord!

BEATRICE: [*aside*] Thank you, but I don't mean to die just yet.

DR. LOMBARDI: Sir, I must beg to inform you that you are too late. Signora Clarice is to marry my son. The law, the law, sir, is clear on the point. *Prior in tempore, potior in jure.*

[*Exeunt* DR. LOMBARDI *and* SILVIO.]

BEATRICE: [*to* CLARICE] And you, madam bride, do you say nothing?

CLARICE: I say—I say—I'd sooner marry the hangman.

[*Exit.*]

PANTALONE: What, you minx! What did you say?

[*starts to run after her*]

BEATRICE: Stay, Signor Pantalone; I am sorry for her. It is not the moment for severity. In course of time I hope I may deserve her favor. Meanwhile let us go into our accounts together, for, as you know, that is one of the two reasons that have brought me to Venice.

PANTALONE: Everything is in order for your inspection. You shall see the books; your money is ready for you, and we will make up the account whenever you like.

BEATRICE: I will call on you at some more convenient time. Now, if you will allow me, I will go with Brighella to settle some little business which I have to do.

PANTALONE: You shall do as you please, and if you have need of anything, I am at your service.

BEATRICE: Well, if you could give me a little money, I should be greatly obliged; I did not bring any with me, for fear of being robbed on the way.

PANTALONE: I am delighted to serve you; but the cashier is not here just now. The moment he comes I will send the money to your lodgings. Are you not staying at my friend Brighella's?

BEATRICE: Yes, I lie there. But I will send my servant; he is entirely honest. You can trust him with anything.

PANTALONE: Very well. I will carry out your wishes, and if you may be pleased to take pot luck with me, I am yours to command.

BEATRICE: For today I thank you. Another day I shall be happy to wait upon you.

PANTALONE: Then I shall expect you.

[*Enter* SMERALDINA.]

SMERALDINA: [*to* PANTALONE] Sir, you are asked for.

PANTALONE: Who is it?

SMERALDINA: I couldn't say, sir.

PANTALONE: I will come directly. Sir, I beg you to excuse me. Brighella, you are at home here; be good enough to attend Signor Federigo.

BEATRICE: Pray do not put yourself about for me, sir.

PANTALONE: I must go. Farewell, sir.

[*aside*]

I don't want to have trouble in my house.

[*Exit with* SMERALDINA.]

BRIGHELLA: May I ask, Signora Beatrice—?

BEATRICE: Hush, for the love of Heaven, don't betray me. My poor brother is dead. 'Twas thought Florindo Aretusi killed him in a duel. You remember, Florindo loved me, and my brother would not have it. They fought, Federigo fell, and Florindo fled from justice. I heard he was making for Venice, so I put on my brother's clothes and followed him. Thanks to the letters of credit, which are my brother's, and thanks still more to you, Signor Pantalone takes me for Federigo. We are to make up our accounts; I shall draw the money, and then I shall be able to help Florindo too, if he has need of it. Be my friend, dear Brighella, help me, please! You shall be generously rewarded.

BRIGHELLA: That's all very well, but I don't want to be responsible for Signor Pantalone paying you out money in good faith and then finding himself made a fool of.

BEATRICE: Made a fool of? If my brother is dead, am I not his heir?

BRIGHELLA: Very true. Then why not say so?

BEATRICE: If I do that, I can do nothing. Pantalone will begin by treating me as if he were my guardian; then they will all worry me and say my conduct is unbecoming and all that sort of thing. I want my liberty. Help me to it. 'Twill not last long.

BRIGHELLA : Well, well, you were always one for having your own way. Trust me, and I'll do my best for you.

BEATRICE: Thank you. And now let us go to your inn.

BRIGHELLA: Where is your servant?

BEATRICE: I told him to wait for me in the street.

BRIGHELLA: Wherever did you get hold of that idiot? He cannot even speak plain.

BEATRICE: I picked him up on the journey. He seems a fool at times; but he isn't really a fool and I can rely on his loyalty.

BRIGHELLA: Yes, loyalty's a fine thing. Well, I am at your service. To think what love will make people do!

BEATRICE: Oh, this is nothing. Love makes people do far worse things than this.

BRIGHELLA: Well, here's a good beginning. If you go on that way, Lord knows what may come of it!

[*Exeunt* BEATRICE *and* BRIGHELLA.]

SCENE II————*A Street with* BRIGHELLA'S *Inn.*

TRUFFALDINO: I'm sick of waiting; I can hold out no longer. With this master of mine there's not enough to eat, and the less there is the more I want it. The town clock struck twelve half an hour ago, and my belly struck two hours ago at least. If I only knew where we were going to lodge! With my other masters the first thing they did, as soon as they came to a town, was to go to a tavern. This gentleman—Lord no! He leaves his trunks in the boat at the landing stage, goes off to pay visits, and forgets all about his poor servant. When they say we ought to serve our masters with love, they ought to tell the masters to have a little charity toward their servants.

     Here's an inn. I've half a mind to go in and see if I could find something to tickle my teeth; but what if my master comes to look for me? His own fault; he ought to know better. I'll go in—but now I come to think of it, there's another little difficulty that I hadn't remembered; I haven't a penny. Oh poor Truffaldin'! Rather than be a servant, devil take me, I'd—what indeed? By the grace of Heaven there's nothing I can do.

[*Enter* FLORINDO *in traveling dress with a* PORTER *carrying a trunk on his shoulder.*]

PORTER: I tell you, sir, I can go no farther; the weight's enough to kill me.

FLORINDO: Here is the sign of an inn. Can't you carry it these few steps?

PORTER: Help! The trunk is falling.

FLORINDO: I told you you could not carry it; you're too weak; you have no strength at all.

> [FLORINDO *rearranges the trunk on the* PORTER'S *shoulder.*]

TRUFFALDINO: Here's a chance for sixpence.

> [*to* FLORINDO]

Sir, can I do anything for you?

FLORINDO: My good man, be so good as to carry this trunk into the inn there.

TRUFFALDINO: Yes, sir, let me take it, sir. See how I do it.

> [*to the* PORTER]

You be off!

> [TRUFFALDINO *puts his shoulder under the trunk and takes it by himself, knocking the* PORTER *down at the same time.*]

FLORINDO: Well done!

TRUFFALDINO: It weighs nothing. A mere trifle.

> [*goes into the inn with the trunk*]

FLORINDO: [*to* PORTER] There! You see how it's done.

PORTER: I can do no more. I work as a porter for my misfortune, but I am the son of a respectable person.

FLORINDO: What did your father do?

PORTER: My father? He skinned lambs in the town.

FLORINDO: The fellow's mad.

> [*to* PORTER]

That will do.

> [*going towards the inn*]

PORTER: Please your honor—

FLORINDO: What do you want?

PORTER: The money for the porterage.

FLORINDO: How much am I to give you for ten yards? There's the landing stage!

> [*pointing off*]

PORTER: I didn't count them. I want my pay.

> [*holds out his hand*]

FLORINDO: There's twopense.

> [*gives money*]

PORTER: I want my pay.

> [*still holding out his hand*]

FLORINDO: Lord, what obstinacy! Here's twopense more.

> [*gives money*]

PORTER: I want my pay.

FLORINDO: [*kicks him*] Go and be hanged!

PORTER: Thank you, sir, that's enough.

> [*Exit.*]

FLORINDO: There's a humorous fellow! He was positively waiting for me to kick him. Well, let us go and see what the inn is like—

> [*Reenter* TRUFFALDINO.]

TRUFFALDINO: Sir, everything is ready for you.

FLORINDO: What lodging is there here?

TRUFFALDINO: 'Tis a very good place, sir. Good beds, fine looking glasses, and a
    grand kitchen with a smell to it that is very comforting. I have talked with
    the waiter. You will be served like a king.

FLORINDO: What's *your* trade?

TRUFFALDINO: Servant.

FLORINDO: Are you a Venetian?

TRUFFALDINO: Not from Venice, but of the State. I'm from Bergamo, at your
    service.

FLORINDO: Have you a master now?

TRUFFALDINO: At the moment—to tell the truth, I have not.

FLORINDO: You are without a master?

TRUFFALDINO: You see me, sir. I am without a master.
       [aside]
    My master is not here, so I tell no lies.

FLORINDO: Will you come and be *my* servant?

TRUFFALDINO: Why not?
       [aside]
    If his terms are better.

FLORINDO: At any rate, for as long as I stay in Venice.

TRUFFALDINO: Very good, sir. How much will you give me?

FLORINDO: How much do you want?

TRUFFALDINO: I'll tell you: another master I had, who is here no more, he gave
    me a shilling a day and all found.

FLORINDO: Good, I will give you as much.

TRUFFALDINO: You must give me a little more than that.

FLORINDO: How much more do you want?

TRUFFALDINO: A halfpenny a day for a snuff.

FLORINDO: Oh, I'll give you that and welcome.

TRUFFALDINO: If that's so, I'm your man, sir.

FLORINDO: But I should like to know a little more about you.

TRUFFALDINO: If you want to know all about me, you go to Bergamo; anyone
    there will tell you who I am.

FLORINDO: Have you nobody in Venice who knows you?

TRUFFALDINO: I only arrived this morning, sir.

FLORINDO: Well, well, I take you for an honest man. I will give you a trial.

TRUFFALDINO: You give me a trial and you shall see.

FLORINDO: First of all, I am anxious to know if there are letters at the Post for
    me. Here is half a crown; go to the Turin Post and ask if there are letters for
    Florindo Aretusi; if there are, take them and bring them at once. I shall wait
    for you.

TRUFFALDINO: Meanwhile you will order dinner, sir?

FLORINDO: Yes, well said! I will order it.
       [aside]
    He is a wag, I like him. I'll give him a trial.
      [FLORINDO goes into the inn.]

TRUFFALDINO: A halfpenny more a day, that's fifteen pence a month. 'Tis not
    true that the other gentleman gave me a shilling; he gives me six pennies.
    Maybe six pennies make a shilling, but I'm not quite sure. And this gentle-

man from Turin is nowhere to be seen. He's mad. He's a young fellow without a beard and without any sense neither. He may go about his business; I shall go to the Post for my new gentleman.

[*As he is going,* BEATRICE *enters with* BRIGHELLA *and meets him.*]

BEATRICE: That's a nice way to behave! Is that the way you wait for me?

TRUFFALDINO: Here I am, sir. I am still waiting for you.

BEATRICE: And how do you come to be waiting for me here, and not in the street where I told you? 'Tis a mere accident that I have found you.

TRUFFALDINO: I went for a bit of a walk to take away my appetite.

BEATRICE: Well, go at once to the landing stage; fetch my trunk and take it to the inn of Master Brighella.

BRIGHELLA: There's my inn, you cannot mistake it.

BEATRICE: Very well, then, make haste, and I will wait for you.

TRUFFALDINO: The devil! In *that* inn?

BEATRICE: Here, you will go at the same time to the Turin Post and ask if there are any letters for me. You may ask if there are letters for Federigo Rasponi and also for Beatrice Rasponi. That's my sister. Some friends of hers might perhaps write to her; so be sure to see if there are letters either for her or for me.

TRUFFALDINO: [*aside*] What *am* I to do? Here's a pretty kettle of fish!

BRIGHELLA: [*to* BEATRICE] Why do you expect letters in your real name if you left home secretly?

BEATRICE: I told the steward to write to me; and I don't know which name he may use. I'll tell you more later.

[*to* TRUFFALDINO]

Make haste, be off with you to the Post and the landing stage. Fetch the letters and have the trunk brought to the inn; I shall be there.

[*Exit* BEATRICE *into the inn.*]

TRUFFALDINO: Are you the landlord?

BRIGHELLA: Yes, I am. You behave properly and you need have no fear, I will do you well.

[*Exit* BRIGHELLA *into the inn.*]

TRUFFALDINO: There's luck! There are many that look in vain for a master, and I have found two. What the devil am I to do? I cannot wait upon them both. No? Why not? Wouldn't it be a fine thing to wait upon both of them, earn two men's wages and eat and drink for two? 'Twould be a fine thing indeed, if neither of them found out. And if they did? What then? No matter! If one sends me away, I stay with the other. I swear I'll try it. If it last but a day, I'll try it. Whatever happens I shall have done a fine thing. Here goes. Let's go to the Post for both of 'em.

[*Enter* SILVIO *and meets* TRUFFALDINO.]

SILVIO: [*aside*] That is the servant of Federigo Rasponi.

[*To* TRUFFALDINO.]

My good man.

TRUFFALDINO: Sir?

SILVIO: Where is your master?

TRUFFALDINO: My master? He's in that inn there.

SILVIO: Go at once and tell your master that I wish to speak to him; if he be a man of honor let him come down; I wait for him.

TRUFFALDINO: My dear sir—

SILVIO: [*angrily*] Go at once.

TRUFFALDINO: But I must tell you, my master—

SILVIO: Don't answer me; or, by Heaven, I'll—

TRUFFALDINO: But which do you want?

SILVIO: At once, I say, or I'll beat you.

TRUFFALDINO: [*aside*] Well, I don't know—I'll send the first I can find.

[*Exit* TRUFFALDINO *into the inn.*]

SILVIO: No, I will never suffer the presence of a rival. Federigo may have got off once with his life, but he shall not always have the same fortune. Either he shall renounce all claims to Clarice, or he shall give me the satisfaction of a gentleman. Here are some more people coming out of the inn. I don't want to be disturbed.

[*retires to the opposite side*]

[*Enter* TRUFFALDINO *with* FLORINDO.]

TRUFFALDINO: [*points out* SILVIO *to* FLORINDO] There's the fire-eating gentleman, sir.

FLORINDO: I do not know him. What does he want with me?

TRUFFALDINO: I don't know. I go to fetch the letters, with your good leave, sir.

[*aside*]

I don't want any more trouble.

[*Exit.*]

SILVIO: [*aside*] Federigo does not come?

FLORINDO: [*aside*] I must find out what the truth is.

[*to* SILVIO]

Sir, are you the gentleman who inquired for me?

SILVIO: I, sir? I have not even the honor of your acquaintance.

FLORINDO: But that servant who has just gone told me that with a loud and threatening voice you made bold to challenge me.

SILVIO: He misunderstood. I said I wished to speak to his master.

FLORINDO: Very well, I am his master.

SILVIO: You his master?

FLORINDO: Certainly. He is in my service.

SILVIO: Then I ask your pardon. Either your servant is exactly like another whom I saw this morning, or he waits on another person.

FLORINDO: You may set your mind at rest; he waits on me.

SILVIO: If that be so, I ask your pardon again.

FLORINDO: No harm done. Mistakes often occur.

SILVIO: Are you a stranger here, sir?

FLORINDO: From Turin, sir, at your service.

SILVIO: The man whom I would have provoked was from Turin.

FLORINDO: Then perhaps I may know him; if he has given you offence, I shall gladly assist you to obtain just satisfaction.

SILVIO: Do you know one Federigo Rasponi?

FLORINDO: Ah! I knew him only too well.

SILVIO: He makes claim, on the strength of her father's word, to the lady who this morning swore to be my wife.

FLORINDO: My good friend, Federigo Rasponi cannot take your wife away from you. He is dead.

SILVIO: Yes, we all believed that he was dead; but this morning to my disgust he arrived in Venice safe and sound.

FLORINDO: Sir, you petrify me.

SILVIO: No wonder! I was petrified myself.

FLORINDO: I assure you Federigo Rasponi is dead.

SILVIO: I assure you that Federigo Rasponi is alive.

FLORINDO: Take care you are not deceived.

SILVIO: Signor Pantalone dei Bisognosi, the young lady's father, has made all possible inquiries to assure himself and is in possession of incontestable proofs that he is here in person.

FLORINDO: [*aside*] Then he was not killed in the duel, as everybody believed!

SILVIO: Either he or I must renounce claim to the love of Clarice or to life.

FLORINDO: [*aside*] Federigo here?

SILVIO: I am surprised that you have not seen him. He was to lodge at this very inn.

FLORINDO: I have not seen him. They told me that there was no one else at all staying there.

SILVIO: He must have changed his mind. Forgive me, sir, if I have troubled you. If you see him, tell him that for his own welfare he must abandon the idea of this marriage. Silvio Lombardi is my name; I am your most obedient servant, sir.

FLORINDO: I shall be greatly pleased to have the honor of your friendship.
[*aside*]
I am confounded.

SILVIO: May I beg to know your name, sir?

FLORINDO: [*aside*] I must not discover myself.
[*to* SILVIO]
Your servant, sir, Orazio Ardenti.

SILVIO: Signor Orazio, I am yours to command.
[*Exit* SILVIO.]

FLORINDO: I was told he died on the spot. Yet I fled so hurriedly when accused of the crime that I had no chance of finding out the truth. Then, since he is not dead, it will be better for me to go back to Turin and console my beloved Beatrice, who is perhaps in suffering and sorrow for my absence.
[*Enter* TRUFFALDINO, *with another* PORTER *who carries* BEATRICE'S *trunk.* TRUFFALDINO *comes forward a few steps, sees* FLORINDO *and, fearing to be seen himself, makes the* PORTER *retire.*]

TRUFFALDINO: Come along. This way—The devil! There's my other master. Go back, friend, and wait for me at that corner.
[*Exit* PORTER.]

FLORINDO: [*continuing to himself*] Yes, without delay. I will go back to Turin.

TRUFFALDINO: Here I am, sir.

FLORINDO: Truffaldino, will you come to Turin with me?

TRUFFALDINO: When?

FLORINDO: Now; at once.

TRUFFALDINO: Before dinner?

FLORINDO: No, we will have dinner, and then we will go.

TRUFFALDINO: Very good, sir. I'll think it over at dinner.

FLORINDO: Have you been to the Post?

TRUFFALDINO: Yes, sir.

FLORINDO: Have you found my letters?

TRUFFALDINO: I have, sir.

FLORINDO: Where are they?

TRUFFALDINO: I will give you them.

> [*Takes three letters out of his pocket. Aside.*]

> The devil! I have mixed up one master's letters with the other's. How shall I find out which are his? I cannot read.

FLORINDO: Come, give me my letters.

TRUFFALDINO: Directly, sir.

> [*aside*]

> Here's a muddle.

> [*to* FLORINDO]

> I must tell you, sir; these three letters are not all for your honor. I met another servant, who knows me; we were in service together in Bergamo; I told him I was going to the Post, and he asked me to see whether there was anything for *his* master. I think there was one letter, but I don't know which of them it was.

FLORINDO: Let me see; I will take mine and give you the other back.

TRUFFALDINO: There, sir; I only wanted to do my friend a good turn.

FLORINDO: [*aside*] What is this? A letter addressed to Beatrice Rasponi? To Beatrice Rasponi at Venice?

TRUFFALDINO: Did you find the one that belongs to my mate?

FLORINDO: Who is this mate of yours who asked you to do this for him?

TRUFFALDINO: He is a servant—his name is Pasqual'—

FLORINDO: Whom does he wait upon?

TRUFFALDINO: I do not know, sir.

FLORINDO: But if he told you to fetch his master's letters, he must have told you his name.

TRUFFALDINO: Of course he did.

> [*aside*]

> The muddle's getting thicker.

FLORINDO: Well, what name did he tell you?

TRUFFALDINO: I don't remember.

FLORINDO: What?

TRUFFALDINO: He wrote it down on a bit of paper.

FLORINDO: And where is the paper?

TRUFFALDINO: I left it at the Post.

FLORINDO: [*aside*] Confusion! What does this mean?

TRUFFALDINO: [*aside*] I am learning my part as I go along.

FLORINDO: Where does this fellow Pasquale live?

TRUFFALDINO: Indeed, sir, I haven't the slightest idea.

FLORINDO: How will you be able to give him the letter?

TRUFFALDINO: He said he would meet me in the Piazza.

FLORINDO: [*aside*] I don't know what to make of it.

TRUFFALDINO: [*aside*] If I get through this business clean 'twill be a miracle. ·
[*to* FLORINDO]
Pray give me the letter, sir, and I shall find him somewhere.

FLORINDO: No; I mean to open this letter.

TRUFFALDINO: Oh, sir, do not do that, sir. Besides, you know how wrong it is to open letters.

FLORINDO: I care not; this letter interests me too much. It is addressed to a person on whom I have a certain claim. I can open it without scruple.
[*opens letter*]

TRUFFALDINO: As you will, sir.
[*aside*]
He has opened it.

FLORINDO: [*reads*] "Madam, your departure from this city has given rise to much talk, and all understand that you have gone to join Signor Florindo. The Court of Justice has discovered that you have fled in man's dress and intends to have you arrested. I have not sent this letter by the courier from Turin to Venice, so as not to reveal the place whither you were bound, but I have sent it to a friend at Genoa to be forwarded to Venice. If I have any more news to tell you, I will not fail to send it by the same means. Your most humble servant, Antonio."

TRUFFALDINO: That's a nice way to behave! Reading other people's letters!

FLORINDO: [*aside*] What is all this? Beatrice has left home? In man's dress? To join me? Indeed she loves me. Heaven grant I may find her in Venice.
[*to* TRUFFALDINO]
Here, my good Truffaldino, go and do all you can to find Pasquale; find out from him who his master is, and if he be man or woman. Find out where he lodges, and if you can, bring him here to me, and both he and you shall be handsomely rewarded.

TRUFFALDINO: Give me the letter; I will try to find him.

FLORINDO: There it is. I count upon you. This matter is of infinite importance to me.

TRUFFALDINO: But am I to give him the letter open like this?

FLORINDO: Tell him it was a mistake, an accident. Don't make difficulties.

TRUFFALDINO: And are you going to Turin now?

FLORINDO: No, not for the present. Lose no time. Go and find Pasquale.
[*aside*]
Beatrice in Venice, Federigo in Venice! If her brother finds her, unhappy woman! I will do all I can to discover her first.
[*Exit toward the town.*]

TRUFFALDINO: Upon my word, I hope he is not going away. I want to see how my two jobs will work out. I'm on my mettle. This letter, now, which I have to take to my other master—I don't like to have to give it to him opened. I must try to fold it again.
[*tries various awkward folds*]
And now it must be sealed. If I only knew how to do it! I have seen my grandmother sometimes seal letters with chewed bread. I'll try it.
[*takes a piece of bread out of his pocket*]

It's a pity to waste this little piece of bread, but still something must be done.

[*chews a little bread to seal the letter and accidentally swallows it*]

The devil! It has gone down. I must chew another bit.

[*same business*]

No good, nature rebels. I'll try once more.

[*chews again; would like to swallow the bread, but restrains himself and with great difficulty removes the bread from his mouth*]

Ah, here it is; I'll seal the letter.

[*seals the letter with the bread*]

I think that looks quite well. I'm always a great man for doing things cleanly. Lord! I had forgotten the porter.

[*calls off*]

Friend, come hither; take the trunk on your shoulder.

[*Reenter* PORTER.]

PORTER: Here I am; where am I to carry it?

TRUFFALDINO: Take it into that inn; I am coming directly.

[BEATRICE *comes out of the inn.*]

BEATRICE: Is this my trunk?

TRUFFALDINO: Yes, sir.

BEATRICE: [*to* PORTER] Carry it into my room.

PORTER: Which is your room?

BEATRICE: Ask the waiter.

PORTER: There's one and threepence to pay.

BEATRICE: Go on, I will pay you.

PORTER: Please be quick about it.

BEATRICE: Don't bother me.

PORTER: I've half a mind to throw the trunk down in the middle of the street.

[*goes into the inn*]

TRUFFALDINO: Great folk for politeness, these porters!

BEATRICE: Have you been to the Post?

TRUFFALDINO: Yes, sir.

BEATRICE: Any letters for me?

TRUFFALDINO: One for your sister.

BEATRICE: Good; where is it?

TRUFFALDINO: Here.

[*gives letter*]

BEATRICE: This letter has been opened.

TRUFFALDINO: Opened? No! Impossible!

BEATRICE: Yes, opened, and then sealed with bread.

TRUFFALDINO: I can't think how that can have happened.

BEATRICE: You cannot think, eh? Rascal, who has opened this letter? I must know.

TRUFFALDINO: Sir, I'll tell you, I'll confess the truth. We are all liable to make mistakes. At the Post there was a letter for me; I can't read very much, and by mistake, instead of opening my letter, I opened yours. I ask your pardon—

BEATRICE: If that was all, there's no great harm done.

TRUFFALDINO: 'Tis true, on the word of a poor man.

BEATRICE: Have you read this letter? Do you know what is in it?

TRUFFALDINO: Not a word. I can't read the handwriting.

BEATRICE: Has anyone else seen it?

TRUFFALDINO: [*with an air of great indignation*] Oh!

BEATRICE: Take care now—

TRUFFALDINO: [*same business*] Sir!

BEATRICE: [*aside*] I hope he is not deceiving me.
    [*reads to herself*]

TRUFFALDINO: That's all put straight.

BEATRICE: [*aside*] Antonio is a faithful servant and I am obliged to him.
    [*to* TRUFFALDINO]
Listen; I have some business to do close by. You go into the inn, open the trunk—here are my keys—and unpack my things. When I come back, we will have dinner.
    [*aside*]
I have seen nothing of Signor Pantalone, and I am anxious to have my money.
    [*Exit.*]

TRUFFALDINO: Come, that all went well; it couldn't have gone better. I'm a great fellow; I think a deal more of myself than I did before.
    [*Enter* PANTALONE.]

PANTALONE: Tell me, my good man, is your master in the house?

TRUFFALDINO: No, sir, he is not there.

PANTALONE: Do you know where he may be?

TRUFFALDINO: Not that neither.

PANTALONE: Is he coming home to dinner?

TRUFFALDINO: Yes, I should think so.

PANTALONE: Here, as soon as he comes home give him this purse with these hundred guineas. I cannot stay, I have business. Good day to you.
    [*Exit* PANTALONE.]

TRUFFALDINO: And a good day to you, sir! He never told me to which of my masters I was to give it.
    [*Enter* FLORINDO.]

FLORINDO: Well, did you find Pasquale?

TRUFFALDINO: No sir, I did not find Pasqual', but I found a gentleman who gave me a purse with a hundred guineas in it.

FLORINDO: A hundred guineas? What for?

TRUFFALDINO: Tell me truly, sir, were you expecting money from anyone?

FLORINDO: Yes; I had presented a letter of credit to a merchant.

TRUFFALDINO: Then this money will be for you.

FLORINDO: What did he say when he gave it to you?

TRUFFALDINO: He told me to give it to my master.

FLORINDO: Then of course it is mine. Am I not your master? What doubt could you have?

TRUFFALDINO: [*aside*] Yes, but what about t'other one?

FLORINDO: And you do not know who gave you the money?

TRUFFALDINO: No, sir; I think I have seen his face somewhere, but I don't remember exactly.

FLORINDO: It will have been the merchant to whom I had a letter.

TRUFFALDINO: Yes, of course, sir.

FLORINDO: You won't forget Pasquale.

TRUFFALDINO: I'll find him after dinner.

FLORINDO: Then let us go and order our meal.
     [*goes into the inn*]

TRUFFALDINO: We will. Lucky I made no mistake this time. I've given the purse to the right one.
     [*goes into the inn*]

SCENE III————*A Room in the House of* PANTALONE.

PANTALONE: That's the long and short of it; Signor Federigo is to be your husband. I have given my word and I am not to be cozened.

CLARICE: You have my obedience, sir; but I beseech you, this is tyranny.

PANTALONE: When Signor Federigo first asked for your hand, I told you; you never replied that you did not wish to marry him. You should have spoken then; now it is too late.

CLARICE: My fear of you, sir, and my respect, made me dumb.

PANTALONE: Then your fear and respect should do the same now.

CLARICE: Indeed I cannot marry him, sir.

PANTALONE: No? And why not?

CLARICE: Nothing shall induce me to marry Federigo.

PANTALONE: You dislike him so much?

CLARICE: He is odious in my eyes.

PANTALONE: And supposing I were to show you how you might begin to like him a little?

CLARICE: What do you mean, sir?

PANTALONE: Put Signor Silvio out of your mind, and you will soon like Federigo well enough.

CLARICE: Silvio is too firmly stamped upon my heart; and your own approval, sir, has rooted him there the more securely.

PANTALONE: [*aside*] In some ways I am sorry for her.
     [*to* CLARICE]
You have got to make a virtue of necessity.

CLARICE: My heart is not capable of so great an effort.

PANTALONE: Come, come; you shall!
     [*Enter* SMERALDINA.]

SMERALDINA: Sir, Signor Federigo is here and desires to speak with you.

PANTALONE: Tell him to come in; I am at his service.

CLARICE: [*weeping*] Alas! What torture!

SMERALDINA: What is it, madam? You are weeping? Truly you do wrong. Have you not noticed how handsome Signor Federigo is? If I had such luck, I would not cry; no, I would laugh with the whole of my mouth.
     [*Exit* SMERALDINA.]

PANTALONE: There, there, my child; you must not be seen crying.

CLARICE: But if I feel my heart bursting!

[*Enter* BEATRICE *in man's dress.*]

BEATRICE: My respects to Signor Pantalone.

PANTALONE: Your servant, sir. Did you receive a purse with a hundred guineas in it?

BEATRICE: No.

PANTALONE: But I gave it to your servant just now. You told me he was a trustworthy man.

BEATRICE: Yes, indeed; there is no danger. I did not see him. He will give me the money when I come home again.

[*aside to* PANTALONE]

What ails Signora Clarice that she is weeping?

PANTALONE: [*aside to* BEATRICE] Dear Signor Federigo, you must have pity on her. The news of your death was the cause of this trouble. I hope it will pass away in time.

BEATRICE: [*to* PANTALONE] Do me a kindness, Signor Pantalone, and leave me alone with her a moment, to see if I cannot obtain a kind word from her.

PANTALONE: With pleasure, sir. I will go, and come back again.

[*to* CLARICE]

My child, stay here, I will be back directly. You must entertain your promised husband awhile.

[*softly to* CLARICE]

Now, be careful.

[*Exit* PANTALONE.]

BEATRICE: Signora Clarice, I beg you—

CLARICE: Stand away, and do not dare to importune me.

BEATRICE: So severe with him who is your destined husband?

CLARICE: They may drag me by force to the altar, but you will have only my hand, never my heart.

BEATRICE: You disdain me, but I hope to appease you.

CLARICE: I shall abhor you to all eternity.

BEATRICE: But if you knew me, you would not say so.

CLARICE: I know you well enough as the destroyer of my happiness.

BEATRICE: But I can find a way to comfort you.

CLARICE: You deceive yourself; there is no one who can comfort me but Silvio.

BEATRICE: 'Tis true, I cannot give you the same comfort as your Silvio might, but I can at least contribute to your happiness.

CLARICE: I think it is quite enough, sir, that although I speak to you as harshly as I can, you should continue to torture me.

BEATRICE: [*aside*] Poor girl! I can't bear to see her suffer.

CLARICE: [*aside*] I'm so angry, I don't care how rude I am.

BEATRICE: Signora Clarice, I have a secret to tell you.

CLARICE: I make no promise to keep it; you had better not tell it me.

BEATRICE: Your severity deprives me of the means to make you happy.

CLARICE: You can never make me anything but miserable.

BEATRICE: You are wrong, and to convince you I will speak plainly. You have no desire for me; I have no use for you. You have promised your hand to another, I to another have already pledged my heart.

CLARICE: Oh! Now you begin to please me.

BEATRICE: Did I not tell you that I knew how to comfort you?

CLARICE: Ah, I feared you would deceive me.

BEATRICE: Nay, madam, I speak in all sincerity; and if you promise me that discretion which you refused me just now, I will confide to you a secret, which will ensure your peace of mind.

CLARICE: I vow I will observe the strictest silence.

BEATRICE: I am not Federigo Rasponi, but his sister Beatrice.

CLARICE: What! I am amazed. You a woman?

BEATRICE: I am indeed. Imagine my feelings when I claimed you as my bride!

CLARICE: And what news have you of your brother?

BEATRICE: He died indeed by the sword. A lover of mine was thought to have killed him, and 'tis he whom I am seeking now in these clothes. I beseech you by all the holy laws of friendship and of love not to betray me.

CLARICE: Won't you let me tell Silvio?

BEATRICE: No; on the contrary I forbid you absolutely.

CLARICE: Well, I will say nothing.

BEATRICE: Remember I count upon you.

CLARICE: You have my promise. I will be silent.

BEATRICE: Now, I hope, you will treat me more kindly.

CLARICE: I will be your friend indeed; and if I can be of service to you, dispose of me.

BEATRICE: I too swear eternal friendship to you. Give me your hand.

CLARICE: I don't quite like to—

BEATRICE: Are you afraid I am not a woman after all? I will give you proof positive.

CLARICE: It all seems just like a dream.

BEATRICE: Yes. 'Tis a strange business.

CLARICE: 'Tis indeed fantastic.

BEATRICE: Come, I must be going. Let us embrace in sign of honest friendship and loyalty.

CLARICE: There! I doubt you no longer.

    [*Enter* PANTALONE.]

PANTALONE: Well done, well done; I congratulate you.

    [*to* CLARICE]

My child, you have been very quick in adapting yourself.

BEATRICE: Did I not tell you, Signor Pantalone, that I should win her round?

PANTALONE: Magnificent! You have done more in four minutes than I should have done in four years.

CLARICE: [*aside*] Now I am in a worse tangle than ever.

PANTALONE: [*to* CLARICE] Then we will have the wedding at once.

CLARICE: Pray do not be in too much haste, sir.

PANTALONE: What? Holding hands on the sly and kissing, and then in no haste about it? No, no, I don't want you to get yourself into trouble. You shall be married tomorrow.

BEATRICE: Signor Pantalone, 'twill be necessary first of all to arrange the settlement and to go into our accounts.

PANTALONE: We will do all that. These things can be done in a couple of hours.

CLARICE: Sir, I beseech you—
PANTALONE: Madam, I am going straight away to say a word to Signor Silvio.
CLARICE: For the love of Heaven do not anger him.
PANTALONE: What, what? Do you want two husbands?
CLARICE: Not exactly—but—
PANTALONE: Butt me no buts. 'Tis all settled. Your servant, sir.
    [*going*]
BEATRICE: [*to* PANTALONE] Listen, sir—
PANTALONE: You are husband and wife.
    [*going*]
CLARICE: Had you not better—
PANTALONE: We will talk about it this evening.
    [*Exit.*]
CLARICE: Oh, Signora Beatrice, 'tis worse than it was before!

ACT II

SCENE I————*The Courtyard of* PANTALONE'S *House.*

SILVIO: Sir, I entreat you to leave me alone.
DR. LOMBARDI: Stay, answer me.
SILVIO: I am beside myself.
DR. LOMBARDI: What are you doing in the courtyard of Signor Pantalone?
SILVIO: I intend either that he should keep his word that he has given me, or that he should render me account for this intolerable insult.
DR. LOMBARDI: But you cannot do this in Pantalone's own house. You are a fool to let yourself be so transported with anger.
SILVIO: A man who behaves so abominably deserves no consideration.
DR. LOMBARDI: True; but that is no reason why you should be so rash. Leave him to me, my dear boy, leave him to me; let me talk to him; maybe I can bring him to reason and make him see where his duty lies. Go away somewhere and wait for me; leave this courtyard; do not let us make a scene. I will wait for Signor Pantalone.
SILVIO: But sir, I—
DR. LOMBARDI: But, sir, I will have you obey me.
SILVIO: I obey you, sir. I will go. Speak to him. I wait for you at the apothecary's. But if Signor Pantalone persists, he will have to settle with me.
    [*Exit* SILVIO.]
DR. LOMBARDI: Poor dear boy, I feel truly sorry for him. Signor Pantalone ought never to have led him on so far before he was quite certain that man from Turin was dead. I must see him quietly; I must not let my temper get the better of me.
    [*Enter* PANTALONE.]
PANTALONE: [*aside*] What is the doctor doing in my house?
DR. LOMBARDI: Oh, Signor Pantalone, your servant.
PANTALONE: Your servant, Doctor. I was just going to look for you and your son.
DR. LOMBARDI: Indeed? Good! I suppose you were coming to give us your assurance that Signora Clarice is to be Silvio's wife.
PANTALONE: [*much embarrassed*] Well, the fact is, I was coming to tell you—

DR. LOMBARDI: No, no; there is no need for explanations. You have my sympathy in a very awkward situation. But we are old friends and we will let bygones be bygones.

PANTALONE: [*still hesitating*] Yes, of course, in view of the promise made to
Signor Federigo—

DR. LOMBARDI: He took you by surprise, and you had no time for reflection; you
did not think of the affront you were giving to our family.

PANTALONE: You can hardly talk of an affront, when a previous contract—

DR. LOMBARDI: I know what you are going to say. It seemed at first sight out of
the question that your promise to the Turin gentleman could be repudiated,
because it was a formal contract. But that was a contract merely between
you and him; whereas ours is confirmed by the girl herself.

PANTALONE: Very true, but—

DR. LOMBARDI: And as you know, in matrimonial cases, *consensus, et non concubi-
tus, facit virum.*

PANTALONE: I am no Latin scholar; but I must tell you—

DR. LOMBARDI: And girls must not be sacrificed.

PANTALONE: Have you anything more to say?

DR. LOMBARDI: I have nothing more to say.

PANTALONE: Have you finished?

DR. LOMBARDI: I have finished.

PANTALONE: May I speak?

DR. LOMBARDI: You may.

PANTALONE: My dear Doctor, with all your learning—

DR. LOMBARDI: As regards the dowry, we can easily arrange matters. A little more
or a little less, I will make no difficulties.

PANTALONE: I must begin all over again. Will you allow me to speak?

DR. LOMBARDI: With pleasure.

PANTALONE: I must tell you; I have the greatest respect for your legal learning,
but in this case it does not apply.

DR. LOMBARDI: And you mean to tell me that this other marriage is to take place?

PANTALONE: For my part I have given my word and I cannot go back upon it. My
daughter is content; what impediment can there be? I was just coming to
look for you or Signor Silvio, to tell you this. I am extremely sorry, but I see
no help for it.

DR. LOMBARDI: I am not surprised at your daughter's behavior. But I am surprised at yours, sir, at your treating me in this disgraceful way. If you were
not perfectly certain about the death of Signor Federigo, you had no business to enter into an engagement with my son; and having entered into an
engagement with him, you are bound to maintain that engagement whatever it may cost you. The news of Federigo's death was quite sufficient to
justify, even to Federigo, your new intention; he could have no right to reproach you, still less to demand compensation. The marriage which was
contracted this morning between Signora Clarice and my son *coram testibus*
cannot be dissolved by a mere word given by you to another party. If I were
to listen to my son I should insist upon the annulment of the new contract
and compel your daughter to marry him; but I should be ashamed to receive
into my house so disreputable a daughter-in-law, the daughter of a man

who breaks his word as you do. Signor Pantalone, you have done me an injury, you have done an injury to the house of Lombardi. The time will come when you will have to pay for it; yes, sir, the time will come—*omnia tempus habent.*

[*Exit* DOCTOR.]

PANTALONE: You may go to the devil for all I care. I don't care a fig, I'm not afraid of you. The Rasponis are worth a hundred of the Lombardis. An only son, and as rich as he is—you won't find that every day. It has got to be.

[*Enter* SILVIO.]

SILVIO: [*aside*] 'Tis all very fine for my father to talk. Let him keep his temper who can.

PANTALONE: [*seeing* SILVIO, *aside*] Here comes the other.

SILVIO: [*rudely*] Your servant, sir.

PANTALONE: Yours to command, sir.

[*aside*]

He is boiling.

SILVIO: I have just heard something from my father; am I to believe that it is true?

PANTALONE: If your father said it, it must certainly be true.

SILVIO: Then the marriage is settled between Signora Clarice and Signor Federigo?

PANTALONE: Yes, sir, settled and concluded.

SILVIO: I am amazed that you should have the face to tell me so. You are a man of no reputation; you are no gentleman.

PANTALONE: What is all this? Is that the way you speak to a man of my age?

SILVIO: I don't care how old you are; I have a mind to run you straight through the body.

PANTALONE: I am not a frog, sir, to be spitted. Do you come into my own house to make all this turmoil?

SILVIO: Come outside then.

PANTALONE: I am surprised at you, sir.

SILVIO: Come on, if you are a man of honor.

PANTALONE: I am accustomed to be treated with respect.

SILVIO: You are a low fellow, a coward, and a villain.

PANTALONE: You are a most impertinent young puppy.

SILVIO: I swear to Heaven—

[*lays his hand to his sword*]

PANTALONE: Help! Murder!

[*draws a pistol*]

[*Enter* BEATRICE *with a drawn sword.*]

BEATRICE: [*to* PANTALONE] I am here to defend you.

PANTALONE: My dear son-in-law, I am much obliged to you.

SILVIO: [*to* BEATRICE] You are the very man I want to fight.

BEATRICE: [*aside*] I am in for it now.

SILVIO: [*to* BEATRICE] Come on, sir.

PANTALONE: [*frightened*] My dear son-in-law—

BEATRICE: It is not the first time that I have been in danger.

[*to* SILVIO]

I am not afraid of you.

[presents sword]

PANTALONE: Help! Help!

> [PANTALONE *runs toward the street.* BEATRICE *and* SILVIO *fight.* SILVIO *falls and drops his sword.* BEATRICE *holds her point to his heart.*]

CLARICE: [*to* BEATRICE] Stop, stop!

BEATRICE: Fair Clarice, at your request I grant Silvio his life, and in consideration of my mercy, I beg you to remember your oath.

> [*Exit* BEATRICE.]

CLARICE: Dear Silvio, are you hurt?

SILVIO: Dear Silvio! Faithless deceiver! Dear Silvio! To a lover disdained, to a betrayed husband!

CLARICE: No, Silvio, I do not deserve your reproaches. I love you, I adore you, I am indeed faithful.

SILVIO: Oh, lying jade! Faithful to me, forsooth! You call that fidelity, to plight your troth to another?

CLARICE: I never did so, nor will I ever. I will die rather than desert you.

SILVIO: I heard just now that you have given your oath.

CLARICE: My oath does not bind me to marry him.

SILVIO: Then what did you swear?

CLARICE: Dear Silvio, have mercy on me; I cannot tell you.

SILVIO: Why not?

CLARICE: Because I am sworn to silence.

SILVIO: That proves your guilt.

CLARICE: No, I am innocent.

SILVIO: Innocent people have no secrets.

CLARICE: Indeed I should be guilty if I spoke.

SILVIO: And to whom have you sworn this silence?

CLARICE: To Federigo.

SILVIO: And you will observe it so jealously?

CLARICE: I will observe it, rather than be a perjuress.

SILVIO: And you tell me you do not love him? He's a fool that believes you. I do not believe you, cruel, deceiver! Begone from my sight!

CLARICE: If I did not love you, I should not have run hither in all haste to save your life.

SILVIO: Then I loathe my life, if I must owe it to one so ungrateful.

CLARICE: I love you with all my heart.

SILVIO: I abhor you with all my soul.

CLARICE: I will die, if you are not to be appeased.

SILVIO: I would sooner see you dead than unfaithful.

CLARICE: Then you shall have that satisfaction.

> [*Picks up his sword.*]

SILVIO: Yes, that sword should avenge my wrongs.

CLARICE: Are you so cruel to your Clarice?

SILVIO: 'Twas you that taught me cruelty.

CLARICE: Then you desire my death?

SILVIO: I know not what I desire.

CLARICE: I do.

> *[points the sword at her breast]*

[*Enter* SMERALDINA.]

SMERALDINA: Stop, stop! What on earth are you doing?

[*takes the sword away from* CLARICE.]

And you, you dog, you would have let her die?

[*to* SILVIO]

Have you the heart of a tiger, of a hyena, of a devil? Look at you, you're a pretty little fellow, that expects ladies to disembowel themselves for you! You are much too kind to him, madam. He doesn't want you any more, I suppose? The man that doesn't want you doesn't deserve you. Let this murderer go to the devil; and you come along with me. There's no shortage of men; I'll promise to find you a dozen before evening.

[*She throws down the sword.* SILVIO *picks it up.*]

CLARICE: [*weeping*] Ungrateful! Can it be that my death should cost you not a single sigh? But I *shall* die, and die of grief. I shall die, and you will be content. But one day you will know that I am innocent, and then, when it is too late, you will be sorry you did not believe me; you will weep for my misfortune and for your own barbarous cruelty.

[*Exit* CLARICE.]

SMERALDINA: Here's something I really don't understand. Here's a girl on the point of killing herself, and you sit there looking on, just as if you were at a play.

SILVIO: Nonsense, woman! Do you suppose she really meant to kill herself?

SMERALDINA: How should I know? I know that if I had not arrived in time, she would have been gone, poor thing.

SILVIO: The point was nowhere near her heart.

SMERALDINA: Did you ever hear such a lie? It was just ready to pierce her.

SILVIO: You women always invent things.

SMERALDINA: We should indeed, if we were like you. It's as the old saw says; we get the kicks and you the halfpence. They say women are unfaithful, but men are committing infidelities all day long. People talk about the women, and they never say a word about the men. We get all the blame, and you are allowed to do as you please. Do you know why? Because 'tis the men who have made the laws. If the women had made them, things would be just the other way. If I were a queen, I'd make every man who was unfaithful carry a branch of a tree in his hand, and I know all the towns would look like forests.

[*Exit* SMERALDINA.]

SILVIO: Clarice faithless! Clarice a traitress! Her pretense at suicide was a trick to deceive me, to move my compassion. But though fate made me fall before my rival, I will never give up the thought of revenge. That wretch shall die, and my ungrateful Clarice shall see her lover wallowing in his own gore.

[*Exit* SILVIO.]

SCENE II————*A Room in* BRIGHELLA'S *Inn, with a door at each side and two doors at the back, facing the audience.*

TRUFFALDINO: Just my luck! Two masters and neither of them comes home to dinner. 'Tis two o'clock, and not one to be seen. Sure enough they will both come at the same time, and I shall be in a mess; I shall not be able to wait on both together, and the whole thing will be found out. Hush, here comes one. All the better.

[*Enter* FLORINDO.]

FLORINDO: Well, did you find that fellow Pasquale?

TRUFFALDINO: Didn't we say, sir, that I was to look for him after dinner?

FLORINDO: I am impatient to see him.

TRUFFALDINO: You should have come back to dinner a little sooner.

FLORINDO: [*aside*] I can find no way of making certain whether Beatrice is here.

TRUFFALDINO: You told me to go and order dinner, and then you go out. The dinner will have been spoiled.

FLORINDO: I don't want to eat anything.

[*aside*]

I shall go to the Post; I must go myself; then perhaps I shall find out something.

TRUFFALDINO: You know, sir, at Venice you must eat; if you do not, you will fall sick.

FLORINDO: I must go out; I have important business. If I come back to dinner, well and good; if not, I shall eat in the evening. You can get yourself some food, if you like.

TRUFFALDINO: Very good, sir; just as you please, sir; you're the master.

FLORINDO: This money is heavy; here, put it in my trunk. There is the key.

[*gives* TRUFFALDINO *the purse and his keys*]

TRUFFALDINO: Certainly, sir; I'll bring the key back at once.

FLORINDO: No, no, you can give it me later. I can't stop. If I do not come back to dinner come to the Piazza; I can't rest till you have found Pasquale.

[*Exit* FLORINDO.]

TRUFFALDINO: Well, anyway, he said I could get myself some food; we are agreed about that. If he won't eat his dinner, he can leave it. My complexion was not made for fasting. I'll just put away this purse, and then—

[*Enter* BEATRICE.]

BEATRICE: Oh, Truffaldino!

TRUFFALDINO: [*aside*] The devil!

BEATRICE: Did Signor Pantalone dei Bisognosi give you a purse of a hundred guineas?

TRUFFALDINO: Yes, indeed he did.

BEATRICE: Then why did you not give it to me?

TRUFFALDINO: Was it meant for your honor?

BEATRICE: Was it meant for me? What did he say when he gave you the purse?

TRUFFALDINO: He told me I was to give it to my master.

BEATRICE: Well, and who is your master?

TRUFFALDINO: Your honor.

BEATRICE: Then why do you ask if the purse is mine?

TRUFFALDINO: Then it will be yours.

BEATRICE: Where is it?

TRUFFALDINO: Here, sir.

[*gives* BEATRICE *the purse*]

BEATRICE: Is the money all there?

TRUFFALDINO: I never touched it, sir.

BEATRICE: [*aside*] I shall count it.

TRUFFALDINO: [*aside*] I made a mistake over the purse; but that puts it straight. I wonder what the other gentleman will say? Oh well, if the money wasn't his, he'll say nothing at all.

BEATRICE: Is the landlord in?

TRUFFALDINO: Yes, sir.

BEATRICE: Tell him I shall have a friend to dinner with me, and he must get it ready as soon as he can.

TRUFFALDINO: What do you want for dinner, sir? How many dishes?

BEATRICE: Oh, Signor Pantalone dei Bisognosi is not a man who expects a great deal. Tell him to give us five or six dishes; something good.

TRUFFALDINO: You leave it all to me, sir?

BEATRICE: Yes, you order it; do the best you can. I am going to fetch the gentleman; he is not far off; see that all is ready by the time we come back.
[*going*]

TRUFFALDINO: You shall see how they serve you here.

BEATRICE: Look! Take this paper; put it in my trunk. Be careful with it; 'tis a bill of exchange for four thousand crowns.

TRUFFALDINO: Be sure of it, sir, I'll put it away at once.

BEATRICE: See that everything is ready.
[*aside*]
Poor old Signor Pantalone—I gave him a terrible fright! I must cheer him up a little.
[*Exit* BEATRICE.]

TRUFFALDINO: Now's the time to do myself proud. 'Tis the first time this master of mine has told me to order him a dinner. I'll show him I am a man of good taste. I'll just put away this paper and then—no, I'll put it away afterward; I must not waste time. Ho there! Is nobody at home?
[*calling into the inn*]
Call Master Brighella, tell him I want to talk to him.
[*returning*]
Now with a really good dinner 'tis not the having such and such dishes, but the way it is served. A properly laid table is worth more than a mountain of dishes.
[*Enter* BRIGHELLA.]

BRIGHELLA: What is it, Si'or Truffaldin'? What can I do for you?

TRUFFALDINO: My master has got a gentleman to dine with him. He wants a good dinner, and that quickly. Have you got enough in the kitchen?

BRIGHELLA: I always have plenty of everything. In half an hour I can put on any sort of dinner you like.

TRUFFALDINO: Very well, then. Tell me what you can give us.

BRIGHELLA: For two persons, we will have two courses of four dishes each; will that do?

TRUFFALDINO: He said five or six dishes—better say six or eight. That will do. What will you give us?

BRIGHELLA: For the first course, I shall give you soup, fried, boiled, and a fricandeau.

TRUFFALDINO: Three of the dishes I know, but I do not know the last.

BRIGHELLA: 'Tis a French dish—a ragout—very tasty indeed.

TRUFFALDINO: Very well, that will do for the first course; now the second.

BRIGHELLA: For the second course the roast, the salad, a meat pie—and a trifle.

TRUFFALDINO: [*indignant*] What's that? A trifle? My master and his guest are
     gentlemen of substance; they won't be satisfied with a mere trifle. A trifle
     indeed!

BRIGHELLA: You don't understand. I said
     [*impressively*]
     a trifle! That's an English dish, a pudding, my very own speciality; there's
     not another man in Venice knows how to make it!

TRUFFALDINO: [*nonchalantly*] Oh well, I dare say it will do. But how are you go-
     ing to arrange the table?

BRIGHELLA: Oh, that's easy enough. The waiter will see to that.

TRUFFALDINO: No, my good friend, laying the table is a very important matter;
     that's the first thing about a dinner, to have the table properly laid.

BRIGHELLA: Well, you might put the soup here, the fried there, there the boiled
     and here the fricandeau.
     [*makes an imaginary arrangement*]

TRUFFALDINO: I don't like that. Don't you put something in the middle?

BRIGHELLA: Then we should want five dishes.

TRUFFALDINO: Good, then let us have five.

BRIGHELLA: We can put the gravy in the middle.

TRUFFALDINO: No, no, friend, you know nothing about laying a table; you can't
     put the gravy in the middle; soup always goes in the middle.

BRIGHELLA: Then the meat on one side, and the gravy on the other.

TRUFFALDINO: Lord, lord, that won't do at all. You innkeepers may know how to
     cook, but you have no idea of butlering. Now I'll show you.
     [*kneels down on one knee and points to the floor*]
     Suppose this is the table. Now you look how we arrange the five dishes.
     Like this: here in the middle the soup.
     [*He tears off a piece of the bill of exchange and puts in on the floor to repre-
     sent a dish.*]
     Now the boiled meat.
     [*same business*]
     Here we put the fried opposite,
     [*same business*]
     here the gravy and here that—what-d'ye-call-it. There now! Won't that
     look fine?

BRIGHELLA: H'm, 'twill do; but you have put the gravy too far away from the
     meat.

TRUFFALDINO: Very well, we must see if we can't put it a little nearer.
     [*Enter* BEATRICE *and* PANTALONE.]

BEATRICE: What are you doing on your knees?

TRUFFALDINO: [*stands up*] I was just planning how to have the table laid.

BEATRICE: What is that paper?

TRUFFALDINO: [*aside*] The devil! The letter that he gave me!

BEATRICE: That is my bill of exchange.

TRUFFALDINO: I am very sorry, sir; I will stick it together again.

BEATRICE: You rascal! Is that the way you look after my things? Things of such
value too! You deserve a good thrashing. What say you, Signor Pantalone?
Did you ever see such a piece of folly?

PANTALONE: To tell the truth, I cannot help laughing. 'Twould be a serious matter if it could not be mended, but I will write you out another and then all
will be in order.

BEATRICE: But just think if the bill had been made out not here but in some place
a long way off!
[*to* TRUFFALDINO]
You ignorant fool!

TRUFFALDINO: This has all come about because Brighella doesn't know how to
lay a table.

BRIGHELLA: He finds fault with everything I do.

TRUFFALDINO: I am a man that knows his business.

BEATRICE: [*to* TRUFFALDINO] Go away.

TRUFFALDINO: Things must be done properly.

BEATRICE: Be off, I tell you.

TRUFFALDINO: In the matter of pantry work I won't give way to the first butler
in the land.
[*Exit* TRUFFALDINO.]

BRIGHELLA: I don't understand that fellow; sometimes he is a knave and sometimes a fool.

BEATRICE: This tomfoolery is all put on. Well, is dinner ready?

BRIGHELLA: If you will have five dishes to each course, 'twill take a little time.

PANTALONE: What's this about courses of five dishes? We'll take pot luck—a
risotto, a couple of other dishes, and I shall be most obliged to you. My
tastes are simple.

BEATRICE: [*to* BRIGHELLA] You hear that? That will do nicely.

BRIGHELLA: Very good, sir; but will you please to tell me if there might be anything you would particularly fancy?

PANTALONE: I should like some rissoles if you have them; my teeth are not very
good nowadays.

BEATRICE: You hear? Rissoles.

BRIGHELLA: Very good, sir. If you will sit down here for a moment, gentlemen,
dinner will be ready directly.

BEATRICE: Tell Truffaldino to come and wait on us.

BRIGHELLA: I'll tell him, sir.
[*Exit* BRIGHELLA.]

BEATRICE: Signor Pantalone, I fear you will indeed have to be content with pot
luck.

PANTALONE: My dear sir, I am overcome with all the attention you show me; in
fact you are doing for me what I ought to be doing for you. But, you see, I
have that girl of mine at home, and until everything is finally settled it
would not be proper for you to be together. So I accept your kind hospitality to raise my spirits a little; indeed I still feel quite upset. Had it not been
for you, that young scoundrel would have done for me.

BEATRICE: I am glad that I arrived in time.

[WAITERS *enter from the kitchen and carry glasses, wine, bread, etc., into the room where* BEATRICE *and* PANTALONE *are to dine.*]

PANTALONE: They are very quick about their business here.

BEATRICE: Brighella is a smart fellow. He was servant to a great nobleman at Turin, and still wears his livery.

PANTALONE: There's a very good tavern on the other side of the Grand Canal opposite the Rialto where you can eat very well; I have often been there with various good friends of mine, very sound men, too; I often think of that place. They had some wonderful Burgundy wine there to—'twas a wine for the gods.

BEATRICE: There's nothing one enjoys more than good wine in good company.

PANTALONE: Good company! Ah, if you had known them! That was good company! Good honest fellows, with many a good story to tell. God bless them. Seven or eight of them there were, and there wasn't the like of them in all the world.

[*The* WAITERS *come out of the room and return to the kitchen.*]

BEATRICE: You often had a merry time with these gentlemen, eh?

PANTALONE: And I hope I may live to have many more.

[*Enter* TRUFFALDINO *carrying the soup tureen.*]

TRUFFALDINO: [*to* BEATRICE] Dinner is ready for you in that room, sir.

BEATRICE: Go and put the soup on the table.

TRUFFALDINO: [*makes a bow*] After you, sir.

PANTALONE: A queer fellow, that servant of yours.

[*goes in*]

BEATRICE: [*to* TRUFFALDINO] I want less wit and more attention.

[*goes in*]

TRUFFALDINO: Call that a dinner! One dish at a time! They have money to spend, but they get nothing good for it. I wonder if this soup is worth eating; I'll try it.

[*takes a spoon out of his pocket and tastes the soup*]

I always carry my weapons about me. Not bad; it might be worse.

[*goes into room with soup*]

[*Enter* FIRST WAITER *with a dish.*]

FIRST WAITER: When is that man coming to take the dishes?

TRUFFALDINO: [*reentering*] Here I am, friend. What have you got for me?

FIRST WAITER: Here's the boiled meat. There's another dish to follow.

[*Exit* FIRST WAITER.]

TRUFFALDINO: Mutton? Or veal? Mutton, I think. Let's taste it.

[*tastes*]

No, 'tis neither mutton nor veal; 'tis lamb, and very good, too.

[*goes toward* BEATRICE'S *room*]

[*Enter* FLORINDO.]

FLORINDO: Where are you going?

TRUFFALDINO: [*aside*] Oh dear, oh dear!

FLORINDO: What are you doing with that dish?

TRUFFALDINO: I was just putting it on the table, sir.

FLORINDO: For whom?

TRUFFALDINO: For you, sir.

FLORINDO: Why do you serve dinner before I come in?

TRUFFALDINO: I saw you from the window.

>[*aside*]

I must find some excuse.

FLORINDO: And you begin with boiled meat instead of soup?

TRUFFALDINO: You must know, sir, at Venice soup is always taken last.

FLORINDO: I have other habits. I want my soup. Take that back to the kitchen.

TRUFFALDINO: Yes, sir, as you wish, sir.

FLORINDO: Make haste; afterward I want to have a nap.

TRUFFALDINO: Yes, sir.

>[*makes as if going to the kitchen*]

FLORINDO: [*aside*] Shall I never find Beatrice again?

>[FLORINDO *goes into the other room. As soon as he is in,* TRUFFALDINO *quickly takes the dish in to* BEATRICE. *Enter* FIRST WAITER *with another dish.* FLORINDO *calls from his room.*]

FLORINDO: Truffaldino! Truffaldino! Am I always to be kept waiting?

TRUFFALDINO: [*coming out of* BEATRICE'S *room*] Coming, sir.

>[*to* FIRST WAITER]

Quick, go and lay the table in that other room; the other gentleman has arrived; bring the soup at once.

FIRST WAITER: Directly.

>[*Exit* FIRST WAITER.]

TRUFFALDINO: What may this dish be? This must be the "fricandeau."

>[*tastes it*]

That's good, upon my word.

>[*takes it in to* BEATRICE]

>[WAITERS *enter and carry glasses, wine, bread, etc., into* FLORINDO'S *room.*]

TRUFFALDINO: [*to* WAITERS] Good lads, that's right.

>[*aside*]

They're as lively as kittens. Well, if I can manage to wait at table on two masters at once, 'twill be a great accomplishment indeed.

>[*The* WAITERS *come back out of* FLORINDO'S *room and go toward the kitchen.*]

TRUFFALDINO: Hurry up, lads, the soup!

FIRST WAITER: You look after your own table; we'll take care of this one.

>[*Exeunt* WAITERS.]

TRUFFALDINO: I want to look after both, if I can.

>[*Reenter* FIRST WAITER *with* FLORINDO'S *soup.*]

TRUFFALDINO: Here, give me that; I'll take it. Go and get the stuff for the other room.

>[*takes soup from* FIRST WAITER *and carries it into* FLORINDO'S *room*]

FIRST WAITER: That's a strange fellow. He wants to wait on everyone. Let him. They will have to give me *my* tip all the same.

>[TRUFFALDINO *comes out of* FLORINDO'S *room.*]

BEATRICE: [*calling from her room*] Truffaldino!

FIRST WAITER: [*to* TRUFFALDINO] Your master's calling.

TRUFFALDINO: Coming, sir.

[*goes into* BEATRICE'S *room*]

[SECOND WAITER *brings the boiled meat for* FLORINDO. TRUFFALDINO *brings the dirty plates out of* BEATRICE'S *room.*]

TRUFFALDINO: Here, give it to me.

[*Exit* SECOND WAITER.]

FLORINDO: [*calls*] Truffaldino!

TRUFFALDINO: [*wishes to take the meat from* WAITER] Give it to me.

FIRST WAITER: No, I'm taking this.

TRUFFALDINO: Didn't you hear him call for me?

[*Takes meat from him and carries it in to* FLORINDO.]

FIRST WAITER: Well, that's fine! He wants to do everything.

[SECOND WAITER *brings in a dish of rissoles, gives it to the* FIRST WAITER *and exit.*]

I would take this in myself, but I don't want to have words with that fellow.

[*Reenter* TRUFFALDINO *from* FLORINDO'S *room with dirty plates.*]

Here, master Jack-of-all-trades; take these rissoles to your master.

TRUFFALDINO: [*takes dish*] Rissoles?

FIRST WAITER: Yes, the rissoles he ordered.

[*Exit* FIRST WAITER.]

TRUFFALDINO: Oh, fine! Now which table are these to go to? I wonder which the devil of my two masters can have ordered them? If I go to the kitchen and ask, they'll begin to suspect; if I make a mistake and carry them to the one who didn't order them, then the other will ask for them and I shall be found out. I know what I'll do; I'll divide them on two plates, take half to each, and then I shall see who ordered them.

[*takes plates and divides the rissoles*]

That's four and that's four. There's one over. Who's to have that? We mustn't cause ill-feeling; I'll eat that one myself.

[*eats it*]

Now. We'll take the rissoles to this gentleman.

[TRUFFALDINO *puts one plate of rissoles on the floor and takes the other in to* BEATRICE. FIRST WAITER *enters with an English pudding (trifle).*]

FIRST WAITER: Truffaldino!

TRUFFALDINO: [*comes out of* BEATRICE'S *room*] Coming!

FIRST WAITER: Take this pudding—

TRUFFALDINO: Wait a moment, I'm coming.

[*Takes the other dish of rissoles and is going to* FLORINDO'S *room.*]

FIRST WAITER: That's not right, the rissoles belong there.

TRUFFALDINO: I know they do, sir; I have carried them there; and my master sends these four as a courtesy to this gentleman.

[*Goes into* FLORINDO'S *room.*]

FIRST WAITER: I see, they know each other—friends, you might say? They might as well have dined together.

TRUFFALDINO: [*reentering*] What's this affair?

FIRST WAITER: That's an English pudding.

TRUFFALDINO: Who is it for?

FIRST WAITER: For your master.

[*Exit* FIRST WAITER.]

TRUFFALDINO: What the devil is this "pudding"? It smells delicious, and looks like polenta. Oh! If it is polenta, that would be good indeed. I'll taste it.
> [*brings a fork out of his pocket and tries the pudding*]

It's not polenta, but it's very much like it.
> [*eats*]

Much better than polenta.
> [*goes on eating*]

BEATRICE: [*calling*] Truffaldino!

TRUFFALDINO: [*with mouth full*] Coming, sir.

FLORINDO: [*calling*] Truffaldino!

TRUFFALDINO: [*with mouth full*] Coming, sir.
> [*to himself*]

Oh what wonderful stuff! Just another mouthful and then I'll go.
> [*goes on eating*]
> [BEATRICE *comes out of her room, sees* TRUFFALDINO *eating, kicks him, and says:*]

BEATRICE: You come and wait on me.
> [*She goes back to her room.*]

Truffaldino!

TRUFFALDINO: Coming!
> [TRUFFALDINO *puts the pudding on the floor and goes into* BEATRICE'S *room.* FLORINDO *comes out of his.*]

FLORINDO: [*calling*] Truffaldino! Where the devil is he?
> [TRUFFALDINO *comes out of* BEATRICE'S *room.*]

TRUFFALDINO: Here, sir.
> [*seeing* FLORINDO]

FLORINDO: What are you doing? Where have you been?

TRUFFALDINO: I just went to fetch the next course, sir.

FLORINDO: Is there anything more to eat?

TRUFFALDINO: I'll go and see.

FLORINDO: Make haste, I tell you, because I want to have a nap afterward.
> [*goes back into his room*]

TRUFFALDINO: Very good, sir.
> [*calling*]

Waiter, is there anything more to come?
> [*aside*]

I'll put this pudding aside for myself.
> [*hides it*]
> [*Enter* FIRST WAITER *with dish.*]

FIRST WAITER: Here's the roast.

TRUFFALDINO: [*takes the roast*] Quick, the dessert!

FIRST WAITER: Lord, what a fluster! In a minute.
> [*Exit* FIRST WAITER.]

TRUFFALDINO: I'll take the roast to this gentleman.
> [*takes it to* FLORINDO]
> [*Reenter* FIRST WAITER.]

FIRST WAITER: [*with plate of fruit*] Here's the dessert; where are you?

TRUFFALDINO: [*reentering from* FLORINDO'S *room*] Here.

FIRST WAITER: [*gives him the fruit*] There. Anything more?
TRUFFALDINO: Wait.
     [*takes the dessert to* BEATRICE]
FIRST WAITER: He jumps about here and there like the devil himself.
TRUFFALDINO: [*reentering*] That will do. Nobody wants any more.
FIRST WAITER: I'm glad to hear it.
TRUFFALDINO: And now lay the table for *me*.
FIRST WAITER: In a moment.
     [*Exit* FIRST WAITER.]
TRUFFALDINO: Now for my pudding! Hurrah! I've got through it all, they are
    all content, they want nothing more, they've had a very good dinner. I
    have waited at table on two masters at once, and neither of 'em knew any-
    thing about the other. But if I have waited for two, now I am going to eat
    for four.

SCENE III———*A Street with* BRIGHELLA'S *Inn.*

     [*Enter* SMERALDINA.]
SMERALDINA: A very proper sort of young lady my mistress is! To send me all
    alone with a letter to a tavern, a young girl like me! Waiting on a woman in
    love is a sad business. This young lady of mine does a thousand crazy things,
    and what I cannot understand is this—if she is so much in love with Signor
    Silvio as to be ready to disembowel herself for him, why does she send let-
    ters to another gentleman? One for summer and one for winter, I suppose!
    Well, there it is!
       I am not going inside that tavern. I'll call; somebody will come out.
    Hey there! Anyone at home?
     [FIRST WAITER *comes out of the inn.*]
FIRST WAITER: Now, young woman, what do you want?
SMERALDINA: [*aside*] I feel thoroughly ashamed.
     [*to* WAITER]
    Tell me—a certain Signor Federigo Rasponi lodges here, does he not?
FIRST WAITER: Yes, indeed. He has just this moment finished dinner.
SMERALDINA: I have something to say to him.
FIRST WAITER: A message? You can come inside.
SMERALDINA: And what sort of a girl do you take me for? I am the waiting maid
    of the lady he is to marry.
FIRST WAITER: [*more politely*] Well then, pray step this way.
SMERALDINA: Oh, but I don't like to go in there.
FIRST WAITER: Do you expect me to bring him out into the street for you? That
    would not be at all the right thing; more especially as he has Signor Pan-
    talone dei Bisognosi with him.
SMERALDINA: What, my master? Worse and worse! I'll not come in.
FIRST WAITER: I can send his servant, if you like.
SMERALDINA: The little dark man?
FIRST WAITER: Exactly so.
SMERALDINA: Yes, do send him.

FIRST WAITER: [*aside*] I understand. She fancies the little dark man, and is ashamed to come inside. She is not ashamed to be seen with him in the middle of the street.
  [*goes in*]
SMERALDINA: If the master sees me, whatever shall I say? I'll tell him I came to look for *him;* that will do nicely. I'm never short of an answer.
  [*Enter* TRUFFALDINO *with a glass, a napkin, and a bottle in his hand.*]
TRUFFALDINO: Who sent for me?
SMERALDINA: I did, sir. I ask pardon if I have troubled you.
TRUFFALDINO: Not a bit of it. I am here to receive your commands.
SMERALDINA: I fear I must have taken you from your dinner.
TRUFFALDINO: I was having dinner, but I can go back to it.
SMERALDINA: I am truly sorry.
TRUFFALDINO: I am delighted. The fact is, I have had my bellyful, and your bright eyes are just the right thing to make me digest it.
SMERALDINA: [*aside*] Very gallant!
TRUFFALDINO: I'll just set down this bottle, and then I'm with you, my dear.
SMERALDINA: [*aside*] He called me "my dear"!
  [*to* TRUFFALDINO]
  My mistress sends this letter to Signor Federigo Rasponi; I do not like to come into the tavern, so I thought I might put you to this trouble, as you are his man.
TRUFFALDINO: I'll take it with pleasure; but first, you must know that I have a message for *you.*
SMERALDINA: From whom?
TRUFFALDINO: From a very honest man. Tell me, are you acquainted with one Truffaldin' Battocchio?
SMERALDINA: I think I have heard him spoken of, but I am not sure.
  [*aside*]
  It must be himself.
TRUFFALDINO: He's a good-looking man; short, thickset, with plenty of wit to his talk. Understands butlering too—
SMERALDINA: I don't know him from Adam.
TRUFFALDINO: Yes, you do; and what's more, he's in love with you.
SMERALDINA: Oh! You are making fun of me.
TRUFFALDINO: And if he could only have just a little hope that his affections were returned, he would make himself known.
SMERALDINA: Well, sir, if I were to see him, and he took my fancy, it might possibly be that I should return his affection.
TRUFFALDINO: Shall I show him to you?
SMERALDINA: I should like to see him.
TRUFFALDINO: Just a moment.
  [*goes into the inn*]
SMERALDINA: Then 'tis not he.
  [TRUFFALDINO *comes out of the inn, makes low bows to* SMERALDINA, *passes close to her, sighs, and goes back into the inn.*]
SMERALDINA: I do not understand this play-acting.

TRUFFALDINO: [*reentering*] Did you see him?

SMERALDINA: See whom?

TRUFFALDINO: The man who is in love with your beauty.

SMERALDINA: I saw no one but you.

TRUFFALDINO: [*sighs*] Well!

SMERALDINA: It is you, then, who profess to be in love with me?

TRUFFALDINO: It is.
      [*sighs*]

SMERALDINA: Why did you not say so before?

TRUFFALDINO: Because I am rather shy.

SMERALDINA: [*aside*] He would make a stone fall in love with him.

TRUFFALDINO: Well, and what do you say?

SMERALDINA: I say—

TRUFFALDINO: Come, tell me.

SMERALDINA: Oh—I am rather shy too.

TRUFFALDINO: Then if we were joined up, 'twould be a marriage of two people
    who are rather shy.

SMERALDINA: I must say, you are just my fancy.

TRUFFALDINO: Are you a maid?

SMERALDINA: Need you ask?

TRUFFALDINO: I suppose that means "certainly not."

SMERALDINA: On the contrary, it means "certainly I am."

TRUFFALDINO: I am a bachelor too.

SMERALDINA: I could have been married fifty times, but I never found the man I
    really fancied.

TRUFFALDINO: Do you think there is any hope for me?

SMERALDINA: Well—to tell the truth—really—I must say—there's a—some-
    thing about you—No, I won't say another word.

TRUFFALDINO: If somebody wanted to marry you, what would he have to do?

SMERALDINA: I have neither father nor mother. He would have to speak to my
    master, or to my mistress.

TRUFFALDINO: And if I speak to them, what will they say?

SMERALDINA: They will say, that if I am content—

TRUFFALDINO: And what will you say?

SMERALDINA: I shall say—that if they are content too—

TRUFFALDINO: That will do. We shall all be content. Give me the letter and when
    I bring you back the answer, we will have a talk.

SMERALDINA: Here's the letter.

TRUFFALDINO: Do you know what is in it?

SMERALDINA: No—if you only knew how curious I am to know!

TRUFFALDINO: I hope it is not a disdainful letter, or I shall get my face spoiled.

SMERALDINA: Who knows? It can't be a love letter.

TRUFFALDINO: I don't want to get into trouble. If I don't know what is in the let-
    ter, I am not going to take it.

SMERALDINA: We could open it—but how are we to seal it again?

TRUFFALDINO: Leave it to me; sealing letters is just my job. No one will ever
    know anything.

SMERALDINA: Then let us open it.

TRUFFALDINO: Can you read?

SMERALDINA: A little. But you can read quite well, I'm sure.

TRUFFALDINO: Yes, I too can read just a little.

SMERALDINA: Then let us hear.

TRUFFALDINO: We must open it cleanly.
[*tears off a piece*]

SMERALDINA: Oh! What have you done?

TRUFFALDINO: Nothing. I've a secret way to mend it. Here it is, open.

SMERALDINA: Quick, read it.

TRUFFALDINO: *You* read it. You will know your young lady's handwriting better than I do.

SMERALDINA: [*looking at the letter*] Really, I can't make out a word.

TRUFFALDINO: [*same business*] Nor I neither.

SMERALDINA: Then what was the good of opening it?

TRUFFALDINO: [*takes the letter*] Wait; let me think; I can make out some of it.

SMERALDINA: Oh I know some of the letters too.

TRUFFALDINO: Let us try one by one. Isn't that an M?

SMERALDINA: No! That's an R!

TRUFFALDINO: Between R and M there is very little difference.

SMERALDINA: *Ri, ri, o.* No, no: keep quiet; I think it *is* an M—*Mi, mi, o—mio!*

TRUFFALDINO: It's not *mio*, it's *mia*.

SMERALDINA: But it is, there's the hook—

TRUFFALDINO: That proves it is *mia*.
[BEATRICE *comes out of the inn with* PANTALONE.]

PANTALONE: [*to* SMERALDINA] What are you doing here?

SMERALDINA: [*frightened*] Nothing sir; I came to look for you.

PANTALONE: [*to* SMERALDINA] What do you want with me?

SMERALDINA: The mistress wants you, sir.

BEATRICE: [*to* TRUFFALDINO] What is this paper?

TRUFFALDINO: [*frightened*] Nothing, just a bit of paper—

BEATRICE: Let me see.

TRUFFALDINO: [*gives paper, trembling*] Yes, sir.

BEATRICE: What? This is a letter addressed to me. Villain, will you open all my letters?

TRUFFALDINO: I know nothing about it, sir—

BEATRICE: Look, Signor Pantalone, here is a letter from Signora Clarice, in which she tells me of Silvio's insane jealousy—and this rascal has the impudence to open it!

PANTALONE: [*to* SMERALDINA] And you helped him to do so?

SMERALDINA: I know nothing about it, sir.

BEATRICE: Who opened this letter?

TRUFFALDINO: Not I.

SMERALDINA: Nor I.

PANTALONE: Well, who brought it?

SMERALDINA: Truffaldino brought it to his master.

TRUFFALDINO: And Smeraldina brought it to Truffaldino.

SMERALDINA: [*aside*] Sneak! I don't like you any more.

PANTALONE: You meddlesome little hussy, so you are the cause of all this trouble, are you? I've a good mind to smack your face.

SMERALDINA: I've never had my face smacked by any man; I'm surprised at you.

PANTALONE: [*coming near her*] Is that the way you answer me?

SMERALDINA: You won't catch me. You're too rheumatic; you can't run.
     [*Exit running.*]

PANTALONE: You saucy minx, I'll show you if I can run; I'll catch you.
     [*runs after her*]

TRUFFALDINO: [*aside*] If I only knew how to get out of this!

BEATRICE: [*looking at the letter, aside*] Poor Clarice! She is in despair over Silvio's jealousy; 'twill be best for me to discover myself and set her mind at rest.

TRUFFALDINO: [*tries to steal away quietly*] I don't think he is looking. I'll try to get away.

BEATRICE: Where are you off to?

TRUFFALDINO: Nowhere.
     [*stops*]

BEATRICE: Why did you open this letter?

TRUFFALDINO: It was Smeraldina; I had nothing to do with it.

BEATRICE: Smeraldina, forsooth! You did it, you rascal. One and one make two. That's the second letter of mine you have opened today. Come here.

TRUFFALDINO: [*approaching timidly*] Oh, for mercy's sake, sir—

BEATRICE: Come here, I say.

TRUFFALDINO: [*same business*] Oh, for the love of Heaven—
     [BEATRICE *takes the stick which* TRUFFALDINO *has at his flank (i.e., Harlequin's wooden sword or baton) and beats him well, she standing with her back to the inn.* FLORINDO *appears at the window and sees the beating.*]

FLORINDO: What's this? Beating my servant?
     [*leaves window*]

TRUFFALDINO: Stop, stop, sir, for pity's sake.

BEATRICE: Take that, rascal, and learn to open my letters.
     [*throws stick on the ground, and exit to street*]

TRUFFALDINO: [*after* BEATRICE *has gone*] My blood! My body! Is that the way to treat a man of my sort? Beat a man like me? If a servant is no good, you can send him away, but you don't beat him.
     [FLORINDO *comes out, unseen by* TRUFFALDINO.]

FLORINDO: What's that?

TRUFFALDINO: [*seeing* FLORINDO] Oh! I said people had no business to beat other people's servants like that. This is an insult to my master.
     [*looking toward direction of* BEATRICE'S *exit*]

FLORINDO: Yes, 'tis an affront put upon *me*. Who was it gave you a thrashing?

TRUFFALDINO: I couldn't say, sir; I do not know him.

FLORINDO: Why did he thrash you?

TRUFFALDINO: Because I—I spat on his shoe.

FLORINDO: And you let yourself be beaten like that? Did nothing? Made no attempt to defend yourself? And you expose your master to insult, with perhaps serious consequences? Ass! Poltroon!
     [*picks up the stick*]

Since you enjoy being thrashed, I'll give you your pleasure, I'll thrash you myself as well.

[*thrashes him and exit into inn*]

TRUFFALDINO: Well, there's no mistake about my being the servant of two masters. They have both paid me my wages.

[*Exit into the inn.*]

ACT III

SCENE I————*A Room in* BRIGHELLA'S *inn.*

TRUFFALDINO: I don't care that for my beating! I have eaten well, I've dined well, and this evening I shall sup still better; and as long as I can serve two masters, there's this at least, that I draw double wages.

And now what's to be done? Master number one is out of doors, master number two is fast asleep; why, it's just the moment to give those clothes an airing—take them out of the trunks and see if there's anything wants doing. Here are the keys. This room will do nicely. I'll get the trunks out and make a proper job of it. I must have someone to help me though.

[*calls*]

Waiter!

[*Enter* WAITERS.]

FIRST WAITER: What do you want?

TRUFFALDINO: I want you to lend a hand to bring some trunks out of those rooms, to give the clothes an airing.

FIRST WAITER: [*to* SECOND WAITER] Go and help him.

TRUFFALDINO: [*to* SECOND WAITER] Come along, and I'll give you a good handful of what my masters gave me.

[TRUFFALDINO *and* SECOND WAITER *go into* BEATRICE'S *room.*]

FIRST WAITER: He looks like a rare good servant—quick, ready, and most attentive; but I'll warrant he has his faults somewhere. I've been a servant myself and I know the ropes. Nobody does anything just for love. Whatever they do, either they are robbing their masters or they are throwing dust in their eyes.

[TRUFFALDINO *comes out of the room with the* SECOND WAITER *carrying a trunk.*]

TRUFFALDINO: Gently! Let's put it down here.

[*They put the trunk in the middle of the room.*]

Now let's fetch the other. But quietly, for my master is in there asleep.

[TRUFFALDINO *and* SECOND WAITER *go into* FLORINDO'S *room.*]

FIRST WAITER: Either he's a real first-rate fellow, or he's a real knave; I never saw anybody wait on two gentlemen at once like that. I shall just keep my eyes open; maybe, under the pretense of waiting on two gentlemen at once, he means to rob them both.

[TRUFFALDINO *and* SECOND WAITER *reenter with the other trunk.*]

TRUFFALDINO: And we'll put this one here.

[*They put it down a little way off from the other.*]

[*to* SECOND WAITER]

There! You can run along now, if you like. I don't want anything more.

FIRST WAITER: [*to* SECOND WAITER] Go on; off with you to the kitchen.
    [*Exit* SECOND WAITER.]
    [*to* TRUFFALDINO]
Can I help you?
TRUFFALDINO: No, thank you; I can do my work myself.
FIRST WAITER: I must say, you are a giant for work; it's a marvel to me how you
    get through it all.
    [*Exit* FIRST WAITER.]
TRUFFALDINO: Now I'm going to do my work properly, in peace and quiet, with
    no one to worry me.
    [*takes a key out of his pocket*]
Now which key is this, I wonder? Which trunk does it fit? Let's try.
    [*opens one trunk*]
I guessed right at once. I'm the cleverest man on earth. And this other will
open t'other trunk.
    [*takes out second key and opens second trunk*]
Now they are both open. Let's take everything out.
    [*He takes all the clothes out of both trunks and puts them on the table. In
    each trunk there must be a black suit, books and papers, and anything else
    ad lib.*]
I'll just see if there is anything in the pockets. You never know, sometimes
they leave biscuits or sweets in them.
    [*searches the pockets of* BEATRICE'S *suit and finds a portrait*]
My word, what a pretty picture! There's a handsome man! Who can it be?
A queer thing, I seem to know him, but yet I can't remember. He is just the
least little bit like my other master; but no, *he* never wears clothes like that,
nor that wig neither.
    [FLORINDO *calls from his room.*]
FLORINDO: Truffaldino!
TRUFFALDINO: Oh, plague take him! He was woken up. If the devil tempts him
    to come out and he sees this other trunk, he'll want to know—quick,
    quick—I'll lock it up and say I don't know whose it is.
    [*begins putting clothes in again*]
FLORINDO: [*calling*] Truffaldino!
TRUFFALDINO: Coming, sir!
    [*aside*]
I must put these things away first. But I can't remember which trunk this
coat came from, nor these papers neither.
FLORINDO: [*calling*] Come here, I say; or must I fetch a stick to you?
TRUFFALDINO: In a minute, sir.
    [*aside*]
Quick, before he comes! I'll put all straight when he goes out.
    [*Stuffs the things into the trunks anyhow and locks them.* FLORINDO *comes
    out in a dressing gown.*]
FLORINDO: What the devil are you doing?
TRUFFALDINO: Pray, sir, didn't you tell me to give your clothes an airing? I was
    just about to do it here.
FLORINDO: And this other trunk, whose is that?

TRUFFALDINO: I couldn't say, sir; 'twill belong to some other gentleman.

FLORINDO: Give me my black coat.

TRUFFALDINO: Very good, sir.

> [*Opens* FLORINDO'S *trunk and gives him the black suit.* FLORINDO *takes off his dressing gown with* TRUFFALDINO'S *help and puts on the black coat; then puts his hand into the pockets and finds the portrait.*]

FLORINDO: [*much surprised*] What is this?

TRUFFALDINO: [*aside*] Oh Lord, I've made a mistake. I ought to have put it into the other gentleman's pocket. 'Tis the color made me go wrong.

FLORINDO: [*aside*] Heavens! There can be no mistake. This is my own portrait; the one I gave to my beloved Beatrice.

> [*to* TRUFFALDINO]

Tell me, how ever did this portrait come to be in the pocket of my coat? It wasn't there before.

TRUFFALDINO: [*aside*] Now what's the answer to that? I don't know. Let me think—

FLORINDO: Come on, out with it, answer me. How did this portrait come to be in my pocket?

TRUFFALDINO: Sir, be kind and forgive me for taking a liberty. The portrait belongs to me, and I hid it there for safety, for fear I might lose it.

FLORINDO: How did you come by this portrait?

TRUFFALDINO: My master left it to me.

FLORINDO: Left it to you?

TRUFFALDINO: Yes, sir; I had a master who died, and he left me a few trifles which I sold, all except this portrait, sir.

FLORINDO: Great heavens! And how long is it since this master of yours died?

TRUFFALDINO: 'Twill be just about a week ago, sir.

> [*aside*]

I say the first thing that comes into my head.

FLORINDO: What was your master's name?

TRUFFALDINO: I do not know, sir; he lived incognito.

FLORINDO: Incognito? How long were you in his service?

TRUFFALDINO: Only a short time, sir; ten or twelve days.

FLORINDO: [*aside*] Heavens! More and more do I fear that it was Beatrice. She escaped in man's dress; she concealed her name—Oh, wretched me, if it be true!

TRUFFALDINO: [*aside*] As he believes it all, I may as well go on with the fairy tale.

FLORINDO: [*despairingly*] Tell me, was your master young?

TRUFFALDINO: Yes, sir, quite a young gentleman.

FLORINDO: Without a beard?

TRUFFALDINO: Without a beard, sir.

FLORINDO: [*aside, with a sigh*] 'Twas she, doubtless.

TRUFFALDINO: [*aside*] I hope I'm not in for another thrashing.

FLORINDO: At least, you know where your late master came from?

TRUFFALDINO: I did know, sir, but I can't now call it to mind.

FLORINDO: Was it from Turin?

TRUFFALDINO: Turin it was, sir.

FLORINDO: [*aside*] Every word he speaks is a sword thrust in my heart.

[*to* TRUFFALDINO]

Tell me again, this young gentleman from Turin, is he really dead?

TRUFFALDINO: He is dead indeed, sir.

FLORINDO: Of what did he die?

TRUFFALDINO: He met with an accident, and that was the end of him.

[*aside*]

That seems to be the best way out.

FLORINDO: Where was he buried?

TRUFFALDINO: [*aside*] I wasn't ready for that one.

[*to* FLORINDO]

He wasn't buried, sir.

FLORINDO: What!

TRUFFALDINO: No, sir, another servant from the same place got permission to have him put into a coffin and sent home, sir.

FLORINDO: And was it, by any chance, the same servant who got you to fetch his letters for him from the Post this morning?

TRUFFALDINO: Exactly so, sir; it was Pasqual'.

FLORINDO: [*aside*] Then all hope is lost. Beatrice is dead. Unhappy Beatrice! The discomforts of the journey and the tortures of her heart must have killed her. Oh! I can no longer endure the agony of my grief!

[*Exit into his room.*]

TRUFFALDINO: That portrait has touched him in the guts. He must have known the gentleman. Well, I had better take the trunks back to the rooms again, or I shall be in for more trouble of the same sort. Oh dear! Here comes my other master.

[*Enter* BEATRICE *and* PANTALONE.]

BEATRICE: I assure you, Signor Pantalone, the last consignment of mirrors and wax candles has been put down twice over.

PANTALONE: Maybe my young men have made a mistake. We will go through the books again, and then we shall find out exactly how things stand.

BEATRICE: I too have a list copied from my own books. We will compare them. Perhaps that may decide the point either in your favor or mine. Truffaldino!

TRUFFALDINO: Here, sir.

BEATRICE: Have you the key of my trunk?

TRUFFALDINO: Yes, sir; here it is.

BEATRICE: Why have you brought my trunk in here?

TRUFFALDINO: To air your clothes, sir.

BEATRICE: Have you aired them?

TRUFFALDINO: I have, sir.

BEATRICE: Open the trunk and give me—Whose is that other trunk?

TRUFFALDINO: It belongs to another gentleman who has just come.

BEATRICE: Give me the memorandum book which you will find there.

TRUFFALDINO: Yes, sir.

[*aside*]

The Lord help me this time!

[*opens trunk and looks for the book*]

PANTALONE: As I say, they may have made a mistake; of course, if there is a mistake, you will not have to pay.

BEATRICE: We may find that all is in order; we shall see.

TRUFFALDINO: Is this the book, sir?

> [*holding out a book to* BEATRICE]

BEATRICE: I expect so.

> [*takes the book without looking carefully and opens it*]

No, this is not it—Whose is this book?

TRUFFALDINO: [*aside*] I've done it now!

BEATRICE: [*aside*] These are two letters which I wrote to Florindo. Alas, these notes, these accounts belong to him. I tremble, I am in a cold sweat, I know not where I am.

PANTALONE: What ails you, Signor Federigo? Are you unwell?

BEATRICE: 'Tis nothing.

> [*aside to* TRUFFALDINO]

Truffaldino, how did this book come to be in my trunk? It is not mine.

TRUFFALDINO: I hardly know, sir—

BEATRICE: Come, out with it—tell me the truth.

TRUFFALDINO: I ask your pardon for the liberty I took, sir, putting the book into your trunk. It belongs to me, and I put it there for safety.

> [*aside*]

That was a good enough story for the other gentleman, I hope 'twill do for this one too.

BEATRICE: The book is your own, you say, and yet you gave it to me instead of mine, without noticing?

TRUFFALDINO: [*aside*] He's much too clever.

> [*to* BEATRICE]

I'll tell you, sir; I have only had the book a very short time, so I did not recognize it at once.

BEATRICE: And how came you by this book?

TRUFFALDINO: I was in service with a gentleman at Venice, and he died and left the book to me.

BEATRICE: How long ago?

TRUFFALDINO: I don't remember exactly—ten or twelve days.

BEATRICE: How can that be, when I met you at Verona?

TRUFFALDINO: I had just come away from Venice on account of my poor master's death.

BEATRICE: [*aside*] Alas for me!

> [*to* TRUFFALDINO]

Your master—was his name—Florindo?

TRUFFALDINO: Yes, sir; Florindo.

BEATRICE: And his family name Aretusi?

TRUFFALDINO: That was it, sir; Aretusi.

BEATRICE: And you are sure he is dead?

TRUFFALDINO: As sure as I stand here.

BEATRICE: Of what did he die? Where was he buried?

TRUFFALDINO: He tumbled into the canal and was drowned and never seen again.

BEATRICE: Oh, wretched that I am! Florindo is dead, my beloved is dead; my one and only hope is dead. All is lost. Love's stratagems are fruitless! I leave my home, I leave my relatives, I dress as a man, I confront danger, I hazard my very life, all for Florindo—and Florindo is dead. Unhappy Beatrice! Was the loss of my brother so little to me that Fate must make me lose my lover as well? Oh! Grief overwhelms me, I can no longer bear the light of day. My adored one, my beloved, I will follow you to the tomb.

> [*Exits into her room raving.*]

PANTALONE: [*who has listened to her speech with astonishment*] Truffaldino!

TRUFFALDINO: Si'or Pantalon'?

PANTALONE: A woman!

TRUFFALDINO: A female!

PANTALONE: Most extraordinary!

TRUFFALDINO: Who'd have thought it?

PANTALONE: I'm struck all of a heap.

TRUFFALDINO: You might knock me down with a feather.

PANTALONE: I shall go straight home and tell my daughter.

> [*Exit.*]

TRUFFALDINO: It seems I am not the servant of two masters but of a master and a mistress.

> [*Exit.*]

SCENE II————*A Street.*

[*Enter* DR. LOMBARDI *meeting* PANTALONE.]

DR. LOMBARDI: [*aside*] This doddering old villain Pantalone sticks in my gizzard. The more I think about him, the more I abominate him.

PANTALONE: [*cheerfully*] Good day, my dear Doctor, your servant.

DR. LOMBARDI: I am surprised that you have the effrontery to address me.

PANTALONE: I have news for you. Do you know—

DR. LOMBARDI: You are going to tell me that the marriage has already been performed? I care not a fig if it has.

PANTALONE: The whole story is untrue. Let me speak, plague take you.

DR. LOMBARDI: Speak on then, pox on you.

PANTALONE: [*aside*] I should like to give him a good doctoring with my fists.

> [*to* DR. LOMBARDI]

My daughter shall marry your son whenever you please.

DR. LOMBARDI: I am vastly obliged to you. Pray do not put yourself to inconvenience. My son is not prepared to stomach that, sir. You may give her to the Turin gentleman.

PANTALONE: If you knew who the Turin gentleman is, you would say differently.

DR. LOMBARDI: He may be who he will. Your daughter has been seen with him, *et hoc sufficit.*

PANTALONE: But 'tis not true that he is—

DR. LOMBARDI: I will not hear another word.

PANTALONE: If you won't hear me, 'twill be the worse for you.

DR. LOMBARDI: We shall see for whom it will be the worse.

PANTALONE: My daughter is a girl of unblemished reputation, and—

DR. LOMBARDI: The devil take you.

PANTALONE: The devil take you, sir.

DR. LOMBARDI: You disreputable old villain!
> [*Exit* DR. LOMBARDI.]

PANTALONE: Damn you! He is more like a beast than a man. Why, how could I ever tell him that the man was a woman? Not a bit of it, he wouldn't let me speak. But here comes that young lout of a son of his; now I shall be in for more impertinence.
> [*Enter* SILVIO.]

SILVIO: [*aside*] There is Pantalone. I should like to run a sword through his paunch.

PANTALONE: Signor Silvio, if you will give me leave, I should like to give you a piece of good news, if you will condescend to allow me to speak, and not behave like that windmill of a father of yours.

SILVIO: What have you to say to me? Pray speak, sir.

PANTALONE: You must know, sir, that the marriage of my daughter to Signor Federigo has come to nothing.

SILVIO: Indeed? Do not deceive me.

PANTALONE: 'Tis true indeed, and if you are still of your former mind, my daughter is ready to give you her hand.

SILVIO: Oh, heavens! You bring me back from death to life.

PANTALONE: [*aside*] Well, well, he is not quite such a bear as his father.

SILVIO: But heavens! How can I clasp to my bosom her who has for so long been the bride of another?

PANTALONE: To cut a long story short, Federigo Rasponi has turned into Beatrice his sister.

SILVIO: What? I do not understand you.

PANTALONE: Then you are very thickheaded. The person whom we thought to be Federigo has been discovered to be Beatrice.

SILVIO: Dressed as a man?

PANTALONE: Dressed as a man.

SILVIO: At last I understand.

PANTALONE: About time you did.

SILVIO: How did it happen? Tell me.

PANTALONE: Let us go to my house. My daughter knows nothing of it. I need only tell the story once to satisfy you both.

SILVIO: I will come, sir; and I must humbly beg your forgiveness, for having allowed myself to be transported by passion—

PANTALONE: 'Twas a mere nothing; I appreciate your feelings. I know what love is. Now, my dear boy, come along with me.
> [*going*]

SILVIO: [*aside*] Who is happier than I am? What heart could be more contended?
> [*Exit with* PANTALONE.]

SCENE III————*A Room in* BRIGHELLA'S *Inn.*

[BEATRICE *and* FLORINDO *come out of their rooms simultaneously; each holds a sword or dagger and is on the point of committing suicide.* BRIGHELLA *is restraining* BEATRICE *and the* FIRST WAITER *restraining* FLORINDO. *They all come forward in such a way that* BEATRICE *and* FLORINDO *are unaware of each other's presence.*]

BRIGHELLA: [*seizing* BEATRICE'S *hand*] Stop, stop!

BEATRICE: [*trying to break loose*] For pity's sake, let me go.

FIRST WAITER: [*holding* FLORINDO] This is madness.

FLORINDO: [*breaks away from* WAITER] Go to the devil.

BEATRICE: [*breaking away from* BRIGHELLA] You shall not hinder me.

[*Both come forward, determined to kill themselves, they see each other, recognize each other, and stand dazed.*]

FLORINDO: What do I see?

BEATRICE: Florindo!

FLORINDO: Beatrice!

BEATRICE: Are you alive?

FLORINDO: Are you too living?

BEATRICE: Oh, destiny!

FLORINDO: Oh, my adored one!

[*They drop their weapons and embrace.*]

BRIGHELLA: [*jokingly to the* WAITER] You had better mop up the blood; we don't want a mess here.

[*Exit* BRIGHELLA.]

FIRST WAITER: [*aside*] Anyway I'll pick up the weapons and I shall not give them back again.

[*picks up the daggers and exits*]

FLORINDO: What brought you to attempt such an act of madness?

BEATRICE: The false news of your death.

FLORINDO: Who told you that I was dead?

BEATRICE: My servant.

FLORINDO: And mine gave me to believe that you were dead; and I too, carried away by the same agony of grief, intended to take my life.

BEATRICE: It was this book caused me to believe the story.

FLORINDO: That book was in my trunk. How came it into your hands? Ah, now I know. By the same means, no doubt, as the portrait I found in my coat pocket. Here it is. The one I gave you in Turin.

BEATRICE: Those rascally servants of ours—Heaven only knows what they have been up to.

FLORINDO: Where are they, I wonder?

BEATRICE: Nowhere to be seen.

FLORINDO: Let us find them and confront them.

[*calling*]

Ho there! Is nobody there?

[*Enter* BRIGHELLA.]

BRIGHELLA: Did you call, sir?

FLORINDO: Where are our servants?

BRIGHELLA: I don't know, sir. Shall I send to look for them?

FLORINDO: Find them at once if you can and send them to us here.

BRIGHELLA: For myself I only know one of them; I will ask the waiters, they will know them both. I congratulate you, sir, and madam, on having made such a satisfactory end of yourselves; if you want to get yourselves buried, you must try some other establishment; that's more than we can undertake. Your servant, madam and sir.

[*Exit* BRIGHELLA.]

FLORINDO: Then you too are lodged in this inn?

BEATRICE: I arrived this morning.

FLORINDO: I too this morning. And yet we never saw each other.

BEATRICE: Fate has been pleased to torment us a little.

FLORINDO: Tell me: your brother Federigo—is he dead?

BEATRICE: Have you any doubt? He died on the spot.

FLORINDO: I was told he was alive and here in Venice.

BEATRICE: It was I who traveled in his name and in these clothes to follow—

FLORINDO: To follow me—I know, my dearest; I read it in a letter from your servant in Turin.

BEATRICE: How came it into your hands?

FLORINDO: My servant gave it me by mistake and seeing it was addressed to you, I could not help opening it.

BEATRICE: I suppose a lover's curiosity is always legitimate.

FLORINDO: But where are these servants of ours? Ah!

> [*Sees* TRUFFALDINO *approaching.*]

Here is one.

BEATRICE: He looks like the worse knave of the two.

FLORINDO: I think you are not far wrong.

> [*Enter* TRUFFALDINO *brought in by force by* BRIGHELLA *and the* FIRST WAITER.]

FLORINDO: Come here, come here, don't be frightened.

BEATRICE: We shall do you no harm.

TRUFFALDINO: [*aside*] H'm, I still remember the thrashing.

BRIGHELLA: We have found this one; if we can find the other, we will bring him.

FLORINDO: Yes, we must have them both here together.

BRIGHELLA: [*aside to* WAITER] Do you know the other?

FIRST WAITER: [*to* BRIGHELLA] Not I.

BRIGHELLA: We'll ask in the kitchen. Someone there will know him.

FIRST WAITER: If he had been there, I should have known him too.

> [*Exeunt* FIRST WAITER *and* BRIGHELLA.]

FLORINDO: [*to* TRUFFALDINO] Come, now, tell us what happened about that changing of the portrait and the book, and why you and that other rascal conspired to drive us distracted.

TRUFFALDINO: [*signs to both with his finger to keep silence*] Hush!

> [*to* FLORINDO]

Pray, sir, a word with you in private.

> [*to* BEATRICE *just as he turns to speak to* FLORINDO]

I will tell you everything directly.

> [*to* FLORINDO]

You must know, sir, I am not to blame for anything that has happened; it's all Pasqual's fault, the servant of that lady there.

> [*cautiously pointing at* BEATRICE]

It was he mixed up the things, and put into one trunk what belonged to the other, without my knowledge. The poor man begged and prayed me to take the blame, for fear his master should send him away, and as I am a kind-hearted fellow that would let himself be drawn and quartered for his friends, I made up all these stories to see if I could help him. I never dreamed it was a portrait of you or that you would be so much upset at hearing of the death of the owner. Now I have told you the whole truth, sir, as an honest man and a faithful servant.

BEATRICE: [*aside*] 'Tis a very long story he is telling. I am curious to know what the mystery is about.

FLORINDO: [*aside to* TRUFFALDINO] Then the man who got you to fetch that letter from the Post was the servant of Signora Beatrice?

TRUFFALDINO: [*aside to* FLORINDO] Yes, sir, that was Pasqual'.

FLORINDO: Then why conceal from me a fact I so urgently desired to know?

TRUFFALDINO: He begged me not to tell anyone, sir.

FLORINDO: Who?

TRUFFALDINO: Pasqual'.

FLORINDO: Why didn't you obey your master?

TRUFFALDINO: For the love of Pasqual'.

FLORINDO: You and Pasquale deserve a sound thrashing together.

TRUFFALDINO: [*aside to himself*] In that case I should get both.

BEATRICE: Have you not yet finished this long cross-examination?

FLORINDO: This fellow has been telling me—

TRUFFALDINO: [*aside to* FLORINDO] For the love of Heaven, your honor, do not say it was Pasqual'. I'd rather you told the lady it was me. You can give me a beating if you like, but don't, don't let any trouble come to Pasqual'.

FLORINDO: [*aside to* TRUFFALDINO] Are you so devoted a friend to Pasquale?

TRUFFALDINO: I love him as if he were my very own self. Now I am going to the lady, and I am going to tell her that it was all my fault; she may scold me as she pleases and do what she will to me, but I will protect Pasqual'.

[TRUFFALDINO *moves toward* BEATRICE.]

FLORINDO: [*aside*] Well, he's certainly a very loyal and affectionate character.

TRUFFALDINO: [*to* BEATRICE] Here I am, madam.

BEATRICE: [*aside to* TRUFFALDINO] What is all this long story you've been telling Signor Florindo?

TRUFFALDINO: [*aside to* BEATRICE] You must know, madam, that that gentleman has a servant called Pasqual'; he is the most arrant noddy in the world; it was he made all that mess of things; but because the poor man was afraid his master would send him away, I made up all the story about the book and the master who was dead and drowned, and all the rest of it. And just now I've been telling Si'or Florindo that I was the cause of it all.

BEATRICE: But why accuse yourself of faults which you have never committed?

TRUFFALDINO: Madam, 'tis all for the love I bear Pasqual'.

FLORINDO: [*aside*] This seems a very long business.

TRUFFALDINO: [*to* BEATRICE *as before*] Dear madam, I beg of you, don't get him into trouble.

BEATRICE: Whom?

TRUFFALDINO: Pasqual'.

BEATRICE: Pasquale and you are a pretty pair of rascals.

TRUFFALDINO: [*aside to himself*] I fear I'm the only one.

FLORINDO: Come. That's enough. Signora Beatrice, our servants certainly deserve to be punished; but in consideration of our own great happiness, we surely may forgive what is past.

BEATRICE: True; but your servant—

TRUFFALDINO: [*aside to* BEATRICE] For the love of Heaven don't mention Pasqual'.

BEATRICE: [*to* FLORINDO] Well, I must go and call upon Signor Pantalone dei Bisognosi; will you accompany me?

FLORINDO: I would do so with pleasure, but I have to wait here and see my banker. I will come later, if you are in haste.

BEATRICE: I am; I must go at once. I shall expect you at Signor Pantalone's; and shall stay there till you come.

FLORINDO: I don't know where he lives.

TRUFFALDINO: I know, sir, I'll show you the way.

BEATRICE: Very well, and now I must go to my room and tidy myself up.

TRUFFALDINO: [*aside to* BEATRICE] Very good, madam; I am at your service directly.

BEATRICE: Dear Florindo! What torments have I not endured for love of you!

[BEATRICE *goes into her room.*]

FLORINDO: Mine have been no less.

TRUFFALDINO: Sir, Pasqual' is not here, and Si'ora Beatrice has no one to help her dress; will you give me leave to wait upon her instead of Pasqual'?

FLORINDO: Yes, by all means. Wait upon her with diligence; I am delighted.

TRUFFALDINO: [*aside*] For invention, for promptness and for intrigue I will challenge the attorney general.

[TRUFFALDINO *goes into* BEATRICE'S *room.*]

FLORINDO: What strange things have happened in the course of this one day! Tears, lamentations, and anguish, and then at last consolation and happiness. From tears to laughter is a happy step, which makes us forget our agonies, but when we pass from pleasure to pain the change is even yet more acutely perceptible.

[*Reenter* BEATRICE *followed by* TRUFFALDINO.]

BEATRICE: Here I am, have I not been quick?

FLORINDO: When will you change these clothes?

BEATRICE: Do I not look well in them?

FLORINDO: I long to see you in a woman's dress. Your beauties ought not to be so completely disguised.

BEATRICE: Well, I shall expect you at Signor Pantalone's; make Truffaldino show you the way.

FLORINDO: I must wait for the banker; if he does not come soon another time will do.

BEATRICE: Show me your love in your anxiety to attend me.

[*about to go*]

TRUFFALDINO: [*aside to* BEATRICE] Do you wish me to stay and wait upon this gentleman?

BEATRICE: Yes, you will show him the way to Signor Pantalone's.

TRUFFALDINO: Yes, madam, certainly, as Pasqual' is not here.

BEATRICE: Wait upon him, I shall be pleased indeed.
> [*aside to herself*]
> I love him more than my very self.
> [*Exit* BEATRICE.]

TRUFFALDINO: The fellow's nowhere to be seen. His master wants to dress, and he goes out on his own and is nowhere to be found.

FLORINDO: Of whom are you speaking?

TRUFFALDINO: Of Pasqual'. I love him, he is a good friend of mine, but he's a lazy dog. Now I am a servant worth two.

FLORINDO: Come and dress my wig. The banker will be here directly.

TRUFFALDINO: Please your honor, I hear your honor has to go to Si'or Pantalon's.

FLORINDO: Yes, what then?

TRUFFALDINO: I want to ask a favor of you.

FLORINDO: Well, you deserve it after all you have done.

TRUFFALDINO: If there has been any trouble, you know, sir, 'tis all the fault of Pasqual'.

FLORINDO: But where on earth is this cursed Pasquale? Can't one see him?

TRUFFALDINO: He'll come, the knave. And so, sir, I want to ask you this favor.

FLORINDO: What do you want?

TRUFFALDINO: You see, sir, I'm in love too.

FLORINDO: In love?

TRUFFALDINO: Yes, sir, and my young woman is maidservant to Si'or Pantalon'; and it would be very kind if your honor—

FLORINDO: How do I come into it?

TRUFFALDINO: I won't say, sir, that you come into it; but I being your servant, you might say a word for me to Si'or Pantalon'.

FLORINDO: We must see first whether the girl wants you.

TRUFFALDINO: The girl wants me, no mistake. All I want is a word to Si'or Pantalon'; I beg you, sir, of your charity.

FLORINDO: Certainly, I will speak for you, but how can you keep a wife?

TRUFFALDINO: I shall do what I can. I shall ask for help from Pasqual'.

FLORINDO: You had better ask help from someone with more sense.
> [FLORINDO *goes into his room.*]

TRUFFALDINO: Well, if I don't show sense this time, I shall never show it again.
> [TRUFFALDINO *follows* FLORINDO *into his room.*]

SCENE IV————*A Room in the House of* PANTALONE.

PANTALONE: Come, Clarice, pull yourself together. You see that Signor Silvio has repented and asks your foregiveness. If he acted foolishly, it was all for love of you; I have forgiven him his extravagances, you ought to forgive him too.

SILVIO: Measure my agony by your own, Signora Clarice, and rest assured that I most truly love you, since 'twas the fear of losing you that rendered me distracted. Heaven desires our happiness; do not be ungrateful for the blessings of Providence. Do not let the idea of revenge spoil the most beautiful day of your life.

DR. LOMBARDI: I join my prayers to those of my son; Signora Clarice, my dear daughter-in-law, have pity on the poor young man; he nearly went out of his mind.

SMERALDINA: Come, dear madam, what would you? Men are all cruel to us, some more, some less. They demand the most absolute fidelity, and on the least shadow of suspicion they bully us, ill-treat us and are like to murder us. Well, you have got to marry one or another of them some day, so I say to you as one says to sick people—since you have got to take your nasty medicine, take it.

PANTALONE: There, do you hear that? Smeraldina calls matrimony medicine. You must not think it is poison.

[*aside to* DR. LOMBARDI]

We must try to cheer her up.

DR. LOMBARDI: Certainly, 'tis not poison, nor even nasty medicine. Matrimony is a lollipop, a jujube, a lozenge!

SILVIO: But dear Clarice, won't you say a word? I know I deserve to be punished by you, but, of your mercy, punish me with hard words rather than with silence. Behold me at your feet; have pity upon me.

CLARICE: [*to* SILVIO *with a sigh*] Cruel!

PANTALONE: [*aside to* DR. LOMBARDI] You heard that little sigh? A good sign.

DR. LOMBARDI: [*aside to* SILVIO] Strike while the iron is hot.

SMERALDINA: [*aside*] A sigh is like lightning; it promises rainfall.

SILVIO: If I could think that you desired my blood to avenge my supposed cruelty, I give it you with all my heart. But, oh God! instead of the blood of my veins, accept, I beg you, that which gushes from my eyes.

[*weeps*]

PANTALONE: Bravo! Bravo! Well said!

DR. LOMBARDI: Capital! Capital!

CLARICE: [*sighing as before, but more tenderly*] Cruel!

DR. LOMBARDI: [*aside to* PANTALONE] She's done to a turn.

PANTALONE: Here, come up with you.

[*He raises* SILVIO, *takes him by the hand.*]

Stand over there.

[*takes* CLARICE'S *hand*]

And you come here too, madam. Now, join your hands together again; and make peace. So no more tears, be happy, no more nonsense and Heaven bless you both.

DR. LOMBARDI: There; 'tis done.

SMERALDINA: 'Tis done, 'tis done.

SILVIO: [*holding* CLARICE'S *hand*] Oh, Signora Clarice, for pity's sake—

CLARICE: Ungrateful!

SILVIO: Dearest!

CLARICE: Inhuman!

SILVIO: Beloved!

CLARICE: Monster!

SILVIO: Angel!

CLARICE: [*sighs*] Ah!

PANTALONE: [*aside*] Going, going—

SILVIO: Forgive me, for the love of Heaven.

CLARICE: [*sighs*] I forgive you.

PANTALONE: [*aside*] Gone!

DR. LOMBARDI: Come, Silvio, she has forgiven you.

SMERALDINA: The patient is ready; give her her medicine.
    [*Enter* BRIGHELLA.]

BRIGHELLA: By your leave, sir, may I come in?

PANTALONE: Pray come in, good friend Brighella. 'Twas you, was it not, that told me all these pretty stories, who assured me that that party was Signor Federigo—eh?

BRIGHELLA: My dear sir, who would not have been deceived? They were twin brother and sister, as like as two peas. In those clothes I would have wagered my head that it was he.

PANTALONE: Enough. That's all done with. What is the news?

BRIGHELLA: Signora Beatrice is here, and desires to pay her respects.

PANTALONE: Let her come in; she is most welcome.

CLARICE: Poor Signora Beatrice, I am happy to think that her troubles are over.

SILVIO: You are sorry for her?

CLARICE: I am indeed.

SILVIO: And for me?

CLARICE: Oh, cruel!

PANTALONE: [*aside to* DR. LOMBARDI] You hear these loving words?

DR. LOMBARDI: [*aside to* PANTALONE] Ah, my son has a way with him.

PANTALONE: My daughter, poor dear child, has a very good heart.

SMERALDINA: Yes, they will both of them do their duty by each other.
    [*Enter* BEATRICE.]

BEATRICE: Ladies and gentlemen, I come to ask your pardon and forgiveness, that you should on my account have been put to inconvenience—

CLARICE: No, no, my dear; come to me.
    [*embraces her*]

SILVIO: [*annoyed at the embrace*] How now?

BEATRICE: [*to* SILVIO] What! May she not even embrace a woman?

SILVIO: [*aside*] 'Tis those clothes again.

PANTALONE: Well, well, Signora Beatrice, I must say, for a young woman of your age you have a wonderful courage.

DR. LOMBARDI: [*to* BEATRICE] Too much spirit, madam.

BEATRICE: Love makes one do great things.

PANTALONE: And you have found your young gentleman at last? So I hear.

BEATRICE: Yes, Heaven has made us happy.

DR. LOMBARDI: A nice reputation you have made yourself!

BEATRICE: Sir, you have no business in my affairs.

SILVIO: [*to* DR. LOMBARDI] Sir, I beg you, let everyone do as they will; do not be so put out about it. Now that I am happy, I want all the world to be happy too. Is anyone else going to be married? Let them all get married!

SMERALDINA: [*to* SILVIO] What about me, sir?

SILVIO: Whom are you going to marry?

SMERALDINA: The first man that comes along, sir.

SILVIO: Find him then, here am I.

CLARICE: [*to* SILVIO] You? What for?

SILVIO: To give her a wedding present.

CLARICE: That is no affair of yours.

SMERALDINA: [*aside*] She's afraid everybody will eat him. She likes the taste of
him, I see.

[*Enter* TRUFFALDINO.]

TRUFFALDINO: My respects to the company.

BEATRICE: [*to* TRUFFALDINO] Where is Signor Florindo?

TRUFFALDINO: He is here and would like to come in, by your leave.

BEATRICE: Signor Pantalone, will you give Signor Florindo leave?

PANTALONE: Is that your young gentleman?

BEATRICE: He is going to marry me.

PANTALONE: I shall be pleased to meet him.

BEATRICE: [*to* TRUFFALDINO] Show him in.

TRUFFALDINO: [*aside to* SMERALDINA] Young woman, my respects to you.

SMERALDINA: [*aside to* TRUFFALDINO] Pleased to see you, my little darkie.

TRUFFALDINO: We will have to talk.

SMERALDINA: What about?

TRUFFALDINO: [*makes as though giving her a wedding ring*] Are you willing?

SMERALDINA: Why not?

TRUFFALDINO: We'll have a talk.

[*Exit* TRUFFALDINO.]

SMERALDINA: [*to* CLARICE] Madam, with the company's leave, I want a favor of
you.

CLARICE: [*going aside to listen to* SMERALDINA] What is it?

SMERALDINA: [*to* CLARICE] I too am a poor young girl that would like to settle
myself; there's the servant of Signora Beatrice who wants to marry me; now
if you would say a kind word to his mistress, and get her to allow him to
take me to wife, I should be the happiest girl in the world.

CLARICE: Dear Smeraldina, with all the pleasure in life; as soon as I can speak
freely to Beatrice, I will certainly do so.

PANTALONE: [*to* CLARICE] What is all this whispering about?

CLARICE: Nothing, sir. She had something to say to me.

SILVIO: [*to* CLARICE] May I not know?

CLARICE: How inquisitive they all are! And then they talk about us women!

[*Enter* FLORINDO *shown in by* TRUFFALDINO.]

FLORINDO: Your most humble servant, ladies and gentlemen.

[*All bow and curtsy.*]

[*to* PANTALONE]

Are you the master of the house, sir?

PANTALONE: Yours to command, sir.

FLORINDO: Allow me, sir, to have the honor of waiting upon you this evening; I
present myself by command of the Signora Beatrice, whose adventures will
be known to you, and mine too.

PANTALONE: I am happy to know you, sir, and to see you here; I congratulate you most heartily on your good fortune.

FLORINDO: Signora Beatrice is to be my wife, and if you will not disdain to do us the honor, I hope you will give away the bride.

PANTALONE: Whatever has to be done, let it be done at once. Give her your hand.

FLORINDO: Signora Beatrice, I am willing.

BEATRICE: Here is my hand, Signor Florindo.

SMERALDINA: [*aside*] *They* don't want pressing.

PANTALONE: Afterward we will settle up our accounts. You will put yours in order; then we will settle ours.

CLARICE: [*to* BEATRICE] Dear friend, I congratulate you.

BEATRICE: [*to* CLARICE] And I you, with all my heart.

SILVIO: [*to* FLORINDO] Sir, do you know me again?

FLORINDO: [*to* SILVIO] Indeed I do, sir; you would have provoked me to a duel.

SILVIO: 'Twas to my own disaster. Here is the adversary
          [*Pointing to* BEATRICE.]
      who disarmed me and very nearly killed me.

BEATRICE: And gave you your life too, you might say.

SILVIO: 'Tis true.

CLARICE: At my entreaty.

SILVIO: That is very true.

PANTALONE: Everything is in order; everything is settled.

TRUFFALDINO: The best is yet to come, ladies and gentlemen.

PANTALONE: What is yet to come?

TRUFFALDINO: [*to* FLORINDO, *taking him apart*] With your good leave, sir, one word.

FLORINDO: What do you want?

TRUFFALDINO: You remember what you promised me, sir?

FLORINDO: What did I promise? I do not recollect.

TRUFFALDINO: To ask Si'or Pantalon' for Smeraldina as my wife.

FLORINDO: Of course, now I remember; I will do so at once.

TRUFFALDINO: [*aside*] I, too, poor man, want to put myself right with the world.

FLORINDO: Signor Pantalone, although this is the first occasion on which I have had the honor of knowing you, I make bold to desire a favor of you.

PANTALONE: You may command me, sir; I will serve you the best of my powers.

FLORINDO: My manservant desires to marry your maid; have you any objection to giving your consent?

SMERALDINA: [*aside*] Wonderful! Here's another who wants to marry me! Who the devil can he be? I wish I knew him.

PANTALONE: For my part I am agreed.
          [*to* SMERALDINA]
      What say you, girl?

SMERALDINA: If I thought he would make a good husband—

PANTALONE: Is he a good honest man, this servant of yours?

FLORINDO: For the short time he has been with me he has certainly proved himself trusty, and he seems to be intelligent.

CLARICE: Signor Florindo, you have anticipated me in something that *I* ought to have done. I was to propose the marriage of my maid with the manservant of Signora Beatrice. You have asked for her for *your* servant, I can say no more.

FLORINDO: No, no; since you so earnestly desire this, I withdraw altogether and leave you completely free.

CLARICE: Indeed, sir, I could never permit myself to have my own wishes preferred to yours. Besides, I must admit that I am not fully authorized. Pray continue in your proposal.

FLORINDO: You say so out of courtesy, madam. Signor Pantalone, I withdraw all that I have said. I will not say another word on behalf of my servant; on the contrary, I am absolutely opposed to his marrying her.

CLARICE: If *your* man is not to marry her, no more shall the other man. We must be fair on both sides.

TRUFFALDINO: [*aside*] Here's a state of things! They pay each other compliments, and meanwhile I am left without a wife at all.

SMERALDINA: [*aside*] It looks as if I should have neither one nor the other.

PANTALONE: Come, we *must* settle it somehow; this poor girl wants to get married, let us give her either to the one or the other.

FLORINDO: Not to *my* man. Nothing shall induce me to do Signora Clarice an injustice.

CLARICE: Nor will I ever tolerate an injustice to Signor Florindo.

TRUFFALDINO: Sir, madam, I can settle the matter myself.
    [*with his usual air of great ingenuity*]
Si'or Florindo, did you not ask the hand of Smeraldina for your servant?

FLORINDO: I did; did you not hear me?

TRUFFALDINO: And you, Si'ora Clarice, did you not intend Smeraldina to marry the servant of Si'ora Beatrice?

CLARICE: Most certainly I was to do so.

TRUFFALDINO: Good; then if that is so, give me your hand, Smeraldina.

PANTALONE: And pray what right have *you* to ask for her hand?

TRUFFALDINO: Because I am the servant of Si'or Florindo and of Si'ora Beatrice too.

FLORINDO: What?

BEATRICE: What do you say?

TRUFFALDINO: Pray be calm. Si'or Florindo, who asked you to ask Si'or Pantalon' for Smeraldina?

FLORINDO: You did.

TRUFFALDINO: And you, Si'ora Clarice, whom had you in mind as the intended husband of Smeraldina?

CLARICE: Yourself.

TRUFFALDINO: *Ergo*, Smeraldina is mine.

FLORINDO: Signora Beatrice, where is your servant?

BEATRICE: Why, here! Truffaldino, of course.

FLORINDO: Truffaldino? He is *my* servant!

BEATRICE: Is not yours called Pasquale?

FLORINDO: Pasquale? I thought Pasquale was *yours!*

BEATRICE: [*to* TRUFFALDINO] How do you explain this?
    [TRUFFALDINO *makes silent gestures asking for forgiveness.*]

FLORINDO: You rascal!

BEATRICE: You knave!

FLORINDO: So you waited on two masters at once?

TRUFFALDINO: Yes, sir, I did; that was the very trick. I took on the job without
thinking; just to see what I could do. It did not last long, 'tis true; but at any
rate I can boast that nobody would ever have found me out, if I had not
given myself away for love of this girl here. I have done a hard day's work,
and I dare say I had my shortcomings, but I hope that in consideration of
the fun of the thing, all these ladies and gentlemen will forgive me.

Molière (Jean-Baptiste Poquelin, 1622–1673)

Tartuffe (1664, 1667, 1669)

While English drama of Shakespeare's time owed much to medieval conventions, French dramatists after the 1630s looked back to Greece and Rome for their standards. This conscious imitation of the classics gave rise to a set of literary standards summed up in the term *neoclassicism*. These included the unities of time, place, and action; strict distinction between tragedy and comedy, with no intermingling of the two; the use of universalized character types; and the demand that drama teach moral lessons. Many of the plays written in compliance with these demands now seem lifeless, but the tragedies of Racine and the comedies of Molière, written in France during the last half of the seventeenth century, reached a peak of artistry in the neoclassical mode. Unlike plays of earlier eras, these were written for the proscenium-arch stage and for perspective settings composed of wings, drops, and borders.

Molière is one of the most skillful and inventive comic dramatists of all times, and *Tartuffe* is one of his most admired plays. Within the restricted frame of one room, one day, and one main story, using a limited number of characters and little physical action, Molière creates an excellent comedy of character. The action of *Tartuffe*, divided into five acts, develops through five stages: the demonstration of Tartuffe's complete hold over Orgon; the unmasking of Tartuffe; Tartuffe's attempted revenge; the foiling of Tartuffe's plan; and the happy resolution. Molière has been criticized for delaying Tartuffe's first appearance until the third act, but he makes skillful use of this delay by having all the other characters establish his hypocrisy and Orgon's gullibility in trusting Tartuffe. The resolution, in which Tartuffe is suddenly discovered to be a notorious criminal, has also been criticized as overly contrived, but it is emotionally satisfying because it punishes Tartuffe and reestablishes the norm.

In *Tartuffe* Molière uses the verse form that by that time had become standard in French tragedy—the alexandrine (twelve-syllable lines, with each pair of adjacent lines rhyming). Richard Wilbur's translation, used here, is generally considered one of the finest now available both for its accuracy and for its rendition of Molière's verse.

When *Tartuffe* was written in 1664, it was immediately denounced as an attack on religious piety. The controversy was so intense that Louis XIV forbade the play's production. Molière rewrote it in 1667, only to have it banned once more. Finally, in 1669 he was able to gain permission for its production. It has remained in the repertory continuously since that time. It is still performed more often than any other play by Molière.

Molière

Tartuffe

Translated into English Verse by Richard Wilbur

CHARACTERS

MME. PERNELLE, *Orgon's mother*
ORGON, *Elmire's husband*
ELMIRE, *Orgon's wife*
DAMIS, *Orgon's son, Elmire's stepson*
MARIANE, *Orgon's daughter, Elmire's stepdaughter, in love with Valère*
VALÈRE, *in love with Mariane*
CLÉANTE, *Orgon's brother-in-law*
TARTUFFE, *a hypocrite*
DORINE, *Mariane's lady's-maid*
M. LOYAL, *a bailiff*
A POLICE OFFICER
FLIPOTE, *Mme. Pernelle's maid*

The scene throughout: ORGON'S *house in Paris*

ACT I

SCENE I

MADAME PERNELLE: Come, come, Flipote; it's time I left this place.
ELMIRE: I can't keep up, you walk at such a pace.
MADAME PERNELLE: Don't trouble, child; no need to show me out.
    It's not your manners I'm concerned about.
ELMIRE: We merely pay you the respect we owe.
    But, Mother, why this hurry? Must you go?
MADAME PERNELLE: I must. This house appals me. No one in it
    Will pay attention for a single minute.
    Children, I take my leave much vexed in spirit.
    I offer good advice, but you won't hear it.
    You all break in and chatter on and on.
    It's like a madhouse with the keeper gone.
DORINE: If . . .
MADAME PERNELLE: Girl, you talk too much, and I'm afraid
    You're far too saucy for a lady's-maid.
    You push in everywhere and have your say.
DAMIS: But . . .

MADAME PERNELLE: You, boy, grow more foolish every day.
    To think my grandson should be such a dunce!
    I've said a hundred times, if I've said it once,
    That if you keep the course on which you've started,
    You'll leave your worthy father broken-hearted.
MARIANE: I think . . .
MADAME PERNELLE: And you, his sister, seem so pure,
    So shy, so innocent, and so demure.
    But you know what they say about still waters.
    I pity parents with secretive daughters.
ELMIRE: Now, Mother . . .
MADAME PERNELLE: And as for you, child, let me add
    That your behavior is extremely bad,
    And a poor example for these children, too.
    Their dear, dead mother did far better than you.
    You're much too free with money, and I'm distressed
    To see you so elaborately dressed.
    When it's one's husband that one aims to please,
    One has no need of costly fripperies.
CLÉANTE: Oh, Madam, really . . .
MADAME PERNELLE: You are her brother, Sir,
    And I respect and love you; yet if I were
    My son, this lady's good and pious spouse,
    I wouldn't make you welcome in my house.
    You're full of worldly counsels which, I fear,
    Aren't suitable for decent folk to hear.
    I've spoken bluntly, Sir; but it behooves us
    Not to mince words when righteous fervor moves us.
DAMIS: Your man Tartuffe is full of holy speeches . . .
MADAME PERNELLE: And practices precisely what he preaches.
    He's a fine man, and should be listened to.
    I will not hear him mocked by fools like you.
DAMIS: Good God! Do you expect me to submit
    To the tyranny of that carping hypocrite?
    Must we forgo all joys and satisfactions
    Because that bigot censures all our actions?
DORINE: To hear him talk—and he talks all the time—
    There's nothing one can do that's not a crime.
    He rails at everything, your dear Tartuffe.
MADAME PERNELLE: Whatever he reproves deserves reproof.
    He's out to save your souls, and all of you
    Must love him, as my son would have you do.
DAMIS: Ah no, Grandmother, I could never take
    To such a rascal, even for my father's sake.
    That's how I feel, and I shall not dissemble.
    His every action makes me seethe and tremble
    With helpless anger, and I have no doubt
    That he and I will shortly have it out.

DORINE: Surely it is a shame and a disgrace
    To see this man usurp the master's place—
    To see this beggar who, when first he came,
    Had not a shoe or shoestring to his name
    So far forget himself that he behaves
    As if the house were his, and we his slaves.
MADAME PERNELLE: Well, mark my words, your souls would fare far better
    If you obeyed his precepts to the letter.
DORINE: You see him as a saint. I'm far less awed;
    In fact, I see right through him. He's a fraud.
MADAME PERNELLE: Nonsense!
DORINE: His man Laurent's the same, or worse;
    I'd not trust either with a penny purse.
MADAME PERNELLE: I can't say what his servant's morals may be;
    His own great goodness I can guarantee.
    You all regard him with distaste and fear
    Because he tells you what you're loath to hear,
    Condemns your sins, points out your moral flaws,
    And humbly strives to further Heaven's cause.
DORINE: If sin is all that bothers him, why is it
    He's so upset when folk drop in to visit?
    Is Heaven so outraged by a social call
    That he must prophesy against us all?
    I'll tell you what I think: if you ask me,
    He's jealous of my mistress' company.
MADAME PERNELLE: Rubbish! [*to* ELMIRE] He's not alone, child, in complaining
    Of all of your promiscuous entertaining.
    Why, the whole neighborhood's upset, I know,
    By all these carriages that come and go,
    With crowds of guests parading in and out
    And noisy servants loitering about.
    In all of this, I'm sure there's nothing vicious;
    But why give people cause to be suspicious?
CLÉANTE: They need no cause, they'll talk in any case.
    Madam, this world would be a joyless place
    If, fearing what malicious tongues might say,
    We locked our doors and turned our friends away.
    And even if one did so dreary a thing,
    D'you think those tongues would cease their chattering?
    One can't fight slander; it's a losing battle;
    Let us instead ignore their tittle-tattle.
    Let's strive to live by conscience's clear decrees,
    And let the gossips gossip as they please.
DORINE: If there is talk against us, I know the source:
    It's Daphne and her little husband, of course.
    Those who have greatest cause for guilt and shame
    Are quickest to besmirch a neighbor's name.
    When there's a chance for libel, they never miss it;

When something can be made to seem illicit
They're off at once to spread the joyous news,
Adding to fact what fantasies they choose.
By talking up their neighbor's indiscretions
They seek to camouflage their own transgressions,
Hoping that others' innocent affairs
Will lend a hue of innocence to theirs,
Or that their own black guilt will come to seem
Part of a general shady color-scheme.

MADAME PERNELLE: All that is quite irrelevant. I doubt
That anyone's more virtuous and devout
Than dear Orante; and I'm informed that she
Condemns your mode of life most vehemently.

DORINE: Oh, yes, she's strict, devout, and has no taint
Of worldliness; in short, she seems a saint.
But it was time which taught her that disguise;
She's thus because she can't be otherwise.
So long as her attractions could enthrall,
She flounced and flirted and enjoyed it all,
But now that they're no longer what they were
She quits a world which fast is quitting her,
And wears a veil of virtue to conceal
Her bankrupt beauty and her lost appeal.
That's what becomes of old coquettes today:
Distressed when all their lovers fall away,
They see no recourse but to play the prude,
And so confer a style on solitude.
Thereafter, they're severe with everyone,
Condemning all our actions, pardoning none,
And claiming to be pure, austere, and zealous
When, if the truth were known, they're merely jealous,
And cannot bear to see another know
The pleasures time has forced them to forgo.

MADAME PERNELLE: [*initially* to ELMIRE] That sort of talk is what you like to
      hear;
Therefore you'd have us all keep still, my dear,
While Madam rattles on the livelong day.
Nevertheless, I mean to have my say.
I tell you that you're blest to have Tartuffe
Dwelling, as my son's guest, beneath this roof;
That Heaven has sent him to forestall its wrath
By leading you, once more, to the true path;
That all he reprehends is reprehensible,
And that you'd better heed him, and be sensible.
These visits, balls, and parties in which you revel
Are nothing but inventions of the Devil.
One never hears a word that's edifying:
Nothing but chaff and foolishness and lying,

As well as vicious gossip in which one's neighbor
Is cut to bits with épée, foil, and saber.
People of sense are driven half-insane
At such affairs, where noise and folly reign
And reputations perish thick and fast.
As a wise preacher said on Sunday last,
Parties are Towers of Babylon, because
The guests all babble on with never a pause;
And then he told a story which, I think . . .
[*to* CLÉANTE] I heard that laugh, Sir, and I saw that wink!
Go find your silly friends and laugh some more!
Enough; I'm going; don't show me to the door.
I leave this household much dismayed and vexed;
I cannot say when I shall see you next.
[*slapping* FLIPOTE] Wake up, don't stand there gaping into space!
I'll slap some sense into that stupid face.
Move, move, you slut.

SCENE II

CLÉANTE: I think I'll stay behind;
    I want no further pieces of her mind.
    How that old lady . . .
DORINE: Oh, what wouldn't she say
    If she could hear you speak of her that way!
    She'd thank you for the *lady*, but I'm sure
    She'd find the *old* a little premature.
CLÉANTE: My, what a scene she made, and what a din!
    And how this man Tartuffe has taken her in!
DORINE: Yes, but her son is even worse deceived;
    His folly must be seen to be believed.
    In the late troubles, he played an able part
    And served his king with wise and loyal heart,
    But he's quite lost his senses since he fell
    Beneath Tartuffe's infatuating spell.
    He calls him brother, and loves him as his life,
    Preferring him to mother, child, or wife.
    In him and him alone will he confide;
    He's made him his confessor and his guide;
    He pets and pampers him with love more tender
    Than any pretty mistress could engender,
    Gives him the place of honor when they dine,
    Delights to see him gorging like a swine,
    Stuffs him with dainties till his guts distend,
    And when he belches, cries "God bless you, friend!"
    In short, he's mad; he worships him; he dotes;
    His deeds he marvels at, his words he quotes;
    Thinking each act a miracle, each word

Oracular as those that Moses heard.
Tartuffe, much pleased to find so easy a victim,
Has in a hundred ways beguiled and tricked him,
Milked him of money, and with his permission
Established here a sort of Inquisition.
Even Laurent, his lackey, dares to give
Us arrogant advice on how to live;
He sermonizes us in thundering tones
And confiscates our ribbons and colognes.
Last week he tore a kerchief into pieces
Because he found it pressed in a *Life of Jesus:*
He said it was a sin to juxtapose
Unholy vanities and holy prose.

SCENE III

ELMIRE: [*to* CLÉANTE] You did well not to follow; she stood in the door
And said *verbatim* all she'd said before.
I saw my husband coming. I think I'd best
Go upstairs now, and take a little rest.
CLÉANTE: I'll wait and greet him here; then I must go.
I've really only time to say hello.
DAMIS: Sound him about my sister's wedding, please.
I think Tartuffe's against it, and that he's
Been urging Father to withdraw his blessing.
As you well know, I'd find that most distressing.
Unless my sister and Valère can marry,
My hopes to wed *his* sister will miscarry,
And I'm determined . . .
DORINE: He's coming.

SCENE IV

ORGON: Ah, Brother, good-day.
CLÉANTE: Well, welcome back. I'm sorry I can't stay.
How was the country? Blooming, I trust, and green?
ORGON: Excuse me, Brother; just one moment.
[*to* DORINE] Dorine . . .
[*to* CLÉANTE] To put my mind at rest, I always learn
The household news the moment I return.
[*to* DORINE] Has all been well, these two days I've been gone?
How are the family? What's been going on?
DORINE: Your wife, two days ago, had a bad fever,
And a fierce headache which refused to leave her.
ORGON: Ah. And Tartuffe?
DORINE: Tartuffe? Why, he's round and red,
Bursting with health, and excellently fed.
ORGON: Poor fellow!

DORINE: That night, the mistress was unable
　　　　To take a single bite at the dinner-table.
　　　　Her headache-pains, she said, were simply hellish.
ORGON: Ah. And Tartuffe?
DORINE: He ate his meal with relish,
　　　　And zealously devoured in her presence
　　　　A leg of mutton and a brace of pheasants.
ORGON: Poor fellow!
DORINE: Well, the pains continued strong,
　　　　And so she tossed and tossed the whole night long,
　　　　Now icy-cold, now burning like a flame.
　　　　We sat beside her bed till morning came.
ORGON: Ah. And Tartuffe?
DORINE: Why, having eaten, he rose
　　　　And sought his room, already in a doze,
　　　　Got into his warm bed, and snored away
　　　　In perfect peace until the break of day.
ORGON: Poor fellow!
DORINE: After much ado, we talked her
　　　　Into dispatching someone for the doctor.
　　　　He bled her, and the fever quickly fell.
ORGON: Ah. And Tartuffe?
DORINE: He bore it very well.
　　　　To keep his cheerfulness at any cost,
　　　　And make up for the blood *Madame* had lost,
　　　　He drank, at lunch, four beakers full of port.
ORGON: Poor fellow!
DORINE: Both are doing well, in short.
　　　　I'll go and tell *Madame* that you've expressed
　　　　Keen sympathy and anxious interest.

SCENE V

CLÉANTE: That girl was laughing in your face, and though
　　　　I've no wish to offend you, even so
　　　　I'm bound to say that she had some excuse.
　　　　How can you possibly be such a goose?
　　　　Are you so dazed by this man's hocus-pocus
　　　　That all the world, save him, is out of focus?
　　　　You've given him clothing, shelter, food, and care;
　　　　Why must you also . . .
ORGON: Brother, stop right there.
　　　　You do not know the man of whom you speak.
CLÉANTE: I grant you that. But my judgment's not so weak
　　　　That I can't tell, by his effect on others . . .
ORGON: Ah, when you meet him, you two will be like brothers!
　　　　There's been no loftier soul since time began.
　　　　He is a man who . . . a man who . . . an excellent man.

To keep his precepts is to be reborn,
And view this dunghill of a world with scorn.
Yes, thanks to him I'm a changed man indeed.
Under his tutelage my soul's been freed
From earthly loves, and every human tie:
My mother, children, brother, and wife could die,
And I'd not feel a single moment's pain.
CLÉANTE: That's a fine sentiment, Brother; most humane.
ORGON: Oh, had you seen Tartuffe as I first knew him,
Your heart, like mine, would have surrendered to him.
He used to come into our church each day
And humbly kneel nearby, and start to pray.
He'd draw the eyes of everybody there
By the deep fervor of his heartfelt prayer;
He'd sigh and weep, and sometimes with a sound
Of rapture he would bend and kiss the ground;
And when I rose to go, he'd run before
To offer me holy-water at the door.
His serving-man, no less devout than he,
Informed me of his master's poverty;
I gave him gifts, but in his humbleness
He'd beg me every time to give him less.
"Oh, that's too much," he'd cry, "too much by twice!
I don't deserve it. The half, Sir, would suffice."
And when I wouldn't take it back, he'd share
Half of it with the poor, right then and there.
At length, Heaven prompted me to take him in
To dwell with us, and free our souls from sin.
He guides our lives, and to protect my honor
Stays by my wife, and keeps an eye upon her;
He tells me whom she sees, and all she does,
And seems more jealous than I ever was!
And how austere he is! Why, he can detect
A mortal sin where you would least suspect;
In smallest trifles, he's extremely strict.
Last week, his conscience was severely pricked
Because, while praying, he had caught a flea
And killed it, so he felt, too wrathfully.
CLÉANTE: Good God, man! Have you lost your common sense—
Or is this all some joke at my expense?
How can you stand there and in all sobriety . . .
ORGON: Brother, your language savors of impiety.
Too much free-thinking's made your faith unsteady,
And as I've warned you many times already,
'Twill get you into trouble before you're through.
CLÉANTE: So I've been told before by dupes like you:
Being blind, you'd have all others blind as well;
The clear-eyed man you call an infidel,

And he who sees through humbug and pretense
Is charged, by you, with want of reverence.
Spare me your warnings, Brother; I have no fear
Of speaking out, for you and Heaven to hear,
Against affected zeal and pious knavery.
There's true and false in piety, as in bravery,
And just as those whose courage shines the most
In battle, are the least inclined to boast,
So those whose hearts are truly pure and lowly
Don't make a flashy show of being holy.
There's a vast difference, so it seems to me,
Between true piety and hypocrisy:
How do you fail to see it, may I ask?
Is not a face quite different from a mask?
Cannot sincerity and cunning art,
Reality and semblance, be told apart?
Are scarecrows just like men, and do you hold
That a false coin is just as good as gold?
Ah, Brother, man's a strangely fashioned creature
Who seldom is content to follow Nature,
But recklessly pursues his inclination
Beyond the narrow bounds of moderation,
And often, by transgressing Reason's laws,
Perverts a lofty aim or noble cause.
A passing observation, but it applies.

ORGON: I see, dear Brother, that you're profoundly wise;
You harbor all the insight of the age.
You are our one clear mind, our only sage,
The era's oracle, its Cato, too,
And all mankind are fools compared to you.

CLÉANTE: Brother, I don't pretend to be a sage,
Nor have I all the wisdom of the age.
There's just one insight I would dare to claim:
I know that true and false are not the same;
And just as there is nothing I more revere
Than a soul whose faith is steadfast and sincere,
Nothing that I more cherish and admire
Than honest zeal and true religious fire,
So there is nothing that I find more base
Than specious piety's dishonest face—
Than these bold mountebanks, these histrios
Whose impious mummeries and hollow shows
Exploit our love of Heaven, and make a jest
Of all that men think holiest and best;
These calculating souls who offer prayers
Not to their Maker, but as public wares,
And seek to buy respect and reputation
With lifted eyes and sighs of exaltation;

These charlatans, I say, whose pilgrim souls
Proceed, by way of Heaven, toward earthly goals,
Who weep and pray and swindle and extort,
Who preach the monkish life, but haunt the court,
Who make their zeal the partner of their vice—
Such men are vengeful, sly, and cold as ice,
And when there is an enemy to defame
They cloak their spite in fair religion's name,
Their private spleen and malice being made
To seem a high and virtuous crusade,
Until, to mankind's reverent applause,
They crucify their foe in Heaven's cause.
Such knaves are all too common; yet, for the wise,
True piety isn't hard to recognize,
And happily, these present times provide us
With bright examples to instruct and guide us.
Consider Ariston and Périandre;
Look at Oronte, Alcidamas, Clitandre;
Their virtue is acknowledged; who could doubt it?
But you won't hear them beat the drum about it.
They're never ostentatious, never vain,
And their religion's moderate and humane;
It's not their way to criticize and chide:
They think censoriousness a mark of pride,
And therefore, letting others preach and rave,
They show, by deeds, how Christians should behave.
They think no evil of their fellow man,
But judge of him kindly as they can.
They don't intrigue and wangle and conspire;
To lead a good life is their one desire;
The sinner wakes no rancorous hate in them;
It is the sin alone which they condemn;
Nor do they try to show a fiercer zeal
For Heaven's cause than Heaven itself could feel.
These men I honor, these men I advocate
As models for us all to emulate.
Your man is not their sort at all, I fear:
And, while your praise of him is quite sincere,
I think that you've been dreadfully deluded.
ORGON: Now then, dear Brother, is your speech concluded?
CLÉANTE: Why, yes.
ORGON: Your servant, Sir. [*He turns to go.*]
CLÉANTE: No, Brother; wait.
    There's one more matter. You agreed of late
    That young Valère might have your daughter's hand.
ORGON: I did.
CLÉANTE: And set the date, I understand.
ORGON: Quite so.

CLÉANTE: You've now postponed it; is that true?
ORGON: No doubt.
CLÉANTE: The match no longer pleases you?
ORGON: Who knows?
CLÉANTE: D'you mean to go back on your word?
ORGON: I won't say that.
CLÉANTE: Has anything occurred
       Which might entitle you to break your pledge?
ORGON: Perhaps.
CLÉANTE: Why must you hem and haw, and hedge?
       The boy asked me to sound you in this affair . . .
ORGON: It's been a pleasure.
CLÉANTE: But what shall I tell Valère?
ORGON: Whatever you like.
CLÉANTE: But what have you decided?
       What are your plans?
ORGON: I plan, Sir, to be guided
       By Heaven's will.
CLÉANTE: Come, Brother, don't talk rot.
       You've given Valère your word; will you keep it, or not?
ORGON: Good day.
CLÉANTE: This looks like poor Valère's undoing;
       I'll go and warn him that there's trouble brewing.

ACT II

SCENE I

ORGON: Mariane.
MARIANE: Yes, Father?
ORGON: A word with you; come here.
MARIANE: What are you looking for?
ORGON: [*peering into a small closet*] Eavesdroppers, dear.
       I'm making sure we shan't be overheard.
       Someone in there could catch our every word.
       Ah, good, we're safe. Now, Mariane, my child,
       You're a sweet girl who's tractable and mild,
       Whom I hold dear, and think most highly of.
MARIANE: I'm deeply grateful, Father, for your love.
ORGON: That's well said, Daughter; and you can repay me
       If, in all things, you'll cheerfully obey me.
MARIANE: To please you, Sir, is what delights me best.
ORGON: Good, good. Now, what d'you think of Tartuffe, our guest?
MARIANE: I, Sir?
ORGON: Yes. Weigh your answer; think it through.
MARIANE: Oh, dear. I'll say whatever you wish me to.
ORGON: That's wisely said, my Daughter. Say of him, then,

That he's the very worthiest of men,
And that you're fond of him, and would rejoice
In being his wife, if that should be my choice.
Well?
MARIANE: What?
ORGON: What's that?
MARIANE: I . . .
ORGON: Well?
MARIANE: Forgive me, pray.
ORGON: Did you not hear me?
MARIANE: Of *whom*, Sir, must I say
    That I am fond of him, and would rejoice
    In being his wife, if that should be your choice?
ORGON: Why, of Tartuffe.
MARIANE: But, Father, that's false, you know.
    Why would you have me say what isn't so?
ORGON: Because I am resolved it shall be true.
    That it's my wish should be enough for you.
MARIANE: You can't mean, Father . . .
ORGON: Yes, Tartuffe shall be
    Allied by marriage to this family,
    And he's to be your husband, is that clear?
    It's a father's privilege . . .

SCENE II

ORGON: [*to* DORINE] What are you doing in here?
    Is curiosity so fierce a passion
    With you, that you must eavesdrop in this fashion?
DORINE: There's lately been a rumor going about—
    Based on some hunch or chance remark, no doubt—
    That you mean Mariane to wed Tartuffe.
    I've laughed it off, of course, as just a spoof.
ORGON: You find it so incredible?
DORINE: Yes, I do.
    I won't accept that story, even from you.
ORGON: Well, you'll believe it when the thing is done.
DORINE: Yes, yes, of course. Go on and have your fun.
ORGON: I've never been more serious in my life.
DORINE: Ha!
ORGON: Daughter, I mean it; you're to be his wife.
DORINE: No, don't believe your father; it's all a hoax.
ORGON: See here, young woman . . .
DORINE: Come, Sir, no more jokes;
    You can't fool us.
ORGON: How dare you talk that way?
DORINE: All right, then: we believe you, sad to say.

But how a man like you, who looks so wise
And wears a moustache of such splendid size,
Can be so foolish as to . . .

ORGON: Silence, please!
My girl, you take too many liberties.
I'm master here, as you must not forget.

DORINE: Do let's discuss this calmly; don't be upset.
You can't be serious, Sir, about this plan.
What should that bigot want with Mariane?
Praying and fasting ought to keep him busy.
And then, in terms of wealth and rank, what is he?
Why should a man of property like you
Pick out a beggar son-in-law?

ORGON: That will do.
Speak of his poverty with reverence.
His is pure and saintly indigence
Which far transcends all worldly pride and pelf.
He lost his fortune, as he says himself,
Because he cared for Heaven alone, and so
Was careless of his interests here below.
I mean to get him out of his present straits
And help him to recover his estates—
Which, in his part of the world, have no small fame.
Poor though he is, he's a gentleman just the same.

DORINE: Yes, so he tells us; and, Sir, it seems to me
Such pride goes very ill with piety.
A man whose spirit spurns this dungy earth
Ought not to brag of lands and noble birth;
Such worldly arrogance will hardly square
With meek devotion and the life of prayer.
. . . But this approach, I see, has drawn a blank;
Let's speak, then, of his person, not his rank.
Doesn't it seem to you a trifle grim
To give a girl like her to a man like him?
When two are so ill-suited, can't you see
What the sad consequence is bound to be?
A young girl's virtue is imperilled, Sir,
When such a marriage is imposed on her;
For if one's bridegroom isn't to one's taste,
It's hardly an inducement to be chaste,
And many a man with horns upon his brow
Has made his wife the thing that she is now.
It's hard to be a faithful wife, in short,
To certain husbands of a certain sort,
And he who gives his daughter to a man she hates
Must answer for her sins at Heaven's gates.
Think, Sir, before you play so risky a role.

ORGON: This servant-girl presumes to save my soul!

DORINE: You would do well to ponder what I've said.
ORGON: Daughter, we'll disregard this dunderhead.
   Just trust your father's judgment. Oh, I'm aware
   That I once promised you to young Valère;
   But now I hear he gambles, which greatly shocks me;
   What's more, I've doubts about his orthodoxy.
   His visits to church, I note, are very few.
DORINE: Would you have him go at the same hours as you,
   And kneel nearby, to be sure of being seen?
ORGON: I can dispense with such remarks, Dorine.
      [*to* MARIANE]
   Tartuffe, however, is sure of Heaven's blessing,
   And that's the only treasure worth possessing.
   This match will bring you joys beyond all measure;
   Your cup will overflow with every pleasure;
   You two will interchange your faithful loves
   Like two sweet cherubs, or two turtle-doves.
   No harsh word shall be heard, no frown be seen,
   And he shall make you happy as a queen.
DORINE: And she'll make him a cuckold, just wait and see.
ORGON: What language!
DORINE: Oh, he's a man of destiny;
   He's *made* for horns, and what the stars demand
   Your daughter's virtue surely can't withstand.
ORGON: Don't interrupt me further. Why can't you learn
   That certain things are none of your concern?
DORINE: It's for your own sake that I interfere.
      [*She repeatedly interrupts* ORGON *just as he is turning to speak to his
      daughter.*]
ORGON: Most kind of you. Now, hold your tongue, d'you hear?
DORINE: If I didn't love you . . .
ORGON: Spare me your affection.
DORINE: I'll love you, Sir, in spite of your objection.
ORGON: Blast!
DORINE: I can't bear, Sir, for your honor's sake,
   To let you make this ludicrous mistake.
ORGON: You mean to go on talking?
DORINE: If I didn't protest
   This sinful marriage, my conscience couldn't rest.
ORGON: If you don't hold your tongue, you little shrew . . .
DORINE: What, lost your temper? A pious man like you?
ORGON: Yes! Yes! You talk and talk. I'm maddened by it.
   Once and for all, I tell you to be quiet.
DORINE: Well, I'll be quiet. But I'll be thinking hard.
ORGON: Think all you like, but you had better guard
   That saucy tongue of yours, or I'll . . . [*turning back to* MARIANE] Now,
      child,
   I've weighed this matter fully.

DORINE: [*aside*] It drives me wild
    That I can't speak.
        [ORGON *turns his head, and she is silent.*]
ORGON: Tartuffe is no young dandy,
    But, still, his person . . .
DORINE: [*aside*] Is as sweet as candy.
ORGON: Is such that, even if you shouldn't care
    For his other merits . . .
        [*He turns and stands facing* DORINE, *arms crossed.*]
DORINE: [*aside*] They'll make a lovely pair.
    If I were she, no man would marry me
    Against my inclination, and go scot-free.
    He'd learn, before the wedding-day was over,
    How readily a wife can find a lover.
ORGON: [*to* DORINE] It seems you treat my orders as a joke.
DORINE: Why, what's the matter? 'Twas not to you I spoke.
ORGON: What *were* you doing?
DORINE: Talking to myself, that's all.
ORGON: Ah! [*aside*] One more bit of impudence and gall,
    And I shall give her a good slap in the face.
        [*He puts himself in position to slap her;* DORINE, *whenever he glances at*
        her, stands immobile and silent.]
    Daughter, you shall accept, and with good grace,
    The husband I've selected . . . Your wedding-day . . .
    [*to* DORINE] Why don't you talk to yourself?
DORINE: I've nothing to say.
ORGON: Come, just one word.
DORINE: No thank you, Sir. I pass.
ORGON: Come, speak; I'm waiting.
DORINE: I'd not be such an ass.
ORGON: [*turning to* MARIANE] In short, dear Daughter, I mean to be obeyed,
    And you must bow to the sound choice I've made.
DORINE: [*moving away*] I'd not wed such a monster, even in jest.
        [ORGON *attempts to slap her, but misses.*]
ORGON: Daughter, that maid of yours is a thorough pest;
    She makes me sinfully annoyed and nettled.
    I can't speak further; my nerves are too unsettled.
    She's so upset me by her insolent talk,
    I'll calm myself by going for a walk.

SCENE III

DORINE: [*returning*] Well, have you lost your tongue, girl? Must I play
    Your part, and say the lines you ought to say?
    Faced with a fate so hideous and absurd,
    Can you not utter one dissenting word?
MARIANE: What good would it do? A father's power is great.

DORINE: Resist him now, or it will be too late.

MARIANE: But . . .

DORINE: Tell him one cannot love at a father's whim;
That you shall marry for yourself, not him;
That since it's you who are to be the bride,
It's you, not he, who must be satisfied;
And that if his Tartuffe is so sublime,
He's free to marry him at any time.

MARIANE: I've bowed so long to Father's strict control,
I couldn't oppose him now, to save my soul.

DORINE: Come, come, Mariane. Do listen to reason, won't you?
Valère has asked your hand. Do you love him, or don't you?

MARIANE: Oh, how unjust of you! What can you mean
By asking such a question, dear Dorine?
You know the depth of my affection for him;
I've told you a hundred times how I adore him.

DORINE: I don't believe in everything I hear;
Who knows if your professions were sincere?

MARIANE: They were, Dorine, and you do me wrong to doubt it;
Heaven knows that I've been all too frank about it.

DORINE: You love him, then?

MARIANE: Oh, more than I can express.

DORINE: And he, I take it, cares for you no less?

MARIANE: I think so.

DORINE: And you both, with equal fire,
Burn to be married?

MARIANE: That is our one desire.

DORINE: What of Tartuffe, then? What of your father's plan?

MARIANE: I'll kill myself, if I'm forced to wed that man.

DORINE: I hadn't thought of that recourse. How splendid!
Just die, and all your troubles will be ended!
A fine solution. Oh, it maddens me
To hear you talk in that self-pitying key.

MARIANE: Dorine, how harsh you are! It's most unfair.
You have no sympathy for my despair.

DORINE: I've none at all for people who talk drivel
And, faced with difficulties, whine and snivel.

MARIANE: No doubt I'm timid, but it would be wrong . . .

DORINE: True love requires a heart that's firm and strong.

MARIANE: I'm strong in my affection for Valère,
But coping with my father is his affair.

DORINE: But if your father's brain has grown so cracked
Over his dear Tartuffe that he can retract
His blessing, though your wedding-day was named,
It's surely not Valère who's to be blamed.

MARIANE: If I defied my father, as you suggest,
Would it not seem unmaidenly, at best?
Shall I defend my love at the expense

Of brazenness and disobedience?
Shall I parade my heart's desires, and flaunt . . .
DORINE: No, I ask nothing of you. Clearly you want
    To be Madame Tartuffe, and I feel bound
    Not to oppose a wish so very sound.
    What right have I to criticize the match?
    Indeed, my dear, the man's a brilliant catch.
    Monsieur Tartuffe! Now, there's a man of weight!
    Yes, yes, Monsieur Tartuffe, I'm bound to state,
    Is quite a person; that's not to be denied;
    'Twill be no little thing to be his bride.
    The world already rings with his renown;
    He's a great noble—in his native town;
    His ears are red, he has a pink complexion,
    And all in all, he'll suit you to perfection.
MARIANE: Dear God!
DORINE: Oh, how triumphant you will feel
    At having caught a husband so ideal!
MARIANE: Oh, do stop teasing, and use your cleverness
    To get me out of this appalling mess.
    Advise me, and I'll do whatever you say.
DORINE: Ah no, a dutiful daughter must obey
    Her father, even if he weds her to an ape.
    You've a bright future; why struggle to escape?
    Tartuffe will take you back where his family lives,
    To a small town aswarm with relatives—
    Uncles and cousins whom you'll be charmed to meet.
    You'll be received at once by the elite,
    Calling upon the bailiff's wife, no less—
    Even, perhaps, upon the mayoress,
    Who'll sit you down in the *best* kitchen chair.
    Then, once a year, you'll dance at the village fair
    To the drone of bagpipes—two of them, in fact—
    And see a puppet-show, or an animal act.
    Your husband . . .
MARIANE: Oh, you turn my blood to ice!
    Stop torturing me, and give me your advice.
DORINE: [*threatening to go*] Your servant, Madam.
MARIANE: Dorine, I beg of you . . .
DORINE: No, you deserve it; this marriage must go through.
MARIANE: Dorine!
DORINE: No.
MARIANE: Not Tartuffe! You know I think him . . .
DORINE: Tartuffe's your cup of tea, and you shall drink him.
MARIANE: I've always told you everything, and relied . . .
DORINE: No. You deserve to be tartuffified.
MARIANE: Well, since you mock me and refuse to care,
    I'll henceforth seek my solace in despair:

Despair shall be my counsellor and friend,
And help me bring my sorrows to an end.
    [*She starts to leave.*]
DORINE: There now, come back; my anger has subsided.
    You do deserve some pity, I've decided.
MARIANE: Dorine, if Father makes me undergo
    This dreadful martyrdom, I'll die, I know.
DORINE: Don't fret; it won't be difficult to discover
    Some plan of action . . . But here's Valère, your lover.

SCENE IV

VALÈRE: Madam, I've just received some wondrous news
    Regarding which I'd like to hear your views.
MARIANE: What news?
VALÈRE: You're marrying Tartuffe.
MARIANE: I find
    That Father does have such a match in mind.
VALÈRE: Your father, Madam . . .
MARIANE: . . . has just this minute said
    That it's Tartuffe he wishes me to wed.
VALÈRE: Can he be serious?
MARIANE: Oh, indeed he can;
    He's clearly set his heart upon the plan.
VALÈRE: And what position do you propose to take,
    Madam?
MARIANE: Why—I don't know.
VALÈRE: For heaven's sake—
    You don't know?
MARIANE: No.
VALÈRE: Well, well!
MARIANE: Advise me, do.
VALÈRE: Marry the man. That's my advice to you.
MARIANE: That's your advice?
VALÈRE: Yes.
MARIANE: Truly?
VALÈRE: Oh, absolutely.
    You couldn't choose more wisely, more astutely.
MARIANE: Thanks for this counsel; I'll follow it, of course.
VALÈRE: Do, do; I'm sure 'twill cost you no remorse.
MARIANE: To give it didn't cause your heart to break.
VALÈRE: I gave it, Madam, only for your sake.
MARIANE: And it's for your sake that I take it, Sir.
DORINE: [*withdrawing to the rear of the stage*]
    Let's see which fool will prove the stubborner.
VALÈRE: So! I am nothing to you, and it was flat
    Deception when you . . .

MARIANE: Please, enough of that.
> You've told me plainly that I should agree
> To wed the man my father's chosen for me,
> And since you've deigned to counsel me so wisely,
> I promise, Sir, to do as you advise me.

VALÈRE: Ah, no 'twas not by me that you were swayed.
> No, your decision was already made;
> Though now, to save appearances, you protest
> That you're betraying me at my behest.

MARIANE: Just as you say.

VALÈRE: Quite so. And I now see
> That you were never truly in love with me.

MARIANE: Alas, you're free to think so if you choose.

VALÈRE: I choose to think so, and here's a bit of news:
> You've spurned my hand, but I know where to turn
> For kinder treatment, as you shall quickly learn.

MARIANE: I'm sure you do. Your noble qualities
> Inspire affection . . .

VALÈRE: Forget my qualities, please.
> They don't inspire you overmuch, I find.
> But there's another lady I have in mind
> Whose sweet and generous nature will not scorn
> To compensate me for the loss I've borne.

MARIANE: I'm no great loss, and I'm sure that you'll transfer
> Your heart quite painlessly from me to her.

VALÈRE: I'll do my best to take it in my stride.
> The pain I feel at being cast aside
> Time and forgetfulness may put an end to.
> Or if I can't forget, I shall pretend to.
> No self-respecting person is expected
> To go on loving once he's been rejected.

MARIANE: Now, that's fine, high-minded sentiment.

VALÈRE: One to which any sane man would assent.
> Would you prefer it if I pined away
> In hopeless passion till my dying day?
> Am I to yield you to a rival's arms
> And not console myself with other charms?

MARIANE: Go then: console yourself; don't hesitate.
> I wish you to; indeed, I cannot wait.

VALÈRE: You wish me to?

MARIANE: Yes.

VALÈRE: That's the final straw.
> Madam, farewell. Your wish shall be my law.
>> [*He starts to leave, and then returns: this repeatedly.*]

MARIANE: Splendid.

VALÈRE: [*coming back again*] This breach, remember, is of your making;
> It's you who've driven me to the step I'm taking.

MARIANE: Of course.

VALÈRE: [*coming back again*] Remember, too, that I am merely
Following your example.

MARIANE: I see that clearly.

VALÈRE: Enough. I'll go and do your bidding, then.

MARIANE: Good.

VALÈRE: [*coming back again*] You shall never see my face again.

MARIANE: Excellent.

VALÈRE: [*walking to the door, then turning about*] Yes?

MARIANE: What?

VALÈRE: What's that? What did you say?

MARIANE: Nothing. You're dreaming.

VALÈRE: Ah. Well, I'm on my way.
Farewell, *Madame*.
[*He moves slowly away.*]

MARIANE: Farewell.

DORINE: [*to* MARIANE] If you ask me,
Both of you are as mad as mad can be.
Do stop this nonsense, now. I've only let you
Squabble so long to see where it would get you.
Whoa there, Monsieur Valère!
[*She goes and seizes Valère by the arm; he makes a great show of resistance.*]

VALÈRE: What's this, Dorine?

DORINE: Come here.

VALÈRE: No, no, my heart's too full of spleen.
Don't hold me back; her wish must be obeyed.

DORINE: Stop!

VALÈRE: It's too late now; my decision's made.

DORINE: Oh, pooh!

MARIANE: [*aside*] He hates the sight of me, that's plain.
I'll go, and so deliver him from pain.

DORINE: [*leaving* VALÈRE, *running after* MARIANE] And now *you* run away!
Come back.

MARIANE: No, no.
Nothing you say will keep me here. Let go!

VALÈRE: [*aside*] She cannot bear my presence, I perceive.
To spare her further torment, I shall leave.

DORINE: [*leaving* MARIANE, *running after* VALÈRE] Again! You'll not escape, Sir;
don't you try it.
Come here, you two. Stop fussing, and be quiet.
[*She takes* VALÈRE *by the hand, then* MARIANE, *and draws them together.*]

VALÈRE: [*to* DORINE] What do you want of me?

MARIANE: [*to* DORINE] What is the point of this?

DORINE: We're going to have a little armistice.
[*to* VALÈRE] Now, weren't you silly to get so overheated?

VALÈRE: Didn't you see how badly I was treated?

DORINE: [*to* MARIANE] Aren't you a simpleton, to have lost your head?

MARIANE: Didn't you hear the hateful things he said?
DORINE: [*to* VALÈRE] You're both great fools. Her sole desire, Valère,
    Is to be yours in marriage. To that I'll swear.
    [*to* MARIANE] He loves you only, and he wants no wife
    But you, Mariane. On that I'll stake my life.
MARIANE: [*to* VALÈRE] Then why you advised me so, I cannot see.
VALÈRE: [*to* MARIANE] On such a question, why ask advice of *me?*
DORINE: Oh, you're impossible. Give me your hands, you two.
    [*to* VALÈRE] Yours first.
VALÈRE: [*giving* DORINE *his hand*] But why?
DORINE: [*to* MARIANE] And now a hand from you.
MARIANE: [*also giving* DORINE *her hand*] What are you doing?
DORINE: There: a perfect fit.
    You suit each other better than you'll admit.
        [VALÈRE *and* MARIANE *hold hands for some time without looking at each
        other.*]
VALÈRE: [*turning toward* MARIANE] Ah, come, don't be so haughty. Give a man
    A look of kindness, won't you, Mariane?
        [MARIANE *turns toward* VALÈRE *and smiles.*]
DORINE: I'll tell you, lovers are completely mad!
VALÈRE: [*to* MARIANE] Now come, confess that you were very bad
    To hurt my feelings as you did just now.
    I have a just complaint, you must allow.
MARIANE: *You* must allow that you were most unpleasant . . .
DORINE: Let's table that discussion for the present;
    Your father has a plan which must be stopped.
MARIANE: Advise us, then; what means must we adopt?
DORINE: We'll use all manner of means, and all at once.
    [*to* MARIANE] Your father's addled; he's acting like a dunce.
    Therefore you'd better humor the old fossil.
    Pretend to yield to him, be sweet and docile,
    And then postpone, as often as necessary,
    The day on which you have agreed to marry.
    You'll thus gain time, and time will turn the trick.
    Sometimes, for instance, you'll be taken sick,
    And that will seem good reason for delay;
    Or some bad omen will make you change the day—
    You'll dream of muddy water, or you'll pass
    A dead man's hearse, or break a looking-glass
    If all else fails, no man can marry you
    Unless you take his ring and say "I do."
    But now, let's separate. If they should find
    Us talking here, our plot might be divined.
    [*to* VALÈRE] Go to your friends, and tell them what's occurred,
    And have them urge her father to keep his word.
    Meanwhile, we'll stir her brother into action,
    And get Elmire, as well, to join our faction.
    Good-bye.

VALÈRE: [*to* MARIANE] Though each of us will do his best,
    It's your true heart on which my hopes shall rest.
MARIANE: [*to* VALÈRE] Regardless of what Father may decide,
    None but Valère shall claim me as his bride.
VALÈRE: Oh, how those words content me! Come what will . . .
DORINE: Oh, lovers, lovers! Their tongues are never still.
    Be off, now.
VALÈRE: [*turning to go, then turning back*] One last word . . .
DORINE: No time to chat:
    You leave by this door; and *you* leave by that.
        [DORINE *pushes them, by the shoulders, toward opposing doors.*]

ACT III

SCENE I

DAMIS: May lightning strike me even as I speak,
    May all men call me cowardly and weak,
    If any fear or scruple holds me back
    From settling things, at once, with that great quack!
DORINE: Now, don't give way to violent emotion.
    Your father's merely talked about this notion,
    And words and deeds are far from being one.
    Much that is talked about is left undone.
DAMIS: No, I must stop that scoundrel's machinations;
    I'll go and tell him off; I'm out of patience.
DORINE: Do calm down and be practical. I had rather
    My mistress dealt with him—and with your father.
    She has some influence with Tartuffe, I've noted.
    He hangs upon her words, seems most devoted,
    And may, indeed, be smitten by her charm.
    Pray Heaven it's true! 'Twould do our cause no harm.
    She sent for him, just now, to sound him out
    On this affair you're so incensed about;
    She'll find out where he stands, and tell him, too,
    What dreadful strife and trouble will ensue
    If he lends countenance to your father's plan.
    I couldn't get in to see him, but his man
    Says that he's almost finished with his prayers.
    Go, now. I'll catch him when he comes downstairs.
DAMIS: I want to hear this conference, and I will.
DORINE: No, they must be alone.
DAMIS: Oh, I'll keep still.
DORINE: Not you. I know your temper. You'd start a brawl,
    And shout and stamp your foot and spoil it all.
    Go on.
DAMIS: I won't; I have a perfect right . . .

DORINE: Lord, you're a nuisance! He's coming; get out of sight.
  [DAMIS *conceals himself in a closet at the rear of the stage.*]

SCENE II

TARTUFFE: [*observing* DORINE, *and calling to his manservant offstage*] Hang up my
  hair-shirt, put my scourge in place,
  And pray, Laurent, for Heaven's perpetual grace.
  I'm going to the prison now, to share
  My last few coins with the poor wretches there.
DORINE: [*aside*] Dear God, what affectation! What a fake!
TARTUFFE: You wished to see me?
DORINE: Yes . . .
TARTUFFE: [*taking a handkerchief from his pocket*] For mercy's sake,
  Please take this handkerchief, before you speak.
DORINE: What?
TARTUFFE: Cover that bosom, girl. The flesh is weak,
  And unclean thoughts are difficult to control.
  Such sights as that can undermine the soul.
DORINE: Your soul, it seems, has very poor defenses,
  And flesh makes quite an impact on your senses.
  It's strange that you're so easily excited;
  My own desires are not so soon ignited,
  And if I saw you naked as a beast,
  Not all your hide would tempt me in the least.
TARTUFFE: Girl, speak more modestly; unless you do,
  I shall be forced to take my leave of you.
DORINE: Oh, no, it's I who must be on my way;
  I've just one little message to convey.
  Madame is coming down, and begs you, Sir,
  To wait and have a word or two with her.
TARTUFFE: Gladly.
DORINE: [*aside*] *That* had a softening effect!
  I think my guess about him was correct.
TARTUFFE: Will she be long?
DORINE: No: that's her step I hear.
  Ah, here she is, and I shall disappear.

SCENE III

TARTUFFE: May heaven, whose infinite goodness we adore,
  Preserve your body and soul forevermore,
  And bless your days, and answer thus the plea
  Of one who is its humblest votary.
ELMIRE: I thank you for that pious wish. But please,
  Do take a chair and let's be more at ease.
   [*They sit down.*]

TARTUFFE: I trust that you are once more well and strong?
ELMIRE: Oh, yes: the fever didn't last for long.
TARTUFFE: My prayers are too unworthy, I am sure,
　　　To have gained from Heaven this most gracious cure;
　　　But lately, Madam, my every supplication
　　　Has had for object your recuperation.
ELMIRE: You shouldn't have troubled so. I don't deserve it.
TARTUFFE: Your health is priceless, Madam, and to preserve it
　　　I'd gladly give my own, in all sincerity.
ELMIRE: Sir, you outdo us all in Christian charity.
　　　You've been most kind. I count myself your debtor.
TARTUFFE: 'Twas nothing, Madam. I long to serve you better.
ELMIRE: There's a private matter I'm anxious to discuss.
　　　I'm glad there's no one here to hinder us.
TARTUFFE: I, too, am glad; it floods my heart with bliss
　　　To find myself alone with you like this.
　　　For just this chance I've prayed with all my power—
　　　But prayed in vain, until this happy hour.
ELMIRE: This won't take long, Sir, and I hope you'll be
　　　Entirely frank and unconstrained with me.
TARTUFFE: Indeed, there's nothing I had rather do
　　　Than bare my inmost heart and soul to you.
　　　First, let me say that what remarks I've made
　　　About the constant visits you are paid
　　　Were prompted not by any mean emotion,
　　　But rather by a pure and deep devotion,
　　　A fervent zeal . . .
ELMIRE: No need for explanation.
　　　Your sole concern, I'm sure, was my salvation.
TARTUFFE: [*taking* ELMIRE'S *hand and pressing her fingertips*] Quite so; and such
　　　great fervor do I feel . . .
ELMIRE: Ooh! Please! You're pinching!
TARTUFFE: 'Twas from excess of zeal.
　　　I never meant to cause you pain, I swear.
　　　I'd rather . . . [*He places his hand on* ELMIRE'S *knee.*]
ELMIRE: What can your hand be doing there?
TARTUFFE: Feeling your gown; what soft, fine-woven stuff!
ELMIRE: Please, I'm extremely ticklish. That's enough.
　　　　　[*She draws her chair away;* TARTUFFE *pulls his after her.*]
TARTUFFE: [*fondling the lace collar of her gown*] My, my, what lovely lacework on
　　　your dress!
　　　The workmanship's miraculous, no less.
　　　I've not seen anything to equal it.
ELMIRE: Yes, quite. But let's talk business for a bit.
　　　They say my husband means to break his word
　　　And give his daughter to you, Sir. Had you heard?
TARTUFFE: He did once mention it. But I confess

> I dream of quite a different happiness.
> It's elsewhere, Madam, that my eyes discern
> The promise of that bliss for which I yearn.

ELMIRE: I see: you care for nothing here below.

TARTUFFE: Ah, well—my heart's not made of stone, you know.

ELMIRE: All your desires mount heavenward, I'm sure,
> In scorn of all that's earthly and impure.

TARTUFFE: A love of heavenly beauty does not preclude
> A proper love for earthly pulchritude;
> Our senses are quite rightly captivated
> By perfect works our Maker has created.
> Some glory clings to all that Heaven has made;
> In you, all Heaven's marvels are displayed.
> On that fair face, such beauties have been lavished,
> The eyes are dazzled and the heart is ravished;
> How could I look on you, O flawless creature,
> And not adore the Author of all Nature,
> Feeling a love both passionate and pure
> For you, this triumph of self-portraiture?
> At first, I trembled lest that love should be
> A subtle snare that Hell had laid for me;
> I vowed to flee the sight of you, eschewing
> A rapture that might prove my soul's undoing;
> But soon, fair being, I became aware
> That my deep passion could be made to square
> With rectitude, and with my bounden duty.
> I thereupon surrendered to your beauty.
> It is, I know, presumptuous on my part
> To bring you this poor offering of my heart,
> And it is not my merit, Heaven knows,
> But your compassion on which my hopes repose.
> You are my peace, my solace, my salvation;
> On you depends my bliss—or desolation;
> I bide your judgment and, as you think best,
> I shall be either miserable or blest.

ELMIRE: Your declaration is most gallant, Sir,
> But don't you think it's out of character?
> You'd have done better to restrain your passion
> And think before you spoke in such a fashion.
> It ill becomes a pious man like you . . .

TARTUFFE: I may be pious, but I'm human, too:
> With your celestial charms before his eyes,
> A man has not the power to be wise.
> I know such words sound strangely, coming from me,
> But I'm no angel, nor was meant to be,
> And if you blame my passion, you must needs
> Reproach as well the charms on which it feeds.
> Your loveliness I had no sooner seen

Than you became my soul's unrivalled queen;
Before your seraph glance, divinely sweet,
My heart's defenses crumbled in defeat,
And nothing fasting, prayer, or tears might do
Could stay my spirit from adoring you.
My eyes, my sighs have told you in the past
What now my lips make bold to say at last,
And if, in your great goodness, you will deign
To look upon your slave, and ease his pain—
If, in compassion for my soul's distress,
You'll stoop to comfort my unworthiness,
I'll raise to you, in thanks for that sweet manna,
An endless hymn, an infinite hosanna.
With me, of course, there need be no anxiety,
No fear of scandal or of notoriety.
These young court gallants, whom all the ladies fancy,
Are vain in speech, in action rash and chancy;
When they succeed in love, the world soon knows it;
No favor's granted them but they disclose it
And by the looseness of their tongues profane
The very altar where their hearts have lain.
Men of my sort, however, love discreetly,
And one may trust our reticence completely.
My keen concern for my good name insures
The absolute security of yours;
In short, I offer you, my dear Elmire,
Love without scandal, pleasure without fear.

ELMIRE: I've heard your well-turned speeches to the end,
And what you urge I clearly apprehend.
Aren't you afraid that I may take a notion
To tell my husband of your warm devotion,
And that, supposing he were duly told,
His feelings toward you might grow rather cold?

TARTUFFE: I know, dear lady, that your exceeding charity
Will lead your heart to pardon my temerity;
That you'll excuse my violent affection
As human weakness, human imperfection;
And that—O fairest!—you will bear in mind
That I'm but flesh and blood, and am not blind.

ELMIRE: Some women might do otherwise, perhaps,
But I shall be discreet about your lapse;
I'll tell my husband nothing of what's occurred
If, in return, you'll give your solemn word
To advocate as forcefully as you can
The marriage of Valère and Mariane,
Renouncing all desire to dispossess
Another of his rightful happiness,
And . . .

SCENE IV

DAMIS: [*emerging from the closet where he has been hiding*] No! We'll not hush up
    this vile affair;
    I heard it all inside that closet there,
    Where Heaven, in order to confound the pride
    Of this great rascal, prompted me to hide.
    Ah, now I have my long-awaited chance
    To punish his deceit and arrogance,
    And give my father clear and shocking proof
    Of the black character of his dear Tartuffe.
ELMIRE: Ah no, Damis; I'll be content if he
    Will study to deserve my leniency.
    I've promised silence—don't make me break my word;
    To make a scandal would be too absurd.
    Good wives laugh off such trifles, and forget them;
    Why should they tell their husbands, and upset them?
DAMIS: You have your reasons for taking such a course,
    And I have reasons, too, of equal force.
    To spare him now would be insanely wrong.
    I've swallowed my just wrath for far too long
    And watched this insolent bigot bringing strife
    And bitterness into our family life.
    Too long he's meddled in my father's affairs,
    Thwarting my marriage-hopes, and poor Valère's.
    It's high time that my father was undeceived,
    And now I've proof that can't be disbelieved—
    Proof that was furnished me by Heaven above.
    It's too good not to take advantage of.
    This is my chance, and I deserve to lose it
    If, for one moment, I hesitate to use it.
ELMIRE: Damis . . .
DAMIS: No, I must do what I think right.
    Madam, my heart is bursting with delight,
    And, say whatever you will, I'll not consent
    To lose the sweet revenge on which I'm bent.
    I'll settle matters without more ado;
    And here, most opportunely, is my cue.

SCENE V

DAMIS: Father, I'm glad you've joined us. Let us advise you
    Of some fresh news which doubtless will surprise you.
    You've just now been repaid with interest
    For all your loving-kindness to our guest.
    He's proved his warm and grateful feelings toward you;
    It's with a pair of horns he would reward you.
    Yes, I surprised him with your wife, and heard

His whole adulterous offer, every word.
She, with her all-too-gentle disposition,
Would not have told you of his proposition;
But I shall not make terms with brazen lechery,
And feel that not to tell you would be treachery.
ELMIRE: And I hold that one's husband's peace of mind
Should not be spoilt by tattle of this kind.
One's honor doesn't require it: to be proficient
In keeping men at bay is quite sufficient.
These are my sentiments, and I wish, Damis,
That you had heeded me and held your peace. [*Exit.*]

SCENE VI

ORGON: Can it be true, this dreadful thing I hear?
TARTUFFE: Yes, Brother, I'm a wicked man, I fear:
A wretched sinner, all depraved and twisted,
The greatest villain that has ever existed.
My life's one heap of crimes, which grows each minute;
There's naught but foulness and corruption in it;
And I perceive that Heaven, outraged by me,
Has chosen this occasion to mortify me.
Charge me with any deed you wish to name;
I'll not defend myself, but take the blame.
Believe what you are told, and drive Tartuffe
Like some base criminal from beneath your roof;
Yes, drive me hence, and with a parting curse:
I shan't protest, for I deserve far worse.
ORGON: [*to* DAMIS] Ah, you deceitful boy, how dare you try
To stain his purity with so foul a lie?
DAMIS: What! are you taken in by such a bluff?
Did you not hear . . . ?
ORGON: Enough, you rogue, enough!
TARTUFFE: Ah. Brother, let him speak: you're being unjust.
Believe his story; the boy deserves your trust.
Why, after all, should you have faith in me?
How can you know what I might do, or be?
Is it on my good actions that you base
Your favor? Do you trust my pious face?
Ah, no, don't be deceived by hollow shows;
I'm far, alas, from being what men suppose;
Though the world takes me for a man of worth,
I'm truly the most worthless man on Earth.
[*to* DAMIS] Yes, my dear son, speak out now: call me the chief
Of sinners, a wretch, a murderer, a thief;
Load me with all the names men most abhor;
I'll not complain; I've earned them all, and more;

I'll kneel here while you pour them on my head
As a just punishment for the life I've led.
ORGON: [*to* TARTUFFE] This is too much, dear Brother.
    [*to* DAMIS] Have you no heart?
DAMIS: Are you so hoodwinked by this rascal's art . . . ?
ORGON: Be still, you monster.
    [*to* TARTUFFE] Brother, I pray you, rise.
    [*to* DAMIS] Villain!
DAMIS: But . . .
ORGON: Silence!
DAMIS: Can't you realize . . . ?
ORGON: Just one word more, and I'll tear you limb from limb.
TARTUFFE: In God's name, Brother, don't be harsh with him.
    I'd rather far be tortured at the stake
    Than see him bear one scratch for my poor sake.
ORGON: [*to* DAMIS] Ingrate!
TARTUFFE: If I must beg you, on bended knee,
    To pardon him . . .
ORGON: [*falling to his knees, addressing* TARTUFFE] Such goodness cannot be!
    [*to* DAMIS] Now, *there's* true charity!
DAMIS: What, you . . . ?
ORGON: Villain, be still!
    I know your motives; I know you wish him ill:
    Yes, all of you—wife, children, servants, all—
    Conspire against him and desire his fall,
    Employing every shameful trick you can
    To alienate me from this saintly man.
    Ah, but the more you seek to drive him away,
    The more I'll do to keep him. Without delay,
    I'll spite this household and confound its pride
    By giving him my daughter as his bride.
DAMIS: You're going to force her to accept his hand?
ORGON: Yes, and this very night, d'you understand?
    I shall defy you all, and make it clear
    That I'm the one who gives the orders here.
    Come, wretch, kneel down and clasp his blessed feet,
    And ask his pardon for your black deceit.
DAMIS: I ask that swindler's pardon? Why, I'd rather . . .
ORGON: So! You insult him, and defy your father!
    A stick! A stick! [*to* TARTUFFE] No, no—release me, do.
        [*to* DAMIS]
    Out of my house this minute! Be off with you,
    And never dare set foot in it again.
DAMIS: Well, I shall go, but . . .
ORGON: Well, go quickly, then.
    I disinherit you; an empty purse
    Is all you'll get from me—except my curse!

SCENE VII

ORGON: How he blasphemed your goodness! What a son!

TARTUFFE: Forgive him, Lord, as I've already done.

[*to* ORGON] You can't know how it hurts when someone tries
To blacken me in my dear Brother's eyes.

ORGON: Ahh!

TARTUFFE: The mere thought of such ingratitude
Plunges my soul into so dark a mood . . .
Such horror grips my heart . . . I gasp for breath,
And cannot speak, and feel myself near death.

ORGON: [*He runs, in tears, to the door through which he has just driven his son.*]
You blackguard! Why did I spare you? Why did I not
Break you in little pieces on the spot?
Compose yourself, and don't be hurt, dear friend.

TARTUFFE: These scenes, these dreadful quarrels, have got to end.
I've much upset your household, and I perceive
That the best thing will be for me to leave.

ORGON: What are you saying!

TARTUFFE: They're all against me here;
They'd have you think me false and insincere.

ORGON: Ah, what of that? Have I ceased believing in you?

TARTUFFE: Their adverse talk will certainly continue,
And charges which you now repudiate
You may find credible at a later date.

ORGON: No, Brother, never.

TARTUFFE: Brother, a wife can sway
Her husband's mind in many a subtle way.

ORGON: No, no.

TARTUFFE: To leave at once is the solution;
Thus only can I end their persecution.

ORGON: No, no, I'll not allow it; you shall remain.

TARTUFFE: Ah, well; 'twill mean much martyrdom and pain,
But if you wish it . . .

ORGON: Ah!

TARTUFFE: Enough; so be it.
But one thing must be settled, as I see it.
For your dear honor, and for our friendship's sake,
There's one precaution I feel bound to take.
I shall avoid your wife, and keep away . . .

ORGON: No, you shall not, whatever they may say.
It pleases me to vex them, and for spite
I'd have them see you with her day and night.
What's more, I'm going to drive them to despair
By making you my only son and heir;
This very day, I'll give to you alone
Clear deed and title to everything I own.
A dear, good friend and son-in-law-to-be

     Is more than wife, or child, or kin to me.
     Will you accept my offer, dearest son?
TARTUFFE: In all things, let the will of Heaven be done.
ORGON: Poor fellow! Come, we'll go draw up the deed.
     Then let them burst with disappointed greed!

ACT IV

SCENE I

CLÉANTE: Yes, all the town's discussing it, and truly,
     Their comments do not flatter you unduly.
     I'm glad we've met, Sir, and I'll give my view
     Of this sad matter in a word or two.
     As for who's guilty, that I shan't discuss;
     Let's say it was Damis who caused the fuss;
     Assuming, then, that you have been ill-used
     By young Damis, and groundlessly accused,
     Ought not a Christian to forgive, and ought
     He not to stifle every vengeful thought?
     Should you stand by and watch a father make
     His only son an exile for your sake?
     Again I tell you frankly, be advised:
     The whole town, high and low, is scandalized;
     This quarrel must be mended, and my advice is
     Not to push matters to a further crisis.
     No, sacrifice your wrath to God above,
     And help Damis regain his father's love.
TARTUFFE: Alas, for my part I should take great joy
     In doing so. I've nothing against the boy.
     I pardon all, I harbor no resentment;
     To serve him would afford me much contentment.
     But Heaven's interest will not have it so:
     If he comes back, then I shall have to go.
     After his conduct—so extreme, so vicious—
     Our further intercourse would look suspicious.
     God knows what people would think! Why, they'd describe
     My goodness to him as a sort of bribe;
     They'd say that out of guilt I made pretense
     Of loving-kindness and benevolence—
     That, fearing my accuser's tongue, I strove
     To buy his silence with a show of love.
CLÉANTE: Your reasoning is badly warped and stretched,
     And these excuses, Sir, are most farfetched.
     Why put yourself in charge of Heaven's cause?
     Does Heaven need our help to enforce its laws?
     Leave vengeance to the Lord, Sir; while we live,
     Our duty's not to punish, but forgive;

And what the Lord commands, we should obey
Without regard to what the world may say.
What! Shall the fear of being misunderstood
Prevent our doing what is right and good?
No, no; let's simply do what Heaven ordains,
And let no other thoughts perplex our brains.

TARTUFFE: Again, Sir, let me say that I've forgiven
Damis, and thus obeyed the laws of Heaven;
But I am not commanded by the Bible
To live with one who smears my name with libel.

CLÉANTE: Were you commanded, Sir, to indulge the whim
Of poor Orgon, and to encourage him
In suddenly transferring to your name
A large estate to which you have no claim?

TARTUFFE: 'Twould never occur to those who know me best
To think I acted from self-interest.
The treasures of this world I quite despise;
Their specious glitter does not charm my eyes;
And if I have resigned myself to taking
The gift which my dear Brother insists on making,
I do so only, as he well understands,
Lest so much wealth fall into wicked hands,
Lest those to whom it might descend in time
Turn it to purposes of sin and crime,
And not, as I shall do, make use of it
For Heaven's glory and mankind's benefit.

CLÉANTE: Forget these trumped-up fears. Your argument
Is one the rightful heir might well resent;
It *is* a moral burden to inherit
Such wealth, but give Damis a chance to bear it.
And would it not be worse to be accused
Of swindling, than to see that wealth misused?
I'm shocked that you allowed Orgon to broach
This matter, and that you feel no self-reproach;
Does true religion teach that lawful heirs
May freely be deprived of what is theirs?
And if the Lord has told you in your heart
That you and young Damis must dwell apart,
Would it not be the decent thing to beat
A generous and honorable retreat,
Rather than let the son of the house be sent,
For your convenience, into banishment?
Sir, if you wish to prove the honesty
Of your intentions . . .

TARTUFFE: Sir, it is half-past three.
I've certain pious duties to attend to,
And hope my prompt departure won't offend you.

CLÉANTE: [*alone*] Damn.

SCENE II

DORINE: Stay, Sir, and help Mariane, for Heaven's sake!
    She's suffering so, I fear her heart will break.
    Her father's plan to marry her off tonight
    Has put the poor child in a desperate plight.
    I hear him coming. Let's stand together, now,
    And see if we can't change his mind, somehow,
    About this match we all deplore and fear.

SCENE III

ORGON: Hah! Glad to find you all assembled here.
    [*to* MARIANE] This contract, child, contains your happiness,
    And what it says I think your heart can guess.
MARIANE: [*falling to her knees*] Sir, by that Heaven which sees me here distressed,
    And by whatever else can move your breast,
    Do not employ a father's power, I pray you,
    To crush my heart and force it to obey you,
    Nor by your harsh commands oppress me so
    That I'll begrudge the duty which I owe—
    And do not so embitter and enslave me
    That I shall hate the very life you gave me.
    If my sweet hopes must perish, if you refuse
    To give me to the one I've dared to choose,
    Spare me at least—I beg you, I implore—
    The pain of wedding one whom I abhor;
    And do not, by a heartless use of force,
    Drive me to contemplate some desperate course.
ORGON: [*feeling himself touched by her*] Be firm, my soul. No human weakness, now.
MARIANE: I don't resent your love for him. Allow
    Your heart free rein, Sir; give him your property,
    And if that's not enough, take mine from me;
    He's welcome to my money; take it, do,
    But don't, I pray, include my person, too.
    Spare me, I beg you; and let me end the tale
    Of my sad days behind a convent veil.
ORGON: A convent! Hah! When crossed in their amours,
    All lovesick girls have the same thought as yours.
    Get up! The more you loathe the man, and dread him,
    The more ennobling it will be to wed him.
    Marry Tartuffe, and mortify your flesh!
    Enough; don't start that whimpering afresh.
DORINE: But why . . . ?
ORGON: Be still, there. Speak when you're spoken to.
    Not one more bit of impudence out of you.
CLÉANTE: If I may offer a word of counsel here . . .

ORGON: Brother, in counseling you have no peer;
    All your advice is forceful, sound, and clever;
    I don't propose to follow it, however.
ELMIRE: [*to* ORGON] I am amazed, and don't know what to say;
    Your blindness simply takes my breath away.
    You are indeed bewitched, to take no warning
    From our account of what occurred this morning.
ORGON: Madam, I know a few plain facts and one
    Is that you're partial to my rascal son;
    Hence, when he sought to make Tartuffe the victim
    Of a base lie, you dared not contradict him.
    Ah, but you underplayed your part, my pet;
    You should have looked more angry, more upset.
ELMIRE: When men make overtures, must we reply
    With righteous anger and a battle-cry?
    Must we turn back their amorous advances
    With sharp reproaches and with fiery glances?
    Myself, I find such offers merely amusing,
    And make no scenes and fusses in refusing;
    My taste is for good-natured rectitude,
    And I dislike the savage sort of prude
    Who guards her virtue with her teeth and claws,
    And tears men's eyes out for the slightest cause:
    The Lord preserve me from such honor as that,
    Which bites and scratches like an alley-cat!
    I've found that a polite and cool rebuff
    Discourages a lover quite enough.
ORGON: I know the facts, and I shall not be shaken.
ELMIRE: I marvel at your power to be mistaken.
    Would it, I wonder, carry weight with you
    If I could *show* you that our tale was true?
ORGON: Show me?
ELMIRE: Yes.
ORGON: Rot.
ELMIRE: Come, what if I found a way
    To make you see the facts as plain as day?
ORGON: Nonsense.
ELMIRE: Do answer me; don't be absurd.
    I'm not now asking you to trust our word.
    Suppose that from some hiding-place in here
    You learned the whole sad truth by eye and ear—
    What would you say of your good friend, after that?
ORGON: Why, I'd say . . . nothing, by Jehoshaphat!
    It can't be true.
ELMIRE: You've been too long deceived,
    And I'm quite tired of being disbelieved.
    Come now: let's put my statements to the test,
    And you shall see the truth made manifest.

ORGON: I'll take that challenge. Now do your uttermost.
    We'll see how you make good your empty boast.
ELMIRE: [*to* DORINE] Send him to me.
DORINE: He's crafty; it may be hard
    To catch the cunning scoundrel off his guard.
ELMIRE: No, amorous men are gullible. Their conceit
    So blinds them that they're never hard to cheat.
    Have him come down. [*to* CLÉANTE *and* MARIANE] Please leave us, for
    a bit.

SCENE IV

ELMIRE: Pull up this table, and get under it.
ORGON: What?
ELMIRE: It's essential that you be well-hidden.
ORGON: Why there?
ELMIRE: Oh, Heavens! Just do as you are bidden.
    I have my plans; we'll soon see how they fare.
    Under the table, now; and once you're there,
    Take care that you are neither seen nor heard.
ORGON: Well, I'll indulge you, since I gave my word
    To see you through this infantile charade.
ELMIRE: Once it is over, you'll be glad we played.
       [*to her husband, who is now under the table*]
    I'm going to act quite strangely, now, and you
    Must not be shocked at anything I do.
    Whatever I may say, you must excuse
    As part of that deceit I'm forced to use.
    I shall employ sweet speeches in the task
    Of making that impostor drop his mask;
    I'll give encouragement to his bold desires,
    And furnish fuel to his amorous fires.
    Since it's for your sake, and for his destruction,
    That I shall seem to yield to his seduction,
    I'll gladly stop whenever you decide
    That all your doubts are fully satisfied.
    I'll count on you, as soon as you have seen
    What sort of man he is, to intervene,
    And not expose me to his odious lust
    One moment longer than you feel you must.
    Remember: you're to save me from my plight
    Whenever . . . He's coming! Hush! Keep out of sight!

SCENE V

TARTUFFE: You wish to have a word with me, I'm told.
ELMIRE: Yes. I've a little secret to unfold.
    Before I speak, however, it would be wise
    To close that door, and look for spies.

[TARTUFFE *goes to the door, closes it, and returns.*]
The very last thing that must happen now
Is a repetition of this morning's row.
I've never been so badly caught off guard.
Oh, how I feared for you! You saw how hard
I tried to make that troublesome Damis
Control his dreadful temper, and hold his peace.
In my confusion, I didn't have the sense
Simply to contradict his evidence;
But as it happened, that was for the best,
And all has worked out in our interest.
This storm has only bettered your position;
My husband doesn't have the least suspicion,
And now, in mockery of those who do,
He bids me be continually with you.
And that is why, quite fearless of reproof,
I now can be alone with my Tartuffe,
And why my heart—perhaps too quick to yield—
Feels free to let its passion be revealed.
TARTUFFE: Madam, your words confuse me. Not long ago,
You spoke in quite a different style, you know.
ELMIRE: Ah, Sir, if that refusal made you smart,
It's little that you know of woman's heart,
Or what that heart is trying to convey
When it resists in such a feeble way!
Always, at first, our modesty prevents
The frank avowal of tender sentiments;
However high the passion which inflames us,
Still, to confess its power somehow shames us.
Thus we reluct, at first, yet in a tone
Which tells you that our heart is overthrown,
That what our lips deny, our pulse confesses,
And that, in time, all noes will turn to yesses.
I fear my words are all too frank and free,
And a poor proof of woman's modesty;
But since I'm started, tell me, if you will—
Would I have tried to make Damis be still,
Would I have listened, calm and unoffended,
Until your lengthy offer of love was ended,
And be so very mild in my reaction,
Had your sweet words not given me satisfaction?
And when I tried to force you to undo
The marriage-plans my husband has in view,
What did my urgent pleading signify
If not that I admired you, and that I
Deplored the thought that someone else might own
Part of a heart I wished for mine alone?
TARTUFFE: Madam, no happiness is so complete

As when, from lips we love, come words so sweet;
Their nectar floods my every sense, and drains
In honeyed rivulets through all my veins.
To please you is my joy, my only goal;
Your love is the restorer of my soul;
And yet I must beg leave, now, to confess
Some lingering doubts as to my happiness.
Might this not be a trick? Might not the catch
Be that you wish me to break off the match
With Mariane, and so have feigned to love me?
I shan't quite trust your fond opinion of me
Until the feelings you've expressed so sweetly
Are demonstrated somewhat more concretely,
And you have shown, by certain kind concessions,
That I may put my faith in your professions.

ELMIRE: [*She coughs, to warn her husband.*] Why be in such a hurry? Must my
    heart
Exhaust its bounty at the very start?
To make that sweet admission cost me dear,
But you'll not be content, it would appear,
Unless my store of favors is disbursed
To the last farthing, and at the very first.

TARTUFFE: The less we merit, the less we dare to hope,
And with our doubts, mere words can never cope.
We trust no promised bliss till we receive it;
Not till a joy is ours can we believe it.
I, who so little merit your esteem,
Can't credit this fulfillment of my dream,
And shan't believe it, Madam, until I savor
Some palpable assurance of your favor.

ELMIRE: My, how tyrannical your love can be,
And how it flusters and perplexes me!
How furiously you take one's heart in hand,
And make your every wish a fierce command!
Come, must you hound and harry me to death?
Will you not give me time to catch my breath?
Can it be right to press me with such force,
Give me no quarter, show me no remorse,
And take advantage, by your stern insistence,
Of the fond feelings which weaken my resistance?

TARTUFFE: Well, if you look with favor upon my love,
Why, then, begrudge me some clear proof thereof?

ELMIRE: But how can I consent without offense
To Heaven, toward which you feel such reverence?

TARTUFFE: If Heaven is all that holds you back, don't worry.
I can remove that hindrance in a hurry.
Nothing of that sort need obstruct our path.

ELMIRE: Must one not be afraid of Heaven's wrath?
TARTUFFE: Madam, forget such fears, and be my pupil,
  And I shall teach you how to conquer scruple.
  Some joys, it's true, are wrong in Heaven's eyes;
  Yet Heaven is not averse to compromise;
  There is a science, lately formulated,
  Whereby one's conscience may be liberated,
  And any wrongful act you care to mention
  May be redeemed by purity of intention.
  I'll teach you, Madam, the secrets of that science;
  Meanwhile, just place on me your full reliance.
  Assuage my keen desires, and feel no dread:
  The sin, if any, shall be on my head.
      [ELMIRE *coughs, this time more loudly.*]
  You've a bad cough.
ELMIRE: Yes, yes. It's bad indeed.
TARTUFFE: [*producing a little paper bag*] A bit of licorice may be what you need.
ELMIRE: No, I've a stubborn cold, it seems. I'm sure it
  Will take much more than licorice to cure it.
TARTUFFE: How aggravating.
ELMIRE: Oh, more than I can say.
TARTUFFE: If you're still troubled, think of things this way:
  No one shall know our joys, save us alone,
  And there's no evil till the act is known;
  It's scandal, Madam, which makes it an offense,
  And it's no sin to sin in confidence.
ELMIRE: [*having coughed once more*] Well, clearly I must do as you require,
  And yield to your importunate desire.
  It is apparent, now, that nothing less
  Will satisfy you, and so I acquiesce.
  To go so far is much against my will;
  I'm vexed that it should come to this; but still,
  Since you are so determined on it, since you
  Will not allow mere language to convince you,
  And since you ask for concrete evidence, I
  See nothing for it, now, but to comply.
  If this is sinful, if I'm wrong to do it,
  So much the worse for him who drove me to it.
  The fault can surely not be charged to me.
TARTUFFE: Madam, the fault is mine, if fault there be,
  And . . .
ELMIRE: Open the door a little, and peek out;
  I wouldn't want my husband poking about.
TARTUFFE: Why worry about the man? Each day he grows
  More gullible; one can lead him by the nose.
  To find us here would fill him with delight,
  And if he saw the worst, he'd doubt his sight.

ELMIRE: Nevertheless, do step out for a minute
    Into the hall, and see that no one's in it.

SCENE VI

ORGON: [*coming out from under the table*] That man's a perfect monster, I must
    admit!
    I'm simply stunned. I can't get over it.
ELMIRE: What, coming out so soon? How premature!
    Get back in hiding, and wait until you're sure.
    Stay till the end, and be convinced completely;
    We mustn't stop till things are proved concretely.
ORGON: Hell never harbored anything so vicious!
ELMIRE: Tut, don't be hasty. Try to be judicious.
    Wait, and be certain that there's no mistake.
    No jumping to conclusions, for Heaven's sake!
       [*She places* ORGON *behind her, as* TARTUFFE *reenters.*]

SCENE VII

TARTUFFE: [*not seeing* ORGON] Madam, all things have worked out to perfection;
    I've given the neighboring rooms a full inspection;
    No one's about; and now I may at last . . .
ORGON: [*intercepting him*] Hold on, my passionate fellow, not so fast!
    I should advise a little more restraint.
    Well, so you thought you'd fool me, my dear saint!
    How soon you wearied of the saintly life—
    Wedding my daughter, and coveting my wife!
    I've long suspected you, and had a feeling
    That soon I'd catch you at your double-dealing.
    Just now, you've given me evidence galore;
    It's quite enough; I have no wish for more.
ELMIRE: [*to* TARTUFFE] I'm sorry to have treated you so slyly,
    But circumstances forced me to be wily.
TARTUFFE: Brother, you can't think . . .
ORGON: No more talk from you;
    Just leave this household, without more ado.
TARTUFFE: What I intended . . .
ORGON: That seems fairly clear.
    Spare me your falsehoods and get out of here.
TARTUFFE: No, I'm the master, and you're the one to go!
    This house belongs to me, I'll have you know,
    And I shall show you that you can't hurt *me*
    By this contemptible conspiracy,
    That those who cross me know not what they do,
    And that I've means to expose and punish you,
    Avenge offended Heaven, and make you grieve
    That ever you dared order me to leave.
       [TARTUFFE *exits.*]

SCENE VIII

ELMIRE: What was the point of all that angry chatter?
ORGON: Dear God, I'm worried. This is no laughing matter.
ELMIRE: How so?
ORGON: I fear I understood his drift.
    I'm much disturbed about that deed of gift.
ELMIRE: You gave him . . . ?
ORGON: Yes, it's all been drawn and signed.
    But one thing more is weighing on my mind.
ELMIRE: What's that?
ORGON: I'll tell you; but first let's see if there's
    A certain strong-box in his room upstairs.

ACT V

SCENE I

CLÉANTE: Where are you going so fast?
ORGON: God knows!
CLÉANTE: Then wait;
    Let's have a conference, and deliberate
    On how this situation's to be met.
ORGON: That strong-box has me utterly upset;
    This is the worst of many, many shocks.
CLÉANTE: Is there some fearful mystery in that box?
ORGON: My poor friend Argas brought that box to me
    With his own hands, in utmost secrecy;
    'Twas on the very morning of his flight.
    It's full of papers which, if they came to light,
    Would ruin him—or such is my impression.
CLÉANTE: Then why did you let it out of your possession?
ORGON: Those papers vexed my conscience, and it seemed best
    To ask the counsel of my pious guest.
    The cunning scoundrel got me to agree
    To leave the strong-box in his custody,
    So that, in case of an investigation,
    I could employ a slight equivocation
    And swear I didn't have it, and thereby,
    At no expense to conscience, tell a lie.
CLÉANTE: It looks to me as if you're out on a limb.
    Trusting him with that box, and offering him
    That deed of gift, were actions of a kind
    Which scarcely indicate a prudent mind.
    With two such weapons, he has the upper hand,
    And since you're vulnerable, as matters stand,
    You erred once more in bringing him to bay.
    You should have acted in some subtler way.

ORGON: Just think of it: behind that fervent face,
    A heart so wicked, and a soul so base!
    I took him in, a hungry beggar, and then . . .
    Enough, by God! I'm through with pious men:
    Henceforth I'll hate the whole false brotherhood,
    And persecute them worse than Satan could.
CLÉANTE: Ah, there you go—extravagant as ever!
    Why can you not be rational? You never
    Manage to take the middle course, it seems,
    But jump, instead, between absurd extremes.
    You've recognized your recent grave mistake
    In falling victim to a pious fake;
    Now, to correct that error, must you embrace
    An even greater error in its place,
    And judge our worthy neighbors as a whole
    By what you've learned of one corrupted soul?
    Come, just because one rascal made you swallow
    A show of zeal which turned out to be hollow,
    Shall you conclude that all men are deceivers,
    And that, today, there are no true believers?
    Let atheists make that foolish inference;
    Learn to distinguish virtue from pretense,
    Be cautious in bestowing admiration,
    And cultivate a sober moderation.
    Don't humor fraud, but also don't asperse
    True piety; the latter fault is worse,
    And it is best to err, if err one must,
    As you have done, upon the side of trust.

SCENE II

DAMIS: Father, I hear that scoundrel's uttered threats
    Against you; that he pridefully forgets
    How, in his need, he was befriended by you,
    And means to use your gifts to crucify you.
ORGON: It's true, my boy. I'm too distressed for tears.
DAMIS: Leave it to me, Sir; let me trim his ears.
    Faced with such insolence, we must not waver.
    I shall rejoice in doing you the favor
    Of cutting short his life, and your distress.
CLÉANTE: What a display of young hotheadedness!
    Do learn to moderate your fits of rage.
    In this just kingdom, this enlightened age,
    One does not settle things by violence.

SCENE III

MADAME PERNELLE: [*entering with* ELMIRE *and* MARIANE]
    I hear strange tales of very strange events.

ORGON: Yes, strange events which these two eyes beheld.
    The man's ingratitude is unparalleled.
    I save a wretched pauper from starvation,
    House him, and treat him like a blood relation,
    Shower him every day with my largesse,
    Give him my daughter, and all that I possess;
    And meanwhile the unconscionable knave
    Tries to induce my wife to misbehave;
    And not content with such extreme rascality,
    Now threatens me with my own liberality,
    And aims, by taking base advantage of
    The gifts I gave him out of Christian love,
    To drive me from my house, a ruined man,
    And make me end a pauper, as he began.
DORINE: Poor fellow!
MADAME PERNELLE: No, my son, I'll never bring
    Myself to think him guilty of such thing.
ORGON: How's that?
MADAME PERNELLE: The righteous always were maligned.
ORGON: Speak clearly, Mother. Say what's on your mind.
MADAME PERNELLE: I mean that I can smell a rat, my dear.
    You know how everybody hates him, here.
ORGON: That has no bearing on the case at all.
MADAME PERNELLE: I told you a hundred times, when you were small,
    That virtue in this world is hated ever;
    Malicious men may die, but malice never.
ORGON: No doubt that's true, but how does it apply?
MADAME PERNELLE: They've turned you against him by a clever lie.
ORGON: I've told you, I was there and saw it done.
MADAME PERNELLE: Ah, slanderers will stop at nothing, Son.
ORGON: Mother, I'll lose my temper . . . For the last time,
    I tell you I was witness to the crime.
MADAME PERNELLE: The tongues of spite are busy night and noon,
    And to their venom no man is immune.
ORGON: You're talking nonsense. Can't you realize
    I saw it; saw it; saw it with my eyes?
    Saw, do you understand me? Must I shout it
    Into your ears before you'll cease to doubt it?
MADAME PERNELLE: Appearances can deceive, my son. Dear me,
    We cannot always judge by what we see.
ORGON: Drat! Drat!
MADAME PERNELLE: One often interprets things awry;
    Good can seem evil to a suspicious eye.
ORGON: Was I to see his pawing at Elmire
    As an act of charity?
MADAME PERNELLE: Till his guilt is clear
    A man deserves the benefit of the doubt.
    You should have waited, to see how things turned out.

ORGON: Great God in Heaven, what more proof did I need?
　　　Was I to sit there, watching, until he'd . . .
　　　You drive me to the brink of impropriety.
MADAME PERNELLE: No, no, a man of such surpassing piety
　　　Could not do such a thing. You cannot shake me.
　　　I don't believe it, and you shall not make me.
ORGON: You vex me so that, if you weren't my mother,
　　　I'd say to you . . . some dreadful thing or other.
DORINE: It's your turn now, Sir, not to be listened to;
　　　You'd not trust us, and now she won't trust you.
CLÉANTE: My friends, we're wasting time which should be spent
　　　In facing up to our predicament.
　　　I fear that scoundrel's threats weren't made in sport.
DAMIS: Do you think he'd have the nerve to go to court?
ELMIRE: I'm sure he won't: they'd find it all too crude
　　　A case of swindling and ingratitude.
CLÉANTE: Don't be too sure. He won't be at a loss
　　　To give his claims a high and righteous gloss;
　　　And clever rogues with far less valid cause
　　　Have trapped their victims in a web of laws.
　　　I say again that to antagonize
　　　A man so strongly armed was most unwise.
ORGON: I know it; but the man's appalling cheek
　　　Outraged me so, I couldn't control my pique.
CLÉANTE: I wish to Heaven that we could devise
　　　Some truce between you, or some compromise.
ELMIRE: If I had known what cards he held, I'd not
　　　Have roused his anger by my little plot.
ORGON: [*to* DORINE, *as* M. LOYAL *enters*] What is that fellow looking for? Who
　　　is he?
Go talk to him—and tell him that I'm busy.

SCENE IV

MONSIEUR LOYAL: Good day, dear sister. Kindly let me see
　　　Your master.
DORINE: He's involved with company,
　　　And cannot be disturbed just now, I fear.
MONSIEUR LOYAL: I hate to intrude; but what has brought me here
　　　Will not disturb your master, in any event.
　　　Indeed, my news will make him most content.
DORINE: Your name?
MONSIEUR LOYAL: Just say that I bring greetings from
　　　Monsieur Tartuffe, on whose behalf I've come.
DORINE: [*to* ORGON] Sir, he's a very gracious man, and bears
　　　A message from Tartuffe, which, he declares,
　　　Will make you most content.
CLÉANTE: Upon my word,

I think this man had best be seen, and heard.
ORGON: Perhaps he has some settlement to suggest.
    How shall I treat him? What manner would be best?
CLÉANTE: Control your anger, and if he should mention
    Some fair adjustment, give him your full attention.
MONSIEUR LOYAL: Good health to you, good Sir. May Heaven confound
    Your enemies, and may your joys abound.
ORGON: [*aside, to* CLÉANTE] A gentle salutation: it confirms
    My guess that he is here to offer terms.
MONSIEUR LOYAL: I've always held your family most dear;
    I served your father, Sir, for many a year.
ORGON: Sir, I must ask your pardon; to my shame,
    I cannot now recall your face or name.
MONSIEUR LOYAL: Loyal's my name; I come from Normandy,
    And I'm a bailiff, in all modesty.
    For forty years, praise God, it's been my boast
    To serve with honor in that vital post,
    And I am here, Sir, if you will permit
    The liberty, to serve you with this writ . . .
ORGON: To—*what?*
MONSIEUR LOYAL: Now, please, Sir, let us have no friction:
    It's nothing but an order of eviction.
    You are to move your goods and family out
    And make way for new occupants, without
    Deferment or delay, and give the keys . . .
ORGON: I? Leave this house?
MONSIEUR LOYAL: Why yes, Sir, if you please.
    This house, Sir, from the cellar to the roof,
    Belongs now to the good Monsieur Tartuffe,
    And he is lord and master of your estate
    By virtue of a deed of present date,
    Drawn in due form, with clearest legal phrasing . . .
DAMIS: Your insolence is utterly amazing!
MONSIEUR LOYAL: Young man, my business here is not with you,
    But with your wise and temperate father, who,
    Like every worthy citizen, stands in awe
    Of justice, and would never obstruct the law.
ORGON: But . . .
MONSIEUR LOYAL: Not for a million, Sir, would you rebel
    Against authority; I know that well.
    You'll not make trouble, Sir, or interfere
    With the execution of my duties here.
DAMIS: Someone may execute a smart tattoo
    On that black jacket of yours, before you're through.
MONSIEUR LOYAL: Sir, bid your son be silent. I'd much regret
    Having to mention such a nasty threat
    Of violence, in writing my report.
DORINE: [*aside*] This man Loyal's a most disloyal sort!

MONSIEUR LOYAL: I love all men of upright character,
      And when I agreed to serve these papers, Sir,
      It was your feelings that I had in mind.
      I couldn't bear to see the case assigned
      To someone else, who might esteem you less
      And so subject you to unpleasantness.
ORGON: What's more unpleasant than telling a man to leave
      His house and home?
MONSIEUR LOYAL: You'd like a short reprieve?
      If you desire it, Sir, I shall not press you,
      But wait until tomorrow to dispossess you.
      Splendid. I'll come and spend the night here, then,
      Most quietly, with half a score of men.
      For form's sake, you might bring me, just before
      You go to bed, the keys to the front door.
      My men, I promise, will be on their best
      Behavior, and will not disturb your rest.
      But bright and early, Sir, you must be quick
      And move out all your furniture, every stick:
      The men I've chosen are both young and strong,
      And with their help it shouldn't take you long.
      In short, I'll make things pleasant and convenient,
      And since I'm being so extremely lenient,
      Please show me, Sir, a like consideration,
      And give me your entire cooperation.
ORGON: [*aside*] I may be all but bankrupt, but I vow
      I'd give a hundred louis, here and now,
      Just for the pleasure of landing one good clout
      Right on the end of that complacent snout.
CLÉANTE: Careful; don't make things worse.
DAMIS: My bootsole itches
      To give that beggar a good kick in the breeches.
DORINE: Monsieur Loyal, I'd love to hear the whack
      Of a stout stick across your fine broad back.
MONSIEUR LOYAL: Take care: a woman, too, may go to jail if
      She uses threatening language to a bailiff.
CLÉANTE: Enough, enough, Sir. This must not go on.
      Give me that paper, please, and then begone.
MONSIEUR LOYAL: Well, *au revoir.* God give you all good cheer!
ORGON: May God confound you, and him who sent you here!

SCENE V

ORGON: Now, Mother, was I right or not? This writ
      Should change your notion of Tartuffe a bit.
      Do you perceive his villainy at last?
MADAME PERNELLE: I'm thunderstruck. I'm utterly aghast.

DORINE: Oh, come, be fair. You mustn't take offense
   At this new proof of his benevolence.
   He's acting out of selfless love, I know.
   Material things enslave the soul, and so
   He kindly has arranged your liberation
   From all that might endanger your salvation.
ORGON: Will you not ever hold your tongue, you dunce?
CLÉANTE: Come, you must take some action, and at once.
ELMIRE: Go tell the world of the low trick he's tried.
   The deed of gift is surely nullified
   By such behavior, and public rage will not
   Permit the wretch to carry out his plot.

SCENE VI

VALÈRE: Sir, though I hate to bring you more bad news,
   Such is the danger that I cannot choose.
   A friend who is extremely close to me
   And knows my interest in your family
   Has, for my sake, presumed to violate
   The secrecy that's due to things of state,
   And sends me word that you are in a plight
   From which your salvation lies in flight.
   That scoundrel who's imposed upon you so
   Denounced you to the King an hour ago
   And, as supporting evidence, displayed
   The strong-box of a certain renegade
   Whose secret papers, so he testified,
   You had disloyally agreed to hide.
   I don't know just what charges may be pressed,
   But there's a warrant out for your arrest;
   Tartuffe has been instructed, furthermore,
   To guide the arresting officer to your door.
CLÉANTE: He's clearly done this to facilitate
   His seizure of your house and your estate.
ORGON: That man, I must say, is a vicious beast!
VALÈRE: Quick, Sir; you mustn't tarry in the least.
   My carriage is outside, to take you hence;
   This thousand louis should cover all expense.
   Let's lose no time, or you shall be undone;
   The sole defense, in this case, is to run.
   I shall go with you all the way, and place you
   In a safe refuge to which they'll never trace you.
ORGON: Alas, dear boy, I wish that I could show you
   My gratitude for everything I owe you.
   But now is not the time; I pray the Lord
   That I may live to give you your reward.
   Farewell, my dears; be careful . . .

CLÉANTE: Brother, hurry.
>   We shall take care of things; you needn't worry.

SCENE VII

TARTUFFE: Gently, Sir, gently; stay right where you are.
>   No need for haste; your lodging isn't far.
>   You're off to prison, by order of the Prince.
ORGON: This is the crowning blow, you wretch; and since
>   It means my total ruin and defeat,
>   Your villainy is now at last complete.
TARTUFFE: You needn't try to provoke me; it's no use.
>   Those who serve Heaven must expect abuse.
CLÉANTE: You are indeed most patient, sweet, and blameless.
DORINE: How he exploits the name of Heaven! It's shameless.
TARTUFFE: Your taunts and mockeries are all for naught;
>   To do my duty is my only thought.
MARIANE: Your love of duty is most meritorious,
>   And what you've done is little short of glorious.
TARTUFFE: All deeds are glorious, Madam, which obey
>   The sovereign Prince who sent me here today.
ORGON: I rescued you when you were destitute;
>   Have you forgotten that, you thankless brute?
TARTUFFE: No, no, I well remember everything;
>   But my first duty is to serve my King.
>   That obligation is so paramount
>   That other claims, beside it, do not count;
>   And for it I would sacrifice my wife,
>   My family, my friend, or my life.
ELMIRE: Hypocrite!
DORINE: All that we most revere, he uses
>   To cloak his plots and camouflage his ruses.
CLÉANTE: If it is true that you are animated
>   By pure and loyal zeal, as you have stated,
>   Why was this zeal not roused until you'd sought
>   To make Orgon a cuckold, and been caught?
>   Why weren't you moved to give your evidence
>   Until your outraged host had driven you hence?
>   I shan't say that the gift of all his treasure
>   Ought to have damped your zeal in any measure;
>   But if he is a traitor, as you declare,
>   How could you condescend to be his heir?
TARTUFFE: [*to the* OFFICER] Sir, spare me all this clamor; it's growing shrill.
>   Please carry out your orders, if you will.
OFFICER: Yes, I've delayed too long, Sir. Thank you kindly.
>   You're just the proper person to remind me.
>   Come, you are off to join the other boarders
>   In the King's prison, according to his orders.

TARTUFFE: Who? I, Sir?

OFFICER: Yes.

TARTUFFE: To prison? This can't be true!

OFFICER: I owe an explanation, but not to you.
    [*to* ORGON] Sir, all is well; rest easy, and be grateful.
We serve a Prince to whom all sham is hateful,
A Prince who sees into our inmost hearts,
And can't be fooled by any trickster's arts.
His royal soul, though generous and human,
Views all things with discernment and acumen;
His sovereign reason is not lightly swayed,
And all his judgments are discreetly weighed.
He honors righteous men of every kind,
And yet his zeal for virtue is not blind,
Nor does his love of piety numb his wits
And make him tolerant of hypocrites.
'Twas hardly likely that this man could cozen
A King who's foiled such liars by the dozen.
With one keen glance, the King perceived the whole
Perverseness and corruption of his soul,
And thus high Heaven's justice was displayed:
Betraying you, the rogue stood self-betrayed.
The King soon recognized Tartuffe as one
Notorious by another name, who'd done
So many vicious crimes that one could fill
Ten volumes with them, and be writing still.
But to be brief: our sovereign was appalled
By this man's treachery toward you, which he called
The last, worst villainy of a vile career,
And bade me follow the impostor here
To see how gross his impudence could be,
And force him to restore your property.
Your private papers, by the King's command,
I hereby seize and give into your hand.
The King, by royal order, invalidates
The deed which gave this rascal your estates,
And pardons, furthermore, your grave offense
In harboring an exile's documents.
By these decrees, our Prince rewards you for
Your loyal deeds in the late civil war,
And shows how heartfelt is his satisfaction
In recompensing any worthy action,
How much he prizes merit, and how he makes
More of men's virtues than of their mistakes.

DORINE: Heaven be praised!

MADAME PERNELLE: I breathe again, at last.

ELMIRE: We're safe.

MARIANE: I can't believe the danger's past.

ORGON: [*to* TARTUFFE] Well, traitor, now you see . . .
CLÉANTE: Ah, Brother, please,
      Let's not descend to such indignities.
      Leave the poor wretch to his unhappy fate,
      And don't say anything to aggravate
      His present woes; but rather hope that he
      Will soon embrace an honest piety,
      And mend his ways, and by a true repentance
      Move our just King to moderate his sentence.
      Meanwhile, go kneel before your sovereign's throne
      And thank him for the mercies he has shown.
ORGON: Well said: let's go at once and, gladly kneeling,
      Express the gratitude which all are feeling.
      Then, when that first great duty has been done,
      We'll turn with pleasure to a second one,
      And give Valère, whose love has proven so true,
      The wedded happiness which is his due.

Henrik Ibsen (1828–1906)

A Doll's House (1879)

Ibsen's early plays (beginning in 1850) were poetic dramas about Norwegian legend or history. In the 1870s, he deliberately abandoned his earlier approach to write prose plays about contemporary life. *A Doll's House* and *Ghosts* made Ibsen the most controversial playwright in Europe, for the former was thought to attack the institution of marriage and the family, and the latter brought the taboo subject of venereal disease to the stage. Ibsen's prose plays were thought to epitomize realism, a new movement then under way. Subsequently, his prose works were said to have initiated the modern drama.

Undergirding *A Doll's House* is the basic assumption that character and action are determined by hereditary and environmental forces. What each character is and does is explained by information about background, upbringing, and experience. During the course of the action, we learn enough about all the characters to understand how they have arrived at where they are. Ibsen could have made his play melodramatic by depicting Krogstad as villain and Nora as persecuted heroine. Instead, all of the characters strive for what they consider right. Thus instead of a type, each character appears to be a complex, fallible human being.

A Doll's House is usually read today as a play about the status of women in the late nineteenth century. It pleases Torvald to think of Nora as incapable of making decisions, even about what she should wear to a party. The play also shows that women were legally reduced to the state of childhood (or doll) because a wife was required to have her husband's consent in almost all matters, whereas her husband could act wholly independently, even disposing of property originally hers without her consent or knowledge. At the end of the play, Nora's alienation is not only from her husband but also from society in general. She chooses to leave her husband and children because, finding herself in disagreement with both law and public opinion and not yet certain of her own convictions, she does not believe herself ready to meet her responsibilities as a wife and mother. It was this ending that made the play so controversial, for it challenged the status quo.

A Doll's House could serve as a model of cause-to-effect dramatic structure. The first act sets up masterfully and with seeming naturalness all of the conditions out of which the subsequent action grows logically and seemingly inexorably.

Henrik Ibsen

A Doll's House

Translated by William Archer (with emendations by Oscar G. Brockett)

CHARACTERS

TORVALD HELMER
NORA, *his wife*
DOCTOR RANK
MRS. LINDE
NILS KROGSTAD
THE HELMERS' THREE YOUNG CHILDREN
ANNE, *their nurse*
A HOUSEMAID
A PORTER

The action of the play takes place in the Helmers' house.

ACT I

SCENE————*A room furnished comfortably and tastefully but not extravagantly. At the back, a door to the right leads to the entrance-hall, another to the left leads to* HELMER's *study. Between the doors stands a piano. In the middle of the left-hand wall is a door, and beyond it a window. Near the window are a round table, armchairs, and a small sofa. In the right-hand wall, at the farther end, another door; and on the same side, nearer the footlights, a stove, two easy chairs, and a rocking chair; between the stove and the door, a small table. Engravings on the walls; a cabinet with china and other small objects; a small book-case with well-bound books. The floors are carpeted, and a fire burns in the stove. It is winter.*

A bell rings in the hall; shortly afterwards the door is heard to open. Enter NORA, *humming a tune and in high spirits. She is in out-door dress and carries a number of parcels; these she lays on the table to the right. She leaves the outer door open after her, and through it is seen a* PORTER *who is carrying a Christmas tree and a basket, which he gives to the* MAID, *who has opened the door.*

NORA: Hide the Christmas tree carefully, Helen. Be sure the children don't see it till this evening, when it is trimmed [*to the* PORTER *taking out her purse*] How much?

PORTER: A half-crown.

NORA: There's a crown. No, keep the change. [*The* PORTER *thanks her, and goes out.* NORA *shuts the door. She is laughing to herself, as she takes off her hat and coat. She takes a packet of macaroons from her pocket and eats one or two; then goes cautiously to her husband's door and listens*] Yes, he is in. [*Still humming, she goes to the table on the right.*]

HELMER: [*calls out from his room*] Is that my little lark twittering out there?

NORA: [*busy opening some of the parcels*] Yes, it is!

HELMER: Is it my little squirrel bustling about?

NORA: Yes!

HELMER: When did my squirrel come home?

NORA: Just now. [*puts the bag of macaroons into her pocket and wipes her mouth*] Come in here, Torvald, and see what I have bought.

HELMER: Don't disturb me. [*A little later he opens the door and looks into the room, pen in hand*] Bought, did you say? All these things? Has my little spend-thrift been wasting money again?

NORA: Yes, but, Torvald, this year we really can let ourselves go a little. This is the first Christmas that we have not needed to economise.

HELMER: Still, you know, we can't spend money recklessly.

NORA: Yes, Torvald, we may be a wee bit more reckless now, mayn't we? Just a tiny wee bit! You are going to have a big salary and earn lots and lots of money.

HELMER: Yes, after the New Year; but then it will be a whole quarter before the salary is due.

NORA: Pooh! We can borrow till then.

HELMER: Nora! [*goes up to her and takes her playfully by the ear*] The same little featherhead! Suppose, now, that I borrowed one thousand crowns to-day, and you spent it all in the Christmas week, and then on New Year's Eve a roof tile fell on my head and killed me, and—

NORA: [*putting her hands over his mouth*] Oh! don't say such horrid things.

HELMER: Still, suppose that happened—what then?

NORA: If that were to happen, I don't suppose I should care whether I owed money or not.

HELMER: Yes, but what about the people who had lent it?

NORA: They? Who would care about them? I wouldn't know who they were.

HELMER: How like a woman! But seriously, Nora, you know what I think about that. No debt, no borrowing. There can be no freedom or beauty about a home that depends on borrowing and debt. We two have kept bravely on the straight road so far, and we will go on the same way for the short time left.

NORA: [*moving towards the stove*] As you please, Torvald.

HELMER: [*following her*] Come, come, my little skylark must not droop her wings. What is this! Is my little squirrel sulking? [*taking out his purse*] Nora, what do you think I've got here?

NORA: [*turning round quickly*] Money!

HELMER: There you are. [*gives her some money*] Do you think I don't know what a lot is needed for housekeeping at Christmas-time?

NORA: [*counting*] One-two-three! Thank you, thank you, Torvald; that will keep me going for a long time.

HELMER: Indeed it must.

NORA: Yes, yes, it will. But come here and let me show you what I have bought. And all so cheap! Look, here is a new suit for Ivar, and a sword; and a horse and trumpet for Bob; and a doll and a doll's bed for Emmy—they are very plain, but anyway she'll soon break them. And here are dress materials and handkerchiefs for the maids; old Anne ought really to have something better.

HELMER: And what is in this parcel?

NORA: [*crying out*] No, no! You mustn't see that till this evening.

HELMER: Very well. But now tell me, you extravagant little person, what would you like for yourself?

NORA: For myself? Oh, I'm sure I don't want anything.

HELMER: Yes, but you must. Tell me something reasonable that you would particularly like to have.

NORA: No, I really can't think of anything—unless, Torvald—

HELMER: Well?

NORA: [*playing with his coat buttons, and without raising her eyes to his*] if you really want to give me something, you might—you might—

HELMER: Well, out with it!

NORA: [*speaking quickly*] You might give me money, Torvald. Only just as much as you can afford; and then one of these days I will buy something with it.

HELMER: But, Nora—

NORA: Oh, do! dear Torvald; please, please do! Then I will wrap it up in beautiful gold paper and hang it on the Christmas tree. Wouldn't that be fun?

HELMER: What are little people called that are always wasting money?

NORA: Spendthrifts—I know. Let's do what you suggest, Torvald, and then I shall have time to think what I need most. That is a very sensible plan, isn't it?

HELMER: [*smiling*] Indeed it is—that is to say, if you were really to save out of the money I give you, and then really buy something for yourself. But if you spend it all on the housekeeping and any number of unnecessary things, then I merely have to pay up again.

NORA: Oh but, Torvald—

HELMER: You can't deny it, my dear little Nora. [*puts his arm around her waist*] It's a sweet little spendthrift, but she uses up a lot of money. One would hardly believe how expensive such little persons are!

NORA: It's a shame to say that. I do really save all I can.

HELMER: [*laughing*] That's very true—all you can. But you can't save anything!

NORA: [*smiling quietly and happily*] You haven't any idea how many expenses we skylarks and squirrels have, Torvald.

HELMER: You are an odd little soul. Very like your father. You always find some new way of wheedling money out of me, and, as soon as you have got it, it seems to melt in your hands. You never know where it has gone. Still, one must take you as you are. It is in the blood; for indeed it is true that you can inherit these things, Nora.

NORA: Ah, I wish I had inherited many of papa's qualities.

HELMER: And I would not wish you to be anything but just what you are, my sweet little skylark. But, do you know, it strikes me that you are looking rather—what shall I say—rather guilty to-day?

NORA: Do I?

HELMER: You do, really. Look straight at me.

NORA: [*looks at him*] Well?

HELMER: [*wagging his finger at her*] Hasn't Miss Sweet-Tooth been breaking rules in town to-day?

NORA: No; what makes you think that?

HELMER: Hasn't she paid a visit to the pastry shop?

NORA: No, I assure you, Torvald—

HELMER: Not been nibbling sweets?

NORA: No, certainly not.

HELMER: Not even taken a bite at a macaroon or two?

NORA: No, Torvald, I assure you really—

HELMER: There, there, of course I was only joking.

NORA: [*going to the table on the right*] I wouldn't think of going against your wishes.

HELMER: No, I am sure of that; besides, you gave me your word—[*going up to her*] Keep your little Christmas secrets to yourself, my darling. They will all be revealed to-night when the Christmas tree is lit, no doubt.

NORA: Did you remember to invite Doctor Rank?

HELMER: No. But there is no need; he will come to dinner with us as he always does. However, I will ask him when he comes in this morning. I have ordered some good wine. Nora, you can't think how I am looking forward to this evening.

NORA: So am I! And how the children will enjoy themselves, Torvald!

HELMER: It is splendid to feel that one has a secure job and a big enough income. It's delightful to think of, isn't it?

NORA: It's wonderful.

HELMER: Do you remember last Christmas? For a full three weeks beforehand you shut yourself up every evening till long after midnight, making ornaments for the Christmas tree and all the other fine things that were to be a surprise to us. It was the dullest three weeks I ever spent!

NORA: I didn't find it dull.

HELMER: [*smiling*] But there was precious little to show for it, Nora.

NORA: Oh, you shouldn't tease me about that again. How could I help the cat's getting in and tearing everything to pieces?

HELMER: Of course you couldn't, poor little girl. You had the best of intentions to please us all, and that's the main thing. But it is a good thing that our hard times are over.

NORA: Yes, it is really wonderful.

HELMER: This time I needn't be all alone and bored and you needn't ruin your dear eyes and your pretty little hands—

NORA: [*clapping her hands*] No, Torvald, I don't have to any longer, do I! It's wonderful to hear you say so! [*taking his arm*] Now I will tell you how I have been thinking we ought to arrange things, Torvald. As soon as Christmas is over—[*A bell rings in the hall.*] There's the doorbell. [*She tidies the room a little.*] There's someone at the door. What a nuisance!

HELMER: If it is a caller, remember I am not at home.

MAID: [*in the doorway*] A lady to see you, ma'am—a stranger.

NORA: Ask her to come in.

MAID: [*to* HELMER] The doctor came at the same time, sir.

HELMER: Did he go straight into my study?

MAID: Yes, sir.

> [HELMER *goes into his room. The* MAID *ushers in* MRS. LINDE, *who is in travelling clothes and shuts the door.*]

MRS. LINDE: [*in a dejected and timid voice*] How do you do, Nora?

NORA: [*doubtfully*] How do you do—

MRS. LINDE: You don't recognise me, I suppose.

NORA: No, I'm afraid—yes, to be sure, I seem to—[*suddenly*] Yes! Christine! Is it really you?

MRS. LINDE: Yes, it is I.

NORA: Christine! To think of my not recognising you! And yet how could I—[*in a gentle voice*] How you've changed, Christine!

MRS. LINDE: Yes, I have indeed. In nine, ten long years—

NORA: Is it so long since we met? I suppose it is. The last eight years have been a happy time for me, I can tell you. And so now you have come into town, and have taken this long journey in winter—that was brave of you.

MRS. LINDE: I arrived by boat this morning.

NORA: To have some fun at Christmas-time, of course. How delightful! We will have such fun together! But take off your things. You are not cold, I hope. [*helps her*] Now we will sit down by the stove, and be comfortable. No, take this armchair; I will sit here in the rocking chair. [*takes her hands*] Now you look like your old self again; it was only the first moment—You are a little paler, Christine, and perhaps a little thinner.

MRS. LINDE: And much, much older, Nora.

NORA: Perhaps a little older; very, very little; certainly not much. [*stops suddenly and speaks seriously*] What a thoughtless creature I am, chattering away like this. My poor, dear Christine, do forgive me.

MRS. LINDE: What do you mean, Nora?

NORA: [*gently*] Poor Christine, you are a widow.

MRS. LINDE: Yes; it is three years ago now.

NORA: Yes, I know; I saw it in the papers. I assure you, Christine, I meant to write to you at the time, but I always put it off and something always prevented me.

MRS. LINDE: I quite understand, dear.

NORA: It was very bad of me, Christine. Poor thing, how you must have suffered. And he left you nothing?

MRS. LINDE: No.

NORA: And no children?

MRS. LINDE: No.

NORA: Nothing at all, then?

MRS. LINDE: Not even sorrow or grief to live upon.

NORA: [*looking incredulously at her*] But, Christine, is that possible?

MRS. LINDE: [*smiles sadly and strokes her hair*] It sometimes happens, Nora.

NORA: So you are quite alone. How dreadfully sad that must be. I have three lovely children. You can't see them just now, for they are out with their nurse. But now you must tell me everything.

MRS. LINDE: No, no; I want to hear about you.

NORA: No, you must begin. I mustn't be selfish to-day; to-day I must only think of your affairs. But there is one thing I must tell you. Have you heard about our great piece of good luck?

MRS. LINDE: No, what is it?

NORA: Just imagine, my husband has been made manager of the Bank!

MRS. LINDE: Your husband? What good luck!

NORA: Yes, tremendous! A lawyer's profession is such an uncertain thing, especially if he won't undertake unsavoury cases; and naturally Torvald has never been willing to do that, and I quite agree with him. You may imagine how pleased we are! He'll begin his job in the Bank at the New Year, and then he'll have a big salary and lots of commissions. For the future we can live quite differently—we can do just as we like. I feel so relieved and so happy, Christine! It will be splendid to have heaps of money and not need to have any anxiety, won't it?

MRS. LINDE: Yes, anyhow I think it would be delightful to have what one needs.

NORA: No, not only what one needs, but heaps and heaps of money.

MRS. LINDE: [*smiling*] Nora, Nora, haven't you learnt sense yet? In our schooldays you were a great spendthrift.

NORA: [*laughing*] Yes, that is what Torvald says now. [*wags her finger at her*] But "Nora, Nora" isn't so silly as you think. We have not been in a position for me to waste money. We have both had to work.

MRS. LINDE: You, too!

NORA: Yes; odds and ends, needlework, crochetings, embroidery, and that kind of thing. [*dropping her voice*] And other things as well. You know Torvald left his office when we were married? There was no prospect of promotion there, and he had to try and earn more than before. But during the first year he overworked himself dreadfully. You see, he had to make money every way he could, and he worked early and late; but he couldn't stand it, and fell dreadfully ill, and the doctors said it was necessary for him to go south.

MRS. LINDE: You spent a whole year in Italy, didn't you?

NORA: Yes. It was no easy matter to get away, I can tell you. It was just after Ivar was born; but naturally we had to go. It was a wonderfully beautiful trip and it saved Torvald's life. But it cost a tremendous lot of money, Christine.

MRS. LINDE: So I should think.

NORA: It cost about forty-eight hundred crowns. That's a lot, isn't it?

MRS. LINDE: Yes, and in emergencies like that it is lucky to have the money.

NORA: We got the money from papa.

MRS. LINDE: Oh, I see. It was just about that time that he died, wasn't it?

NORA: Yes; and just think of it, I couldn't go and nurse him. I was expecting little Ivar's birth every day and I had my poor sick Torvald to look after. My dear, kind father—I never saw him again, Christine. That was the saddest time I have known since our marriage.

MRS. LINDE: I know how fond you were of him. And then you went off to Italy?

NORA: Yes; you see, we had money then, and the doctors insisted on our going, so we started a month later.

MRS. LINDE: And your husband came back quite well?

NORA: As sound as a bell!

MRS. LINDE: But—the doctor?

NORA: What doctor?

MRS. LINDE: I thought your maid said the gentleman who arrived here just as I
did, was the doctor?

NORA: Yes, that was Doctor Rank, but he doesn't come here professionally. He is
our closest friend, and comes in at least once every day. No, Torvald has not
had an hour's illness since then, and our children are strong and healthy and
so am I. [*jumps up and claps her hands*] Christine! Christine! it's good to be
alive and happy!—But how horrid of me; I am talking of nothing but
my own affairs. [*sits on a stool near her, and rests her arms on her knees*] You
mustn't be angry with me. Tell me, is it really true that you did not love your
husband? Why did you marry him?

MRS. LINDE: My mother was alive then, and was bedridden and helpless, and I
had to provide for my two younger brothers; so I didn't think I was justified
in refusing his offer.

NORA: No, perhaps you were quite right. He was rich at that time, then?

MRS. LINDE: I believe he was quite well off. But his business was a precarious one;
and, when he died, it all went to pieces and there was nothing left.

NORA: And then?—

MRS. LINDE: Well, I had to turn my hand to anything I could find—first a small
shop, then a small school, and so on. The last three years have seemed like
one long working-day, with no rest. Now it is at an end, Nora. My poor
mother needs me no more, for she is gone; and the boys don't need me either; they have got jobs and can shift for themselves.

NORA: What a relief you must feel—

MRS. LINDE: No, indeed; I only feel my life unspeakably empty. No one to live for
any more. [*gets up restlessly*] That was why I could not stand the life in my
little backwater any longer. I hope it may be easier here to find something
which will busy me and occupy my thoughts. If only I could have the good
luck to get some regular work—office work of some kind—

NORA: But, Christine, that is so frightfully tiring, and you look tired out now. You
had far better go away to some watering-place.

MRS. LINDE: [*walking to the window*] I have no father to give me money for a
journey, Nora.

NORA: [*rising*] Oh, don't be angry with me.

MRS. LINDE: [*going up to her*] It is you that mustn't be angry with me, dear. The
worst of a position like mine is that it makes one so bitter. No one to work
for, and yet obliged to be always on the look-out for chances. One must live,
and so one becomes selfish. When you told me of the happy turn your fortunes have taken—you will hardly believe it—I was delighted not so much
on your account as on my own.

NORA: How do you mean?—Oh, I understand. You mean that perhaps Torvald
could get you something to do.

MRS. LINDE: Yes, that was what I was thinking of.

NORA: He must, Christine. Just leave it to me; I will broach the subject very clev-
erly—I will think of something that will please him very much. It will make
me so happy to be of some use to you.

MRS. LINDE: How kind you are, Nora, to be so anxious to help me! It is doubly kind in you, for you know so little of the burdens and troubles of life.

NORA: I—? I know so little of them?

MRS. LINDE: [*smiling*] My dear! Small household cares and that sort of thing! You are a child, Nora.

NORA: [*tosses her head and crosses the stage*] You ought not to be so superior.

MRS. LINDE: No!

NORA: You are just like the others. They all think that I am incapable of anything really serious—

MRS. LINDE: Come, come—

NORA: —that I have gone through nothing in this world of cares.

MRS. LINDE: But, my dear Nora, you have just told me all your troubles.

NORA: Pooh!—Those were trifles. [*lowering her voice*] I have not told you the important thing.

MRS. LINDE: The important thing! What do you mean?

NORA: You look down on me, Christine—but you shouldn't. You are proud, aren't you, of having worked so hard and so long for your mother?

MRS. LINDE: Indeed, I don't look down on any one. But it is true that I am proud and glad to think that I was privileged to make the end of my mother's life almost free from care.

NORA: And you are proud to think of what you have done for your brothers.

MRS. LINDE: I think I have the right to be.

NORA: I think so, too. But now, listen to this; I, too, have something to be proud and glad of.

MRS. LINDE: I have no doubt you have. But what do you refer to?

NORA: Speak low. Suppose Torvald were to hear! He mustn't on any account—no one in the world must know, Christine, except you.

MRS. LINDE: But what is it?

NORA: Come here. [*pulls her down on the sofa beside her*] Now I'll show you that I also have something to be proud and glad of. It was I who saved Torvald's life.

MRS. LINDE: "Saved"? How?

NORA: I told you about our trip to Italy. Torvald would never have recovered if he had not gone there—

MRS. LINDE: Yes, but your father gave you the necessary funds.

NORA: [*smiling*] Yes, that is what Torvald and all the others think, but—

MRS. LINDE: But—

NORA: Papa didn't give us a crown. It was I who procured the money.

MRS. LINDE: You? All that large sum?

NORA: Forty-eight hundred crowns. What do you think of that?

MRS. LINDE: But, Nora, how could you possibly do it? Did you win a prize in the Lottery?

NORA: [*contemptuously*] In the Lottery? There would have been no credit in that.

MRS. LINDE: But where did you get it then?

NORA: [*humming and smiling with an air of mystery*] Hm, hm! Aha!

MRS. LINDE: Because you couldn't have borrowed it.

NORA: Couldn't I? Why not?

MRS. LINDE: No, a wife cannot borrow without her husband's consent.

NORA: [*tossing her head*] Oh, if it's a wife who has any head for business—a wife who has the wit to be a little bit clever—

MRS. LINDE: I don't understand it at all, Nora.

NORA: There is no need you should. I never said I had borrowed the money. I may have got it some other way. [*lies back on the sofa*] Perhaps I got it from some admirer. When you're as attractive as I am—

MRS. LINDE: You're mad.

NORA: Now, you know you're full of curiosity, Christine.

MRS. LINDE: Listen to me, Nora dear. Haven't you been a little bit foolish?

NORA: [*sits up straight*] Is it foolish to save your husband's life?

MRS. LINDE: It seems to me foolish without his knowledge, to—

NORA: But it was absolutely necessary that he not know! My goodness, can't you understand that? It was necessary he should have no idea what a dangerous condition he was in. It was to me that the doctors came and said that his life was in danger, and that the only thing to save him was to live in the south. Do you suppose I didn't try, first of all, to get what I wanted as if it were for myself? I told him how much I should love to travel abroad like other young wives; I tried tears and entreaties with him; I told him that he ought to remember the condition I was in, and that he ought to be kind and indulgent to me; I even hinted that he might raise a loan. That nearly made him angry, Christine. He said I was thoughtless, and that it was his duty as my husband not to indulge me in my whims and caprices—as I believe he called them. Very well, I thought, you must be saved—and that was how I came to devise a way out of the difficulty—

MRS. LINDE: And did your husband never find out from your father that the money hadn't come from him?

NORA: No, never. Papa died just at that time. I had meant to let him into the secret and beg him never to reveal it. But he was so ill then—unfortunately there was no need to tell him.

MRS. LINDE: And since then have you never told your secret to your husband?

NORA: Good Heavens, no! How could you think that? A man who has such strong opinions about these things! And besides, how painful and humiliating it would be for Torvald, with his male pride, to know that he owed me anything! It would upset our relationship altogether; our beautiful happy home would no longer be the same.

MRS. LINDE: Do you mean never to tell him about it?

NORA: [*meditatively, and with a half smile*] Yes—some day, perhaps, after many years, when I'm no longer as attractive as I am now. Don't laugh at me! I mean, of course, when Torvald is no longer as devoted to me as he is now; when my dancing and dressing-up and reciting have palled on him; then it may be a good thing to have something in reserve—[*breaking off*] What nonsense! That time will never come. Now, what do you think of my great secret, Christine? Do you still think I am of no use? I can tell you, too, that this affair has caused me a lot of worry. It has been by no means easy for me to meet my payments punctually. I may tell you that there is something that is called, in business, quarterly interest, and another thing called payment in installments, and it is always so dreadfully difficult to manage them. I have had to save a little here and there, where I could, you understand. I have not been able to put aside much from my housekeeping money, for Torvald must have a good table. I couldn't let my children be shabbily dressed; I have felt obliged to use up all he gave me for them, the sweet little darlings!

MRS. LINDE: So it has all had to come out of your own expenses, poor Nora?

NORA: Of course. Besides, I was the one responsible for it. Whenever Torvald has given me money for new dresses and such things, I have never spent more than half of it; I have always bought the simplest and cheapest things. Thank Heaven, any clothes look good on me, and so Torvald has never noticed it. But it was often very hard on me, Christine—because it is delightful to be really well dressed, isn't it?

MRS. LINDE: Quite so.

NORA: Well, then I have found other ways of earning money. Last winter I was lucky enough to get a lot of copying to do; so I locked myself up and sat writing every evening until quite late at night. Many a time I was desperately tired; but all the same it was a tremendous pleasure to sit there working and earning money. It was like being a man.

MRS. LINDE: How much have you been able to pay off in that way?

NORA: I can't tell you exactly. You see, it is very difficult to keep an account of a business matter of that kind. I only know that I have paid every penny that I could scrape together. Many a time I was at my wits' end. [*smiles*] Then I used to sit here and imagine that a rich old gentleman had fallen in love with me—

MRS. LINDE: What! Who was it?

NORA: —that he had died; and that when his will was opened it contained, written in big letters, the instruction: "The lovely Mrs. Nora Helmer is to have all I possess paid over to her at once in cash."

MRS. LINDE: But, my dear Nora—who could the man be!

NORA: Good gracious, can't you understand? There was no old gentleman at all; it was only something that I used to sit here and imagine, when I couldn't think of any way of getting money. But it's all the same now; the tiresome old person can stay where he is, as far as I am concerned; I don't care about him or his will, either, for I am free from care now. [*jumps up*] My goodness, it's delightful to think of, Christine! Free from care! To be able to be free from care, quite free from care; to be able to play and romp with the children; to be able to keep the house beautifully and have everything just as Torvald likes it! And, think of it, soon the spring will come and the big blue sky! Perhaps we shall be able to take a little trip—perhaps I shall see the sea again! Oh, it's a wonderful thing to be alive and be happy. [*a bell is heard in the hall*]

MRS. LINDE: [*rising*] There's the doorbell; perhaps I had better go.

NORA: No, don't go; no one will come in here; it is sure to be for Torvald.

SERVANT: [*at the hall door*] Excuse me, ma'am—there is a gentleman to see the master, and as the doctor is with him—

NORA: Who is it?

KROGSTAD: [*at the door*] It is I, Mrs. Helmer. [MRS. LINDE *starts, trembles, and turns to the window.*]

NORA: [*takes a step towards him, and speaks in a strained, low voice*] You? What is it? What do you want to see my husband about?

KROGSTAD: Bank business—in a way. I have a small post in the Bank, and I hear your husband is to be our chief now—

NORA: Then it is—

KROGSTAD: Nothing but dry business matters, Mrs. Helmer; absolutely nothing else.

NORA: Be so good as to go into the study, then. [*She bows indifferently to him and shuts the door into the hall; then comes back and makes up the fire in the stove.*]

MRS. LINDE: Nora—who was that man?

NORA: A lawyer named Krogstad.

MRS. LINDE: Then it really was he.

NORA: Do you know the man?

MRS. LINDE: I used to—many years ago. At one time he was a solicitor's clerk in our town.

NORA: Yes, he was.

MRS. LINDE: He is greatly altered.

NORA: He made a very unhappy marriage.

MRS. LINDE: He is a widower now isn't he?

NORA: With several children. There now, it's burning. [*shuts the door of the stove and moves the rocking chair aside*]

MRS. LINDE: They say he carried on various kinds of business.

NORA: Really! Perhaps he does; I don't know anything about it. But don't let's think of business: it is so boring.

DOCTOR RANK: [*Comes out of* HELMER's *study. Before he shuts the door he calls to him.*] No, my dear fellow, I won't disturb you; I would rather go in to your wife for a little while. [*shuts the door and sees* MRS. LINDE] I beg your pardon; I'm afraid I'm disturbing you, too.

NORA: No, not at all. [*introducing him*] Doctor Rank, Mrs. Linde.

RANK: I have often heard Mrs. Linde's name mentioned here. I think I passed you on the stairs when I arrived, Mrs. Linde?

MRS. LINDE: Yes, I go up very slowly; I can't manage stairs well.

RANK: Ah! Some slight internal weakness?

MRS. LINDE: No, the fact is I have been overworking myself.

RANK: Nothing more than that? Then I suppose you have come to town to amuse yourself with our entertainments?

MRS. LINDE: I have come to look for work.

RANK: Is that a good cure for overwork?

MRS. LINDE: One must live, Doctor Rank.

RANK: Yes, the general opinion seems to be that it's necessary.

NORA: Look here, Doctor Rank—you know you want to live.

RANK: Certainly. However wretched I may feel, I want to prolong the agony as long as possible. All my patients are like that. And so are those who are morally sick—one of them, and a bad case, too, is at this very moment with Helmer—

MRS. LINDE: [*sadly*]. Ah!

NORA: Whom do you mean?

RANK: A lawyer, Krogstad, a fellow you don't know at all. He suffers from a diseased moral character, Mrs. Helmer; but even he began talking about it being highly important that he should live.

NORA: Did he? What did he want to speak to Torvald about?

RANK: I have no idea; I only heard that it was something about the Bank.

NORA: I didn't know this—what's his name—Krogstad had anything to do with the Bank.

RANK: Yes, he has some sort of appointment there. [*to* MRS. LINDE] I don't know whether you find also in your part of the world that there are certain people who go zealously sniffing about to smell out moral corruption, and, as soon as they have found some, put the person concerned into some lucrative position where they can keep their eye on him. Healthy natures are left out in the cold.

MRS. LINDE: Still I think the sick are those who most need taking care of.

RANK: [*shrugging his shoulders*] Yes, there you are. That is the sentiment that is turning Society into a hospital.

[NORA, *who has been absorbed in her thoughts, breaks out into smothered laughter and claps her hands.*]

RANK: Why do you laugh at that? Have you any notion what Society really is?

NORA: What do I care about tiresome Society? I am laughing at something quite different, something extremely amusing. Tell me, Doctor Rank, are all the people who are employed in the Bank dependent on Torvald now?

RANK: Is that what you find so extremely amusing?

NORA: [*smiling and humming*] That's my affair! [*walking about the room*] It's perfectly glorious to think that we have—that Torvald has so much power over so many people. [*takes the packet from her pocket*] Doctor Rank, what do you say to a macaroon?

RANK: What, macaroons? I thought they were forbidden here.

NORA: Yes, but these are some Christine gave me.

MRS. LINDE: What! I?

NORA: Oh, well, don't be alarmed! You couldn't know that Torvald had forbidden them. I must tell you that he's afraid they will spoil my teeth. But—once in a while—That's so, isn't it, Doctor Rank? Here [*puts a macaroon into his mouth*] you must have one, too, Christine. And I shall have one, just a little one—or at most two. [*walking about*] I am tremendously happy. There is just one thing in the world now that I should dearly love to do.

RANK: Well, what is that?

NORA: It's something I should dearly love to say so Torvald could hear me.

RANK: Well, why can't you say it?

NORA: No, I daren't; it's so shocking.

MRS. LINDE: Shocking?

RANK: Well, I should not advise you to say it. Still, with us you might. What is it you would so much like to say so Torvald could hear?

NORA: I should just love to say—Well, I'm damned!

RANK: Are you mad?

MRS. LINDE: Nora, dear—!

RANK: Say it, here he is!

NORA: [*hiding the packet*] Hush! Hush! Hush! [HELMER *comes out of his room, with his coat over his arm and his hat in his hand.*]

NORA: Well, Torvald dear, have you got rid of him?

HELMER: Yes, he's gone.

NORA: Let me introduce you—this is Christine, who has come to town.

HELMER: Christine—? Excuse me, but I don't know—

NORA: Mrs. Linde, dear; Christine Linde.

HELMER: Of course. A school friend of my wife, I presume?

MRS. LINDE: Yes, we've known each other since then.

NORA: And just think, she's taken a long journey in order to see you.

HELMER: What do you mean?

MRS. LINDE: No, really I—

NORA: Christine is tremendously clever at office work and she's frightfully anxious to work under some clever man, so as to improve—

HELMER: Very sensible, Mrs. Linde.

NORA: And when she heard you had been appointed manager of the Bank—the news was telegraphed, you know—she travelled here as quick as she could, Torvald, I'm sure you will be able to do something for Christine, for my sake, won't you?

HELMER: Well, it is not altogether impossible. I presume you are a widow, Mrs. Linde?

MRS. LINDE: Yes.

HELMER: And have had some experience of office work?

MRS. LINDE: Yes, a fair amount.

HELMER: Ah! well, it's very likely I may be able to find something for you.

NORA: [*clapping her hands*] What did I tell you? What did I tell you?

HELMER: You have just come at a fortunate moment, Mrs. Linde.

MRS. LINDE: How am I to thank you?

HELMER: There's no need. [*puts on his coat*] But to-day you must excuse me—

RANK: Wait a minute, I'll come with you. [*brings his fur coat from the hall and warms it at the fire*]

NORA: Don't be long away, Torvald dear.

HELMER: About an hour, not more.

NORA: Are you going, too, Christine?

MRS. LINDE: [*putting on her cloak*] Yes, I must go and look for a room.

HELMER: Oh, well then, we can walk together.

NORA: [*helping her*] What a pity it is we are so short of space here; I am afraid it is impossible for us—

MRS. LINDE: Please don't think of it! Good-bye, Nora dear, and many thanks.

NORA: Good-bye for the present. Of course you will come back this evening. And you, too, Doctor Rank. What do you say? If you are well enough? Oh, you must be! Wrap yourself up well. [*They go to the door all talking together. Children's voices are heard on the staircase.*]

NORA: There they are. There they are! [*She runs to open the door. The* NURSE *comes in with the children.*] Come in! Come in! [*stoops and kisses them*] Oh, you sweet blessings! Look at them, Christine! Aren't they darlings?

RANK: Don't let's stand here in the draught.

HELMER: Come along, Mrs. Linde; the place will only be bearable for a mother now! [RANK, HELMER, *and* MRS. LINDE *go downstairs. The* NURSE *comes forward with the children;* NORA *shuts the hall door.*]

NORA: How fresh and well you look! Such red cheeks!—like apples and roses. [*The children all talk at once while she speaks to them.*] Have you had great fun? That's splendid! What, you pulled both Emmy and Bob along on the sled?—both at once?—that *was* good. You are a clever boy, Ivar. Let me take her for a little, Anne. My sweet little baby doll! [*takes the baby from the* MAID *and dances it up and down*] Yes, yes, mother will dance with Bob, too. What! Have you been snowballing? I wish I had been there, too! No, no, I will take their things off, Anne; please let me do it, it's such fun. Go in now, you look half frozen. There's some hot coffee for you on the stove.

[*The* NURSE *goes into the room on the left.* NORA *takes off the children's things and throws them about, while they all talk to her at once.*]

NORA: Really! Did a big dog run after you? But it didn't bite you? No, dogs don't bite nice little dolly children. You mustn't look at the parcels, Ivar. What are they? Ah, I daresay you would like to know. No, no—it's something nasty! Come, let us have a game! What shall we play? Hide-and-Seek? Yes, we'll play Hide-and-Seek. Bob shall hide first. Must I hide? Very well, I'll hide first. [*She and the children laugh and shout, and romp in and out of the room; at last* NORA *hides under the table, the children rush in and look for her, but do not see her; they hear her smothered laughter, run to the table, lift up the cloth and find her. Shouts of laughter. She crawls forward and pretends to frighten them. Fresh laughter. Meanwhile there has been a knock at the hall door, but none of them has noticed it. The door is half opened, and* KROGSTAD *appears. He waits a little; the game goes on.*]

KROGSTAD: Excuse me, Mrs. Helmer.

NORA: [*with a stifled cry, turns round and gets up on to her knees*] Ah! What do you want?

KROGSTAD: Excuse me, the outer door was ajar; I suppose someone forgot to shut it.

NORA: [*rising*] My husband is out, Mr. Krogstad.

KROGSTAD: I know that.

NORA: What do you want here, then?

KROGSTAD: A word with you.

NORA: With me?—[*to the children, gently*] Go in to nurse. What? No, the strange man won't do mother any harm. When he's gone we will have another game. [*She takes the children into the room on the left, and shuts the door after them.*] You want to speak to me?

KROGSTAD: Yes, I do.

NORA: To-day? It is not the first of the month yet.

KROGSTAD: No, it is Christmas Eve, and it will depend on yourself what sort of a Christmas you will spend.

NORA: What do you want? To-day it is absolutely impossible for me—

KROGSTAD: We won't talk about that till later on. This is something different. I presume you can give me a moment?

NORA: Yes—yes, I can—although—

KROGSTAD: Good. I was in Olsen's Restaurant and saw your husband going down the street—

NORA: Yes?

KROGSTAD: With a lady.

NORA: What then?

KROGSTAD: May I make so bold as to ask if it was a Mrs. Linde?

NORA: It was.

KROGSTAD: Just arrived in town?

NORA: Yes, to-day.

KROGSTAD: She's a great friend of yours, isn't she?

NORA: She is. But I don't see—

KROGSTAD: I knew her, too, once upon a time.

NORA: I'm aware of that.

KROGSTAD: Are you? So you know all about it; I thought as much. Then I can ask you, without beating about the bush—is Mrs. Linde to have an appointment in the Bank?

NORA: What right have you to question me, Mr. Krogstad?—You, one of my husband's subordinates! But since you ask, you shall know. Yes, Mrs. Linde *is* to have an appointment. And it was I who pleaded her cause, Mr. Krogstad, let me tell you that.

KROGSTAD: I was right in what I thought, then.

NORA: [*walking up and down*] Sometimes one has a tiny little bit of influence, I should hope. Because one is a woman, it doesn't necessarily follow that—. When anyone is in a subordinate position, Mr. Krogstad, they should really be careful to avoid offending anyone who—who—

KROGSTAD: Who has influence?

NORA: Exactly.

KROGSTAD: [*changing his tone*] Mrs. Helmer, you will be so good as to use your influence on my behalf.

NORA: What? What do you mean?

KROGSTAD: You will be so kind as to see that I am allowed to keep my subordinate position in the Bank.

NORA: What do you mean by that? Who proposes to take your post away from you?

KROGSTAD: Oh, there is no necessity to keep up the pretence of ignorance. I can quite understand that your friend is not very anxious to expose herself to the chance of rubbing shoulders with me; and I quite understand, too, whom I have to thank for being discharged.

NORA: But I assure you—

KROGSTAD: Very likely; but, to come to the point, the time has come when I should advise you to use your influence to prevent that.

NORA: But, Mr. Krogstad, I *have* no influence.

KROGSTAD: Haven't you? I thought you said yourself just now—

NORA: Naturally I didn't mean you to put that construction on it. I! What should make you think I have any influence of that kind with my husband?

KROGSTAD: Oh, I have known your husband from our student days. I don't suppose he's any more unassailable than other husbands.

NORA: If you speak slightingly of my husband, I shall turn you out of the house.

KROGSTAD: You are bold, Mrs. Helmer.

NORA: I'm not afraid of you any longer. As soon as the New Year comes, I shall in a very short time be free of the whole thing.

KROGSTAD: [*controlling himself*] Listen to me, Mrs. Helmer. If necessary, I am prepared to fight for my small post in the Bank as if I were fighting for my life.

NORA: So it seems.

KROGSTAD: It's not only for the sake of the money; indeed, that weighs least with me in the matter. There's another reason—well, I may as well tell you. My position is this. I daresay you know, like everybody else, that once, many years ago, I was guilty of an indiscretion.

NORA: I think I've heard something of the kind.

KROGSTAD: The matter never came into court; but every way seemed to be closed to me after that. So I took to the business that you know of. I had to do something; and, honestly, I don't think I've been one of the worst. But now I must cut myself free from all that. My sons are growing up; for their sake I must try and win back as much respect as I can in the town. This post in the Bank was like the first step up for me—and now your husband is going to kick me downstairs again into the mud.

NORA: But you must believe me, Mr. Krogstad; it's not in my power to help you at all.

KROGSTAD: Then it's because you haven't the will; but I have means to compel you.

NORA: You don't mean that you will tell my husband that I owe you money?

KROGSTAD: Hm!—Suppose I were to tell him?

NORA: It would be shameful of you. [*sobbing*] To think of his learning my secret, which has been my joy and pride, in such an ugly, clumsy way—that he should learn it from you! And it would put me in a horribly disagreeable position—

KROGSTAD: Only disagreeable?

NORA: [*impetuously*] Well, do it, then!—and it will be the worse for you. My husband will see for himself what a blackguard you are, and you certainly won't keep your post then.

KROGSTAD: I asked you if it was only a disagreeable scene at home that you were afraid of?

NORA: If my husband does get to know of it, of course he will at once pay you what is still owing, and we shall have nothing more to do with you.

KROGSTAD: [*coming a step nearer*] Listen to me, Mrs. Helmer. Either you have a very bad memory or you know very little of business. I shall be obliged to remind you of a few details.

NORA: What do you mean?

KROGSTAD: When your husband was ill, you came to me to borrow forty-eight hundred crowns.

NORA: I didn't know any one else to go to.

KROGSTAD: I promised to get you that amount—

NORA: Yes, and you did so.

KROGSTAD: I promised to get you that amount, on certain conditions. Your mind was so taken up with your husband's illness, and were so anxious to get the money for your journey, that you seem to have paid no attention to the conditions of our bargain. Therefore it will not be amiss if I remind you of them. Now, I promised to get the money on the security of a bond which I drew up.

NORA: Yes, and which I signed.

KROGSTAD: Good. But below your signature there were a few lines constituting your father a surety for the money; those lines your father should have signed.

NORA: Should? He did sign them.

KROGSTAD: I had left the date blank; that is to say your father should himself have inserted the date on which he signed the paper. Do you remember that?

NORA: Yes, I think I remember—

KROGSTAD: Then I gave you the bond to send by post to your father. Is that not so?

NORA: Yes.

KROGSTAD: And you naturally did so at once, because five or six days afterwards you brought me the bond with your father's signature. And then I gave you the money.

NORA: Well, haven't I been paying it off regularly?

KROGSTAD: Fairly so, yes. But—to come back to the matter in hand—that must have been a very trying time for you, Mrs. Helmer?

NORA: It was, indeed.

KROGSTAD: Your father was very ill, wasn't he?

NORA: He was very near his end.

KROGSTAD: And died soon afterwards?

NORA: Yes.

KROGSTAD: Tell me, Mrs. Helmer, can you by any chance remember what day your father died?—on what day of the month, I mean.

NORA: Papa died on the 29th of September.

KROGSTAD: That is correct; I have ascertained it for myself. And, as that is so, there is a discrepancy [*taking a paper from his pocket*] which I cannot account for.

NORA: What discrepancy? I don't know—

KROGSTAD: The discrepancy consists, Mrs. Helmer, in the fact that your father signed this bond three days after his death.

NORA: What do you mean? I don't understand—

KROGSTAD: Your father died on the 29th of September. But, look here; your father has dated his signature the 2nd of October. It is a discrepancy, isn't it? [NORA *is silent.*] Can you explain it to me? [NORA *is still silent.*] It is a remarkable thing, too, that the words "2nd of October," as well as the year, are not written in your father's handwriting but in one that I think I know. Well, of course it can be explained; your father may have forgotten to date his signature, and someone else may have dated it before they knew of his death. There is no harm in that. It all depends on the signature of the name; and *that* is genuine, I suppose, Mrs. Helmer? It was your father himself who signed his name here?

NORA: [*after a short pause, throws her head up and looks defiantly at him*] No, it was not. It was I that wrote papa's name.

KROGSTAD: Are you aware that is a dangerous confession?

NORA: In what way? You'll have your money soon.

KROGSTAD: Let me ask you a question; why did you not send the paper to your father?

NORA: It was impossible; papa was so ill. If I'd asked him for his signature, I should have had to tell him what the money was to be used for; and when he was so ill himself I couldn't tell him that my husband's life was in danger—it was impossible.

KROGSTAD: It would have been better for you if you had given up your trip abroad.

NORA: No, that was impossible. That trip was to save my husband's life; I couldn't give that up.

KROGSTAD: But did it never occur to you that you were committing a fraud on me?

NORA: I couldn't take that into account; I didn't trouble myself about you at all. I couldn't bear you, because you put so many heartless difficulties in my way, although you knew what a dangerous condition my husband was in.

KROGSTAD: Mrs. Helmer, you evidently do not realise clearly what it is that you have been guilty of. But I can assure you that my one false step, which lost me all my reputation, was nothing more or nothing worse than what you have done.

NORA: You? Do you ask me to believe that you were brave enough to run a risk to save your wife's life?

KROGSTAD: The law cares nothing about motives.

NORA: Then it must be a very foolish law.

KROGSTAD: Foolish or not, it is the law by which you will be judged, if I produce this paper in court.

NORA: I don't believe it. Is a daughter not to be allowed to spare her dying father anxiety and care? Is a wife not to be allowed to save her husband's life? I don't know much about law; but I am certain that there must be laws permitting such things as that. Have you no knowledge of such laws—you who are a lawyer? You must be a very poor lawyer, Mr. Krogstad.

KROGSTAD: Maybe. But matters of business—such business as you and I have had together—do you think I don't understand that? Very well. Do as you please. But let me tell you this—if I lose my position a second time, you shall lose yours with me. [*He bows, and goes out through the hall.*]

NORA: [*appears buried in thought for a short time, then tosses her head*] Nonsense! Trying to frighten me like that!—I am not so silly as he thinks. [*begins to busy herself putting the children's things in order*] And yet—? No, it's impossible! I did it for love's sake.

THE CHILDREN: [*in the doorway on the left*] Mother, the stranger has gone out through the gate.

NORA: Yes, dears, I know. But, don't tell anyone about the stranger. Do you hear? Not even papa.

CHILDREN: No, mother; but will you come and play again?

NORA: No, no—not now.

CHILDREN: But, mother, you promised.

NORA: Yes, but I can't now. Go in; I have such a lot to do. Go in, my sweet little darlings. [*She gets them into the room by degrees and shuts the door on them; then sits down on the sofa, takes up a piece of needlework and sews a few stitches, but soon stops.*] No! [*throws down the work, gets up, goes to the hall door and calls out*] Helen! bring the tree in. [*goes to the table on the left, opens a drawer, and stops again*] No, no! it is quite impossible!

MAID: [*coming in with the tree*] Where shall I put it, ma'am?

NORA: Here, in the middle of the floor.

MAID: Shall I get you anything else?

NORA: No, thank you. I have all I want.
    [*Exit* MAID.]

NORA: [*begins dressing the tree*] A candle here—and flowers here—. The horrible man! It's all nonsense—there's nothing wrong. The tree shall be splendid! I'll do everything I can think of to please you, Torvald!—I'll sing for you, dance for you—[HELMER *comes in with some papers under his arm.*] Oh! are you back already?

HELMER: Yes. Has anyone been here?

NORA: Here? No.

HELMER: That's strange. I saw Krogstad going out of the gate.

NORA: Did you? Oh yes, I forgot, Krogstad was here for a moment.

HELMER: Nora, I can see from your manner that he has been here begging you to say a good word for him.

NORA: Yes.

HELMER: And you were to appear to do it of your own accord; you were to conceal from me the fact of his having been here; didn't he beg that of you, too?

NORA: Yes, Torvald, but—

HELMER: Nora, Nora, and you would be a party to that sort of thing? To have any talk with a man like that, and give him any sort of promise? And to tell me a lie into the bargain?

NORA: A lie—?

HELMER: Didn't you tell me no one had been here? [*shakes his finger at her*] My little song-bird must never do that again. A song-bird must have a clean beak to chirp with—no false notes! [*puts his arm round her waist*] That's so, isn't it? Yes, I'm sure it is. [*lets her go*] We will say no more about it. [*sits down by the stove*] How warm and snug it is here! [*turns over his papers*]

NORA: [*after a short pause, during which she busies herself with the Christmas tree*] Torvald!

HELMER: Yes.

NORA: I am looking forward tremendously to the fancy dress ball at the Stenborgs' the day after to-morrow.

HELMER: And I'm tremendously curious to see what you're going to surprise me with.

NORA: It was very silly of me to want to do that.

HELMER: What do you mean?

NORA: I can't hit upon anything that will do; everything I think of seems so silly and insignificant.

HELMER: Does my little Nora acknowledge that at last?

NORA: [*standing behind his chair with her arms on the back of it*] Are you very busy, Torvald?

HELMER: Well—

NORA: What are all those papers?

HELMER: Bank business.

NORA: Already?

HELMER: I have got authority from the retiring manager to undertake the necessary changes in the staff and in the reorganization of the work; and I must make use of the Christmas week for that, so as to have everything in order for the new year.

NORA: Then that was why this poor Krogstad—

HELMER: Hm!

NORA: [*leans against the back of his chair and strokes his hair*] If you hadn't been so busy I should have asked you a tremendously big favour, Torvald.

HELMER: What's that? Tell me.

NORA: There is no one has such good taste as you. And I do so want to look nice at the costume ball. Torvald, couldn't you take me in hand and decide what I shall go as, and what sort of a dress I shall wear?

HELMER: Aha! So my obstinate little woman is obliged to get someone to come to her rescue?

NORA: Yes, Torvald, I can't get along at all without your help.

HELMER: Very well, I'll think it over, we shall manage to hit on something.

NORA: That *is* nice of you. [*Goes to the Christmas tree. A short pause.*] How pretty the red flowers look—. But, tell me, was it really something very bad that this Krogstad was guilty of?

HELMER: He forged someone's name. Have you any idea what that means?

NORA: Isn't it possible that he was driven to do it by necessity?

HELMER: Yes; or, as in so many cases, by imprudence. I am not so heartless as to condemn a man altogether because of a single false step of that kind.

NORA: No, you wouldn't, would you, Torvald?

HELMER: Many a man has been able to retrieve his character, if he has openly confessed his fault and taken his punishment.

NORA: Punishment—?

HELMER: But Krogstad did nothing of that sort; he got himself out of it by a cunning trick, and that is why he has gone under altogether.

NORA: But do you think it would—?

HELMER: Just think how a guilty man like that has to lie and play the hypocrite with everyone, how he has to wear a mask in the presence of those near and dear to him, even before his own wife and children. And about the children—that's the most terrible part of it all, Nora.

NORA: How?

HELMER: Because such an atmosphere of lies infects and poisons the whole life of a home. Each breath the children take in such a house is full of the germs of evil.

NORA: [*coming nearer him*] Are you sure of that?

HELMER: My dear, I have often seen it in the course of my life as a lawyer. Almost everyone who has gone to the bad early in life has had a deceitful mother.

NORA: Why do you only say—mother?

HELMER: It seems most commonly to be the mother's influence, though naturally a bad father's would have the same result. Every lawyer is familiar with the fact. This Krogstad, now, has been persistently poisoning his own children with lies and dissimulation; that's why I say he has lost all moral character. [*holds out his hands to her*] That's why my sweet little Nora must promise me not to plead his cause. Give me your hand on it. Come, come, what's this? Give me your hand. There now, that's settled. I assure you it would be quite impossible for me to work with him; I literally feel physically ill when I am in the company of such people.

NORA: [*takes her hand out of his and goes to the opposite side of the Christmas tree*] How hot it is in here; and I have such a lot to do.

HELMER: [*getting up and putting his papers in order*] Yes, and I must try and read through some of these before dinner; and I must think about your costume, too. And it's just possible I may have something ready in gold paper to hang up on the tree. [*puts his hand on her head*] My precious little singing-bird! [*He goes into his room and shuts the door after him.*]

NORA: [*after a pause, whispers*] No, no—it isn't true. It's impossible; it must be impossible.

[*The* NURSE *opens the door on the left.*]

NURSE: The little ones are begging so hard to be allowed to come in to mamma.

NORA: No, no, no! Don't let them come in to me! You stay with them, Anne.

NURSE: Very well, ma'am. [*shuts the door*]

NORA: [*pale with terror*] Deprave my little children? Poison my home? [*A short pause. Then she tosses her head.*] It's not true. It can't possibly be true.

ACT II

THE SAME SCENE————*The Christmas tree is in the corner by the piano, stripped of its ornaments and with burnt-down candle-ends on its dishevelled branches.* NORA's *cloak and hat are lying on the sofa. She is alone in the room, walking about uneasily. She stops by the sofa and takes up her cloak.*

NORA: [*drops the cloak*] Someone is coming now! [*goes to the door and listens*] No—it's no one. Of course, no one will come to-day, Christmas Day—nor to-morrow, either. But, perhaps—[*opens the door and looks out*] No, nothing in the mail box; it's quite empty. [*comes forward*] What rubbish! Of course he can't be in earnest about it. Such a thing couldn't happen; it's impossible— I have three little children.

[*Enter the* NURSE *from the room on the left, carrying a big cardboard box.*]

NURSE: At last I've found the box with the fancy dress.

NORA: Thanks; put it on the table.

NURSE: [*doing so*] But it's very much in want of mending.

NORA: I should like to tear it into a hundred thousand pieces.

NURSE: What an idea! It can easily be put in order—just a little patience.

NORA: Yes, I'll go and get Mrs. Linde to come and help me with it.

NURSE: What, out again? In this horrible weather? You'll catch cold, ma'am, and make yourself ill.

NORA: Well, worse than that might happen. How are the children?

NURSE: The poor little souls are playing with their Christmas presents, but—

NORA: Do they ask much for me?

NURSE: You see, they're so accustomed to have their mamma with them.

NORA: Yes, but nurse, I shan't be able to be so much with them now as I was before.

NURSE: Oh well, young children easily get accustomed to anything.

NORA: Do you think so? Do you think they would forget their mother if she went away altogether?

NURSE: Good heavens!—went away altogether?

NORA: Nurse, I want you to tell me something I have often wondered about—how could you have the heart to put your own child out among strangers?

NURSE: I was obliged to, if I wanted to be little Nora's nurse.

NORA: Yes, but how could you be willing to do it?

NURSE: What, when I was going to get such a good place by it? A poor girl who has got into trouble should be glad to. Besides, that wicked man didn't do a single thing for me.

NORA: But I suppose your daughter has quite forgotten you.

NURSE: No, indeed she hasn't. She wrote to me when she was confirmed, and when she was married.

NORA: [*putting her arms around her neck*] Dear old Anne, you were a good mother to me when I was little.

NURSE: Little Nora, poor dear, had no other mother but me.

NORA: And if my little ones had no other mother, I'm sure you would—. What nonsense I'm talking! [*opens the box*] Go in to them. Now I must—. You will see to-morrow how charming I'll look.

NURSE: I'm sure there will be no one at the ball so charming as you, ma'am. [*goes into the room on the left*]

NORA: [*begins to unpack the box, but soon pushes it away from her*] If only I dared go out. If only no one would come. If only I could be sure nothing would happen here in the meantime. Stuff and nonsense! No one will come. Only I mustn't think about it. I'll brush my muff. What lovely, lovely gloves! Out of my thoughts, out of my thoughts! One, two, three, four, five, six—[*screams*] Ah! there is someone coming—. [*makes a movement towards the door, but stands irresolute*]

[*Enter* MRS. LINDE *from the hall, where she has taken off her cloak and hat.*]

NORA: Oh, it's you, Christine. There is no one else out there, is there? How good of you to come!

MRS. LINDE: I heard you were up asking for me.

NORA: Yes, I was passing by. As a matter of fact, it's something you could help me with. Let us sit down here on the sofa. Look here. To-morrow evening there is to be a costume ball at the Stenborgs', who live above us; and Torvald wants me to go as a Neapolitan fisher-girl, and dance the Tarantella that I learned on Capri.

MRS. LINDE: I see; you're going to perform a character.

NORA: Yes, Torvald wants me to. Look, here's the dress; Torvald had it made for me there, but now it's all so torn, and I haven't any idea—.

MRS. LINDE: We'll easily put that right. It's only some of the trimming come unsewn here and there. Needle and thread? Now then, that's all we need.

NORA: It *is* nice of you.

MRS. LINDE: [*sewing*] So you're going to be dressed up to-morrow, Nora. I'll tell you what—I'll come in for a moment and see you in your fine feathers. But

I have completely forgotten to thank you for a delightful evening yesterday.

NORA: [*gets up, and crosses the stage*] Well, I don't think yesterday was as pleasant as usual. You ought to have come to town a little earlier, Christine. Certainly Torvald does understand how to make a house attractive.

MRS. LINDE: And so do you, it seems to me; you are not your father's daughter for nothing. But tell me, is Doctor Rank always as depressed as he was yesterday?

NORA: No; yesterday it was very noticeable. I must tell you that he suffers from a very dangerous disease. He has tuberculosis of the spine, poor creature. His father was a horrible man who committed all sorts of excesses; and that's why his son was sickly from childhood, do you understand?

MRS. LINDE: [*dropping her sewing*] But my dearest Nora, how do you know anything about such things?

NORA: [*walking about*] Pooh! When you have three children, you get visits now and then from—from married women, who know something of medical matters, and they talk about one thing and another.

MRS. LINDE: [*goes on sewing. A short silence*] Does Doctor Rank come here every day?

NORA: Every day regularly. He's Torvald's best friend, and a great friend of mine, too. He's just like one of the family.

MRS. LINDE: But tell me this—is he perfectly sincere? I mean, isn't he the kind of man that is very anxious to make himself agreeable?

NORA: Not in the least. What makes you think that?

MRS. LINDE: When you introduced him to me yesterday, he declared he had often heard my name mentioned in this house; but afterwards I noticed that your husband hadn't the slightest idea who I was. So how could Doctor Rank—?

NORA: That's quite right, Christine. Torvald is so absurdly fond of me that he wants me absolutely to himself, as he says. At first he used to seem almost jealous if I mentioned any of my friends back home, so naturally I gave up doing so. But I often talk about such things with Doctor Rank, because he likes hearing about them.

MRS. LINDE: Listen to me, Nora. You are still very like a child in many things, and I'm older than you in many ways and have a little more experience. Let me tell you this—you ought to make an end of it with Doctor Rank.

NORA: What ought I to make an end of?

MRS. LINDE: Of two things, I think. Yesterday you talked some nonsense about a rich admirer who was to leave you money—

NORA: An admirer who doesn't exist, unfortunately! But what then?

MRS. LINDE: Is Doctor Rank well off?

NORA: Yes, he is.

MRS. LINDE: And has no one to provide for?

NORA: No, no one; but—

MRS. LINDE: And comes here every day?

NORA: Yes, I told you so.

MRS. LINDE: But how can this well-bred man be so tactless?

NORA: I don't understand you at all.

MRS. LINDE: Don't pretend, Nora. Do you suppose I don't guess who lent you the forty-eight hundred crowns?

NORA: Are you out of your senses? How can you think of such a thing! A friend of ours, who comes here every day! Do you realize what a horribly painful position that would be?

MRS. LINDE: Then it really isn't he?

NORA: No certainly not. It would never have entered my head for a moment. Besides, he had no money to lend then; he came into his money afterwards.

MRS. LINDE: Well, I think that was lucky for you, my dear Nora.

NORA: No, it would never have come into my head to ask Doctor Rank. Although I am quite sure that if I had asked him—

MRS. LINDE: But of course you won't.

NORA: Of course not. I have no reason to think it could possibly be necessary. But I'm quite sure that if I told Doctor Rank—

MRS. LINDE: Behind your husband's back?

NORA: I must make an end of it with the other one, and that will be behind his back, too. I must make an end of it with him.

MRS. LINDE: Yes, that's what I told you yesterday, but—

NORA: [*walking up and down*] A man can put a thing like that straight much easier than a woman—

MRS. LINDE: One's husband, yes.

NORA: Nonsense! [*standing still*] When you pay off a debt you get your bond back, don't you?

MRS. LINDE: Yes, as a matter of course.

NORA: And can tear it into a hundred thousand pieces, and burn it—the nasty dirty paper!

MRS. LINDE: [*looks hard at her, lays down her sewing and gets up slowly*] Nora, you are keeping something from me.

NORA: Do I look as if I were?

MRS. LINDE: Something has happened to you since yesterday morning. Nora, what is it?

NORA: [*going nearer to her*] Christine! [*listens*] Hush! There's Torvald come home. Do you mind going in to the children for the present? Torvald can't bear to see dressmaking going on. Let Anne help you.

MRS. LINDE: [*gathering some of the things together*] Certainly—but I'm not leaving till we've had it out with one another. [*She goes into the room on the left, as Helmer comes in from the hall.*]

NORA: [*going up to* HELMER] I have wanted you so much, Torvald dear.

HELMER: Was that the dressmaker?

NORA: No, it was Christine; she is helping me to put my costume in order. You will see I shall look quite smart.

HELMER: Wasn't that a happy thought of mine, now?

NORA: Splendid! But don't you think it's nice of me, too, to do as you wish?

HELMER: Nice?—because you do as your husband wishes? Well, well, you little rogue, I'm sure you did not mean it in that way. But I'm not going to disturb you; you will want to be trying on your costume, I expect.

NORA: I suppose you're going to work.

HELMER: Yes. [*shows her a bundle of papers*] Look at that. I have just been to the Bank. [*turns to go into his room*]

NORA: Torvald.

HELMER: Yes.

NORA: If your little squirrel were to ask you something very, very prettily—?

HELMER: What then?

NORA: Would you do it?

HELMER: I should like to hear what it is, first.

NORA: Your squirrel would run about and do all her tricks if you would be nice, and do what she wants.

HELMER: Speak plainly.

NORA: Your skylark would chirp about in every room, with her song rising and falling—

HELMER: Well, my skylark does that anyhow.

NORA: I'd be a fairy and dance for you in the moonlight, Torvald.

HELMER: Nora—you surely don't mean that request you made of me this morning?

NORA: [*going near him*] Yes, Torvald, I beg you so earnestly—

HELMER: Have you really the nerve to bring up that question again?

NORA: Yes, dear, you *must* do as I ask; you *must* let Krogstad keep his post in the Bank.

HELMER: My dear Nora, it is his post that I have arranged for Mrs. Linde to have.

NORA: Yes, you've been awfully kind about that; but you could just as well dismiss some other clerk instead of Krogstad.

HELMER: This is simply incredible obstinacy! Because you chose to give him a thoughtless promise that you would speak for him, I am expected to—

NORA: That isn't the reason, Torvald. It is for your own sake. This fellow writes in the most scurrilous newspapers; you've told me so yourself. He can do you an unspeakable amount of harm. I am frightened to death of him—

HELMER: Ah, I understand; it is recollections of the past that scare you.

NORA: What do you mean?

HELMER: Naturally you are thinking of your father.

NORA: Yes—yes, of course. Just recall in your mind what these malicious creatures wrote in the papers about papa, and how horribly they slandered him. I believe they would have procured his dismissal if the Department had not sent you over to inquire into it, and if you had not been so kindly disposed and helpful to him.

HELMER: My little Nora, there is an important difference between your father and me. Your father's reputation as a public official was not above suspicion. Mine is, and I hope it will continue to be so, as long as I hold my office.

NORA: You never can tell what mischief these men may contrive. We ought to be so well off, so snug and happy here in our peaceful home, and have no cares—you and I and the children, Torvald! That's why I beg you so earnestly—

HELMER: And it's just by interceding for him that you make it impossible for me to keep him. It's already known at the Bank that I mean to dismiss Krogstad. Is it to get about now that the new manager has changed his mind at his wife's bidding—

NORA: And what if it did?

HELMER: Of course!—if only this obstinate little person can get her way! Do you suppose I'm going to make myself ridiculous before my entire staff, to let people think that I am a man to be swayed by all sorts of outside influence? I should very soon feel the consequences of that, I can tell you! And besides, there is something that makes it quite impossible for me to have Krogstad in the Bank as long as I am manager.

NORA: Whatever is that?

HELMER: His moral failings I might perhaps have overlooked, if necessary—

NORA: Yes, you could—couldn't you?

HELMER: And I hear he is a good worker, too. But I knew him when we were boys. It was one of those rash friendships that so often prove an embarrassment later in life. I may as well tell you plainly, we were once on first-name terms with one another. But this tactless fellow lays no restraint on himself when other people are present. On the contrary, he thinks it gives him the right to adopt a familiar tone with me, and every minute it is "I say, Helmer, old fellow!" and that sort of thing. It's extremely painful for me. He would make my position in the Bank intolerable.

NORA: Torvald, I don't believe you mean that.

HELMER: Don't you? Why not?

NORA: Because it is such a petty way of looking at things.

HELMER: What are you saying? Petty? Do you think I'm petty?

NORA: No, just the opposite, dear—it's exactly for that reason.

HELMER: It's the same thing. You say my point of view is petty, so I must be so, too. Petty. Very well—I must put an end to this. [*goes to the hall door and calls*] Helen!

NORA: What are you going to do?

HELMER: [*looking among his papers*] Settle it. [*Enter* MAID.] Look here; take this letter and go downstairs with it at once. Find a messenger and tell him to deliver it, and be quick. The address is on it, and here is the money.

MAID: Very well, sir. [*exit with the letter*]

HELMER: [*putting his papers together*] Now then, little Miss Obstinate.

NORA: [*breathless*] Torvald—what was that letter?

HELMER: Krogstad's dismissal.

NORA: Call her back, Torvald! There is still time. Oh Torvald, call her back! Do it for my sake—for your own sake—for the children's sake! Do you hear me, Torvald? Call her back! You don't know what that letter can bring upon us.

HELMER: It's too late.

NORA: Yes, it's too late.

HELMER: My dear Nora, I can forgive the anxiety you are in, although really it is an insult to me. It is, indeed. Isn't it an insult to think that I should be afraid of a starving journalist's vengeance? But I forgive you nevertheless, because it's such eloquent witness to your great love for me. [*takes her in his arms*] And that's as it should be, my own darling Nora. Come what will, you may be sure I'll have both courage and strength if they be needed. You'll see I am man enough to take everything upon myself.

NORA: [*in a horror-stricken voice*] What do you mean by that?

HELMER: Everything, I say—

NORA: [*recovering herself*] You'll never have to do that.

HELMER: That's right. Well, we'll share it, Nora, as man and wife should. That's how it should be. [*caressing her*] Are you happy now? There, there!—not

these frightened dove's eyes! The whole thing is only the wildest fantasy—
Now, you must go and play through the Tarantella and practise with your
tambourine. I'll go into the inner office and shut the door, and I'll hear
nothing, you can make as much noise as you please. [*turns back at the door*]
And when Rank comes, tell him where he can find me. [*nods to her, takes his
papers and goes into his room and shuts the door after him*]

NORA: [*bewildered with anxiety, stands as if rooted to the spot, and whispers*] He was
capable of doing it. He will do it. He will do it in spite of everything—No,
not that! Never, never! Anything rather than that! Oh, for some help, some
way out of it! [*the doorbell rings*] Doctor Rank! Anything rather than
that—anything, whatever it is! [*She puts her hands over her face, pulls herself
together, goes to the door and opens it.* RANK *is standing without, hanging up his
coat. During the following dialogue it begins to grow dark.*]

NORA: Good-day, Doctor Rank. I knew your ring. But you mustn't go into Torvald now; I think he is busy with something.

RANK: And you?

NORA: [*brings him in and shuts the door after him*] Oh, you know very well I always
have time for you.

RANK: Thank you. I shall make use of as much of it as I can.

NORA: What do you mean by that? As much of it as you can?

RANK: Well, does that alarm you?

NORA: It was such a strange way of putting it. Is anything likely to happen?

RANK: Nothing but what I've long been prepared for. But I certainly didn't expect
it to happen so soon.

NORA: [*gripping him by the arm*] What have you found out? Doctor Rank, you
must tell me.

RANK: [*sitting down by the stove*] It's all up with me. And it can't be helped.

NORA: [*with a sigh of relief*] Is it about yourself?

RANK: Who else? It's no use lying to one's self. I am the most wretched of all
my patients, Mrs. Helmer. Lately I've been taking stock of my internal
economy. Bankrupt! Probably within a month I shall lie rotting in the
churchyard.

NORA: What an ugly thing to say!

RANK: The thing itself is cursedly ugly, and the worst of it is that I'll have to face
so much more that is ugly before that. I'll only make one more examination
of myself; when I have done that, I'll know pretty certainly when the horrors of dissolution will begin. There's something I want to tell you. Helmer's
sensitivity makes him disgusted at everything that is ugly; I won't have him
in my sickroom.

NORA: Oh, but, Doctor Rank—

RANK: I won't have him there. Not on any account. I bar my door to him. As soon
as I'm quite certain that the worst has come, I'll send you my card with a
black cross on it, and then you will know that the loathsome end has begun.

NORA: You are quite absurd to-day. And I wanted you so much to be in a really
good humour.

RANK: With death stalking beside me?—To have to pay this penalty for another
man's sin! Is there any justice in that? And in every single family, in one way
or another, some such inexorable retribution is being exacted—

NORA: [*putting her hands over her ears*] Rubbish! Do talk of something cheerful.

RANK: Oh, it's a mere laughing matter, the whole thing. My poor innocent spine has to suffer for my father's youthful amusements.

NORA: [*sitting at the table on the left*] I suppose you mean that he was too partial to asparagus and paté de foie gras, don't you?

RANK: Yes, and to truffles.

NORA: Truffles, yes. And oysters, too, I suppose?

RANK: Oysters, of course, that goes without saying.

NORA: And heaps of port and champagne. It is sad that all these nice things should take their revenge on our bones.

RANK: Especially that they should revenge themselves on the unlucky bones of those who have not had the satisfaction of enjoying them.

NORA: Yes, that's the saddest part of it all.

RANK: [*with a searching look at her*] Hm!—

NORA: [*after a short pause*] Why did you smile?

RANK: No, it was you that laughed.

NORA: No, it was you that smiled, Doctor Rank!

RANK: [*rising*] You're a bigger tease than I thought.

NORA: I'm in a silly mood to-day.

RANK: So it seems.

NORA: [*putting her hands on his shoulders*] Dear, dear Doctor Rank, death mustn't take you away from Torvald and me.

RANK: It's a loss you would easily recover from. Those who are gone are soon for-gotten.

NORA: [*looking at him anxiously*] Do you believe that?

RANK: People form new ties, and then—

NORA: Who will form new ties?

RANK: Both you and Helmer, when I'm gone. You yourself are already on the high road to it, I think. What did Mrs. Linde want here last night?

NORA: Oho!—you don't mean to say you're jealous of poor Christine?

RANK: Yes, I am. She'll be my successor in this house. When I'm done for, this woman will—

NORA: Hush! don't speak so loud. She's in that room.

RANK: To-day again. There, you see.

NORA: She's only come to sew my costume for me. Bless my soul, how unrea-sonable you are! [*sits down on the sofa*] Be nice now, Doctor Rank, and to-morrow you will see how beautifully I shall dance, and you can imagine I'm doing it all for you—and for Torvald, too, of course. [*takes various things out of the box*] Doctor Rank, come and sit down here, and I'll show you something.

RANK: [*sitting down*] What is it?

NORA: Just look at those!

RANK: Silk stockings.

NORA: Flesh-coloured. Aren't they lovely? It is so dark here now, but to-mor-row—. No, no, no! you must only look at the feet. Oh well, you may have leave to look at the legs, too.

RANK: Hm!—

NORA: Why are you looking so critical? Don't you think they will fit me?

RANK: I have no means of forming an opinion about that.

NORA: [*looks at him for a moment*] For shame! [*hits him lightly on the ear with the stockings*] That's to punish you. [*folds them up again*]

RANK: And what other nice things am I to be allowed to see?

NORA: Not a single thing more, for being so naughty. [*She looks among the things, humming to herself.*]

RANK: [*after a short silence*] When I'm sitting here, talking to you as intimately as this, I can't imagine for a moment what would have become of me if I had never come into this house.

NORA: [*smiling*] I believe you do feel thoroughly at home with us.

RANK: [*in a lower voice, looking straight in front of him*] And to be obliged to leave it all—

NORA: Nonsense, you're not going to leave it.

RANK: [*as before*] And not be able to leave behind one the slightest token of one's gratitude, scarcely even a fleeting regret—nothing but an empty place which the first comer can fill as well as any other.

NORA: And if I asked you now for a—? No!

RANK: For what?

NORA: For a big proof of your friendship—

RANK: Yes, yes!

NORA: I mean a tremendously big favour—

RANK: Would you really make me so happy for once?

NORA: Ah, but you don't know what it is yet.

RANK: No—but tell me.

NORA: I really can't, Doctor Rank. It's something out of all reason; it means advice, and help, and a favour—

RANK: The bigger the better. I can't conceive what it is you mean. Do tell me. Haven't I your confidence?

NORA: More than anyone else. I know you are my truest and best friend, and so I'll tell you what it is. Well, Doctor Rank, it's something you must help me to prevent. You know how devotedly, how inexpressibly deeply Torvald loves me; he would never for a moment hesitate to give his life for me.

RANK: [*leaning towards her*] Nora—do you think he is the only one—?

NORA: [*with a slight start*] The only one—?

RANK: The only one who would gladly give his life for your sake.

NORA: [*sadly*] Is that it?

RANK: I was determined you should know it before I went away, and there'll never be a better opportunity than this. Now you know it, Nora. And now you know, too, that you can trust me as you would trust no one else.

NORA: [*rises, deliberately and quietly*] Let me pass.

RANK: [*makes room for her to pass him, but sits still*] Nora!

NORA: [*at the hall door*] Helen, bring in the lamp. [*goes over to the stove*] Dear Doctor Rank, that was really horrid of you.

RANK: To have loved you as much as anyone else does? Was that horrid?

NORA: No, but to go and tell me so. There was really no need—

RANK: What do you mean? Did you know—? [MAID *enters with lamp, puts it down on the table, and goes out.*] Nora—Mrs. Helmer—tell me, had you any idea of this?

NORA: Oh, how do I know whether I had or whether I hadn't? I really can't tell you—To think you could be so clumsy, Doctor Rank! We were getting on so nicely.

RANK: Well, at all events you know now that you can command me, body and soul. So won't you speak out?

NORA: [*looking at him*] After what happened?

RANK: I beg you to let me know what it is.

NORA: I can't tell you anything now.

RANK: Yes, yes. You mustn't punish me in that way. Let me have permission to do for you whatever a man may do.

NORA: You can do nothing for me now. Besides, I really don't need any help at all. You will find the whole thing is merely fancy on my part. It really is so—of course it is! [*Sits down in the rocking chair, and looks at him with a smile.*] You are a nice man, Doctor Rank!—don't you feel ashamed of yourself, now the lamp has come!

RANK: Not a bit. But perhaps I had better go—for ever?

NORA: No, indeed, you shall not. Of course you must come here just as before. You know very well Torvald can't do without you.

RANK: Yes, but you?

NORA: Oh I'm always tremendously pleased when you come.

RANK: It's just that, that put me on the wrong track. You are a riddle to me. I've often thought that you'd almost as soon be in my company as in Helmer's.

NORA: Yes—you see there are some people one loves best, and others whom one would almost always rather have as companions.

RANK: Yes, there is something in that.

NORA: When I was at home, of course I loved papa best. But I always thought it tremendous fun if I could steal down into the maids' room, because they never moralised at all, and talked to each other about such entertaining things.

RANK: I see—it is *their* place I have taken.

NORA: [*jumping up and going to him*] Oh, dear, nice Doctor Rank, I never meant that at all. But surely you can understand that being with Torvald is a little like being with papa—

[*Enter* MAID *from the hall.*]

MAID: If you please, ma'am. [*whispers and hands her a card*]

NORA: [*glancing at the card*] Oh! [*puts it in her pocket*]

RANK: Is there anything wrong?

NORA: No, no, not in the least. It's only something—it's my new dress—

RANK: What? Your dress is lying there.

NORA: Oh, yes, that one; but this is another. I ordered it. Torvald mustn't know about it—

RANK: Oho! Then that was the great secret.

NORA: Of course. Just go in to him; he is sitting in the inner room. Keep him as long as—

RANK: Make your mind easy; I won't let him escape. [*goes into* HELMER'*s room*]

NORA: [*to the* MAID] And he's waiting in the kitchen?

MAID: Yes; he came up the back stairs.

NORA: But didn't you tell him no one was in?

MAID: Yes, but it was no good.

NORA: He won't go away?

MAID: No; he says he won't until he has seen you, ma'am.

NORA: Well, let him come in—but quietly. Helen, you mustn't say anything about it to anyone. It's a surprise for my husband.

MAID: Yes, ma'am, I quite understand. [*exit*]

NORA: This dreadful thing is going to happen! It will happen in spite of me! No, no, no, it can't happen—it shan't happen! [*She bolts the door of* HELMER's *room. The* MAID *opens the hall door for* KROGSTAD *and shuts it after him. He is wearing a fur coat, high boots, and a fur cap.*]

NORA: [*advancing towards him*] Speak low—my husband is at home.

KROGSTAD: No matter about that!

NORA: What do you want of me?

KROGSTAD: An explanation.

NORA: Make haste then. What is it?

KROGSTAD: You know, I suppose, that I've got my dismissal.

NORA: I couldn't prevent it, Mr. Krogstad. I fought as hard as I could on your side, but it was no good.

KROGSTAD: Does your husband love you so little, then? He knows what I can expose you to, and yet he ventures—

NORA: How can you suppose that he has any knowledge of the sort?

KROGSTAD: I didn't suppose so at all. It would not be the least like our dear Torvald Helmer to show so much courage—

NORA: Mr. Krogstad, a little respect for my husband, please.

KROGSTAD: Certainly—all the respect he deserves. But since you have kept the matter so carefully to yourself, I make bold to suppose that you have a little clearer idea, than you had yesterday, of what it actually is that you have done?

NORA: More than you could ever teach me.

KROGSTAD: Yes, bad lawyer that I am.

NORA: What is it you want of me?

KROGSTAD: Only to see how you were, Mrs. Helmer. I have been thinking about you all day long. A mere cashier, hackwriter, a—well, a man like me—even he has a little of what is called feeling, you know.

NORA: Show it, then; think of my little children.

KROGSTAD: Have you and your husband thought of mine? But never mind about that. I only wanted to tell you that you need not take this matter too seriously. In the first place there will be no accusation made on my part.

NORA: No, of course not; I was sure of that.

KROGSTAD: The whole thing can be arranged amicably; there is no reason why anyone should know anything about it. It will remain a secret between us three.

NORA: My husband must never get to know anything about it.

KROGSTAD: How will you be able to prevent it? Am I to understand that you can pay the balance that's owing?

NORA: No, not just at present.

KROGSTAD: Or perhaps that you have some means of raising the money soon?

NORA: None that I mean to make use of.

KROGSTAD: Well, in any case, it would've been of no use to you now. If you stood there with ever so much money in your hand, I would never part with your bond.

NORA: Tell me what purpose you mean to put it to.

KROGSTAD: I shall only preserve it—keep it in my possession. No one who is not concerned in the matter shall have the slightest hint of it. So that if the thought of it has driven you to any desperate resolution—

NORA: It has.

KROGSTAD: If you had it in your mind to run away from your home—

NORA: I had.

KROGSTAD: Or even something worse—

NORA: How could you know that?

KROGSTAD: Give up the idea.

NORA: How did you know I had thought of *that?*

KROGSTAD: Most of us think of that at first. I did, too—but I hadn't the courage.

NORA: [*faintly*] No more had I.

KROGSTAD: [*in a tone of relief*] No, that's it, isn't it—you hadn't the courage, either?

NORA: No, I haven't—I haven't.

KROGSTAD: Besides, it would have been a great piece of folly. Once the first storm at home is over—. I have a letter for your husband in my pocket.

NORA: Telling him everything?

KROGSTAD: In as lenient a manner as I possibly could.

NORA: [*quickly*] He mustn't get that letter. Tear it up. I will find some means of getting money.

KROGSTAD: Excuse me, Mrs. Helmer, but I think I told you just now—

NORA: I am not speaking of what I owe you. Tell me what sum you are asking my husband for, and I will get the money.

KROGSTAD: I am not asking your husband for a penny.

NORA: What do you want, then?

KROGSTAD: I will tell you. I want to rehabilitate myself, Mrs. Helmer; I want to get on; and in that your husband must help me. For the last year and a half I have not had a hand in anything dishonourable, and all that time I have been struggling in most restricted circumstances. I was content to work my way up step by step. Now I'm turned out, and I'm not going to be satisfied with merely being taken into favour again. I want to get on, I tell you. I want to get into the Bank again, in a higher position. Your husband must make a place for me—

NORA: That he will never do!

KROGSTAD: He will; I know him; he dare not protest. And as soon as I'm in there again with him, then you will see! Within a year I shall be the manager's right hand. It will be Nils Krogstad and not Torvald Helmer who manages the Bank.

NORA: That's a thing you will never see!

KROGSTAD: Do you mean that you will—?

NORA: I have courage enough for it now.

KROGSTAD: Oh, you can't frighten me. A fine, spoilt lady like you—

NORA: You'll see, you'll see.

KROGSTAD: Under the ice, perhaps? Down into the cold, coal-black water? And
  then, in the spring, to float up to the surface, all horrible and unrecognis-
  able, with your hair fallen out—

NORA: You can't frighten me.

KROGSTAD: Nor you me. People don't do such things, Mrs. Helmer. Besides, what
  use would it be? I should have him completely in my power all the same.

NORA: Afterwards? When I am no longer—

KROGSTAD: Have you forgotten that it is I who have the keeping of your reputation? [*Nora stands speechlessly looking at him.*] Well, now, I've warned you.
  Don't do anything foolish. When Helmer has received my letter, I shall expect a message from him. And be sure you remember that it's your husband
  himself who has forced me into such ways as this again. I'll never forgive
  him for that. Good-bye, Mrs. Helmer. [*exit through the hall*]

NORA: [*goes to the hall door, opens it slightly and listens*] He's going. He's not
  putting the letter in the box. Oh no, no! that's impossible! [*opens the door by
  degrees*] What's that? He's standing outside. He's not going downstairs. Is
  he hesitating? Can he—? [*A letter drops into the box; then* KROGSTAD's *footsteps are heard, till they die away as he goes downstairs.* NORA *utters a stifled cry,
  and runs across the room to the table by the sofa. A short pause.*]

NORA: In the mail box. [*steals across to the hall door*] There it lies—Torvald, Torvald, there is no hope for us now!

       [MRS. LINDE *comes in from the room on the left, carrying the dress.*]

MRS. LINDE: There, I can't see anything more to mend now. Would you like to try
  it on—?

NORA: [*in a hoarse whisper*] Christine, come here.

MRS. LINDE: [*throwing the dress down on the sofa*] What's the matter with you?
  You look so upset.

NORA: Come here. Do you see that letter? There, look—you can see it through
  the glass in the box.

MRS. LINDE: Yes, I see it.

NORA: That letter is from Krogstad.

MRS. LINDE: Nora—it was Krogstad who lent you the money!

NORA: Yes, and now Torvald will know all about it.

MRS. LINDE: Believe me, Nora, that's the best thing for both of you.

NORA: You don't know all. I forged a name.

MRS. LINDE: Good heavens—!

NORA: I only want to say this to you, Christine—you must be my witness.

MRS. LINDE: Your witness? What do you mean? What am I to—?

NORA: If I should go out of my mind—and it might easily happen—

MRS. LINDE: Nora!

NORA: Or if anything else should happen to me—anything, for instance, that
  might prevent my being here—

MRS. LINDE: Nora! Nora! You're quite out of your mind.

NORA: And if it should happen that there were someone who wanted to take all
  the responsibility, all the blame, you understand—

MRS. LINDE: Yes, yes—but how can you suppose—?

NORA: Then you must be my witness, that it's not true, Christine. I'm not out of
  my mind at all. I'm in my right senses now, and I tell you no one else has

known anything about it; I, and I alone, did the whole thing. Remember that.

MRS. LINDE: I will, indeed. But I don't understand all this.

NORA: How should you understand it? A miracle is going to happen.

MRS. LINDE: A miracle?

NORA: Yes, a miracle.—But it's so terrible, Christine; it *mustn't* happen, not for all the world.

MRS. LINDE: I will go at once and see Krogstad.

NORA: Don't go to him; he will do you some harm.

MRS. LINDE: There was a time when he would gladly do anything for my sake.

NORA: He?

MRS. LINDE: Where does he live?

NORA: How should I know—? Yes [*feeling in her pocket*] here is his card. But the letter, the letter—!

HELMER: [*calls from his room, knocking at the door*] Nora!

NORA: [*cries out anxiously*] Oh, what's that? What do you want?

HELMER: Don't be so frightened. We are not coming in; you have locked the door. Are you trying on your dress?

NORA: Yes, that's it. I look so nice, Torvald.

MRS. LINDE: [*who has read the card*] I see he lives at the corner here.

NORA: Yes, but it's no use. It's hopeless. The letter is lying there in the box.

MRS. LINDE: And your husband keeps the key?

NORA: Yes, always.

MRS. LINDE: Krogstad must ask for his letter back unread, he must find some pretence—

NORA: But it's just at this time that Torvald generally—

MRS. LINDE: You must delay him. Go in to him in the meantime. I'll come back as soon as I can. [*She goes out hurriedly through the hall door.*]

NORA: [*goes to* HELMER's *door, opens it and peeps in*] Torvald!

HELMER: [*from the inner room*] Well? May I venture at last to come into my own room again? Come along, Rank, now you'll see—[*halting in the doorway*] But what is this?

NORA: What is what, dear?

HELMER: Rank led me to expect a splendid transformation.

RANK: [*in the doorway*] I understood so, but evidently I was mistaken.

NORA: Yes, nobody is to have the chance of admiring me in my costume until to-morrow.

HELMER: But, my dear Nora, you look so worn out. Have you been practising too much?

NORA: No, I have not practised at all.

HELMER: But you will need to—

NORA: Yes, indeed I shall, Torvald. But I can't get on a bit without you to help me; I have absolutely forgotten the whole thing.

HELMER: Oh, we'll soon work it up again.

NORA: Yes, help me, Torvald. Promise that you will! I'm so nervous about it—all the people—. You must give yourself up to me entirely this evening. Not the tiniest bit of business—you mustn't even take a pen in your hand. Will you promise, Torvald dear?

HELMER: I promise: This evening I'll be wholly and absolutely at your service, you helpless little thing. But, first of all I'll just—[*goes towards the hall door*]

NORA: What are you going to do there?

HELMER: Only see if any letters have come.

NORA: No, no! Don't do that, Torvald!

HELMER: Why not?

NORA: Torvald, please don't. There is nothing there.

HELMER: Well, let me look. [*Turns to go to the letterbox.* NORA, *at the piano, plays the first bars of the Tarantella.* HELMER *stops in the doorway.*] Aha!

NORA: I can't dance to-morrow if I don't practise with you.

HELMER: [*going up to her*] Are you really so afraid of it, dear?

NORA: Yes, so dreadfully afraid of it. Let me practise at once; there is time now, before we go to dinner. Sit down and play for me, Torvald dear; coach me, and correct me as you play.

HELMER: With great pleasure, if you wish me to. [*sits down at the piano*]

NORA: [*Takes out of the box a tambourine and a long variegated shawl. She hastily drapes the shawl round her. Then she springs to the front of the stage and calls out.*] Now play for me! I'm going to dance!

[HELMER *plays and* NORA *dances.* RANK *stands by the piano behind* HELMER, *and looks on.*]

HELMER: [*as he plays*] Slower, slower!

NORA: I can't do it any other way.

HELMER: Not so violently, Nora!

NORA: This is the way.

HELMER: [*stops playing*] No, no—that's not a bit right.

NORA: [*laughing and swinging the tambourine*] Didn't I tell you so?

RANK: Let me play for her.

HELMER: [*getting up*] Yes, do. I can correct her better then.

[RANK *sits down at the piano and plays.* NORA *dances more and more wildly.* HELMER *has taken up a position beside the stove, and during her dance gives her frequent instructions. She does not seem to hear him; her hair comes down and falls over her shoulders; she pays no attention to it, but goes on dancing. Enter* MRS. LINDE.]

MRS. LINDE: [*standing as if spellbound in the doorway*] Oh!—

NORA: [*as she dances*] Such fun, Christine!

HELMER: My dear darling Nora, you are dancing as if your life depended on it.

NORA: So it does.

HELMER: Stop, Rank; this is sheer madness. Stop, I tell you! [RANK *stops playing, and* NORA *suddenly stands still.* HELMER *goes up to her.*] I could never have believed it. You have forgotten everything I taught you.

NORA: [*throwing away the tambourine*] There, you see.

HELMER: You'll want a lot of coaching.

NORA: Yes, you see how much I need it. You must coach me up to the last minute. Promise me that, Torvald!

HELMER: You can depend on me.

NORA: You must not think of anything but me, either to-day or to-morrow; you mustn't open a single letter—not even open the mail box—

HELMER: Ah, you're still afraid of that fellow—

NORA: Yes, indeed I am.

HELMER: Nora, I tell from your looks that there is a letter from him lying there.

NORA: I don't know; I think there is; but you must not read anything of that kind now. Nothing horrid must come between us till this is all over.

RANK: [*whispers to* HELMER] You mustn't contradict her.

HELMER: [*taking her in his arms*] The child shall have her way. But to-morrow night, after you've danced—

NORA: Then you will be free. [*The* MAID *appears in the doorway to the right.*]

MAID: Dinner is served, ma'am.

NORA: We will have champagne, Helen.

MAID: Very good, ma'am. [*exit*]

HELMER: Hullo!—are we going to have a banquet?

NORA: Yes, a champagne banquet till the small hours. [*calls out*] And a few macaroons, Helen—lots, just for once!

HELMER: Come, come, don't be so wild and nervous. Be my own little skylark.

NORA: Yes, dear, I will. But go in now and you, too, Doctor Rank. Christine, you must help me to do up my hair.

RANK: [*whispers to* HELMER *as they go out*] I suppose there's nothing—she is not expecting anything?

HELMER: Far from it, my dear fellow; it is simply nothing more than this childish nervousness I was telling you of. [*They go into the right-hand room.*]

NORA: Well!

MRS. LINDE: Gone out of town.

NORA: I could tell from your face.

MRS. LINDE: He's coming home to-morrow evening. I wrote a note for him.

NORA: You should have let it alone; you must prevent nothing. After all, it is splendid to be waiting for a wonderful thing to happen.

MRS. LINDE: What is it that you are waiting for?

NORA: Oh, you wouldn't understand. Go in to them, I will come in a moment. [MRS. LINDE *goes into the dining room.* NORA *stands still for a little while, as if to compose herself. Then she looks at her watch.*] Five o'clock. Seven hours till midnight; and then twenty-four hours till the next midnight. Then the Tarantella will be over. Twenty-four and seven? Thirty-one hours to live.

HELMER: [*from the doorway on the right*] Where's my little skylark?

NORA: [*going to him with her arms outstretched*] Here she is!

ACT III

THE SAME SCENE————*The table has been placed in the middle of the stage, with chairs round it. A lamp is burning on the table. The door into the hall stands open. Dance music is heard in the room above.* MRS. LINDE *is sitting at the table idly turning over the leaves of a book she tries to read, but does not seem able to collect her thoughts. Every now and then she listens intently for a sound at the outer door.*

MRS. LINDE: [*looking at her watch*] Not yet—and the time is nearly up. If only he doesn't—. [*listens again*] Ah, there he is. [*Goes into the hall and opens the outer door carefully. Light footsteps are heard on the stairs. She whispers.*] Come in. There's no one here.

KROGSTAD: [*in the doorway*] I found a note from you at home. What does this mean?

MRS. LINDE: It's absolutely necessary that I have a talk with you.

KROGSTAD: Really! And is it absolutely necessary that it should be here?

MRS. LINDE: It's impossible where I live; there's no private entrance to my rooms. Come in; we're quite alone. The maid's asleep and the Helmers are at the dance upstairs.

KROGSTAD: [*coming into the room*] Are the Helmers really at a dance to-night?

MRS. LINDE: Yes, why not?

KROGSTAD: Certainly—why not?

MRS. LINDE: Now, Nils, let's have a talk.

KROGSTAD: Can we two have anything to talk about.

MRS. LINDE: We have a great deal to talk about.

KROGSTAD: I shouldn't have thought so.

MRS. LINDE: No, you have never properly understood me.

KROGSTAD: Was there anything else to understand except what was obvious to all the world—a heartless woman jilts a man when a better catch turns up.

MRS. LINDE: Do you believe I'm as absolutely heartless as all that? And do you believe that I did it with a light heart?

KROGSTAD: Didn't you?

MRS. LINDE: Nils, did you really think that?

KROGSTAD: If it were as you say, why did you write to me as you did at that time?

MRS. LINDE: I could do nothing else. As I had to break with you, it was my duty also to put an end to all that you felt for me.

KROGSTAD: [*wringing his hands*] So that was it. And all this—only for the sake of money!

MRS. LINDE: You must not forget that I had a helpless mother and two little brothers. We couldn't wait for you, Nils; your prospects seemed hopeless then.

KROGSTAD: That may be so, but you had no right to throw me over for any one else's sake.

MRS. LINDE: Indeed I don't know. Many a time did I ask myself if I had the right to do it.

KROGSTAD: [*more gently*] When I lost you, it was as if all the solid ground went from under my feet. Look at me now—I'm a shipwrecked man clinging to a bit of wreckage.

MRS. LINDE: But help may be near.

KROGSTAD: It *was* near; but then you came and stood in my way.

MRS. LINDE: Unintentionally, Nils. It was only to-day that I learned it was your place I was going to take in the Bank.

KROGSTAD: I believe you, if you say so. But now that you know it, are you not going to give it up to me?

MRS. LINDE: No, because that would not benefit you in the least.

KROGSTAD: Oh, benefit, benefit—I would have done it whether or no.

MRS. LINDE: I have learned to act prudently. Life, and hard, bitter necessity have taught me that.

KROGSTAD: And life has taught me not to believe in fine speeches.

MRS. LINDE: Then life has taught you something very reasonable. But deeds you must believe in?

KROGSTAD: What do you mean by that?

MRS. LINDE: You said you were like a shipwrecked man clinging to some wreckage.

KROGSTAD: I had good reason to say so.

MRS. LINDE: Well, I am like a shipwrecked woman clinging to some wreckage—no one to mourn for, no one to care for.

KROGSTAD: It was your own choice.

MRS. LINDE: There was no other choice—then.

KROGSTAD: Well, what now?

MRS. LINDE: Nils, how would it be if we two shipwrecked people could join forces?

KROGSTAD: What are you saying?

MRS. LINDE: Two on the same piece of wreckage would stand a better chance than each on their own.

KROGSTAD: Christine!

MRS. LINDE: What do you suppose brought me to town?

KROGSTAD: Do you mean that you gave me a thought?

MRS. LINDE: I couldn't endure life without work. All my life, as long as I can remember, I have worked, and it's been my greatest and only pleasure. But now I'm quite alone in the world—my life is so dreadfully empty and I feel so forsaken. There is not the least pleasure in working for one's self. Nils, give me someone and something to work for.

KROGSTAD: I don't trust that. It's nothing but a woman's overstrained sense of generosity that prompts you to make such an offer of yourself.

MRS. LINDE: Have you ever noticed anything of the sort in me?

KROGSTAD: Could you really do it? Tell me—do you know all about my past life?

MRS. LINDE: Yes.

KROGSTAD: And do you know what they think of me here?

MRS. LINDE: You seemed to me to imply that with me you might have been quite another man.

KROGSTAD: I'm certain of it.

MRS. LINDE: Is it too late now?

KROGSTAD: Christine, are you saying this deliberately? Yes, I'm sure you are. I see it in your face. Have you really the courage, then—?

MRS. LINDE: I want to be a mother to someone, and your children need a mother. We two need each other. Nils, I have faith in your real character—I can dare anything together with you.

KROGSTAD: [*grasps her hand*] Thanks, thanks, Christine! Now I shall find a way to clear myself in the eyes of the world. Ah, but I forgot—

MRS. LINDE: [*listening*] Hush! The Tarantella! Go, go!

KROGSTAD: Why? What is it?

MRS. LINDE: Do you hear them up there? When that is over, we may expect them back.

KROGSTAD: Yes, yes—I will go. But it's all no use. Of course you're not aware what steps I've taken in the matter of the Helmers.

MRS. LINDE: Yes, I know all about that.

KROGSTAD: And in spite of that have you the courage to—?

MRS. LINDE: I understand very well to what lengths a man like you might be driven by despair.

KROGSTAD: If I could only undo what I've done!

MRS. LINDE: You cannot. Your letter is lying in the mail box now.

KROGSTAD: Are you sure of that?

MRS. LINDE: Quite sure, but—

KROGSTAD: [*with a searching look at her*] Is that what it all means?—that you want to save your friend at any cost? Tell me frankly. Is that it?

MRS. LINDE: Nils, a woman who has once sold herself for another's sake, doesn't do it a second time.

KROGSTAD: I'll ask for my letter back.

MRS. LINDE: No, no.

KROGSTAD: Yes, of course I will. I'll wait here till Torvald comes; I will tell him he must give me my letter back—that it only concerns my dismissal—that he's not to read it.

MRS. LINDE: No, Nils, you must not recall your letter.

KROGSTAD: But, tell me, wasn't it for that very purpose that you asked me to meet you here?

MRS. LINDE: In my first moment of fright, it was. But twenty-four hours have elapsed since then, and in that time I've witnessed incredible things in this house. Torvald must know all about it. This unhappy secret must be disclosed; they must have a complete understanding between them, which is impossible with all this concealment and falsehood going on.

KROGSTAD: Very well, if you will take the responsibility. But there's one thing I can do in any case, and I shall do it at once.

MRS. LINDE: [*listening*] You must be quick and go! The dance is over; we are not safe a moment longer.

KROGSTAD: I'll wait for you below.

MRS. LINDE: Yes, do. You must see me back to my door.

KROGSTAD: I have never had such an amazing piece of good fortune in my life! [*Goes out through the outer door. The door between the room and the hall remains open.*]

MRS. LINDE: [*tidying up the room and laying her hat and cloak ready*] What a difference! What a difference! Someone to work for and live for—a home to bring comfort into. That I will do, indeed. I wish they would be quick and come—[*listens*] Ah, there they are now. I must put on my things. [*Takes up her hat and cloak.* HELMER'*s and* NORA'*s voices are heard outside; a key is turned, and* HELMER *brings* NORA *almost by force into the hall. She is in an Italian costume with a large black shawl around her; he is in evening dress, and a black cloak which is flying open.*]

NORA: [*hanging back in the doorway, and struggling with him*] No, no, no!—don't take me in. I want to go upstairs again; I don't want to leave so early.

HELMER: But, my dearest Nora—

NORA: Please, Torvald dear—please, *please*—only an hour more.

HELMER: Not a single minute, my sweet Nora. You know that was our agreement. Come along into the room; you are catching cold standing there. [*He brings her gently into the room, in spite of her resistance.*]

MRS. LINDE: Good-evening.

NORA: Christine!

HELMER: You here, so late, Mrs. Linde?

MRS. LINDE: Yes, you must excuse me; I was so anxious to see Nora in her dress.

NORA: Have you been sitting here waiting for me?

MRS. LINDE: Yes, unfortunately I came too late; you had already gone upstairs, and I thought I couldn't go away again without having seen you.

HELMER: [*taking off* NORA's *shawl*] Yes, take a good look at her. I think she's worth looking at. Isn't she charming, Mrs. Linde?

MRS. LINDE: Yes, indeed she is.

HELMER: Doesn't she look remarkably pretty? Everyone thought so at the dance. But she is terribly self-willed, this sweet little person. What are we to do with her? You will hardly believe that I had almost to bring her away by force.

NORA: Torvald, you will repent not having let me stay, even if it were only for half an hour.

HELMER: Listen to her, Mrs. Linde! She had danced her Tarantella, and it had been a tremendous success, as it deserved—although possibly the performance was a trifle too realistic—a little more so, I mean, than was strictly compatible with propriety. But never mind about that! The chief thing is, she had made a success—she had made a tremendous success. Do you think I was going to let her remain there after that, and spoil the effect? No, indeed! I took my charming little Capri maiden—my capricious little Capri maiden, I should say—on my arm; took one quick turn around the room; a curtsy on either side, and, as they say in novels, the beautiful apparition disappeared. An exit ought always to be effective, Mrs. Linde; but that's what I cannot make Nora understand. Pooh! this room is hot. [*throws his cloak on a chair, and opens the door of his room*] Hullo! it's all dark in here. Oh, of course—excuse me—[*He goes in, and lights some candles.*]

NORA: [*in a hurried and breathless whisper*] Well?

MRS. LINDE: [*in a low voice*] I have had a talk with him.

NORA: Yes, and—

MRS. LINDE: Nora, you must tell your husband all about it.

NORA: [*in an expressionless voice*] I knew it.

MRS. LINDE: You have nothing to be afraid of as far as Krogstad is concerned; but you must tell him.

NORA: I won't tell him.

MRS. LINDE: Then the letter will.

NORA: Thank you, Christine. Now I know what I must do. Hush—!

HELMER: [*coming in again*] Well, Mrs. Linde, have you admired her?

MRS. LINDE: Yes, and now I will say good-night.

HELMER: What, already? Is this yours, this knitting?

MRS. LINDE: [*taking it*] Yes, thank you, I had very nearly forgotten it.

HELMER: So you knit?

MRS. LINDE: Of course.

HELMER: Do you know, you ought to embroider.

MRS. LINDE: Really? Why?

HELMER: Yes, it's far more becoming. Let me show you. You hold the embroidery thus in your left hand, and use the needle with the right—like this—with a long, easy sweep. Do you see?

MRS. LINDE: Yes, perhaps—

HELMER: But in the case of knitting—that can never be anything but ungraceful; look here—the arms close together, the knitting-needles going up and down—it has a sort of Chinese effect—. That was really excellent champagne they gave us.

MRS. LINDE: Well—good-night, Nora, and don't be stubborn any more.

HELMER: That's right, Mrs. Linde.

MRS. LINDE: Good-night, Mr. Helmer.

HELMER: [*accompanying her to the door*] Good-night, good-night. I hope you'll get home all right. I should be very happy to—but you haven't any great distance to go. Good-night, good-night. [*She goes out; he shuts the door after her, and comes in again.*] Ah!—at last we have got rid of her. She is a frightful bore, that woman.

NORA: Aren't you very tired, Torvald?

HELMER: No, not in the least.

NORA: Nor sleepy?

HELMER: Not a bit. On the contrary, I feel extraordinarily lively. And you?—you really look both tired and sleepy.

NORA: Yes, I'm very tired. I want to go to sleep at once.

HELMER: There, you see it was quite right of me not to let you stay there any longer.

NORA: Everything you do is quite right, Torvald.

HELMER: [*kissing her on the forehead*] Now my little skylark is speaking reasonably. Did you notice what good spirits Rank was in this evening?

NORA: Really? Was he? I didn't speak to him at all.

HELMER: And I very little, but I haven't seen him in such good form for a long time. [*looks for a while at her and then goes nearer to her*] It's delightful to be at home by ourselves again, to be all alone with you—you fascinating, charming little darling!

NORA: Don't look at me like that, Torvald.

HELMER: Why shouldn't I look at my dearest treasure?—at all the beauty that's mine, all mine?

NORA: [*going to the other side of the table*] You mustn't say things like that to me to-night.

HELMER: [*following her*] You have still got the Tarantella in your blood, I see. And it makes you more captivating than ever. Listen—the guests are beginning to leave now. [*in a lower voice*] Nora—soon the whole house will be quiet.

NORA: Yes, I hope so.

HELMER: Yes, my own darling Nora. Do you know when I'm out at a party with you like this, why I speak so little to you, keep away from you, and only send a stolen glance in your direction now and then?—do you know why I do that? It's because I make believe that we are secretly in love, and you are my secretly promised bride, and that no one suspects there is anything between us.

NORA: Yes, yes—I know very well you're thinking about me all the time.

HELMER: And when we are leaving, and I am putting the shawl over your beautiful young shoulders—on your lovely neck—then I imagine that you are my bride and that we have just come from the wedding, and I am bringing you for the first time into our home—to be alone with you for the first time—quite alone with my shy little darling! All this evening I have longed for nothing but you. When I watched the seductive figures of the Tarantella, my blood was on fire; I could endure it no longer, and that was why I brought you down so early—

NORA: Go away, Torvald! You must let me go. I won't—

HELMER: What's that? You're teasing, my little Nora! You won't—you won't? Am I not your husband—? [*A knock is heard at the outer door.*]

NORA: [*starting*] Did you hear—?

HELMER: [*going into the hall*] Who is it?

RANK: [*outside*] It is I. May I come in for a moment?

HELMER: [*in a fretful whisper*]. Oh, what does he want now? [*aloud*] Wait a minute? [*unlocks the door*] Come, that's kind of you not to pass by our door.

RANK: I thought I heard your voice, and felt as if I should like to look in. [*with a swift glance round*] Ah, yes!—these dear familiar rooms. You are very happy and cozy in here, you two.

HELMER: It seems to me that you looked after yourself pretty well upstairs, too.

RANK: Excellently. Why shouldn't I? Why shouldn't one enjoy everything in this world?—at any rate as much as one can, and as long as one can. The wine was capital—

HELMER: Especially the champagne.

RANK: So you noticed that, too? It's almost incredible how much I managed to put away!

NORA: Torvald drank a great deal of champagne to-night, too.

RANK: Did he?

NORA: Yes, and he is always in such good spirits afterwards.

RANK: Well, why should one not enjoy a merry evening after a well-spent day?

HELMER: Well spent: I'm afraid I can't take credit for that.

RANK: [*clapping him on the back*] But I can, you know!

NORA: Doctor Rank, you must have been occupied with some scientific investigation to-day.

RANK: Exactly.

HELMER: Just listen!—little Nora talking about scientific investigations!

NORA: And may I congratulate you on the result?

RANK: Indeed you may.

NORA: Was it favourable, then?

RANK: The best possible, for both doctor and patient—certainty.

NORA: [*quickly and searchingly*] Certainty?

RANK: Absolute certainty. So wasn't I entitled to make a merry evening of it after that?

NORA: Yes, you certainly were, Doctor Rank.

HELMER: I think so, too, so long as you don't have to pay for it in the morning.

RANK: Oh well, one can't have anything in this life without paying for it.

NORA: Doctor Rank—are you fond of masked balls?

RANK: Yes, if there's a fine lot of pretty costumes.

NORA: Tell me—what shall we two wear at the next?

HELMER: Little featherbrain!—are you thinking of the next already?

RANK: We two? Yes. I can tell you. You shall go as a good fairy—

HELMER: Yes, but what do you suggest as an appropriate costume for that?

RANK: Let your wife go dressed just as she is in everyday life.

HELMER: That was really very prettily turned. But can't you tell us what you'll be?

RANK: Yes, my dear friend, I have quite made up my mind about that.

HELMER: Well?

RANK: At the next fancy-dress ball I shall be invisible.

HELMER: That's a good joke!

RANK: There is a big black hat—have you never heard of hats that make you invisible? If you put one on, no one can see you.

HELMER: [*suppressing a smile*] Yes, you're quite right.

RANK: But I am clean fogetting what I came for. Helmer, give me a cigar—one of the dark Havanas.

HELMER: With the greatest pleasure. [*offers him his case*]

RANK: [*takes a cigar and cuts off the end*] Thanks.

NORA: [*striking a match*] Let me give you a light.

RANK: Thank you. [*She holds the match for him to light his cigar.*] And now good-bye!

HELMER: Good-bye, good-bye, dear old man!

NORA: Sleep well, Doctor Rank.

RANK: Thank you for that wish.

NORA: Wish me the same.

RANK: You? Well, if you want me to sleep well! And thanks for the light. [*He nods to them both and goes out.*]

HELMER: [*in a subdued voice*] He has drunk more than he ought.

NORA: [*absently*] Maybe. [HELMER *takes a bunch of keys out of his pocket and goes into the hall.*] Torvald! what are you going to do there?

HELMER: Empty the mail box; it's quite full; there will be no room for the newspaper, to-morrow morning.

NORA: Are you going to work to-night?

HELMER: You know quite well I'm not. What is this? Some one has been at the lock.

NORA: At the lock—?

HELMER: Yes, someone has. What can it mean? I should never have thought the maid—. Here is a broken hairpin. Nora, it is one of yours.

NORA: [*quickly*] Then it must have been the children—

HELMER: Then you must get them out of those ways. There, at last I have got it open. [*takes out the contents of the mail box, and calls to the kitchen*] Helen!— Helen, put out the light over the front door. [*Goes back into the room and shuts the door into the hall. He holds out his hand full of letters.*] Look at that—look what a heap of them there are. [*turning them over*] What on earth is that?

NORA: [*at the window*] The letter—No! Torvald, no!

HELMER: Two cards—of Rank's.

NORA: Of Doctor Rank's?

HELMER: [*looking at them*] Doctor Rank. They were on the top. He must have put them in when he went out.

NORA: Is there anything written on them?

HELMER: There is a black cross over the name. Look there—what an uncomfortable idea! It looks as if he were announcing his own death.

NORA: It's just what he's doing.

HELMER: What? Do you know anything about it? Has he said anything to you?

NORA: Yes. He told me that when the cards came it would be his leave-taking from us. He means to shut himself up and die.

HELMER: My poor old friend. Certainly I knew we should not have him very long with us. But so soon! And so he hides himself away like a wounded animal.

NORA: If it has to happen, it's best it should be without a word—don't you think so, Torvald?

HELMER: [*walking up and down*] He had so grown into our lives. I can't think of him as having gone out of them. He, with his sufferings and his loneliness, was like a cloudy background to our sunlit happiness. Well, perhaps it's best so. For him, anyway. [*standing still*] And perhaps for us, too, Nora. We two are thrown quite upon each other now. [*puts his arms round her*] My darling wife, I don't feel as if I could hold you tight enough. Do you know, Nora, I've often wished that you might be threatened by some great danger, so I might risk my life's blood, and everything, for your sake.

NORA: [*disengages herself, and says firmly and decidedly*] Now you must read your letters, Torvald.

HELMER: No, no; not to-night. I want to be with you, my darling wife.

NORA: With the thought of your friend's death—

HELMER: You are right, it has affected us both. Something ugly has come between us—the thought of the horrors of death. We must try and rid our minds of that. Until then—we'll each go to our own room.

NORA: [*hanging on his neck*] Good-night, Torvald—Good-night!

HELMER: [*kissing her on the forehead*] Good-night, my little singing-bird. Sleep sound, Nora. Now I'll read my letters through. [*He takes his letters and goes into his room, shutting the door after him.*]

NORA: [*gropes distractedly about, seizes* HELMER's *cloak, throws it round her, while she says in quick, hoarse, spasmodic whispers*] Never to see him again. Never! Never! [*puts her shawl over her head*] Never to see my children again, either—never again. Never! Never!—Ah! the icy, black water—the unfathomable depths—if only it were over! He has got it now—now he is reading it. Good-bye, Torvald and my children! [*She is about to rush out through the hall, when* HELMER *opens his door hurriedly and stands with an open letter in his hand.*]

HELMER: Nora!

NORA: Ah!—

HELMER: What's this? Do you know what's in this letter?

NORA: Yes, I know. Let me go! Let me get out!

HELMER: [*holding her back*] Where are you going?

NORA: [*trying to get free*] You shan't save me, Torvald!

HELMER: [*reeling*] True? Is this true, that I read here? Horrible! No, no—it's impossible that it can be true.

NORA: It's true. I have loved you above everything else in the world.

HELMER: Oh, don't let us have any silly excuses.

NORA: [*taking a step towards him*] Torvald—!

HELMER: Miserable creature—what have you done?

NORA: Let me go. You shall not suffer for my sake. You shall not take it upon yourself.

HELMER: No tragedy airs, please. [*locks the hall door*] Here you shall stay and give me an explanation. Do you understand what you've done? Answer me? Do you understand what you've done?

NORA: [*looks steadily at him and says with a growing look of coldness in her face*] Yes, now I am beginning to understand thoroughly.

HELMER: [*walking about the room*] What a horrible awakening! All these eight years—she who was my joy and pride—a hypocrite, a liar—worse, worse—a criminal! The unutterable ugliness of it all!—For shame! For shame! [NORA *is silent and looks steadily at him. He stops in front of her.*] I ought to have suspected that something of the sort would happen. I ought to have foreseen it. All your father's lack of principle—be silent!—all your father's lack of principle has come out in you. No religion, no morality, no sense of duty—. How I'm punished for having winked at what he did! I did it for your sake, and this is how you repay me.

NORA: Yes, that's just it.

HELMER: Now you have destroyed all my happiness. You've ruined my entire future. It is horrible to think of! I'm in the power of an unscrupulous man; he can do what he likes with me, ask anything he likes of me, give me any orders he pleases—I dare not refuse. And I must sink to such miserable depths because of a silly woman!

NORA: When I'm out of the way, you'll be free.

HELMER: No fine speeches, please. Your father had always plenty of those ready, too. What good would it be to me if you were out of the way, as you say? Not the slightest. He can make the affair known everywhere; and if he does, I may be falsely suspected of having been a party to your criminal action. Very likely people will think I was behind it all—that it was I who prompted you! and I have to thank you for all this—you whom I have cherished during the whole of our married life. Do you understand now what it is you have done to me?

NORA: [*coldly and quietly*] Yes.

HELMER: It's so incredible that I can't take it in. But we must come to some understanding. Take off that shawl. Take it off, I tell you. I must try and appease him some way or another. The matter must be hushed up at any cost. And as for you and me, it must appear as if everything between us were just as before—but naturally only in the eyes of the world. You will still remain in my house, that is a matter of course. But I shall not allow you to bring up the children; I dare not trust them to you. To think that I should be obliged to say so to one whom I have loved dearly, and whom I still—. No, that's all over. From this moment happiness is not the question; all that concerns us is to save the remains, the fragments, the appearance—

[*A ring is heard at the front-door bell.*]

HELMER: [*with a start*] What's that? So late? Can the worst—? Can he—? Hide yourself, Nora. Say you are ill.

[NORA *stands motionless.* HELMER *goes and unlocks the hall door.*]

MAID: [*half-dressed, comes to the door*] A letter for the mistress.

HELMER: Give it to me. [*takes the letter, and shuts the door*] Yes, it's from him. You shall not have it; I will read it myself.

NORA: Yes, read it.

HELMER: [*standing by the lamp*] I scarcely have the courage to do it. It may mean ruin for both of us. No, I must know. [*tears open the letter, runs his eye over a few lines, looks at a paper enclosed, and gives a shout of joy*] Nora! [*She looks at him questioningly.*] Nora!—No, I must read it once again—. Yes, it's true! I'm saved! Nora, I'm saved!

NORA: And I?

HELMER: You, too, of course; we are both saved, both you and I. Look, he sends you your bond back. He says he regrets and repents—that a happy change in his life—never mind what he says! We are saved, Nora! No one can do anything to you. Oh, Nora, Nora!—no, first I must destroy these hateful things. Let me see—. [*takes a look at the bond*] No, no, I won't look at it. The whole thing shall be nothing but a bad dream to me. [*tears up the bond and both letters, throws them all into the stove, and watches them burn*] There—now it doesn't exist any longer. He says that since Christmas Eve you—. These must have been three dreadful days for you, Nora.

NORA: I have fought a hard fight these three days.

HELMER: And suffered agonies, and seen no way out but—. No, we won't call any of the horrors to mind. We'll only shout with joy, and keep saying, "It's all over! It's all over!" Listen to me, Nora. You don't seem to realise that it is all over. What is this?—such a cold, set face! My poor little Nora, I quite understand; you don't feel that I have forgiven you. But it's true, Nora, I swear it; I've forgiven you everything. I know that what you did, you did out of love for me.

NORA: That's true.

HELMER: You have loved me as a wife ought to love her husband. Only you hadn't sufficient knowledge to judge of the means you used. But do you suppose you are any the less dear to me, because you don't understand how to act on your own responsibility? No, no; only lean on me; I will advise you and direct you. I should not be a man if this womanly helplessness did not just give you a double attractiveness in my eyes. You mustn't think any more about the hard things I said in my first moment of consternation, when I thought everything was going to overwhelm me. I've forgiven you, Nora; I swear to you I've forgiven you.

NORA: Thank you for your forgiveness. [*She goes out through to the door to the right.*]

HELMER: No, don't go—[*looks in*] What are you doing in there?

NORA: [*from within*] Taking off my costume.

HELMER: [*standing at the open door*] Yes, do. Try and calm yourself, and make your mind easy again, my frightened little singing-bird. Be at rest, and feel secure; I have broad wings to shelter you under. [*walks up and down by the door*] How warm and cozy our home is, Nora. Here is shelter for you; here I'll protect you like a hunted dove that I have saved from a hawk's claws: I'll bring peace to your poor beating heart. It will come, little by little, Nora, believe me. To-morrow morning you will look upon it all quite differently; soon everything will be just as it was before. Very soon you won't need me to assure you that I've forgiven you; you will feel the certainty that I've done so. Can you suppose I should ever think of such a thing as repudiating you, or even reproaching you? You have no idea what a true man's heart is like, Nora. There is something so inde-scribably sweet and satisfying, to a man, in the knowledge that he has for-given his wife—forgiven her freely, and with all his heart. It seems as if that had made her, as it were, doubly his own; he has given her a new life, so to speak; and she has in a way become both wife and child to him. So you shall be for me after this, my little scared, helpless darling. Have no anxiety about anything, Nora; only be frank and open with me, and I'll serve as will and conscience both to you—. What's this? Not gone to bed? Have you changed your clothes?

NORA: [*in everyday dress*] Yes, Torvald, I have changed my clothes now.

HELMER: But what for?—so late as this.

NORA: I shall not sleep to-night.

HELMER: But, my dear Nora—

NORA: [*looking at her watch*] It's not so very late. Sit down here, Torvald. You and I have much to say to one another. [*She sits down at one side of the table.*]

HELMER: Nora—what's this?—this cold, set face!

NORA: Sit down. It'll take some time; I have a lot to talk over with you.

HELMER: [*sits down at the opposite side of the table*] You alarm me, Nora!—and I don't understand you.

NORA: No, that's just it. You don't understand me, and I've never understood you either—before to-night. No, you mustn't interrupt me. You must simply lis-ten to what I say. Torvald, this is a settling of accounts.

HELMER: What do you mean by that?

NORA: [*after a short silence*] Isn't there any thing that strikes you as strange in our sitting here like this?

HELMER: What is that?

NORA: We've been married now eight years. Doesn't it occur to you that this is the first time we two, you and I, husband and wife, have had a serious con-versation?

HELMER: What do you mean by "serious"?

NORA: In all these eight years—longer than that—from the beginning of our ac-quaintance, we've never exchanged a word on any serious subject.

HELMER: Was it likely that I would be continually and for ever telling you about worries that you couldn't help me with?

NORA: I'm not speaking about business matters. I say that we have never sat down in earnest together to try and get at the bottom of anything.

HELMER: But, dearest Nora, would it have been any good to you?

NORA: That's just it; you've never understood me. I have been greatly wronged, Torvald—first by papa and then by you.

HELMER: What! By us two—by us two, who've loved you better than anyone else in the world?

NORA: [*shaking her head*] You've never loved me. You've only thought it pleasant to be in love with me.

HELMER: Nora, what do I hear you saying?

NORA: It's perfectly true, Torvald. When I was at home with papa, he told me his opinion about everything, and so I had the same opinions; and if I differed from him I concealed the fact, because he wouldn't have liked it. He called me his doll-child, and he played with me just as I used to play with my dolls. And when I came to live with you—

HELMER: What sort of an expression is that to use about our marriage?

NORA: [*undisturbed*] I mean that I was simply transferred from papa's hands into yours. You arranged everything according to your own taste, and so I got the same tastes as you—or else I pretended to. I'm really not quite sure which—I think sometimes the one and sometimes the other. When I look back on it, it seems to me as if I'd been living here like a poor woman—just from hand to mouth. I've existed merely to perform tricks for you, Torvald. But you would have it so. You and papa have committed a great sin against me. It's your fault that I have made nothing of my life.

HELMER: How unreasonable and how ungrateful you are, Nora! Have you not been happy here?

NORA: No, I have never been happy. I thought I was, but it's never really been so.

HELMER: Not—not happy!

NORA: No, only merry. And you've always been so kind to me. But our home has been nothing but a playroom. I've been your doll-wife, just as at home I was papa's doll-child; and here the children have been my dolls. I thought it great fun when you played with me, just as they thought it great fun when I played with them. That's what our marriage has been, Torvald.

HELMER: There is some truth in what you say—exaggerated and strained as your view of it is. But for the future it'll be different. Playtime shall be over, and lesson-time shall begin.

NORA: Whose lessons? Mine, or the children's?

HELMER: Both yours and the children's, my darling Nora.

NORA: Alas, Torvald, you're not the man to educate me into being a proper wife for you.

HELMER: And you can say that?

NORA: And I—how am I fitted to bring up the children?

HELMER: Nora!

NORA: Didn't you say so yourself a little while ago—that you dare not trust me to bring them up?

HELMER: In a moment of anger! Why do you pay any heed to that?

NORA: Indeed, you were perfectly right. I'm not fit for the task. There is another task I must undertake first. I must try and educate myself—you're not the man to help me in that. I must do that for myself. And that's why I'm going to leave you now.

HELMER: [*springing up*] What do you say?

NORA: I must stand quite alone, if I'm to understand myself and everything about me. It's for that reason that I cannot remain with you any longer.

HELMER: Now, Nora!

NORA: I'm going away from here now, at once. I'm sure Christine will take me in for the night—

HELMER: You're out of your mind! I won't allow it! I forbid you!

NORA: It's no use forbidding me anything any longer. I'll take with me what belongs to myself. I'll take nothing from you, either now or later.

HELMER: What sort of madness is this!

NORA: To-morrow I'll go home—I mean, to my old home. It will be easiest for me to find something to do there.

HELMER: You blind, foolish woman!

NORA: I must try and get some sense, Torvald.

HELMER: To desert your home, your husband, and your children! And you don't consider what people will say!

NORA: I can't consider that at all. I only know that it is necessary for me.

HELMER: It's shocking. This is how you would neglect your most sacred duties.

NORA: What do you consider my most sacred duties?

HELMER: Do I need to tell you that? Are they not your duties to your husband and your children?

NORA: I have other duties just as sacred.

HELMER: That you have not. What duties could those be?

NORA: Duties to myself.

HELMER: Before all else, you are a wife and a mother.

NORA: I don't believe that any longer. I believe that before all else I'm a reasonable human being, just as you are—or, at all events, that I must try and become one. I know quite well, Torvald, that most people would think you right, and that views of that kind are to be found in books; but I can no longer content myself with what most people say, or with what's found in books. I must think over things for myself and get to understand them.

HELMER: Can't you understand your place in your own home? Haven't you a reliable guide in such matters as that?—have you no religion?

NORA: I'm afraid, Torvald, I do not exactly know what religion is.

HELMER: What're you saying?

NORA: I know nothing but what the clergyman said, when I went to be confirmed. He told us that religion was this, and that, and the other. When I'm away from all this, and am alone, I'll look into that matter, too. I'll see if what the clergyman said is true, or at all events if it is true for me.

HELMER: This is unheard of in a woman of your age! But if religion cannot touch you, let me try and awaken your conscience. I suppose you have some moral sense? Or—answer me—am I to think you have none?

NORA: I assure you, Torvald, that is not an easy question to answer. I really don't know. The thing puzzles me altogether. I only know that you and I look at it in quite a different light. I'm learning, too, that the law is quite another thing from what I supposed; but I find it impossible to convince myself that the law is right. According to it a woman has no right to spare her old dying father, or to save her husband's life. I can't believe that.

HELMER: You talk like a child. You don't understand the conditions of the world in which you live.

NORA: No, I don't. But now I'm going to try. I'm going to see if I can make out who is right, the world or I.

HELMER: You're ill, Nora; you're delirious; I almost think you're out of your mind.

NORA: I've never felt my mind so clear and certain as to-night.

HELMER: And is it with a clear and certain mind that you forsake your husband and your children?

NORA: Yes, it is.

HELMER: Then there is only one possible explanation.

NORA: What is that?

HELMER: You don't love me any more.

NORA: No, that's just it.

HELMER: Nora!—and you can say that?

NORA: It gives me great pain, Torvald, for you have always been so kind to me, but I can't help it. I don't love you any more.

HELMER: [*regaining his composure*] Is that a clear and certain conviction, too?

NORA: Yes, absolutely clear and certain. That's the reason why I'll not stay here any longer.

HELMER: And can you tell me what I've done to forfeit your love?

NORA: Yes, indeed I can. It was to-night, when the wonderful thing did not happen; then I saw you were not the man I had thought you.

HELMER: Explain yourself better—I don't understand you.

NORA: I've waited so patiently for eight years; for, goodness knows, I knew very well that wonderful things don't happen every day. Then this horrible misfortune came upon me; and then I felt quite certain that the wonderful thing was going to happen at last. When Krogstad's letter was lying out there, never for a moment did I imagine that you would consent to accept this man's conditions. I was so absolutely certain that you would say to him: Publish the thing to the whole world. And when that was done—

HELMER: Yes, what then?—when I had exposed my wife to shame and disgrace?

NORA: When that was done, I was so absolutely certain, you would come forward and take everything upon yourself, and say I'm the guilty one.

HELMER: Nora—!

NORA: You mean that I would never have accepted such a sacrifice on your part? No, of course not. But what would my assurances have been worth against yours? That was the wonderful thing which I hoped for and feared; and it was to prevent that, that I wanted to kill myself.

HELMER: I would gladly work night and day for you, Nora—bear sorrow and want for your sake. But no man would sacrifice his honour for the one he loves.

NORA: Millions of women have done it.

HELMER: Oh, you think and talk like a heedless child.

NORA: Maybe. But you neither think nor talk like the man I could bind myself to. As soon as your fear was over—and it was not fear for what threatened me, but for what might happen to you—when the whole thing was past, as far as you were concerned it was exactly as if nothing at all had happened. Exactly as before, I was your little skylark, your doll, which you would in future treat with doubly gentle care, because it was so brittle and fragile. [*getting up*] Torvald—it was then it dawned on me that for eight years I'd been living here with a strange man, and had borne him three children—. Oh, I can't bear to think of it! I could tear myself into little bits!

HELMER: [*sadly*] I see, I see. An abyss has opened between us—there's no denying it. But, Nora, wouldn't it be possible to fill it up?

NORA: As I am now, I'm no wife for you.

HELMER: I have it in me to become a different man.

NORA: Perhaps—if your doll is taken away from you.

HELMER: But to part!—to part from you! No, no. Nora, I can't understand that idea.

NORA: [*going out to the right*] That makes it all the more certain that it must be done. [*She comes back with her cloak and hat and a small bag, which she puts on a chair by the table.*]

HELMER: Nora, Nora, not now! Wait till to-morrow.

NORA: [*putting on her cloak*] I can't spend the night in a strange man's room.

HELMER: But can't we live here like brother and sister—?

NORA: [*putting on her hat*] You know very well that wouldn't last long. [*puts the shawl round her*] Good-bye, Torvald. I won't see the little ones. I know they are in better hands than mine. As I am now, I can be of no use to them.

HELMER: But some day, Nora—some day?

NORA: How can I tell? I have no idea what is going to become of me.

HELMER: But you are my wife, whatever becomes of you.

NORA: Listen, Torvald. I have heard that when a wife deserts her husband's house, as I'm doing now, he is legally freed from all obligations towards her. In any case I set you free from all your obligations. You're not to feel yourself bound in the slightest way, any more than I shall. There must be perfect freedom on both sides. See, here is your ring back. Give me mine.

HELMER: That, too?

NORA: That, too.

HELMER: Here it is.

NORA: That's right. Now it's all over. I've put the keys here. The maids know all about everything in the house—better than I do. To-morrow, after I've left her, Christine will come here and pack up my own things that I brought with me from home. I'll have them sent to me.

HELMER: All over! all over!—Nora, shall you never think of me again?

NORA: I know I'll often think of you and the children and this house.

HELMER: May I write to you, Nora?

NORA: No—never. You must not do that.

HELMER: But at least let me send you—

NORA: Nothing—nothing—

HELMER: Let me help you if you're in want.

NORA: No. I can receive nothing from a stranger.

HELMER: Nora—can I never be anything more than a stranger to you?

NORA: [*taking her bag*] Ah, Torvald, the most miraculous thing of all would have to happen.

HELMER: Tell me what that would be!

NORA: Both you and I would have to be so changed that—Oh, Torvald, I don't believe any longer in miracles happening.

HELMER: But I will believe in it. Tell me? So changed that—?

NORA: That our life together would be a real wedlock. Good-bye. [*She goes out through the hall.*]

HELMER: [*sinks down on a chair at the door and buries his face in his hands*] Nora! Nora! [*looks round, and rises*] Empty. She is gone. [*A hope flashes across his mind.*] The most miraculous thing of all—?

[*The sound of a door shutting is heard from below.*]

Eugene O'Neill (1888–1953)

"The Hairy Ape" (1921)

Eugene O'Neill was the first American dramatist to win widespread international fame. He experimented with many dramatic forms and styles in his twenty-five full-length plays. In *The Hairy Ape* he adopted many conventions of expressionism, an artistic movement that emerged in Germany just prior to World War I. The expressionists proclaimed the supreme importance of the human spirit, which they believed was being crushed or distorted by materialism and industrialism.

"The Hairy Ape" shows the influence of expressionism on American drama. The unity of the play derives from a central theme: humanity's frustrated search for identity in a hostile environment. In the first scene, Yank is confident that he and his fellow stokers are the only ones who belong because it is they who make the ship go (and by extension the factories and machines of modern industrialized society). But when Yank is told that the pampered, anemic daughter of one of the shipowners (who represents power, money, and influence) has called him "a hairy ape," his confidence is shattered. Seeking to reestablish his identity, he first visits Fifth Avenue, the home territory of the rich and powerful, where he proclaims his superiority by physically attacking the men, only to have his very existence go unacknowledged. Thrown into jail, he decides that the answer lies in destroying the steel and machinery over which he originally thought he had power. In jail he learns that the International Workers of the World (IWW) opposes the owners of factories and ships and, when he is released, he offers to blow up the IWW's enemies. Rejected there, too, Yank visits the apes in the zoo, but when he releases a gorilla it crushes him, and he dies without having achieved a sense of belonging. Yank is symbolic of modern humanity in an industrialized society—cut off from a past when human beings had an integral relationship with the natural environment and now little better than cogs in the industrial machine.

"The Hairy Ape" is representative of the outlook and techniques of expressionism. The episodic structure and distorted visual elements are typical of the movement, as is the longing for fulfillment, which suggests the need to change society so that the individual can find a coherent, satisfying relationship with the environment.

Eugene O'Neill

"The Hairy Ape"

CHARACTERS

ROBERT SMITH, "YANK"
PADDY
LONG
MILDRED DOUGLAS
HER AUNT
SECOND ENGINEER
A GUARD
A SECRETARY OF AN ORGANIZATION
STOKERS, LADIES, GENTLEMEN, ETC.

SCENES

Scene I: The firemen's forecastle of an ocean liner—an hour after sailing from
  New York.
Scene II: Section of promenade deck, two days out—morning.
Scene III: The stokehole. A few minutes later.
Scene IV: Same as Scene I. Half an hour later.
Scene V: Fifth Avenue, New York. Three weeks later.
Scene VI: An island near the city. The next night.
Scene VII: In the city. About a month later.
Scene VIII: In the city. Twilight of the next day.

SCENE I

*The firemen's forecastle of a transatlantic liner an hour after sailing from New York for
the voyage across. Tiers of narrow, steel bunks, three deep, on all sides. An entrance in
rear. Benches on the floor before the bunks. The room is crowded with men, shouting, cursing, laughing, singing—a confused, inchoate uproar swelling into a sort of unity, a
meaning—the bewildered, furious, baffled defiance of a beast in a cage. Nearly all the
men are drunk. Many bottles are passed from hand to hand. All are dressed in dungaree
pants, heavy, ugly shoes. Some wear singlets, but the majority are stripped to the waist.*

    *The treatment of this scene, or of any other scene in the play, should by no means
be naturalistic. The effect sought after is a cramped space in the bowels of a ship, im-
prisoned by white steel. The lines of bunks, the uprights supporting them, cross each other
like the steel framework of a cage. The ceiling crushes down upon the men's heads. They
cannot stand upright. This accentuates the natural stooping posture which shoveling coal
and the resultant overdevelopment of back and shoulder muscles have given them. The*

men themselves should resemble those pictures in which the appearance of Neanderthal Man is guessed at. All are hairy-chested, with long arms of tremendous power, and low, receding brows above their small, fierce, resentful eyes. All the civilized white races are represented, but except for the slight differentiation in color of hair, skin, eyes, all these men are alike.

The curtain rises on a tumult of sound. YANK *is seated in the foreground. He seems broader, fiercer, more truculent, more powerful, more sure of himself than the rest. They respect his superior strength—the grudging respect of fear. Then, too, he represents to them a self-expression, the very last word in what they are, their most highly developed individual.*

VOICES: Gif me trink dere, you!
    'Ave a wet!
    Salute!
    Gesundheit!
    Skoal!
    Drunk as a lord, God stiffen you!
    Here's how!
    Luck!
    Pass back that bottle, damn you!
    Pourin' it down his neck!
    Ho, Froggy! Where the devil have you been?
    La Touraine.
    I hit him smash in yaw, py Gott!
    Jenkins—the First—he's a rotten swine—
    And the coppers nabbed him—and I run—
    I like peer better. It don't pig head gif you.
    A slut, I'm sayin'! She robbed me aslape—
    To hell with 'em all!
    Your're a bloody liar!
    Say dot again!
    [*Commotion. Two men about to fight are pulled apart.*]
    No scrappin' now!
    Tonight—
    See who's the best man!
    Bloody Dutchman!
    Tonight on the for'ard square.
    I'll bet on Dutchy.
    He packa da wallop, I tella you!
    Shut up, Wop!
    No fightin', maties. We're all chums, ain't we?
    [*A voice starts bawling a song.*]
        Beer, beer, glorious beer!
        Fill yourselves right up to here.
YANK: [*for the first time seeming to take notice of the uproar about him, turns around threateningly—in a tone of contemptuous authority*] Choke off dat noise! Where d'yuh get dat beer stuff? Beer, hell! Beer's for goils—and Dutchmen. Me for somep'n wit a kick to it! Gimme a drink, one of youse guys.

[*Several bottles are eagerly offered. He takes a tremendous gulp at one of them; then, keeping the bottle in his hand, glares belligerently at the owner, who hastens to acquiesce in this robbery by saying.*] All righto, Yank. Keep it and have another. [YANK *contemptuously turns his back on the crowd again. For a second there is an embarrassed silence. Then*—]

VOICES: We must be passing the Hook.
　　　　She's beginning to roll to it.
　　　　Six days in hell—and then Southampton.
　　　　Py Yesus, I vish somepody take my first vatch for me!
　　　　Gittin seasick, Square-head?
　　　　Drink up and forget it!
　　　　What's in your bottle?
　　　　Gin.
　　　　Dot's nigger trink.
　　　　Absinthe? It's doped. You'll go off your chump, Froggy!
　　　　Cochon!
　　　　Whisky, that's the ticket!
　　　　Where's Paddy?
　　　　Going asleep.
　　　　Sing us that whisky song, Paddy.
　　　　　　[*They all turn to an old, wizened Irishman who is dozing, very drunk, on the benches forward. His face is extremely monkey-like with all the sad, patient pathos of that animal in his small eyes.*]
　　　　Singa da song, Caruso Pat!
　　　　He's gettin' old. The drink is too much for him.
　　　　He's too drunk.
PADDY: [*blinking about him, starts to his feet resentfully, swaying, holding on to the edge of a bunk*] I'm never too drunk to sing. 'Tis only when I'm dead to the world I'd be wishful to sing at all. [*with a sort of sad contempt*] "Whisky Johnny," ye want? A chanty, ye want? Now that's a queer wish from the ugly like of you, God help you. But no matther. [*He starts to sing in a thin, nasal, doleful tone.*]
　　　　　　　　Oh, whisky is the life of man!
　　　　　　　　　Whisky! O Johnny! [*They all join in on this.*]
　　　　　　　　Oh, whisky is the life of man!
　　　　　　　　　Whisky for my Johnny! [*Again chorus.*]
　　　　　　　　Oh, whisky drove my old man mad!
　　　　　　　　　Whisky! O Johnny!
　　　　　　　　Oh, whisky drove my old man mad!
　　　　　　　　　Whisky for my Johnny!
YANK: [*again turning around scornfully*] Aw hell! Nix on dat old sailing ship stuff! All dat bull's dead, see? And you're dead, too, yuh damned old Harp, on'y yuh don't know it. Take it easy, see. Give us a rest. Nix on de loud noise. [*with a cynical grin*] Can't youse see I'm tryin to t'ink?
ALL: [*repeating the word after him as one with the same cynical amused mockery*] Think! [*The chorused word has a brazen metallic quality as if their throats were phonograph horns. It is followed by a general uproar of hard, barking laughter.*]
VOICES: Don't be cracking your head wit ut, Yank!

You gat headache, py yingo!
One thing about it—it rhymes with drink!
Ha, ha, ha!
Drink, don't think!
Drink, don't think!
Drink, don't think!

[*A whole chorus of voices has taken up this refrain, stamping on the floor, pounding on the benches with fists.*]

YANK: [*taking a gulp from his bottle—good-naturedly*] Aw right. Can de noise. I got yuh de foist time. [*The uproar subsides. A very drunken sentimental tenor begins to sing.*]

> Far away in Canada,
> Far across the sea,
> There's a lass who fondly waits
> Making a home for me—

YANK: [*fiercely contemptuous*] Shut up, yuh lousy boob! Where d'yuh get dat tripe? Home? Home, hell! I'll make a home for yuh! I'll knock yuh dead. Home! T'hell wit home! Where d'yuh get dat tripe? Dis is home, see? What d'yuh want wit home? [*proudly*] I runned away from mine when I was a kid. On'y too glad to beat it, dat was me. Home was lickings for me, dat's all. But yuh can bet your shoit no one ain't never licked me since! Wanter try it, any of youse? Huh! I guess not. [*in a more placated but still contemptuous tone*] Goils waitin' for yuh, huh? Aw, hell! Dat's all tripe. Dey don't wait for no one. Dey'd double-cross yuh for a nickel. Dey're all tarts, get me? Treat 'em rough, dat's me. To hell wit 'em. Tarts, dat's what, de whole bunch of 'em.

LONG: [*very drunk, jumps on a bench excitedly, gesticulating with a bottle in his hand*] Listen 'ere, Comrades! Yank 'ere is right. 'E says this 'ere stinkin' ship is our 'ome. And 'e says as 'ome is 'ell. And 'e's right! This is 'ell. We lives in 'ell, Comrades—and right enough we'll die in it. [*raging*] And who's ter blame, I arsks yer? We ain't. We wasn't born this rotten way. All men is born free and ekal. That's in the bleedin' Bible, maties. But what d'they care for the Bible—them lazy, bloated swine what travels first cabin? Them's the ones. They dragged us down 'til we're on'y wage slaves in the bowels of a bloody ship, sweatin', burnin' up, eatin' coal dust! Hit's them's ter blame—the damned Capitalist clarss!

[*There had been a gradual murmur of contemptuous resentment rising among the men until now he is interrupted by a storm of catcalls, hisses, boos, hard laughter.*]

VOICES: Turn it off!
Shut up!
Sit down!
Closa da face!
Tamn fool! [*Etc.*]

YANK: [*standing up and glaring at* LONG] Sit down before I knock yuh down! [LONG *makes haste to efface himself.* YANK *goes on contemptuously.*] De Bible, huh? De Cap'tlist class, huh? Aw nix on dat Salvation Army–Socialist bull. Git a soapbox! Hire a hall! Come and be saved, huh? Jerk us to Jesus, huh? Aw g'wan! I've listened to lots of guys like you, see. Yuh're all wrong. Wanter know what I t'ink? Yuh ain't no good for no one. Yuh're de bunk. Yuh ain't got no noive, get me? Yuh're yellow, dat's what. Yellow, dat's you. Say! What's dem slobs in de foist cabin got to do wit us? We're better men dan dey are, ain't we? Sure! One of us guys could clean up de whole mob wit one mitt. Put one of 'em down here for one watch in de stokehole, what'd happen? Dey'd carry him off on a stretcher. Dem boids don't amount to nothin'. Dey're just baggage. Who makes dis old tub run? Ain't it us guys? Well den, we belong, don't we? We belong and dey don't. Dat's all. [*A loud chorus of approval.* YANK *goes on.*] As for dis bein' hell—aw, nuts! Yuh lost your noive, dat's what. Dis is a man's job, get me? It belongs. It runs dis tub. No stiffs need apply. But yuh're a stiff, see? Yuh're yellow, dat's you.

VOICES: [*with a great hard pride in them*]
  Righto!
  A man's job!
  Talk is cheap, Long.
  He never could hold up his end.
  Divil take him!
  Yank's right. We make it go.
  Py Gott, Yank say right ting!
  We don't need no one cryin' over us.
  Makin' speeches.
  Throw him out!
  Yellow!
  Chuck him overboard!
  I'll break his jaw for him!
    [*They crowd around* LONG *threateningly.*]

YANK: [*half good-natured again—contemptuously*] Aw, take it easy. Leave him alone. He ain't woith a punch. Drink up. Here's how, whoever owns dis. [*He takes a long swallow from his bottle. All drink with him. In a flash all is hilarious amiability again, back-slapping, loud talk, etc.*]

PADDY: [*who has been sitting in a blinking, melancholy daze—suddenly cries out in a voice full of old sorrow*] We belong to this, you're saying? We make the ship to go, you're saying? Yerra then, that Almighty God have pity on us! [*His voice runs into the wail of a keen, he rocks back and forth on his bench. The men stare at him, startled and impressed in spite of themselves.*] Oh, to be back in the fine days of my youth, ochone! Oh, there was fine beautiful ships them days—clippers wid tall masts touching the sky—fine strong men in them—men that was sons of the sea as if 'twas the mother that bore them. Oh, the clean skins of them, and the clear eyes, the straight backs and full chests of them! Brave men they was, and bold men surely! We'd be sailing out, bound down round the Horn maybe. We'd be making sail in the dawn, with a fair breeze, singing a chanty song wid no care to it. And astern the land would be sinking low and dying out, but we'd give it no heed but a laugh, and never a look behind. For the day that was, was enough, for we was free men—and I'm thinking 'tis only slaves do be giving heed to the day that's gone or the day to come—until they're old like me. [*with a sort of religious exaltation*] Oh, to be scudding south again wid the power of the Trade Wind driving her on steady through the nights and the days! Full sail on her! Nights and days! Nights when the foam of the wake would be flaming wid fire, when the sky'd be blazing and winking wid stars. Or the full of the moon maybe. Then you'd see her driving through the gray night, her sails stretching aloft all silver and white, not a sound on the deck, the lot of us dreaming dreams, till you'd believe 'twas no real ship at all you was on but a ghost ship like the *Flying Dutchman* they say does be roaming the seas forevermore widout touching a port. And there was the days, too. A warm sun on the clean decks. Sun warming the blood of you, and wind over the miles of shiny green ocean like strong drink to your lungs. Work—aye, hard work—but who'd mind that at all? Sure, you worked under the sky and 'twas work wid skill and daring to it. And wid the day done, in the dog watch, smoking me pipe at ease, the lookout would be raising land maybe, and we'd see the mountains of South Americy wid the red fire of the setting sun painting their white tops and the clouds floating by them! [*His tone of exaltation ceases. He goes on mournfully.*] Yerra, what's the use of talking? 'Tis a dead man's whisper. [*to* YANK *resentfully*] 'Twas them days men belonged to ships, not now. 'Twas them days a ship was part of the sea, and a man was part of a ship, and the sea joined all together and made it one. [*scornfully*] Is it one wid this you'd be, Yank—black smoke from the funnels smudging the sea, smudging the decks—the bloody engines pounding and throbbing and shaking—wid divil a sight of sun or a breath of clean air—choking our lungs wid coal dust—breaking our backs and hearts in the hell of the stokehole—feeding the bloody furnace—feeding our lives along wid the coal, I'm thinking—caged in by steel from a sight of the sky like bloody apes in the zoo! [*with a harsh laugh*] Ho-ho, divil mend you! Is it to belong to that you're wishing? Is it a flesh and blood wheel of the engines you'd be?

YANK: [*who has been listening with a contemptuous sneer, barks out the answer*] Sure ting! Dat's me. What about it?

PADDY: [*as if to himself—with great sorrow*] Me time is past due. That a great wave wid sun in the heart of it may sweep me over the side sometime I'd be dreaming of the days that's gone!

YANK: Aw, yuh crazy Mick! [*He springs to his feet and advances on* PADDY *threateningly—then stops, fighting some queer struggle within himself—lets his hands fall to his sides—contemptuously.*] Aw, take it easy. Yuh're aw right, at dat. Yuh're bugs, dat's all—nutty as a cuckoo. All dat tripe yuh been pullin'—Aw, dat's all right. On'y it's dead, get me? Yuh don't belong no more, see. Yuh don't got de stuff. Yuh're too old. [*disgustedly*] But aw say, come up for air onct in a while, can't yuh? See what's happened since yuh croaked. [*He suddenly bursts forth vehemently, growing more and more excited.*] Say! Sure! Sure I meant it! What de hell—Say, lemme talk! Hey! Hey, you old Harp! Hey, youse guys! Say, listen to me—wait a moment—I gotter talk, see. I belong and he don't. He's dead but I'm livin'. Listen to me! Sure I'm part of de engines! Why de hell not! Dey move, don't dey? Dey're speed, ain't dey? Dey smash trou, don't dey! Twenty-five knots a hour! Dat's goin' some! Dat's new stuff! Dat belongs! But him, he's too old. He gets dizzy. Say, listen. All dat crazy tripe about nights and days; all dat crazy tripe about stars and moons; all dat crazy tripe about suns and winds, fresh air and de rest of it—Aw hell, dat's all a dope dream! Hittin' de pipe of de past, dat's what he's doin'. He's old and don't belong no more. But me, I'm young! I'm in de pink! I move wit it! It, get me! I mean de ting dat's de guts of all dis. It ploughs trou all de tripe he's been sayin'. It blows dat up! It knocks dat dead! It slams dat offen de face of de Oith! It, get me! De engines and de coal and de smoke and all de rest of it! He can't breathe and swallow coal dust, but I kin, see? Dat's fresh air for me! Dat's food for me! I'm new, get me? Hell in de stokehole? Sure! It takes a man to work in hell. Hell, sure, dat's my fav'rite climate. I eat it up! I git fat on it! It's me makes it hot! It's me makes it roar! It's me makes it move! Sure, on'y for me everyting stops. It all goes dead, get me? De noise and smoke and all de engines movin' de woild, dey stop. Dere ain't nothin' no more! Dat's what I'm sayin'. Everyting else dat makes de woild move, somep'n makes it move. It can't move without somep'n else, see? Den yuh get down to me. I'm at de bottom, get me! Dere ain't nothin' foither. I'm de end! I'm de start! I start somep'n and de woild moves! It—dat's me!—de new dat's moiderin' de old! I'm de ting in coal dat makes it boin; I'm steam and oil for de engines; I'm de ting in noise dat makes yuh hear it; I'm smoke and express trains and steamers and factory whistles; I'm de ting in gold dat makes it money! And I'm what makes iron into steel! Steel, dat stands for de whole ting! And I'm steel—steel—steel! I'm de muscles in steel, de punch behind it! [*As he says this he pounds with his fist against the steel bunks. All the men, roused to a pitch of frenzied self-glorification by his speech, do likewise. There is a deafening metallic roar, through which* YANK's *voice can be heard bellowing.*] Slaves, hell. We run de whole woiks. All de rich guys dat tink dey're somep'n, dey ain't nothin'! Dey don't belong. But us guys, we're in de move, we're at de bottom, de whole ting is us! [PADDY *from the start of* YANK's *speech has been taking one gulp after another from his bottle, at first frightenedly, as if he were afraid to listen, then desperately, as if to drown his senses, but finally has achieved complete indifferent, even amused, drunkenness.* YANK *sees his lips moving. He quells the uproar with a shout.*] Hey, youse guys, take it easy! Wait a moment! De nutty Harp is sayin' somep'n.

PADDY: [*is heard now—throws his head back a mocking burst of laughter*] Ho-ho-ho-ho-ho—

YANK: [*drawing back his fist, with a snarl*] Aw! Look out who yuh're givin' the bark!

PADDY: [*begins to sing the "Miller of Dee" with enormous good nature*]
> *I care for nobody, no, not I,*
> *And nobody cares for me.*

YANK: [*good-natured himself in a flash, interrupts* PADDY *with a slap on the bare back like a report*] Dat's de stuff! Now yuh're gettin' wise to somep'n. Care for nobody, dat's de dope! To hell wit 'em all. And nix on nobody else carin'. I kin care for myself, get me! [*Eight bells sound, muffled, vibrating through the steel walls as if some enormous brazen gong were imbedded in the heart of the ship. All the men jump up mechanically, file through the door silently close upon each other's heels in what is very like a prisoners' lockstep.* YANK *slaps* PADDY *on the back.*] Our watch, yuh old Harp! [*mockingly*] Come on down in hell. Eat up de coal dust. Drink in de heat. It's it, see! Act like yuh liked it, yuh better—or croak yuhself.

PADDY: [*with jovial defiance*] To the divil wid it! I'll not report this watch. Let thim log me and be damned. I'm no slave the like of you. I'll be sittin' here at me ease, and drinking, and thinking, and dreaming dreams.

YANK: [*contemptuously*] Tinkin' and dreamin', what'll that get yuh? What's tinkin' got to do wit it? We move, don't we? Speed, ain't it? Fog, dat's all you stand for. But we drive trou dat, don't we? We split dat up and smash trou— twenty-five knots a hour! [*turns his back on* PADDY *scornfully*] Aw, yuh make me sick! Yuh don't belong! [*He strides out the door in rear.* PADDY *hums to himself, blinking drowsily.*]

CURTAIN

SCENE II

Two days out. A section of the promenade deck, MILDRED DOUGLAS *and her aunt are discovered reclining in deck chairs. The former is a girl of twenty, slender, delicate, with a pale, pretty face marred by a self-conscious expression of disdainful superiority. She looks fretful, nervous, and discontented, bored by her own anemia. Her aunt is a pompous and proud—and fat—old lady. She is a type even to the point of a double chin and lorgnettes. She is dressed pretentiously, as if afraid her face alone would never indicate her position in life.* MILDRED *is dressed all in white.*

The impression to be conveyed by this scene is one of the beautiful, vivid life of the sea all about—sunshine on the deck in a great flood, the fresh sea wind blowing across it. In the midst of this, these two incongruous, artificial figures, inert and disharmonious, the elder like a gray lump of dough touched up with rouge, the younger looking as if the vitality of her stock had been sapped before she was conceived, so that she is the expression not of its life energy but merely of the artificialities that energy had won for itself in the spending.

MILDRED: [*looking up with affected dreaminess*] How the black smoke swirls back against the sky! Is it not beautiful?

AUNT: [*without looking up*] I dislike smoke of any kind.

MILDRED: My great-grandmother smoked a pipe—a clay pipe.

AUNT: [*ruffling*] Vulgar!

MILDRED: She was too distant a relative to be vulgar. Time mellows pipes.

AUNT: [*pretending boredom but irritated*] Did the sociology you took up at college teach you that—to play the ghoul on every possible occasion, excavating old bones? Why not let your great-grandmother rest in her grave?

MILDRED: [*dreamily*] With her pipe beside her—puffing in Paradise.

AUNT: [*with spite*] Yes, you are a natural-born ghoul. You are even getting to look like one, my dear.

MILDRED: [*in a passionless tone*] I detest you, Aunt. [*looking at her critically*] Do you know what you remind me of? Of a cold pork pudding against a background of linoleum tablecloth in the kitchen of a—but the possibilities are wearisome. [*She closes her eyes*]

AUNT: [*with a bitter laugh*] Merci for your candor. But since I am and must be your chaperon—in appearance, at least—let us patch up some sort of armed truce. For my part you are quite free to indulge any pose of eccentricity that beguiles you—as long as you observe the amenities—

MILDRED: [*drawling*] The inanities?

AUNT: [*going on as if she hadn't heard*] After exhausting the morbid thrills of social service work on New York's East Side—how they must have hated you, by the way, the poor that you made so much poorer in their own eyes!—you are now bent on making your slumming international. Well, I hope Whitechapel will provide the needed nerve tonic. Do not ask me to chaperon you there, however. I told your father I would not. I loathe deformity. We will hire an army of detectives and you may investigate everything—they allow you to see.

MILDRED: [*protesting with a trace of genuine earnestness*] Please do not mock at my attempts to discover how the other half lives. Give me credit for some sort of groping sincerity in that at least. I would like to help them. I would like to be some use in the world. Is it my fault I don't know how? I would like to be sincere, to touch life somewhere. [*with weary bitterness*] But I'm afraid I have neither the vitality nor integrity. All that was burnt out in our stock before I was born. Grandfather's blast furnaces, flaming to the sky, melting steel, making millions—then father keeping those home fires burning, making more millions—and little me at the tail-end of it all. I'm a waste product in the Bessemer process—like the millions. Or rather, I inherit the acquired trait of the by-product, wealth, but none of the energy, none of the strength of the steel that made it. I am sired by gold and damned by it, as they say at the race track—damned in more ways than one. [*She laughs mirthlessly.*]

AUNT: [*unimpressed—superciliously*] You seem to be going in for sincerity today. It isn't becoming to you, really—except as an obvious pose. Be as artificial as you are, I advise. There's a sort of sincerity in that, you know. And, after all, you must confess you like that better.

MILDRED: [*again affected and bored*] Yes, I suppose I do. Pardon me for my outburst. When a leopard complains of its spots, it must sound rather grotesque. [*in a mocking tone*] Purr, little leopard. Purr, scratch, tear, kill, gorge yourself and be happy—only stay in the jungle where your spots are camouflage. In a cage they make you conspicuous.

AUNT: I don't know what you are talking about.

MILDRED: It would be rude to talk about anything to you. Let's just talk. [*She looks at her wristwatch.*] Well, thank goodness, it's about time for them to come for me. That ought to give me a new thrill, Aunt.

AUNT: [*affectedly troubled*] You don't mean to say you're really going? The dirt—the heat must be frightful—

MILDRED: Grandfather started as a puddler. I should have inherited an immunity to heat that would make a salamander shiver. It will be fun to put it to the test.

AUNT: But don't you have to have the captain's—or someone's—permission to visit the stokehole?

MILDRED: [*with a triumphant smile*] I have it—both his and the chief engineer's. Oh, they didn't want to at first, in spite of my social service credentials. They didn't seem a bit anxious that I should investigate how the other half lives and works on a ship. So I had to tell them that my father, the president of Nazareth Steel, chairman of the board of directors of this line, had told me it would be all right.

AUNT: He didn't.

MILDRED: How naïve age makes one! But I said he did, Aunt. I even said he had given me a letter to them—which I had lost. And they were afraid to take the chance that I might be lying. [*excitedly*] So it's ho! for the stokehole. The second engineer is to escort me. [*looking at her watch again*] It's time. And here he comes, I think.

    [*The* SECOND ENGINEER *enters. He is a husky, fine-looking man of thirty-five or so. He stops before the two and tips his cap, visibly embarrassed and ill-at-ease.*]

SECOND ENGINEER: Miss Douglas?

MILDRED: Yes. [*throwing off her rugs and getting to her feet*] Are we all ready to start?

SECOND ENGINEER: In just a second, ma'am. I'm waiting for the Fourth. He's coming along.

MILDRED: [*with a scornful smile*] You don't care to shoulder this responsibility alone, is that it?

SECOND ENGINEER: [*forcing a smile*] Two are better than one. [*disturbed by her eyes, glances out to sea—blurts out*] A fine day we're having.

MILDRED: Is it?

SECOND ENGINEER: A nice warm breeze—

MILDRED: It feels cold to me.

SECOND ENGINEER: But it's hot enough in the sun—

MILDRED: Not hot enough for me. I don't like Nature. I was never athletic.

SECOND ENGINEER: [*forcing a smile*] Well, you'll find it hot enough where you're going.

MILDRED: Do you mean hell?

SECOND ENGINEER: [*flabbergasted, decides to laugh*] Ho-ho! No, I mean the stokehole.

MILDRED: My grandfather was a puddler. He played with boiling steel.

SECOND ENGINEER: [*all at sea—uneasily*] Is that so? Hum, you'll excuse me, ma'am, but are you intending to wear that dress?

MILDRED: Why not?

SECOND ENGINEER: You'll likely rub against oil and dirt. It can't be helped.

MILDRED: It doesn't matter. I have lots of white dresses.

SECOND ENGINEER: I have an old coat you might throw over—

MILDRED: I have fifty dresses like this. I will throw this one into the sea when I come back. That ought to wash it clean, don't you think?

SECOND ENGINEER: [*doggedly*] There's ladders to climb down that are none too clean—and dark alleyways—

MILDRED: I will wear this very dress and none other.

SECOND ENGINEER: No offense meant. It's none of my business. I was only warning you—

MILDRED: Warning? That sounds thrilling.

SECOND ENGINEER: [*looking down the deck—with a sigh of relief*] There's the Fourth now. He's waiting for us. If you'll come—

MILDRED: Go on. I'll follow you. [*He goes.* MILDRED *turns a mocking smile on her aunt.*] An oaf—but a handsome, virile oaf.

AUNT: [*scornfully*] Poser!

MILDRED: Take care. He said there were dark alleyways—

AUNT: [*in the same tone*] Poser!

MILDRED: [*biting her lips angrily*] You are right. But would that my millions were not so anemically chaste!

AUNT: Yes, for a fresh pose I have no doubt you would drag the name of Douglas in the gutter!

MILDRED: From which it sprang. Good-by, Aunt. Don't pray too hard that I may fall into the fiery furnace.

AUNT: Poser!

MILDRED: [*viciously*] Old hag! [*She slaps her aunt insultingly across the face and walks off, laughing gaily.*]

AUNT: [*screams after her*] I said "poser"!

CURTAIN

SCENE III

The stokehole. In the rear, the dimly-outlined bulks of the furnaces and boilers. High overhead one hanging electric bulb sheds just enough light through the murky air laden with coal dust to pile up masses of shadows everywhere. A line of men, stripped to the waist, is before the furnace doors. They bend over, looking neither to right nor left, handling their shovels as if they were part of their bodies, with a strange, awkward, swinging rhythm. They use the shovels to throw open the furnace doors. Then from these fiery round holes in the black a flood of terrific light and heat pours full upon the men who are outlined in silhouette in the crouching, inhuman attitudes of chained gorillas. The men shovel with a rhythmic motion, swinging as on a pivot from the coal which lies in heaps on the floor behind to hurl it into the flaming mouths before them. There is a tumult of noise—the brazen clang of the furnace doors as they are flung open or slammed shut, the grating, teeth-gritting grind of steel against steel, of crunching coal. This clash of sounds stuns one's ears with its rending dissonance. But there is order in it, rhythm, a mechanical regulated recurrence, a tempo. And rising above all, making the air hum with the quiver of liberated energy, the roar of leaping flames in the furnaces, the monotonous throbbing beat of the engines.

As the curtain rises, the furnace doors are shut. The men are taking a breathing spell. One or two are arranging the coal behind them, pulling it into more accessible heaps. The others can be dimly made out leaning on their shovels in relaxed attitudes of exhaustion.

PADDY: [*from somewhere in the line—plaintively*] Yerra, will this divil's own watch nivir end? Me back is broke. I'm destroyed entirely.

YANK: [*from the center of the line—with exuberant scorn*] Aw, yuh make me sick! Lie down and croak, why don't yuh? Always beefin', dat's you! Say, dis is a cinch! Dis was made for me! It's my meat, get me! [*A whistle is blown—a thin, shrill note from somewhere overhead in the darkness. YANK curses without resentment.*] Dere's de damn engineer crackin' de whip. He tinks we're loafin'.

PADDY: [*vindictively*] God stiffen him!

YANK: [*in an exultant tone of command*] Come on, youse guys! Git into de game! She's gittin' hungry. Pile some grub in her. Trow it into her belly! Come on now, all of youse! Open her up!

[*At this last all the men, who have followed his movements of getting into position, throw open their furnace doors with a deafening clang. The fiery light floods over their shoulders as they bend round for the coal. Rivulets of sooty sweat have traced maps on their backs. The enlarged muscles form bunches of highlight and shadow.*]

YANK: [*chanting a count as he shovels without seeming effort*] One—two—tree—[*his voice rising exultantly in the joy of battle*] Dat's de stuff! Let her have it! All togedder now! Sling it into her! Let her ride! Shoot de piece now! Call de toin on her! Drive her into it! Feel her move! Watch her smoke! Speed, dat's her middle name! Give her coal, youse guys! Coal, dat's her booze! Drink it up, baby! Let's see yuh sprint! Dig in and gain a lap! Dere she go-o-es.

[*This last in the chanting formula of the gallery gods at the six-day bike race. He slams his furnace door shut. The others do likewise with as much unison as their wearied bodies will permit. The effect is of one fiery eye after another, being blotted out with a series of accompanying bangs.*]

PADDY: [*groaning*] Me back is broke. I'm bate out—bate—

[*There is a pause. Then the inexorable whistle sounds again from the dim regions above the electric light. There is a growl of cursing rage from all sides.*]

YANK: [*shaking his fist upward—contemptuously*] Take it easy dere, you! Who d'yuh tink's runnin' dis game, me or you? When I git ready, we move. Not before! When I git ready, get me!

VOICES: [*approvingly*]
That's the stuff!
Yank tal him, py golly!
Yank ain't affeerd.
Goot poy, Yank!
Give 'im hell!
Tell 'im 'e's a bloody swine!
Bloody slave-driver!

YANK: [*contemptuously*] He ain't got no noive. He's yellow, get me? All de engineers is yellow. Dey got streaks a mile wide. Aw, to hell wit him! Let's move, youse guys. We had a rest. Come on, she needs it! Give her pep! It ain't for him. Him and his whistle, dey don't belong. But we belong, see! We gotter feed de baby! Come on!

[*He turns and flings his furnace door open. They all follow his lead. At this instant the* SECOND *and* FOURTH ENGINEERS *enter from the darkness on the left with* MILDRED *between them. She starts, turns paler, her pose is crumbling, she shivers with fright in spite of the blazing heat, but forces herself to leave the* ENGINEERS *and take a few steps nearer the men. She is right behind* YANK. *All this happens quickly while the men have their backs turned.*]

YANK: Come on, youse guys! [*He is turning to get coal when the whistle sounds again in a peremptory, irritating note. This drives* YANK *into a sudden fury. While the other men have turned full around and stopped dumbfounded by the spectacle of* MILDRED *standing there in her white dress,* YANK *does not turn far enough to see her. Besides, his head is thrown back, he blinks upward through the murk trying to find the owner of the whistle, he brandishes his shovel murderously over his*

head in one hand, pounding on his chest, gorilla-like, with the other, shouting.]
Toin off dat whistle! Come down outa dere, yuh yellow, brass-buttoned,
Belfast bum, yuh! Come down and I'll knock yer brains out! Yuh lousy,
stinkin', yellow mutt of a Catholic-moiderin' bastard! Come down and I'll
moider yuh! Pullin' dat whistle on me, huh? I'll show yuh! I'll crash yer skull
in! I'll drive yer teet' down yer troat! I'll slam yer nose trou de back of yer
head! I'll cut yer guts out for a nickel, yuh lousy boob, yuh dirty crummy,
muck-eatin' son of a—[*Suddenly he becomes conscious of all the other men staring at something directly behind his back. He whirls defensively with a snarling,
murderous growl, crouching to spring, his lips drawn back over his teeth, his small
eyes gleaming ferociously. He sees* MILDRED, *like a white apparition in the full
light from the open furnace doors. He glares into her eyes, turned to stone. As for
her, during his speech she has listened, paralyzed with horror, terror, her whole
personality crushed, beaten in, collapsed, by the terrific impact of this unknown,
abysmal brutality, naked and shameless. As she looks at his gorilla face, as his eyes
bore into hers, she utters a low, choking cry and shrinks away from him, putting
both hands up before her eyes to shut out the sight of his face, to protect her own.
This startles* YANK *to a reaction. His mouth falls open, his eyes grow bewildered.*]
MILDRED: [*about to faint—to the* ENGINEERS, *who now have her one by each
arm—whimperingly*] Take me away! Oh, the filthy beast!
[*She faints. They carry her quickly back, disappearing in the darkness at the
left, rear. An iron door clangs shut. Rage and bewildered fury rush back on*
YANK. *He feels himself insulted in some unknown fashion in the very heart
of his pride. He roars.*]
YANK: God damn yuh! [*And hurls his shovel after them at the door which has just
closed. It hits the steel bulkhead with a clang and falls clattering on the steel floor.
From overhead the whistle sounds again in a long, angry, insistent command.*]
CURTAIN

SCENE IV

The firemen's forecastle. YANK'*s watch has just come off duty and had dinner. Their faces
and bodies shine from a soap-and-water scrubbing but around their eyes, where a hasty
dousing does not touch, the coal dust sticks like black makeup, giving them a queer, sin-
ister expression.* YANK *has not washed either face or body. He stands out in contrast to
them, a blackened, brooding figure. He is seated forward on a bench in the exact attitude
of Rodin's "The Thinker." The others, most of them smoking pipes, are staring at* YANK
*half-apprehensively, as if fearing an outburst; half-amusedly as if they saw a joke some-
where that tickled them.*

VOICES: He ain't ate nothin'
Py golly, a fallar gat to gat grub in him.
Divil a lie.
Yank feeda da fire, no feeda da face.
Ha-ha.
He ain't even washed hisself.
He's forgot.
Hey, Yank you forgot to wash.

YANK: [*sullenly*] Forgot nothin'! To hell wit washin'.

VOICES: It'll stick to you.

> It'll get under your skin.
> Give yer the bleedin' itch, that's wot.
> It makes spots on you—like a leopard.
> Like a piebald nigger, you mean.
> Better wash up, Yank.
> You sleep better.
> Wash up, Yank.
> Wash up! Wash up!

YANK: [*resentfully*] Aw say, youse guys. Lemme alone. Can't youse see I'm tryin' to tink?

ALL: [*repeating the word after him as one with cynical mockery*] Think! [*The word has a brazen, metallic quality as if their throats were phonograph horns. It is followed by a chorus of hard, barking laughter.*]

YANK: [*springing to his feet and glaring at them belligerently*] Yes, tink! Tink, dat's what I said! What about it?

> [*They are silent, puzzled by his sudden resentment at what used to be one of his jokes.* YANK *sits down again in the same attitude of "The Thinker."*]

VOICES: Leave him alone.

> He's got a grouch on.
> Why wouldn't he?

PADDY: [*with a wink at the others*] Sure I know what's the matther. 'Tis aisy to see. He's fallen in love, I'm telling you.

ALL: [*repeating the word after him as one with cynical mockery*] Love! [*The word has a brazen, metallic quality as if their throats were phonograph horns. It is followed by a chorus of hard, barking laughter.*]

YANK: [*with a contemptuous snort*] Love, hell! Hate, dat's what. I've fallen in hate, get me?

PADDY: [*philosophically*] 'Twould take a wise man to tell one from the other. [*with a bitter, ironical scorn, increasing as he goes on*] But I'm telling you it's love that's in it. Sure what else but love for us poor bastes in the stokehole would be bringing a fine lady, dressed like a white quane, down a mile of ladders and steps to be havin' a look at us? [*A growl of anger goes up from all sides.*]

LONG: [*jumping on a bench—hectically*] Hinsultin' us! Hinsultin' us, the bloody cow! And them bloody engineers! What right 'as they got to be exhibitin' us's if we was bleedin' monkeys in a menagerie? Did we sign for hinsults to our dignity as 'onest workers? Is that in the ship's articles? You kin bloody well bet it ain't! But I knows why they done it. I arsked a deck steward 'o she was and 'e told me. 'Er old man's a bleedin' millionaire, a bloody Capitalist! 'E's got enuf bloody gold to sink this bleedin' ship! 'E makes arf the bloody steel in the world! 'E owns this bloody boat! And you and me, Comrades, we're 'is slaves! And the skipper and mates and engineers, they're 'is slaves! And she's 'is bloody daughter and we're all 'er slaves, too! And she gives 'er orders as 'ow she wants to see the bloody animals below decks and down they takes 'er!

> [*There is a roar of rage from all sides.*]

YANK: [*blinking at him bewilderedly*] Say! Wait a moment! Is all dat straight goods?

LONG: Straight as string! The bleedin' steward as waits on 'em, 'e told me about 'er. And what're we goin' ter do, I arsks yer? 'Ave we got ter swaller 'er hinsults like dogs? It ain't in the ship's articles. I tell yer we got a case. We kin go to law—

YANK: [*with abysmal contempt*] Hell! Law!

ALL: [*repeating the word after him as one with cynical mockery*] Law! [*The word has a brazen, metallic quality as if their throats were phonograph horns. It is followed by a chorus of hard, barking laughter.*]

LONG: [*feeling the ground slipping from under his feet—desperately*] As voters and citizens we kin force the bloody governments—

YANK: [*with abysmal contempt*] Hell! Governments!

ALL: [*repeating the word after him as one with cynical mockery*] Governments! [*The word has a brazen, metallic quality as if their throats were phonograph horns. It is followed by a chorus of hard, barking laughter.*]

LONG: [*hysterically*] We're free and equal in the sight of God—

YANK: [*with abysmal contempt*] Hell! God!

ALL: [*repeating the word after him as one with cynical mockery*] God! [*The word has a brazen, metallic quality as if their throats were phonograph horns. It is followed by a chorus of hard, barking laughter.*]

YANK: [*witheringly*] Aw, join de Salvation Army!

ALL: Sit down! Shut up! Damn fool! Sea-lawyer!

        [LONG *slinks back out of sight.*]

PADDY: [*continuing the trend of his thoughts as if he had never been interrupted—bitterly*] And there she was standing behind us, and the Second pointing at us like a man you'd hear in a circus would be saying: In this cage is a queerer kind of baboon than ever you'd find in darkest Africy. We roast them in their own sweat—and be damned if you won't hear some of thim saying they like it! [*He glances scornfully at* YANK.]

YANK: [*with a bewildered uncertain growl*] Aw!

PADDY: And there was Yank roarin' curses and turning round wid his shovel to brain her—and she looked at him, and him at her—

YANK: [*slowly*] She was all white. I tought she was a ghost. Sure.

PADDY: [*with heavy, biting sarcasm*] 'Twas love at first sight, divil a doubt of it! If you'd seen the endearin' look on her pale mug when she shriveled away with her hands over her eyes to shut out the sight of him! Sure, 'twas as if she'd seen a great hairy ape escaped from the Zoo!

YANK: [*stung—with a growl of rage*] Aw!

PADDY: And the loving way Yank heaved his shovel at the skull of her, only she was out the door! [*a grin breaking over his face*] 'Twas touching, I'm telling you! It put the touch of home, swate home in the stokehole. [*There is a roar of laughter from all.*]

YANK: [*glaring at* PADDY *menacingly*] Aw, choke dat off, see!

PADDY: [*not heeding him—to the others*] And her grabbin' at the Second's arm for protection. [*with a grotesque imitation of a woman's voice*] Kiss me, Engineer dear, for it's dark down here and me old man's in Wall Street making money! Hug me tight, darlin', for I'm afeerd in the dark and me mother's on deck makin' eyes at the skipper! [*Another roar of laughter.*]

YANK: [*threateningly*] Say! What yuh tryin' to do, kid me, yuh old Harp?

PADDY: Divil a bit! Ain't I wishin' myself you'd brained her?

YANK: [*fiercely*] I'll brain her! I'll brain her yet, wait 'n' see! [*coming over to PADDY—slowly*] Say, is dat what she called me—a hairy ape?

PADDY: She looked it at you if she didn't say the word itself.

YANK: [*grinning horribly*] Hairy ape, huh? Sure! Dat's de way she looked at me, aw right. Hairy ape! So dat's me, huh? [*bursting into rage—as if she were still in front of him*] Yuh skinny tart! Yuh white-faced bum, yuh! I'll show yuh who's a ape! [*turning to the others, bewilderment seizing him again*] Say, youse guys. I was bawlin' him out for pullin' de whistle on us. You heard me. And den I seen youse lookin' at somep'n and I tought he'd sneaked down to come up in back of me, and I hopped round to knock him dead wit de shovel. And dere she was wit de light on her! Christ, yuh coulda pushed me over with a finger! I was scared, get me? Sure! I tought she was a ghost, see? She was all in white like dey wrap around stiffs. You seen her. Kin yuh blame me? She didn't belong, dat's what. And den when I come to and seen it was a real skoit and seen de way she was lookin' at me—like Paddy said—Christ, I was sore, get me? I don't stand for dat stuff from nobody. And I flung de shovel—on'y she'd beat it. [*furiously*] I wished it'd banged her! I wished it'd knocked her block off!

LONG: And be 'anged for murder or 'lectrocuted? She ain't bleedin' well worth it.

YANK: I don't give a damn what! I'd be square wit her, wouldn't I? Tink I wanter let her put somep'n over on me? Tink I'm goin' to let her git away wit dat stuff? Yuh don't know me! No one ain't never put nothin' over on me and got away wit it, see!—not dat kind of stuff—no guy and no skoit neither! I'll fix her! Maybe she'll come down again—

VOICE: No chance, Yank. You scared her out of a year's growth.

YANK: I scared her? Why de hell should I scare her? Who de hell is she? Ain't she de same as me? Hairy ape, huh? [*with his old confident bravado*] I'll show her I'm better'n her, if she on'y knew it. I belong and she don't, see! I move and she's dead! Twenty-five knots a hour, dat's me! Dat carries her but I make dat. She's on'y baggage. Sure! [*again bewilderedly*] But, Christ, she was funny lookin'! Did yuh pipe her hands? White and skinny. Yuh could see de bones through 'em. And her mush, dat was dead white, too. And her eyes, dey was like dey'd seen a ghost. Me, dat was! Sure! Hairy ape! Ghost, huh? Look at dat arm! [*He extends his right arm, swelling out the great muscles.*] I coulda took her wit dat, wit just my little finger even, and broke her in two. [*again bewilderedly*] Say, who is dat skoit, huh? What is she? What's she come from? Who made her? Who give her de noive to look at me like dat? Dis ting's got my goat right. I don't get her. She's new to me. What does a skoit like her mean, huh? She don't belong, get me! I can't see her. [*with growing anger*] But one ting I'm wise to, aw right, aw right! Youse all kin bet your shoits I'll git even wit her. I'll show her if she tinks she—She grinds de organ and I'm on de string, huh? I'll fix her! Let her come down again and I'll fling her in de furnace! She'll move den! She won't shiver at nothin', den! Speed, dat'll be her! She'll belong den! [*He grins horribly.*]

PADDY: She'll never come. She's had her bellyful, I'm telling you. She'll be in bed now, I'm thinking, wid ten doctors and nurses feedin' her salts to clean the fear out of her.

YANK: [*enraged*] Yuh tink I made her sick, too, do yuh? Just lookin' at me, huh? Hairy ape, huh? [*in a frenzy of rage*] I'll fix her! I'll tell her where to git off! She'll git down on her knees and take it back or I'll bust de face offen her! [*shaking one fist upward and beating on his chest with the other*] I'll find yuh! I'm comin', d'yuh hear? I'll fix yuh, God damn yuh! [*He makes a rush for the door.*]

VOICES: Stop him!
> He'll get shot!
> He'll murder her!
> Trip him up!
> Hold him!
> He's gone crazy!
> Gott, he's strong!
> Hold him down!
> Look out for a kick!
> Pin his arms!
>> [*They have all piled on him and, after a fierce struggle, by sheer weight of numbers have borne him to the floor just inside the door.*]

PADDY: [*who has remained detached*] Kape him down till he's cooled off. [*scornfully*] Yerra, Yank, you're a great fool. Is it payin' attention at all you are to the like of that skinny sow widout one drop of rale blood in her?

YANK: [*frenziedly, from the bottom of the heap*] She done me doit! She done me doit, didn't she? I'll get square wit her! I'll get her some way! Git offen me, youse guys! Lemme up! I'll show her who's a ape!

CURTAIN

SCENE V

Three weeks later. A corner of Fifth Avenue in the Fifties on a fine Sunday morning. A general atmosphere of clean, well-tidied, wide street; a flood of mellow, tempered sunshine; gentle, genteel breezes. In the rear, the show windows of two shops, a jewelry establishment on the corner, a furrier's next to it. Here the adornments of extreme wealth are tantalizingly displayed. The jeweler's window is gaudy with glittering diamonds, emeralds, rubies, pearls, etc., fashioned in ornate tiaras, crowns, necklaces, collars, etc. From each piece hangs an enormous tag from which a dollar sign and numerals in intermittent electric lights wink out the incredible prices. The same in the furrier's. Rich furs of all varieties hang there bathed in a downpour of artificial light. The general effect is of a background of magnificence cheapened and made grotesque by commercialism, a background in tawdry disharmony with the clear light and sunshine on the street itself.

Up the side street YANK *and* LONG *come swaggering.* LONG *is dressed in shore clothes, wears a black Windsor tie, cloth cap.* YANK *is in his dirty dungarees. A fireman's cap with black peak is cocked defiantly on the side of his head. He has not shaved for days and around his fierce, resentful eyes—as around those of* LONG *to a lesser degree—the black smudge of coal dust still sticks like makeup. They hesitate and stand together at the corner, swaggering, looking about them with a forced, defiant contempt.*

LONG: [*indicating it all with an oratorical gesture*] Well, 'ere we are, Fif' Avenoo. This 'ere's their bleedin private lane, as yer might say. [*bitterly*] We're trespassers 'ere. Proletarians keep orf the grass!

YANK: [*dully*] I don't see no grass, yuh boob. [*staring at the sidewalk*] Clean, ain't it? Yuh could eat a fried egg offen it. The white wings got some job sweepin' dis up. [*looking up and down the avenue—surlily*] Where's all de white-collar stiffs yuh said was here—and de skoits—*her* kind?

LONG: In church, blast 'em! Arskin' Jesus to give 'em more money.

YANK: Choich, huh? I uster go to choich onct—sure—when I was a kid. Me old man and woman, dey made me. Dey never went demselves, dough. Always got too big a head on Sunday mornin', dat was dem. [*with a grin*] Dey was scrappers for fair, bot' of dem. On Satiday nights when dey bot' got a skinful dey could put up a bout oughter been staged at de Garden. When dey got trough dere wasn't a chair or table wit a leg under it. Or else dey bot' jumped on me for somep'n. Dat was where I loined to take punishment. [*with a grin and a swagger*] I'm a chip offen de old block, get me?

LONG: Did yer old man follow the sea?

YANK: Naw. Worked along shore. I runned away when me old lady croaked wit de tremens. I helped at truckin' and in de market. Den I shipped in de stokehole. Sure. Dat belongs. De rest was nothin'. [*looking around him*] I ain't never seen dis before. De Brooklyn waterfront, dat was where I was dragged up. [*taking a deep breath*] Dis ain't so bad at dat, huh?

LONG: Not bad? Well, we pays for it wiv our bloody sweat, if yer wants to know!

YANK: [*with sudden angry disgust*] Aw, hell! I don't see no one, see—like her. All dis gives me a pain. It don't belong. Say, ain't dere a back room around dis dump? Let's go shoot a ball. All dis is too clean and quiet and dolled-up, get me! It gives me a pain.

LONG: Wait and yer'll bloody well see—

YANK: I don't wait for no one. I keep on de move. Say, what yuh drag me up here for, anyway? Tryin' to kid me, yuh simp, yuh?

LONG: Yer wants to get back at 'er, don't yer? That's what yer been sayin' every bloomin' hour since she hinsulted yer.

YANK: [*vehemently*] Sure ting I do! Didn't I try to get even wit her in Southampton? Didn't I sneak on de dock and wait for her by de gangplank? I was goin' to spit in her pale mug, see! Sure, right in her pop-eyes! Dat woulda made me even, see? But no chanct. Dere was a whole army of plainclothes bulls around. Dey spotted me and gimme de bum's rush. I never seen her. But I'll git square wit her yet, you watch! [*furiously*] De lousy tart! She tinks she kin get away wit moider—but not wit me! I'll fix her! I'll tink of a way!

LONG: [*as disgusted as he dares to be*] Ain't that why I brought yer up 'ere—to show yer? Yer been lookin' at this 'ere 'ole affair wrong. Yer been actin' an' talkin' 's if it was all a bleedin' personal matter between yer and that bloody cow. I wants to convince yer she was on'y a representative of 'er clarss. I wants to awaken yer bloody clarss consciousness. Then yer'll see it's 'er clarss yer've got to fight, not 'er alone. There's a 'ole mob of 'em like 'er, Gawd blind 'em!

YANK: [*spitting on his hands—belligerently*] De more de merrier when I gits started. Bring on de gang!

LONG: Yer'll see 'em in arf a mo', when that church lets out. [*He turns and sees the window display in the two stores for the first time.*] Blimey! Look at that, will yer? [*They both walk back and stand looking in the jeweler's.* LONG *flies into a fury.*] Just look at this 'ere bloomin' mess! Just look at it! Look at the bleedin' prices on 'em—more 'n our 'ole bloody stokehole makes in ten voyages sweatin' in 'ell! And they—'er and 'er bloody clarss—buys 'em for toys to dangle on 'em! One of these 'ere would buy scoff for a starvin' family for a year!

YANK: Aw, cut de sob stuff! T'hell wit de starvin' family. Yuh'll be passin' de hat to me next. [*with naïve admiration*] Say, dem tings is pretty, huh? Bet yuh dey'd hock for a piece of change aw right. [*then turning away, bored*] But, aw hell, what good are dey? Let her have 'em. Dey don't belong no more'n she does. [*with a gesture of sweeping the jeweler's into oblivion*] All dat don't count, get me?

LONG: [*who has moved to the furrier's—indignantly*] And I s'pose this 'ere don't, neither—skins of poor, 'armless animals slaughtered so as 'er and 'ers can keep their bleedin' noses warm!

YANK: [*who has been staring at something inside—with queer excitement*] Take a slant at dat! Give it de once-over! Monkey fur—two t'ousand bucks! [*bewilderedly*] Is dat straight goods—monkey fur? What de hell—?

LONG: [*bitterly*] It's straight enuf. [*with grim humor*] They wouldn't bloody well pay that for a 'airy ape's skin—no, nor for the 'ole livin' ape with all 'is 'ead, and body, and soul thrown in!

YANK: [*clenching his fists, his face growing pale with rage as if the skin in the window were a personal insult*] Trowin' it up in my face! Christ! I'll fix her!

LONG: [*excitedly*] Church is out. 'Ere they come, the bleedin' swine. [*after a glance at* YANK'*s lowering face—uneasily*] Easy goes, Comrade. Keep yer bloomin' temper. Remember force defeats itself. It ain't our weapon. We must impress our demands through peaceful means—the votes of the onmarching proletarians of the bloody world!

YANK: [*with abysmal contempt*] Votes, hell! Votes is a joke, see. Votes for women! Let dem do it!

LONG: [*still more uneasily*] Calm, now. Treat 'em wiv the proper contempt. Observe the bleedin' parasites but 'old yer 'orses.

YANK: [*angrily*] Git away from me! Yuh're yellow, dat's what. Force, dat's me! De punch, dat's me every time, see!

> [*The crowd from church enter from the right, sauntering slowly and affectedly, their heads held stiffly up, looking neither to right nor left, talking in toneless, simpering voices. The women are rouged, calcimined, dyed, overdressed to the nth degree. The men are in Prince Alberts, high hats, spats, canes, etc. A procession of gaudy marionettes, yet with something of the relentless horror of Frankensteins in their detached, mechanical unawareness.*]

VOICES: Dear Doctor Caiaphas! He is so sincere!

What was the sermon? I dozed off.

About the radicals, my dear—and the false doctrines that are being preached.

We must organize a hundred percent American bazaar.

And let everyone contribute one one-hundredth percent of their income tax.

What an original idea!

We can devote the proceeds to rehabilitating the veil of the temple.

But that has been done so many times.

YANK: [*glaring from one to the other of them—with an insulting snort of scorn*] Huh! Huh! [*Without seeming to see him, they make wide detours to avoid the spot where he stands in the middle of the sidewalk.*]

LONG: [*frightenedly*] Keep yer bloomin' mouth shut, I tells yer.

YANK: [*viciously*] G'wan! Tell it to Sweeney! [*He swaggers away and deliberately lurches into a top-hatted gentleman, then glares at him pugnaciously.*] Say, who d'yuh tink yuh're bumpin'? Tink yuh own de Oith?

GENTLEMAN: [*coldly and affectedly*] I beg your pardon. [*He has not looked at* YANK *and passes on without a glance, leaving him bewildered.*]

LONG: [*rushing up and grabbing* YANK's *arm*] 'Ere! Come away! This wasn't what I meant. Yer'll 'ave the bloody coppers down on us.

YANK: [*savagely—giving him a push that sends him sprawling*] G'wan!

LONG: [*picks himself up—hysterically*] I'll pop orf then. This ain't what I meant. And whatever 'appens, yer can't blame me. [*He slinks off left.*]

YANK: T' hell wit youse! [*He approaches a lady—with a vicious grin and a smirking wink.*] Hello, Kiddo. How's every little ting? Got anyting on for tonight? I know an old boiler down to de docks we kin crawl into. [*The lady stalks by without a look, without a change of pace.* YANK *turns to others—insultingly.*] Holy smokes, what a mug! Go hide yuhself before de horses shy at yuh. Gee, pipe de heinie on dat one! Say, youse, yuh look like de stoin of a ferryboat. Paint and powder! All dolled up to kill! Yuh look like stiffs laid out for de boneyard! Aw, g'wan, de lot of youse! Yuh give me de eye-ache. Yuh don't belong, get me! Look at me, why don't youse dare? I belong, dat's me! [*pointing to a skyscraper across the street which is in process of construction—with bravado*] See dat building goin' up dere? See de steel work? Steel, dat's me! Youse guys lives on it and tink yuh're somep'n. But I'm *in* it, see! I'm de hoistin' engine dat makes it go up! I'm it—de inside and bottom of it! Sure! I'm steel and steam and smoke and de rest of it! It moves—speed—twenty-five stories up—and me at de top and bottom—movin'! Youse simps don't move. Yuh're on'y dolls I winds up to see 'm spin. Yuh're de garbage, get me—de leavins—de ashes we dump over de side! Now, what 'a' yuh gotta say? [*But as they seem neither to see nor hear him, he flies into a fury.*] Bums! Pigs! Tarts! Bitches! [*He turns in a rage on the men, bumping viciously into them but not jarring them the least bit. Rather it is he who recoils after each collision. He keeps growling.*] Git off de Oith! G'wan, yuh bum! Look where yuh're goin', can't yuh? Git outa here! Fight, why don't yuh? Put up yer mitts! Don't be a dog! Fight or I'll knock yuh dead!

[*But, without seeming to see him, they all answer with mechanical affected politeness:*]

I beg your pardon. [*Then at a cry from one of the women, they all scurry to the furrier's window.*]

THE WOMAN: [*ecstatically, with a gasp of delight*] Monkey fur! [*The whole crowd of men and women chorus after her in the same tone of affected delight.*] Monkey fur!

YANK: [*with a jerk of his head back on his shoulders, as if he had received a punch full in the face—raging*] I see yuh, all in white! I see yuh, yuh white-faced tart, yuh! Hairy ape, huh? I'll hairy ape yuh!

[*He bends down and grips at the street curbing as if to pluck it out and hurl it. Foiled in this, snarling with passion, he leaps to the lamppost on the corner and tries to pull it up for a club. Just at that moment a bus is heard rumbling up. A fat, high-hatted, spatted gentleman runs out from the side street. He calls out plaintively:*] Bus! Bus! Stop there! [*and runs full tilt into the bending, straining* YANK, *who is bowled off his balance*]

YANK: [*seeing a fight—with a roar of joy as he springs to his feet*] At last! Bus, huh? I'll bust yuh! [*He lets drive a terrific swing, his fist landing full on the fat gentleman's face. But the gentleman stands unmoved as if nothing had happened.*]

GENTLEMAN: I beg your pardon. [*then irritably*] You have made me lose my bus. [*He claps his hands and begins to scream.*] Officer! Officer!

[*Many police whistles shrill out on the instant and a whole platoon of policemen rush in on* YANK *from all sides. He tries to fight but is clubbed to the pavement and fallen upon. The crowd at the window have not moved or noticed this disturbance. The clanging gong of the patrol wagon approaches with a clamoring din.*]

CURTAIN

SCENE VI

Night of the following day. A row of cells in the prison on Blackwells Island. The cells extend back diagonally from right front to left rear. They do not stop, but disappear in the dark background as if they ran on, numberless, into infinity. One electric bulb from the low ceiling of the narrow corridor sheds its light through the heavy steel bars of the cell at the extreme front and reveals part of the interior. YANK *can be seen within, crouched on the edge of his cot in the attitude of Rodin's "The Thinker." His face is spotted with black and blue bruises. A blood-stained bandage is wrapped around his head.*

YANK: [*suddenly starting as if awakening from a dream, reaches out and shakes the bars—aloud to himself, wonderingly*] Steel. Dis is de zoo, huh? [*A burst of hard, barking laughter comes from the unseen occupants of the cells, runs back down the tier, and abruptly ceases.*]

VOICES: [*mockingly*] The zoo? That's a new name for this coop—a damn good name!
Steel, eh? You said a mouthful. This is the old iron house.
Who is that boob talkin'?
He's the bloke they brung in out of his head. The bulls had beat him up fierce.

YANK: [*dully*] I musta been dreamin'. I tought I was in a cage at de zoo—but de apes don't talk, do dey?

VOICES: [*with mocking laughter*] You're in a cage aw right.
A coop!
A pen!
A sty!
A kennel! [*hard laughter—a pause*]
Say, guy! Who are you? No, never mind lying. What are you?
Yes, tell us your sad story. What's your game?

What did they jug yuh for?

YANK: [*dully*] I was a fireman—stokin' on de liners. [*then with sudden rage, rattling his cell bars*] I'm a hairy ape, get me? And I'll bust youse all in de jaw if yuh don't lay off kiddin' me.

VOICES: Huh! You're a hard-boiled duck, ain't you!

When you spit, it bounces! [*laughter*]

Aw, can it. He's a regular guy. Ain't you?

What did he say he was—a ape?

YANK: [*defiantly*] Sure ting! Ain't dat what youse all are—apes?

[*A silence. Then a furious rattling of bars from down the corridor.*]

A VOICE: [*thick with rage*] I'll show yuh who's a ape, yuh bum!

VOICES: Ssshh! Nix!

Can de noise!

Piano!

You'll have the guard down on us!

YANK: [*scornfully*] De guard? Yuh mean de keeper, don't yuh?

[*angry exclamations from all the cells*]

VOICE: [*placatingly*] Aw, don't pay no attention to him. He's off his nut from the beatin'-up he got. Say, you guy! We're waitin' to hear what they landed you for—or ain't yuh tellin'?

YANK: Sure, I'll tell youse. Sure! Why de hell not? On'y—youse won't get me. Nobody gets me but me, see? I started to tell de judge and all he says was: "Toity days to tink it over." Tink it over! Christ, dat's all I been doin' for weeks! [*after a pause*] I was tryin' to git even wit someone, see?—someone dat done me doit.

VOICES: [*cynically*] De old stuff, I bet. Your goil, huh?

Give yuh the double-cross, huh?

That's them every time!

Did yuh beat up de odder guy?

YANK: [*disgustedly*] Aw, yuh're all wrong! Sure dere was a skoit in it—but not what youse mean, not dat old tripe. Dis was a new kind of skoit. She was dolled up all in white—in de stokehole. I tought she was a ghost. Sure. [*A pause.*]

VOICES: [*whispering*] Gee, he's still nutty.

Let him rave. It's fun listenin'.

YANK: [*unheeding—groping in his thoughts*] Her hands—dey was skinny and white like dey wasn't real but painted on somep'n. Dere was a million miles from me to her—twenty-five knots a hour. She was like some dead ting de cat brung in. Sure, dat's what. She didn't belong. She belonged in de window of a toy store, or on de top of a garbage can, see! Sure! [*He breaks out angrily.*] But would yuh believe it, she had de noive to do me doit. She lamped me like she was seein' somep'n broke loose from de menagerie. Christ, yuh'd oughter seen her eyes! [*He rattles the bars of his cell furiously.*] But I'll get back at her yet, you watch! And if I can't find her I'll take it out on de gang she runs wit. I'm wise to where dey hangs out now. I'll show her who belongs! I'll show her who's in de move and who ain't. You watch my smoke!

VOICES: [*serious and joking*] Dat's de talkin'!
    Take her for all she's got!
    What was this dame anyway? Who was she, eh?

YANK: I dunno. First cabin stiff. Her old man's a millionaire, dey says—name of
    Douglas.

VOICES: Douglas? That's the president of the Steel Trust, I bet.
    Sure. I seen his mug in de papers.
    He's filthy with dough.

VOICE: Hey, feller, take a tip from me. If you want to get back at that dame, you
    better join the Wobblies. You'll get some action then.

YANK: Wobblies? What de hell's dat?

VOICE: Ain't you ever heard of the I.W.W.?

YANK: Naw. What is it?

VOICE: A gang of blokes—a tough gang. I been readin' about 'em today in the pa-
    per. The guard give me the *Sunday Times*. There's a long spiel about 'em. It's
    from a speech made in the Senate by a guy named Senator Queen. [*He is
    in the cell next to* YANK'*s. There is a rustling of paper.*] Wait'll I see if I got light
    enough and I'll read you. Listen. [*He reads.*] "There is a menace existing in
    the country today which threatens the vitals of our fair Republic—as foul a
    menace against the very life-blood of the American Eagle as was the foul
    conspiracy of Cataline against the eagles of ancient Rome!"

VOICE: [*disgustedly*] Aw, hell! Tell him to salt de tail of dat eagle!

VOICE: [*reading*] "I refer to that devil's brew of rascals, jailbirds, murderers and
    cutthroats who libel all honest working men by calling themselves the In-
    dustrial Workers of the World; but in the light of their nefarious plots, I call
    them the Industrious *Wreckers* of the World!"

YANK: [*with vengeful satisfaction*] Wreckers, dat's de right dope! Dat belongs! Me
    for dem!

VOICE: Ssshh! [*reading*] "This fiendish organization is a foul ulcer on the fair
    body of our Democracy—"

VOICE: Democracy, hell! Give him the boid, fellers—the raspberry! [*They do.*]

VOICE: Ssshh! [*reading*] "Like Cato I say to this Senate, the I.W.W. must be de-
    stroyed! For they represent an ever-present dagger pointed at the heart of
    the greatest nation the world has ever known, where all men are born free
    and equal, with equal opportunities to all, where the Founding Fathers have
    guaranteed to each one happiness, where Truth, Honor, Liberty, Justice, and
    the Brotherhood of Man are a religion absorbed with one's mother's milk,
    taught at our father's knee, sealed, signed, and stamped upon the glorious
    Constitution of these United States!" [*a perfect storm of hisses, catcalls, boos,
    and hard laughter*]

VOICES: [*scornfully*] Hurrah for de Fort' of July!
    Pass de hat!
    Liberty!
    Justice!
    Honor!
    Opportunity!
    Brotherhood!

ALL: [*with abysmal scorn*] Aw, hell!

VOICE: Give that Queen Senator guy the bark! All togedder now—one—two—tree—[*a terrific chorus of barking and yapping*]

GUARD: [*from a distance*] Quiet there, youse—or I'll git the hose.
[*The noise subsides.*]

YANK: [*with growling rage*] I'd like to catch dat senator guy alone for a second. I'd loin him some trute!

VOICE: Ssshh! Here's where he gits down to cases on the Wobblies. [*reads*] "They plot with fire in one hand and dynamite in the other. They stop not before murder to gain their ends, nor at the outraging of defenseless womanhood. They would tear down society, put the lowest scum in the seats of the mighty, turn Almighty God's revealed plan for the world topsy-turvy, and make of our sweet and lovely civilization a shambles, a desolation where man, God's masterpiece, would soon degenerate back to the ape!"

VOICE: [*to* YANK] Hey, you guy. There's your ape stuff again.

YANK: [*with a growl of fury*] I got him. So dey blow up tings, do dey? Dey turn tings round, do dey? Hey, lend me dat paper, will yuh?

VOICE: Sure. Give it to him. On'y keep it to yourself, see. We don't wanter listen to no more of that slop.

VOICE: Here you are. Hide it under your mattress.

YANK: [*reaching out*] Tanks. I can't read much but I kin manage. [*He sits, the paper in the hand at his side, in the attitude of Rodin's "The Thinker." A pause. Several snores from down the corridor. Suddenly* YANK *jumps to his feet with a furious groan as if some appalling thought had crashed on him—bewilderedly.*] Sure—her old man—president of de Steel Trust—makes half de steel in de world—steel—where I tought I belonged—drivin' trou—movin'—in dat—to make *her*—and cage me in for her to spit on! Christ! [*He shakes the bars of his cell door till the whole tier trembles. Irritated, protesting exclamations from those awakened or trying to get to sleep.*] He made dis—dis cage! Steel! *It* don't belong, dat's what! Cages, cells, locks, bolts, bars—dat's what it means!—holdin' me down wit him at de top! But I'll drive trou! Fire, dat melts it! I'll be fire—under de heap—fire dat never goes out—hot as hell—breakin' out in de night—[*While he has been saying this last he has shaken his cell door to a clanging accompaniment. As he comes to the "breakin' out" he seizes one bar with both hands and, putting his two feet up against the others so that his position is parallel to the floor like a monkey's, he gives a great wrench backwards. The bar bends like a licorice stick under his tremendous strength. Just at this moment the* PRISON GUARD *rushes in, dragging a hose behind him.*]

GUARD: [*angrily*] I'll loin youse bums to wake me up! [*sees* YANK] Hello, it's you, huh? Got the D. Ts., hey? Well, I'll cure 'em. I'll drown your snakes for yuh! [*noticing the bar*] Hell, look at dat bar bended! On'y a bug is strong enough for dat!

YANK: [*glaring at him*] Or a hairy ape, yuh big yellow bum! Look out! Here I come! [*He grabs another bar.*]

GUARD: [*scared now—yelling off left*] Toin de hose on, Ben—Full pressure! And call de others—and a straitjacket!
[*The curtain is falling. As it hides* YANK *from view, there is a splattering smash as the stream of water hits the steel of* YANK's *cell.*]

CURTAIN

SCENE VII

Nearly a month later. An I.W.W. local near the waterfront, showing the interior of a front room on the ground floor, and the street outside. Moonlight on the narrow street, buildings massed in black shadow. The interior of the room, which is general assembly room, office, and reading room, resembles some dingy settlement boys' club. A desk and high stool are in one corner. A table with papers, stacks of pamphlets, chairs about it, is at center. The whole is decidedly cheap, banal, commonplace and unmysterious as a room could well be. The SECRETARY *is perched on the stool making entries in a large ledger. An eye shade casts his face into shadows. Eight or ten men, longshoremen, ironworkers, and the like, are grouped about the table. Two are playing checkers. One is writing a letter. Most of them are smoking pipes. A big signboard is on the wall at the rear, "Industrial Workers of the World—Local No. 57."*

> [YANK *comes down the street outside. He is dressed as in Scene Five. He moves cautiously, mysteriously. He comes to a point opposite the door; tiptoes softly up to it, listens, is impressed by the silence within, knocks carefully, as if he were guessing at the password to some secret rite. Listens. No answer. Knocks again a bit louder. No answer. Knocks impatiently, much louder.*]

SECRETARY: [*turning around on his stool*] What the hell is that—someone knocking? [*shouts*] Come in, why don't you?

> [*All the men in the room look up.* YANK *opens the door slowly, gingerly, as if afraid of an ambush. He looks around for secret doors, mystery, is taken aback by the commonplaceness of the room and the men in it, thinks he may have gotten in the wrong place, then sees the signboard on the wall and is reassured.*]

YANK: [*blurts out*] Hello.

MEN: [*reservedly*] Hello.

YANK: [*more easily*] I tought I'd bumped into de wrong dump.

SECRETARY: [*scrutinizing him carefully*] Maybe you have. Are you a member?

YANK: Naw, not yet. Dat's what I come for—to join.

SECRETARY: That's easy. What's your job—longshore?

YANK: Naw. Fireman—stoker on de liners.

SECRETARY: [*with satisfaction*] Welcome to our city. Glad to know you people are waking up at last. We haven't got many members in your line.

YANK: Naw. Dey're all dead to de woild.

SECRETARY: Well, you can help to wake 'em. What's your name? I'll make out your card.

YANK: [*confused*] Name? Lemme tink.

SECRETARY: [*sharply*] Don't you know your own name?

YANK: Sure; but I been just Yank for so long—Bob, dat's it—Bob Smith.

SECRETARY: [*writing*] Robert Smith. [*fills out the rest of card*] Here you are. Cost you half a dollar.

YANK: Is dat all—four bits? Dat's easy. [*gives the* SECRETARY *the money*]

SECRETARY: [*throwing it in drawer*] Thanks. Well, make yourself at home. No introductions needed. There's literature on the table. Take some of those pamphlets with you to distribute aboard ship. They may bring results. Sow the seed, only go about it right. Don't get caught and fired. We got plenty out of work. What we need is men who can hold their jobs—and work for us at the same time.

YANK: Sure. [*But he still stands, embarrassed and uneasy.*]

SECRETARY: [*looking at him—curiously*] What did you knock for? Think we had a coon in uniform to open doors?

YANK: Naw. I tought it was locked—and dat yuh'd wanter give me the once-over trou a peep-hole or somep'n to see if I was right.

SECRETARY: [*alert and suspicious but with an easy laugh*] Think we were running a crap game? That door is never locked. What put that in your nut?

YANK: [*with a knowing grin, convinced that this is all camouflage, a part of the secrecy*] Dis burg is full of bulls, ain't it?

SECRETARY: [*sharply*] What have the cops got to do with us? We're breaking no laws.

YANK: [*with a knowing wink*] Sure. Youse wouldn't for woilds. Sure. I'm wise to dat.

SECRETARY: You seem to be wise to a lot of stuff none of us knows about.

YANK: [*with another wink*] Aw, dat's aw right, see. [*then made a bit resentful by the suspicious glances from all sides*] Aw, can it! Youse needn't put me trou de toid degree. Can't youse see I belong? Sure! I'm reg'lar. I'll stick, get me? I'll shoot de woiks for youse. Dat's why I wanted to join in.

SECRETARY: [*breezily, feeling him out*] That's the right spirit. Only are you sure you understand what you've joined? It's all plain and above board; still, some guys get a wrong slant on us. [*sharply*] What's your notion of the purpose of the I.W.W.?

YANK: Aw, I know all about it.

SECRETARY: [*sarcastically*] Well, give us some of your valuable information.

YANK: [*cunningly*] I know enough not to speak outa my toin. [*then resentfully again*] Aw, say! I'm reg'lar. I'm wise to de game. I know yuh got to watch your step wit a stranger. For all youse know, I might be a plainclothes dick, or somep'n, dat's what yuh're tinkin', huh? Aw, forget it! I belong, see? Ask any guy down to de docks if I don't

SECRETARY: Who said you didn't?

YANK: After I'm 'nitiated, I'll show yuh.

SECRETARY: [*astounded*] Initiated? There's no initiation.

YANK: [*disappointed*] Ain't there no password—no grip nor nothin'?

SECRETARY: What'd you think this is—the Elks—or the Black Hand?

YANK: De Elks, hell! De Black Hand, dey're a lot of yellow back-stickin' Ginees. Naw. Dis is a man's gang, ain't it?

SECRETARY: You said it! That's why we stand on our two feet in the open. We got no secrets.

YANK: [*surprised but admiringly*] Yuh mean to say yuh always run wide open—like dis?

SECRETARY: Exactly.

YANK: Den yuh sure got your noive wit youse!

SECRETARY: [*sharply*] Just what was it made you want to join us? Come out with that straight.

YANK: Yuh call me? Well, I got noive, too! Here's my hand. Yuh wanter blow tings up, don't yuh? Well, dat's me! I belong!

SECRETARY: [*with pretended carelessness*] You mean change the unequal conditions of society by legitimate direct action—or with dynamite?

YANK: Dynamite! Blow it offen de Oith—steel—all de cages—all de factories, steamers, buildings, jails—de Steel Trust and all dat makes it go.

SECRETARY: So—that's your idea, eh? And did you have any special job in that line you wanted to propose to us? [*He makes a sign to the men, who get up cautiously one by one and group behind* YANK.]

YANK: [*boldly*] Sure, I'll come out wit it. I'll show youse I'm one of de gang. Dere's dat millionaire guy, Douglas—

SECRETARY: President of the Steel Trust, you mean? Do you want to assassinate him?

YANK: Naw, dat don't get yuh nothin'. I mean blow up de factory, de woiks, where he makes de steel. Dat's what I'm after—to blow up de steel, knock all de steel in de woild up to de moon. Dat'll fix tings! [*eagerly, with a touch of bravado*] I'll do it by me lonesome! I'll show yuh! Tell me where his woiks is, how to get there, all de dope. Gimme de stuff, de old butter—and watch me do de rest! Watch de smoke and see it move! I don't give a damn if dey nab me—long as it's done! I'll soive life for it—and give 'em de laugh! [*half to himself*] And I'll write her a letter and tell her de hairy ape done it. Dat'll square tings.

SECRETARY: [*stepping away from* YANK] Very interesting. [*He gives a signal. The men, huskies all, throw themselves on* YANK *and before he knows it they have his legs and arms pinioned. But he is too flabbergasted to make a struggle, anyway. They feel him over for weapons.*]

MAN: No gat, no knife. Shall we give him what's what and put the boots to him?

SECRETARY: No. He isn't worth the trouble we'd get into. He's too stupid. [*He comes closer and laughs mockingly in* YANK's *face.*] Ho-ho! By God, this is the biggest joke they've put up on us yet. Hey, you Joke! Who sent you—Burns or Pinkerton? No, by God, you're such a bonehead I'll bet you're in the Secret Service! Well, you dirty spy, you rotten agent-provocator, you can go back and tell whatever skunk is paying you blood-money for betraying your brothers that he's wasting his coin. You couldn't catch a cold. And tell him that all he'll ever get on us, or ever has got, is just his own sneaking plots that he's framed up to put us in jail. We are what our manifesto says we are, neither more nor less—and we'll give him a copy of that any time he calls. And as for you—[*He glares scornfully at* YANK, *who is sunk in an oblivious stupor.*] Oh, hell, what's the use of talking? You're a brainless ape.

YANK: [*aroused by the word to fierce-but-futile struggles*] What's dat, yuh Sheeny bum, yuh!

SECRETARY: Throw him out, boys.

[*In spite of his struggles, this is done with gusto and éclat. Propelled by several parting kicks,* YANK *lands sprawling in the middle of the narrow cobbled street. With a growl he starts to get up and storm the closed door, but stops bewildered by the confusions in his brain, pathetically impotent. He sits there brooding, in as near to the attitude of Rodin's "The Thinker" as he can get in his position.*]

YANK: [*bitterly*] So dem boids don't tink I belong, neider. Aw, to hell wit 'em! Dey're in de wrong pew—de same old bull—soapboxes and Salvation Army—no guts! Cut out an hour offen de job a day and make me happy! Gimme a dollar more a day and make me happy! Tree square a day, and cauliflowers in de front yard—ekal rights—a woman and kids—a lousy vote—and I'm all fixed for Jesus, huh? Aw, hell! What does dat get yuh? Dis ting's in your inside, but it ain't your belly. Feedin' your face—sinkers and coffee—dat don't touch it. It's way down—at de bottom. Yuh can't grab it, and yuh can't stop it. It moves, and everything moves. It stops and de whole woild stops. Dat's me now—I don't tick, see?—I'm a busted Ingersoll, dat's what. Steel was me, and I owned de woild. Now I ain't steel, and de woild owns me. Aw, hell! I can't see—it's all dark, get me? It's all wrong! [*He turns a bitter mocking face up like an ape gibbering at the moon.*] Say, youse up dere, Man in de Moon, yuh look so wise, gimme de answer, huh? Slip me de inside dope, de information right from de stable—where do I get off at, huh?

A POLICEMAN: [*who has come up the street in time to hear this last—with grim humor*] You'll get off at the station, you boob, if you don't get up out of that and keep movin'.

YANK: [*looking up at him—with a hard, bitter laugh*] Sure! Lock me up! Put me in a cage! Dat's de on'y answer yuh know. G'wan, lock me up!

POLICEMAN: What you been doin'?

YANK: Enuf to gimme life for! I was born, see? Sure, dat's de charge. Write it in de blotter. I was born, get me!

POLICEMAN: [*jocosely*] God pity your old woman! [*then matter-of-fact*] But I've no time for kidding. You're soused. I'd run you in but it's too long a walk to the station. Come on now, get up, or I'll fan your ears with this club! Beat it now! [*He hauls* YANK *to his feet.*]

YANK: [*in a vague mocking tone*] Say, where do I go from here?

POLICEMAN: [*giving him a push—with a grin, indifferently*] Go to hell.

CURTAIN

SCENE VIII

Twilight of the next day. The monkey house at the zoo. One spot of clear gray light falls on the front of one cage so that the interior can be seen. The other cages are vague, shrouded in shadow from which chatterings pitched in a conversational tone can be heard. On the one cage a sign from which the word "gorilla" stands out. The gigantic animal himself is seen squatting on his haunches on a bench in much the same attitude as Rodin's "The Thinker." YANK enters from the left. Immediately a chorus of angry chattering and screeching breaks out. The gorilla turns his eyes but makes no sound or move.

YANK: [*with a hard, bitter laugh*] Welcome to your city, huh? Hail, hail, de gang's all here! [*At the sound of his voice the chattering dies away into an attentive silence.* YANK *walks up to the gorilla's cage and, leaning over the railing, stares in at its occupant, who stares back at him, silent and motionless. There is a pause of dead stillness. Then* YANK *begins to talk in a friendly, confidential tone, half-mockingly, but with a deep undercurrent of sympathy.*] Say, yuh're some hard-lookin' guy, ain't yuh? I seen lots of tough nuts dat de gang called gorillas, but yuh're de foist real one I ever seen. Some chest yuh got, and shoulders, and dem arms and mitts! I bet yuh got a punch in eider fist dat'd knock 'em silly! [*This with genuine admiration. The gorilla, as if he understood, stands upright, swelling out his chest and pounding on it with his fist.* YANK *grins sympathetically.*] Sure, I get yuh. Yuh challenge de whole woild, huh? Yuh got what I was sayin' even if yuh muffed de woids. [*then bitterness creeping in*] And why wouldn't yuh get me? Ain't we both members of de same club—de Hairy Apes? [*They stare at each other—a pause—then* YANK *goes on slowly and bitterly.*] So yuh're what she seen when she looked at me, de white-faced tart! I was you to her, get me? On'y outa de cage—broke out—free to moider her, see? Sure! Dat's what she tought. She wasn't wise dat I was in a cage, too—worser'n yours—sure—a damn sight—'cause you got some chanct to bust loose—but me—[*He grows confused.*] Aw, hell! It's all wrong, ain't it? [*a pause*] I s'pose yuh wanter know what I'm doin' here, huh? I been warmin' a bench down to de Battery—ever since last night. Sure. I seen de sun come up. Dat was pretty, too—all red and pink and green. I was lookin' at de skyscrapers—steel—and all de ships comin' in, sailin' out, all over de Oith—and dey was steel, too. De sun was warm, dey wasn't no clouds, and dere was a breeze blowin'. Sure, it was great stuff. I got it aw right—what Paddy said about dat bein' de right dope—on'y I couldn't get *in* it, see? I couldn't belong in dat. It was over my head. And I kept tinkin'—and den I beat it up here to see what youse was like. And I waited till dey was all gone to git yuh alone. Say, how d'yuh feel sittin' in dat pen all de time, havin' to stand for 'em comin' and starin' at yuh—de white-faced, skinny tarts and de boobs what marry 'em—makin' fun of yuh, laughin' at yuh, gittin' scared of yuh—damn 'em! [*He pounds on the rail with his fist. The gorilla rattles the bars of his cage and snarls. All the other monkeys set up an angry chattering in the darkness.* YANK *goes on excitedly.*] Sure! Dat's de way it hits me, too. On'y yuh're lucky, see? Yuh don't belong wit 'em and yuh know it. But me, I belong wit 'em—but I don't, see? Dey don't belong wit me, dat's what. Get me? Tinkin' is hard—[*He passes one hand across his forehead with a painful gesture. The gorilla growls impatiently.* YANK *goes on gropingly.*] It's dis way, what I'm drivin' at. Youse can sit and dope dream in de past, green woods, de jungle, and de rest of it. Den yuh belong and dey don't. Den yuh kin laugh at 'em, see? Yuh're de champ of de woild. But me—I ain't got no past to tink in, nor nothin' dat's comin', on'y what's now—and dat don't belong. Sure, you're de best off! Yuh can't tink, can yuh? Yuh can't talk, neider. But I kin make a bluff at talkin' and tinkin'—a'most git away wit it— a'most!—and dat's where de joker comes in. [*He laughs.*] I ain't on Oith and I ain't in heaven, get me? I'm in de middle tryin' to separate 'em, takin' all de woise punches from bot' of 'em. Maybe dat's what dey call hell, huh? But you, yuh're at de bottom. You belong! Sure! Yuh're de on'y one in de woild dat does, yuh lucky stiff! [*The gorilla growls proudly.*] And dat's why dey gotter put yuh in a cage, see? [*The gorilla roars angrily.*] Sure! Yuh get me. It beats it when you try to tink it or talk it—it's way down—deep—behind—you 'n' me we feel it. Sure! Bot' members of dis club! [*He laughs—then in a savage tone.*] What de hell! T' hell wit it! A little action, dat's our meat! Dat belongs! Knock 'em down and keep bustin' 'em till dey croak yuh wit a gat—wit steel! Sure! Are yuh game? Dey've looked at youse, ain't dey—in a cage? Wanter git even? Wanter wind up like a sport 'stead of croakin' slow in dere? [*The gorilla roars an emphatic affirmative.* YANK *goes on with a sort of furious exultation.*] Sure! Yuh're reg'lar! You'll stick to de finish! Me 'n' you, huh?—bot' members of this club! We'll put up one last star bout dat'll knock 'em offen deir seats! Dey'll have to make de cages stronger after we're trou! [*The gorilla is straining at his bars, growling, hopping from one foot to the other.* YANK *takes a jimmy from under his coat and forces the lock on the cage door. He throws this open.*] Pardon from de governor! Step out and shake hands. I'll take yuh for a walk down Fif' Avenoo. We'll knock 'em offen de Oith and croak wit' de band playin'. Come on, Brother. [*The gorilla scrambles gingerly out of his cage. Goes to* YANK *and stands looking at him.* YANK *keeps his mocking tone—holds out his hand.*] Shake—de secret grip of our order. [*Something, the tone of mockery, perhaps, suddenly outrages the animal. With a spring he wraps his huge arms around* YANK *in a murderous hug. There is a cracking snap of crushed ribs—a gasping cry, still mocking, from* YANK.] Hey, I didn't say kiss me! [*The gorilla lets the crushed body slip to the floor, stands over it uncertainly, considering; then picks it up, throws it in the cage, shuts the door, and shuffles off menacingly into the darkness at left. A great uproar of frightened chattering and whimpering comes from the other cages. Then* YANK *moves, groaning, opening his eyes, and there is silence. He mutters painfully.*] Say—dey oughter match him—wit Zybszko. He got me, aw right. I'm trou. Even him didn't tink I belonged. [*then, with sudden passionate despair*] Christ, where do I get off at? Where do I fit in? [*checking himself as suddenly*] Aw, what de hell! No squawkin', see! No quittin', get me! Croak wit your boots on! [*He grabs hold of the bars of the cage and hauls himself painfully to his feet—looks around him bewilderedly—forces a mocking laugh.*] In de cage, huh? [*in the strident tones of a circus broker*] Ladies and gents, step forward and take a slant at de one and only—[*his voice weakening*]—one and original—Hairy Ape from de wilds of—

[*He slips in a heap on the floor and dies. The monkeys set up a chattering, whimpering wail. And, perhaps, the Hairy Ape at last belongs.*]

CURTAIN

Bertolt Brecht (1891–1956)

The Good Woman of Setzuan (1940)

The expressionists' idealistic dream of transforming humanity foundered in disillusionment during the 1920s. Some writers came to believe that society could be improved only by adopting a program of concrete political action, and in the theatre they sought to focus attention on the great difference between human needs and existing conditions. Attempts to use the theatre as a weapon took several forms, but the most significant was Epic Theatre, exemplified in the plays of Bertolt Brecht. Brecht used many of the devices of expressionist drama, such as episodic structure, unity derived from theme or thesis, and nonillusionistic visual elements. But Brecht, unlike the expressionists, did not suggest that external appearance is untruthful or insignificant; rather, he wished to provoke audiences to reflect on the immediate world and its injustices, and he believed that he could do so most effectively if his audience remained conscious that it was in a theatre. Rejecting the theatre of illusion on the basis that it merely lulls the spectator's critical faculties, Brecht devised several techniques (such as projected captions, songs, and presentational acting) to interrupt the empathetic response and intensify the spectator's awareness of social, economic, and political injustices. It was his hope that the spectator would become aware of the need for change outside the theatre.

The Good Woman of Setzuan is a parable about the difficulties of remaining good under existing social and economic conditions. The "good" person, Shen Te, is generous and well-intentioned, but she soon finds herself exploited and betrayed. Her solution is to disguise herself as her cousin Shui Ta—that is, to let the exploitative side of her character direct her actions. As time passes, she finds herself more and more frequently forced into taking on the role of the ruthless capitalist. Brecht uses this device to suggest the progressive deterioration of morality. The play ends in a stalemate, for the gods leave Shen Te with the same simplistic message they delivered in the prologue—"Be good"—and she is no nearer to knowing how to accomplish this under the present economic system. Throughout the play Brecht skillfully and persistently reminds the audience that Shen Te's predicament is a universal human condition—and one that might be solved by taking the right economic and political action.

Bertolt Brecht

The Good Woman of Setzuan

Revised English Version by Eric Bentley

CHARACTERS

WONG, *a water seller*
THREE GODS
SHEN TE, *a prostitute, later a shopkeeper*
MRS. SHIN, *former owner of Shen Te's shop*
A FAMILY OF EIGHT (*husband, wife, brother, sister-in-law, grandfather, nephew, niece, boy*)
AN UNEMPLOYED MAN
A CARPENTER
MRS. MI TZU, *Shen Te's landlady*
YANG SUN, *an unemployed pilot, later a factory manager*
AN OLD WHORE
A POLICEMAN
AN OLD MAN
AN OLD WOMAN, *his wife*
MR. SHU FU, *a barber*
MRS. YANG, *mother of Yang Sun*
GENTLEMEN, VOICES, CHILDREN (*three*), etc.

PROLOGUE

At the gates of the half-Westernized city of Setzuan. Evening.

[WONG *the water seller introduces himself to the audience.*]
WONG: I sell water here in the city of Setzuan. It isn't easy. When water is scarce, I have long distances to go in search of it, and when it is plentiful, I have no income. But in our part of the world there is nothing unusual about poverty. Many people think only the gods can save the situation. And I hear from a cattle merchant—who travels a lot—that some of the highest gods are on their way at this very moment. Informed sources have it that heaven is quite disturbed at all the complaining. I've been coming out here to the city gates for three days now to bid these gods welcome. I want to be the

first to greet them. What about those fellows over there? No, no, they *work*. And that one there has ink on his fingers, he's no god, he must be a clerk from the cement factory. *Those* two are another story. They look as though they'd like to beat you. But gods don't need to beat you, do they?

[THREE GODS *appear.*]

What about those three? Old-fashioned clothes—dust on their feet—they *must be gods!* [*He throws himself at their feet.*] Do with me what you will, illustrious ones!

FIRST GOD: [*with an ear trumpet*] Ah! [*He is pleased.*] So we are expected?

WONG: [*giving them water*] Oh, yes. And I *knew* you'd come.

FIRST GOD: We need somewhere to stay the night. You know of a place?

WONG: The whole town is at your service, illustrious ones! What sort of a place would you like?

[*The* GODS *eye each other.*]

FIRST GOD: Just try the first house you come to, my son.

WONG: That would be Mr. Fo's place.

FIRST GOD: Mr. Fo.

WONG: One moment! [*He knocks at the first house.*]

VOICE FROM MR. FO'S: No!

[WONG *returns a little nervously.*]

WONG: It's too bad. Mr. Fo isn't in. And his servants don't dare do a thing without his consent. He'll have a fit when he finds out who they turned away, won't he?

FIRST GOD: [*smiling*] He will, won't he?

WONG: One moment! The next house is Mr. Cheng's. Won't he be thrilled!

FIRST GOD: Mr. Cheng.

[WONG *knocks.*]

VOICE FROM MR. CHENG'S: Keep your gods. We have our own troubles!

WONG: [*back with the* GODS] Mr. Cheng is very sorry, but he has a houseful of relations. I think some of them are a bad lot, and naturally, he wouldn't like you to see them.

THIRD GOD: Are we so terrible?

WONG: Well, only with bad people, of course. Everyone knows the province of Kwan is always having floods.

SECOND GOD: Really? How's that?

WONG: Why, because they're so irreligious.

SECOND GOD: Rubbish. It's because they neglected the dam.

FIRST GOD: [*to* SECOND] Sh! [*to* WONG] You're still in hopes, aren't you, my son?

WONG: Certainly. All Setzuan is competing for the honor! What happened up to now is pure coincidence. I'll be back. [*He walks away, but then stands undecided.*]

SECOND GOD: What did I tell you?

THIRD GOD: It *could* be pure coincidence.

SECOND GOD: The same coincidence in Shun, Kwan, and Setzuan? People just aren't religious any more, let's face the fact. Our mission has failed!

FIRST GOD: Oh come, we might run into a good person any minute.

THIRD GOD: How did the resolution read? [*unrolling a scroll and reading from it*] "The world can stay as it is if enough people are found [*at the word "found" he unrolls it a little more*] living lives worthy of human beings." Good people, that is. Well, what about this water seller himself? *He's* good, or I'm very much mistaken.

SECOND GOD: You're very much mistaken. When he gave us a drink, I had the impression there was something odd about the cup. Well, look! [*He shows the cup to the* FIRST GOD.]

FIRST GOD: A false bottom!

SECOND GOD: The man is a swindler.

FIRST GOD: Very well, count *him* out. That's one man among millions. And as a matter of fact, we only need one on *our* side. These atheists are saying, "The world must be changed because no one can *be* good and *stay* good." No one, eh? I say: let us find one—just one—and we have those fellows where we want them!

THIRD GOD: [*to* WONG] Water seller, is it so hard to find a place to stay?

WONG: Nothing could be easier. It's just me. I don't go about it right.

THIRD GOD: Really?

  [*He returns to the others. A* GENTLEMAN *passes by.*]

WONG: Oh dear, they're catching on. [*He accosts the* GENTLEMAN.] Excuse the intrusion, dear sir, but three gods have just turned up. Three of the very highest. They need a place for the night. Seize this rare opportunity—to have real gods as your guests!

GENTLEMAN: [*laughing*] A new way of finding free rooms for a gang of crooks.
  [*Exit* GENTLEMAN.]

WONG: [*shouting at him*] Godless rascal! Have you no religion, gentleman of Setzuan? [*pause*] Patience, illustrious ones! [*pause*] There's only one person left. Shen Te, the prostitute. She *can't* say no. [*calls up to a window*] Shen Te!
  [SHEN TE *opens the shutters and looks out.*]

WONG: Shen Te, it's Wong. *They're* here, and nobody wants them. Will you take them?

SHEN TE: Oh, no, Wong, I'm expecting a gentleman.

WONG: Can't you forget about him for tonight?

SHEN TE: The rent has to be paid by tomorrow or I'll be out on the street.

WONG: This is no time for calculation, Shen Te.

SHEN TE: Stomachs rumble even on the Emperor's birthday, Wong.

WONG: Setzuan is one big dunghill!

SHEN TE: Oh, very well! I'll hide till my gentleman has come and gone. Then I'll take them. [*She disappears.*]

WONG: They mustn't see her gentleman or they'll know what she is.

FIRST GOD: [*who hasn't heard any of this*] I think it's hopeless.
  [*They approach* WONG.]

WONG: [*jumping, as he finds them behind him*] A room has been found, illustrious ones! [*He wipes sweat off his brow.*]

SECOND GOD: Oh, good.

THIRD GOD: Let's see it.

WONG: [*nervously*] Just a minute. It has to be tidied up a bit.

THIRD GOD: Then we'll sit down here and wait.

WONG: [*still more nervous*] No, no! [*holding himself back*] Too much traffic, you know.

THIRD GOD: [*with a smile*] Of course, if you *want* us to move.

>[*They retire a little. They sit on a doorstep.* WONG *sits on the ground.*]

WONG: [*after a deep breath*] You'll be staying with a single girl—the finest human being in Setzuan!

THIRD GOD: That's nice.

WONG: [*to the audience*] They gave me such a look when I picked up my cup just now.

THIRD GOD: You're worn out, Wong.

WONG: A little, maybe.

FIRST GOD: Do people have a hard time of it?

WONG: The good ones do.

FIRST GOD: What about yourself?

WONG: You mean I'm not good. That's true. And I don't have an easy time, either!

>[*During this dialogue, a* GENTLEMAN *has turned up in front of* SHEN TE's *house, and has whistled several times. Each time* WONG *has given a start.*]

THIRD GOD: [*to* WONG, *softly*] Psst! I think he's gone now.

WONG: [*confused and surprised*] Ye-e-es.

>[*The* GENTLEMAN *has left now, and* SHEN TE *has come down in the street.*]

SHEN TE: [*softly*] Wong!

>[*Getting no answer, she goes off down the street.* WONG *arrives just too late, forgetting his carrying pole.*]

WONG: [*softly*] Shen Te! Shen Te! [*to himself*] So she's gone off to earn the rent. Oh dear, I can't go to the gods *again* with no room to offer them. Having failed in the service of the gods, I shall run to my den in the sewer pipe down by the river and hide from their sight!

>[*He rushes off.* SHEN TE *returns, looking for him, but finding the* GODS. *She stops in confusion.*]

SHEN TE: You are the illustrious ones? My name is Shen Te. It would please me very much if my simple room could be of use to you.

THIRD GOD: Where is the water seller, Miss . . . Shen Te?

SHEN TE: I missed him, somehow.

FIRST GOD: Oh, he probably thought you weren't coming, and was afraid of telling us.

THIRD GOD: [*picking up the carrying pole*] We'll leave this with you. He'll be needing it.

>[*Led by* SHEN TE, *they go into the house. It grows dark, then light. Dawn. Again escorted by* SHEN TE, *who leads them through the half-light with a little lamp, the* GODS *take their leave.*]

FIRST GOD: Thank you, thank you, dear Shen Te, for your elegant hospitality! We shall not forget! And give our thanks to the water seller—he showed us a good human being.

SHEN TE: Oh, *I'm* not good. Let me tell you something: when Wong asked me to put you up, I hesitated.

FIRST GOD: It's all right to hesitate if you then go ahead! And in giving us that room you did much more than you knew. You proved that good people still exist, a point that has been disputed of late—even in heaven. Farewell!

SECOND GOD: Farewell!

THIRD GOD: Farewell!

SHEN TE: Stop, illustrious ones! I'm not sure you're right. I'd like to be good, it's true, but there's the rent to pay. And that's not all: I sell myself for a living. Even so I can't make ends meet, there's too much competition. I'd like to honor my father and mother and speak nothing but the truth and not covet my neighbor's house. I should love to stay with one man. But how? How is it done? Even breaking a few of your commandments, I can hardly manage.

FIRST GOD: [*clearing his throat*] These thoughts are but, um, the misgivings of an unusually good woman!

THIRD GOD: Good-bye, Shen Te! Give our regards to the water seller!

SECOND GOD: And above all: be good! Farewell!

FIRST GOD: Farewell!

THIRD GOD: Farewell!

[*They start to wave good-bye.*]

SHEN TE: But everything is so expensive. I don't feel sure I can do it!

SECOND GOD: That's not in our sphere. We never meddle with economics.

THIRD GOD: One moment. [*They stop.*] Isn't it true she might do better if she had more money?

SECOND GOD: Come, come! How could we ever account for it Up Above?

FIRST GOD: Oh, there are ways. [*They put their heads together and confer in dumb show. To* SHEN TE, *with embarrassment:*] As you say you can't pay your rent, well, um, we're not paupers, so of course we *insist* on paying for our room. [*Awkwardly thrusting money into her hand.*] There! [*quickly*] But don't tell anyone! The incident is open to misinterpretation.

SECOND GOD: It certainly is!

FIRST GOD: [*defensively*] But there's no law against it! It was never decreed that a god mustn't pay hotel bills!

[*The* GODS *leave.*]

SCENE I————*A small tobacco shop. The shop is not as yet completely furnished and hasn't started doing business.*

SHEN TE: [*to the audience*] It's three days now since the gods left. When they wanted to pay for the room, I looked down at my hand, and there was more than a thousand silver dollars! I bought a tobacco shop with the money, and moved in yesterday. I don't own the building, of course, but I can pay the rent, and I hope to do a lot of good here. Beginning with Mrs. Shin, who's just coming across the square with her pot. She had the shop before me, and yesterday she dropped in to ask for rice for her children. [*Enter* MRS. SHIN. *Both women bow.*] How do you do, Mrs. Shin.

MRS. SHIN: How do you do, Miss Shen Te. You like your new home?

SHEN TE: Indeed, yes. Did your children have a good night?

MRS. SHIN: In that hovel? The youngest is coughing already.

SHEN TE: Oh, dear!

MRS. SHIN: You're going to learn a thing or two in these slums.

SHEN TE: Slums? That's not what you said when you sold me the shop!

MRS. SHIN: Now don't start nagging! Robbing me and my innocent children of their home and then calling it a slum! That's the limit! [*She weeps.*]

SHEN TE: [*tactfully*] I'll get your rice.

MRS. SHIN: And a little cash while you're at it.

SHEN TE: I'm afraid I haven't sold anything yet.

MRS. SHIN: [*screeching*] I've got to have it. Strip the clothes from my back and then cut my throat, will you? I know what I'll do: I'll dump my children on your doorstep! [*She snatches the pot out of* SHEN TE'S *hands.*]

SHEN TE: Please don't be angry. You'll spill the rice.

[*Enter an elderly* HUSBAND *and* WIFE *with their shabbily dressed* NEPHEW.]

WIFE: Shen Te, dear! You've come into money, they tell me. And we haven't a roof over our heads! A tobacco shop. We had one, too. But it's gone. Could we spend the night here, do you think?

NEPHEW: [*appraising the shop*] Not bad!

WIFE: He's our nephew. We're inseparable!

MRS. SHIN: And who are these . . . ladies and gentlemen?

SHEN TE: They put me up when I first came in from the country. [*to the audience*] Of course, when my small purse was empty, they put me out on the street, and they may be afraid I'll do the same to them. [*to the newcomers, kindly*] Come in, and welcome, though I've only one little room for you—it's behind the shop.

HUSBAND: That'll do. Don't worry.

WIFE: [*bringing* SHEN TE *some tea*] We'll stay over here, so we won't be in your way. Did you make it a tobacco shop in memory of your first real home? We can certainly give you a hint or two! That's one reason we came.

MRS. SHIN: [*to* SHEN TE] Very nice! As long as you have a few customers, too!

HUSBAND: Sh! A customer!

[*Enter an* UNEMPLOYED MAN, *in rags.*]

UNEMPLOYED MAN: Excuse me. I'm unemployed.

[MRS. SHIN *laughs.*]

SHEN TE: Can I help you?

UNEMPLOYED MAN: Have you any damaged cigarettes? I thought there might be some damage when you're unpacking.

WIFE: What nerve, begging for tobacco! [*rhetorically*] Why don't they ask for bread?

UNEMPLOYED MAN: Bread is expensive. One cigarette butt and I'll be a new man.

SHEN TE: [*giving him cigarettes*] That's very important—to be a new man. You'll be my first customer and bring me luck.

[*The* UNEMPLOYED MAN *quickly lights a cigarette, inhales, and goes off, coughing.*]

WIFE: Was that right, Shen Te, dear?

MRS. SHIN: If this is the opening of a shop, you can hold the closing at the end of the week.

HUSBAND: I bet he had money on him.

SHEN TE: Oh, no, he said he hadn't!

NEPHEW: How d'you know he wasn't lying?

SHEN TE: [*angrily*] How do you know he was?

WIFE: [*wagging her head*] You're too good, Shen Te, dear. If you're going to keep this shop, you'll have to learn to say no.

HUSBAND: Tell them the place isn't yours to dispose of. Belongs to . . . some relative who insists on all accounts being strictly in order. . . .

MRS. SHIN: That's right! What do you think you are—a philanthropist?

SHEN TE: [*laughing*] Very well, suppose I ask you for my rice back, Mrs. Shin?

WIFE: [*combatively, at* MRS. SHIN] So that's *her* rice?

[*Enter the* CARPENTER, *a small man.*]

MRS. SHIN: [*who, at the sight of him, starts to hurry away*] See you tomorrow, Miss Shen Te! [*Exit* MRS. SHIN.]

CARPENTER: Mrs. Shin, it's you I want!

WIFE: [*to* SHEN TE] Has she some claim on you?

SHEN TE: She's hungry. That's a claim.

CARPENTER: Are you the new tenant? And filling up the shelves already? Well, they're not yours till they're paid for, ma'am. I'm the carpenter, so I should know.

SHEN TE: I took the shop "furnishings included."

CARPENTER: You're in league with that Mrs. Shin, of course. All right. I demand my hundred silver dollars.

SHEN TE: I'm afraid I haven't got a hundred silver dollars.

CARPENTER: Then you'll find it. Or I'll have you arrested.

WIFE: [*whispering to* SHEN TE] That relative, make it a cousin.

SHEN TE: Can't it wait till next month?

CARPENTER: No!

SHEN TE: Be a little patient, Mr. Carpenter, I can't settle all claims at once.

CARPENTER: Who's patient with me? [*He grabs a shelf from the wall.*] Pay up—or I take the shelves back!

WIFE: Shen Te! Dear! Why don't you let your . . . cousin settle this affair? [*to* CARPENTER] Put your claim in writing. Shen Te's cousin will see you get paid.

CARPENTER: [*derisively*] Cousin, eh?

HUSBAND: Cousin, yes.

CARPENTER: I know these cousins!

NEPHEW: Don't be silly. He's a personal friend of mine.

HUSBAND: What a man! Sharp as a razor!

CARPENTER: All right. I'll put my claim in writing. [*Puts shelf on floor, sits on it, writes out bill.*]

WIFE: [*to* SHEN TE] He'd tear the dress off your back to get his shelves. Never recognize a claim. That's my motto.

SHEN TE: He's done a job, and wants something in return. It's shameful that I can't give it to him. What will the gods say?

HUSBAND: You did your bit when you took *us* in.

[*Enter the* BROTHER, *limping, and the* SISTER-IN-LAW, *pregnant.*]

BROTHER: [*to* HUSBAND *and* WIFE] So this is where you're hiding out! There's family feeling for you! Leaving us on the corner!

WIFE: [*embarrassed, to* SHEN TE] It's my brother and his wife. [*to them*] Now stop grumbling, and sit quietly in that corner. [*to* SHEN TE] It can't be helped. She's in her fifth month.

SHEN TE: Oh yes. Welcome!

WIFE: [*to the couple*] Say "thank you." [*They mutter something.*] The cups are there. [*to* SHEN TE] Lucky you bought this shop when you did!

SHEN TE: [*laughing and bringing tea*] Lucky indeed!

[*Enter* MRS. MI TZU, *the landlady.*]

MRS. MI TZU: Miss Shen Te? I am Mrs. Mi Tzu, your landlady. I hope our relationship will be a happy one. I like to think I give my tenants modern, personalized service. Here is your lease. [*to the others, as* SHEN TE *reads the lease*] There's nothing like the opening of a little shop, is there? A moment of true beauty! [*she is looking around*] Not very much on the shelves, of course. But everything in the gods' good time! Where are your references, Miss Shen Te?

SHEN TE: Do I *have* to have references?

MRS. MI TZU: After all, I haven't a notion who you are!

HUSBAND: Oh, *we'd* be glad to vouch for Miss Shen Te! We'd go through fire for her!

MRS. MI TZU: And who may you be?

HUSBAND: [*stammering*] Ma Fu, tobacco dealer.

MRS. MI TZU: Where is your shop, Mr. . . . Ma Fu?

HUSBAND: Well, um, I haven't got a shop—I've just sold it.

MRS. MI TZU: I see. [*to* SHEN TE] Is there no one else that knows you?

WIFE: [*whispering to* SHEN TE] Your cousin! Your cousin!

MRS. MI TZU: This is a respectable house, Miss Shen Te. I never sign a lease without certain assurances.

SHEN TE: [*slowly, her eyes downcast*] I have . . . a cousin.

MRS. MI TZU: On the square? Let's go over and see him. What does he do?

SHEN TE: [*as before*] He lives . . . in another city.

WIFE: [*prompting*] Didn't you say he was in Shung?

SHEN TE: That's right. Shung.

HUSBAND: [*prompting*] I had his name on the tip of my tongue, Mr. . . .

SHEN TE: [*with an effort*] Mr. . . . Shui . . . Ta.

HUSBAND: That's it! Tall, skinny fellow!

SHEN TE: Shui Ta!

NEPHEW: [*to* CARPENTER] *You* were in touch with him, weren't you? About the shelves?

CARPENTER: [*surlily*] Give him this bill. [*He hands it over.*] I'll back in the morning. [*Exit* CARPENTER.]

NEPHEW: [*calling after him, but with his eyes on* MRS. MI TZU] Don't worry! Mr. Shui Ta pays on the nail!

MRS. MI TZU: [*looking closely at* SHEN TE] I'll be happy to make his acquaintance, Miss Shen Te. [*Exit* MRS. MI TZU.]

[*pause*]

WIFE: By tomorrow morning she'll know more about you than you do yourself.

SISTER-IN-LAW: [*to* NEPHEW] This thing isn't built to last.

[*Enter* GRANDFATHER.]

WIFE: It's Grandfather! [*to* SHEN TE] Such a good old soul!

[*The* BOY *enters.*]

BOY: [*over his shoulder*] Here they are!

WIFE: And the boy, how he's grown! But he always could eat enough for
    [*Enter the* NIECE.]
WIFE: [*to* SHEN TE] Our little niece from the country. There are more of u
    than in your time. The less we had, the more there were of us; the more
    there were of us, the less we had. Give me the key. We must protect our-
    selves from unwanted guests. [*She takes the key and locks the door.*] Just make
    yourself at home. I'll light the little lamp.
NEPHEW: [*a big joke*] I hope her cousin doesn't drop in tonight! The strict Mr.
    Shui Ta!
    [SISTER-IN-LAW *laughs.*]
BROTHER: [*reaching for a cigarette*] One cigarette more or less . . .
HUSBAND: One cigarette more or less.
    [*They pile into the cigarettes. The* BROTHER *hands a jug of wine round.*]
NEPHEW: Mr. Shui Ta'll pay for it!
GRANDFATHER: [*gravely, to* SHEN TE] How do you do?
    [SHEN TE, *a little taken aback by the belatedness of the greeting, bows. She
    has the* CARPENTER's *bill in one hand, the landlady's lease in the other.*]
WIFE: How about a bit of song? To keep Shen Te's spirits up?
NEPHEW: Good idea. Grandfather, you start!

SONG OF THE SMOKE

GRANDFATHER:
> *I used to think (before old age beset me)*
> *That brains could fill the pantry of the poor.*
> *But where did all my cerebration get me?*
> *I'm just as hungry as I was before.*
>   *So what's the use?*
>   *See the smoke float free*
>   *Into ever colder coldness!*
>   *It's the same with me.*

HUSBAND:
> *The straight and narrow path leads to disaster*
> *And so the crooked path I tried to tread.*
> *That got me to disaster even faster.*
> *(They say we shall be happy when we're dead.)*
>   *So what's the use?*
>   *See the smoke float free*
>   *Into ever colder coldness!*
>   *It's the same with me.*

NIECE:
> *You older people, full of expectation,*
> *At any moment now you'll walk the plank!*
> *The future's for the younger generation!*
> *Yes, even if that future is a blank.*
>   *So what's the use?*
>   *See the smoke float free*
>   *Into ever colder coldness!*
>   *It's the same with me.*

NEPHEW: [*to the* BROTHER] Where'd you get that wine?

SISTER-IN-LAW: [*answering for the* BROTHER] He pawned the sack of tobacco.

HUSBAND: [*stepping in*] What? That tobacco was all we had to fall back on! You pig!

BROTHER: *You'd* call a man a pig because your wife was frigid! Did you refuse to drink it?

[*They fight. The shelves fall over.*]

SHEN TE: [*imploringly*] Oh don't! Don't break everything! Take it, take it, take it all, but don't destroy a gift from the gods!

WIFE: [*disparagingly*] This shop isn't big enough. I should never have mentioned it to Uncle and the others. When *they* arrive, it's going to be disgustingly overcrowded.

SISTER-IN-LAW: And did you hear our gracious hostess? She cools off quick!

[*Voices outside. Knocking at the door.*]

UNCLE'S VOICE: Open the door!

WIFE: Uncle! Is that you, Uncle?

UNCLE'S VOICE: Certainly, it's me. Auntie says to tell you she'll have the children here in ten minutes.

WIFE: [*to* SHEN TE] I'll have to let him in.

SHEN TE: [*who scarcely hears her*]
The little lifeboat is swiftly sent down
Too many men too greedily
Hold on to it as they drown.

SCENE Ia————WONG's *den in a sewer pipe.*

WONG: [*crouching there*] All quiet! It's four days now since I left the city. The gods passed this way on the second day. I heard their steps on the bridge over there. They must be a long way off by this time, so I'm safe. [*Breathing a sigh of relief, he curls up and goes to sleep. In his dream the pipe becomes transparent, and the* GODS *appear. Raising an arm, as if in self-defense:*] I know, I know, illustrious ones! I found no one to give you a room—not in all Setzuan! There, it's out. Please continue on your way!

FIRST GOD: [*mildly*] But you did find someone. Someone who took us in for the night, watched over us in our sleep, and in the early morning lighted us down to the street with a lamp.

WONG: It was . . . Shen Te that took you in?

THIRD GOD: Who else?

WONG: And I ran away! "She isn't coming," I thought, "she just can't afford it."

GODS: [*singing*]
O you feeble, well-intentioned, and yet feeble chap
Where there's need the fellow thinks there is no goodness!
When there's danger he thinks courage starts to ebb away!
Some people only see the seamy side!
What hasty judgment! What premature desperation!

WONG: I'm *very* ashamed, illustrious ones.

FIRST GOD: Do us a favor, water seller. Go back to Setzuan. Find Shen Te, and give us a report on her. We hear that she's come into a little money. Show interest in her goodness—for no one can be good for long if goodness is not in demand. Meanwhile we shall continue the search, and find other good people. After which, the idle chatter about the impossibility of goodness will stop!

[*The* GODS *vanish.*]

SCENE II

[*a knocking*]

WIFE: Shen Te! Someone at the door. Where is she, anyway?

NEPHEW: She must be getting the breakfast. Mr. Shui Ta will pay for it.

[*The* WIFE *laughs and shuffles to the door. Enter* MR. SHUI TA *and the* CARPENTER.]

WIFE: Who is it?

SHUI TA: I am Miss Shen Te's cousin.

WIFE: What?

SHUI TA: My name is Shui Ta.

WIFE: Her cousin?

NEPHEW: Her cousin?

NIECE: But that was a joke. She hasn't got a cousin.

HUSBAND: So early in the morning?

BROTHER: What's all the noise?

SISTER-IN-LAW: This fellow says he's her cousin.

BROTHER: Tell him to prove it.

NEPHEW: Right. If you're Shen Te's cousin, prove it by getting the breakfast.

SHUI TA: [*whose regime begins as he puts out the lamp to save oil; loudly, to all present, asleep or awake*] Would you all please get dressed! Customers will be coming! I wish to open my shop!

HUSBAND: *Your* shop? Doesn't it belong to our good friend Shen Te?

[SHUI TA *shakes his head.*]

SISTER-IN-LAW: So we've been cheated. Where is the little liar?

SHUI TA: Miss Shen Te has been delayed. She wishes me to tell you there will be nothing she can do—now I am here.

WIFE: [*bowled over*] I thought she was good!

NEPHEW: Do you have to believe *him?*

HUSBAND: I don't.

NEPHEW: Then do something.

HUSBAND: Certainly! I'll send out a search party at once. You, you, you, and you, go out and look for Shen Te. [*as the* GRANDFATHER *rises and makes for the door*] Not you, Grandfather, you and I will hold the fort.

SHUI TA: You won't find Miss Shen Te. She has suspended her hospitable activity for an unlimited period. There are too many of you. She asked me to say: this is a tobacco shop, not a gold mine.

HUSBAND: Shen Te never said a thing like that. Boy, food! There's a bakery on the corner. Stuff your shirt full when they're not looking!

SISTER-IN-LAW: Don't overlook the raspberry tarts.

HUSBAND: And don't let the policeman see you.

[*The* BOY *leaves.*]

SHUI TA: Don't you depend on this shop now? Then why give it a bad name by stealing from the bakery?

NEPHEW: Don't listen to him. Let's find Shen Te. She'll give him a piece of her mind.

SISTER-IN-LAW: Don't forget to leave us some breakfast.

[BROTHER, SISTER-IN-LAW, *and* NEPHEW *leave.*]

SHUI TA: [*to the* CARPENTER] You see, Mr. Carpenter, nothing has changed since the poet, eleven hundred years ago, penned these lines:
A governor was asked what was needed
To save the freezing people in the city.
He replied:
"A blanket ten thousand feet long
to cover the city and all its suburbs."

[*He starts to tidy up the shop.*]

CARPENTER: Your cousin owes me money. I've got witnesses. For the shelves.

SHUI TA: Yes, I have your bill. [*He takes it out of his pocket.*] Isn't a hundred silver dollars rather a lot?

CARPENTER: No deductions! I have a wife and children.

SHUI TA: How many children?

CARPENTER: Three.

SHUI TA: I'll make you an offer. Twenty silver dollars.

[*The* HUSBAND *laughs.*]

CARPENTER: You're crazy. Those shelves are real walnut.

SHUI TA: Very well, take them away.

CARPENTER: What?

SHUI TA: They cost too much. Please take them away.

WIFE: Not bad! [*And she, too, is laughing.*]

CARPENTER: [*a little bewildered*] Call Shen Te, someone! [*to* SHUI TA] She's *good!*

SHUI TA: Certainly. She's ruined.

CARPENTER: [*provoked into taking some of the shelves*] All right, you can keep your tobacco on the floor.

SHUI TA: [*to the* HUSBAND] Help him with the shelves.

HUSBAND: [*grins and carries one shelf over to the door where the* CARPENTER *now is*] Good-bye, shelves!

CARPENTER: [*to the* HUSBAND] You dog! You want my family to starve?

SHUI TA: I repeat my offer. I have no desire to keep my tobacco on the floor. Twenty silver dollars.

CARPENTER: [*with desperate aggressiveness*] One hundred!

[SHUI TA *shows indifference, looks through the window. The* HUSBAND *picks up several shelves.*]

CARPENTER: [*to* HUSBAND] You needn't smash them against the doorposts, you idiot! [*to* SHUI TA] These shelves were made to measure. They're no use anywhere else!

SHUI TA: Precisely.

[*The* WIFE *squeals with pleasure.*]

CARPENTER: [*giving up, sullenly*] Take the shelves. Pay what you want to pay.

SHUI TA: [*smoothly*] Twenty silver dollars.

[*He places two large coins on the table. The* CARPENTER *picks them up.*]

HUSBAND: [*brings the shelves in*] And quite enough, too!

CARPENTER: [*slinking off*] Quite enough to get drunk on.

HUSBAND: [*happily*] Well, we got rid of him!

WIFE: [*weeping with fun, gives a rendition of the dialogue just spoken*] "Real walnut," says he. "Very well, take them away," says his lordship. "I have three children," says he. "Twenty silver dollars," says his lordship. "They're no use anywhere else," says he. "Pre-cisely," said his lordship! [*She dissolves into shrieks of merriment.*]

SHUI TA: And now: go!

HUSBAND: What's that?

SHUI TA: You're thieves, parasites. I'm giving you this chance. Go!

HUSBAND: [*summoning all his ancestral dignity*] That sort deserves no answer. Besides, one should never shout on an empty stomach.

WIFE: Where's that boy?

SHUI TA: Exactly. The boy. I want no stolen goods in this shop. [*very loudly*] I strongly advise you to leave! [*But they remain seated, noses in the air. Quietly.*] As you wish. [SHUI TA *goes to the door.* A POLICEMAN *appears.* SHUI TA *bows.*] I am addressing the officer in charge of this precinct?

POLICEMAN: That's right, Mr., um, what was the name, sir?

SHUI TA: Mr. Shui Ta.

POLICEMAN: Yes, of course, sir.

[*They exchange a smile.*]

SHUI TA: Nice weather we're having.

POLICEMAN: A little on the warm side, sir.

SHUI TA: Oh, a little on the warm side.

HUSBAND: [*whispering to the* WIFE] If he keeps it up till the boy's back, we're done for. [*Tries to signal* SHUI TA.]

SHUI TA: [*ignoring the signal*] Weather, of course, is one thing indoors, another out on the dusty street!

POLICEMAN: Oh, quite another, sir!

WIFE: [*to the* HUSBAND] It's all right as long as he's standing in the doorway—the boy will see him.

SHUI TA: Step inside for a moment! It's quite cool indoors. My cousin and I have just opened the place. And we attach the greatest importance to being on good terms with the, um, authorities.

POLICEMAN: [*entering*] Thank you, Mr. Shui Ta. It *is* cool.

HUSBAND: [*whispering to the* WIFE] And now the boy won't see him.

SHUI TA: [*showing* HUSBAND *and* WIFE *to the* POLICEMAN] Visitors, I think my cousin knows them. They were just leaving.

HUSBAND: [*defeated*] Ye-e-es, we were . . . just leaving.

SHUI TA: I'll tell my cousin you couldn't wait.

[*Noise from the street. Shouts of* "Stop, Thief!"]

POLICEMAN: What's that?

[*The* BOY *is in the doorway with cakes and buns and rolls spilling out of his shirt. The* WIFE *signals desperately to him to leave. He gets the idea.*]

POLICEMAN: No, you don't! [*he grabs the* BOY *by the collar*] Where's all this from?

BOY: [*vaguely pointing*] Down the street.

POLICEMAN: [*grimly*] So that's it. [*prepares to arrest the* BOY]

WIFE: [*stepping in*] And we knew nothing about it. [*to the* BOY] Nasty little thief!

POLICEMAN: [*dryly*] Can you clarify the situation, Mr. Shui Ta?

> [SHUI TA *is silent.*]

POLICEMAN: [*who understands silence*] Aha. You're all coming with me—to the station.

SHUI TA: I can hardly say how sorry I am that my establishment . . .

WIFE: Oh, he saw the boy leave not ten minutes ago!

SHUI TA: And to conceal the theft asked a policeman in?

POLICEMAN: Don't listen to her, Mr. Shui Ta. I'll be happy to relieve you of their presence one and all! [*to all three*] Out! [*He drives them before him.*]

GRANDFATHER: [*leaving last, gravely*] Good morning!

POLICEMAN: Good morning!

> [SHUI TA, *left alone, continues to tidy up.* MRS. MI TZU *breezes in.*]

MRS. MI TZU: You're her cousin, are you? Then have the goodness to explain what all this means—police dragging people from a respectable house! By what right does your Miss Shen Te turn my property into a house of assignation? Well, as you see, I know all!

SHUI TA: Yes. My cousin has the worst possible reputation: that of being poor.

MRS. MI TZU: No sentimental rubbish, Mr. Shui Ta. Your cousin was a common . . .

SHUI TA: Pauper. Let's use the uglier word.

MRS. MI TZU: I'm speaking of her conduct, not her earnings. But there must have *been* earnings, or how did she buy all this? Several elderly gentlemen took care of it, I suppose. I repeat: this is a respectable house! I have tenants who prefer not to live under the same roof with such a person.

SHUI TA: [*quietly*] How much do you want?

MRS. MI TZU: [*he is ahead of her now*] I beg your pardon.

SHUI TA: To reassure yourself. To reassure your tenants. How much will it cost?

MRS. MI TZU: You're a cool customer.

SHUI TA: [*picking up the lease*] The rent is high. [*He reads on.*] I assume it's payable by the month?

MRS. MI TZU: Not in her case.

SHUI TA: [*looking up*] What?

MRS. MI TZU: Six months' rent payable in advance. Two hundred silver dollars.

SHUI TA: Six . . . ! Sheer usury! And where am I to find it?

MRS. MI TZU: You should have thought of that before.

SHUI TA: Have you no heart, Mrs. Mi Tzu? It's true Shen Te acted foolishly, being kind to all those people, but she'll improve with time. I'll see to it she does. She'll work her fingers to the bone to pay her rent, and all the time be as quiet as a mouse, as humble as a fly.

MRS. MI TZU: Her social background . . .

SHUI TA: Out of the depths! She came out of the depths! And before she'll go back there, she'll work, sacrifice, shrink from nothing. . . . Such a tenant is worth her weight in gold, Mrs. Mi Tzu.

MRS. MI TZU: It's silver dollars we were talking about, Mr. Shui Ta. Two hundred silver dollars or . . .

> [*Enter the* POLICEMAN.]

POLICEMAN: Am I intruding, Mr. Shui Ta?

MRS. MI TZU: This tobacco shop is well known to the police, I see.

POLICEMAN: Mr. Shui Ta has done us a service, Mrs. Mi Tzu. I am here to present our official felicitations!

MRS. MI TZU: That means less than nothing to me, sir. Mr. Shui Ta, all I can say is: I hope your cousin will find my terms acceptable. Good day, gentlemen. [*Exit.*]

SHUI TA: Good day, ma'am.
　　　[*pause*]

POLICEMAN: Mrs. Mi Tzu a bit of a stumbling block, sir?

SHUI TA: She wants six months' rent in advance.

POLICEMAN: And you haven't got it, eh? [SHUI TA *is silent.*] But surely you can get it, sir? A man like you?

SHUI TA: What about a woman like Shen Te?

POLICEMAN: You're not staying, sir?

SHUI TA: No, and I won't be back. Do you smoke?

POLICEMAN: [*taking two cigars, and placing them both in his pocket*] Thank you, sir—I see your point. Miss Te—let's mince no words—Miss Shen Te lived by selling herself. "What else could she have done?" you ask. "How else was she to pay the rent?" True. But the fact remains, Mr. Shui Ta, it is not respectable. Why not? A very deep question. But, in the first place, love—love isn't bought and sold like cigars, Mr. Shui Ta. In the second place, it isn't respectable to go waltzing off with someone that's paying his way, so to speak—it must be for love! Thirdly, and lastly, as the proverb has it: not for a handful of rice but for love! [*Pause. He is thinking hard.*] "Well," you may say, "and what good is all this wisdom if the milk's already spilt?" Miss Shen Te is what she is. Is *where* she is. We have to face the fact that if she doesn't get hold of six months' rent pronto, she'll be back on the streets. The question then as I see it—everything in this world is a matter of opinion—the question as I see it is: *how* is she to get hold of this rent? How? Mr. Shui Ta: I don't know. [*pause*] I take that back, sir. It's just come to me. A husband. We must find her a husband!
　　　[*Enter a little* OLD WOMAN.]

OLD WOMAN: A good cheap cigar for my husband; we'll have been married forty years tomorrow and we're having a little celebration.

SHUI TA: Forty years? And you still want to celebrate?

OLD WOMAN: As much as we can afford to. We have the carpet shop across the square. We'll be good neighbors, I hope?

SHUI TA: I hope so, too.

POLICEMAN: [*who keeps making discoveries*] Mr. Shui Ta, you know what we need? We need capital. And how do we acquire capital? We get married.

SHUI TA: [*to* OLD WOMAN] I'm afraid I've been pestering this gentleman with my personal worries.

POLICEMAN: [*lyrically*] We can't pay six months' rent, so what do we do? We marry money.

SHUI TA: That might not be easy.

POLICEMAN: Oh, I don't know. She's a good match. Has a nice, growing business. [*to the* OLD WOMAN] What do you think?

OLD WOMAN: [*undecided*] Well—

POLICEMAN: Should she put an ad in the paper?

OLD WOMAN: [*not eager to commit herself*] Well, if *she* agrees—

POLICEMAN: I'll write it for her. *You* lend us a hand, and *we* write an ad for you!
> [*He chuckles away to himself, takes out his notebook, wets the stump of a pencil between his lips, and writes away.*]

SHUI TA: [*slowly*] Not a bad idea.

POLICEMAN: "What . . . *respectable* . . . man . . . with small capital . . . widower . . . not excluded . . . desires . . . marriage . . . into flourishing . . . tobacco shop?" And now let's add: "Am . . . pretty . . ." No! . . . "Prepossessing appearance."

SHUI TA: If you don't think that's an exaggeration?

OLD WOMAN: Oh, not a bit. I've seen her.
> [*The* POLICEMAN *tears the page out of his notebook, and hands it over to* SHUI TA.]

SHUI TA: [*with horror in his voice*] How much luck we need to keep our heads above water! How many ideas! How many friends! [*to the* POLICEMAN] Thank you, sir, I think I see my way clear.

SCENE III————*Evening in the municipal park. Noise of a plane overhead.*

> [YANG SUN, *a young man in rags, is following the plane with his eyes: one can tell that the machine is describing a curve above the park.* YANG SUN *then takes a rope out of his pocket, looking anxiously about him as he does so. He moves toward a large willow. Enter two prostitutes, one the* OLD WHORE, *the other the* NIECE *whom we have already met.*]

NIECE: Hello. Coming with me?

YANG SUN: [*taken aback*] If you'd like to buy me a dinner.

OLD WHORE: Buy you a dinner! [*to the* NIECE] Oh, we know him—it's the unemployed pilot. Waste no time on him!

NIECE: But he's the only man left in the park. And it's going to rain.

OLD WHORE: Oh, how do you know?
> [*As they pass by,* YANG SUN *again looks about him, again takes his rope, and this time throws it round a branch of the willow tree. Again he is interrupted. It is the two prostitutes returning—and in such a hurry they don't notice him.*]

NIECE: It's going to pour!
> [*Enter* SHEN TE.]

OLD WHORE: There's that *gorgon* Shen Te! That *drove* your family out into the cold!

NIECE: It wasn't her. It was that cousin of hers. She offered to pay for the cakes. I've nothing against her.

OLD WHORE: I have, though. [*so that* SHEN TE *can hear*] Now where would the little lady be off to? She may be rich now but that won't stop her snatching our young men, will it?

SHEN TE: I'm going to the tearoom by the pond.

NIECE: Is it true what they say? You're marrying a widower—with three children?

SHEN TE: Yes. I'm just going to see him.

YANG SUN: [*his patience at breaking point*] Move on there! This is a park, not a whorehouse!

OLD WHORE: Shut your mouth!

> [*But the two prostitutes leave.*]

YANG SUN: Even in the farthest corner of the park, even when it's raining, you can't get rid of them! [*He spits.*]

SHEN TE: [*overhearing this*] And what right have you to scold them? [*But at this point she sees the rope.*] Oh!

YANG SUN: Well, what are you staring at?

SHEN TE: That rope. What is it for?

YANG SUN: Think! Think! I haven't a penny. Even if I had, I wouldn't spend it on you. I'd buy a drink of water.

> [*The rain starts.*]

SHEN TE: [*still looking at the rope*] What is the rope for? You mustn't!

YANG SUN: What's it to you? Clear out!

SHEN TE: [*irrelevantly*] It's raining.

YANG SUN: Well, don't try to come under this tree.

SHEN TE: Oh, no. [*She stays in the rain.*]

YANG SUN: Now go away. [*pause*] For one thing, I don't like your looks, you're bowlegged.

SHEN TE: [*indignantly*] That's not true!

YANG SUN: Well, don't show 'em to me. Look, it's raining. You better come under this tree.

> [*Slowly, she takes shelter under the tree.*]

SHEN TE: Why did you want to do it?

YANG SUN: You really want to know? [*pause*] To get rid of you! [*pause*] You know what a flyer is?

SHEN TE: Oh yes, I've met a lot of pilots. At the tearoom.

YANG SUN: You call *them* flyers? Think they know what a machine is? Just 'cause they have leather helmets? They gave the airfield director a bribe, that's the way *those* fellows got up in the air! Try one of them out sometime. "Go up to two thousand feet," tell them, "then let it fall, then pick it up again with a flick of the wrist at the last moment." Know what he'll say to that? "It's not in my contract." Then again, there's the landing problem. It's like landing on your own backside. It's no different, planes are human. Those fools don't understand. [*pause*] And I'm the biggest fool for reading the book on flying in the Peking school and skipping the page where it says, "We've got enough flyers and we don't need you." I'm a mail pilot with no mail. You understand that?

SHEN TE: [*shyly*] Yes. I do.

YANG SUN: No, you don't. You'd never understand that.

SHEN TE: When we were little we had a crane with a broken wing. He made friends with us and was very good-natured about our jokes. He would strut along behind us and call out to stop us going too fast for him. But every spring and autumn when the cranes flew over the villages in great swarms, he got quite restless. [*pause*] I understand that. [*She bursts out crying.*]

YANG SUN: Don't!

SHEN TE: [*quieting down*] No.

YANG SUN: It's bad for the complexion.

SHEN TE: [*sniffing*] I've stopped.

[*She dries her tears on her big sleeve. Leaning against the tree, but not look-ing at her, he reaches for her face.*]

YANG SUN: You can't even wipe your own face. [*He is wiping it for her with his handkerchief. Pause.*]

SHEN TE: [*still sobbing*] I don't know *anything!*

YANG SUN: You interrupted me! What for?

SHEN TE: It's such a rainy day. You only wanted to do . . . *that* because it's such a rainy day. [*To the audience:*]
In our country
The evenings should never be somber
High bridges over rivers
The gray hour between night and morning
And the long, long winter:
Such things are dangerous
For, with all the misery,
A very little is enough
And men throw away an unbearable life.
      [*pause*]

YANG SUN: Talk about yourself for a change.

SHEN TE: What about me? I have a shop.

YANG SUN: [*incredulous*] You have a shop, have you? Never thought of walking the streets?

SHEN TE: I did walk the streets. Now I have a shop.

YANG SUN: [*ironically*] A gift of the gods, I suppose!

SHEN TE: How did you know?

YANG SUN: [*even more ironically*] One fine evening the gods turned up saying: here's some money!

SHEN TE: [*quickly*] One fine morning.

YANG SUN: [*fed up*] This isn't much of an entertainment.
      [*pause*]

SHEN TE: I can play the zither a little. [*pause*] And I can mimic men. [*pause*] I got the shop, so the first thing I did was to give my zither away. So I can be as stupid as a fish now, I said to myself, and it won't matter.
I'm rich now, I said
I walk alone, I sleep alone
For a whole year, I said
I'll have nothing to do with a man.

YANG SUN: And now you're marrying one! The one at the tearoom by the pond?
      [SHEN TE *is silent.*]

YANG SUN: What do you know about love?

SHEN TE: Everything.

YANG SUN: Nothing. [*pause*] Or d'you just mean you enjoyed it?

SHEN TE: No.

YANG SUN: [*again without turning to look at her, he strokes her cheek with his hand*] You like that?

SHEN TE: Yes.

YANG SUN: [*breaking off*] You're easily satisfied, I must say. [*pause*] What a town!

SHEN TE: You have no friends?

YANG SUN: [*defensively*] Yes, I have! [*change of tone*] But they don't want to hear I'm still unemployed. "What?" they ask. "Is there still water in the sea?" You have friends?

SHEN TE: [*hesitating*] Just a . . . cousin.

YANG SUN: Watch him carefully.

SHEN TE: He only came once. Then he went away. He won't be back. [YANG SUN *is looking away.*] But to be without hope, they say, is to be without goodness!

    [*pause*]

YANG SUN: Go on talking. A voice is a voice.

SHEN TE: Once, when I was a little girl, I fell, with a load of brushwood. An old man picked me up. He gave me a penny, too. Isn't it funny how people who don't have very much like to give some of it away? They must like to show what they can do, and how could they show it better than by being kind? Being wicked is just like being clumsy. When we sing a song, or build a machine, or plant some rice, we're being kind. You're kind.

YANG SUN: You make it sound easy.

SHEN TE: Oh, no. [*little pause*] Oh! A drop of rain!

YANG SUN: Where'd you feel it?

SHEN TE: Right between the eyes.

YANG SUN: Near the right eye? Or the left?

SHEN TE: Near the left eye.

YANG SUN: Oh, good. [*He is getting sleepy.*] So you're through with men, eh?

SHEN TE: [*with a smile*] But I'm not bowlegged.

YANG SUN: Perhaps not.

SHEN TE: Definitely not.

    [*pause*]

YANG SUN: [*leaning wearily against the willow*] I haven't had a drop to drink all day, I haven't eaten anything for *two* days. I couldn't love you if I tried.

    [*pause*]

SHEN TE: I like it in the rain.

    [*Enter* WONG *the water seller, singing.*]

THE SONG OF THE WATER SELLER IN THE RAIN

> *"Buy my water," I am yelling*
> *And my fury restraining*
> *For no water I'm selling*
> *'Cause it's raining, 'cause it's raining!*
>   *I keep yelling: "Buy my water!"*
>   *But no one's buying*
>   *Athirst and dying*
>   *And drinking and paying!*
>   *Buy water!*
>   *Buy water, you dogs!*
>
> *Nice to dream of lovely weather!*
> *Think of all the consternation*

> Were there no precipitation
> Half a dozen years together!
>> Can't you hear them shrieking: "Water!"
>> Pretending they adore me?
>> They all would go down on their knees before me!
>> Down on your knees!
>> Go down on your knees, you dogs!
>
> What are lawns and hedges thinking?
> What are fields and forests saying?
> "At the cloud's breast we are drinking!
> And we've no idea who's paying!"
>> I keep yelling: "Buy my water!"
>> But no one's buying
>> Athirst and dying
>> And drinking and paying!
>> Buy water
>> Buy water, you dogs!

[*The rain has stopped now.* SHEN TE *sees* WONG *and runs toward him.*]

SHEN TE: Wong! You're back! Your carrying pole's at the shop.

WONG: Oh, thank you, Shen Te. And how is life treating *you*?

SHEN TE: I've just met a brave and clever man. And I want to buy him a cup of your water.

WONG: [*bitterly*] Throw back your head and open your mouth and you'll have all the water you need—

SHEN TE: [*tenderly*]

> I want your water, Wong
> That water that has tired you so
> The water that you carried all this way
> The water that is hard to sell because
>> it's been raining.
> I need it for the young man over there—he's a flyer!
>> A flyer is a bold man:
>> Braving the storms
>> In company with the clouds
>> He crosses the heavens
>> And brings to friends in faraway lands
>> The friendly mail!

[*She pays* WONG, *and runs over to* YANG SUN *with the cup. But* YANG SUN *is fast asleep.*]

SHEN TE: [*calling to* WONG, *with a laugh*] He's fallen asleep! Despair and rain and I have worn him out!

SCENE IIIa————WONG's den.

[*The sewer pipe is transparent, and the* GODS *again appear to* WONG *in a dream.*]

WONG: [*radiant*] I've seen her, illustrious ones! And she hasn't changed!

FIRST GOD: That's good to hear.

WONG: She loves someone.

FIRST GOD: Let's hope the experience gives her the strength to stay good!

WONG: It does. She's doing good deeds all the time.

FIRST GOD: Ah? What sort? What sort of good deeds, Wong?

WONG: Well, she has a kind word for everybody.

FIRST GOD: [*eagerly*] And then?

WONG: Hardly anyone leaves her shop without tobacco in his pocket—even if he can't pay for it.

FIRST GOD: Not bad at all. Next?

WONG: She's putting up a family of eight.

FIRST GOD: [*gleefully, to the* SECOND GOD] Eight! [*to* WONG] And that's not all, of course!

WONG: She bought a cup of water from me even though it was raining.

FIRST GOD: Yes, yes, yes, all these smaller good deeds!

WONG: Even they run into money. A little tobacco shop doesn't make so much.

FIRST GOD: [*sententiously*] A prudent gardener works miracles on the smallest plot.

WONG: She hands out rice every morning. That eats up half her earnings.

FIRST GOD: [*a little disappointed*] Well, as a beginning . . .

WONG: They call her the Angel of the Slums—whatever the carpenter may say!

FIRST GOD: What's this? A carpenter speaks ill of her?

WONG: Oh, he only says her shelves weren't paid for in full.

SECOND GOD: [*who has a bad cold and can't pronounce his* n's *and* m's] What's this? Not paying a carpenter? Why was that?

WONG: I suppose she didn't have the money.

SECOND GOD: [*severely*] One pays what one owes, that's in our book of rules! First the letter of the law, then the spirit.

WONG: But it wasn't Shen Te, illustrious ones, it was her cousin. She called *him* in to help.

SECOND GOD: Then her cousin must never darken her threshold again!

WONG: Very well, illustrious ones! But in fairness to Shen Te, let me say that her cousin is a businessman.

FIRST GOD: Perhaps we should inquire what is customary? I find business quite unintelligible. But everybody's doing it. Business! Did the Seven Good Kings do business? Did King the Just sell fish?

SECOND GOD: In any case, such a thing must not occur again!

[*The* GODS *start to leave.*]

THIRD GOD: Forgive us for taking this tone with you, Wong, we haven't been getting enough sleep. The rich recommended us to the poor, and the poor tell us they haven't enough room.

SECOND GOD: Feeble, feeble, the best of them!

FIRST GOD: No great deeds! No heroic daring!

THIRD GOD: On such a *small* scale.

SECOND GOD: Sincere, yes, but what is actually *achieved*?

[*One can no longer hear them.*]

WONG: [*calling after them*] I've thought of something, illustrious ones: Perhaps you shouldn't ask—too—much—all—at—once!

SCENE IV————*The square in front of* SHEN TE's *tobacco shop. Besides* SHEN TE's *place, two other shops are seen: the carpet shop and a barber's. Morning.*

> [*Outside* SHEN TE's *the* GRANDFATHER, *the* SISTER-IN-LAW, *the* UNEM-PLOYED MAN, *and* MRS. SHIN *stand waiting.*]

SISTER-IN-LAW: She's been out all night again.

MRS. SHIN: No sooner did we get rid of that crazy cousin of hers than Shen Te herself starts carrying on! Maybe she does give us an ounce of rice now and then, but can you depend on her? Can you depend on her?

> [*loud voices from the barber's*]

VOICE OF SHU FU: What are you doing in my shop? Get out—at once!

VOICE OF WONG: But, sir. They all let me sell . . .

> [WONG *comes staggering out of the barber's shop pursued by* MR. SHU FU, *the barber, a fat man carrying a heavy curling iron.*]

SHU FU: Get out, I said! Pestering my customers with your slimy old water! Get out! Take your cup!

> [*He holds out the cup.* WONG *reaches out for it.* MR. SHU FU *strikes his hand with the curling iron, which is hot.* WONG *howls.*]

SHU FU: You had it coming, my man!

> [*Puffing, he returns to his shop. The* UNEMPLOYED MAN *picks up the cup and gives it to* WONG.]

UNEMPLOYED MAN: You can report that to the police.

WONG: My hand! It's smashed up!

UNEMPLOYED MAN: Any bones broken?

WONG: I can't move my fingers.

UNEMPLOYED MAN: Sit down. I'll put some water on it.

> [WONG *sits.*]

MRS. SHIN: The water won't cost you anything.

SISTER-IN-LAW: You might have got a bandage from Miss Shen Te till she took to staying out all night. It's a scandal.

MRS. SHIN: [*despondently*] If you ask me, she's forgotten we ever existed!

> [*Enter* SHEN TE *down the street, with a dish of rice.*]

SHEN TE: [*to the audience*] How wonderful to see Setzuan in the early morning! I always used to stay in bed with my dirty blanket over my head afraid to wake up. This morning I saw the newspapers being delivered by little boys, the streets being washed by strong men, and fresh vegetables coming in from the country on ox carts. It's a long walk from where Yang Sun lives, but I feel lighter at every step. They say you walk on air when you're in love, but it's even better walking on the rough earth, on the hard cement. In the early morning, the old city looks like a great heap of rubbish! Nice, though, with all its little lights. And the sky, so pink, so transparent, before the dust comes and muddies it! What a lot you miss if you never see your city rising from its slumbers like an honest old craftsman pumping his lungs full of air and reaching for his tools as the poet says! [*cheerfully, to her waiting guests*] Good morning, everyone, here's your rice! [*Distributing the rice, she comes upon* WONG.] Good morning, Wong, I'm quite lightheaded today. On my way over, I looked at myself in all the shop windows. I'd love to be beautiful.

[*She slips into the carpet shop.* MR. SHU FU *has just emerged from his shop.*]

SHU FU: [*to the audience*] It surprises me how beautiful Miss Shen Te is looking today! I never gave her a passing thought before. But now I've been gazing upon her comely form for exactly three minutes! I begin to suspect I am in love with her. She is overpoweringly attractive! [*crossly, to* WONG] Be off with you, rascal!

[*He returns to his shop.* SHEN TE *comes back out of the carpet shop with the* OLD MAN, *its proprietor, and his wife—whom we have already met—the* OLD WOMAN. SHEN TE *is wearing a shawl. The* OLD MAN *is holding up a looking glass for her.*]

OLD WOMAN: Isn't it lovely? We'll give you a reduction because there's a little hole in it.

SHEN TE: [*looking at another shawl on the* OLD WOMAN'*s arm*] The other one's nice, too.

OLD WOMAN: [*smiling*] Too bad there's no hole in that!

SHEN TE: That's right. My shop doesn't make very much.

OLD WOMAN: And your good deeds eat it all up! Be more careful, my dear. . . .

SHEN TE: [*trying on the shawl with the hole*] Just now, I'm lightheaded! Does the color suit me?

OLD WOMAN: You'd better ask a man.

SHEN TE: [*to the* OLD MAN] Does the color suit me?

OLD MAN: You'd better ask your young friend.

SHEN TE: I'd like to have your opinion.

OLD MAN: It suits you very well. But wear it this way: the dull side out.

[SHEN TE *pays up.*]

OLD WOMAN: If you decide you don't like it, you can exchange it. [*She pulls* SHEN TE *to one side.*] Has he got money?

SHEN TE: [*with a laugh*] Yang Sun? Oh, no.

OLD WOMAN: Then how're you going to pay your rent?

SHEN TE: I'd forgotten about that.

OLD WOMAN: And next Monday is the first of the month! Miss Shen Te, I've got something to say to you. After we [*indicating her husband*] got to know you, we had our doubts about that marriage ad. We thought it would be better if you'd let *us* help you. Out of our savings. We reckon we could lend you two hundred silver dollars. We don't need anything in writing—you could pledge us your tobacco stock.

SHEN TE: You're prepared to lend money to a person like me?

OLD WOMAN: It's folks like you that need it. We'd think twice about lending anything to your cousin.

OLD MAN: [*coming up*] All settled, my dear?

SHEN TE: I wish the gods could have heard what your wife was just saying, Mr. Ma. They're looking for good people who're happy—and helping me makes you happy because you know it was love that got me into difficulties!

[*The* OLD COUPLE *smile knowingly at each other.*]

OLD MAN: And here's the money, Miss Shen Te.

[*He hands her an envelope.* SHEN TE *takes it. She bows. They bow back. They return to their shop.*]

SHEN TE: [*holding up her envelope*] Look, Wong, here's six months' rent! Don't you
     believe in miracles now? And how do you like my new shawl?
WONG: For the young fellow I saw you with in the park?
          [SHEN TE *nods.*]
MRS. SHIN: Never mind all that. It's time you took a look at his hand!
SHEN TE: Have you hurt your hand?
MRS. SHIN: That barber smashed it with his curling iron. Right in front of our
     eyes.
SHEN TE: [*shocked at herself*] And I never noticed! We must get you to a doctor
     this minute or who knows what will happen?
UNEMPLOYED MAN: It's not a doctor he should see, it's a judge. He can ask for
     compensation. The barber's filthy rich.
WONG: You think I have a chance?
MRS. SHIN: [*with relish*] If it's really good and smashed. But is it?
WONG: I think so. It's very swollen. Could I get a pension?
MRS. SHIN: You'd need a witness.
WONG: Well, you all saw it. You could all testify.
          [*He looks around. The* UNEMPLOYED MAN, *the* GRANDFATHER, *and the*
          SISTER-IN-LAW *are all sitting against the wall of the shop eating rice. Their
          concentration on eating is complete.*]
SHEN TE: [*to* MRS. SHIN] You saw it yourself.
MRS. SHIN: I want nothing to do with the police. It's against my principles.
SHEN TE: [*to* SISTER-IN-LAW] What about you?
SISTER-IN-LAW: Me? I wasn't looking.
SHEN TE: [*to the* GRANDFATHER, *coaxingly*] Grandfather, *you'll* testify, won't you?
SISTER-IN-LAW: And a lot of good that will do. He's simple-minded.
SHEN TE: [*to the* UNEMPLOYED MAN] You seem to be the only witness left.
UNEMPLOYED MAN: My testimony would only hurt him. I've been picked up
     twice for begging.
SHEN TE: Your brother is assaulted, and you shut your eyes?
     He is hit, cries out in pain, and you are silent?
     The beast prowls, chooses, and seizes his victim, and you say:
     "Because we showed no displeasure, he has spared us."
     If no one present will be a witness, I will. I'll say
     I saw it.
MRS. SHIN: [*solemnly*] The name for that is perjury.
WONG: I don't know if I can accept that. Though maybe I'll have to. [*looking at
     his hand*] Is it swollen enough, do you think? The swelling's not going
     down?
UNEMPLOYED MAN: No, no. The swelling's holding up well.
WONG: Yes. It's *more* swollen if anything. Maybe my wrist is broken after all. I'd
     better see a judge at once.
          [*Holding his hand very carefully, and fixing his eyes on it, he runs off.* MRS.
          SHIN *goes quickly into the barber's shop.*]
UNEMPLOYED MAN: [*seeing her*] She is getting on the right side of Mr. Shu Fu.
SISTER-IN-LAW: You and I can't change the world, Shen Te.
SHEN TE: Go away! Go away, all of you!

[*The* UNEMPLOYED MAN, *the* SISTER-IN-LAW, *and the* GRANDFATHER *stalk off, eating and sulking.*]

[*To the audience:*]

They've stopped answering
They stay put
They do as they're told
They don't care
Nothing can make them look up
But the smell of food.

[*Enter* MRS. YANG, YANG SUN's *mother, out of breath.*]

MRS. YANG: Miss Shen Te. My son has told me everything. I am Mrs. Yang, Sun's mother. Just think. He's got an offer. Of a job as a pilot. A letter has just come. From the director of the airfield in Peking!

SHEN TE: So he can fly again? Isn't that wonderful!

MRS. YANG: [*less breathlessly all the time*] They won't give him the job for nothing. They want five hundred silver dollars.

SHEN TE: We can't let money stand in his way, Mrs. Yang!

MRS. YANG: If only you could help him out!

SHEN TE: I have the shop. I can try! [*She embraces* MRS. YANG.] I happen to have two hundred with me now. Take it. [*She gives her the old couple's money.*] It was a loan but they said I could repay it with my tobacco stock.

MRS. YANG: And they were calling Sun the Dead Pilot of Setzuan! A friend in need!

SHEN TE: We must find another three hundred.

MRS. YANG: How?

SHEN TE: Let me think. [*slowly*] I know someone who can help. I didn't want to call on his services again, he's hard and cunning. But a flyer must fly. And I'll make this the last time.

[*distant sound of a plane*]

MRS. YANG: If the man you mentioned can do it . . . Oh, look, there's the morning mail plane, heading for Peking!

SHEN TE: The pilot can see us, let's wave!

[*They wave. The noise of the engine is louder.*]

MRS. YANG: You know that pilot up there?

SHEN TE: Wave, Mrs. Yang! I know the pilot who will be up there. He gave up hope. But he'll do it now. One man to raise himself above the misery, above us all.

[*To the audience:*]

Yang Sun, my lover:
Braving the storms
In company with the clouds
Crossing the heavens
And bringing to friends in faraway lands
The friendly mail!

SCENE IVa————*In front of the inner curtain.*

[*Enter* SHEN TE, *carrying* SHUI TA's *mask. She sings:*]

THE SONG OF DEFENSELESSNESS

> *In our country*
> *A useful man needs luck*
> *Only if he finds strong backers*
> *Can he prove himself useful.*
> *The good can't defend themselves and*
> *Even the gods are defenseless.*
>
> *Oh, why don't the gods have their own ammunition*
> *And launch against badness their own expedition*
> *Enthroning the good and preventing sedition*
> *And bringing the world to a peaceful condition?*
>
> *Oh, why don't the gods do the buying and selling*
> *Injustice forbidding, starvation dispelling*
> *Give bread to each city and joy to each dwelling?*
> *Oh, why don't the gods do the buying and selling?*
> [*She puts on* SHUI TA's *mask and sings in his voice.*]
> *You can only help one of your luckless brothers*
> *By trampling down a dozen others.*
>
> *Why is it the gods do not feel indignation*
> *And come down in fury to end exploitation*
> *Defeat all defeat and forbid desperation*
> *Refusing to tolerate such toleration?*
>
> *Why is it?*

SCENE V————SHEN TE's *tobacco shop.*

> [*Behind the counter,* MR. SHUI TA, *reading the paper.* MRS. SHIN *is cleaning up. She talks and he takes no notice.*]

MRS. SHIN: And when certain rumors get about, what *happens* to a little place like this? It goes to pot. *I* know. So, if you want my advice, Mr. Shui Ta, find out just what has been going on between Miss Shen Te and that Yang Sun from Yellow Street. And remember: a certain interest in Miss Shen Te has been expressed by the barber next door, a man with twelve houses and only one wife, who, for that matter, is likely to drop off at any time. A certain interest has been expressed. He was even inquiring about her means and, if *that* doesn't prove a man is getting serious, what would? [*Still getting no response, she leaves with her bucket.*]

YANG SUN'S VOICE: Is that Miss Shen Te's tobacco shop?

MRS. SHIN'S VOICE: Yes, it is, but it's Mr. Shui Ta who's here today.

> [SHUI TA *runs to the mirror with the short, light steps of* SHEN TE, *and is just about to start primping, when he realizes his mistake, and turns away, with a short laugh. Enter* YANG SUN. MRS. SHIN *enters behind him and slips into the back room to eavesdrop.*]

YANG SUN: I am Yang Sun. [SHUI TA *bows*] Is Shen Te in?

SHUI TA: No.

YANG SUN: I guess you know our relationship? [*He is inspecting the stock.*] Quite a place! And I thought she was just talking big. I'll be flying again, all right. [*He takes a cigar, solicits and receives a light from* SHUI TA.] You think we can squeeze the other three hundred out of the tobacco stock?

SHUI TA: May I ask if it is your intention to sell at once?

YANG SUN: It was decent of her to come out with the two hundred, but they aren't much use with the other three hundred still missing.

SHUI TA: Shen Te was overhasty promising so much. She might have to sell the shop itself to raise it. Haste, they say, is the wind that blows the house down.

YANG SUN: Oh, she isn't a girl to keep a man waiting. For one thing or the other, if you take my meaning.

SHUI TA: I take your meaning.

YANG SUN: [*leering*] Uh, huh.

SHUI TA: Would you explain what the five hundred silver dollars are for?

YANG SUN: Want to sound me out? Very well. The director of the Peking airfield is a friend of mine from flying school. I give him five hundred: he gets me the job.

SHUI TA: The price is high.

YANG SUN: Not as these things go. He'll have to fire one of the present pilots—for negligence. Only the man he has in mind isn't negligent. Not easy, you understand. You needn't mention that part of it to Shen Te.

SHUI TA: [*looking intently at* YANG SUN] Mr. Yang Sun, you are asking my cousin to give up her possessions, leave her friends, and place her entire fate in your hands. I presume you intend to marry her?

YANG SUN: I'd be prepared to.

[*slight pause*]

SHUI TA: Those two hundred silver dollars would pay the rent here for six months. If you were Shen Te wouldn't you be tempted to continue in business?

YANG SUN: What? Can you imagine Yang Sun the flyer behind a counter? [*in an oily voice*] "A strong cigar or a mild one, worthy sir?" Not in this century!

SHUI TA: My cousin wishes to follow the promptings of her heart, and, from her own point of view, she may even have what is called the right to love. Accordingly, she has commissioned me to help you to this post. There is nothing here that I am not empowered to turn immediately into cash. Mrs. Mi Tzu, the landlady, will advise me about the sale.

[*Enter* MRS. MI TZU.]

MRS. MI TZU: Good morning, Mr. Shui Ta, you wish to see me about the rent? As you know it falls due the day after tomorrow.

SHUI TA: Circumstances have changed, Mrs. Mi Tzu: my cousin is getting married. Her future husband here, Mr. Yang Sun, will be taking her to Peking. I am interested in selling the tobacco stock.

MRS. MI TZU: How much are you asking, Mr. Shui Ta?

YANG SUN: Three hundred sil—

SHUI TA: Five hundred silver dollars.

MRS. MI TZU: How much did she pay for it, Mr. Shui Ta?

SHUI TA: A thousand. And very little has been sold.

MRS. MI TZU: She was robbed. But I'll make you a special offer if you'll promise to be out by the day after tomorrow. Three hundred silver dollars.

YANG SUN: [*shrugging*] Take it, man, take it.

SHUI TA: It is not enough.

YANG SUN: Why not? Why not? Certainly, it's enough.

SHUI TA: Five hundred silver dollars.

YANG SUN: But why? We only need three!

SHUI TA: [*to* MRS. MI TZU] Excuse me. [*takes* YANG SUN *on one side*] The tobacco stock is pledged to the old couple who gave my cousin the two hundred.

YANG SUN: Is it in writing?

SHUI TA: No.

YANG SUN: [*to* MRS. MI TZU] Three hundred will do.

MRS. MI TZU: Of course, I need an assurance that Miss Shen Te is not in debt.

YANG SUN: Mr. Shui Ta?

SHUI TA: She is not in debt.

YANG SUN: When can you let us have the money?

MRS. MI TZU: The day after tomorrow. And remember: I'm doing this because I have a soft spot in my heart for young lovers! [*Exit.*]

YANG SUN: [*calling after her*] Boxes, jars, and sacks—three hundred for the lot and the pain's over! [*to* SHUI TA] Where else can we raise money by the day after tomorrow?

SHUI TA: Nowhere. Haven't you enough for the trip and the first few weeks?

YANG SUN: Oh, certainly.

SHUI TA: How much, exactly.

YANG SUN: Oh, I'll dig it up, even if I have to steal it.

SHUI TA: I see.

YANG SUN: Well, don't fall off the roof. I'll get to Peking somehow.

SHUI TA: Two people can't travel for nothing.

YANG SUN: [*not giving* SHUI TA *a chance to answer*] I'm leaving *her* behind. No millstones round *my* neck!

SHUI TA: Oh.

YANG SUN: Don't look at me like that!

SHUI TA: How precisely is my cousin to live?

YANG SUN: Oh, you'll think of something.

SHUI TA: A small request, Mr. Yang Sun. Leave the two hundred silver dollars here until you can show me two tickets for Peking.

YANG SUN: You learn to mind your own business, Mr. Shui Ta.

SHUI TA: I'm afraid Miss Shen Te may not wish to sell the shop when she discovers that . . .

YANG SUN: You don't know women. She'll want to. Even then.

SHUI TA: [*a slight outburst*] She is a human being, sir! And not devoid of common sense!

YANG SUN: Shen Te is a woman: she *is* devoid of common sense. I only have to lay my hand on her shoulder, and church bells ring.

SHUI TA: [*with difficulty*] Mr. Yang Sun!

YANG SUN: Mr. Shui Whatever-it-is!

SHUI TA: My cousin is devoted to you . . . because . . .

YANG SUN: Because I have my hands on her breasts. Give me a cigar. [*He takes one for himself, stuffs a few more in his pocket, then changes his mind and takes the whole box.*] Tell her I'll marry her, then bring me the three hundred. Or let her bring it. One or the other. [*Exit.*]

MRS. SHIN: [*sticking her head out of the back room*] Well, he has your cousin under his thumb, and doesn't care if all Yellow Street knows it!

SHUI TA: [*crying out*] I've lost my shop! And he doesn't love me! [*He runs berserk through the room, repeating these lines incoherently. Then stops suddenly, and addresses* MRS. SHIN.] Mrs. Shin, you grew up in the gutter, like me. Are we lacking in hardness? I doubt it. If you steal a penny from me, I'll take you by the throat till you spit it out! You'd do the same to me. The times are bad, this city is hell, but we're like ants, we keep coming, up and up the walls, however smooth! Till bad luck comes. Being in love, for instance. One weakness is enough, and love is the deadliest.

MRS. SHIN: [*emerging from the back room*] You should have a little talk with Mr. Shu Fu, the barber. He's a real gentleman and just the thing for your cousin. [*She runs off.*]

SHUI TA: A caress becomes a stranglehold
A sigh of love turns to a cry of fear
Why are there vultures circling in the air?
A girl is going to meet her lover.
    [SHUI TA *sits down and* MR. SHU FU *enters with* MRS. SHIN.]

SHUI TA: Mr. Shu Fu?

SHU FU: Mr. Shui Ta.
    [*They both bow.*]

SHUI TA: I am told that you have expressed a certain interest in my cousin Shen Te. Let me set aside all propriety and confess: she is at this moment in grave danger.

SHU FU: Oh, dear!

SHUI TA: She has lost her shop, Mr. Shu Fu.

SHU FU: The charm of Miss Shen Te, Mr. Shui Ta, derives from the goodness, not of her shop, but of her heart. Men call her the Angel of the Slums.

SHUI TA: Yet her goodness has cost her two hundred silver dollars in a single day: we must put a stop to it.

SHU FU: Permit me to differ, Mr. Shui Ta. Let us, rather, open wide the gates to such goodness! Every morning, with pleasure tinged by affection, I watch her charitable ministrations. For they are hungry, and she giveth them to eat! Four of them, to be precise. Why only four? I ask. Why not four hundred? I hear she has been seeking shelter for the homeless. What about my humble cabins behind the cattle run? They are at her disposal. And so forth. And so on. Mr. Shui Ta, do you think Miss Shen Te could be persuaded to listen to certain ideas of mine? Ideas like these?

SHUI TA: Mr. Shu Fu, she would be honored.
    [*Enter* WONG *and the* POLICEMAN. MR. SHU FU *turns abruptly away and studies the shelves.*]

WONG: Is Miss Shen Te here?

SHUI TA: No.

WONG: I am Wong the water seller. You are Mr. Shui Ta?

SHUI TA: I am.

WONG: I am a friend of Shen Te's.

SHUI TA: An intimate friend, I hear.

WONG: [*to the* POLICEMAN] You see? [*to* SHUI TA] It's because of my hand.

POLICEMAN: He hurt his hand, sir, that's a fact.

SHUI TA: [*quickly*] You need a sling, I see. [*He takes a shawl from the back room, and throws it to* WONG.]

WONG: But that's her new shawl!

SHUI TA: She has no more use for it.

WONG: But she bought it to please someone!

SHUI TA: It happens to be no longer necessary.

WONG: [*making the sling*] She is my only witness.

POLICEMAN: Mr. Shui Ta, your cousin is supposed to have seen the barber hit the water seller with a curling iron.

SHUI TA: I'm afraid my cousin was not present at the time.

WONG: But she was, sir! Just ask her! Isn't she in?

SHUI TA: [*gravely*] Mr. Wong, my cousin has her own troubles. You wouldn't wish her to add to them by committing perjury?

WONG: But it was she that told me to go to the judge!

SHUI TA: Was the judge supposed to heal your hand?

　　　　　[MR. SHU FU *turns quickly around.* SHUI TA *bows to* SHU FU, *and vice versa.*]

WONG: [*taking the sling off, and putting it back*] I see how it is.

POLICEMAN: Well, I'll be on my way. [*to* WONG] And you be careful. If Mr. Shu Fu wasn't a man who tempers justice with mercy, as the saying is, you'd be in jail for libel. Be off with you!

　　　　　[*Exit* WONG, *followed by* POLICEMAN.]

SHUI TA: Profound apologies, Mr. Shu Fu.

SHU FU: Not at all, Mr. Shui Ta. [*pointing to the shawl*] The episode is over?

SHUI TA: It may take her time to recover. There are some fresh wounds.

SHU FU: We shall be discreet. Delicate. A short vacation could be arranged. . . .

SHUI TA: First, of course, you and she would have to talk things over.

SHU FU: At a small supper in a small, but high-class, restaurant.

SHUI TA: I'll go and find her. [*Exit into back room.*]

MRS. SHIN: [*sticking her head in again*] Time for congratulations, Mr. Shu Fu?

SHU FU: Ah, Mrs. Shin! Please inform Miss Shen Te's guests they may take shelter in the cabins behind the cattle run!

　　　　　[MRS. SHIN *nods, grinning.*]

SHU FU: [*to the audience*] Well? What do you think of me, ladies and gentlemen? What could a man do more? Could he be less selfish? More farsighted? A small supper in a small but . . . Does that bring rather vulgar and clumsy thoughts into your mind? Ts, ts, ts. Nothing of the sort will occur. She won't even be touched. Not even accidentally while passing the salt. An exchange of ideas only. Only the flowers on the table—white chrysanthemums, by the way [*he writes down a note of this*]—yes, over the white chrysanthemums, two young souls will . . . shall I say "find each other"? We shall *not* exploit the misfortune of others. Understanding? Yes. An offer of assistance? Certainly. But quietly. Almost inaudibly. Perhaps with a single glance. A glance that could also—also mean more.

MRS. SHIN: [*coming forward*] Everything under control, Mr. Shu Fu?

SHU FU: Oh, Mrs. Shin, what do you know about this worthless rascal Yang Sun?

MRS. SHIN: Why, he's the most worthless rascal. . . .

SHU FU: Is he really? You're sure? [*as she opens her mouth*] From now on, he doesn't exist! Can't be found anywhere!

    [*Enter* YANG SUN.]

YANG SUN: What's been going on here?

MRS. SHIN: Shall I call Mr. Shui Ta, Mr. Shu Fu? He wouldn't want strangers in here!

SHU FU: Mr. Shui Ta is in conference with Miss Shen Te. Not to be disturbed.

YANG SUN: Shen Te here? I didn't see her come in. What kind of conference?

SHU FU: [*not letting him enter the back room*] Patience, dear sir! And if by chance I have an inkling who you are, pray take note that Miss Shen Te and I are about to announce our engagement.

YANG SUN: What?

MRS. SHIN: You didn't expect that, did you?

    [YANG SUN *is trying to push past the barber into the back room when* SHEN TE *comes out.*]

SHU FU: My dear Shen Te, ten thousand apologies! Perhaps you . . .

YANG SUN: What is it, Shen Te? Have you gone crazy?

SHEN TE: [*breathless*] My cousin and Mr. Shu Fu have come to an understanding. They wish me to hear Mr. Shu Fu's plans for helping the poor.

YANG SUN: Your cousin wants to part us.

SHEN TE: Yes.

YANG SUN: And you've agreed to it?

SHEN TE: Yes.

YANG SUN: They told you I was bad. [SHEN TE *is silent.*] And suppose I am. Does that make me need you less? I'm low, Shen Te, I have no money, I don't do the right thing but at least I put up a fight! [*He is near her now, and speaks in an undertone.*] Have you no eyes? Look at him. Have you forgotten already?

SHEN TE: No.

YANG SUN: How it was raining?

SHEN TE: No.

YANG SUN: How you cut me down from the willow tree? Bought me water? Promised me money to fly with?

SHEN TE: [*shakily*] Yang Sun, what do you want?

YANG SUN: I want you to come with me.

SHEN TE: [*in a small voice*] Forgive me, Mr. Shu Fu, I want to go with Mr. Yang Sun.

YANG SUN: We're lovers you know. Give me the key to the shop. [SHEN TE *takes the key from around her neck.* YANG SUN *puts it on the counter. To* MRS. SHIN:] Leave it under the mat when you're through. Let's go, Shen Te.

SHU FU: But this is rape! Mr. Shui Ta!

YANG SUN: [*to* SHEN TE] Tell him not to shout.

SHEN TE: Please don't shout for my cousin, Mr. Shu Fu. He doesn't agree with
me, I know, but he's wrong. [*To the audience:*]
I want to go with the man I love
I don't want to count the cost
I don't want to consider if it's wise
I don't want to know if he loves me
I want to go with the man I love.
YANG SUN: That's the spirit.
[*And the couple leave.*]

SCENE Va————*In front of the inner curtain.*

[SHEN TE *in her wedding clothes, on the way to her wedding.*]
SHEN TE: Something terrible has happened. As I left the shop with Yang Sun, I
found the old carpet dealer's wife waiting on the street, trembling all over.
She told me her husband had taken to his bed sick with all the worry and
excitement over the two hundred silver dollars they lent me. She said it
would be best if I gave it back now. Of course, I had to say I would. She said
she couldn't quite trust my cousin Shui Ta or even my fiancé Yang Sun.
There were tears in her eyes. With my emotions in an uproar, I threw myself into Yang Sun's arms, I couldn't resist him. The things he'd said to Shui
Ta had taught Shen Te nothing. Sinking into his arms, I said to myself:

To let no one perish, not even oneself
To fill everyone with happiness, even oneself
Is so good

How could I have forgotten those two old people? Yang Sun swept me away
like a small hurricane. But he's not a bad man, and he loves me. He'd rather
work in the cement factory than owe his flying to a crime. Though, of
course, flying *is* a great passion with Sun. Now, on the way to my wedding,
I waver between fear and joy.

SCENE VI————*The "private dining room" on the upper floor of a cheap restaurant in
a poor section of town.*

[*With* SHEN TE: *the* GRANDFATHER, *the* SISTER-IN-LAW, *the* NIECE, MRS.
SHIN, *the* UNEMPLOYED MAN. *In a corner, alone, a* PRIEST. *A* WAITER
pouring wine. Downstage, YANG SUN *talking to his* MOTHER. *He wears a
dinner jacket.*]
YANG SUN: Bad news, Mamma. She came right out and told me she can't sell the
shop for me. Some idiot is bringing a claim because he lent her the two
hundred she gave you.
MRS. YANG: What did you say? Of course, you can't marry her now.
YANG SUN: It's no use saying anything to *her.* I've sent for her cousin, Mr. Shui
Ta. He said there was nothing in writing.
MRS. YANG: Good idea. I'll go and look for him. Keep an eye on things.
[*Exit* MRS. YANG. SHEN TE *has been pouring wine.*]

SHEN TE: [*to the audience, pitcher in hand*] I wasn't mistaken in him. He's bearing up well. Though it must have been an awful blow—giving up flying. I do love him so. [*calling across the room to him*] Sun, you haven't drunk a toast with the bride!

YANG SUN: What do we drink to?

SHEN TE: Why, to the future!

YANG SUN: When the bridegroom's dinner jacket won't be a hired one!

SHEN TE: But when the bride's dress will still get rained on sometimes!

YANG SUN: To everything we ever wished for!

SHEN TE: May all our dreams come true!

    [*They drink.*]

YANG SUN: [*with loud conviviality*] And now, friends, before the wedding gets under way, I have to ask the bride a few questions. I've no idea what kind of wife she'll make, and it worries me. [*wheeling on* SHEN TE] For example. Can you make five cups of tea with three tea leaves?

SHEN TE: No.

YANG SUN: So I won't be getting very much tea. Can you sleep on a straw mattress the size of that book? [*He points to the large volume the* PRIEST *is reading.*]

SHEN TE: The two of us?

YANG SUN: The one of you.

SHEN TE: In that case, no.

YANG SUN: What a wife! I'm shocked!

    [*While the audience is laughing, his* MOTHER *returns. With a shrug of her shoulders, she tells* YANG SUN *the expected guest hasn't arrived. The* PRIEST *shuts the book with a bang, and makes for the door.*]

MRS. YANG: Where are *you* off to? It's only a matter of minutes.

PRIEST: [*watch in hand*] Time goes on, Mrs. Yang, and I've another wedding to attend to. Also a funeral.

MRS. YANG: [*irately*] D'you think we planned it this way? I was hoping to manage with one pitcher of wine, and we've run through two already. [*Points to empty pitcher. Loudly*] My dear Shen Te, I don't know where your cousin can be keeping himself!

SHEN TE: My cousin?!

MRS. YANG: Certainly. I'm old-fashioned enough to think such a close relative should attend the wedding.

SHEN TE: Oh, Sun, is it the three hundred silver dollars?

YANG SUN: [*not looking her in the eye*] Are you deaf? Mother says she's old-fashioned. And I say I'm considerate. We'll wait another fifteen minutes.

HUSBAND: Another fifteen minutes.

MRS. YANG: [*addressing the company*] Now you all know, don't you, that my son is getting a job as a mail pilot?

SISTER-IN-LAW: In Peking, too, isn't it?

MRS. YANG: In Peking, too! The two of us are moving to Peking!

SHEN TE: Sun, tell your mother Peking is out of the question now.

YANG SUN: Your cousin'll tell her. If he agrees. I don't agree.

SHEN TE: [*amazed, and dismayed*] Sun!

YANG SUN: I hate this godforsaken Setzuan. What people! Know what they look like when I half close my eyes? Horses! Whinnying, fretting, stamping, screwing their necks up! [*loudly*] And what is it the thunder says? They are su-per-flu-ous! [*He hammers out the syllables.*] They've run their last race! They can go trample themselves to death! [*pause*] I've got to get out of here.

SHEN TE: But I've promised the money to the old couple.

YANG SUN: And since you always do the wrong thing, it's lucky your cousin's coming. Have another drink.

SHEN TE: [*quietly*] My cousin can't be coming.

YANG SUN: How d'you mean?

SHEN TE: My cousin can't be where I am.

YANG SUN: Quite a conundrum!

SHEN TE: [*desperately*] Sun, I'm the one that loves you. Not my cousin. He was thinking of the job in Peking when he promised you the old couple's money—

YANG SUN: Right. And that's why he's bringing the three hundred silver dollars. Here—to my wedding.

SHEN TE: He is not bringing the three hundred silver dollars.

YANG SUN: Huh? What makes you think that?

SHEN TE: [*looking into his eyes*] He says you only bought one ticket to Peking.
          [*short pause*]

YANG SUN: That was yesterday. [*He pulls two tickets part way out of his inside pocket, making her look under his coat.*] Two tickets. I don't want Mother to know. She'll get left behind. I sold her furniture to buy these tickets, so you see . . .

SHEN TE: But what's to become of the old couple?

YANG SUN: What's to become of me? Have another drink. Or do you believe in moderation? If I drink, I fly again. If you drink, you may learn to understand me.

SHEN TE: You want to fly. But I can't help you.

YANG SUN: "Here's a plane, my darling—but it's only got one wing!"
          [*The* WAITER *enters.*]

WAITER: Mrs. Yang!

MRS. YANG: Yes?

WAITER: Another pitcher of wine, ma'am?

MRS. YANG: We have enough, thanks. Drinking makes me sweat.

WAITER: Would you mind paying, ma'am?

MRS. YANG: [*to everyone*] Just be patient a few moments longer, everyone, Mr. Shui Ta is on his way over! [*to the* WAITER] Don't be a spoilsport.

WAITER: I can't let you leave till you've paid your bill, ma'am.

MRS. YANG: But they know me here!

WAITER: That's just it.

PRIEST: [*ponderously getting up*] I humbly take my leave. [*And he does.*]

MRS. YANG: [*to the others, desperately*] Stay where you are, everybody! The priest says he'll be back in two minutes!

YANG SUN: It's no good, Mamma. Ladies and gentlemen, Mr. Shui Ta still hasn't arrived and the priest has gone home. We won't detain you any longer.

[*They are leaving now.*]

GRANDFATHER: [*in the doorway, having forgotten to put his glass down*] To the bride! [*He drinks, puts down the glass, and follows the others.*]

[*pause*]

SHEN TE: Shall I go, too?

YANG SUN: You? Aren't you the bride? Isn't this your wedding? [*He drags her across the room, tearing her wedding dress.*] If we can wait, you can wait. Mother calls me her falcon. She wants to see me in the clouds. But I think it may be St. Nevercome's Day before she'll go to the door and see my plane thunder by. [*Pause. He pretends the guests are still present.*] Why such a lull in the conversation, ladies and gentlemen? Don't you like it here? The ceremony is only slightly postponed—because an important guest is expected at any moment. Also because the bride doesn't know what love is. While we're waiting, the bridegroom will sing a little song. [*He does so:*]

THE SONG OF ST. NEVERCOME'S DAY

> *On a certain day, as is generally known,*
> *One and all will be shouting: Hooray, hooray!*
> *For the beggar maid's son has a solid-gold throne*
> *And the day is St. Nevercome's Day*
> *On St. Nevercome's, Nevercome's, Nevercome's Day*
> *He'll sit on his solid-gold throne*
>
> *Oh, hooray, hooray! That day goodness will pay!*
> *That day badness will cost you your head!*
> *And merit and money will smile and be funny*
> *While exchanging salt and bread*
> *On St. Nevercome's, Nevercome's, Nevercome's Day*
> *While exchanging salt and bread*
>
> *And the grass, oh, the grass will look down at the sky*
> *And the pebbles will roll up the stream*
> *And all men will be good without batting an eye*
> *They will make of our Earth a dream*
> *On St. Nevercome's, Nevercome's, Nevercome's Day*
> *They will make of our Earth a dream*
>
> *And as for me, that's the day I shall be*
> *A flyer and one of the best*
> *Unemployed man, you will have work to do*
> *Washerwoman, you'll get your rest*
> *On St. Nevercome's, Nevercome's, Nevercome's Day*
> *Washerwoman you'll get your rest*

MRS. YANG: It looks like he's not coming.

[*The three of them sit looking at the door.*]

SCENE VIa————WONG's *den.*

> [*The sewer pipe is again transparent and again the* GODS *appear to*
> WONG *in a dream.*]

WONG: I'm so glad you've come, illustrious ones. It's Shen Te. She's in great trouble from following the rule about loving thy neighbor. Perhaps she's *too* good for this world!

FIRST GOD: Nonsense! You are eaten up by lice and doubts!

WONG: Forgive me, illustrious one, I only meant you might deign to intervene.

FIRST GOD: Out of the question! My colleague here intervened in some squabble or other only yesterday. [*He points to the* THIRD GOD, *who has a black eye.*] The results are before us!

WONG: She had to call on her cousin again. But not even he could help. I'm afraid the shop is done for.

THIRD GOD: [*a little concerned*] Perhaps we should help after all?

FIRST GOD: The gods help those that help themselves.

WONG: What if we *can't* help ourselves, illustrious ones?
> [*slight pause*]

SECOND GOD: Try, anyway! Suffering ennobles!

FIRST GOD: Our faith in Shen Te is unshaken!

THIRD GOD: We certainly haven't found any *other* good people. You can see where we spend our nights from the straw on our clothes.

WONG: You might help her find her way by—

FIRST GOD: The good man finds his own way here below!

SECOND GOD: The good woman, too.

FIRST GOD: The heavier the burden, the greater her strength!

THIRD GOD: We're only onlookers, you know.

FIRST GOD: And everything will be all right in the end, O ye of little faith!
> [*They are gradually disappearing through these last lines.*]

SCENE VII————*The yard behind* SHEN TE's *shop. A few articles of furniture on a cart.*

> [SHEN TE *and* MRS. SHIN *are taking the washing off the line.*]

MRS. SHIN: If you ask me, you should fight tooth and nail to keep the shop.

SHEN TE: How can I? I have to sell the tobacco to pay back the two hundred silver dollars today.

MRS. SHIN: No husband, no tobacco, no house and home! What are you going to live on?

SHEN TE: I can work. I can sort tobacco.

MRS. SHIN: Hey, look. Mr. Shui Ta's trousers! He must have left here stark naked!

SHEN TE: Oh, he may have another pair, Mrs. Shin.

MRS. SHIN: But if he's gone for good as you say, why has he left his pants behind?

SHEN TE: Maybe he's thrown them away.

MRS. SHIN: Can I take them?

SHEN TE: Oh, no.
> [*Enter* MR. SHU FU, *running.*]

SHU FU: Not a word! Total silence! I know all. You have sacrificed your own love and happiness so as not to hurt a dear old couple who had put their trust in you! Not in vain does this district—for all its malevolent tongues—call you the Angel of the Slums! That young man couldn't rise to your level, so you left him. And now, when I see you closing up the little shop, that veritable heaven of rest for the multitude, well, I cannot, I cannot let it pass. Morning after morning I have stood watching in the doorway not un-moved—while you graciously handed out rice to the wretched. Is that never to happen again? Is the good woman of Setzuan to disappear? If only you would allow *me* to assist you! Now don't say anything! No assurances, no ex-clamations of gratitude! [*He has taken out his checkbook.*] Here! A blank check. [*He places it on the cart.*] Just my signature. Fill it out as you wish. Any sum in the world. I herewith retire from the scene, quietly, unobtrusively, making no claims, on tiptoe, full of veneration, absolutely selflessly . . . [*He has gone.*]

MRS. SHIN: Well! You're saved. There's always some idiot of a man. . . . Now hurry! Put down a thousand silver dollars and let me fly to the bank before he comes to his senses.

SHEN TE: I can pay you for the washing without any check.

MRS. SHIN: What? You're not going to cash it just because you might have to marry him? Are you crazy? Men like him *want* to be led by the nose! Are you still thinking of that flyer? All Yellow Street knows how he treated you!

SHEN TE: When I heard his cunning laugh, I was afraid
But when I saw the holes in his shoes, I loved him dearly.

MRS. SHIN: Defending that good-for-nothing after all that's happened!

SHEN TE: [*staggering as she holds some of the washing*] Oh!

MRS. SHIN: [*taking the washing from her, dryly*] So you feel dizzy when you stretch and bend? There couldn't be a little visitor on the way? If that's it, you can forget Mr. Shu Fu's blank check: it wasn't meant for a christening present!

[*She goes to the back with a basket.* SHEN TE's *eyes follow* MRS. SHIN *for a moment. Then she looks down at her own body, feels her stomach, and a great joy comes into her eyes.*]

SHEN TE: O joy! A new human being is on the way. The world awaits him. In the cities the people say: he's got to be reckoned with, this new human being! [*She imagines a little boy to be present, and introduces him to the audience.*] This is my son, the well-known flyer!
Say: "Welcome"
To the conqueror of unknown mountains and unreachable regions
Who brings us our mail across the impassable deserts!

[*She leads him up and down by the hand.*]

Take a look at the world, my son. That's a tree. Tree, yes. Say: "Hello, tree!" And bow. Like this. [*She bows.*] Now you know each other. And, look, here comes the water seller. He's a friend, give him your hand. A cup of fresh wa-ter for my little son, please. Yes, it *is* a warm day. [*handing the cup*] Oh dear, a policeman, we'll have to make a circle round *him.* Perhaps we can pick a few cherries over there in the rich Mr. Pung's garden. But we mustn't be seen. You want cherries? Just like children with fathers. No, no, you can't go straight at them like that. Don't pull. We must learn to be reasonable. Well, have it your own way. [*She has let him make for the cherries.*] Can you reach? Where to put them? Your mouth is the best place. [*She tries one herself.*]

Mmm, they're good. But the policeman, we must run! [*They run.*] Yes, back
to the street. Calm now, so no one will notice us. [*Walking the street with her
child, she sings.*]

> Once a plum—'twas in Japan—
> Made a conquest of a man
> But the man's turn soon did come
> For he gobbled up the plum

[*Enter* WONG, *with a* CHILD *by the hand. He coughs.*]

SHEN TE: Wong!

WONG: It's about the carpenter, Shen Te. He's lost his shop, and he's been drinking. His children are on the streets. This is one. Can you help?

SHEN TE: [*to the* CHILD] Come here, little man. [*Takes him down to the footlights.
To the audience:*]

You there! A man is asking you for shelter!
A man of tomorrow says: what about today?
His friend the conqueror, whom you know,
Is his advocate!

[*to* WONG] He can live in Mr. Shu Fu's cabins. I may have to go there myself. I'm going to have a baby. That's a secret—don't tell Yang Sun—we'd
only be in his way. Can you find the carpenter for me?

WONG: I knew you'd think of something. [*to the* CHILD] Good-bye, son, I'm going for your father.

SHEN TE: What about your hand, Wong? I wanted to help, but my cousin . . .

WONG: Oh, I can get along with one hand, don't worry. [*He shows how he can handle his pole with his left hand alone.*]

SHEN TE: But your right hand! Look, take this cart, sell everything that's on it,
and go to the doctor with the money . . .

WONG: She's still good. But first I'll bring the carpenter. I'll pick up the cart
when I get back. [*Exit* WONG.]

SHEN TE: [*to the* CHILD] Sit down over here, son, till your father comes. [*The*
CHILD *sits cross-legged on the ground. Enter the* HUSBAND *and* WIFE, *each
dragging a large, full sack.*]

WIFE: [*furtively*] You're alone, Shen Te, dear?

[SHEN TE *nods. The* WIFE *beckons to the* NEPHEW *offstage. He comes on
with another sack.*]

WIFE: Your cousin's away? [SHEN TE *nods*] He's not coming back?

SHEN TE: No. I'm giving up the shop.

WIFE: That's why we're here. We want to know if we can leave these things in
your new home. Will you do us this favor?

SHEN TE: Why, yes, I'd be glad to.

HUSBAND: [*cryptically*] And if anyone asks about them, say they're yours.

SHEN TE: Would anyone ask?

WIFE: [*with a glance at her husband*] Oh, someone might. The police, for instance.
They don't seem to like us. Where can we put it?

SHEN TE: Well, I'd rather not get in any more trouble . . .

WIFE: Listen to her. The good woman of Setzuan!

[SHEN TE *is silent.*]

HUSBAND: There's enough tobacco in those sacks to give us a new start in life. We could have our own tobacco factory!

SHEN TE: [*slowly*] You'll have to put them in the back room.

[*The sacks are taken offstage, while the* CHILD *is alone. Shyly glancing about him, he goes to the garbage can, starts playing with the contents, and eating some of the scraps. The others return.*]

WIFE: We're counting on you, Shen Te!

SHEN TE: Yes. [*She sees the* CHILD *and is shocked.*]

HUSBAND: We'll see you in Mr. Shu Fu's cabins.

NEPHEW: The day after tomorrow.

SHEN TE: Yes. Now, go. Go! I'm not feeling well.

[*Exeunt all three, virtually pushed off.*]

He is eating the refuse in the garbage can!
Only look at his little gray mouth!

[*Pause. Music.*]

As this is the world *my* son will enter
I will study to defend him.
To be good to you, my son,
I shall be a tigress to all others
If I have to.
And I shall have to.

[*She starts to go.*]

One more time, then. I hope really the last.

[*Exit* SHEN TE, *taking* SHUI TA's *trousers.* MRS. SHIN *enters and watches her with marked interest. Enter the* SISTER-IN-LAW *and the* GRANDFATHER.]

SISTER-IN-LAW: So it's true, the shop has closed down. And the furniture's in the back yard. It's the end of the road!

MRS. SHIN: [*pompously*] The fruit of high living, selfishness, and sensuality! Down the primrose path to Mr. Shu Fu's cabins—with you!

SISTER-IN-LAW: Cabins? Rat holes! He gave them to us because his soap supplies only went moldy there!

[*Enter the* UNEMPLOYED MAN.]

UNEMPLOYED MAN: Shen Te is moving?

SISTER-IN-LAW: Yes. She was sneaking away.

MRS. SHIN: She's ashamed of herself, and no wonder!

UNEMPLOYED MAN: Tell her to call Mr. Shui Ta or she's done for this time!

SISTER-IN-LAW: Tell her to call Mr. Shui Ta or *we're* done for this time.

[*Enter* WONG *and* CARPENTER, *the latter with a* CHILD *on each hand.*]

CARPENTER: So we'll have a roof over our heads for a change!

MRS. SHIN: Roof? Whose roof?

CARPENTER: Mr. Shu Fu's cabins. And we have little Feng to thank for it. [FENG, *we find, is the name of the* CHILD *already there; his* FATHER *now takes him. To the other two:*] Bow to your little brother, you two!

[*The* CARPENTER *and the two new arrivals bow to* FENG. *Enter* SHUI TA.]

UNEMPLOYED MAN: Sst! Mr. Shui Ta!

[*pause*]

SHUI TA: And what is this crowd here for, may I ask?

WONG: How do you do, Mr. Shui Ta? This is the carpenter. Miss Shen Te promised him space in Mr. Shu Fu's cabins.

SHUI TA: That will not be possible.

CARPENTER: We can't go there after all?

SHUI TA: All the space is needed for other purposes.

SISTER-IN-LAW: You mean we have to get out? But we've got nowhere to go.

SHUI TA: Miss Shen Te finds it possible to provide employment. If the proposition interests you, you may stay in the cabins.

SISTER-IN-LAW: [*with distaste*] You mean *work*? Work for Miss Shen Te?

SHUI TA: Making tobacco, yes. There are three bales here already. Would you like to get them?

SISTER-IN-LAW: [*trying to bluster*] We have our own tobacco! We were in the tobacco business before you were born!

SHUI TA: [*to the* CARPENTER *and the* UNEMPLOYED MAN] You *don't* have your own tobacco. What about you?

> [*The* CARPENTER *and the* UNEMPLOYED MAN *get the point, and go for the sacks. Enter* MRS. MI TZU.]

MRS. MI TZU: Mr. Shui Ta? I've brought you your three hundred silver dollars.

SHUI TA: I'll sign your lease instead. I've decided not to sell.

MRS. MI TZU: What? You don't need the money for that flyer?

SHUI TA: No.

MRS. MI TZU: And you can pay six months' rent?

SHUI TA: [*takes the barber's blank check from the cart and fills it out*] Here is a check for ten thousand silver dollars. On Mr. Shu Fu's account. Look! [*He shows her the signature on the check.*] Your six months' rent will be in your hands by seven this evening. And now, if you'll excuse me.

MRS. MI TZU: So it's Mr. Shu Fu now. The flyer has been given his walking papers. These modern girls! In my day they'd have said she was flighty. That poor, deserted Mr. Yang Sun!

> [*Exit* MRS. MI TZU. *The* CARPENTER *and the* UNEMPLOYED MAN *drag the three sacks back on the stage.*]

CARPENTER: [*to* SHUI TA] I don't know why I'm doing this for you.

SHUI TA: Perhaps your children want to eat, Mr. Carpenter.

SISTER-IN-LAW: [*catching sight of the sacks*] Was my brother-in-law here?

MRS. SHIN: Yes, he was.

SISTER-IN-LAW: I thought as much. I know those sacks! That's our tobacco!

SHUI TA: Really? I thought it came from my back room! Shall we consult the police on the point?

SISTER-IN-LAW: [*defeated*] No.

SHUI TA: Perhaps you will show me the way to Mr. Shu Fu's cabins?

> [*Taking* FENG *by the hand,* SHUI TA *goes off, followed by the* CARPENTER *and his two older children, the* SISTER-IN-LAW, *the* GRANDFATHER, *and the* UNEMPLOYED MAN. *Each of the last three drags a sack. Enter* OLD MAN *and* OLD WOMAN.]

MRS. SHIN: A pair of pants—missing from the clothesline one minute—and next minute on the honorable backside of Mr. Shui Ta.

OLD WOMAN: We thought Miss Shen Te was here.

MRS. SHIN: [*preoccupied*] Well, she's not.

OLD MAN: There was something she was going to give us.

WONG: She was going to help me, too. [*looking at his hand*] It'll be too late soon. But she'll be back. This cousin has never stayed long.

MRS. SHIN: [*approaching a conclusion*] No, he hasn't, has he?

SCENE VIIa————*The sewer pipe.*

[WONG *asleep. In his dream, he tells the* GODS *his fears. The* GODS *seem tired from all their travels. They stop for a moment and look over their shoulders at the water seller.*]

WONG: Illustrious ones. I've been having a bad dream. Our beloved Shen Te was in great distress in the rushes down by the river—the spot where the bodies of suicides are washed up. She kept staggering and holding her head down as if she was carrying something and it was dragging her down into the mud. When I called out to her, she said she had to take your book of rules to the other side, and not get it wet, or the ink would all come off. You had talked to her about the virtues, you know, the time she gave you shelter in Setzuan.

THIRD GOD: Well, but what do you suggest, my dear Wong?

WONG: Maybe a little relaxation of the rules, Benevolent One, in view of the bad times.

THIRD GOD: As for instance?

WONG: Well, um, goodwill, for instance, might do instead of love?

THIRD GOD: I'm afraid that would create new problems.

WONG: Or instead of justice, good sportsmanship?

THIRD GOD: That would only mean more work.

WONG: Instead of honor, outward propriety?

THIRD GOD: Still more work! No, no! The rules will have to stand, my dear Wong!

[*Wearily shaking their heads, all three journey on.*]

SCENE VIII————SHUI TA's *tobacco factory in* SHU FU's *cabins.*

[*Huddled together behind bars, several families, mostly women and children. Among these people the* SISTER-IN-LAW, *the* GRANDFATHER, *the* CARPEN-TER, *and his* THREE CHILDREN. *Enter* MRS. YANG *followed by* YANG SUN.]

MRS. YANG: [*to the audience*] There's something I just *have* to tell you: strength and wisdom are wonderful things. The strong and wise Mr. Shui Ta has transformed my son from a dissipated good-for-nothing into a model citizen. As you may have heard, Mr. Shui Ta opened a small tobacco factory near the cattle runs. It flourished. Three months ago—I shall never forget it—I asked for an appointment, and Mr. Shui Ta agreed to see us—me and my son. I can see him now as he came through the door to meet us. . . .

[*Enter* SHUI TA *from a door.*]

SHUI TA: What can I do for you, Mrs. Yang?

MRS. YANG: This morning the police came to the house. We find you've brought an action for breach of promise of marriage. In the name of Shen Te. You also claim that Sun came by two hundred silver dollars by improper means.

SHUI TA: That is correct.

MRS. YANG: Mr. Shui Ta, the money's all gone. When the Peking job didn't materialize, he ran through it all in three days. I know he's a good-for-nothing. He sold my furniture. He was moving to Peking without me. Miss Shen Te thought highly of him at one time.

SHUI TA: What do *you* say, Mr. Yang Sun?

YANG SUN: The money's gone.

SHUI TA: [*to* MRS. YANG] Mrs. Yang, in consideration of my cousin's incomprehensible weakness for your son, I am prepared to give him another chance. He can have a job—here. The two hundred silver dollars will be taken out of his wages.

YANG SUN: So it's the factory or jail?

SHUI TA: Take your choice.

YANG SUN: May I speak with Shen Te?

SHUI TA: You may not.

     [*pause*]

YANG SUN: [*sullenly*] Show me where to go.

MRS. YANG: Mr. Shui Ta, you are kindness itself: the gods will reward you! [*to* YANG SUN] And honest work will make a man of you, my boy. [YANG SUN *follows* SHUI TA *into the factory.* MRS. YANG *comes down again to the footlights.*] Actually, honest work didn't agree with him—at first. And he got no opportunity to distinguish himself till—in the third week—when the wages were being paid . . .

    [SHUI TA *has a bag of money. Standing next to his foreman—the former* UNEMPLOYED MAN—*he counts out the wages. It is* YANG SUN'*s turn.*]

UNEMPLOYED MAN: [*reading*] Carpenter, six silver dollars. Yang Sun, six silver dollars.

YANG SUN: [*quietly*] Excuse me, sir. I don't think it can be more than five. May I see? [*He takes the foreman's list.*] It says six working days. But that's a mistake, sir. I took a day off for court business. And I won't take what I haven't earned, however miserable the pay is!

UNEMPLOYED MAN: Yang Sun. Five silver dollars. [*to* SHUI TA] A rare case, Mr. Shui Ta!

SHUI TA: How is it the book says six when it should say five?

UNEMPLOYED MAN: I must've made a mistake, Mr. Shui Ta. [*with a look at* YANG SUN] It won't happen again.

SHUI TA: [*taking* YANG SUN *aside*] You don't hold back, do you? You give your all to the firm. You're even honest. Do the foreman's mistakes always favor the workers?

YANG SUN: He does have . . . friends.

SHUI TA: Thank you. May I offer you any little recompense?

YANG SUN: Give me a trial period of one week, and I'll prove my intelligence is worth more to you than my strength.

MRS. YANG: [*still down at the footlights*] Fighting words, fighting words! That evening, I said to Sun: "If you're a flyer, then fly, my falcon! Rise in the world!" And he got to be foreman. Yes, in Mr. Shui Ta's tobacco factory, he worked real miracles.

[*We see* YANG SUN *with his legs apart standing behind the workers who are handing along a basket of raw tobacco above their heads.*]

YANG SUN: Faster! Faster! You, there, d'you think you can just stand around, now you're not foreman any more? It'll be your job to lead us in song. Sing!

[UNEMPLOYED MAN *starts singing. The others join in the refrain.*]

SONG OF THE EIGHTH ELEPHANT

> *Chang had seven elephants—all much the same—*
>> *But then there was Little Brother*
> *The seven, they were wild, Little Brother, he was tame*
>> *And to guard them Chang chose Little Brother*
>>> *Run faster!*
>>> *Mr. Chang has a forest park*
>>> *Which must be cleared before tonight*
>>> *And already it's growing dark!*
>
> *When the seven elephants cleared that forest park*
>> *Mr. Chang rode high on Little Brother*
> *While the seven toiled and moiled till dark*
>> *On his big behind sat Little Brother*
>>> *Dig faster!*
>>> *Mr. Chang has a forest park*
>>> *Which must be cleared before tonight*
>>> *And already it's growing dark!*
>
> *And the seven elephants worked many an hour*
>> *Till none of them could work another*
> *Old Chang, he looked sour, on the seven he did glower*
>> *But gave a pound of rice to Little Brother*
>>> *What was that?*
>>> *Mr. Chang has a forest park*
>>> *Which must be cleared before tonight*
>>> *And already it's growing dark!*
>
> *And the seven elephants hadn't any tusks*
>> *The one that had the tusks was Little Brother*
> *Seven are no match for one, if the one has a gun!*
>> *How old Chang did laugh at Little Brother!*
>>> *Keep on digging!*
>>> *Mr. Chang has a forest park*
>>> *Which must be cleared before tonight*
>>> *And already it's growing dark!*

[*Smoking a cigar,* SHUI TA *strolls by* YANG SUN, *laughing, has joined in the refrain of the third stanza and speeded up the tempo of the last stanza by clapping his hands.*]

MRS. YANG: And that's why I say: strength and wisdom are wonderful things. It took the strong and wise Mr. Shui Ta to bring out the best in Yang Sun. A real superior man is like a bell. If you ring it, it rings, and if you don't, it don't, as the saying is.

SCENE IX————SHEN TE's *shop, now an office with club chairs and fine carpets. It is raining.*

> [SHUI TA, *now fat, is just dismissing the* OLD MAN *and* OLD WOMAN. MRS. SHIN, *in obviously new clothes, looks on, smirking.*]

SHUI TA: No! I can *not* tell you when we expect her back.

OLD WOMAN: The two hundred silver dollars came today. In an envelope. There was no letter, but it must be from Shen Te. We want to write and thank her. May we have her address?

SHUI TA: I'm afraid I haven't got it.

OLD MAN: [*pulling* OLD WOMAN's *sleeve*] Let's be going.

OLD WOMAN: She's got to come back some time!

> [*They move off, uncertainly, worried.* SHUI TA *bows.*]

MRS. SHIN: They lost the carpet shop because they couldn't pay their taxes. The money arrived too late.

SHUI TA: They could have come to me.

MRS. SHIN: People don't like coming to you.

SHUI TA: [*sits suddenly, one hand to his head*] I'm dizzy.

MRS. SHIN: After all, you *are* in your seventh month. But old Mrs. Shin will be there in your hour of trial! [*She cackles feebly.*]

SHUI TA: [*in a stifled voice*] Can I count on that?

MRS. SHIN: We all have our price, and mine won't be too high for the great Mr. Shui Ta! [*She opens* SHUI TA's *collar.*]

SHUI TA: It's for the child's sake. All of this.

MRS. SHIN: "All for the child," of course.

SHUI TA: I'm so fat. People must notice.

MRS. SHIN: Oh no, they think it's 'cause you're rich.

SHUI TA: [*more feelingly*] What will happen to the child?

MRS. SHIN: You ask that nine times a day. Why, it'll have the best that money can buy!

SHUI TA: He must never see Shui Ta.

MRS. SHIN: Oh, no. Always Shen Te.

SHUI TA: What about the neighbors? There are rumors, aren't there?

MRS. SHIN: As long as Mr. Shu Fu doesn't find out, there's nothing to worry about. Drink this.

> [*Enter* YANG SUN *in a smart business suit, and carrying a businessman's briefcase.* SHUI TA *is more or less in* MRS. SHIN's *arms.*]

YANG SUN: [*surprised*] I guess I'm in the way.

SHUI TA: [*ignoring this, rises with an effort*] Till tomorrow, Mrs. Shin.

> [MRS. SHIN *leaves with a smile, putting her new gloves on.*]

YANG SUN: Gloves now! She couldn't be fleecing you? And since when did you have a private life? [*taking a paper from the briefcase*] You haven't been at your desk lately, and things are getting out of hand. The police want to close us

down. They say that at the most they can only permit twice the lawful number of workers.

SHUI TA: [*evasively*] The cabins are quite good enough.

YANG SUN: For the workers maybe, not for the tobacco. They're too damp. We
must take over some of Mrs. Mi Tzu's buildings.

SHUI TA: Her price is double what I can pay.

YANG SUN: Not unconditionally. If she has me to stroke her knees she'll come
down.

SHUI TA: I'll never agree to that.

YANG SUN: What's wrong? Is it the rain? You get so irritable whenever it rains.

SHUI TA: Never! I will never . . .

YANG SUN: Mrs. Mi Tzu'll be here in five minutes. *You* fix it. And Shu Fu will be
with her. . . . What's all that noise?

[*During the above dialogue,* WONG *is heard offstage, calling:* "The good
Shen Te, where is she? Which of you has seen Shen Te, good people?
Where is Shen Te?" *A knock. Enter* WONG.]

WONG: Mr. Shui Ta, I've come to ask when Miss Shen Te will be back, it's six
months now. . . . There are rumors. People say something's happened to her.

SHUI TA: I'm busy. Come back next week.

WONG: [*excited*] In the morning there was always rice on her doorstep—for the
needy. It's been there again lately!

SHUI TA: And what do people conclude from this?

WONG: That Shen Te is still in Setzuan! She's been . . . [*He breaks off.*]

SHUI TA: She's been what? Mr. Wong, if you're Shen Te's friend, talk a little less
about her, that's my advice to you.

WONG: I don't want your advice! Before she disappeared, Miss Shen Te told me
something very important—she's pregnant!

YANG SUN: What? What was that?

SHUI TA: [*quickly*] The man is lying.

WONG: A good woman isn't so easily forgotten, Mr. Shui Ta.

[*He leaves.* SHUI TA *goes quickly into the back room.*]

YANG SUN: [*to the audience*] Shen Te's pregnant? So that's why. Her cousin sent
her away, so I wouldn't get wind of it. I have a son, a Yang appears on the
scene, and what happens? Mother and child vanish into thin air! That
scoundrel, that unspeakable . . . [*The sound of sobbing is heard from the back
room.*] What was that? Someone sobbing? Who was it? Mr. Shui Ta the Tobacco King doesn't weep his heart out. And where does the rice come from
that's on the doorstep in the morning? [SHUI TA *returns. He goes to the door
and looks out into the rain.*] Where is she?

SHUI TA: Sh! It's nine o'clock. But the rain's so heavy, you can't hear a thing.

YANG SUN: What do you want to hear?

SHUI TA: The mail plane.

YANG SUN: What?!

SHUI TA: I've been told *you* wanted to fly at one time. Is that all forgotten?

YANG SUN: Flying mail is night work. I prefer the daytime. And the firm is very
dear to me—after all, it belongs to my ex-fiancée, even if she's not around.
And she's not, is she?

SHUI TA: What do you mean by that?

YANG SUN: Oh, well, let's say I haven't altogether—lost interest.

SHUI TA: My cousin might like to know that.

YANG SUN: I might not be indifferent—if I found she was being kept under lock and key.

SHUI TA: By whom?

YANG SUN: By you.

SHUI TA: What could you do about it?

YANG SUN: I could submit for discussion—my position in the firm.

SHUI TA: You are now my manager. In return for a more . . . appropriate position, you might agree to drop the inquiry into your ex-fiancée's whereabouts?

YANG SUN: I might.

SHUI TA: What position *would* be more appropriate?

YANG SUN: The one at the top.

SHUI TA: My own? [*silence*] And if I preferred to throw you out on your neck?

YANG SUN: I'd come back on my feet. With suitable escort.

SHUI TA: The police?

YANG SUN: The police.

SHUI TA: And when the police found no one?

YANG SUN: I might ask them not to overlook the back room. [*ending the pretense*] In short, Mr. Shui Ta, my interest in this young woman has not been officially terminated. I should like to see more of her. [*into* SHUI TA's *face*] Besides, she's pregnant and needs a friend. [*He moves to the door.*] I shall talk about it with the water seller.

> [*Exit.* SHUI TA *is rigid for a moment, then he quickly goes into the back room. He returns with* SHEN TE's *belongings: underwear, etc. He takes a long look at the shawl of the previous scene. He then wraps the things in a bundle, which, upon hearing a noise, he hides under the table. Enter* MRS. MI TZU *and* MR. SHU FU. *They put away their umbrellas and galoshes.*]

MRS. MI TZU: I thought your manager was here, Mr. Shui Ta. He combines charm with business in a way that can only be to the advantage of all of us.

SHU FU: You sent for us, Mr. Shui Ta?

SHUI TA: The factory is in trouble.

SHU FU: It always is.

SHUI TA: The police are threatening to close us down unless I can show that the extension of our facilities is imminent.

SHU FU: Shui Ta, I'm sick and tired of your constantly expanding projects. I place cabins at your cousin's disposal; you make a factory of them. I hand your cousin a check; you present it. Your cousin disappears; you find the cabins too small and start talking of yet more—

SHUI TA: Mr. Shu Fu, I'm authorized to inform you that Miss Shen Te's return is now imminent.

SHU FU: Imminent? It's becoming his favorite word.

MRS. MI TZU: Yes, what does it mean?

SHUI TA: Mrs. Mi Tzu, I can pay you exactly half what you asked for your buildings. Are you ready to inform the police that I am taking them over?

MRS. MI TZU: Certainly, if I can take over your manager.

SHU FU: What?

MRS. MI TZU: He's so efficient.

SHUI TA: I'm afraid I need Mr. Yang Sun.

MRS. MI TZU: So do I.

SHUI TA: He will call on you tomorrow.

SHU FU: So much the better. With Shen Te likely to turn up at any moment, the presence of that young man is hardly in good taste.

SHUI TA: So we have reached a settlement. In what was once the good Shen Te's little shop we are laying the foundation for the great Mr. Shui Ta's twelve magnificent super tobacco markets. You will bear in mind that though they call me the Tobacco King of Setzuan, it is my cousin's interests that have been served . . .

VOICES: [*off*] The police, the police! Going to the tobacco shop! Something must have happened!

[*Enter* YANG SUN, WONG, *and the* POLICEMAN.]

POLICEMAN: Quiet there, quiet, quiet! [*They quiet down.*] I'm sorry, Mr. Shui Ta, but there's a report that you've been depriving Miss Shen Te of her freedom. Not that I believe all I hear, but the whole city's in an uproar.

SHUI TA: That's a lie.

POLICEMAN: Mr. Yang Sun has testified that he heard someone sobbing in the back room.

SHU FU: Mrs. Mi Tzu and myself will testify that no one here has been sobbing.

MRS. MI TZU: We have been quietly smoking our cigars.

POLICEMAN: Mr. Shui Ta, I'm afraid I shall have to take a look at that room. [*He does so. The room is empty.*] No one there, of course, sir.

YANG SUN: But I heard sobbing. What's that? [*He finds the clothes.*]

WONG: Those are Shen Te's things. [*to crowd*] Shen Te's clothes are here!

VOICES: [*off, in sequence*]
—Shen Te's clothes!
—They've been found under the table!
—Body of murdered girl still missing!
—Tobacco King suspected!

POLICEMAN: Mr. Shui Ta, unless you can tell us where the girl is, I'll have to ask you to come along.

SHUI TA: I do not know.

POLICEMAN: I can't say how sorry I am, Mr. Shui Ta. [*He shows him the door.*]

SHUI TA: Everything will be cleared up in no time. There are still judges in Setzuan.

YANG SUN: I heard sobbing!

SCENE IXa————WONG's *den.*

[*For the last time, the* GODS *appear to the water seller in his dream. They have changed and show signs of a long journey, extreme fatigue, and plenty of mishaps. The* FIRST *no longer has a hat; the* THIRD *has lost a leg; all three are barefoot.*]

WONG: Illustrious ones, at last you're here. Shen Te's been gone for months and today her cousin's been arrested. They think he murdered her to get the shop. But I had a dream and in this dream Shen Te said her cousin was keeping her prisoner. You must find her for us, illustrious ones!

FIRST GOD: We've found very few good people anywhere, and even they didn't keep it up. Shen Te is still the only one that stayed good.

SECOND GOD: If she *has* stayed good.

WONG: Certainly she has. But she's vanished.

FIRST GOD: That's the last straw. All is lost!

SECOND GOD: A little moderation, dear colleague!

FIRST GOD: [*plaintively*] What's the good of moderation now? If she can't be found, we'll have to resign! The world is a terrible place! Nothing but misery, vulgarity, and waste! Even the countryside isn't what it used to be. The trees are getting their heads chopped off by telephone wires, and there's such a noise from all the gunfire, and I can't stand those heavy clouds of smoke, and—

THIRD GOD: The place is absolutely unlivable! Good intentions bring people to the brink of the abyss, and good deeds push them over the edge. I'm afraid our book of rules is destined for the scrap heap—

SECOND GOD: It's people! They're a worthless lot!

THIRD GOD: The world is too cold!

SECOND GOD: It's people! They're too weak!

FIRST GOD: Dignity, dear colleagues, dignity! Never despair! As for this world, didn't we agree that we only have to find one human being who can stand the place? Well, we found her. True, we lost her again. We must find her again, that's all. And at once!

[*They disappear.*]

SCENE X————*Courtroom.*

[*Groups:* SHU FU *and* MRS. MI TZU; YANG SUN *and* MRS. YANG; WONG, *the* CARPENTER, *the* GRANDFATHER, *the* NIECE, *the* OLD MAN, *the* OLD WOMAN; MRS. SHIN, *the* POLICEMAN; *the* UNEMPLOYED MAN, *the* SISTER-IN-LAW.]

OLD MAN: So much power isn't good for one man.

UNEMPLOYED MAN: And he's going to open twelve super tobacco markets!

WIFE: One of the judges is a friend of Mr. Shu Fu's.

SISTER-IN-LAW: Another one accepted a present from Mr. Shui Ta only last night. A great fat goose.

OLD WOMAN: [*to* WONG] And Shen Te is nowhere to be found.

WONG: Only the gods will ever know the truth.

POLICEMAN: Order in the court! My lords the judges!

[*Enter the* THREE GODS *in judges' robes. We overhear their conversation as they pass along the footlights to their bench.*]

THIRD GOD: We'll never get away with it, our certificates were so badly forged.

SECOND GOD: My predecessor's "sudden indigestion" will certainly cause comment.

FIRST GOD: But he *had* just eaten a whole goose.

UNEMPLOYED MAN: Look at that! *New* judges.

WONG: New judges. And what good ones!

[*The* THIRD GOD *hears this, and turns to smile at* WONG. *The* GODS *sit. The* FIRST GOD *beats on the bench with his gavel. The* POLICEMAN *brings in* SHUI TA, *who walks with lordly steps. He is whistled at.*]

POLICEMAN: [*to* SHUI TA] Be prepared for a surprise. The judges have been changed.

[SHUI TA *turns quickly round, looks at them, and staggers.*]

NIECE: What's the matter now?

WIFE: The great Tobacco King nearly fainted.

HUSBAND: Yes, as soon as he saw the new judges.

WONG: Does he know who they are?

[SHUI TA *picks himself up, and the proceedings open.*]

FIRST GOD: Defendant Shui Ta, you are accused of doing away with your cousin Shen Te in order to take possession of her business. Do you plead guilty or not guilty?

SHUI TA: Not guilty, my lord.

FIRST GOD: [*thumbing through the documents of the case*] The first witness is the policeman. I shall ask him to tell us something of the respective reputations of Miss Shen Te and Mr. Shui Ta.

POLICEMAN: Miss Shen Te was a young lady who aimed to please, my lord. She liked to live and let live, as the saying goes. Mr. Shui Ta, on the other hand, is a man of principle. Though the generosity of Miss Shen Te forced him at times to abandon half measures, unlike the girl he was always on the side of the law, my lord. One time, he even unmasked a gang of thieves to whom his too-trustful cousin had given shelter. The evidence, in short, my lord, proves that Mr. Shui Ta was *incapable* of the crime of which he stands accused!

FIRST GOD: I see. And are there others who could testify along, shall we say, the same lines?

[SHU FU *rises.*]

POLICEMAN: [*whispering to* GODS] Mr. Shu Fu—a very important person.

FIRST GOD: [*inviting him to speak*] Mr. Shu Fu!

SHU FU: Mr. Shui Ta is a businessman, my lord. Need I say more?

FIRST GOD: Yes.

SHU FU: Very well, I will. He is Vice President of the Council of Commerce and is about to be elected a Justice of the Peace. [*He returns to his seat.*]

[MRS. MI TZU *rises.*]

WONG: Elected! *He* gave him the job!

[*With a gesture the* FIRST GOD *asks who* MRS. MI TZU *is.*]

POLICEMAN: Another very important person. Mrs. Mi Tzu.

MRS. MI TZU: My lord, as Chairman of the Committee on Social Work, I wish to call attention to just a couple of eloquent facts: Mr. Shui Ta not only has erected a model factory with model housing in our city, he is a regular contributor to our home for the disabled. [*She returns to her seat.*]

POLICEMAN: [*whispering*] And she's a great friend of the judge that ate the goose!

FIRST GOD: [*to the* POLICEMAN] Oh, thank you. What's next? [*to the Court, genially*] Oh, yes. We should find out if any of the evidence is less favorable to the defendant.

[WONG, *the* CARPENTER, *the* OLD MAN, *the* OLD WOMAN, *the* UNEMPLOYED MAN, *the* SISTER-IN-LAW, *and the* NIECE *come forward.*]

POLICEMAN: [*whispering*] Just the riffraff, my lord.

FIRST GOD: [*addressing the "riffraff"*] Well, um, riffraff—do you know anything of the defendant, Mr. Shui Ta?

WONG: Too much, my lord.

UNEMPLOYED MAN: What don't we know, my lord.

CARPENTER: He ruined us.

SISTER-IN-LAW: He's a cheat.

NIECE: Liar.

WIFE: Thief.

BOY: Blackmailer.

BROTHER: Murderer.

FIRST GOD: Thank you. We should now let the defendant state his point of view.

SHUI TA: I only came on the scene when Shen Te was in danger of losing what I had understood was a gift from the gods. Because I did the filthy jobs which someone had to do, they hate me. My activities were restricted to the minimum, my lord.

SISTER-IN-LAW: He had us arrested!

SHUI TA: Certainly. You stole from the bakery!

SISTER-IN-LAW: Such concern for the bakery! You didn't want the shop for yourself, I suppose!

SHUI TA: I didn't want the shop overrun with parasites.

SISTER-IN-LAW: We had nowhere else to go.

SHUI TA: There were too many of you.

WONG: What about this old couple. Were *they* parasites?

OLD MAN: We lost our shop because of you!

OLD WOMAN: And we gave your cousin money!

SHUI TA: My cousin's fiancé was a flyer. The money had to go to *him.*

WONG: Did you care whether he flew or not? Did you care whether she married him or not? You wanted her to marry someone else! [*He points at* SHU FU.]

SHUI TA: The flyer unexpectedly turned out to be a scoundrel.

YANG SUN: [*jumping up*] Which was the reason you made him your manager?

SHUI TA: Later on he improved.

WONG: And when he improved, you sold him to her? [*He points out* MRS. MI TZU.]

SHUI TA: She wouldn't let me have her premises unless she had him to stroke her knees!

MRS. MI TZU: What? The man's a pathological liar. [*to him*] Don't mention my property to me as long as you live! Murderer! [*She rustles off, in high dudgeon.*]

YANG SUN: [*pushing in*] My lord, I wish to speak for the defendant.

SISTER-IN-LAW: Naturally. He's your employer.

UNEMPLOYED MAN: And the worst slave driver in the country.

MRS. YANG: That's a lie! My lord, Mr. Shui Ta is a great man. He . . .

YANG SUN: He's this and he's that, but he is not a murderer, my lord. Just fifteen minutes before his arrest I heard Shen Te's voice in his own back room.

FIRST GOD: Oh? Tell us more!

YANG SUN: I heard sobbing, my lord!

FIRST GOD: But lots of women sob, we've been finding.

YANG SUN: Could I fail to recognize her voice?

SHU FU: No, you made her sob so often yourself, young man!

YANG SUN: Yes. But I also made her happy. Till he [*pointing at* SHUI TA] decided to sell her to you!

SHUI TA: Because you didn't love her.

WONG: Oh, no: it was for the money, my lord!

SHUI TA: And what was the money for, my lord? For the poor! And for Shen Te so she could go on being good!

WONG: For the poor? That he sent to his sweatshops? And why didn't you let Shen Te be good when you signed the big check?

SHUI TA: For the child's sake, my lord.

CARPENTER: What about *my* children? What did he do about them?

[SHUI TA *is silent.*]

WONG: The shop was to be a fountain of goodness. That was the gods' idea. You came and spoiled it!

SHUI TA: If I hadn't, it would have run dry!

MRS. SHIN: There's a lot in that, my lord.

WONG: What have you done with the good Shen Te, bad man? She *was* good, my lords, she was, I swear it! [*He raises his hand in an oath.*]

THIRD GOD: What's happened to your hand, water seller?

WONG: [*pointing to* SHUI TA] It's all his fault, my lord, *she* was going to send me to a doctor—[*to* SHUI TA] You were her worst enemy!

SHUI TA: I was her only friend!

WONG: Where is she then? Tell us where your good friend is!

[*The excitement of this exchange has run through the whole crowd.*]

ALL: Yes, where is she? Where is Shen Te? [*etc.*]

SHUI TA: Shen Te . . . had to go.

WONG: Where? Where to?

SHUI TA: I cannot tell you! I cannot tell you!

ALL: Why? Why did she have to go away? [*etc.*]

WONG: [*into the din with the first words, but talking on beyond the others*] Why not, why not? Why did she have to go away?

SHUI TA: [*shouting*] Because you'd all have torn her to shreds, that's why! My lords, I have a request. Clear the court! When only the judges remain, I will make a confession.

ALL: [*except* WONG, *who is silent, struck by the new turn of events*] So he's guilty? He's confessing! [*etc.*]

FIRST GOD: [*using the gavel*] Clear the court!

POLICEMAN: Clear the court!

WONG: Mr. Shui Ta has met his match this time.

MRS. SHIN: [*with a gesture toward the judges*] You're in for a little surprise.

[*The court is cleared. Silence.*]

SHUI TA: Illustrious ones!

[*The* GODS *look at each other, not quite believing their ears.*]

SHUI TA: Yes, I recognize you!

SECOND GOD: [*taking matters in hand, sternly*] What have you done with our good woman of Setzuan?

SHUI TA: I have a terrible confession to make: I am she! [*He takes off his mask, and tears away his clothes.* SHEN TE *stands there.*]

SECOND GOD: Shen Te!

SHEN TE: Shen Te, yes. Shui Ta *and* Shen Te. Both.

Your injunction

To be good and yet to live
Was a thunderbolt:
It has torn me in two
I can't tell how it was
But to be good to others
And myself at the same time
I could not do it
Your world is not an easy one, illustrious ones!
When we extend our hand to a beggar, he tears it off for us
When we help the lost, we are lost ourselves
And so
Since not to eat is to die
Who can long refuse to be bad?
As I lay prostrate beneath the weight of good intentions
Ruin stared me in the face
It was when I was unjust that I ate good meat
And hobnobbed with the mighty
Why?
Why are bad deeds rewarded?
Good ones punished?
I enjoyed giving
I truly wished to be the Angel of the Slums
But washed by a foster mother in the water of the gutter
I developed a sharp eye
The time came when pity was a thorn in my side
And, later, when kind words turned to ashes in my mouth
And anger took over
I became a wolf
Find me guilty, then, illustrious ones,
But know:
All that I have done I did
To help my neighbor
To love my lover
And to keep my little one from want
For your great, godly deeds, I was too poor, too small.
    [*pause*]

FIRST GOD: [*shocked*] Don't go making yourself miserable, Shen Te! We're over-
joyed to have found you!

SHEN TE: I'm telling you I'm the bad man who committed all those crimes!

FIRST GOD: [*using—or failing to use—his ear trumpet*] The good woman who did
all those good deeds?

SHEN TE: Yes, but the bad man, too!

FIRST GOD: [*as if something had dawned*] Unfortunate coincidences! Heartless
neighbors!

THIRD GOD: [*shouting in his ear*] But how is she to continue?

FIRST GOD: Continue? Well, she's a strong, healthy girl . . .

SECOND GOD: You didn't hear what she said!

FIRST GOD: I heard every word! She is confused, that's all! [*He begins to bluster.*] And what about this book of rules—we can't renounce our rules, can we? [*more quietly*] Should the world be changed? How? By whom? The world should *not* be changed! [*At a sign from him, the lights turn pink, and music plays.*][1]
And now the hour of parting is at hand.
Dost thou behold, Shen Te, yon fleecy cloud?
It is our chariot. At a sign from me
'Twill come and take us back from whence we came
Above the azure vault and silver stars. . . .

SHEN TE: No! Don't go, illustrious ones!

FIRST GOD: Our cloud has landed now in yonder field
From which it will transport us back to heaven.
Farewell, Shen Te, let not thy courage fail thee. . . .
    [*Exeunt* GODS.]

SHEN TE: What about the old couple? They've lost their shop! What about the water seller and his hand? And I've got to defend myself against the barber, because I don't love him! And against Sun, because I do love him! How? How?
    [SHEN TE's *eyes follow the* GODS *as they are imagined to step into a cloud which rises and moves forward over the orchestra and up beyond the balcony.*]

FIRST GOD: [*from on high*] We have faith in you, Shen Te!

SHEN TE: There'll be a child. And he'll have to be fed. I can't stay here. Where shall I go?

FIRST GOD: Continue to be good, good woman of Setzuan!

SHEN TE: I need my bad cousin!

FIRST GOD: But not very often!

SHEN TE: Once a week at least!

FIRST GOD: Once a month will be quite enough!

SHEN TE: [*shrieking*] No, no! Help!
    [*But the cloud continues to recede as the* GODS *sing.*]

VALEDICTORY HYMN

> *What a rapture, oh, it is to know*
> *A good thing when you see it*
> *And having seen a good thing, oh,*
> *What rapture 'tis to flee it*
>
> *Be good, sweet maid of Setzuan*
> *Let Shui Ta be clever*
> *Departing, we forget the man*
> *Remember your endeavor*

---

[1] The rest of this scene has been adapted for the many American theatres that do not have "fly-space" to lower things from ropes.

> *Because through all the length of days*
> *Her goodness faileth never*
> *Sing hallelujah! Make Shen Te's*
> *Good name live on forever!*

SHEN TE: Help!

EPILOGUE

You're thinking, aren't you, that this is no right
Conclusion to the play you've seen tonight?[2]
After a tale, exotic, fabulous,
A nasty ending was slipped up on us.
We feel deflated, too. We, too, are nettled
To see the curtain down and nothing settled.
How could a better ending be arranged?
Could one change people? Can the world be changed?
Would new gods do the trick? Will atheism?
Moral rearmament? Materialism?
It is for you to find a way, my friends,
To help good men arrive at happy ends.
You write the happy ending to the play!
There must, there must, there's got to be a way![3]

---

[2] *At afternoon performances:*
We quite agree, our play this afternoon
Collapsed upon us like a pricked balloon
[3] When I first received the German manuscript of *Good Woman* from Brecht in 1945 it had no Epilogue. He wrote it a little later, influenced by misunderstandings of the ending in the press on the occasion of the Viennese première of the play. I believe that the Epilogue has sometimes been spoken by the actress playing Shen Te, but the actor playing Wong might be a shrewder choice, since the audience has already accepted him as a kind of chorus. On the other hand, it is not *Wong* who should deliver the Epilogue: whichever actor delivers it should drop the character he has been playing—E. B.

Tennessee Williams (1911–1983)

Cat on a Hot Tin Roof (1955)

For several years following World War II, the most successful American plays were written in a style that can be called modified realism. Tennessee Williams helped to popularize this style with *The Glass Menagerie* (1944), in which scenes and characters are called up out of the narrator-character's memory. The emphasis in this play, as in Williams' *A Streetcar Named Desire* (1949) and Arthur Miller's *Death of a Salesman* (1949), is on the psychological truth of character and situation played out in minimal and symbolic settings.

Cat on a Hot Tin Roof is in this tradition. The action, which is continuous, takes place in a bed-sitting room in a large plantation house in Mississippi. Within this restricted time and space, the characters are engulfed in mendacity—deception both of themselves and others. Two of the characters, Big Daddy and Brick, are forced to face truths that threaten the very core of their being: that Big Daddy is actually dying of cancer though he has been told he is free of it; and that Brick's friend Skipper loved him and died when Brick rejected him.

Brick's wife Maggie and his brother Gooper (along with Gooper's wife Mae) are primarily concerned with gaining control over Big Daddy's estate. Maggie, whose description of her position gives the play its title, seeks desperately to convince Brick to impregnate her because she believes a child will help overcome the doubts about Brick's reliability raised by his alcoholism. Ironically, it is a new deception, Maggie's false announcement that she is pregnant, that forces her to find the means to make Brick sleep with her (taking away his alcohol until he does so). Despite the play's denunciation of deception, the ending seems to condone Maggie's mendacity.

With its powerful psychological portraits, compelling conflicts, and its insights into a world dominated by self-interest, *Cat on a Hot Tin Roof* is an excellent example of postwar realism.

Tennessee Williams

Cat on a Hot Tin Roof

CHARACTERS

MARGARET
BRICK
MAE, *sometimes called Sister Woman*
BIG MAMA
DIXIE, *a little girl*
BIG DADDY
REVEREND TOOKER
GOOPER, *sometimes called Brother Man*
DOCTOR BAUGH, *pronounced "Baw"*
LACEY, *a Negro servant*
SOOKEY, *another*
Another little girl and two small boys

The set is the bed-sitting room of a plantation house in the Mississippi Delta. It is along an upstairs gallery that probably runs around the entire house; it has two pairs of very wide doors opening onto the gallery, showing white balustrades against a fair summer sky that fades into dusk and night during the course of the play. . . . The bathroom door, showing only pale-blue tile and silver towel racks, is in one side wall; the hall door in the opposite wall. Two articles of furniture need mention: a big double bed . . . ; and against the wall space between the two huge double doors upstage . . . a huge console combination of radio-phonograph (hi-fi with three speakers), TV set, and liquor cabinet, bearing and containing many glasses and bottles. . . . The walls below the ceiling should dissolve mysteriously into air; the set should be roofed by the sky. . . .
An evening in summer. The action is continuous, with two intermissions.

ACT ONE

At the rise of the curtain someone is taking a shower in the bathroom, the door of which is half open. A pretty young woman, with anxious lines in her face, enters the bedroom and crosses to the bathroom door.

MARGARET: [*shouting above roar of water*] One of those no-neck monsters hit me
    with a hot buttered biscuit so I have t' change!
        [MARGARET'S *voice is both rapid and drawling. In her long speeches she has
        the vocal tricks of a priest delivering a liturgical chant, the lines are almost
        sung, always continuing a little beyond her breath so she has to gasp for an-
        other. Sometimes she intersperses the lines with a little wordless singing, such
        as* "DA-DA-DAAAA!"]

[*Water turns off and* BRICK *calls out to her, but is still unseen. A tone of politely feigned interest, masking indifference, or worse, is characteristic of his speech with* MARGARET.]

BRICK: Wha'd you say, Maggie? Water was on s' loud I couldn't hearya. . . .

MARGARET: Well, I!—just remarked that!—one of th' no-neck monsters messed up m' lovely lace dress so I got t'—cha-a-ange. . . .

[*She opens and kicks shut drawers of the dresser.*]

BRICK: Why d'ya call Gooper's kiddies "no-neck monsters"?

MARGARET: Because they've got no necks! Isn't that a good enough reason?

BRICK: Don't they have any necks?

MARGARET: None visible. Their fat little heads are set on their fat little bodies without a bit of connection.

BRICK: That's too bad.

MARGARET: Yes, it's too bad because you can't wring their necks if they've got no necks to wring! Isn't that right, honey?

[*She steps out of her dress, stands in a slip of ivory satin and lace.*]

Yep, they're no-neck monsters, all no-neck people are monsters. . . .

[*Children shriek downstairs.*]

Hear them? Hear them screaming? I don't know where their voice boxes are located since they don't have necks. I tell you I got so nervous at that table tonight I thought I would throw back my head and utter a scream you could hear across the Arkansas border an' parts of Louisiana an' Tennessee. I said to your charming sister-in-law, Mae, honey, couldn't you feed those precious little things at a separate table with an oilcloth cover? They make such a mess an' the lace cloth looks *so* pretty! She made enormous eyes at me and said, "Ohhh, noooooo! On Big Daddy's birthday? Why, he would never forgive me!" Well, I want you to know, Big Daddy hadn't been at the table two minutes with those five no-neck monsters slobbering and drooling over their food before he threw down his fork an' shouted, "Fo' God's sake, Gooper, why don't you put them pigs at a trough in th' kitchen?"—Well, I swear, I simply could have di-eed!

Think of it, Brick, they've got five of them and number six is coming. They've brought the whole bunch down here like animals to display at a county fair. Why they have those children doin' tricks all the time! "Junior, show Big Daddy how you do this, show Big Daddy how you do that, say your little piece fo' Big Daddy, Sister. Show your dimples, Sugar. Brother, show Big Daddy how you stand on your head!"—It goes on all the time along, with constant little remarks and innuendos about the fact that you and I have not produced any children, are totally childless, and therefore totally useless!—Of course it's comical but it's also disgusting since it's so obvious what they're up to!

BRICK: [*without interest*] What are they up to, Maggie?

MARGARET: Why, you know what they're up to!

BRICK: [*appearing*] No, I don't know what they're up to.

[*He stands there in the bathroom doorway drying his hair with a towel and hanging onto the towel rack because one ankle is broken, plastered and bound. He is still slim and firm as a boy. His liquor hasn't started tearing him down outside. He has the additional charm of that cool air of detachment that people have who have given up the struggle. But now and then, when disturbed, something flashes behind it, like lightning in a fair sky, which shows that at some deeper level he is far from peaceful. Perhaps in a stronger light he would show some signs of deliquescence, but the fading, still warm, light from the gallery treats him gently.*]

MARGARET: I'll tell you what they're up to, boy of mine!—They're up to cutting you out of your father's estate, and—

[*She freezes momentarily before her next remark. Her voice drops as if it were somehow a personally embarrassing admission.*]

—Now we know that Big Daddy's dyin' of—*cancer.* . . .

[*There are voices on the lawn below: long-drawn calls across distance. MARGARET raises her lovely bare arms and powders her armpits with a light sigh.*]

[*She adjusts the angle of a magnifying mirror to straighten an eyelash, then rises fretfully saying:*]

There's so much light in the room it—

BRICK: [*softly but sharply*] Do we?

MARGARET: Do we what?

BRICK: Know Big Daddy's dyin' of cancer?

MARGARET: Got the report today.

BRICK: Oh . . .

MARGARET: [*letting down bamboo blinds which cast long, gold-fretted shadows over the room*]

Yep, got th' report just now . . . It didn't surprise me, Baby. . . .

[*Her voice has range and music; sometimes it drops low as a boy's and you have a sudden image of her playing boy's games as a child.*]

I recognized the symptoms soon's we got here last spring and I'm willin' to bet you that Brother Man and his wife were pretty sure of it, too. That more than likely explains why their usual summer migration to the coolness of the Great Smokies was passed up this summer in favor of—hustlin' down here ev'ry whipstitch with their whole screamin' tribe! And why so many allusions have been made to Rainbow Hill lately. You know what Rainbow Hill is? Place that's famous for treatin' alcoholics an' dope fiends in the movies!

BRICK: I'm not in the movies.

MARGARET: No, and you don't take dope. Otherwise you're a perfect candidate for Rainbow Hill, Baby, and that's where they aim to ship you—over my dead body! Yep, over my dead body they'll ship you there, but nothing would please them better. Then Brother Man could get a-hold of the purse strings and dole out remittances to us, maybe get power of attorney and sign checks for us and cut off our credit wherever, whenever he wanted! Son-of-a-bitch!—How'd you like that, Baby?—Well, you've been doin' just about ev'rything in your power to bring it about, you've just been doin' ev'erything you can think of to aid and abet them in this scheme of theirs! Quittin' work, devoting yourself to the occupation of drinkin'!—Breakin' your ankle last night on the high school athletic field: doin' what? Jumpin' hurdles? At two or three in the morning? Just fantastic! Got in the paper. *Clarksdale Register* carried a nice little item about it, human interest story about a well-known former athlete stagin' a one-man track meet on the Glorious Hill High School athletic field last night, but was slightly out of condition and didn't clear the first hurdle! Brother Man Gooper claims he exercised his influence t' keep it from goin' out over AP or UP or every goddam "*P*."

But, Brick? You still have one big advantage!

[*During the above swift flood of words,* BRICK *has reclined with contrapuntal leisure on the snowy surface of the bed and has rolled over carefully on his side or belly.*]

BRICK: [*wryly*] Did you *say* something, Maggie?

MARGARET: Big Daddy dotes on you, honey. And he can't stand Brother Man and Brother Man's wife, that monster of fertility, Mae; she's downright odious to him! Know how I know? By little expressions that flicker over his face when that woman is holding fo'th on one of her choice topics such as—how she refused twilight sleep!—when the twins were delivered! Because she feels motherhood's an experience that a woman ought to experience fully!—in order to fully appreciate the wonder and beauty of it! HAH!

[*This loud* "HAH!" *is accompanied by a violent action such as slamming a drawer shut.*]

—and how she made Brother Man come in an' stand beside her in the delivery room so he would not miss out on the "wonder and beauty" of it, either!—producin' those no-neck monsters . . . .

[*A speech of this kind would be antipathetic from almost anybody but* MARGARET; *she makes it oddly funny, because her eyes constantly twinkle and her voice shakes with laughter which is basically indulgent.*]

—Big Daddy shares my attitude toward those two! As for me, well—I give him a laugh now and then and he tolerates me. In fact!—I sometimes suspect that Big Daddy harbors a little unconscious "lech" fo' me. . . .

BRICK: What makes you think that Big Daddy has a lech for you, Maggie?

MARGARET: Way he always drops his eyes down my body when I'm talkin' to him, drops his eyes to my boobs an' licks his old chops! Ha ha!

BRICK: That kind of talk is disgusting.

MARGARET: Did anyone ever tell you that you're an ass-aching Puritan, Brick?

I think it's mighty fine that that ole fellow, on the doorstep of death, still takes in my shape with what I think is deserved appreciation!

And you wanta know something else? Big Daddy didn't know how many little Maes and Goopers had been produced! "How many kids have you got?" he asked at the table, just like Brother Man and his wife were new acquaintances to him! Big Mama said he was jokin', but that old boy wasn't jokin', Lord, no!

And when they infawmed him that they had five already and were turning out number six!—the news seemed to come as a sort of unpleasant surprise. . . .

[*Children yell below.*]

Scream, monsters!

[*Turns to* BRICK *with a sudden, gay, charming smile which fades as she notices that he is not looking at her but into fading gold space with a troubled expression.*]

[*It is constant rejection that makes her humor "bitchy."*]
Yes, you should of been at that supper table, Baby.
[*Whenever she calls him "Baby" the word is a soft caress.*]
Y'know, Big Daddy, bless his ole sweet soul, he's the dearest ole thing in the
world, but he does hunch over his food as if he preferred not to notice anything else. Well, Mae an' Gooper were side by side at the table, direckly
across from Big Daddy, watchin' his face like hawks while they jawed an'
jabbered about the cuteness an' brilliance of th' no-neck monsters!
[*She giggles with a hand fluttering at her throat and her breast and her long
throat arched.*]
[*She comes downstage and re-creates the scene with voice and gesture.*]
And the no-neck monsters were ranged around the table, some in high
chairs and some on th' *Books of Knowledge*, all in fancy little paper caps in
honor of Big Daddy's birthday, and all through dinner, well, I want you to
know that Brother Man an' his partner never once, for one moment,
stopped exchanging pokes an' pinches an' kicks an' signs an' signals!—Why,
they were like a couple of cardsharps fleecing a sucker.—Even Big Mama,
bless her ole sweet soul, she isn't th' quickest an' brightest thing in the
world, she finally noticed, at last, an' said to Gooper, "Gooper, what are you
an' Mae makin' all these signs at each other about?"—I swear t' goodness, I
nearly choked on my chicken!
[MARGARET, *back at the dressing table, still doesn't see* BRICK. *He is
watching her with a look that is not quite definable—Amused? shocked?
contemptuous?—part of those and part of something else.*]
Y'know—your brother Gooper still cherishes the illusion he took a giant
step up on the social ladder when he married Miss Mae Flynn of the Memphis Flynns.
[MARGARET *moves about the room as she talks, stops before the mirror,
moves on.*]
But I have a piece of Spanish news for Gooper. The Flynns never had a
thing in this world but money and they lost that, they were nothing at all
but fairly successful climbers. Of course, Mae Flynn came out in Memphis
eight years before I made my debut in Nashville, but I had friends at
Ward-Belmont who came from Memphis and they used to come to see me
and I used to go to see them for Christmas and spring vacations, and so I
know who rates an' who doesn't rate in Memphis society. Why, y'know ole
Papa Flynn, he barely escaped doing time in the federal pen for shady ma-
nipulations on th' stock market when his chain stores crashed, and as for
Mae having been a cotton carnival queen, as they remind us so often, lest
we forget, well, that's one honor that I don't envy her for!—Sit on a brass
throne on a tacky float an' ride down Main Street, smilin', bowin', and
blowin' kisses to all the trash on the street—
[*She picks out a pair of jeweled sandals and rushes to the dressing table.*]
Why, year before last, when Susan McPheeters was singled out fo' that
honor, y'know what happened to her? Y'know what happened to poor little Susie McPheeters?
BRICK: [*absently*] No. What happened to little Susie McPheeters?
MARGARET: Somebody spit tobacco juice in her face.

BRICK: [*dreamily*] Somebody spit tobacco juice in her face?

MARGARET: That's right, some old drunk leaned out of a window in the Hotel
   Gayoso and yelled, "Hey, Queen, hey, hey, there, Queenie!" Poor Susie
   looked up and flashed him a radiant smile and he shot out a squirt of tobacco juice right in poor Susie's face.

BRICK: Well, what d'you know about that.

MARGARET: [*gaily*] What do I know about it? I was there, I saw it!

BRICK: [*absently*] Must have been kind of funny.

MARGARET: Susie didn't think so. Had hysterics. Screamed like a banshee. They
   had to stop th' parade an' remove her from her throne an' go on with—
   [*She catches sight of him in the mirror, gasps slightly, wheels about to face
   him. Count ten.*]
   —Why are you looking at me like that?

BRICK: [*whistling softly, now*] Like what, Maggie?

MARGARET: [*intensely, fearfully*] The way y' were looking at me just now, befo' I
   caught your eye in the mirror and you started t' whistle! I don't know how
   t' describe it but it froze my blood!—I've caught you lookin' at me like that
   so often lately. What are you thinkin' of when you look at me like that?

BRICK: I wasn't conscious of lookin' at you, Maggie.

MARGARET: Well, I was conscious of it! What were you thinkin'?

BRICK: I don't remember thinking of anything, Maggie.

MARGARET: Don't you think I know that—? Don't you—?—Think I know
   that—?

BRICK: [*coolly*] Know *what*, Maggie?

MARGARET: [*struggling for expression*] That I've gone through this—*hideous!*—
   transformation, become—*hard!* Frantic!
   [*Then she adds, almost tenderly:*]
   —*cruel!!*
        That's what you've been observing in me lately. How could y' help but
   observe it? That's all right. I'm not—thin-skinned any more, can't afford t'
   be thin-skinned any more.
   [*She is now recovering her power.*]
   —But Brick? Brick?

BRICK: Did you say something?

MARGARET: I was *goin'* t' say something: that I get—lonely. Very!

BRICK: Ev'rybody gets that. . . .

MARGARET: Living with someone you love can be lonelier—than living entirely
   alone!—if the one that y' love doesn't love you. . . .
   [*There is a pause. BRICK hobbles downstage and asks, without looking at
   her:*]

BRICK: Would you like to live alone, Maggie?
   [*Another pause: then—after she has caught a quick, hurt breath:*]

MARGARET: *No!—God!—I wouldn't!*
   [*Another gasping breath. She forcibly controls what must have been an im-
   pulse to cry out. We see her deliberately, very forcibly, going all the way back
   to the world in which you can talk about ordinary matters.*]
   Did you have a nice shower?

BRICK: Uh-huh.

MARGARET: Was the water cool?

BRICK: No.

MARGARET: But it made y' feel fresh, huh?

BRICK: Fresher. . . .

MARGARET: I know something would make y' feel *much* fresher!

BRICK: What?

MARGARET: An alcohol rub. Or cologne, a rub with cologne!

BRICK: That's good after a workout but I haven't been workin' out, Maggie.

MARGARET: You've kept in good shape, though.

BRICK: [*indifferently*] You think so, Maggie?

MARGARET: I always thought drinkin' men lost their looks, but I was plainly mistaken.

BRICK: [*wryly*] Why; thanks, Maggie.

MARGARET: You're the only drinkin' man I know that it never seems t' put fat on.

BRICK: I'm gettin' softer, Maggie.

MARGARET: Well, sooner or later it's bound to soften you up. It was just beginning to soften up Skipper when—

> [*She stops short.*]

I'm sorry. I never could keep my fingers off a sore—I wish you *would* lose your looks. If you did it would make the martyrdom of Saint Maggie a little more bearable. But no such goddam luck. I actually believe you've gotten better looking since you've gone on the bottle. Yeah, a person who didn't know you would think you'd never had a tense nerve in your body or a strained muscle.

> [*There are sounds of croquet on the lawn below: the click of mallets, light voices, near and distant.*]

Of course, you always had that detached quality as if you were playing a game without much concern over whether you won or lost, and now that you've lost the game, not lost but just quit playing, you have that rare sort of charm that usually only happens in very old or hopelessly sick people, the charm of the defeated.—You look so cool, so cool, so enviably cool.

> [*Music is heard.*]

They're playing croquet. The moon has appeared and it's white, just beginning to turn a little bit yellow. . . .

You were a wonderful lover. . . .

Such a wonderful person to go to bed with, and I think mostly because you were really indifferent to it. Isn't that right? Never had any anxiety about it, did it naturally, easily, slowly, with absolute confidence and perfect calm, more like opening a door for a lady or seating her at a table than giving expression to any longing for her. Your indifference made you wonderful at lovemaking—*strange?*—but true. . . .

You know, if I thought you would never, never, *never* make love to me again—I would go downstairs to the kitchen and pick out the longest and sharpest knife I could find and stick it straight into my heart, I swear that I would!

But one thing I don't have is the charm of the defeated, my hat is still in the ring, and I am determined to win!

> [*There is the sound of croquet mallets hitting croquet balls.*]

—What is the victory of a cat on a hot tin roof?—I wish I knew. . . . Just staying on it, I guess, as long as she can. . . .

[*more croquet sounds*]

Later tonight I'm going to tell you I love you an' maybe by that time you'll be drunk enough to believe me. Yes, they're playing croquet. . . .

Big Daddy is dying of cancer. . . .

What were you thinking of when I caught you looking at me like that? Were you thinking of Skipper?

[BRICK *takes up his crutch, rises.*]

Oh, excuse me, forgive me, but laws of silence don't work! No, laws of silence don't work. . . .

[BRICK *crosses to the bar, takes a quick drink, and rubs his head with a towel.*]

Laws of silence don't work. . . .

When something is festering in your memory or your imagination, laws of silence don't work, it's just like shutting a door and locking it on a house on fire in hope of forgetting that the house is burning. But not facing a fire doesn't put it out. Silence about a thing just magnifies it. It grows and festers in silence, becomes malignant. . . .

Get dressed, Brick.

[*He drops his crutch.*]

BRICK: I've dropped my crutch.

[*He has stopped rubbing his hair dry but still stands hanging onto the towel rack in a white towel-cloth robe.*]

MARGARET: Lean on me.

BRICK: No, just give me my crutch.

MARGARET: Lean on my shoulder.

BRICK: *I don't want to lean on your shoulder, I want my crutch!*

[*This is spoken like sudden lightning.*]

Are you going to give me my crutch or do I have to get down on my knees on the floor and—

MARGARET: *Here, here, take it, take it!*

[*She has thrust the crutch at him.*]

BRICK: [*hobbling out*] Thanks. . . .

MARGARET: We mustn't scream at each other, the walls in this house have ears. . . .

[*He hobbles directly to liquor cabinet to get a new drink.*]

—but that's the first time I've heard you raise your voice in a long time, Brick. A crack in the wall?—Of composure?

—I think that's a good sign. . . .

A sign of nerves in a player on the defensive!

[BRICK *turns and smiles at her coolly over his fresh drink.*]

BRICK: It just hasn't happened yet, Maggie.

MARGARET: What?

BRICK: The click I get in my head when I've had enough of this stuff to make me peaceful. . . .

Will you do me a favor?

MARGARET: Maybe I will. What favor?

BRICK: Just, just keep your voice down!

MARGARET: [*in a hoarse whisper*] I'll do you that favor, I'll speak in a whisper, if not shut up completely, if *you* will do *me* a favor and make that drink your last one till after the party.

BRICK: What party?

MARGARET: Big Daddy's birthday party.

BRICK: Is this Big Daddy's birthday?

MARGARET: You know this is Big Daddy's birthday!

BRICK: No, I don't, I forgot it.

MARGARET: Well, I remembered it for you. . . .

> [*They are both speaking as breathlessly as a pair of kids after a fight, drawing deep exhausted breaths and looking at each other with faraway eyes, shaking and panting together as if they had broken apart from a violent struggle.*]

BRICK: Good for you, Maggie.

MARGARET: You just have to scribble a few lines on this card.

BRICK: You scribble something, Maggie.

MARGARET: It's got to be your handwriting; it's your present, I've given him my present; it's got to be your handwriting!

> [*The tension between them is building again, the voices becoming shrill once more.*]

BRICK: I didn't get him a present.

MARGARET: I got one for you.

BRICK: All right. You write the card, then.

MARGARET: And have him know you didn't remember his birthday?

BRICK: I didn't remember his birthday.

MARGARET: You don't have to prove you didn't!

BRICK: I don't want to fool him about it.

MARGARET: Just write "Love, Brick!" for God's—

BRICK: No.

MARGARET: You've *got* to!

BRICK: I don't have to do anything I don't want to do. You keep forgetting the conditions on which I agreed to stay on living with you.

MARGARET: [*out before she knows it*] I'm not living with you. We occupy the same cage.

BRICK: You've got to remember the conditions agreed on.

MARGARET: They're impossible conditions!

BRICK: Then why don't you—?

MARGARET: HUSH! Who is out there? Is somebody at the door?

> [*There are footsteps in hall.*]

MAE: [*outside*] May I enter a moment?

MARGARET: Oh, *you!* Sure. Come in, Mae.

> [MAE *enters bearing aloft the bow of a young lady's archery set.*]

MAE: Brick, is this thing yours?

MARGARET: Why, Sister Woman—that's my Diana Trophy. Won it at the intercollegiate archery contest on the Ole Miss campus.

MAE: It's a mighty dangerous thing to leave exposed round a house full of nawmal rid-blooded children attracted t' weapons.

MARGARET: "Nawmal rid-blooded children attracted t' weapons" ought t' be taught to keep their hands off things that don't belong to them.

MAE: Maggie, honey, if you had children of your own you'd know how funny that is. Will you please lock this up and put the key out of reach?

MARGARET: Sister Woman, nobody is plotting the destruction of your kiddies.— Brick and I still have our special archers' license. We're goin' deer-huntin' on Moon Lake as soon as the season starts. I love to run with dogs through chilly woods, run, run leap over obstructions—

[*She goes into the closet carrying the bow.*]

MAE: How's the injured ankle, Brick?

BRICK: Doesn't hurt. Just itches.

MAE: Oh my! Brick—Brick, you should've been downstairs after supper! Kiddies put on a show. Polly played the piano, Buster an' Sonny drums, an' then they turned out the lights an' Dixie an' Trixie puhfawmed a toe dance in fairy costume with *spahkluhs!* Big Daddy just beamed! He just beamed!

MARGARET: [*from the closet with a sharp laugh*] Oh, I bet. It breaks my heart that we missed it!

[*She reenters.*]

But Mae? Why did y'give dawgs' names to all your kiddies?

MAE: *Dogs'* names?

[MARGARET *has made this observation as she goes to raise the bamboo blinds, since the sunset glare has diminished. In crossing she winks at* BRICK.]

MARGARET: [*sweetly*] Dixie, Trixie, Buster, Sonny, Polly!—Sounds like four dogs and a parrot . . . animal act in a circus!

MAE: Maggie?

[MARGARET *turns with a smile.*]

Why are you so catty?

MARGARET: 'Cause I'm a cat! But why can't *you* take a joke, Sister Woman?

MAE: Nothin' pleases me more than a joke that's funny. You know the real names of our kiddies. Buster's real name is Robert. Sonny's real name is Saunders. Trixie's real name is Marlene and Dixie's—

[*Someone downstairs calls for her.* "HEY, MAE!"—*She rushes to door, saying:*] Intermission is over!

MARGARET: [*as* MAE *closes door*] I wonder what Dixie's real name is?

BRICK: Maggie, being catty doesn't help things any. . . .

MARGARET: I know! *WHY!*—Am I so catty?—'Cause I'm consumed with envy an' eaten up with longing?—Brick, I've laid out your beautiful Shantung silk suit from Rome and one of your monogrammed silk shirts. I'll put your cuff links in it, those lovely star sapphires I get you to wear so rarely. . . .

BRICK: I can't get trousers on over this plaster cast.

MARGARET: Yes, you can, I'll help you.

BRICK: I'm not going to get dressed, Maggie.

MARGARET: Will you just put on a pair of white silk pajamas?

BRICK: Yes, I'll do that, Maggie.

MARGARET: *Thank* you, thank you *so much!*

BRICK: Don't mention it.

MARGARET: *Oh, Brick!* How long does it have t' go on? This punishment? Haven't I done time enough, haven't I served my term, can't I apply for a—pardon?

BRICK: Maggie, you're spoiling my liquor. Lately your voice always sounds like you'd been running upstairs to warn somebody that the house was on fire!

MARGARET: Well, no wonder, no wonder. Y'know what I feel like, Brick?
  [*Children's and grown-ups' voices are blended, below, in a loud-but-uncertain rendition of "My Wild Irish Rose."*]
  I feel all the time like a cat on a hot tin roof!

BRICK: Then jump off the roof, jump off it, cats can jump off roofs and land on their four feet uninjured!

MARGARET: Oh, yes!

BRICK: Do it!—Fo' God's sake, do it. . . .

MARGARET: Do what?

BRICK: Take a lover!

MARGARET: I can't see a man but you! Even with my eyes closed, I just see you! Why don't you get ugly, Brick, why don't you please get fat or ugly or something so I could stand it?
  [*She rushes to hall door, opens it, listens.*]
  The concert is still going on! Bravo, no-necks, bravo!
  [*She slams and locks door fiercely.*]

BRICK: What did you lock the door for?

MARGARET: To give us a little privacy for a while.

BRICK: You know better, Maggie.

MARGARET: No, I don't know better. . . .
  [*She rushes to gallery doors, draws the rose-silk drapes across them.*]

BRICK: Don't make a fool of yourself.

MARGARET: I don't mind makin' a fool of myself over you!

BRICK: I mind, Maggie. I feel embarrassed for you.

MARGARET: Feel embarrassed! But don't continue my torture. I can't live on and on under these circumstances.

BRICK: You agreed to—

MARGARET: I know but—

BRICK: —Accept that condition!

MARGARET: *I CAN'T! CAN'T! CAN'T!*
  [*She seizes his shoulder.*]

BRICK: Let go!
  [*He breaks away from her and seizes the small boudoir chair and raises it like a lion-tamer facing a big circus cat.*]
  [*Count five. She stares at him with her fist pressed to her mouth, then bursts into shrill, almost hysterical laughter. He remains grave for a moment, then grins and puts the chair down.*]
  [BIG MAMA *calls through closed door.*]

BIG MAMA: Son? Son? Son?

BRICK: What is it, Big Mama?

BIG MAMA: [*outside*] Oh, son! We got the most wonderful news about Big Daddy. I just had t' run up an' tell you right this—
  [*She rattles the knob.*]

—What's this door doin', locked, faw? You all think there's robbers in the house?

MARGARET: Big Mama, Brick is dressin', he's not dressed yet.

BIG MAMA: That's all right, it won't be the first time I've seen Brick not dressed. Come on, open this door!

[MARGARET, *with a grimace, goes to unlock and open the hall door, as* BRICK *hobbles rapidly to the bathroom and kicks the door shut.* BIG MAMA *has disappeared from the hall.*]

MARGARET: Big Mama?

[BIG MAMA *appears through the opposite gallery doors behind* MARGARET, *huffing and puffing like an old bulldog. She is a short, stout woman; her sixty years and 170 pounds have left her somewhat breathless most of the time; she's always tensed like a boxer, or rather, a Japanese wrestler. Her "family" was maybe a little superior to* BIG DADDY's, *but not much. She wears a black or silver lace dress and at least half a million in flashy gems. She is very sincere.*]

BIG MAMA: [*loudly, startling* MARGARET] Here—I come through Gooper's and Mae's gall'ry door. Where's Brick? *Brick*—Hurry on out of there, son, I just have a second and want to give you the news about Big Daddy.—I hate locked doors in a house. . . .

MARGARET: [*with affected lightness*] I've noticed you do, Big Mama, but people have got to have *some* moments of privacy, don't they?

BIG MAMA: No, ma'am, not in *my* house. [*without pause*] Whacha took off you' dress faw? I thought that little lace dress was so sweet on yuh, honey.

MARGARET: I thought it looked sweet on me, too, but one of m' cute little table partners used it for a napkin so—!

BIG MAMA: [*picking up stockings on floor*] What?

MARGARET: You know, Big Mama, Mae and Gooper's so touchy about those children—thanks, Big Mama . . .

[BIG MAMA *has thrust the picked-up stockings in* MARGARET's *hand with a grunt.*]

—that you just don't dare to suggest there's any room for improvement in their—

BIG MAMA: Brick, hurry out!—Shoot, Maggie, you just don't like children.

MARGARET: I do SO like children! Adore them!—well brought up!

BIG MAMA: [*gentle—loving*] Well, why don't you have some and bring them up well, then, instead of all the time pickin' on Gooper's an' Mae's?

GOOPER: [*shouting up the stairs*] Hey, hey, Big Mama, Betsy an' Hugh got to go, waitin' t' tell yuh g'by!

BIG MAMA: Tell 'em to hold their hawses, I'll be right down in a jiffy!

[*She turns to the bathroom door and calls out.*]

Son? Can you hear me in there?

[*There is a muffled answer.*]

We just got the full report from the laboratory at the Ochsner Clinic, completely negative, son, ev'rything negative, right on down the line! Nothin' a-tall's wrong with him but some little functional thing called a spastic colon. Can you hear me, son?

MARGARET: He can hear you, Big Mama.

BIG MAMA: Then why don't he say something? God Almighty, a piece of news
like that should make him shout. It made *me* shout, I can tell you. I shouted
and sobbed and fell right down on my knees!—Look!
[*She pulls up her skirt.*]
See the bruises where I hit my kneecaps? Took both doctors to haul me
back on my feet!
[*She laughs—she always laughs like hell at herself.*]
Big Daddy was furious with me! But ain't that wonderful news?
[*Facing bathroom again, she continues:*]
After all the anxiety we been through to git a report like that on Big
Daddy's birthday? Big Daddy tried to hide how much of a load that news
took off his mind, but didn't fool *me*. He was mighty close to crying about
it *himself!*
[*Goodbyes are shouted downstairs, and she rushes to door.*]
Hold those people down there, don't let them go!—Now, git dressed, we're all
comin' up to this room fo' Big Daddy's birthday party because of your
ankle.—How's his ankle, Maggie?

MARGARET: Well, he broke it, Big Mama.

BIG MAMA: I know he broke it.
[*A phone is ringing in hall. A Negro voice answers:* "Mistuh Polly's
res'dence."]
I mean does it hurt him much still.

MARGARET: I'm afraid I can't give you that information, Big Mama. You'll have
to ask Brick if it hurts much still or not.

SOOKEY: [*in the hall*] It's Memphis, Mizz Polly, it's Miss Sally in Memphis.

BIG MAMA: Awright, Sookey.
[BIG MAMA *rushes into the hall and is heard shouting on the phone:*]
Hello, Miss Sally. How are you, Miss Sally?—Yes, well, I was just gonna call
you about it. *Shoot!*—
[*She raises her voice to a bellow.*]
*Miss Sally? Don't ever call me from the Gayoso Lobby, too much talk goes on in
that hotel lobby, no wonder you can't hear me!* Now listen, Miss Sally. They's
nothin' serious wrong with Big Daddy. We got the report just now, they's
nothin' wrong but a thing called a—spastic! *SPASTIC!*—colon. . . .
[*She appears at the hall door and calls to* MARGARET.]
—Maggie, come out here and talk to that fool on the phone. I'm shouted
breathless!

MARGARET: [*goes out and is heard sweetly at phone*] Miss Sally? This is Brick's
wife, Maggie. So nice to hear your voice. Can you hear *mine?* Well,
good!—Big Mama just wanted you to know that they've got the report from
the Ochsner Clinic and what Big Daddy has is a spastic colon. Yes. Spastic
colon, Miss Sally. That's right, spastic colon. *G'bye, Miss Sally, hope I'll see
you real soon!*
[*Hangs up a little before* MISS SALLY *was probably ready to terminate the
talk. She returns through the hall door.*]
She heard me perfectly. I've discovered with deaf people the thing to do is
not shout at them but just enunciate clearly. My rich old Aunt Cornelia was
deaf as the dead but I could make her hear me just by sayin' each word

slowly, distinctly, close to her ear. I read her the *Commercial Appeal* ev'ry night, read her the classified ads in it, even, she never missed a word of it. But was she a mean ole thing! Know what I got when she died? Her unexpired subscriptions to five magazines and the Book-of-the-Month Club and a LIBRARY full of ev'ry dull book ever written! All else went to her hellcat of a sister . . . meaner than she was, even!

> [BIG MAMA *has been straightening things up in the room during this speech.*]

BIG MAMA: [*closing closet door on discarded clothes*] *Miss Sally sure is a case!* Big Daddy says she's always got her hand out fo' something. He's not mistaken. That poor ole thing always has her hand out fo' somethin'. I don't think Big Daddy gives her as much as he should.

> [*Somebody shouts for her downstairs and she shouts:*]

I'm comin'!

> [*She starts out. At the hall door, turns and jerks a forefinger, first toward the bathroom door, then toward the liquor cabinet, meaning:* "Has Brick been drinking?" MARGARET *pretends not to understand, cocks her head and raises her brows as if the pantomimic performance was completely mystifying to her.*]
>
> [BIG MAMA *rushes back to* MARGARET:]

Shoot! Stop playin' so dumb!—I mean has he been drinkin' that stuff much yet?

MARGARET: [*with a little laugh*] Oh! I think he had a highball after supper.

BIG MAMA: Don't laugh about it!—Some single men stop drinkin' when they git married and others start! Brick never touched liquor before he—!

MARGARET: [*crying out*] THAT'S NOT FAIR!

BIG MAMA: Fair or not fair I want to ask you a question, one question: D'you make Brick happy in bed?

MARGARET: Why don't you ask if he makes *me* happy in bed?

BIG MAMA: Because I know that—

MARGARET: *It works both ways!*

BIG MAMA: Something's not right! You're childless and my son drinks!

> [*Someone has called her downstairs and she has rushed to the door on the line above. She turns at the door and points at the bed.*]

—When a marriage goes on the rocks, the rocks are *there*, right *there!*

MARGARET: *That's*—

> [BIG MAMA *has swept out of the room and slammed the door.*]

—not—*fair . . .*

> [MARGARET *is alone, completely alone, and she feels it. She draws in, hunches her shoulders, raises her arms with fists clenched, shuts her eyes tight as a child about to be stabbed with a vaccination needle. When she opens her eyes again, what she sees is the long oval mirror and she rushes straight to it, stares into it with a grimace and says:* "Who are you?"—*Then she crouches a little and answers herself in a different voice which is high, thin, mocking:* "I am Maggie the Cat!"—*Straightens quickly as bathroom door opens a little and* BRICK *calls out to her.*]

BRICK: Has Big Mama gone?

MARGARET: She's gone.

[*He opens the bathroom door and hobbles out, with his liquor glass now empty, straight to the liquor cabinet. He is whistling softly.* MARGARET's *head pivots on her long, slender throat to watch him.*]

[*She raises a hand uncertainly to the base of her throat, as if it was difficult for her to swallow, before she speaks:*]

You know, our sex life didn't just peter out in the usual way, it was cut off short, long before the natural time for it to, and it's going to revive again, just as sudden as that. I'm confident of it. That's what I'm keeping myself attractive for. For the time when you'll see me again like other men see me. Yes, like other men see me. They still see me, Brick, and they like what they see. Uh-huh. Some of them would give their—

    Look, Brick!

[*She stands before the long oval mirror, touches her breast and then her hips with her two hands.*]

How high my body stays on me!—Nothing has fallen on me—not a fraction. . . .

[*Her voice is soft and trembling: a pleading child's. At this moment as he turns to glance at her—a look which is like a player passing a ball to another player, third down and goal to go—she has to capture the audience in a grip so tight that she can hold it till the first intermission without any lapse of attention.*]

Other men still want me. My face looks strained, sometimes, but I've kept my figure as well as you've kept yours, and men admire it. I still turn heads on the street. Why, last week in Memphis everywhere that I went men's eyes burned holes in my clothes, at the country club and in restaurants and department stores, there wasn't a man I met or walked by that didn't just eat me up with his eyes and turn around when I passed him and look back at me. Why, at Alice's party for her New York cousins, the best-lookin' man in the crowd—followed me upstairs and tried to force his way in the powder room with me, followed me to the door and tried to force his way in!

BRICK: Why didn't you let him, Maggie?

MARGARET: Because I'm not that common, for one thing. Not that I wasn't almost tempted to. You like to know who it was? It was Sonny Boy Maxwell, that's who!

BRICK: Oh, yeah, Sonny Boy Maxwell, he was a good end-runner but had a little injury to his back and had to quit.

MARGARET: He has no injury now and has no wife and still has a lech for me!

BRICK: I see no reason to lock him out of a powder room in that case.

MARGARET: And have someone catch me at it? I'm not that stupid. Oh, I might sometime cheat on you with someone, since you're so insultingly eager to have me do it!—But if I do, you can be damned sure it will be in a place and time where no one but me and the man could possibly know. Because I'm not going to give you any excuse to divorce me for being unfaithful or anything else. . . .

BRICK: Maggie, I wouldn't divorce you for being unfaithful or anything else. Don't you know that? Hell. I'd be relieved to know that you'd found yourself a lover.

MARGARET: Well, I'm taking no chances. No, I'd rather stay on this hot tin roof.

BRICK: A hot tin roof's 'n uncomfo'table place t' stay on. . . .

> [*He starts to whistle softly.*]

MARGARET: [*through his whistle*] Yeah, but I can stay on it just as long as I have to.

BRICK: You could leave me, Maggie.

> [*He resumes whistle. She wheels about to glare at him.*]

MARGARET: *Don't want to and will not!* Besides if I did, you don't have a cent to pay for it but what you get from Big Daddy and he's dying of cancer!

> [*For the first time a realization of* BIG DADDY's *doom seems to penetrate to* BRICK's *consciousness, visibly, and he looks at* MARGARET.]

BRICK: Big Mama just said he *wasn't*, that the report was okay.

MARGARET: That's what she thinks because she got the same story that they gave Big Daddy. And was just as taken in by it as he was, poor ole things. . . .

 But tonight they're going to tell her the truth about it. When Big Daddy goes to bed, they're going to tell her that he is dying of cancer.

> [*She slams the dresser drawer.*]

—It's malignant and it's terminal.

BRICK: Does Big Daddy know it?

MARGARET: Hell, do they *ever* know it? Nobody says, "You're dying." You have to fool them. They have to fool *themselves.*

BRICK: Why?

MARGARET: *Why?* Because human beings dream of life everlasting, that's the reason! But most of them want it on earth and not in heaven.

> [*He gives a short, hard laugh at her touch of humor.*]

Well. . . . [*She touches up her mascara.*] That's how it is, anyhow. . . . [*She looks about.*] Where did I put down my cigarette? Don't want to burn up the home place, at least not with Mae and Gooper and their five monsters in it!

> [*She has found it and sucks at it greedily. Blows out smoke and continues:*]

So this is Big Daddy's last birthday. And Mae and Gooper, they know it, oh, *they* know it, all right. They got the first information from the Ochsner Clinic. That's why they rushed down here with their no-neck monsters. Because. Do you know something? Big Daddy's made no will? Big Daddy's never made out any will in his life, and so this campaign's afoot to impress him, forcibly as possible, with the fact that you drink and I've borne no children!

> [*He continues to stare at her a moment, then mutters something sharp but not audible and hobbles rather rapidly out onto the long gallery in the fading, much faded, gold light.*]

MARGARET: [*continuing her liturgical chant*] Y'know, I'm *fond* of Big Daddy, I am genuinely fond of that old man, I really *am*, you know. . . .

BRICK: [*faintly, vaguely*] Yes, I know you are. . . .

MARGARET: I've always sort of admired him in spite of his coarseness, his four-letter words, and so forth. Because Big Daddy *is* what he *is,* and he makes no bones about it. He hasn't turned gentleman farmer, he's still a Mississippi redneck, as much of a redneck as he must have been when he was just overseer here on the old Jack Straw and Peter Ochello place. But he got hold of it an' built it into th' biggest an' finest plantation in the Delta.—I've always *liked* Big Daddy. . . .

[*She crosses to the proscenium.*]

Well, this is Big Daddy's last birthday. I'm sorry about it. But I'm facing the facts. It takes money to take care of a drinker and that's the office that I've been elected to lately.

BRICK: You don't have to take care of me.

MARGARET: Yes, I do. Two people in the same boat have got to take care of each other. At least you want money to buy more Echo Spring when this supply is exhausted, or will you be satisfied with a ten-cent beer?

Mae an' Gooper are plannin' to freeze us out of Big Daddy's estate because you drink and I'm childless. But we can defeat that plan. We're *going* to defeat that plan!

Brick, y'know, I've been so goddam disgustingly poor all my life!—That's the *truth*, Brick!

BRICK: I'm not sayin' it isn't.

MARGARET: Always had to suck up to people I couldn't stand because they had money and I was poor as Job's turkey. You don't know what that's like. Well, I'll tell you, it's like you would feel a thousand miles away from Echo Spring!—And had to get back to it on that broken ankle . . . without a crutch!

That's how it feels to be as poor as Job's turkey and have to suck up to relatives that you hated because they had money and all you had was a bunch of hand-me-down clothes and a few old moldly three-percent government bonds. My daddy loved his liquor, he fell in love with his liquor the way you've fallen in love with Echo Spring!—And my poor Mama, having to maintain some semblance of social position, to keep appearances up, on an income of one hundred and fifty dollars a month on those old government bonds!

When I came out, the year that I made my debut, I had just two evening dresses! One Mother made me from a pattern in *Vogue,* the other a hand-me-down from a snotty rich cousin I hated!

—The dress that I married you in was my grandmother's weddin' gown. . . .

So that's why I'm like a cat on a hot tin roof!

[BRICK *is still on the gallery. Someone below calls up to him in a warm Negro voice,* "Hiya, Mistuh Brick, how yuh feelin'?" BRICK *raises his liquor glass as if that answered the question.*]

MARGARET: You can be young without money, but you can't be old without it. You've got to be old *with* money because to be old without it is just too awful, you've got to be one or the other, either *young* or *with money,* you can't be old and *without* it.—That's the *truth,* Brick. . . .

[BRICK *whistles softly, vaguely.*]

Well, now I'm dressed, I'm all dressed, there's nothing else for me to do.

[*forlornly, almost fearfully*]

I'm dressed, all dressed, nothing else for me to do. . . .

[*She moves about restlessly, aimlessly, and speaks, as if to herself.*]

I know when I made my mistake.—What am I—? Oh!—my bracelets. . . .

[*She starts working a collection of bracelets over her hands onto her wrists, about six on each, as she talks.*]

I've thought a whole lot about it and now I know when I made my mistake. Yes, I made my mistake when I told you the truth about that thing with Skipper. Never should have confessed it, a fatal error, tellin' you about that thing with Skipper.

BRICK: Maggie, shut up about Skipper. I mean it, Maggie; you got to shut up about Skipper.

MARGARET: You ought to understand that Skipper and I—

BRICK: You don't think I'm serious, Maggie? You're fooled by the fact that I am saying this quiet? Look, Maggie. What you're doing is a dangerous thing to do. You're—you're—you're—

MARGARET: This time I'm going to finish what I have to say to you. Skipper and I made love, if love you could call it, because it made both of us feel a little bit closer to you. You see, you son of a bitch, you asked too much of people, of me, of him, of all the unlucky poor damned sons of bitches that happen to love you, and there was a whole pack of them, yes, there was a pack of them besides me and Skipper, you asked too goddam much of people that loved you, you—superior creature!—you godlike being!—And so we made love to each other to dream it was you, both of us! Yes, yes, yes! Truth, truth! What's so awful about it? I like it, I think the truth is—yeah! I shouldn't have told you. . . .

BRICK: [*holding his head unnaturally still and uptilted a bit*] It was Skipper that told me about it. Not you, Maggie.

MARGARET: I told you!

BRICK: After he told me!

MARGARET: What does it matter who—?

[BRICK *turns suddenly out upon the gallery and calls:*]

BRICK: Little girl! Hey, little girl!

LITTLE GIRL: [*at a distance*] What, Uncle Brick?

BRICK: Tell the folks to come up!—Bring everybody upstairs!

MARGARET: I can't stop myself! I'd go on telling you this in front of them all, if I had to!

BRICK: Little girl! Go on, go on, will you? Do what I told you, call them!

MARGARET: Because it's got to be told and you, you!—you never let me!

[*She sobs, then controls herself, and continues almost calmly.*]

It was one of those beautiful, ideal things they tell about in the Greek legends, it couldn't be anything else, you being you, and that's what made it so sad, that's what made it so awful, because it was love that never could be carried through to anything satisfying or even talked about plainly. Brick, I tell you, you got to believe me, Brick, I *do* understand all about it! I—I think it was—*noble!* Can't you tell I'm sincere when I say I respect it? My only point, the only point that I'm making, is life has got to be allowed to continue even after the *dream* of life is—all—over. . . .

[BRICK *is without his crutch. Leaning on furniture, he crosses to pick it up as she continues as if possessed by a will outside herself.*]

Why, I remember when we double-dated at college, Gladys Fitzgerald and I and you and Skipper, it was more like a date between you and Skipper.

Gladys and I were just sort of tagging along as if it was necessary to chaperone you!—to make a good public impression—

BRICK: [*turns to face her, half lifting his crutch*] Maggie, you want me to hit you with this crutch? Don't you know I could kill you with this crutch?

MARGARET: Good Lord, man, d' you think I'd care if you did?

BRICK: One man has one great good true thing in his life. One great good thing which is true!—I had friendship with Skipper.—You are naming it dirty!

MARGARET: I'm not naming it dirty! I am naming it clean.

BRICK: Not love with you, Maggie, but friendship with Skipper was that one great true thing, and you are naming it dirty!

MARGARET: Then you haven't been listenin', not understood what I'm saying! I'm naming it so damn clean that it killed poor Skipper!—You two had something that had to be kept on ice, yes, incorruptible, yes!—and death was the only icebox where you could keep it. . . .

BRICK: I married you, Maggie. Why would I marry you, Maggie, if I was—?

MARGARET: Brick, don't brain me yet, let me finish!—I know, believe me I know, that it was only Skipper that harbored even any *unconscious* desire for anything not perfectly pure between you two!—Now let me skip a little. You married me early that summer we graduated out of Ole Miss, and we were happy, weren't we, we were blissful, yes, hit heaven together ev'ry time that we loved! But that fall you an' Skipper turned down wonderful offers of jobs in order to keep on bein' football heroes—pro football heroes. You organized the Dixie Stars that fall, so you could keep on bein' teammates forever! But somethin' was not right with it!—*Me included!*—between you. Skipper began hittin' the bottle . . . you got a spinal injury—couldn't play the Thanksgivin' game in Chicago, watched it on TV from a traction bed in Toledo. I joined Skipper. The Dixie Stars lost because poor Skipper was drunk. We drank together that night all night in the bar of the Blackstone and when cold day was comin' up over the lake an' we were comin' out drunk to take a dizzy look at it, I said, "SKIPPER! STOP LOVIN' MY HUSBAND OR TELL HIM HE'S GOT TO LET YOU ADMIT IT TO HIM!"—one way or another!

  HE SLAPPED ME HARD ON THE MOUTH!—then turned and ran without stopping once, I am sure, all the way back into his room at the Blackstone. . . .

  —When I came to his room that night, with a little scratch like a shy little mouse at his door, he made that pitiful, ineffectual little attempt to prove that what I had said wasn't true. . . .

  [BRICK *strikes at her with crutch, a blow that shatters the gemlike lamp on the table.*]

—In this way, I destroyed him, by telling him truth that he and his world which he was born and raised in, yours and his world, had told him could not be told?

  —From then on Skipper was nothing at all but a receptacle for liquor and drugs. . . .

  —*Who shot Cock Robin? I with my*—

  [*She throws back her head with tight shut eyes.*]

—*merciful arrow!*

[BRICK *strikes at her; misses.*]

Missed me!—Sorry—I'm not tryin' to whitewash my behavior, Christ, no! Brick, I'm not good. I don't know why people have to pretend to be good, nobody's good. The rich or the well-to-do can afford to respect moral patterns, conventional moral patterns, but I could never afford to, yeah, but—I'm honest! Give me credit for just that, will you *please?*—Born poor, raised poor, expect to die poor unless I manage to get us something out of what Big Daddy leaves when he dies of cancer! But Brick?!—*Skipper is dead! I'm alive!* Maggie the Cat is—

[BRICK *hops awkwardly forward and strikes at her again with his crutch.*]
—alive! I am alive, alive! I am . . .

[*He hurls the crutch at her, across the bed she took refuge behind, and pitches forward on the floor as she completes her speech.*]
—alive!

[*A little girl,* DIXIE, *bursts into the room, wearing an Indian war bonnet and firing a cap pistol at* MARGARET *and shouting:* "Bang, bang, bang!"]
[*Laughter downstairs floats through the open hall door.* MARGARET *had crouched gasping to bed at child's entrance. She now rises and says with cool fury:*]

Little girl, your mother or someone should teach you—[*gasping*]—to knock at a door before you come into a room. Otherwise people might think that you—lack—good breeding. . . .

DIXIE: Yanh, yanh, yanh, what is Uncle Brick doin' on th' floor?

BRICK: I tried to kill your Aunt Maggie, but I failed—and I fell. Little girl, give me my crutch so I can get up off th' floor.

MARGARET: Yes, give your uncle his crutch, he's a cripple, honey, he broke his ankle last night jumping hurdles on the high school athletic field!

DIXIE: What were you jumping hurdles for, Uncle Brick?

BRICK: Because I used to jump them, and people like to do what they used to do, even after they've stopped being able to do it. . . .

MARGARET: That's right, that's your answer, now go away, little girl.

[DIXIE *fires cap pistol at* MARGARET *three times.*]
Stop, you stop that, monster! You little no-neck monster!

[*She seizes the cap pistol and hurls it through gallery doors.*]

DIXIE: [*with a precocious instinct for the cruelest thing*] You're *jealous!*—You're just jealous because you can't have babies!

[*She sticks out her tongue at* MARGARET *as she sashays past her with her stomach stuck out, to the gallery.* MARGARET *slams the gallery doors and leans panting against them. There is a pause.* BRICK *has replaced his spilt drink and sits, faraway, on the great four-poster bed.*]

MARGARET: You see?—they gloat over us being childless, even in front of their five little no-neck monsters!

[*Pause. Voices approach on the stairs.*]

Brick?—I've been to a doctor in Memphis, a—a gynecologist. . . .

I've been completely examined, and there is no reason why we can't have a child whenever we want one. And this is my time by the calendar to conceive. Are you listening to me? Are you? Are you LISTENING TO ME!

BRICK: Yes. I hear you, Maggie.
> [*His attention returns to her inflamed face.*]

—But how in hell on Earth do you imagine—that you're going to have a child by a man that can't stand you?

MARGARET: That's a problem that I will have to work out.
> [*She wheels about to face the hall door.*]
> Here they come!
> [*The lights dim.*]

CURTAIN

ACT TWO

There is no lapse of time. MARGARET *and* BRICK *are in the same positions they held at the end of Act I.*

MARGARET: [*at door*]: Here they come!
> [BIG DADDY *appears first, a tall man with a fierce, anxious look, moving carefully not to betray his weakness even, or especially, to himself.*]

BIG DADDY: Well, Brick.

BRICK: Hello, Big Daddy.—Congratulations!

BIG DADDY: —Crap. . . .
> [*Some of the people are approaching through the hall, others along the gallery: voices from both directions.* GOOPER *and* REVEREND TOOKER *become visible outside gallery doors, and their voices come in clearly.*]
> [*They pause outside as* GOOPER *lights a cigar.*]

REVEREND TOOKER: [*vivaciously*] Oh, but St. Paul's in Grenada has three memorial windows, and the latest one is a Tiffany stained-glass window that cost twenty-five hundred dollars, a picture of Christ the Good Shepherd with a Lamb in His arms.

GOOPER: Who give that window, Preach?

REVEREND TOOKER: Clyde Fletcher's widow. Also presented St. Paul's with a baptismal font.

GOOPER: Y'know what somebody ought t' give your church is a *coolin'* system, Preach.

REVEREND TOOKER: Yes, siree, Bob! And y'know what Gus Hamma's family gave in his memory to the church at Two Rivers? A complete new stone parish-house with a basketball court in the basement and a—

BIG DADDY: [*uttering a loud barking laugh, which is far from truly mirthful*] Hey, Preach! What's all this talk about memorials, Preach? Y' think somebody's about t' kick off around here? 'S that it?
> [*Startled by this interjection,* REVEREND TOOKER *decides to laugh at the question almost as loud as he can.*]
> [*How he would answer the question we'll never know, as he's spared that embarrassment by the voice of* GOOPER's *wife,* MAE, *rising high and clear as she appears with* "DOC" BAUGH, *the family doctor, through the hall door.*]

MAE: [*almost religiously*]—Let's see now, they've had their *tyyy*-phoid shots, and their tetanus shots, their diphtheria shots and their hepatitis shots and their polio shots, they got *those* shots every month from May through September and—Gooper? Hey! Gooper!—What all have the kiddies been shot faw?

MARGARET: [*overlapping a bit*] Turn on the hi-fi, Brick! Let's have some music t' start off th' party with!

> [*The talk becomes so general that the room sounds like a great aviary of chattering birds. Only* BRICK *remains unengaged, leaning upon the liquor cabinet with his faraway smile, an ice cube in a paper napkin with which he now and then rubs his forehead. He doesn't respond to* MARGARET's *command. She bounds forward and stoops over the instrument panel of the console.*]

GOOPER: We gave 'em that thing for a third anniversary present, got three speakers in it.

> [*The room is suddenly blasted by the climax of a Wagnerian opera or a Beethoven symphony.*]

BIG DADDY: *Turn that dam thing off!*

> [*Almost instant silence, almost instantly broken by the shouting charge of* BIG MAMA, *entering through hall door like a charging rhino.*]

BIG MAMA: *Wha's my Brick, wha's mah precious baby!!*

BIG DADDY: *Sorry! Turn it back on!*

> [*Everyone laughs very loud.* BIG DADDY *is famous for his jokes at* BIG MAMA's *expense, and nobody laughs louder at these jokes than* BIG MAMA *herself, though sometimes they're pretty cruel and* BIG MAMA *has to pick up or fuss with something to cover the hurt that the loud laugh doesn't quite cover.*]

> [*On this occasion, a happy occasion because the dread in her heart has also been lifted by the false report on* BIG DADDY's *condition, she giggles, grotesquely, coyly, in* BIG DADDY's *direction and bears down upon* BRICK, *all very quick and alive.*]

BIG MAMA: Here he is, here's my precious baby! What's that you've got in your hand? You put that liquor down, son, your hand was made fo' holdin' somethin' better than that!

GOOPER: Look at Brick put it down!

> [BRICK *has obeyed* BIG MAMA *by draining the glass and handing it to her. Again everyone laughs, some high, some low.*]

BIG MAMA: Oh, you bad boy, you're my bad little boy. Give Big Mama a kiss, you bad boy, you!—Look at him shy away, will you? Brick never liked bein' kissed or made a fuss over, I guess because he's always had too much of it!

> Son, you turn that thing off!

> [BRICK *has switched on the TV set.*]

I can't stand TV, radio was bad enough but TV has gone it one better, I mean—[*plops wheezing in chair*]—one worse, ha ha! Now what'm I sittin' down here faw? I want t' sit next to my sweetheart on the sofa, hold hands with him and love him up a little!

> [BIG MAMA *has on a black-and-white-figured chiffon. The large irregular patterns, like the markings of some massive animal, the luster of her great diamonds and many pearls, the brilliants set in the silver frames of her glasses, her riotous voice, booming laugh, have dominated the room since she entered.* BIG DADDY *has been regarding her with a steady grimace of chronic annoyance.*]

BIG MAMA: [*still louder*] Preacher, Preacher, hey, Preach! Give me you' hand an'
help me up from this chair!

REVEREND TOOKER: None of your tricks, Big Mama!

BIG MAMA: What tricks? You give me you' hand so I can get up an'—

> [REVEREND TOOKER *extends her his hand. She grabs it and pulls him into
> her lap with a shrill laugh that spans an octave in two notes.*]

Ever seen a preacher in a fat lady's lap? Hey, hey, folks! Ever seen a preacher
in a fat lady's lap?

> [BIG MAMA *is notorious throughout the Delta for this sort of inelegant
> horseplay.* MARGARET *looks on with indulgent humor, sipping Dubonnet
> "on the rocks" and watching* BRICK, *but* MAE *and* GOOPER *exchange signs
> of humorless anxiety over these antics, the sort of behavior which* MAE *thinks
> may account for their failure to quite get in with the smartest young married
> set in Memphis, despite all. One of the negroes,* LACY *or* SOOKEY, *peeks in,
> cackling. They are waiting for a sign to bring in the cake and champagne.
> But* BIG DADDY's *not amused. He doesn't understand why, in spite of the in-
> finite mental relief he's received from the doctor's report, he still has these same
> old fox teeth in his guts. "This spastic thing sure is something," he says to
> himself, but aloud he roars at* BIG MAMA:]

BIG DADDY: *BIG MAMA, WILL YOU QUIT HORSIN'?*—You're too old an'
too fat fo' that sort of crazy kid stuff an' besides a woman with your blood
pressure—she had two hundred last spring!—is riskin' a stroke when you
mess around like that. . . .

BIG MAMA: *Here comes Big Daddy's birthday!*

> [*Negroes in white jackets enter with an enormous birthday cake ablaze with
> candles and carrying buckets of champagne with satin ribbons about the bot-
> tle necks.*]

> [MAE *and* GOOPER *strike up song, and everybody, including the Negroes
> and* CHILDREN, *joins in. Only* BRICK *remains aloof.*]

EVERYONE: *Happy birthday to you.*
                             Happy birthday to you.
                             Happy birthday, Big Daddy—
[*Some sing:* "Dear, Big Daddy!"]
                             Happy birthday to you.
[*Some sing:* "How old are you?"]

> [MAE *has come down center and is organizing her children like a chorus. She
> gives them a barely audible:* "One, two, three!" *and they are off in the new
> tune.*]

CHILDREN: *Skinamarinka—dinka—dink*
                             Skinamarinka—do
                             We love you.
                             Skinamarinka—dinka—dink
                             Skinamarinka—do.
[*All together, they turn to* BIG DADDY.]
                             Big Daddy, you!
[*They turn back front, like a musical comedy chorus.*]
                             We love you in the morning;
                             We love you in the night.

> We love you when we're with you,
> And we love you out of sight.
> Skinamarinka—dinka—dink
> Skinamarinka—do.

[MAE *turns to* BIG MAMA.]

Big Mama, too!

[BIG MAMA *bursts into tears. The Negroes leave.*]

BIG DADDY: Now Ida, what the hell is the matter with you?

MAE: She's just so happy.

BIG MAMA: I'm just so happy, Big Daddy, I have to cry or something.

[*Sudden and loud in the hush:*]

Brick, do you know the wonderful news that Doc Baugh got from the clinic about Big Daddy? Big Daddy's one hundred percent!

MARGARET: Isn't that wonderful?

BIG MAMA: He's just one hundred percent. Passed the examination with flying colors. Now that we know there's nothing wrong with Big Daddy but a spastic colon, I can tell you something. I was worried sick, half out of my mind, for fear that Big Daddy might have a thing like—

[MARGARET *cuts through this speech, jumping up and exclaiming shrilly:*]

MARGARET: Brick, honey, aren't you going to give Big Daddy his birthday present?

[*Passing by him, she snatches his liquor glass from him.*]

[*She picks up a fancily wrapped package.*]

Here it is, Big Daddy, this is from Brick!

BIG MAMA: This is the biggest birthday Big Daddy's ever had, a hundred presents and bushels of telegrams from—

MAE: [*at same time*] What is it, Brick?

GOOPER: I bet 500 to 50 that Brick don't *know* what it is.

BIG MAMA: The fun of presents is not knowing what they are till you open the package. Open your present, Big Daddy.

BIG DADDY: Open it you'self. I want to ask Brick somethin! Come here, Brick.

MARGARET: Big Daddy's callin' you, Brick.

[*She is opening the package.*]

BRICK: Tell Big Daddy I'm crippled.

BIG DADDY: I see you're crippled. I want to know how you got crippled.

MARGARET: [*making diversionary tactics*] Oh, look, oh, look, why, it's a cashmere robe!

[*She holds the robe up for all to see.*]

MAE: You sound surprised, Maggie.

MARGARET: I never saw one before.

MAE: That's funny.—*Hah!*

MARGARET: [*turning on her fiercely, with a brilliant smile*] Why is it funny? All my family ever had was family—and luxuries such as cashmere robes still surprise me!

BIG DADDY: [*ominously*] Quiet!

MAE: [*heedless in her fury*] I don't see how you could be so surprised when you bought it yourself at Loewenstein's in Memphis last Saturday. You know how I know?

BIG DADDY: I said, "Quiet!"

MAE: —I know because the salesgirl that sold it to you waited on me and said, "Oh, Mrs. Pollitt, your sister-in-law just bought a cashmere robe for your husband's father!"

MARGARET: Sister Woman! Your talents are wasted as a housewife and mother, you really ought to be with the FBI or—

BIG DADDY: QUIET!

> [REVEREND TOOKER's *reflexes are slower than the others'. He finishes a sentence after the bellow.*]

REVEREND TOOKER: [*to* DOC BAUGH]—the Stork and the Reaper are running neck and neck!

> [*He starts to laugh gaily when he notices the silence and* BIG DADDY's *glare. His laugh dies falsely.*]

BIG DADDY: Preacher, I hope I'm not butting in on more talk about memorial stained-glass windows, am I, Preacher?

> [REVEREND TOOKER *laughs feebly, then coughs dryly in the embarrassed silence.*]

> Preacher?

BIG MAMA: Now, Big Daddy, don't you pick on Preacher!

BIG DADDY: [*raising his voice*] You ever hear that expression "all hawk and no spit"? You bring that expression to mind with that little dry cough of yours, all hawk an' no spit. . . .

> [*The pause is broken only by a short startled laugh from* MARGARET, *the only one there who is conscious of and amused by the grotesque.*]

MAE: [*raising her arms and jangling her bracelets*] I wonder if the mosquitoes are active tonight?

BIG DADDY: What's that, Little Mama? Did you make some remark?

MAE: Yes, I said I wondered if the mosquitoes would eat us alive if we went out on the gallery for a while.

BIG DADDY: Well, if they do, I'll have your bones pulverized for fertilizer!

BIG MAMA: [*quickly*] Last week we had an airplane spraying the place and I think it done some good, at least I haven't had a—

BIG DADDY: [*cutting her speech*] Brick, they tell me, if what they tell me is true, that you done some jumping last night on the high school athletic field?

BIG MAMA: Brick, Big Daddy is talking to you, son.

BRICK: [*smiling vaguely over his drink*] What was that, Big Daddy?

BIG DADDY: They said you done some jumping on the high school track field last night.

BRICK: That's what they told me, too.

BIG DADDY: Was it jumping or humping that you were doing out there? What were you doing out there at three A.M., layin' a woman on that cinder track?

BIG MAMA: Big Daddy, you are off the sick-list, now, and I'm not going to excuse you for talkin' so—

BIG DADDY: Quiet!

BIG MAMA: —*nasty* in front of Preacher and—

BIG DADDY: QUIET!—I ast you, Brick, if you was cuttin' you'self a piece o' poon-tang last night on that cinder track? I thought maybe you were chasin poon-tang on that track an' tripped over something in the heat of the chase—'sthat it?

[GOOPER *laughs, loud and false, others nervously following suit.* BIG MAMA *stamps her foot, and purses her lips, crossing to* MAE *and whispering something to her as* BRICK *meets his father's hard, intent, grinning stare with a slow, vague smile that he offers all situations from behind the screen of his liquor.*]

BRICK: No, sir, I don't think so. . . .

MAE: [*at the same time, sweetly*] Reverend Tooker, let's you and I take a stroll on the widow's walk.

[*She and the preacher go out on the gallery as* BIG DADDY *says:*]

BIG DADDY: Then what the hell were you doing out there at three o'clock in the morning?

BRICK: Jumping the hurdles, Big Daddy, runnin' and jumpin' the hurdles, but those high hurdles have gotten too high for me, now.

BIG DADDY: 'Cause you was drunk?

BRICK: [*his vague smile fading a little*] Sober I wouldn't have tried to jump the *low* ones. . . .

BIG MAMA: [*quickly*] Big Daddy, blow out the candles on your birthday cake!

MARGARET: [*at the same time*] I want to propose a toast to Big Daddy Pollitt on his sixty-fifth birthday, the biggest cotton planter in—

BIG DADDY: [*bellowing with fury and disgust*] I told you to stop it, now stop it, quit this—!

BIG MAMA: [*coming in front of* BIG DADDY *with the cake*] Big Daddy, I will not allow you to talk that way, not even on your birthday, I—

BIG DADDY: I'll talk like I want to on my birthday, Ida, or any other goddam day of the year and anybody here that don't like it knows what they can do!

BIG MAMA: You don't mean that!

BIG DADDY: What makes you think I don't mean it?

[*Meanwhile various discreet signals have been exchanged and* GOOPER *has also gone out on the gallery.*]

BIG MAMA: I just know you don't mean it.

BIG DADDY: You don't know a goddam thing and you never did!

BIG MAMA: Big Daddy, you don't mean that.

BIG DADDY: Oh, yes, I do, oh, yes, I do, I mean it! I put up with a whole lot of crap around here because I thought I was dying. And you thought I was dying and you started taking over, well, you can stop taking over now, Ida, because I'm not gonna die, you can just stop now this business of taking over because you're not taking over because I'm not dying, I went through the laboratory and the goddam exploratory operation and there's nothing wrong with me but a spastic colon. And I'm not dying of cancer which you thought I was dying of. Ain't that so? Didn't you think that I was dying of cancer, Ida?

[*Almost everybody is out on the gallery but the two old people glaring at each other across the blazing cake.*]

[BIG MAMA's *chest heaves and she presses a fat fist to her mouth.*]

[BIG DADDY *continues, hoarsely:*]

Ain't that so, Ida? Didn't you have an idea I was dying of cancer and now you could take control of this place and everything on it? I got that impression, I seemed to get that impression. Your loud voice everywhere, your fat old body butting in here and there!

BIG MAMA: Hush! The preacher!

BIG DADDY: Rut the goddam preacher!

> [BIG MAMA *gasps loudly and sits down on the sofa, which is almost too small for her.*]

Did you hear what I said? I said rut the goddam preacher!

> [*Somebody closes the gallery doors from outside just as there is a burst of fireworks and excited cries from the children.*]

BIG MAMA: I never seen you act like this before and I can't think what's got in you!

BIG DADDY: I went through all that laboratory and operation and all just so I would know if you or me was boss here! Well, now it turns out that I am and you ain't—and that's my birthday present—and my cake and champagne!—because for three years now you been gradually taking over. Bossing. Talking. Sashaying your fat old body around the place I made! I made this place! I was overseer on it! I was the overseer on the old Straw and Ochello plantation. I quit school at ten! I quit school at ten years old and went to work like a nigger in the fields. And I rose to be overseer of the Straw and Ochello plantation. And old Straw died and I was Ochello's partner and the place got bigger and bigger and bigger and bigger and bigger! I did all that myself with no goddam help from you, and now you think you're just about to take over. Well, I am just about to tell you that you are not just about to take over, you are not just about to take over a goddam thing. Is that clear to you, Ida? Is that very plain to you, now? Is that understood completely? I been through the laboratory from A to Z. I've had the goddam exploratory operation, and nothing is wrong with me but a spastic colon—made spastic, I guess, by *disgust!* By all the goddam lies and liars that I have had to put up with, and all the goddam hypocrisy that I lived with all these forty years that we been livin' together!

> Hey! Ida!! Blow out the candles on the birthday cake! Purse up your lips and draw a deep breath and blow out the goddam candles on the cake!

BIG MAMA: Oh, Big Daddy, oh, oh, oh, Big Daddy!

BIG DADDY: What's the matter with you?

BIG MAMA: *In all these years you never believed that I loved you??*

BIG DADDY: Huh?

BIG MAMA: *And I did, I did so much, I did love you!*—I even loved your hate and your hardness, Big Daddy!

> [*She sobs and rushes awkwardly out onto the gallery.*]

BIG DADDY: [*to himself*] *Wouldn't it be funny if that was true. . . .*

> [*A pause is followed by a burst of light in the sky from the fireworks.*]
> *BRICK! HEY, BRICK!*
> [*He stands over his blazing birthday cake.*]
> [*After some moments,* BRICK *hobbles in on his crutch, holding his glass.*]
> [MARGARET *follows him with a bright, anxious smile.*]

I didn't call you, Maggie. I called Brick.

MARGARET: I'm just delivering him to you.

> [*She kisses* BRICK *on the mouth, which he immediately wipes with the back of his hand. She flies girlishly back out.* BRICK *and his father are alone.*]

BIG DADDY: Why did you do that?

BRICK: Do what, Big Daddy?

BIG DADDY: Wipe her kiss off your mouth like she'd spit on you.

BRICK: I don't know. I wasn't conscious of it.

BIG DADDY: That woman of yours has a better shape on her than Gooper's but somehow or other they got the same look about them.

BRICK: What sort of look is that, Big Daddy?

BIG DADDY: I don't know how to describe it but it's the same look.

BRICK: They don't look peaceful, do they?

BIG DADDY: No, they sure in hell don't.

BRICK: They look nervous as cats?

BIG DADDY: That's right, they look nervous as cats.

BRICK: Nervous as a couple of cats on a hot tin roof?

BIG DADDY: That's right, boy, they look like a couple of cats on a hot tin roof. It's funny that you and Gooper being so different would pick out the same type of woman.

BRICK: Both of us married into society, Big Daddy.

BIG DADDY: Crap . . . I wonder what gives them both that look?

BRICK: Well. They're sittin' in the middle of a big piece of land, Big Daddy, twenty-eight thousand acres is a pretty big piece of land and so they're squaring off on it, each determined to knock off a bigger piece of it than the other whenever you let it go.

BIG DADDY: I got a surprise for those women. I'm not gonna let it go for a long time yet if that's what they're waiting for.

BRICK: That's right, Big Daddy. You just sit tight and let them scratch each other's eyes out. . . .

BIG DADDY: You bet your life I'm going to sit tight on it and let those sons of bitches scratch their eyes out, ha ha ha. . . .

But Gooper's wife's a good breeder, you got to admit she's fertile. Hell, at supper tonight she had them all at the table and they had to put a couple of extra leafs in the table to make room for them, she's got five head of them, now, and another one's comin'.

BRICK: Yep, number six is comin'. . . .

BIG DADDY: Brick, you know, I swear to God, I don't know the way it happens?

BRICK: The way what happens, Big Daddy?

BIG DADDY: You git you a piece of land, by hook or crook, an' things start growin' on it, things accumulate on it, and the first thing you know it's completely out of hand, completely out of hand!

BRICK: Well, they say nature hates a vacuum, Big Daddy.

BIG DADDY: That's what they say, but sometimes I think that a vacuum is a hell of a lot better than some of the stuff that nature replaces it with.

Is someone out there by that door?

BRICK: Yep.

BIG DADDY: Who?

[*He has lowered his voice.*]

BRICK: Someone int'rested in what we say to each other.

BIG DADDY: Gooper?—*GOOPER!*

[*After a discreet pause,* MAE *appears in the gallery door.*]

MAE: Did you call Gooper, Big Daddy?

BIG DADDY: Aw, it was you.

MAE: Do you want Gooper, Big Daddy?

BIG DADDY: No, and I don't want you. I want some privacy here, while I'm having a confidential talk with my son Brick. Now it's too hot in here to close
them doors, but if I have to close those rutten doors in order to have a private talk with my son Brick, just let me know and I'll close 'em. Because I
hate eavesdroppers, I don't like any kind of sneakin' an' spyin'.

MAE: Why, Big Daddy—

BIG DADDY: You stood on the wrong side of the moon, it threw your shadow!

MAE: I was just—

BIG DADDY: You was just nothing but *spyin'* an' you *know* it!

MAE: [*begins to sniff and sob*] Oh, Big Daddy, you're so unkind for some reason to
those that really love you!

BIG DADDY: Shut up, shut up, shut up! I'm going to move you and Gooper out of
that room next to this! It's none of your goddam business what goes on in
here at night between Brick an' Maggie. You listen at night like a couple of
rutten peekhole spies and go and give a report on what you hear to Big
Mama an' she comes to me and says they say such and such and so and so
about what they heard goin' on between Brick an' Maggie, and Jesus, it
makes me sick. I'm goin' to move you an' Gooper out of that room, I can't
stand sneakin' an' spyin', it makes me sick. . . .

    [MAE *throws back her head and rolls her eyes heavenward and extends her
    arms as if invoking God's pity for this unjust martyrdom; then she presses a
    handkerchief to her nose and flies from the room with a loud swish of skirts.*]

BRICK: [*now at the liquor cabinet*] They listen, do they?

BIG DADDY: Yeah. They listen and give reports to Big Mama on what goes on in
here between you and Maggie. They say that—

    [*He stops as if embarrassed.*]

—You won't sleep with her, that you sleep on the sofa. Is that true or not
true? If you don't like Maggie, get rid of Maggie!—What are you doin'
there now?

BRICK: Fresh'nin' up my drink.

BIG DADDY: Son, you know you got a real liquor problem?

BRICK: Yes, sir, yes, I know.

BIG DADDY: Is that why you quit sports announcing, because of this liquor
problem?

BRICK: Yes, sir, yes, sir, I guess so.

    [*He smiles vaguely and amiably at his father across his replenished drink.*]

BIG DADDY: Son, don't guess about it, it's too important.

BRICK: [*vaguely*] Yes, sir.

BIG DADDY: And listen to me, don't look at the damn chandelier. . . .

    [*Pause.* BIG DADDY's *voice is husky.*]

—Somethin' else we picked up at th' big fire sale in Europe.

    [*another pause*]

Life is important. There's nothing else to hold onto. A man that drinks is
throwing his life away. Don't do it, hold onto your life. There's nothing else
to hold onto. . . .

Sit down over here so we don't have to raise our voices, the walls have ears in this place.

BRICK: [*hobbling over to sit on the sofa beside him*] All right, Big Daddy.

BIG DADDY: Quit!—how'd that come about? Some disappointment?

BRICK: I don't know. Do you?

BIG DADDY: I'm askin' you, goddam it! How in hell would I know if you don't?

BRICK: I just got out there and found that I had a mouth full of cotton. I was always two or three beats behind what was goin' on on the field and so I—

BIG DADDY: Quit!

BRICK: [*amiably*] Yes, quit.

BIG DADDY: Son?

BRICK: Huh?

BIG DADDY: [*inhales loudly and deeply from his cigar; then bends suddenly a little forward, exhaling loudly and raising a hand to his forehead*]

—Whew!—ha ha!—I took in too much smoke, it made me a little light-headed. . . .

[*The mantel clock chimes.*]

Why is it so damn hard for people to talk?

BRICK: Yeah. . . .

[*The clock goes on sweetly chiming till it has completed the stroke of ten.*]

—Nice peaceful-soundin' clock, I like to hear it all night. . . .

[*He slides low and comfortable on the sofa;* BIG DADDY *sits up straight and rigid with some unspoken anxiety. All his gestures are tense and jerky as he talks. He wheezes and pants and sniffs through his nervous speech, glancing quickly, shyly, from time to time, at his son.*]

BIG DADDY: We got that clock the summer we wint to Europe, me an' Big Mama on that damn Cook's Tour, never had such an awful time in my life, I'm tellin' you, son, those gooks over there, they gouge your eyeballs out in their grand hotels. And Big Mama bought more stuff than you could haul in a couple of boxcars, that's no crap. Everywhere she wint on this whirlwind tour, she bought, bought, bought. Why, half that stuff she bought is still crated up in the cellar, under water last spring!

[*He laughs.*]

That Europe is nothin' on earth but a great big auction, that's all it is, that bunch of worn-out places, it's just a big fire sale, the whole rutten thing, an' Big Mama wint wild in it, why, you couldn't hold that woman with a mule's harness! Bought, bought, bought!—lucky I'm a rich man, yes, siree, Bob, an' half that stuff is mildewin' in th' basement. It's lucky I'm a rich man, it sure is lucky, well, I'm a rich man, Brick, yep, I'm a mighty rich man.

[*His eyes light up for a moment.*]

Y'know how much I'm worth? Guess, Brick! Guess how much I'm worth!

[BRICK *smiles vaguely over his drink.*]

Close on ten million in cash an' blue-chip stocks, outside, mind you, of twenty-eight thousand acres of the richest land this side of the valley Nile!

[*A puff and crackle and the night sky blooms with an eerie greenish glow. Children shriek on the gallery.*]

But a man can't buy his life with it, he can't buy back his life with it when his life has been spent, that's one thing not offered in the Europe fire sale or in the American markets or any markets on earth, a man can't buy his life with it, he can't buy back his life when his life is finished. . . .

That's a sobering thought, a very sobering thought, and that's a thought that I was turning over in my head, over and over and over—until today. . . .

I'm wiser and sadder, Brick, for this experience which I just gone through. They's one thing else that I remember in Europe.

BRICK: What is that, Big Daddy?

BIG DADDY: The hills around Barcelona in the country of Spain and the children running over those bare hills in their bare skins beggin' like starvin' dogs with howls and screeches, and how fat the priests are on the streets of Barcelona, so many of them and so fat and so pleasant, ha ha!—Y'know I could feed that country? I got money enough to feed that goddam country, but the human animal is a selfish beast and I don't reckon the money I passed out there to those howling children in the hills around Barcelona would more than upholster one of the chairs in this room, I mean pay to put a new cover on this chair!

Hell, I threw them money like you'd scatter feed corn for chickens, I threw money at them just to get rid of them long enough to climb back into th' car and—drive away. . . .

And then in Morocco, them Arabs, why, prostitution begins at four or five, that's no exaggeration, why, I remember one day in Marrakech, that old walled Arab city, I set on a broken-down wall to have a cigar, it was fearful hot there and this Arab woman stood in the road and looked at me till I was embarrassed, she stood stock still in the dusty hot road and looked at me till I was embarrassed. But listen to this. She had a naked child with her, a little naked girl with her, barely able to toddle, and after a while she set this child on the ground and give her a push and whispered something to her.

This child come toward me, barely able t' walk, come toddling up to me and—

Jesus, it makes you sick t' remember a thing like this!

It stuck out its hand and tried to unbutton my trousers!

That child was not yet five! Can you believe me? Or do you think that I am making this up? I wint back to the hotel and said to Big Mama, "Git packed! We're clearing out of this country." . . .

BRICK: Big Daddy, you're on a talkin' jag tonight.

BIG DADDY: [*ignoring this remark*] Yes, sir, that's how it is, the human animal is a beast that dies but the fact that he's dying don't give him pity for others, no, sir, it—

—Did you say something?

BRICK: Yes.

BIG DADDY: What?

BRICK: Hand me over that crutch so I can get up.

BIG DADDY: Where you goin'?

BRICK: I'm takin' a little short trip to Echo Spring.

BIG DADDY: To where?

BRICK: Liquor cabinet. . . .

BIG DADDY: Yes, sir, boy—

> [*He hands* BRICK *the crutch.*]

—the human animal is a beast that dies and if he's got money he buys and buys and buys and I think the reason he buys everything he can buy is that in the back of his mind he has the crazy hope that one of his purchases will be life everlasting!—Which it never can be. . . . The human animal is a beast that—

BRICK: [*at the liquor cabinet*] Big Daddy, you sure are shootin' th' breeze here tonight.

> [*There is a pause and voices are heard outside.*]

BIG DADDY: I been quiet here lately, spoke not a word, just sat and stared into space. I had something heavy weighing on my mind but tonight that load was took off me. That's why I'm talking.—The sky looks diff'rent to me. . . .

BRICK: You know what I like to hear most?

BIG DADDY: What?

BRICK: Solid quiet. Perfect unbroken quiet.

BIG DADDY: Why?

BRICK: Because it's more peaceful.

BIG DADDY: Man, you'll hear a lot of that in the grave.

> [*He chuckles agreeably.*]

BRICK: Are you through talkin' to me?

BIG DADDY: Why are you so anxious to shut me up?

BRICK: Well, sir, ever so often you say to me, "Brick, I want to have a talk with you," but when we talk, it never materializes. Nothing is said. You sit in a chair and gas about this and that and I look like I listen. I try to look like I listen, but I don't listen, not much. Communication is—awful hard between people an'—somehow between you and me, it just don't—

BIG DADDY: Have you ever been scared? I mean have you ever felt downright terror of something?

> [*He gets up.*]

Just one moment. I'm going to close these doors. . . .

> [*He closes doors on gallery as if he were going to tell an important secret.*]

BRICK: What?

BIG DADDY: Brick?

BRICK: Huh?

BIG DADDY: Son, I thought I had it!

BRICK: Had what? Had what, Big Daddy?

BIG DADDY: Cancer!

BRICK: Oh . . .

BIG DADDY: I thought the old man made out of bones had laid his cold and heavy hand on my shoulder!

BRICK: Well, Big Daddy, you kept a tight mouth about it.

BIG DADDY: A pig squeals. A man keeps a tight mouth about it, in spite of a man not having a pig's advantage.

BRICK: What advantage is that?

BIG DADDY: Ignorance—of mortality—is a comfort. A man don't have that comfort, he's the only living thing that conceives of death, that knows what it is.

The others go without knowing, which is the way that anything living should go, go without knowing, without any knowledge of it, and yet a pig squeals, but a man sometimes, he can keep a tight mouth about it. Sometimes he—

[*There is a deep, smoldering ferocity in the old man.*]

—can keep a tight mouth about it. I wonder if—

BRICK: What, Big Daddy?

BIG DADDY: A whiskey highball would injure this spastic condition?

BRICK: No, sir, it might do it good.

BIG DADDY: [*grins suddenly, wolfishly*] Jesus, I can't tell you! The sky is open! Christ it's open again! It's open, boy, it's open!

[BRICK *looks down at his drink.*]

BRICK: You feel better, Big Daddy?

BIG DADDY: Better? Hell! I can breathe!—All of my life I been like a doubled-up fist. . . .

[*He pours a drink.*]

—Poundin', smashin', drivin'!—now I'm going to loosen these doubled-up hands and touch things *easy* with them. . . .

[*He spreads his hands as if caressing the air.*]

You know what I'm contemplating?

BRICK: [*vaguely*] No, sir. What are you contemplating?

BIG DADDY: Ha ha!—*Pleasure!*—pleasure with *women!*

[BRICK'*s smile fades a little but lingers.*]

  ` Brick, this stuff burns me!—

    —Yes, boy. I'll tell you something that you might not guess. I still have desire for women and this is my sixty-fifth birthday.

BRICK: I think that's mighty remarkable, Big Daddy.

BIG DADDY: Remarkable?

BRICK: *Admirable,* Big Daddy.

BIG DADDY: You're damn right it is, remarkable and admirable both. I realize now that I never had me enough. I let many chances slip by because of scruples about it, scruples, convention—crap. . . . All that stuff is bull, bull, bull!—It took the shadow of death to make me see it. Now that shadow's lifted, I'm going to cut loose and have, what is it they call it, have me a—ball!

BRICK: A ball, huh?

BIG DADDY: That's right, a ball, a ball! Hell!—I slept with Big Mama till, let's see, five years ago, till I was sixty and she was fifty-eight, and never even liked her, never did!

[*The phone has been ringing down the hall.* BIG MAMA *enters, exclaiming.*]

BIG MAMA: Don't you men hear that phone ring? I heard it way out on the gall'ry.

BIG DADDY: There's five rooms off this front gall'ry that you could go through. Why do you go through this one?

[BIG MAMA *makes a playful face as she bustles out the hall door.*]

Hunh!—Why, when Big Mama goes out of a room, I can't remember what that woman looks like, but when Big Mama comes back into the room, boy, then I see what she looks like, and I wish I didn't!

[*Bends over laughing at this joke till it hurts his guts and he straightens with a grimace. The laugh subsides to a chuckle as he puts the liquor glass a little distrustfully down on the table.*]

[BRICK *has risen and hobbled to the gallery doors.*]
    Hey! Where you goin'?

BRICK: Out for a breather.

BIG DADDY: Not yet you ain't. Stay here till this talk is finished, young fellow.

BRICK: I thought it was finished, Big Daddy.

BIG DADDY: It ain't even begun.

BRICK: My mistake. Excuse me. I just wanted to feel that river breeze.

BIG DADDY: Turn on the ceiling fan and set back down in that chair.
    [BIG MAMA'*s voice rises, carrying down the hall.*]

BIG MAMA: Miss Sally, you're a case! You're a caution, Miss Sally. Why didn't you give me a chance to explain it to you?

BIG DADDY: Jesus, she's talking to my old maid sister again.

BIG MAMA: Well, goodbye, now, Miss Sally. You come down real soon, Big Daddy's dying to see you! Yaisss, goodbye, Miss Sally. . . .
    [*She hangs up and bellows with mirth.* BIG DADDY *groans and covers his ears as she approaches.*]
    [*Bursting in:*]
    Big Daddy, that was Miss Sally callin' from Memphis again! You know what she done, Big Daddy? She called her doctor in Memphis to git him to tell her what that spastic thing is! Ha-*HAAAA!*—And called back to tell me how relieved she was that—Hey! Let me in!
    [BIG DADDY *has been holding the door half closed against her.*]

BIG DADDY: Naw I ain't. I told you not to come and go through this room. You just back out and go through those five other rooms.

BIG MAMA: Big Daddy? Big Daddy? Oh, Big Daddy!—You didn't mean those things you said to me, did you?
    [*He shuts door firmly against her but she still calls.*]
    Sweetheart? Sweetheart? Big Daddy? You didn't mean those awful things you said to me?—I know you didn't. I know you didn't mean those things in your heart. . . .
    [*The childlike voice fades with a sob and her heavy footsteps retreat down the hall.* BRICK *has risen once more on his crutches and starts for the gallery again.*]

BIG DADDY: All I ask of that woman is that she leave me alone. But she can't admit to herself that she makes me sick. That comes of having slept with her too many years. Should of quit much sooner but that old woman she never got enough of it—and I was good in bed. . . . I never should of wasted so much of it on her. . . . They say you got just so many and each one is numbered. Well, I got a few left in me, a few, and I'm going to pick me a good one to spend 'em on! I'm going to pick me a choice one, I don't care how much she costs, I'll smother her in—minks! Ha ha! I'll strip her naked and smother her in minks and choke her with diamonds! Ha ha! I'll strip her naked and choke her with diamonds and smother her with minks and hump her from hell to breakfast. *Ha aha ha ha ha!*

MAE: [*gaily at door*] Who's that laughin' in there?

GOOPER: Is Big Daddy laughin' in there?

BIG DADDY: Crap!—them two—*drips.* . . .
    [*He goes over and touches* BRICK'*s shoulder.*]

Yes, son. Brick, boy.—I'm—*happy!* I'm happy, son, I'm happy!

[*He chokes a little and bites his under lip, pressing his head quickly, shyly against his son's head and then, coughing with embarrassment, goes uncertainly back to the table where he set down the glass. He drinks and makes a grimace as it burns his guts.* BRICK *sighs and rises with effort.*]

What makes you so restless? Have you got ants in your britches?

BRICK: Yes, sir. . . .

BIG DADDY: Why?

BRICK: —Something—hasn't happened. . . .

BIG DADDY: Yeah? What is that!

BRICK: [*sadly*]—the click. . . .

BIG DADDY: Did you say "click"?

BRICK: Yes, click.

BIG DADDY: What click?

BRICK: A click that I get in my head that makes me peaceful.

BIG DADDY: I sure in hell don't know what you're talking about, but it disturbs me.

BRICK: It's just a mechanical thing.

BIG DADDY: What is a mechanical thing?

BRICK: This click that I get in my head that makes me peaceful. I got to drink till I get it. It's just a mechanical thing, something like a—like a—like a—

BIG DADDY: Like a—

BRICK: Switch clicking off in my head, turning the hot light off and the cool night on and—

[*He looks up, smiling sadly.*]

—all of a sudden there's—peace!

BIG DADDY: [*whistles long and soft with astonishment; he goes back to* BRICK *and clasps his son's two shoulders*] Jesus! I didn't know it had gotten that bad with you. Why, boy, you're—*alcoholic!*

BRICK: That's the truth, Big Daddy. I'm alcoholic.

BIG DADDY: This shows how I—let things go!

BRICK: I have to hear that little click in my head that makes me peaceful. Usually I hear it sooner than this, sometimes as early as—noon, but—

—Today it's—dilatory. . . .

—I just haven't got the right level of alcohol in my bloodstream yet!

[*This last statement is made with energy as he freshens his drink.*]

BIG DADDY: Uh—huh. Expecting death made me blind. I didn't have no idea that a son of mine was turning into a drunkard under my nose.

BRICK: [*gently*] Well, now you do, Big Daddy, the news has penetrated.

BIG DADDY: UH-huh, yes, now I do, the news has—penetrated. . . .

BRICK: And so if you'll excuse me—

BIG DADDY: No, I won't excuse you.

BRICK: —I'd better sit by myself till I hear that click in my head, it's just a mechanical thing but it don't happen except when I'm alone or talking to no one. . . .

BIG DADDY: You got a long, long time to sit still, boy, and talk to no one, but now you're talkin' to me. At least I'm talking to you. And you set there and listen until I tell you the conversation is over!

BRICK: But this talk is like all the others we've ever had together in our lives! It's
nowhere, nowhere!—it's—it's *painful,* Big Daddy. . . .

BIG DADDY: All right, then let it be painful, but don't you move from that
chair!—I'm going to remove that crutch. . . .

[*He seizes the crutch and tosses it across room.*]

BRICK: I can hop on one foot, and if I fall, I can crawl!

BIG DADDY: If you ain't careful you're gonna crawl off this plantation and then,
by Jesus, you'll have to hustle your drinks along Skid Row!

BRICK: That'll come, Big Daddy.

BIG DADDY: Naw, it won't. You're my son and I'm going to straighten you out;
now that *I'm* straightened out, I'm going to straighten out you!

BRICK: Yeah?

BIG DADDY: Today the report come in from Ochsner Clinic. Y'know what they
told me?

[*His face glows with triumph.*]

The only thing that they could detect with all the instruments of science in
that great hospital is a little spastic condition of the colon! And nerves torn
to pieces by all that worry about it.

[*A little girl bursts into room with a sparkler clutched in each fist, hops and
shrieks like a monkey gone mad and rushes back out again as* BIG DADDY
strikes at her.]

[*Silence. The two men stare at each other. A woman laughs gaily outside.*]

I want you to know I breathed a sigh of relief almost as powerful as the
Vicksburg tornado!

BRICK: You weren't ready to go?

BIG DADDY: GO WHERE?—crap. . . .

—When you are gone from here, boy, you are long gone and no where! The
human machine is not no different from the animal machine or the fish
machine or the bird machine or the reptile machine or the insect machine!
It's just a whole goddam lot more complicated and consequently more trouble to keep together. Yep. I thought I had it. The earth shook under my
foot, the sky come down like the black lid of a kettle and I couldn't
breathe!—Today!!—that lid was lifted, I drew my first free breath in—how
many years?—*God!—three.* . . .

[*There is laughter outside, running footsteps, the soft, plushy sound and light
of exploding rockets.*]

[BRICK *stares at him soberly for a long moment; then makes a sort of startled
sound in his nostrils and springs up on one foot and hops across the room to
grab his crutch, swinging on the furniture for support. He gets the crutch and
flees as if in horror for the gallery. His father seizes him by the sleeve of his
white silk pajamas.*]

Stay here, you son of a bitch!—till I say go!

BRICK: I can't.

BIG DADDY: You sure in hell will, goddamn it.

BRICK: No, I can't. We talk, you talk, in—circles! We get no where, no where! It's
always the same, you say you want to talk to me and don't have a ruttin'
thing to say to me!

BIG DADDY: Nothin' to say when I'm tellin' you I'm going to live when I thought I was dying?!

BRICK: Oh—*that!*—Is that what you have to say to me?

BIG DADDY: Why, you son of a bitch! Ain't that, ain't that—*important?!*

BRICK: Well, you said that, that's said, and now I—

BIG DADDY: Now you set back down.

BRICK: You're all balled up, you—

BIG DADDY: I ain't balled up!

BRICK: You are, you're all balled up!

BIG DADDY: Don't tell me what I am, you drunken whelp! I'm going to tear this coat sleeve off if you don't set down!

BRICK: Big Daddy—

BIG DADDY: Do what I tell you! I'm the boss here, now! I want you to know I'm back in the driver's seat now!

[BIG MAMA *rushes in, clutching her great heaving bosom.*]

What in hell do you want in here, Big Mama?

BIG MAMA: Oh, Big Daddy! Why are you shouting like that? I just cain't *stainnnnnnnd*—it. . . .

BIG DADDY: [*raising the back of his hand above his head*] GIT!—outa here.

[*She rushes back out, sobbing.*]

BRICK: [*softly, sadly*] Christ. . . .

BIG DADDY: [*fiercely*] Yeah! Christ!—is right. . . .

[BRICK *breaks loose and hobbles toward the gallery.*]

[BIG DADDY *jerks his crutch from under* BRICK *so he steps with the injured ankle. He utters a hissing cry of anguish, clutches a chair and pulls it over on top of him on the floor.*]

Son of a—tub of—hog fat. . . .

BRICK: Big Daddy! Give me my crutch.

[BIG DADDY *throws the crutch out of reach.*]

Give me that crutch, Big Daddy.

BIG DADDY: Why do you drink?

BRICK: Don't know, give me my crutch!

BIG DADDY: You better think why you drink or give up drinking!

BRICK: Will you please give me my crutch so I can get up off this floor?

BIG DADDY: First you answer my question. Why do you drink? Why are you throwing your life away, boy, like somethin' disgusting you picked up on the street?

BRICK: [*getting onto his knees*] Big Daddy, I'm in pain, I stepped on that foot.

BIG DADDY: Good! I'm glad you're not too numb with the liquor in you to feel some pain!

BRICK: You—spilled my—drink. . . .

BIG DADDY: I'll make a bargain with you. You tell me why you drink and I'll hand you one. I'll pour you the liquor myself and hand it to you.

BRICK: Why do I drink?

BIG DADDY: Yea! Why?

BRICK: Give me a drink and I'll tell you.

BIG DADDY: Tell me first!

BRICK: I'll tell you in one word.

BIG DADDY: What word?

BRICK: DISGUST!

> [*The clock chimes softly, sweetly.* BIG DADDY *gives it a short, outraged glance.*]

Now how about that drink?

BIG DADDY: What are you disgusted with? You got to tell me that, first. Otherwise being disgusted don't make no sense!

BRICK: Give me my crutch.

BIG DADDY: You heard me, you got to tell me what I asked you first.

BRICK: I told you, I said to kill my disgust!

BIG DADDY: DISGUST WITH WHAT!

BRICK: You strike a hard bargain.

BIG DADDY: What are you disgusted with?—an' I'll pass you the liquor.

BRICK: I can hop on one foot, and if I fall, I can crawl.

BIG DADDY: You want liquor that bad?

BRICK: [*dragging himself up, clinging to bedstead*] Yeah, I want it that bad.

BIG DADDY: If I give you a drink, will you tell me what it is you're disgusted with, Brick?

BRICK: Yes, sir, I will try to.

> [*The old man pours him a drink and solemnly passes it to him.*]
>
> [*There is silence as* BRICK *drinks.*]

Have you ever heard the word "mendacity"?

BIG DADDY: Sure. Mendacity is one of them five-dollar words that cheap politicians throw back and forth at each other.

BRICK: You know what it means?

BIG DADDY: Don't it mean lying and liars?

BRICK: Yes, sir, lying and liars.

BIG DADDY: Has someone been lying to you?

CHILDREN: [*chanting in chorus offstage*]

> We want Big Dad-dee!
>
> We want Big Dad-dee!
>
> [GOOPER *appears in the gallery door.*]

GOOPER: Big Daddy, the kiddies are shouting for you out there.

BIG DADDY: [*fiercely*] Keep out, Gooper!

GOOPER: 'Scuse *me!*

> [BIG DADDY *slams the doors after* GOOPER.]

BIG DADDY: Who's been lying to you, has Margaret been lying to you, has your wife been lying to you about something, Brick?

BRICK: Not her. That wouldn't matter.

BIG DADDY: Then who's been lying to you, and what about?

BRICK: No one single person and no one lie. . . .

BIG DADDY: Then what, what then, for Christ's sake?

BRICK: —The whole, the whole—thing. . . .

BIG DADDY: Why are you rubbing your head? You got a headache?

BRICK: No, I'm tryin' to—

BIG DADDY: —Concentrate, but you can't because your brain's all soaked with liquor, is that the trouble? Wet brain!

> [*He snatches the glass from* BRICK's *hand.*]

What do you know about this mendacity thing? Hell! I could write a book on it! Don't you know that? I could write a book on it and still not cover the subject? Well, I could, I could write a goddam book on it and still not cover the subject anywhere near enough!!—Think of all the lies I got to put up with!—Pretenses! Ain't that mendacity? Having to pretend stuff you don't think or feel or have any idea of? Having for instance to act like I care for Big Mama!—I haven't been able to stand the sight, sound, or smell of that woman for forty years now!—even when I *laid* her!—regular as a piston. . . .

Pretend to love that son of a bitch of a Gooper and his wife Mae and those five same screechers out there like parrots in a jungle? Jesus! Can't stand to look at 'em!

Church!—it bores the bejesus out of me but I go!—I go an' sit there and listen to the fool preacher!

Clubs!—Elks! Masons! Rotary!—*crap!*

[*A spasm of pain makes him clutch his belly. He sinks into a chair and his voice is softer and hoarser.*]

You I *do* like for some reason, did always have some kind of real feeling for—affection—respect yes, always. . . .

You and being a success as a planter is all I ever had any devotion to in my whole life!—and that's the truth. . . .

I don't know why, but it is!

I've lived with mendacity!—Why can't *you* live with it? Hell, you *got* to live with it, there's nothing *else* to *live* with except mendacity, is there?

BRICK: Yes, sir. Yes, sir, there is something else that you can live with!

BIG DADDY: What?

BRICK: [*lifting his glass*] This!—Liquor. . . .

BIG DADDY: That's not living, that's dodging away from life.

BRICK: I want to dodge away from it.

BIG DADDY: Then why don't you kill yourself, man?

BRICK: I like to drink. . . .

BIG DADDY: Oh, God, I can't talk to you. . . .

BRICK: I'm sorry, Big Daddy.

BIG DADDY: Not as sorry as I am. I'll tell you something. A little while back when I thought my number was up—

[*This speech should have torrential pace and fury.*]

—before I found out it was just this—spastic—colon. I thought about you. Should I or should I not, if the jig was up, give you this place when I go—since I hate Gooper an' Mae an' know that they hate me, and since all five same monkeys are little Maes an' Goopers.—And I thought, No!—Then I thought, Yes!—I couldn't make up my mind. I hate Gooper and his five same monkeys and that bitch Mae! Why should I turn over twenty-eight thousand acres of the richest land this side of the valley Nile to not my kind?—But why in hell, on the other hand, Brick—should I subsidize a goddam fool on the bottle?—Liked or not liked, well, maybe even—*loved!*—Why should I do that?—Subsidize worthless behavior? Rot? Corruption?

BRICK: [*smiling*] I understand.

BIG DADDY: Well, if you do, you're smarter than I am, goddam it, because I don't understand. And this I will tell you frankly. I didn't make up my mind at all on that question and still to this day I ain't made out no will!—Well, now I don't *have* to. The pressure is gone. I can just wait and see if you pull yourself together or if you don't.

BRICK: That's right, Big Daddy.

BIG DADDY: You sound like you thought I was kidding.

BRICK: [*rising*] No, sir, I know you're not kidding.

BIG DADDY: But you don't care—?

BRICK: [*hobbling toward the gallery door*] No, sir, I don't care. . . .
Now how about taking a look at your birthday fireworks and getting some of that cool breeze off the river?
> [*He stands in the gallery doorway as the night sky turns pink and green and gold with successive flashes of light.*]

BIG DADDY: *WAIT!*—Brick. . . .
> [*His voice drops. Suddenly there is something shy, almost tender, in his restraining gesture.*]

Don't let's—leave it like this, like them other talks we've had, we've always—talked around things, we've—just talked around things for some rutten reason, I don't know what, it's always like something was left not spoken, something avoided because neither of us was honest enough with the—other. . . .

BRICK: I never lied to you, Big Daddy.

BIG DADDY: Did I ever to *you?*

BRICK: No, sir. . . .

BIG DADDY: Then there is at least two people that never lied to each other.

BRICK: But we've never *talked* to each other.

BIG DADDY: We can *now.*

BRICK: Big Daddy, there don't seem to be anything much to say.

BIG DADDY: You say that you drink to kill your disgust with lying.

BRICK: You said to give you a reason.

BIG DADDY: Is liquor the only thing that'll kill this disgust?

BRICK: Now. Yes.

BIG DADDY: But not once, huh?

BRICK: Not when I was still young an' believing. A drinking man's someone who wants to forget he isn't still young an' believing.

BIG DADDY: Believing what?

BRICK: Believing. . . .

BIG DADDY: Believing *what?*

BRICK: [*stubbornly evasive*] Believing. . . .

BIG DADDY: I don't know what the hell you mean by "believing" and I don't think you know what you mean by "believing" but if you still got sports in your blood, go back to sports announcing and—

BRICK: Sit in a glass box watching games I can't play? Describing what I can't do while players do it? Sweating out their disgust and confusion in contests I'm not fit for? Drinkin' a Coke, half bourbon, so I can stand it? That's no goddam good any more, no help—time just outran me, Big Daddy—got there first. . . .

BIG DADDY: I think you're passing the buck.

BRICK: You know many drinkin' men?

BIG DADDY: [*with a slight, charming smile*] I have known a fair number of that species.

BRICK: Could any of them tell you why he drank?

BIG DADDY: Yep, you're passin' the buck to things like time and disgust with "mendacity" and—crap!—if you got to use that kind of language about a thing, it's ninety-proof bull, and I'm not buying any.

BRICK: I had to give you a reason to get a drink!

BIG DADDY: You started drinkin' when your friend Skipper died.

[*Silence for five beats. Then* BRICK *makes a startled movement, reaching for his crutch.*]

BRICK: What are you suggesting?

BIG DADDY: I'm suggesting nothing.

[*The shuffle and clop of* BRICK's *rapid hobble away from his father's steady, grave attention.*]

—But Gooper an' Mae suggested that there was something not right exactly in your—

BRICK: [*stopping short downstage as if backed to a wall*] "Not right"?

BIG DADDY: Not, well, exactly *normal* in your friendship with—

BRICK: They suggested that, too? I thought that was Maggie's suggestion.

[BRICK's *detachment is at last broken through. His heart is accelerated; his forehead sweat-beaded; his breath becomes more rapid and his voice hoarse. The thing they're discussing, timidly and painfully on the side of* BIG DADDY, *fiercely, violently on* BRICK's *side, is the inadmissible thing that Skipper died to disavow between them. The fact that if it existed it had to be disavowed to "keep face" in the world they lived in, may be at the heart of the "mendacity" that* BRICK *drinks to kill his disgust with. It may be the root of his collapse. Or maybe it is only a single manifestation of it, not even the most important. The bird that I hope to catch in the net of this play is not the solution of one man's psychological problem. I'm trying to catch the true quality of experience in a group of people, that cloudy, flickering, evanescent— fiercely charged!—interplay of live human beings in the thundercloud of a common crisis. Some mystery should be left in the revelation of character in a play, just as a great deal of mystery is always left in the revelation of character in life, even in one's own character to himself. This does not absolve the playwright of his duty to observe and probe as clearly and deeply as he legitimately can: but it should steer him away from "pat" conclusions, facile definitions which make a play just a play, not a snare for the truth of human experience.*]

[*The following scene should be played with great concentration, with most of the power leashed but palpable in what is left unspoken.*]

Who else's suggestion is it, is it *yours?* How many others thought that Skipper and I were—

BIG DADDY: [*gently*] Now, hold on, hold on a minute, son.—I knocked around in my time.

BRICK: What's that got to do with—

BIG DADDY: I said "Hold on!"—I bummed, I bummed this country till I was—

BRICK: Whose suggestion, who else's suggestion is it?

BIG DADDY: Slept in hobo jungles and railroad Y's and flophouses in all cities before I—

BRICK: Oh, *you* think so, too, you call me your son and a queer. Oh! Maybe that's why you put Maggie and me in this room that was Jack Straw's and Peter Ochello's, in which that pair of old sisters slept in a double bed where both of 'em died!

BIG DADDY: *Now just don't go throwing rocks at—*

> [*Suddenly* REVEREND TOOKER *appears in the gallery doors, his head slightly, playfully, fatuously cocked, with a practiced clergyman's smile, sincere as a bird call blown on a hunter's whistle, the living embodiment of the pious, conventional lie.*]

> [BIG DADDY *gasps a little at this perfectly timed, but incongruous, apparition.*]

—What're you lookin' for, Preacher?

REVEREND TOOKER: The gentleman's lavatory, ha ha!—heh, heh . . .

BIG DADDY: [*with strained courtesy*]—Go back out and walk down to the other end of the gallery, Reverend Tooker, and use the bathroom connected with my bedroom, and if you can't find it, ask them where it is!

REVEREND TOOKER: Ah, thanks.

> [*He goes out with a deprecatory chuckle.*]

BIG DADDY: It's hard to talk in this place. . . .

BRICK: Son of a—!

BIG DADDY: [*leaving a lot unspoken*]—I seen all things and understood a lot of them, till 1910. Christ, the year that—I had worn my shoes through, hocked my—I hopped off a yellow dog freight car half a mile down the road, slept in a wagon of cotton outside the gin—Jack Straw an' Peter Ochello took me in. Hired me to manage this place which grew into this one.—When Jack Straw died—why, old Peter Ochello quit eatin' like a dog does when its master's dead, and died, too!

BRICK: Christ!

BIG DADDY: I'm just saying I understand such—

BRICK: [*violently*] Skipper is dead. I have not quit eating!

BIG DADDY: No, but you started drinking.

> [BRICK *wheels on his crutch and hurls his glass across the room shouting.*]

BRICK: YOU THINK SO, TOO?

BIG DADDY: *Shhh!*

> [*Footsteps run on the gallery. There are women's calls.*]

> [BIG DADDY *goes toward the door.*]

Go way!—Just broke a glass. . . .

> [BRICK *is transformed, as if a quiet mountain blew suddenly up in volcanic flame.*]

BRICK: You think so, too? You think so, too? You think me an' Skipper did, did, did!—*sodomy!*—together?

BIG DADDY: Hold—!

BRICK: That what you—

BIG DADDY: —*ON*—a minute!

BRICK: You think we did dirty things between us, Skipper an'—

BIG DADDY: Why are you shouting like that? Why are you—

BRICK: —Me, is that what you think of Skipper, is that—

BIG DADDY: —so excited? I don't think nothing. I don't know nothing. I'm simply telling you what—

BRICK: You think that Skipper and me were a pair of dirty old men?

BIG DADDY: Now that's—

BRICK: Straw? Ochello? A couple of—

BIG DADDY: Now just—

BRICK: —ducking sissies? Queers? Is that what you—

BIG DADDY: Shhh.

BRICK: —think?

> [*He loses his balance and pitches to his knees without noticing the pain. He
> grabs the bed and drags himself up.*]

BIG DADDY: Jesus!—Whew. . . . Grab my hand!

BRICK: Naw, I don't want your hand. . . .

BIG DADDY: Well, I want yours. Git up!

> [*He draws him up, keeps an arm about him with concern and affection.*]

You broken out in a sweat! You're panting like you'd run a race with—

BRICK: [*freeing himself from his father's hold*] Big Daddy, you shock me, Big
Daddy, you, you—*shock* me! Talkin' so—

> [*He turns away from his father.*]

—casually!—about a—thing like that. . . .

—Don't you know how people *feel* about things like that? How, how
disgusted they are by things like that? Why, at Ole Miss when it was discovered a pledge to our fraternity, Skipper's and mine, did a, *attempted* to do
a, unnatural thing with—

We not only dropped him like a hot rock!—We told him to git off
the campus, and he did, he got!—All the way to—

> [*He halts, breathless.*]

BIG DADDY: —Where?

BRICK: —North Africa, last I heard!

BIG DADDY: Well, I have come back from further away than that, I have just now
returned from the other side of the moon, death's country, son, and I'm not
easy to shock by anything here.

> [*He comes downstage and faces out.*]

Always, anyhow, lived with too much space around me to be infected by
ideas of other people. One thing you can grow on a big place more important than cotton!—is *tolerance!*—I grown it.

> [*He returns toward* BRICK.]

BRICK: Why can't exceptional friendship, *real, real, deep, deep friendship!* between
two men be respected as something clean and decent without being
thought of as—

BIG DADDY: It can, it is, for God's sake.

BRICK: —*Fairies.* . . .

> [*In his utterance of this word, we gauge the wide and profound reach of the
> conventional mores he got from the world that crowned him with early
> laurel.*]

BIG DADDY: I told Mae an' Gooper—

BRICK: Frig Mae and Gooper, frig all dirty lies and liars!—Skipper and me had a clean, true thing between us!—had a clean friendship, practically all our lives, till Maggie got the idea you're talking about. Normal? No!—It was too rare to be normal, any true thing between two people is too rare to be normal. Oh, once in a while he put his hand on my shoulder or I'd put mine on his, oh, maybe even, when we were touring the country in pro football an' shared hotel rooms we'd reach across the space between the two beds and shake hands to say goodnight, yeah, one or two times we—

BIG DADDY: Brick, nobody thinks that that's not normal!

BRICK: Well, they're mistaken, it was! It was a pure an' true thing an' that's not normal.

[*They both stare straight at each other for a long moment. The tension breaks and both turn away as if tired.*]

BIG DADDY: Yeah, it's—hard t'—talk. . . .

BRICK: All right, then, let's—let it go. . . .

BIG DADDY: Why did Skipper crack up? Why have you?

[BRICK *looks back at his father again. He has already decided, without knowing that he has made this decision, that he is going to tell his father that he is dying of cancer. Only this could even the score between them: one inadmissible thing in return for another.*]

BRICK: [*ominously*] All right. You're asking for it, Big Daddy. We're finally going to have that real true talk you wanted. It's too late to stop it, now, we got to carry it through and cover every subject.

[*He hobbles back to the liquor cabinet.*]

Uh-huh.

[*He opens the ice bucket and picks up the silver tongs with slow admiration of their frosty brightness.*]

Maggie declares that Skipper and I went into pro football after we left Ole Miss because we were scared to grow up. . . .

[*He moves downstage with the shuffle and clop of a cripple on a crutch. As* MARGARET *did when her speech became "recitative," he looks out into the house, commanding its attention by his direct, concentrated gaze—a broken, "tragically elegant" figure telling simply as much as he knows of "the Truth":*]

—Wanted to—keep on tossing—those long, long!—high, high!—passes that—couldn't be intercepted except by time, the aerial attack that made us famous! And so we did, we did, we kept it up for one season, that aerial attack, we held it high!—Yeah, but—

—that summer, Maggie, she laid the law down to me, said, Now or never, and so I married Maggie. . . .

BIG DADDY: How was Maggie in bed?

BRICK: [*wryly*] Great! the greatest!

[BIG DADDY *nods as if he thought so.*]

She went on the road that fall with the Dixie Stars. Oh, she made a great show of being the world's best sport. She wore a—wore a—tall bearskin cap! A "shako," they call it, a dyed moleskin coat, a moleskin coat dyed red!—Cut up crazy! Rented hotel ballrooms for victory celebrations, wouldn't cancel them when it—turned out—defeat. . . .

MAGGIE THE CAT! Ha ha!

[BIG DADDY *nods.*]

—But Skipper, he had some fever which came back on him which doctors couldn't explain and I got that injury—turned out to be just a shadow on the X-ray plate—and a touch of bursitis. . . .

I lay in a hospital bed, watched our games on TV, saw Maggie on the bench next to Skipper when he was hauled out of a game for stumbles, fumbles!—Burned me up the way she hung on his arm!—Y'know, I think that Maggie had always felt sort of left out because she and me never got any closer together than two people just get in bed, which is not much closer than two cats on a—fence humping. . . .

So! She took this time to work on poor dumb Skipper. He was a less-than-average student at Ole Miss, you know that, don't you?!—Poured in his mind the dirty, false idea that what we were, him and me, was a frustrated case of that ole pair of sisters that lived in this room, Jack Straw and Peter Ochello!—He, poor Skipper, went to bed with Maggie to prove it wasn't true, and when it didn't work out, he thought it *was* true!—Skipper broke in two like a rotten stick—nobody ever turned so fast to a lush—or died of it so quick. . . .

—Now are you satisfied?

[BIG DADDY *has listened to this story, dividing the grain from the chaff. Now he looks at his son.*]

BIG DADDY: Are *you* satisfied?

BRICK: With what?

BIG DADDY: That half-ass story!

BRICK: What's half-ass about it?

BIG DADDY: Something's left out of that story. What did you leave out?

[*The phone has started ringing in the hall. As if it reminded him of something,* BRICK *glances suddenly toward the sound and says:*]

BRICK: Yes!—I left out a long-distance call which I had from Skipper, in which he made a drunken confession to me and on which I hung up!—last time we spoke to each other in our lives. . . .

[*Muted ring stops as someone answers phone in a soft, indistinct voice in hall.*]

BIG DADDY: You hung up?

BRICK: Hung up. Jesus! Well—

BIG DADDY: Anyhow now!—we have tracked down the lie with which you're disgusted and which you are drinking to kill your disgust with, Brick. You been passing the buck. This disgust with mendacity is disgust with yourself.

You!—dug the grave of your friend and kicked him in it!—before you'd face truth with him!

BRICK: *His* truth, not *mine!*

BIG DADDY: His truth, okay! But you wouldn't face it with him!

BRICK: Who *can* face truth? Can *you?*

BIG DADDY: Now don't start passin' the rotten buck again, boy!

BRICK: *How about these birthday congratulations, these many, many happy returns of the day, when ev'rybody but you knows there won't be any!*

[*Whoever has answered the hall phone lets out a high, shrill laugh; the voice becomes audible saying:* "No, no, you got it all wrong! Upside down! Are you crazy?"]

[BRICK *suddenly catches his breath as he realizes that he has made a shocking disclosure. He hobbles a few paces, then freezes, and without looking at his father's shocked face, says:*]

Let's let's—go out, now, and—

[BIG DADDY *moves suddenly forward and grabs hold of the boy's crutch like it was a weapon for which they were fighting for possession.*]

BIG DADDY: Oh, no, no! No one's going out! What did you start to say?

BRICK: I don't remember.

BIG DADDY: "Many happy returns when they know there won't be any"?

BRICK: Aw, hell, Big Daddy, forget it. Come on out on the gallery and look at the fireworks they're shooting off for your birthday. . . .

BIG DADDY: First you finish that remark you were makin' before you cut off. "Many happy returns when they know there won't be any"?—Ain't that what you just said?

BRICK: Look, now. I can get around without that crutch if I have to but it would be a lot easier on the furniture an' glassware if I didn' have to go swinging along like Tarzan of th'—

BIG DADDY: FINISH! WHAT YOU WAS SAYIN'!

[*An eerie green glow shows in sky behind him.*]

BRICK: [*sucking the ice in his glass, speech becoming thick*] Leave th' place to Gooper and Mae an' their five little same little monkeys. All I want is—

BIG DADDY: "LEAVE TH' PLACE," did you say?

BRICK: [*vaguely*] All twenty-eight thousand acres of the richest land this side of the valley Nile.

BIG DADDY: Who said I was "leaving the place" to Gooper or anybody? This is my sixty-fifth birthday! I got fifteen years or twenty years left in me! I'll outlive *you!* I'll bury you an' have to pay for your coffin!

BRICK: Sure. Many happy returns. Now let's go watch the fireworks, come on, let's—

BIG DADDY: Lying, have they been lying? About the report from th'—clinic? did they, did they—find something?—*Cancer.* Maybe?

BRICK: Mendacity is a system that we live in. Liquor is one way out an' death's the other. . . .

[*He takes the crutch from* BIG DADDY's *loose grip and swings out on the gallery leaving the doors open.*]

[*A song, "Pick a Bale of Cotton," is heard.*]

MAE: [*appearing in door*] Oh, Big Daddy, the field hands are singin' fo' you!

BIG DADDY: [*shouting hoarsely*] BRICK! BRICK!

MAE: He's outside drinkin', Big Daddy.

BIG DADDY: *BRICK!*

[MAE *retreats, awed by the passion of his voice. Children call "Brick" in tones mocking* BIG DADDY. *His face crumbles like broken yellow plaster about to fall into dust.*]

[*There is a glow in the sky.* BRICK *swings back through the doors, slowly, gravely, quite soberly.*]

BRICK: I'm sorry, Big Daddy. My head don't work any more and it's hard for me to understand how anybody could care if he lived or died or was dying or cared about anything but whether or not there was liquor left in the bottle and so I said what I said without thinking. In some ways I'm no better than the others, in some ways worse because I'm less alive. Maybe it's being alive that makes them lie, and being almost *not* alive makes me sort of accidentally truthful—I don't know but—anyway—we've been friends. . . .

—And being friends is telling each other the truth. . . .

[*There is a pause.*]

You told *me!* I told *you!*

[*A child rushes into the room and grabs a fistful of firecrackers and runs out again.*]

CHILD: [*screaming*] Bang, bang, bang, bang, bang, bang, bang, bang, bang!

BIG DADDY: [*slowly and passionately*]

CHRIST—DAMN—ALL—LYING SONS OF—LYING BITCHES!

[*He straightens at last and crosses to the inside door. At the door he turns and looks back as if he had some desperate question he couldn't put into words. Then he nods reflectively and says in a hoarse voice:*]

Yes, all liars, all liars, all lying dying liars!

[*This is said slowly, slowly, with a fierce revulsion. He goes on out.*]

—Lying! Dying! Liars!

[*His voice dies out. There is a sound of a child being slapped. It rushes, hideously bawling, through room and out the hall door.*]

[BRICK *remains motionless as the lights dim out and the curtain falls.*]

CURTAIN

ACT THREE

There is no lapse of time. MAE *enters with* REVEREND TOOKER.

MAE: Where is Big Daddy! Big Daddy?

BIG MAMA: [*entering*] Too much smell of burnt fireworks makes me feel a little bit sick at my stomach.—Where is Big Daddy?

MAE: That's what I want to know, where has Big Daddy gone?

BIG MAMA: He must have turned in, I reckon he went to baid. . . .

[GOOPER *enters.*]

GOOPER: Where is Big Daddy?

MAE: We don't know where he is!

BIG MAMA: I reckon he's gone to baid.

GOOPER: Well, then, now we can talk.

BIG MAMA: What *is* this talk, *what* talk?

[MARGARET *appears on gallery, talking to* DR. BAUGH.]

MARGARET: [*musically*] My family freed their slaves ten years before abolition, my great-great-grandfather gave his slaves their freedom five years before the War between the States started!

MAE: Oh, for God's sake! Maggie's climbed back up in her family tree!

MARGARET: [*sweetly*] What, Mae?—Oh, where's Big Daddy?!

[*The pace must be very quick. Great Southern animation.*]

BIG MAMA: [*addressing them all*] I think Big Daddy was just worn out. He loves his family, he loves to have them around him, but it's a strain on his nerves.

He wasn't himself tonight, Big Daddy wasn't himself, I could tell he was all worked up.

REVEREND TOOKER: I think he's remarkable.

BIG MAMA: Yaisss! Just remarkable. Did you all notice the food he ate at that table? Did you all notice the supper he put away? Why, he ate like a hawss!

GOOPER: I hope he doesn't regret it.

BIG MAMA: Why, that man—ate a huge piece of cawn-bread with molasses on it! Helped himself twice to hoppin' john.

MARGARET: Big Daddy loves hoppin' john.—We had a real country dinner.

BIG MAMA: [*overlapping* MARGARET] Yais, he simply adores it! An' candied yams? That man put away enough food at that table to stuff a nigger *field* hand!

GOOPER: [*with grim relish*] I hope he don't have to pay for it later on. . . .

BIG MAMA: [*fiercely*] What's *that*, Gooper?

MAE: Gooper says he hopes Big Daddy doesn't suffer tonight.

BIG MAMA: Oh, shoot, Gooper says, Gooper says! Why should Big Daddy suffer for satisfying a normal appetite? There's nothin' wrong with that man but nerves, he's sound as a dollar! And now he knows he is an' that's why he ate such a supper. He had a big load off his mind, knowin' he wasn't doomed t'—what he thought he was doomed to. . . .

MARGARET: [*sadly and sweetly*] Bless his old sweet soul. . . .

BIG MAMA: [*vaguely*] Yais, bless his heart, where's Brick?

MAE: Outside.

GOOPER: —Drinkin' . . .

BIG MAMA: I know he's drinkin'. You all don't have to keep tellin' *me* Brick is drinkin'. Cain't I see he's drinkin' without you continually tellin' me that boy's drinkin'?

MARGARET: Good for you, Big Mama!

[*She applauds.*]

BIG MAMA: Other people *drink* and *have* drunk an' will *drink*, as long as they make that stuff an' put it in bottles.

MARGARET: That's the truth. I never trusted a man that didn't drink.

MAE: Gooper never drinks. Don't you trust Gooper?

MARGARET: Why, Gooper, don't you drink? If I'd known you didn't drink, I wouldn't of made that remark—

BIG MAMA: *Brick?*

MARGARET: —at least not in your presence.

[*She laughs sweetly.*]

BIG MAMA: *Brick!*

MARGARET: He's still on the gall'ry. I'll go bring him in so we can talk.

BIG MAMA: [*worriedly*] I don't know what this mysterious family conference is about.

[*Awkward silence.* BIG MAMA *looks from face to face, then belches slightly and mutters, "Excuse me. . . ." She opens an ornamental fan suspended about her throat, a black lace fan to go with her black lace gown, and fans her wilting corsage, sniffing nervously and looking from face to face in the uncomfortable silence as* MARGARET *calls "Brick?" and* BRICK *sings to the moon on the gallery.*]

I don't know what's wrong here, you all have such long faces! Open that door on the hall and let some air circulate through here, will you please, Gooper?

MAE: I think we'd better leave that door closed, Big Mama, till after the talk.

BIG MAMA: Reveren' Tooker, will *you* please open that door?!

REVEREND TOOKER: I sure will, Big Mama.

MAE: I just didn't think we ought t' take any chance of Big Daddy hearin' a word of this discussion.

BIG MAMA: I *swan!* Nothing's going to be said in Big Daddy's house that he cain't hear if he wants to!

GOOPER: Well, Big Mama, it's—

> [MAE *gives him a quick, hard poke to shut him up. He glares at her fiercely as she circles before him like a burlesque ballerina, raising her skinny bare arms over her head, jangling her bracelets, exclaiming:*]

MAE: *A breeze! A breeze!*

REVEREND TOOKER: I think this house is the coolest house in the Delta.—Did you all know that Halsey Banks' widow put air-conditioning units in the church and rectory at Friar's Point in memory of Halsey?

> [*General conversation has resumed; everybody is chatting so that the stage sounds like a big bird cage.*]

GOOPER: Too bad nobody cools your church off for you. I bet you sweat in that pulpit these hot Sundays, Reverend Tooker.

REVEREND TOOKER: Yes, my vestments are drenched.

MAE: [*at the same time to* DR. BAUGH] You think those vitamin B_{12} injections are what they're cracked up t' be, Doc Baugh?

DOCTOR BAUGH: Well, if you want to be stuck with something I guess they're as good to be stuck with as anything else.

BIG MAMA: [*at gallery door*] Maggie, Maggie, aren't you comin' with Brick?

MAE: [*suddenly and loudly, creating a silence*] I have a strange feeling, I have a peculiar feeling!

BIG MAMA: [*turning from gallery*] What feeling?

MAE: That Brick said somethin' he shouldn't of said t' Big Daddy.

BIG MAMA: Now what on earth could Brick of said t' Big Daddy that he shouldn't say?

GOOPER: Big Mama, there's somethin'—

MAE: NOW, WAIT!

> [*She rushes up to* BIG MAMA *and gives her a quick hug and kiss.* BIG MAMA *pushes her impatiently off as the* REVEREND TOOKER'*s voice rises serenely in a little pocket of silence:*]

REVEREND TOOKER: Yes, last Sunday the gold in my chasuble faded into th' purple. . . .

GOOPER: Reveren', you must of been preachin' hell's fire last Sunday!

> [*He guffaws at this witticism but the* REVEREND *is not sincerely amused. At the same time* BIG MAMA *has crossed over to* DR. BAUGH *and is saying to him:*]

BIG MAMA: [*her breathless voice rising high-pitched above the others*]
In my day they had what they call the Keeley cure for heavy drinkers. But now I understand they just take some kind of tablets, they call them "Annie Bust" tablets. But *Brick* don't need to take *nothin'*.

[BRICK *appears in gallery doors with* MARGARET *behind him.*]

BIG MAMA: [*unaware of his presence behind her*] That boy is just broken up over Skipper's death. You know how poor Skipper died. They gave him a big, big dose of that sodium amytal stuff at his home and then they called the ambulance and give him another big, big dose of it at the hospital and that and all of the alcohol in his system fo' months an' months an' months just proved too much for his heart. . . . I'm scared of needles! I'm more scared of a needle than the knife. . . . I think more people have been needled out of this world than—

[*She stops short and wheels about.*]

OH!—here's Brick! My precious baby—

[*She turns upon* BRICK *with short, fat arms extended, at the same time uttering a loud, short sob, which is both comic and touching.*]

[BRICK *smiles and bows slightly, making a burlesque gesture of gallantry for* MAGGIE *to pass before him into the room. Then he hobbles on his crutch directly to the liquor cabinet and there is absolute silence, with everybody looking at* BRICK *as everybody has always looked at* BRICK *when he spoke or moved or appeared. One by one he drops ice cubes in his glass, then suddenly, but not quickly, looks back over his shoulder with a wry, charming smile, and says:*]

BRICK: I'm sorry! Anyone else?

BIG MAMA: [*sadly*] No, son. I *wish* you wouldn't!

BRICK: I wish I didn't have to, Big Mama, but I'm still waiting for that click in my head which makes it all smooth out!

BIG MAMA: Aw, Brick, you—BREAK MY HEART!

MARGARET: [*at the same time*] Brick, go sit with Big Mama!

BIG MAMA: I just cain't *staiiiiiiiii-nnnnnd*—it. . . .

[*She sobs.*]

MAE: Now that we're all assembled—

GOOPER: We kin talk. . . .

BIG MAMA: Breaks my heart. . . .

MARGARET: Sit with Big Mama, Brick, and hold her hand.

[BIG MAMA *sniffs very loudly three times, almost like three drum beats in the pocket of silence.*]

BRICK: You do that, Maggie. I'm a restless cripple. I got to stay on my crutch.

[BRICK *hobbles to the gallery door; leans there as if waiting.* MAE *sits beside* BIG MAMA, *while* GOOPER *moves in front and sits on the end of the couch, facing her.* REVEREND TOOKER *moves nervously into the space between them; on the other side,* DR. BAUGH *stands looking at nothing in particular and lights a cigar.* MARGARET *turns away.*]

BIG MAMA: Why're you all *surroundin'* me—like this? Why're you all starin' at me like this an' makin' signs at each other?

[REVEREND TOOKER *steps back startled.*]

MAE: Calm yourself, Big Mama.

BIG MAMA: Calm you'self, *you'self,* Sister Woman. How could I calm myself with everyone starin' at me as if big drops of blood had broken out on m' face? What's this all about, annh! What?

[GOOPER *coughs and takes a center position.*]

GOOPER: Now, Doc Baugh.

MAE: Doc Baugh?

BRICK: [*suddenly*] SHHH!—
> [*Then he grins and chuckles and shakes his head regretfully.*]
—Naw!—that wasn't th' click.

GOOPER: Brick, shut up or stay out there on the gallery with your liquor! We got to talk about a serious matter. Big Mama wants to know the complete truth about the report we got today from the Ochsner Clinic.

MAE: [*eagerly*]—on Big Daddy's condition!

GOOPER: Yais, on Big Daddy's condition, we got to face it.

DOCTOR BAUGH: Well. . . .

BIG MAMA: [*terrified, rising*] Is there? Something? Something that I? Don't— Know?
> [*In these few words, this startled, very soft, question,* BIG MAMA *reviews the history of her forty-five years with* BIG DADDY, *her great, almost embarrassingly true-hearted and simple-minded devotion to* BIG DADDY, *who must have had something* BRICK *has, who made himself loved so much by the "simple expedient" of not loving enough to disturb his charming detachment, also once coupled, like* BRICK's, *with virile beauty.*]
> [BIG MAMA *has a dignity at this moment: she almost stops being fat.*]

DOCTOR BAUGH: [*after a pause, uncomfortably*] Yes?—Well—

BIG MAMA: *I!!!*—want to—*knowwwwwww.* . . .
> [*Immediately she thrusts her fist to her mouth as if to deny that statement.*]
> [*Then, for some curious reason, she snatches the withered corsage from her breast and hurls it on the floor and steps on it with her short, fat feet.*]
—*Somebody must be lyin'!—I want to know!*

MAE: Sit down, Big Mama, sit down on this sofa.

MARGARET: [*quickly*] Brick, go sit with Big Mama.

BIG MAMA: *What is it, what is it?*

DOCTOR BAUGH: I never have seen a more thorough examination than Big Daddy Pollitt was given in all my experience with the Ochsner Clinic.

GOOPER: It's one of the best in the country.

MAE: It's *THE* best in the country—bar *none!*
> [*For some reason she gives* GOOPER *a violent poke as she goes past him. He slaps at her hand without removing his eyes from his mother's face.*]

DOCTOR BAUGH: Of course, they were ninety-nine and nine-tenths percent sure before they even started.

BIG MAMA: Sure of what, sure of what, sure of—*what?—what!*
> [*She catches her breath in a startled sob.* MAE *kisses her quickly. She thrusts* MAE *fiercely away from her, staring at the doctor.*]

MAE: Mommy, be a brave girl!

BRICK: [*in the doorway, softly*]
> "By the light, by the light,
> Of the sil-ve-ry mo-ooo-n . . ."

GOOPER: Shut up!—Brick.

BRICK: —Sorry. . . .
> [*He wanders out on the gallery.*]

DOCTOR BAUGH: But now, you see, Big Mama, they cut a piece off this growth, a specimen of the tissue and—

BIG MAMA: Growth? You told Big Daddy—

DOCTOR BAUGH: Now wait.

BIG MAMA: [*fiercely*] You told me and Big Daddy there wasn't a thing wrong with him but—

MAE: Big Mama, they always—

GOOPER: Let Doc Baugh talk, will yuh?

BIG MAMA: —little spastic condition of—

[*Her breath gives out in a sob.*]

DOCTOR BAUGH: Yes, that's what we told Big Daddy. But we had this bit of tissue run through the laboratory and I'm sorry to say the test was positive on it. It's—well—malignant. . . .

[*Pause.*]

BIG MAMA: —Cancer?! Cancer?!

[DR. BAUGH *nods gravely.*]

[BIG MAMA *gives a long gasping cry.*]

MAE AND GOOPER: Now, now, now, Big Mama, you had to know. . . .

BIG MAMA: *WHY DIDN'T THEY CUT IT OUT OF HIM? HANH? HANH?*

DOCTOR BAUGH: Involved too much, Big Mama, too many organs affected.

MAE: Big Mama, the liver's affected and so's the kidneys, both! It's gone way past what they call a—

GOOPER: A Surgical risk.

MAE: —Uh-huh. . . .

[BIG MAMA *draws a breath like a dying gasp.*]

REVEREND TOOKER: Tch, tch, tch, tch, tch!

DOCTOR BAUGH: Yes, it's gone past the knife.

MAE: *That's why he's turned yellow, Mommy!*

BIG MAMA: *Git away from me, git away from me, Mae!*

[*She rises abruptly.*]

I want Brick! Where's Brick? Where is my only son?

MAE: Mama! Did she say "*only* son"?

GOOPER: What does that make *me*?

MAE: A sober responsible man with five precious children!—*Six!*

BIG MAMA: I want Brick to tell me! Brick! Brick!

MARGARET: [*rising from her reflections in a corner*] Brick was so upset he went back out.

BIG MAMA: *Brick!*

MARGARET: Mama, let *me* tell you!

BIG MAMA: No, no, leave me alone, you're not my blood!

GOOPER: *Mama, I'm your son!* Listen to *me!*

MAE: Gooper's your son, Mama, he's your first-born!

BIG MAMA: Gooper never liked Daddy.

MAE: [*as if terribly shocked*] *That's not TRUE!*

[*There is a pause. The minister coughs and rises.*]

REVEREND TOOKER: [*to* MAE] I think I'd better slip away at this point.

MAE: [*sweetly and sadly*] Yes, Doctor Tooker, you go.

REVEREND TOOKER: [*discreetly*] Goodnight, goodnight, everybody, and God bless you all . . . on this place. . . .
> [*He slips out.*]

DOCTOR BAUGH: That man is a good man but lacking in tact. Talking about people giving memorial windows—if he mentioned one memorial window, he must have spoke of a dozen, and saying how awful it was when somebody died intestate, the legal wrangles, and so forth.
> [MAE *coughs, and points at* BIG MAMA.]

DOCTOR BAUGH: Well, Big Mama. . . .
> [*He sighs.*]

BIG MAMA: It's all a mistake, I know it's just a bad dream.

DOCTOR BAUGH: We're gonna keep Big Daddy as comfortable as we can.

BIG MAMA: Yes, it's just a bad dream, that's all it is, it's just an awful dream.

GOOPER: In my opinion Big Daddy is having some pain but won't admit that he has it.

BIG MAMA: Just a dream, a bad dream.

DOCTOR BAUGH: That's what lots of them do, they think if they don't admit they're having the pain they can sort of escape the fact of it.

GOOPER: [*with relish*] Yes, they get sly about it, they get real sly about it.

MAE: Gooper and I think—

GOOPER: Shut up, Mae!—Big Daddy ought to be started on morphine.

BIG MAMA: Nobody's going to give Big Daddy morphine.

DOCTOR BAUGH: Now, Big Mama, when that pain strikes it's going to strike mighty hard and Big Daddy's going to need the needle to bear it.

BIG MAMA: I tell you, nobody's going to give him morphine.

MAE: Big Mama, you don't want to see Big Daddy suffer, you know you—
> [GOOPER *standing beside her gives her a savage poke.*]

DOCTOR BAUGH: [*placing a package on the table*] I'm leaving this stuff here, so if there's a sudden attack you all won't have to send out for it.

MAE: I know how to give a hypo.

GOOPER: Mae took a course in nursing during the war.

MARGARET: Somehow I don't think Big Daddy would want Mae to give him a hypo.

MAE: You think he'd want *you* to do it?
> [DR. BAUGH *rises.*]

GOOPER: Doctor Baugh is goin'.

DOCTOR BAUGH: Yes, I got to be goin'. Well, keep your chin up, Big Mama.

GOOPER: [*with jocularity*] She's gonna keep *both* chins up, aren't you, Big Mama?
> [BIG MAMA *sobs.*]

Now stop that, Big Mama.

MAE: Sit down with me, Big Mama.

GOOPER: [*at door with* DR. BAUGH] Well, Doc, we sure do appreciate all you done. I'm telling you, we're surely obligated to you for—
> [DR. BAUGH *has gone out without a glance at him.*]

GOOPER: —I guess that doctor has got a lot on his mind but it wouldn't hurt him to act a little more human. . . .
> [BIG MAMA *sobs.*]

Now be a brave girl, Mommy.

BIG MAMA: It's not true, I know that it's just not true!

GOOPER: Mama, those tests are infallible!

BIG MAMA: Why are you so determined to see your father daid?

MAE: Big Mama!

MARGARET: [*gently*] I know what Big Mama means.

MAE: [*fiercely*] Oh, do you?

MARGARET: [*quietly and very sadly*] Yes, I think I do.

MAE: For a newcomer in the family you sure do show a lot of understanding.

MARGARET: Understanding is needed on this place.

MAE: I guess you must have needed a lot of it in your family, Maggie, with your father's liquor problem and now you've got Brick with his!

MARGARET: Brick does not have a liquor problem at all. Brick is devoted to Big Daddy. This thing is a terrible strain on him.

BIG MAMA: Brick is Big Daddy's boy, but he drinks too much and it worries me and Big Daddy, and, Margaret, you've got to cooperate with us, you've got to cooperate with Big Daddy and me in getting Brick straightened out. Because it will break Big Daddy's heart if Brick don't pull himself together and take hold of things.

MAE: Take hold of *what* things, Big Mama?

BIG MAMA: The place.

[*There is a quick violent look between* MAE *and* GOOPER.]

GOOPER: Big Mama, you've had a shock.

MAE: Yais, we've all had a shock, but . . .

GOOPER: Let's be realistic—

MAE: —Big Daddy would never, would *never*, be foolish enough to—

GOOPER: —put this place in irresponsible hands!

BIG MAMA: Big Daddy ain't going to leave the place in anybody's hands; Big Daddy is *not* going to die. I want you to get that in your heads, all of you!

MAE: Mommy, Mommy, Big Mama, we're just as hopeful an' optimistic as you are about Big Daddy's prospects, we have faith in *prayer*—but nevertheless there are certain matters that have to be discussed an' dealt with, because otherwise—

GOOPER: Eventualities have to be considered and now's the time. . . . Mae, will you please get my briefcase out of our room?

MAE: Yes, honey.

[*She rises and goes out through the hall door.*]

GOOPER: [*standing over* BIG MAMA] Now, Big Mom. What you said just now was not at all true and you know it. I've always loved Big Daddy in my own quiet way. I never made a show of it, and I know that Big Daddy has always been fond of me in a quiet way, too, and he never made a show of it, neither.

[MAE *returns with* GOOPER's *briefcase.*]

MAE: Here's your briefcase, Gooper, honey.

GOOPER: [*handing the briefcase back to her*] Thank you. . . . Of ca'use, my relationship with Big Daddy is different from Brick's.

MAE: You're eight years older'n Brick an' always had t'carry a bigger load of th' responsibilities than Brick ever had t' carry. He never carried a thing in his life but a football or a highball.

GOOPER: Mae, will y' let me talk, please?

MAE: Yes, honey.

GOOPER: Now, a twenty-eight thousand-acre plantation's a mighty big thing t' run.

MAE: Almost singlehanded.

> [MARGARET *has gone out onto the gallery, and can be heard calling softly* BRICK.]

BIG MAMA: You never had to run this place! What are you talking about? As if Big Daddy was dead and in his grave, you had to run it? Why, you just helped him out with a few business details and had your law practice at the same time in Memphis!

MAE: Oh, Mommy, Mommy, Big Mommy! Let's be fair! Why, Gooper has given himself body and soul to keeping this place up for the past five years since Big Daddy's health started failing. Gooper won't say it, Gooper never thought of it as a duty, he just did it. And what did Brick do? Brick kept living in his past glory at college! Still a football player at twenty-seven!

MARGARET: [*returning alone*] Who are you talking about, now? Brick? A football player? He isn't a football player and you know it. Brick is a sports announcer on TV and one of the best-known ones in the country!

MAE: I'm talking about what he was.

MARGARET: Well, I wish you would just stop talking about my husband.

GOOPER: I've got a right to discuss my brother with other members of MY OWN family which don't include *you*. Why don't you go out there and drink with Brick?

MARGARET: I've never seen such malice toward a brother.

GOOPER: How about his for me? Why, he can't stand to be in the same room with me!

MARGARET: This is a deliberate campaign of vilification for the most disgusting and sordid reason on earth, and I know what it is! It's *avarice, avarice, greed, greed!*

BIG MAMA: *Oh, I'll scream! I will scream in a moment unless this stops!*

> [GOOPER *has stalked up to* MARGARET *with clenched fists at his sides as if he would strike her.* MAE *distorts her face again into a hideous grimace behind* MARGARET's *back.*]

MARGARET: We only remain on the place because of Big Mom and Big Daddy. If it is true what they say about Big Daddy we are going to leave here just as soon as it's over. Not a moment later.

BIG MAMA: [*sobs*] Margaret. Child. Come here. Sit next to Big Mama.

MARGARET: Precious Mommy. I'm sorry, I'm so sorry, I—!

> [*She bends her long graceful neck to press her forehead to* BIG MAMA's *bulging shoulder under its black chiffon.*]

GOOPER: How beautiful, how touching, this display of devotion!

MAE: Do you know why she's childless? She's childless because that big beautiful athlete husband of hers won't go to bed with her!

GOOPER: You jest won't let me do this in a nice way, will yah? Aw right—Mae and I have five kids with another one coming! I don't give a goddam if Big Daddy likes me or don't like me or did or never did or will or will never! I'm just appealing to a sense of common decency and fair play. I'll tell you the truth. I've resented Big Daddy's partiality to Brick ever since Brick was born, and the way I've been treated like I was just barely good enough to spit on and sometimes not even good enough for that. Big Daddy is dying of cancer, and it's spread all through him and it's attacked all his vital organs including the kidneys and right now he is sinking into uremia, and you all know what uremia is, it's poisoning of the whole system due to the failure of the body to eliminate its poisons.

MARGARET: [*to herself, downstage, hissingly*] Poisons, poisons! Venomous thoughts and words! In hearts and minds!—That's poisons!

GOOPER: [*overlapping her*] I am asking for a square deal, and I expect to get one. But if I don't get one, if there's any peculiar shenanigans going on around here behind my back, or before me, well, I'm not a corporation lawyer for nothing, I know how to protect my own interests.—*OH! A late arrival!*

[BRICK *enters from the gallery with a tranquil, blurred smile, carrying an empty glass with him.*]

MAE: Behold the conquering hero comes!

GOOPER: The fabulous Brick Pollitt! Remember him?—Who could forget him!

MAE: He looks like he's been injured in a game!

GOOPER: Yep, I'm afraid you'll have to warm the bench at the Sugar Bowl this year, Brick!

[MAE *laughs shrilly.*]

Or was it the Rose Bowl that he made that famous run in?

MAE: The punch bowl, honey. It was in the punch bowl, the cut-glass punch bowl!

GOOPER: Oh, that's right, I'm getting the bowls mixed up!

MARGARET: Why don't you stop venting your malice and envy on a sick boy?

BIG MAMA: *Now you two hush, I mean it, hush, all of you, hush!*

GOOPER: All right, Big Mama. A family crisis brings out the best and the worst in every member of it.

MAE: *That's* the truth.

MARGARET: *Amen!*

BIG MAMA: *I said, "hush!"* I won't tolerate any more catty talk in my house.

[MAE *gives* GOOPER *a sign indicating briefcase.*]

[BRICK's *smile has grown both brighter and vaguer. As he prepares a drink, he sings softly:*]

BRICK: Show me the way to go home,
  I'm tired and I wanta go to bed,
  I had a little drink about an hour ago—

GOOPER: [*at the same time*] Big Mama, you know it's necessary for me t' go back to Memphis in th' mornin' t' represent the Parker estate in a lawsuit.

[MAE *sits on the bed and arranges papers she has taken from the briefcase.*]

BRICK: [*continuing the song*]

  Wherever I may roam,
  On land or sea or foam.

BIG MAMA: Is it, Gooper?

MAE: Yaiss.

GOOPER: That's why I'm forced to—to bring up a problem that—

MAE: Somethin' that's too important t' be put off!

GOOPER: If Brick was sober, he ought to be in on this.

MARGARET: Brick is present; we're here.

GOOPER: Well, good. I will now give you this outline my partner, Tom Bullitt, an' me have drawn up—a sort of dummy—trusteeship.

MARGARET: Oh, that's it! You'll be in charge an' dole out remittances, will you?

GOOPER: This we did as soon as we got the report on Big Daddy from th' Ochsner Laboratories. We did this thing, I mean we drew up this dummy outline with the advice and assistance of the Chairman of the Boa'd of Directors of th' Southern Plantahs Bank and Trust Company in Memphis, C. C. Bellowes, a man who handles estates for all th' prominent fam'lies in West Tennessee and th' Delta.

BIG MAMA: Gooper?

GOOPER: [crouching in front of BIG MAMA] Now this is not—not final, or anything like it. This is just a preliminary outline. But it does provide a basis—a design—a—possible, feasible—plan!

MARGARET: Yes, I'll bet.

MAE: It's a plan to protect the biggest estate in the Delta from irresponsibility an'—

BIG MAMA: Now you listen to me, all of you, you listen here! They's not goin' to be any more catty talk in my house! And Gooper, you put that away before I grab it out of your hand and tear it right up! I don't know what the hell's in it, and I don't want to know what the hell's in it. I'm talkin' in Big Daddy's language now; I'm his *wife*, not his *widow*, I'm still his *wife*! And I'm talkin' to you in his language an'—

GOOPER: Big Mama, what I have here is—

MAE: Gooper explained that it's just a plan. . . .

BIG MAMA: I don't care what you got there. Just put it back where it came from, an' don't let me see it again, not even the outside of the envelope of it! Is that understood? Basis! Plan! Preliminary! Design! I say—what is it Big Daddy always says when he's disgusted?

BRICK: [*from the bar*] Big Daddy says "crap" when he's disgusted.

BIG MAMA: [*rising*] That's right—*CRAP!* I say *CRAP*, too, like Big Daddy!

MAE: Coarse language doesn't seem called for in this—

GOOPER: Somethin' in me is *deeply outraged* by hearin' you talk like this.

BIG MAMA: *Nobody's goin' to take nothin'!*—till Big Daddy lets go of it, and maybe, just possibly, not—not even then! No, not even then!

BRICK: You can always hear me singin' this song,
                                        Show me the way to go home.

BIG MAMA: Tonight Brick looks like he used to look when he was a little boy, just like he did when he played wild games and used to come home all sweaty and pink-cheeked and sleepy, with his—red curls shining. . . .

[*She comes over to him and runs her fat shaky hand through his hair. He draws aside as he does from all physical contact and continues the song in a whisper, opening the ice bucket and dropping in the ice cubes one by one as if he were mixing some important chemical formula.*]

BIG MAMA: [*continuing*] Time goes by so fast. Nothin' can outrun it. Death commences too early—almost before you're half acquainted with life—you meet with the other. . . .

Oh, you know we just got to love each other an' stay together, all of us, just as close as we can, especially now that such a *black* thing has come and moved into this place without invitation.

[*Awkwardly embracing* BRICK, *she presses her head to his shoulder.*]

[GOOPER *has been returning papers to* MAE, *who has restored them to brief-case with an air of severely tried patience.*]

GOOPER: Big Mama? Big Mama?

[*He stands behind her, tense with sibling envy.*]

BIG MAMA: [*oblivious of* GOOPER] Brick, you hear me, don't you?

MARGARET: Brick hears you, Big Mama, he understands what you're saying.

BIG MAMA: Oh, Brick, son of Big Daddy! Big Daddy does so love you! Y'know what would be his fondest dream come true? If before he passed on, if Big Daddy has to pass on, you gave him a child of yours, a grandson as much like his son as his son is like Big Daddy!

MAE: [*zipping briefcase shut: an incongruous sound*] Such a pity that Maggie an' Brick can't oblige!

MARGARET: [*suddenly and quietly but forcefully*] Everybody listen.

[*She crosses to the center of the room, holding her hands rigidly together.*]

MAE: Listen to what, Maggie?

MARGARET: I have an announcement to make.

GOOPER: A sports announcement, Maggie?

MARGARET: Brick and I are going to—*have a child!*

[BIG MAMA *catches her breath in a loud gasp.*]

[*Pause.* BIG MAMA *rises.*]

BIG MAMA: Maggie! Brick! This is too good to believe!

MAE: That's right, too good to believe.

BIG MAMA: Oh, my, my! This is Big Daddy's dream, his dream come true! I'm going to tell him right now before he—

MARGARET: We'll tell him in the morning. Don't disturb him now.

BIG MAMA: I want to tell him before he goes to sleep, I'm going to tell him his dream's come true this minute! And Brick! A child will make you pull your-self together and quit this drinking!

[*She seizes the glass from his hand.*]

The responsibilities of a father will—

[*Her face contorts and she makes an excited gesture; bursting into sobs, she rushes out, crying.*]

I'm going to tell Big Daddy right this minute!

[*Her voice fades out down the hall.*]

[BRICK *shrugs slightly and drops an ice cube into another glass.* MARGARET *crosses quickly to his side, saying something under her breath, and she pours the liquor for him, staring up almost fiercely into his face.*]

BRICK: [*coolly*] Thank you, Maggie, that's a nice big shot.

[MAE *has joined* GOOPER *and she gives him a fierce poke, making a low hissing sound and a grimace of fury.*]

GOOPER: [*pushing her aside*] Brick, could you possibly spare me one small shot of that liquor?

BRICK: Why, help yourself, Gooper boy.

GOOPER: I will.

MAE: [*shrilly*] Of course we know that this is—
GOOPER: *Be still, Mae!*
MAE: I won't be still! I know she's made this up!
GOOPER: Goddam it, I said to shut up!
MARGARET: Gracious! I didn't know that my little announcement was going to provoke such a storm!
MAE: *That* woman isn't *pregnant!*
GOOPER: Who said she was?
MAE: *She* did.
GOOPER: The doctor didn't. Doc Baugh didn't.
MARGARET: I haven't gone to Doc Baugh.
GOOPER: Then who'd you go to, Maggie?
MARGARET: One of the best gynecologists in the South.
GOOPER: Uh huh, uh huh!—I see. . . .
       [*He takes out pencil and notebook.*]
       —May we have his name, please?
MARGARET: No, you may not, Mister Prosecuting Attorney!
MAE: He doesn't have any name, he doesn't exist!
MARGARET: Oh, he exists all right, and so does my child, Brick's baby!
MAE: You can't conceive a child by a man that won't sleep with you unless you think you're—
       [BRICK *has turned on the phonograph. A scat song cuts* MAE's *speech.*]
GOOPER: *Turn that off!*
MAE: We know it's a lie because we hear you in here; he won't sleep with you, we hear you! So don't imagine you're going to put a trick over on us, to fool a dying man with a—
       [*A long drawn cry of agony and rage fills the house.* MARGARET *turns phonograph down to a whisper.*]
       [*The cry is repeated.*]
MAE: [*awed*] Did you hear that, Gooper, did you hear that?
GOOPER: Sounds like the pain has struck.
MAE: Go see, Gooper!
GOOPER: Come along and leave these lovebirds together in their nest!
       [*He goes out first.* MAE *follows but turns at the door, contorting her face and hissing at* MARGARET.]
MAE: *Liar!*
       [*She slams the door.*]
       [MARGARET *exhales with relief and moves a little unsteadily to catch hold of* BRICK's *arm.*]
MARGARET: Thank you for—keeping still. . . .
BRICK: Okay, Maggie.
MARGARET: It was gallant of you to save my face!
BRICK: —It hasn't happened yet.
MARGARET: What?
BRICK: The click. . . .
MARGARET: —the click in your head that makes you peaceful, honey?
BRICK: Uh-huh. It hasn't happened. . . . I've got to make it happen before I can sleep. . . .

MARGARET: —I—know what you—mean. . . .

BRICK: Give me that pillow in the big chair, Maggie.

MARGARET: I'll put it on the bed for you.

BRICK: No, put it on the sofa, where I sleep.

MARGARET: Not tonight, Brick.

BRICK: I want it on the sofa. That's where I sleep.

> [*He has hobbled to the liquor cabinet. He now pours down three shots in quick succession and stands waiting, silent. All at once he turns with a smile and says:*]

> *There!*

MARGARET: What?

BRICK: The *click*. . . .

> [*His gratitude seems almost infinite as he hobbles out on the gallery with a drink. We hear his crutch as he swings out of sight. Then, at some distance, he begins singing to himself a peaceful song.*]

> [MARGARET *holds the big pillow forlornly as if it were her only companion, for a few moments, then throws it on the bed. She rushes to the liquor cabinet, gathers all the bottles in her arms, turns about undecidedly, then runs out of the room with them, leaving the door ajar on the dim yellow hall.* BRICK *is heard hobbling back along the gallery, singing his peaceful song. He comes back in, sees the pillow on the bed, laughs lightly, sadly, picks it up. He has it under his arm as* MARGARET *returns to the room.* MARGARET *softly shuts the door and leans against it, smiling softly at* BRICK.]

MARGARET: Brick, I used to think that you were stronger than me and I didn't want to be overpowered by you. But now, since you've taken to liquor—you know what?—I guess it's bad, but now I'm stronger than you and I can love you more truly!

> Don't move that pillow. I'll move it right back if you do!

> —Brick?

> [*She turns out all the lamps but a single rose-silk-shaded one by the bed.*]

> I really have been to a doctor and I know what to do and—Brick?— this is my time by the calendar to conceive!

BRICK: Yes, I understand, Maggie. But how are you going to conceive a child by a man in love with his liquor?

MARGARET: By locking his liquor up and making him satisfy my desire before I unlock it!

BRICK: Is that what you've done, Maggie?

MARGARET: Look and see. That cabinet's mighty empty compared to before!

BRICK: Well, I'll be a son of a—

> [*He reaches for his crutch but she beats him to it and rushes out on the gallery, hurls the crutch over the rail and comes back in, panting.*]

> [*There are running footsteps.* BIG MAMA *bursts into the room, her face all awry, gasping, stammering.*]

BIG MAMA: Oh, my God, oh, my God, oh, my God, where is it?

MARGARET: Is this what you want, Big Mama?

> [MARGARET *hands her the package left by the doctor.*]

BIG MAMA: I can't bear it, oh, God! Oh, Brick! Brick, baby!

[_She rushes at him. He averts his face from her sobbing kisses._ MARGARET _watches with a tight smile._]

My son, Big Daddy's boy! Little Father!

[_The groaning cry is heard again. She runs out, sobbing._]

MARGARET: And so tonight we're going to make the lie true, and when that's done, I'll bring the liquor back here and we'll get drunk together, here, tonight, in this place that death has come into. . . .

—What do you say?

BRICK: I don't say anything. I guess there's nothing to say.

MARGARET: Oh, you weak people, you weak, beautiful people!—who give up.—What you want is someone to—

[_She turns out the rose-silk lamp._]

—take hold of you.—Gently, gently, with love! And—

[_The curtain begins to fall slowly._]

I _do_ love you, Brick, I _do!_

BRICK: [_smiling with charming sadness_] Wouldn't it be funny if that was true?

THE CURTAIN COMES DOWN

THE END

Samuel Beckett (1906–1989)

Happy Days (1961)

Several postwar dramatists (among them Samuel Beckett, Eugene Ionesco, and Jean Genet) were dubbed "absurdists" by Martin Esslin because their work conveyed "the sense that the certitudes and unshakable basic assumptions of former ages have been swept away, that they have been . . . discredited as cheap and somewhat childish illusions." Or, as Ionesco put it, "cut off from his religious, metaphysical, and transcendental roots, man is lost; all his actions become senseless, absurd and useless." Most absurdist plays, rather than telling a story, explore this human condition, in which characters seek to insulate themselves against the void by indulging in meaningless activities or abortive attempts at communication.

Beckett's *Happy Days* embodies most of the traits of absurdism. It has virtually abandoned action. The first act shows a woman, Winnie, trapped up to her waist in a mound of earth. She does not struggle against her physical entrapment but fills her days with a routine built around objects she keeps in a shopping bag; she speaks often to her husband, who for the most part remains unseen behind the mound and who responds only rarely. In the second act, Winnie is buried up to her neck and able to move only her eyes and mouth; at first she is not even sure that her husband is still alive, but eventually he crawls up the mound into her view. Despite her situation, Winnie remains determinedly cheerful; she speaks often of her blessings and the small things that will make this "another happy day." She never questions why she is in this situation, nor does she wonder at her isolation. She apparently accepts her lot as no more to be questioned than existence itself.

As in others of his plays, in *Happy Days* Beckett uses visual imagery to sum up his vision of the human condition. He shows human beings trapped in a symbolic landscape, cut off from all but the most minimal contact, passing time as best they can while waiting doggedly or hoping desperately for something that will give meaning to the moment or to life itself. Occasionally they reveal flashes of anxiety, but they quickly divert themselves with games, memories, and speculations. The plays explore a state of being rather than show a developing action.

Samuel Beckett

Happy Days

CHARACTERS

WINNIE, *a woman about fifty*
WILLIE, *a man about sixty*

ACT I

Expanse of scorched grass rising centre to low mound. Gentle slopes down to front and either side of stage. Back an abrupter fall to stage level. Maximum of simplicity and symmetry.
Blazing light.
Very pompier trompe-l'oeil backcloth to represent unbroken plain and sky receding to meet in far distance.
Embedded up to above her waist in exact centre of mound, WINNIE. *About fifty, well preserved, blond for preference, plump, arms and shoulders bare, low bodice, big bosom, pearl necklet. She is discovered sleeping, her arms on the ground before her, her head, on her arms. Beside her on ground to her left a capacious black bag, shopping variety and to her right a collapsible collapsed parasol, beak of handle emerging from sheath.*
To her right and rear, lying asleep on ground, hidden by mound, WILLIE.
Long pause. A bell rings piercingly, say ten seconds, stops. She does not move. Pause. Bell more piercingly, say five seconds. She wakes. Bell stops. She raises her head, gazes front. Long pause. She straightens up, lays her hands flat on ground, throws back her head and gazes at zenith. Long pause.

WINNIE: [*gazing at zenith*] Another heavenly day. [*Pause. Head back level, eyes front, pause. She clasps hands to breast, closes eyes. Lips move in unaudible prayer, say ten seconds. Lips still. Hands remain clasped. Low.*] For Jesus Christ sake Amen. [*Eyes open, hands unclasp, return to mound. Pause. She clasps hands to breast again, closes eyes, lips move again in inaudible addendum, say five seconds. Low.*] World without end Amen. [*Eyes open, hands unclasp, return to mound. Pause.*] Begin, Winnie. [*pause*] Begin your day, Winnie. [*Pause. She turns to bag, rummages in it without moving it from its place, brings out toothbrush, rummages again, brings out flat tube of toothpaste, turns back front, unscrews cap of tube, lays cap on ground, squeezes with difficulty small blob of paste on brush, holds tube in one hand and brushes teeth with other. She turns modestly aside and back to her right to spit out behind mound. In this position her eyes rest on* WILLIE. *She spits out. She cranes a little further back and down. Loud.*] Hoo-oo! [*Pause. Louder.*] Hoo-oo! [*Pause. Tender smile as she turns back front, lays down brush.*] Poor Willie—[*examines tube, smile off*]—running out—[*looks for cap*]—ah well—[*finds cap*]—can't be helped—[*screws on cap*]—just one of those old things—[*lays down tube*]—another of those old things—[*turns towards bag*]—just can't be cured—[*rummages in bag*]—cannot be cured—[*brings out small mirror, turns back front*]—ah yes—[*inspects teeth in mirror*]—poor dear Willie—[*testing upper front teeth with thumb, indistinctly*]—good Lord!—[*pulling back upper lip to inspect gums, do.*]—good God!—[*pulling back corner of mouth, mouth open, do.*]—ah well—[*other corner, do.*]—no worse—[*abandons inspection, normal speech*]—no better, no worse—[*lays down mirror*]—no change—[*wipes fingers on grass*]—no pain—[*looks for toothbrush*]—hardly any—[*takes up toothbrush*]—great thing that—[*examines handle of brush*]—nothing like it—[*examines handle, reads*]—pure . . . what?—[*pause*]—what?—[*lays down brush*]—ah yes—[*turns toward bag*]—poor Willie—[*rummages in bag*]—no zest—[*rummages*]—for anything—[*brings out spectacles in case*]—no interest—[*turns back front*]—in life—[*takes spectacles from case*]—poor dear Willie—[*lays down case*]—sleep for ever—[*opens spectacles*]—marvellous gift—[*puts on spectacles*]—nothing to touch it—[*looks for toothbrush*]—in my opinion—[*takes up toothbrush*]—always said so—[*examines handle of brush*]—wish I had it—[*examines handle, reads*]—genuine . . . pure . . . what?—[*lays down brush*]—blind next—[*takes off spectacles*]—ah well—[*lays down spectacles*]—seen enough—[*feels in bodice for handkerchief*]—I suppose—[*takes out folded handkerchief*]—by now—[*shakes out handkerchief*]—what are those wonderful lines—[*wipes one eye*]—woe woe is me—[*wipes the other*]—to see what I see—[*looks for spectacles*]—ah yes—[*takes up spectacles*]—wouldn't miss it—[*starts polishing spectacles, breathing on lenses*]—or would I?—[*polishes*]—holy light—[*polishes*]—bob up out of dark—[*polishes*]—blaze of hellish light. [*stops polishing, raises face to sky, pause, head back level, resumes polishing, stops polishing, cranes back to her right and down*] Hoo-oo! [*Pause. Tender smile as she turns back front and resumes polishing. Smile off.*] Marvelous gift—[*stops polishing, lays down spectacles*]—wish I had it—[*folds handkerchief*]—ah well—[*puts handkerchief back in bodice*]—can't complain—[*looks for spectacles*]—no no—[*takes up spectacles*]—mustn't complain—[*holds up spectacles, looks through lens*]—so much to be thankful for—[*looks through other lens*]—no pain—[*puts on spectacles*]—hardly any—[*looks for toothbrush*]—wonderful thing that—[*takes up toothbrush*]—nothing like it [*examines handle of brush*]—slight headache sometimes—[*examines handle, reads*]—guaranteed . . . genuine . . . pure . . . what?—[*looks closer*]—genuine pure . . . —[*takes handkerchief from bodice*]—ah yes—[*shakes out handkerchief*]—occasional mild migraine—[*starts wiping handle of brush*]—it comes—[*wipes*]—then goes—[*wiping mechanically*]—ah yes—[*wiping*]—many mercies—[*wiping*]—great mercies—[*stops wiping, fixed lost gaze, brokenly*]—prayers perhaps not for naught—[*Pause. Do.*]—first thing—[*Pause. Do.*]—last thing—[*head down, resumes wiping, stops wiping, head up, calmed, wipes eyes, folds handkerchief, puts it back in bodice, examines handle of brush, reads*]—fully guaranteed . . . genuine pure . . . —[*looks closer*]—genuine pure . . . [*takes off spectacles, lays them and brush down, gazes before her*] Old things. [*pause*] Old eyes. [*long pause*] On, Winnie. [*She casts about her, sees parasol, considers it at length, takes it up, and* develops from sheath a handle of surprising length. Holding butt of parasol in right hand she cranes back and down to her right to hand over WILLIE.] Hoo-oo! [*pause*] Willie! [*pause*] Wonderful gift. [*She strikes down at him with beak of parasol.*] Wish I had it. [*She strikes again. The parasol slips from her grasp and falls behind mound. It is immediately restored to her by* WILLIE's *invisible hand.*] Thank you, dear. [*She transfers parasol to left hand, turns back front and examines right palm.*] Damp. [*returns parasol to right hand, examines left palm*] Ah well, no worse. [*head up, cheerfully*] No better, no worse, no change. [*Pause. Do.*] No pain. [*cranes back to look down at* WILLIE, *holding parasol by butt as before*] Don't go off on me again now, dear, will you please, I may need you. [*pause*] No hurry, no hurry, just don't curl up on me again. [*turns back front, lays down parasol, examines palms together, wipes them on grass*] Perhaps a shade off colour just the same. [*turns to bag, rummages in it, brings out revolver, holds it up, kisses it rapidly, puts it back, rummages, brings out almost-empty bottle of red medicine, turns back front, looks for spectacles, puts them on, reads label*] Loss of spirits . . . lack of keenness . . . want of appetite . . . infants . . . children . . . adults . . . six level . . . tablespoonfuls daily—[*head up, smile*]—the old style!—[*smile off, head down, reads*]—daily . . . before and after . . . meals . . . instantaneous . . . [*looks closer*] improvement. [*Takes off spectacles, lays them down, holds up bottle at arm's length to see level, unscrews cap, swigs it off head well back, tosses cap and bottle away in* WILLIE's *direction. Sound of breaking glass.*] Ah that's better! [*turns to bag, rummages in it, brings out lipstick, turns back front, examines lipstick*] Running out. [*looks for spectacles*] Ah well. [*puts on spectacles, looks for mirror*] Musn't complain. [*takes up mirror, starts doing lips*] What is that wonderful line? [*lips*] Oh fleeting joys—[*lips*]—oh something lasting woe. [*Lips. She is interrupted by disturbance from* WILLIE. *He is sitting up. She lowers lipstick and mirror and cranes back and down to look at him. Pause. Top back of* WILLIE's *bald head, trickling blood, rises to view above slope, comes to rest.* WINNIE *pushes up her spectacles. Pause. His hand appears with handkerchief, spreads it on skull, disappears. Pause. The hand appears with boater, club ribbon, settles it on head, rakish angle, disappears. Pause.* WINNIE *cranes a little further back and down.*] Slip on your drawers, dear, before you get singed. [*pause*] No? [*pause*] Oh I see, you still have some of that stuff left. [*pause*] Work it well in, dear. [*pause*] Now the other. [*Pause. She turns back front, gazes before her. Happy expression.*] Oh this is going to be another happy day! [*Pause. Happy expression off. She pulls down spectacles and resumes lips.* WILLIE *opens newspaper, hands invisible. Tops of yellow sheets appear on either side of his head.* WINNIE *finishes lips, inspects them in mirror held a little further away.*] Ensign crimson. [WILLIE *turns page.* WINNIE *lays down lipstick and mirror, turns towards bag.*] Pale flag.

    [WILLIE *turns page.* WINNIE *rummages in bag, brings out small ornate brimless hat with crumpled feather, turns back front, straightens hat, smooths feather, raises it towards head, arrests gesture as* WILLIE *reads.*]

WILLIE: His Grace and Most Reverend Father in God Dr. Carolus Hunter dead in tub.

    [*pause*]

WINNIE: [*gazing front, hat in hand, tone of fervent reminiscence*] Charlie Hunter! [*pause*] I close my eyes—[*She takes off spectacles and does so, hat in one hand, spectacles in other.* WILLIE *turns page.*]—and am sitting on his knees again, in the back garden at Borough Green, under the horse-beech. [*Pause. She opens eyes, puts on spectacles, fiddles with hat.*] Oh the happy memories!

[*Pause. She raises hat towards head, arrests gesture as* WILLIE *reads.*]

WILLIE: Opening for smart youth.

[*Pause. She raises hat towards head, arrests gesture, takes off spectacles, gazes front, hat in one hand, spectacles in other.*]

WINNIE: My first ball! [*long pause*] My second ball! [*Long pause. Closes eyes.*] My first kiss! [*Pause.* WILLIE *turns page.* WINNIE *opens eyes.*] A Mr. Johnson, or Johnston, or perhaps I should say John*stone*. Very bushy moustache, very tawny. [*reverently*] Almost ginger! [*pause*] Within a toolshed, though whose I cannot conceive. We had no toolshed and he most certainly had no toolshed. [*closes eyes*] I see the piles of pots. [*pause*] The tangles of bast. [*pause*] The shadows deepening among the rafters.

[*Pause. She opens eyes, puts on spectacles, raises hat towards head, arrests gesture as* WILLIE *reads.*]

WILLIE: Wanted bright boy.

[*Pause.* WINNIE *puts on hat hurriedly, looks for mirror.* WILLIE *turns page.* WINNIE *takes up mirror, inspects hat, lays down mirror, turns towards bag. Paper disappears.* WINNIE *rummages in bag, brings out magnifying glass, turns back front, looks for toothbrush. Paper reappears, folded, and begins to fan* WILLIE'S *face, hand invisible.* WINNIE *takes up toothbrush and examines handle through glass.*]

WINNIE: Fully guaranteed . . . [WILLIE *stops fanning.*] . . . genuine pure . . . [*Pause.* WILLIE *resumes fanning.* WINNIE *looks closer, reads.*] Fully guaranteed . . . [WILLIE *stops fanning.*] . . . genuine pure . . . [*Pause.* WILLIE *resumes fanning.* WINNIE *lays down glass and brush, takes handkerchief from bodice, takes off and polishes spectacles, puts on spectacles, looks for glass, takes up and polishes glass, lays down glass, looks for brush, takes up brush and wipes handle, lays down brush, puts handkerchief back in bodice, looks for glass, takes up glass, looks for brush, takes up brush and examines handle through glass.*] Fully guaranteed . . . [WILLIE *stops fanning.*] . . . genuine pure . . . [*Pause.* WILLIE *resumes fanning.*] . . . hog's [WILLIE *stops fanning. Pause.*] . . . setae. [*Pause.* WINNIE *lays down glass and brush. Paper disappears.* WINNIE *takes off spectacles, lays them down, gazes front.*] Hog's setae. [*pause*] That is what I find so wonderful, that not a day goes by—[*smile*]—to speak in the old style—[*smile off*]—hardly a day, without some addition to one's knowledge however trifling, the addition I mean, provided one takes the pains. [WILLIE'S *hand reappears with a postcard which he examines close to eyes.*] And if for some strange reason no further pains are possible, why then just close the eyes—[*She does so.*]—and wait for the day to come—[*opens eyes*]—the happy day to come when flesh melts at so many degrees and the night of the moon has so many hundred hours. [*pause*] That is what I find so comforting when I lose heart and envy the brute beast. [*turning towards* WILLIE] I hope you are taking in—[*She sees postcard, bends lower.*] What is that you have there,

Willie, may I see? [*She reaches down with hand and* WILLIE *hands her card.
The hairy forearm appears above slope, raised in gesture of giving, the hand open
to take back, and remains in this position till card is returned.* WINNIE *turns back
front and examines card.*] Heavens, what are they up to! [*She looks for spectacles, puts them on and examines card.*] No *but this is just* genuine pure filth!
[*examines card*] Make any nice-minded person want to vomit! [*Impatience
of* WILLIE'S *fingers. She looks for glass, takes it up and examines card through
glass. Long pause.*] What does the creature in the background think he's doing? [*looks closer*] Oh no really! [*Impatience of fingers. Last long look. She lays
down glass, takes edge of card between right forefinger and thumb, averts head,
takes nose between left forefinger and thumb.*] Pah! [*drops card*] Take it away!
[WILLIE'S *arm disappears. His hand reappears immediately, holding card.*
WINNIE *takes off spectacles, lays them down, gazes before her. During what follows* WILLIE *continues to relish card, varying angles and distance from his eyes.*]
Hog's setae. [*puzzled expression*] What exactly is a hog? [*Pause. Do.*] A sow,
of course, I know, but a hog . . . [*puzzled expression off*] Oh well what does
it matter, that is what I always say, it will come back, that is what I find so
wonderful, all comes back. [*pause*] All? [*pause*] No, not all. [*smile*] No no.
[*smile off*] Not quite. [*pause*] A part. [*pause*] Floats up, one fine day, out of
the blue. [*pause*] That is what I find so wonderful. [*Pause. She turns towards
bag. Hand and card disappear. She makes to rummage in bag, arrests gesture.*]
No. [*She turns back front. Smile.*] No no. [*smile off*] Gently Winnie. [*She
gazes front.* WILLIE'S *hand reappears, takes off hat, disappears with hat.*] What
then? [*Hand reappears, takes handkerchief from skull, disappears with handkerchief. Sharply, as to one not paying attention.*] Winnie! [WILLIE *bows head out
of sight.*] What is the alternative? [*pause*] What *is* the al—[WILLIE *blows
nose loud and long, head and hands invisible. She turns to look at him. Pause.
Head reappears. Pause. Hand reappears with handkerchief, spreads it on skull,
disappears. Pause. Hand reappears with boater, settles it on head, rakish angle,
disappears. Pause.*] Would I had let you sleep on. [*She turns back front. Intermittent plucking at grass, head up and down, to animate following.*] Ah yes, if
only I could bear to be alone, I mean prattle away with not a soul to hear.
[*pause*] Not that I flatter myself you hear much, no Willie, God forbid.
[*pause*] Days perhaps when you hear nothing. [*pause*] But days, too, when
you answer. [*pause*] So that I may say at all times, even when you do not
answer and perhaps hear nothing, something of this is being heard, I am
not merely talking to myself, that is in the wilderness, a thing I could never
bear to do—for any length of time. [*pause*] That is what enables me to go
on, go on talking, that is. [*pause*] Whereas if you were to die—[*smile*]—to
speak in the old style—[*smile off*]—or go away and leave me, then what
would I do, what *could* I do, all day long, I mean between the bell for waking and the bell for sleep? [*pause*] Simply gaze before me with compressed
lips. [*Long pause while she does so. No more plucking.*] Not another word as
long as I drew breath, nothing to break the silence of this place. [*pause*]
Save possibly, now and then, every now and then, a sigh into my looking
glass. [*pause*] Or a brief . . . gale of laughter, should I happen to see the old
joke again. [*Pause. Smile appears, broadens and seems about to culminate in
laugh when suddenly replaced by expression of anxiety.*] My hair! [*pause*] Did

I brush and comb my hair? [*pause*] I may have done. [*pause*] Normally I do. [*pause*] There is so little one *can* do. [*pause*] One does it all. [*pause*] All one can. [*pause*] 'Tis only human. [*pause*] Human nature. [*She begins to inspect mound, looks up.*] Human weakness. [*She resumes inspection of mound, looks up.*] Natural weakness. [*She resumes inspection of mound.*] I see no comb. [*inspects*] Nor any hairbrush. [*Looks up. Puzzled expression. She turns to bag, rummages in it.*] The comb is here. [*Back front. Puzzled expression.*] Perhaps I put them back after use. [*Pause. Do.*] But normally I do not put things back, after use, no, I leave them lying about and put them back all together, at the end of the day. [*smile*] To speak in the old style. [*pause*] The sweet old style. [*smile off*] And yet . . . I seem . . . to remember . . . [*suddenly careless*] Oh well, what does it matter, that is what I always say, I shall simply brush and comb them later on, purely and simply, I have the whole—[*Pause. Puzzled.*] Them? [*pause*] Or it? [*pause*] Brush and comb it? [*pause*] Sounds improper somehow. [*Pause. Turning a little towards* WILLIE.] What would you say, Willie? [*Pause. Turning a little further.*] What would you say, Willie, speaking of your hair, them or it? [*pause*] The hair on your head, I mean. [*Pause. Turning a little further.*] The hair on your head, Willie, what would you say speaking of the hair on your head, them or it?

[*long pause*]

WILLIE: It.

WINNIE: [*turning back front, joyfully*] Oh you are going to talk to me today, this is going to be a happy day! [*Pause. Joy off.*] Another happy day. [*pause*] Ah well, where was I, my hair, yes, later on, I shall be thankful for it later on. [*pause*] I have my—[*raises hand to hat*]—yes, on, my hat on—[*lowers hands*]—I cannot take it off now. [*pause*] To think there are times one cannot take off one's hat, not if one's life were at stake. Times one cannot put it on, times one cannot take it off. [*pause*] How often I have said, Put on your hat now, Winnie, there is nothing else for it, take off your hat now, Winnie, like a good girl, it will do you good, and did not. [*pause*] Could not. [*Pause. She raises hand, frees a strand of hair from under hat, draws it towards eye, squints at it, lets it go, hand down.*] Golden you called it, that day, when the last guest was gone—[*hand up in gesture of raising a glass*]—to your golden . . . may it never . . . [*voice breaks*] . . . may it never . . . [*Hand down. Head down. Pause. Low.*] That day. [*Pause. Do.*] What day? [*Pause. Head up. Normal voice.*] What now? [*pause*] Words fail, there are times when even they fail. [*turning a little towards* WILLIE] Is that not so, Willie? [*Pause. Turning a little further.*] Is not that so, Willie, that even words fail, at times? [*Pause. Back front.*] What is one to do then, until they come again? Brush and comb the hair, if it has not been done, or if there is some doubt, trim the nails if they are in need of trimming, these things tide one over. [*pause*] That is what I mean. [*pause*] That is all I mean. [*pause*] That is what I find so wonderful, that not a day goes by—[*smile*]—to speak in the old style—[*smile off*]—without some blessing—[WILLIE *collapses behind slope, his head disappears.* WINNIE *turns towards event.*]—in disguise. [*She cranes back and down.*] Go back into your hole now, Willie, you've exposed yourself enough. [*pause*] Do as I say, Willie, don't lie sprawling there in this hellish sun, go back into your hole. [*pause*] Go on now, Willie. [WILLIE, *invisible, starts crawling left towards hole.*] That's the man. [*She follows his progress with her eyes.*] Not head first, stupid, how are you going to turn? [*pause*] That's it . . . right round . . . now . . . back in. [*pause*] Oh I know it is not easy, dear, crawling backwards, but it is rewarding in the end. [*pause*] You have left your Vaseline behind. [*She watches as he crawls back for Vaseline.*] The lid! [*She watches as he crawls back towards hole. Irritated.*] Not head first, I tell you! [*pause*] More to the right. [*pause*] The *right*, I said. [*Pause. Irritated.*] Keep your tail down, can't you! [*pause*] Now. [*pause*] There! [*All these directions loud. Now in her normal voice, still turned towards him.*] Can you hear me? [*pause*] I beseech you, Willie, just yes or no, can you hear me, just yes or nothing.

     [*pause*]

WILLIE: Yes.

WINNIE: [*turning front, same voice*] And now?

WILLIE: [*irritated*] Yes.

WINNIE: [*less loud*] And now?

WILLIE: [*more irritated*] Yes.

WINNIE: [*still less loud*] And now? [*A little louder.*] And now?

WILLIE: [*violently*] Yes!

WINNIE: [*same voice*] Fear no more the heat o' the sun. [*pause*] Did you hear that?

WILLIE: [*irritated*] Yes.

WINNIE: [*same voice*] What? [*pause*] What?

WILLIE: [*more irritated*] Fear no more.

     [*pause*]

WINNIE: [*same voice*] No more what? [*pause*] Fear no more what?

WILLIE: [*violently*] Fear no more!

WINNIE: [*normal voice, gabbled*] Bless you Willie I do appreciate your goodness I know what an effort it costs you, now you may relax I shall not trouble you again unless I am obliged to, by that I mean unless I come to the end of my own resources which is most unlikely, just to know that in theory you can hear me even though in fact you don't is all I need, just to feel you there within earshot and conceivably on the qui vive is all I ask, not to say anything I would not wish you to hear or liable to cause you pain, not to be just babbling away on trust as it is were not knowing and something gnawing at me. [*pause for breath*] Doubt. [*places index and second finger on heart area, moves them about, brings them to rest*] Here. [*moves them slightly*] Abouts. [*hand away*] Oh no doubt the time will come when before I can utter a word I must make sure you heard the one that went before and then no doubt another come another time when I must learn to talk to myself a thing I could never bear to do such wilderness. [*pause*] Or gaze before me with compressed lips. [*She does so.*] All day long. [*gaze and lips again*] No. [*smile*] No no. [*smile off*] There is, of course, the bag. [*turns towards it*] There will always be the bag. [*back front*] Yes, I suppose so. [*pause*] Even when you are gone, Willie. [*She turns a little towards him.*] You *are* going, Willie, aren't you? [*Pause. Louder.*] You *will* be going soon, Willie, won't you? [*Pause. Louder.*] Willie! [*Pause. She cranes back and down to look at him.*] So you have taken off your straw, that is wise. [*pause*] You do look snug, I must say, with your chin on your hands and the old blue eyes like saucers in the shadows. [*pause*] Can you see me from there I wonder, I still wonder. [*pause*] No? [*back front*] Oh I know it does not follow when two are gathered together—[*faltering*]—in this way—[*normal*]—that because one sees the other the other sees the one, life has taught me that . . . too. [*pause*] Yes, life I suppose, there is no other word. [*She turns a little towards him.*] Could you see me, Willie, do you think, from where you are, if you were to raise your eyes in my direction? [*turns a little further*] Lift up your eyes to me, Willie, and tell me can you see me, do that for me, I'll lean back as far as I can. [*Does so. Pause.*] No? [*pause*] Well never mind. [*turns back painfully front*] The earth is very tight today, can it be I have put on flesh, I trust not. [*Pause. Absently, eyes lowered.*] The great heat possibly. [*starts to pat and stroke ground*] All things expanding, some more than others. [*Pause. Patting and stroking.*] Some less. [*Pause. Do.*] Oh I can well imagine what is passing through your mind, it is not enough to have to listen to the woman, now I must look at her as well. [*Pause. Do.*] Well it is very understandable. [*Pause. Do.*] One does not appear to be asking a great deal, indeed at times it would seem hardly possible—[*voice breaks, falls to a murmur*]—to ask less—of a fellow creature—to put it mildly—whereas actually—when you think about it—look into your heart—see the other—what he needs—peace—to be left in peace—then perhaps the moon—all this time—asking for the moon. [*Pause. Stroking hand suddenly still. Lively.*] Oh I say, what have we here? [*Bending head to ground, incredulous.*] Looks like life of some kind! [*Looks for spectacles, puts them on, bends closer. Pause.*] An emmet! [*Recoils. Shrill.*] Willie, an emmet, a live emmet! [*Seizes magnifying glass, bends to ground again, inspects through glass.*] Where's it gone? [*inspects*] Ah! [*follows its progress through grass*] Has like a little white ball in its arms. [*Follows progress. Hand still. Pause.*] It's gone in. [*Continues a moment to gaze at spot through glass, then slowly straightens up, lays down glass, takes off spectacles and gazes before her, spectacles in hand. Finally.*] Like a little white ball.

    [*Long pause. Gesture to lay down spectacles.*]

WILLIE: Eggs.

WINNIE: [*arresting gesture*] What?

    [*pause*]

WILLIE: Eggs. [*Pause. Gesture to lay down glass.*] Formication.

WINNIE: [*arresting gesture*] What!

    [*pause*]

WILLIE: Formication.

    [*Pause. She lays down spectacles, gazes before her. Finally.*]

WINNIE: [*murmur*] God. [*Pause.* WILLIE *laughs quietly. After a moment she joins in. They laugh quietly together.* WILLIE *stops. She laughs on a moment alone.* WILLIE *joins in. They laugh together. She stops.* WILLIE *laughs on a moment alone. He stops. Pause. Normal voice.*] Ah well what a joy in any case to hear you laugh again, Willie, I was convinced I never would, you never would. [*pause*] I suppose some people might think us a trifle irreverent, but I doubt it. [*pause*] How can one better magnify the Almighty than by sniggering with him at his little jokes, particularly the poorer ones? [*pause*] I think you would back me up there, Willie. [*pause*] Or were we perhaps diverted by two quite different things? [*pause*] Oh well, what does it matter, that is what

I always say, so long as one . . . you know . . . what is that wonderful line . . . laughing wild . . . something something laughing wild amid severest woe. [*pause*] And now? [*long pause*] Was I lovable once, Willie? [*pause*] Was I ever lovable? [*pause*] Do not misunderstand my question, I am not asking you if you loved me, we know all about that, I am asking you if you found me lovable—at one stage. [*pause*] No? [*pause*] You can't? [*pause*] Well I admit it is a teaser. And you have done more than your bit already, for the time being, just lie back now and relax, I shall not trouble you again unless I am compelled to, just to know you are there within hearing and conceivably on the semi-alert is . . . er . . . paradise enow. [*pause*] The day is now well advanced. [*smile*] To speak in the old style. [*smile off*] And yet it is perhaps a little soon for my song. [*pause*] To sing too soon is a great mistake, I find. [*turning towards bag*] There is, of course, the bag. [*looking at bag*] The bag. [*back front*] Could I enumerate its contents? [*pause*] No. [*pause*] Could I, if some kind person were to come along and ask, What all have you got in that big black bag, Winnie? give an exhaustive answer? [*pause*] No. [*pause*] The depths in particular, who knows what treasures. [*pause*] What comforts. [*turns to look at bag*] Yes, there is the bag. [*back front*] But something tells me, Do not overdo the bag, Winnie, make use of it, of course, let it help you . . . along, when stuck, by all means, but cast your mind forward, something tells me, cast your mind forward, Winnie, to the time when words must fail—[*She closes eyes, pause, opens eyes.*]—and do not overdo the bag. [*Pause. She turns to look at bag.*] Perhaps just one quick dip. [*She turns back front, closes eyes, throws out left arm, plunges hand in bag and brings out revolver. Disgusted.*] You again! [*She opens eyes, brings revolver front and contemplates it. She weighs it in her palm.*] You'd think the weight of this thing would bring it down among the . . . last rounds. But no. It doesn't. Ever uppermost, like Browning. [*pause*] Brownie . . . [*turning a little toward* WILLIE] Remember Brownie, Willie? [*pause*] Remember how you used to keep on at me to take it away from you? Take it away, Winnie, take it away, before I put myself out of my misery. [*Back front. Derisive.*] Your misery! [*to revolver*] Oh I suppose it's a comfort to know you're there, but I'm tired of you. [*pause*] I'll leave you out, that's what I'll do. [*She lays revolver on ground to her right.*] There, that's your home from this day out. [*smile*] The old style! [*smile off*] And now? [*long pause*] Is gravity what it was, Willie, I fancy not. [*pause*] Yes, the feeling more and more that if I were not held—[*gesture*]—in this way, I would simply float up into the blue. [*pause*] And that perhaps some day the earth will yield and let me go, the pull is so great, yes, crack all round me and let me out. [*pause*] Don't you ever have that feeling, Willie, of being sucked up? [*pause*] Don't you have to cling on sometimes, Willie? [*Pause. She turns a little towards him.*] Willie.
    [*pause*]

WILLIE: *Sucked* up?

WINNIE: Yes, love, up into the blue, like gossamer. [*pause*] No? [*pause*] You don't [*pause*] Ah well, natural laws, natural laws, I suppose it's like everything else, it all depends on the creature you happen to be. All I can say for my part is that for me they are not what they were when I was young and . . . foolish and . . . [*faltering, head down*] . . . beautiful . . . possibly . . . lovely . . .

in a way . . . to look at. [*Pause. Head up.*] Forgive me, Willie, sorrow keeps breaking in. [*Normal voice.*] Ah well what a joy in any case to know you are there, as usual, and perhaps awake, and perhaps taking all this in, some of all this, what a happy day for me . . . it will have been. [*pause*] So far. [*pause*] What a blessing nothing grows, imagine if all this stuff were to start growing. [*pause*] Imagine. [*pause*] Ah yes, great mercies. [*long pause*] I can say no more. [*pause*] For the moment. [*Pause. Turns to look at bag. Back front. Smile.*] No no. [*Smile off. Looks at parasol.*] I suppose I might—[*takes up parasol*]—yes, I suppose I might . . . hoist this thing now. [*Begins to unfurl it. Following punctuated by mechanical difficulties overcome.*] One keeps putting off—putting up—for fear of putting up—too soon—and the day goes by—quite by—without one's having put up—at all. [*Parasol now fully open. Turned to her right she twirls it idly this way and that.*] Ah yes, so little to say, so little to do, and the fear so great, certain days, of finding oneself . . . left, with hours still to run, before the bell for sleep, and nothing more to say, nothing more to do, that the days go by, certain days go by, quite by, the bell goes, and little or nothing said, little or nothing done. [*raising parasol*] That is the danger. [*turning front*] To be guarded against. [*She gazes front, holding up parasol with right hand. Maximum pause.*] I used to perspire freely. [*pause*] Now hardly at all. [*pause*] The heat is much greater. [*pause*] The perspiration much less. [*pause*] That is what I find so wonderful. [*pause*] The way man adapts himself. [*pause*] To changing conditions. [*She transfers parasol to left hand. Long pause.*] Holding up wearies the arm. [*pause*] Not if one is going along. [*pause*] Only if one is at rest. [*pause*] That is a curious observation. [*pause*] I hope you heard that, Willie, I should be grieved to think you had not heard that. [*She takes parasol in both hands. Long pause.*] I am weary, holding it up, and I cannot put it down. [*pause*] I am worse off with it up than with it down, and I cannot put it down. [*pause*] Reason says, Put it down, Winnie, it is not helping you, put the thing down and get on with something else. [*pause*] I cannot. [*pause*] I cannot move. [*pause*] No, something must happen, in the world, take place, some change, I cannot, if I am to move again. [*pause*] Willie. [*mildly*] Help. [*pause*] No? [*pause*] Bid me put this thing down, Willie, I would obey you instantly, as I have always done, honoured, and obeyed. [*pause*] Please, Willie. [*mildly*] For pity's sake. [*pause*] No? [*pause*] You can't? [*pause*] Well I don't blame you, no, it would ill become me, who cannot move, to blame my Willie because he cannot speak. [*pause*] Fortunately I am in tongue again. [*pause*] That is what I find so wonderful, my two lamps, when one goes out the other burns brighter. [*pause*] Oh yes, great mercies. [*Maximum pause. The parasol goes on fire. Smoke, flames if feasible. She sniffs, looks up, throws parasol to her right behind mound, cranes back to watch it burning. Pause.*] Ah earth you old extinguisher. [*back front*] I presume this has occurred before, though I cannot recall it. [*pause*] Can you, Willie? [*turns a little towards him*] Can you recall this having occurred before? [*Pause. Cranes to look at him.*] Do you know what has occurred, Willie? [*pause*] Have you gone off on me again? [*pause*] I do not ask if you are alive to all that is going on, I merely ask if you have not gone off on me again. [*pause*] Your eyes appear to be closed, but that has no particular significance, we know. [*pause*]

Raise a finger, dear, will you please, if you are not quite senseless. [*pause*] Do
that for me, Willie, please, just the little finger, if you are still conscious.
[*Pause. Joyful.*] Oh all five, you are a darling today, now I may continue with
an easy mind. [*back front*] Yes, what ever occurred that did not occur before
and yet . . . I wonder, yes, I confess I wonder. [*pause*] With the sun blazing
so much fiercer down, and hourly fiercer, is it not natural things should go
on fire never known to do so, in this way I mean, spontaneous like. [*pause*]
Shall I myself not melt perhaps in the end, or burn, oh I do not mean necessarily burst into flames, no, just little by little be charred to a black cinder,
all this—[*ample gesture of arms*]—visible flesh. [*pause*] On the other hand,
did I ever know a temperate time? [*pause*] No. [*pause*] I speak of temperate
times and torrid times, they are empty words. [*pause*] I speak of when I was
not yet caught—in this way—and had my legs and had the use of my legs,
and could seek out a shady place, like you, when I was tired of the sun, or a
sunny place when I was tired of the shade, like you, and they are all empty
words. [*pause*] It is no hotter today than yesterday, it will be no hotter to-
morrow than today, how could it, and so on back into the far past, forward
into the far future. [*pause*] And should one day the earth cover my breasts,
then I shall never have seen my breasts, no one ever seen my breasts. [*pause*]
I hope you caught something of that, Willie, I should be sorry to think you
had caught nothing of all that, it is not every day I rise to such heights.
[*pause*] Yes, something seems to have occurred, something has seemed to occur, and nothing has occurred, nothing at all, you are quite right, Willie.
[*pause*] The sunshade will be there again tomorrow, beside me on this
mound, to help me through the day. [*Pause. She takes up mirror.*] I take up
this little glass, I shiver it on a stone—[*does so*]—I throw it away—[*does so far
behind her*]—it will be in the bag again tomorrow, without a scratch, to help
me through the day. [*pause*] No, one can do nothing. [*pause*] That is what I
find so wonderful, the way things . . . [*voice breaks, head down*] . . . things . . .
so wonderful. [*Long pause, head down. Finally turns, still bowed, to bag, brings
out unidentifiable odds and ends, stuffs them back, fumbles deeper, brings out finally musical box, winds it up, turns it on, listens for a moment holding it in both
hands, huddled over it, turns back front, straightens up and listens to tune, holding box to breast with both hands. It plays the waltz duet "I Love You So" from*
The Merry Widow. *Gradually happy expression. She sways to the rhythm.
Music stops. Pause. Brief burst of hoarse song without words—musical box
tune—from* WILLIE. *Increase of happy expression. She lays down box.*] Oh this
will have been a happy day! [*She claps hands.*] Again, Willie, again! [*claps*]
Encore, Willie, please! [*Pause. Happy expression off.*] No? You won't do that
for me? [*pause*] Well it is very understandable, very understandable. One
cannot sing just to please someone, however much one loves them, no, song
must come from the heart, that is what I always say, pour out from the inmost, like a thrush. [*pause*] How often I have said, in evil hours, Sing now,
Winnie, sing your song, there is nothing else for it, and did not. [*pause*]
Could not. [*pause*] No, like the thrush, or the bird of dawning, with no
thought of benefit, to oneself or anyone else. [*pause*] And now? [*Long pause.
Low.*] Strange feeling. [*Pause. Do.*] Strange feeling that someone is looking
at me. I am clear, then dim, then gone, then dim again, then clear again, and

so on, back and forth, in and out of someone's eye. [*Pause. Do.*] Strange?
[*Pause. Do.*] No, here all is strange. [*Pause. Normal voice.*] Something says,
Stop talking now, Winnie, for a minute, don't squander all your words for
the day, stop talking and do something for a change, will you? [*She raises
hands and holds them open before her eyes. Apostrophic.*] Do something! [*She
closes hands.*] What claws! [*She turns to bag, rummages in it, brings out finally
a nail file, turns back front and begins to file nails. Files for a time in silence, then
the following punctuated by filing.*] There floats up—into my thoughts—a
Mr. Shower—a Mr. and perhaps a Mrs. Shower—no—they are holding
hands—his fiancée then more likely—or just some—loved one. [*looks closer
at nails*] Very brittle today. [*resumes filing*] Shower—Shower—does the
name mean anything—to you, Willie—evoke any reality, I mean—for
you, Willie—don't answer if you don't—feel up to it—you have done
more—than your bit—already—Shower—Shower. [*inspects filed nails*] Bit
more like it. [*raises head, gazes front*] Keep yourself nice, Winnie, that's what
I always say, come what may, keep yourself nice. [*Pause. Resumes filing.*]
Yes—Shower—Shower—[*stops filing, raises head, gazes front, pause*]—or
Cooker, perhaps I should say Cooker, [*turning a little towards* WILLIE]
Cooker, Willie, does Cooker strike a chord? [*Pause. Turns a little further.
Louder.*] Cooker, Willie, does Cooker ring a bell, the name Cooker? [*Pause.
She cranes back to look at him. Pause.*] Oh really! [*pause*] Have you no handkerchief, darling? [*pause*] Have you no delicacy? [*pause*] Oh, Willie, you're
not eating it! Spit it out, dear, spit it out! [*Pause. Back front.*] Ah well, I suppose it's only natural. [*break in voice*] Human. [*Pause. Do.*] What *is* one to
do? [*Head down. Do.*] All day long. [*Pause. Do.*] Day after day. [*Pause. Head
up. Smile. Calm.*] The old style! [*Smile off. Resumes nails.*] No, done him.
[*passes on to next*] Should have put on my glasses. [*pause*] Too late now.
[*finishes left hand, inspects it.*] Bit more human. [*Starts right hand. Following
punctuated as before.*] Well anyway—this man Shower—or Cooker—no
matter—and the woman—hand in hand—in the other hands bags—kind
of big brown grips—standing there gaping at me—and at last this man
Shower—or Cooker—ends in "er" anyway—stake my life on that—What's
she doing? he says—What's the idea? he says—stuck up to her diddies in
the bleeding ground—coarse fellow—What does it mean? he says—What's
it meant to mean?—and so on—lot more stuff like that—usual drivel—Do
you hear me? he says—I do, she says, God help me—What do you mean,
he says, God help you? [*stops filing, raises head, gazes front*] And you, she
says, what's the idea of you, she says, what are you meant to mean? It is because you're still on your two flat feet, with your old ditty full of tinned
muck and changes of underwear, dragging me up and down this fornicat-
ing wilderness, coarse creature, fit mate—[*with sudden violence*]—let go of
my hand and drop for God's sake, she says, drop! [*Pause. Resumes filing.*]
Why doesn't he dig her out? he says—referring to you, my dear—What
good is she to him like that?—What good is he to her like that?—and so
on—usual tosh—Good! she says, have a heart for God's sake—Dig her out,
he says, dig her out, no sense in her like that—Dig her out with what? she
says—I'd dig her out with my bare hands, he says—must have been man
and—wife. [*files in silence*] Next thing they're away—hand in hand—and

the bags—dim—then gone—last human kind—to stray this way. [*finishes right hand, inspects it, lays down file, gazes front*] Strange thing, time like this, drift up into the mind. [*pause*] Strange? [*pause*]. No, here all is strange. [*pause*] Thankful for it in any case. [*voice breaks*] Most thankful. [*Head down. Pause. Head up. Calm.*] Bow and raise the head, bow and raise, always that. [*pause*] And now? [*Long pause. Starts putting things back in bag, tooth-brush last. This operation, interrupted by pauses as indicated, punctuates follow-ing.*] It is perhaps a little soon—to make ready—for the night—[*stops tidy-ing, head up, smile*]—the old style!—[*smile off, resumes tidying*]—and yet I do—make ready for the night—feeling it at hand—the bell for sleep—say-ing to myself—Winnie—it will not be long now, Winnie—until the bell for sleep. [*stops tidying, head up*] Sometimes I am wrong. [*smile*] But not often. [*smile off*] Sometimes all is over, for the day, all done, all said, all ready for the night, and the day not over, far from over, the night not ready, far, far from ready. [*smile*] But not often. [*smile off*] Yes, the bell for sleep, when I feel it at hand, and so make ready for the night—[*gesture*]—in this way, sometimes I am wrong—[*smile*]—but not often. [*Smile off. Resumes tidy-ing.*] I used to think—I say I used to think—that all these things—put back into the bag—if too soon—put back too soon—could be taken out again—if necessary—if needed—and so on—indefinitely—back into the bag—back out of the bag—until the bell—went. [*Stops tidying, head up, smile.*] But no. [*smile broader*] No no. [*Smile off. Resumes tidying.*] I suppose this—might seem strange—this—what shall I say—this what I have said—yes—[*She takes up revolver.*]—strange—[*She turns to put revolver in bag.*]—were it not—[*about to put revolver in bag she arrests gesture and turns back front*]—were it not—[*She lays down revolver to her right, stops tidying, head up.*]—that all seems strange. [*pause*] Most strange. [*pause*] Never any change. [*pause*] And more and more strange. [*Pause. She bends to mound again, takes up last object, i.e. toothbrush, and turns to put it in bag when her at-tention is drawn to disturbance from* WILLIE. *She cranes back and to her right to see. Pause.*] Weary of your hole, dear? [*pause*] Well I can understand that. [*pause*] Don't forget your straw. [*pause*] Not the crawler you were, poor dar-ling. [*pause*] No, not the crawler I gave my heart to. [*pause*] The hands and knees, love, try the hands and knees. [*pause*] The knees! The knees! [*pause*] What a curse, mobility! [*She follows with eyes his progress towards her behind mound, i.e. towards place he occupied at beginning of act.*] Another foot, Willie, and you're home. [*pause as he observes last foot*] Ah! [*turns back front labori-ously, rubs neck*] Crick in my neck admiring you. [*rubs neck*] But it's worth it, well worth it. [*turns slightly towards him*] Do you know what I dream sometimes? [*pause*] What I dream sometimes, Willie. [*pause*] That you'll come round and live this side where I could see you. [*Pause. Back front.*] I'd be a different woman. [*pause*] Unrecognizable. [*turning slightly toward him*] Or just now and then, come round this side just every now and then and let me feast on you. [*back front*] But you can't, I know. [*head down*] I know. [*Pause. Head up.*] Well anyway—[*looks at toothbrush in her hand*]—can't be long now—[*looks at brush*]—until the bell. [*Top back of* WILLIE's *head appears above slope.* WINNIE *looks closer at brush.*] Fully guaranteed . . . [*head up*] . . . what's this it was? [WILLIE's *hand appears with handkerchief, spreads it on*

skull, disappears.] Genuine pure . . . fully guaranteed . . . [WILLIE's *hand appears with boater, settles it on head, rakish angle, disappears.*] . . . genuine pure . . . ah! hog's setae. [*pause*] What is a hog exactly? [*Pause. Turns slightly towards* WILLIE.] What exactly is a hog, Willie, do you know, I can't remember. [*Pause. Turning a little further, pleading.*] What is a hog, Willie, please!
[*pause*]

WILLIE: Castrated male swine. [*Happy expression appears on* WINNIE's *face.*] Reared for slaughter.
[*Happy expression increases.* WILLIE *opens newspaper, hands invisible. Tops of yellow sheets appear on either side of his head.* WINNIE *gazes before her with happy expression.*]

WINNIE: Oh this *is* a happy day! This will have been another happy day! [*pause*] After all. [*pause*] So far.
[*Pause. Happy expression off.* WILLIE *turns page. Pause. He turns another page. Pause.*]

WILLIE: Opening for smart youth.
[*Pause.* WINNIE *takes off hat, turns to put it in bag, arrests gesture, turns back front. Smile.*]

WINNIE: No. [*smile broader*] No no. [*Smile off. Puts on hat again, gazes front, pause.*] And now? [*pause*] Sing. [*pause*] Sing your song, Winnie. [*pause*] No? [*pause*] Then pray. [*pause*] Pray your prayer, Winnie.
[*Pause.* WILLIE *turns page.*]

WILLIE: Wanted bright boy.
[*Pause.* WINNIE *gazes before her.* WILLIE *turns page. Pause. Newspaper disappears. Long pause.*]

WINNIE: Pray your old prayer, Winnie.
[*Long pause.*]

CURTAIN

ACT II

Scene as before.

WINNIE *embedded up to neck, hat on head, eyes closed. Her head, which she can no longer turn, nor bow, nor raise, faces front motionless throughout act. Movements of eyes as indicated.*

Bag and parasol as before. Revolver conspicuous to her right on mound.
Long pause.
Bell rings loudly. She opens eyes at once. Bell stops. She gazes front. Long pause.

WINNIE: Hail, holy light. [*Long pause. She closes her eyes. Bell rings loudly. She opens eyes at once. Bell stops. She gazes front. Long smile. Smile off. Long pause.*] Someone is looking at me still. [*pause*] Caring for me still. [*pause*] That is what I find so wonderful. [*pause*] Eyes on my eyes. [*pause*] What is that unforgettable line? [*Pause. Eyes right.*] Willie. [*Pause. Louder.*] Willie. [*Pause. Eyes front.*] May one still speak of time? [*pause*] Say it is a long time now, Willie, since I saw you. [*pause*] Since I heard you. [*pause*] May one? [*pause*] One does. [*smile*] The old style! [*smile off*] There is so little one can speak of. [*pause*] One speaks of it all. [*pause*] All one can. [*pause*] I used to think . . . [*pause*] . . . I say I used to think that I would learn to talk alone. [*pause*] By that I mean to myself, the wilderness. [*smile*] But no. [*smile broader*] No no. [*smile off*] Ergo you are there. [*pause*] Oh no doubt you are dead like the others, no doubt you have died, or gone away and left me, like the others, it doesn't matter, you are there. [*Pause. Eyes left.*] The bag, too, is there, the same as ever, I can see it. [*Pause. Eyes right. Louder.*] The bag is there, Willie, as good as ever, the one you gave me that day . . . to go to market. [*Pause. Eyes front.*] That day. [*pause*] What day? [*pause*] I used to pray. [*pause*] I say I used to pray. [*pause*] Yes, I must confess I did. [*smile*] Not now. [*smile broader*] No no. [*Smile off. Pause.*] Then . . . now . . . what difficulties here, for the mind. [*pause*] To have been always what I am—and so changed from what I was. [*pause*] I am the one, I say the one, then the other. [*pause*] Now the one, then the other. [*pause*] Now the one, then the other. [*pause*] There is so little one can say, one says it all. [*pause*] All one can. [*pause*] And no truth in it anywhere. [*pause*] My arms. [*pause*] My breasts. [*pause*] What arms? [*pause*] What breasts? [*pause*] Willie. [*pause*] What Willie? [*sudden vehement affirmation*] My Willie! [*eyes right, calling*] Willie! [*Pause. Louder.*] Willie! [*Pause. Eyes front.*] Ah well, not to know, not to know for sure, great mercy, all I ask. [*pause*] Ah yes . . . then . . . now . . . beechen green . . . this . . . Charlie . . . kisses . . . this . . . all that . . . deep trouble for the mind. [*pause*] But it does not trouble mine. [*smile*] Not now. [*smile broader*] No no. [*Smile off. Long pause. She closes eyes. Bell rings loudly. She opens eyes. Pause.*] Eyes float up that seem to close in peace . . . to see . . . in peace. [*pause*] Not mine. [*smile*] Not now. [*smile broader*] No no. [*Smile off. Long pause.*] Willie. [*pause*] Do you think the earth has lost its atmosphere, Willie? [*pause*] Do you, Willie? [*pause*] You have no opinion? [*pause*] Well that is like you, you never had any opinion about anything. [*pause*] It's understandable. [*pause*] Most. [*pause*] The earth-ball. [*pause*] I sometimes wonder. [*pause*] Perhaps not quite all. [*pause*] There always remains something. [*pause*] Of everything.[*pause*] Some remains. [*pause*] If the mind were to go. [*pause*] It won't, of course. [*pause*] Not quite. [*pause*] Not mine. [*smile*] Now now. [*smile broader*] No no. [*Smile off. Long pause.*] It might be the eternal cold. [*pause*] Everlasting perishing cold. [*pause*] Just chance, I take it, happy chance. [*pause*] Oh yes, great mercies, great mercies. [*pause*] And now? [*Long pause*] The face. [*pause*] The nose. [*She squints down.*] I can see it . . . [*squinting down*] . . . the tip . . . the nostrils . . . breath of life . . . that curve you so admired . . . [*pouts*] . . . a hint of lip . . . [*pouts again*] . . . if I pout them out . . . [*sticks out tongue*] . . . the tongue, of course . . . you so admired . . . if I stick it out . . . [*sticks it out again*] . . . the tip . . . [*eyes up*] . . . suspicion of brow . . . eyebrow . . . imagination possibly . . . [*eyes left*] . . . cheek . . . no . . . [*eyes right*] . . . no . . . [*distends cheeks*] . . . even if I puff them out . . . [*eyes left, distends cheeks again*] . . . no . . . no damask. [*eyes front*] That is all. [*pause*] The bag, of course . . . [*eyes left*] . . . a little blurred perhaps . . . but the bag. [*Eyes front. Offhand.*] The Earth, of course, and sky. [*eyes right*] The sunshade you gave me . . . that day . . . [*pause*] . . . that day . . . the lake . . . the reeds. [*Eyes front. Pause.*] What day? [*pause*] What reeds? [*Long pause. Eyes close. Bell rings loudly. Eyes open. Pause. Eyes right.*] Brownie, of course. [*pause*] You remember Brownie, Willie, I can see him. [*pause*] Brownie is there, Willie, beside me. [*Pause. Eyes front.*] That is all. [*pause*] What would I do without them? [*pause*] What would I do without them, when words fail? [*pause*] Gaze before me, with compressed lips. [*long pause while she does so*] I cannot. [*pause*] Ah yes, great mercies, great mercies. [*Long pause. Low.*] Sometimes I hear sounds. [*Listening expression. Normal voice.*] But not often. [*pause*] They are a boon, sounds are a boon, they help me . . . through the day. [*smile*] The old style! [*smile off*] Yes, those are happy days, when there are sounds. [*pause*] When I hear sounds.[*pause*] I used to think . . . [*pause*] . . . I say I used to think they were in my head. [*smile*] But no. [*smile broader*] No no. [*smile off*] That was just logic. [*pause*] Reason. [*pause*] I have not lost my reason. [*pause*] Not yet. [*pause*] Not all. [*pause*] Some remains. [*pause*] Sounds. [*pause*] Like little . . . sunderings, little falls . . . apart. [*Pause. Low.*] It's things, Willie. [*Pause. Normal voice.*] In the bag, outside the bag. [*pause*] Ah yes, things have their life, that is what I always say, *things* have a life. [*pause*] Take my looking glass, it doesn't need me. [*pause*] The bell. [*pause*] It hurts like a knife. [*pause*] A gouge. [*pause*] One cannot ignore it. [*pause*] How often . . . [*pause*] . . . I say how often I have said, Ignore it, Winnie, ignore the bell, pay no heed, just sleep and wake, sleep and wake, as you please, open and close the eyes, as you please, or in the way you find most helpful. [*pause*] Open and close the eyes, Winnie, open and close, always that. [*pause*] But no. [*smile*] Not now. [*smile broader*] No no. [*Smile off. Pause.*] What now? [*pause*] What now, Willie? [*long pause*] There is my story, of course, when all else fails. [*pause*] A life. [*smile*] A long life. [*smile off*] Beginning in the womb, where life used to begin, Mildred has memories, she will have memories, of the womb, before she dies, the mother's womb. [*pause*] She is now four or five already and has recently been given a big waxen dolly. [*pause*] Fully clothed, complete outfit. [*pause*] Shoes, socks, undies, complete set, frilly frock, gloves. [*pause*] White mesh. [*pause*] A little white straw hat with a chin elastic. [*pause*] Pearly necklet. [*pause*] A little picture book with legends in real print to go under her arm when she takes her walk. [*pause*] China blue eyes that open and shut. [*Pause. Narrative.*] The sun was not well up when Milly rose, descended the steep . . . [*pause*] . . . slipped on her nightgown, descended all along the steep wooden stairs, backwards on all fours, though she had been forbidden to do so, entered the . . . [*pause*] . . . tiptoed down the silent passage, entered the nursery and began to undress Dolly. [*pause*] Crept under the table and began to undress Dolly. [*pause*] Scolding her . . . the while. [*pause*] Suddenly a mouse—[*long pause*] Gently, Winnie. [*Long pause. Calling.*] Willie! [*Pause. Louder.*] Willie! [*Pause. Mild reproach.*] I sometimes find your attitude a little strange, Willie, all this time, it is not like you to be wantonly cruel. [*pause*] Strange? [*pause*] No. [*smile*] Not here. [*smile broader*] Not now. [*smile off*] And yet . . . [*suddenly anxious*] I do hope nothing is amiss. [*eyes right, loud*] Is all well, dear? [*Pause. Eyes front. To herself.*] God grant he did not go in head foremost [*Eyes right, loud.*] You're not stuck, Willie? [*Pause. Do.*] You're not jammed, Willie? [*eyes front, distressed*] Perhaps he is crying out for help all this time and I do not hear him! [*pause*] I do, of course, hear cries. [*pause*] But they are in my head surely. [*pause*] Is it possible that . . . [*Pause. With finality.*] No no, my head

was always full of cries. [*pause*] Faint confused cries. [*pause*] They come.
[*pause*] Then go. [*pause*] As on a wind. [*pause*] That is what I find so wonderful. [*pause*] They cease. [*pause*] Ah yes, great mercies, great mercies.
[*pause*] The day is now well advanced. [*Smile. Smile off.*] And yet it is perhaps a little soon for my song. [*pause*] To sing too soon is fatal, I always
find. [*pause*] On the other hand it is possible to leave it too late. [*pause*] The
bell goes for sleep and one has not sung. [*pause*] The whole day has
flown—[*smile, smile off*]—flown by, quite by, and no song of any class, kind,
or description. [*pause*] There is a problem here. [*pause*] One cannot sing . . .
just like that, no. [*pause*] It bubbles up, for some unknown reason, the time
is ill chosen, one chokes it back. [*pause*] One says, Now is the time, it is now
or never, and one cannot. [*pause*] Simply cannot sing. [*pause*] Not a note.
[*pause*] Another thing, Willie, while we are on this subject. [*pause*] The
sadness after song. [*pause*] Have you run across that, Willie? [*pause*] In the
course of your experience. [*pause*] No? [*pause*] Sadness after intimate sexual intercourse one is familiar with, of course. [*pause*] You would concur
with Aristotle there, Willie, I fancy. [*pause*] Yes, that one knows and is prepared to face. [*pause*] But after song . . . [*pause*] It does not last, of course.
[*pause*] That is what I find so wonderful. [*Pause*] It wears away. [*pause*]
What are those exquisite lines? [*pause*] Go forget me why should something o'er that something shadow fling . . . go forget me . . . why should
sorrow . . . brightly smile . . . go forget me . . . never hear me . . . sweetly
smile . . . brightly sing . . . [*Pause. With a sigh.*] One loses one's classics.
[*pause*] Oh not all. [*pause*] A part. [*pause*] A part remains. [*pause*] That is
what I find so wonderful, a part remains, of one's classics, to help one
through the day. [*pause*] Oh yes, many mercies, many mercies. [*pause*] And
now? [*pause*] And now, Willie? [*long pause*] I call to the eye of the mind . . .
Mr. Shower—or Cooker. [*She closes her eyes. Bell rings loudly. She opens her
eyes. Pause.*] Hand in hand, in the other hands bags. [*pause*] Getting on . . .
in life. [*pause*] No longer young, not yet old. [*pause*] Standing there gaping
at me. [*pause*] Can't have been a bad bosom, he says, in its day. [*pause*] Seen
worse shoulders, he says, in my time. [*pause*] Does she feel her legs? he says.
[*pause*] Is there any life in her legs? he says. [*pause*] Has she anything on
underneath? he says. [*pause*] Ask her, he says, I'm shy. [*pause*] Ask her
what? she says. [*pause*] Is there any life in her legs. [*pause*] Has she anything on underneath. [*pause*] Ask her yourself, she says. [*Pause. With sudden
violence.*] Let go of me for Christ sake and drop! [*Pause. Do.*] Drop dead!
[*smile*] But no. [*smile broader*] No no. [*smile off*] I watch them recede.
[*pause*] Hand in hand—and the bags. [*pause*] Dim. [*pause*] Then gone.
[*pause*] Last human kind—to stray this way. [*pause*] Up to date. [*pause*]
And now? [*Pause. Low.*] Help. [*Pause. Do.*] Help, Willie. [*Pause. Do.*] No?
[*Long pause. Narrative.*] Suddenly a mouse . . . [*pause*] Suddenly a mouse
ran up her little thigh and Mildred, dropping Dolly in her fright, began to
scream—[*Winnie gives a sudden piercing scream.*]—and screamed and
screamed—[*Winnie screams twice.*]—screamed and screamed and screamed
and screamed till all came running, in their night attire, papa, mamma,
Bibby and . . . old Annie, to see what was the matter . . . [*pause*] . . . what
on earth could possibly be the matter. [*pause*] Too late. [*pause*] Too late.

[*Long pause. Just audible.*] Willie. [*Pause. Normal voice.*] Ah well, not long now, Winnie, can't be long now, until the bell for sleep. [*pause*] Then you may close your eyes, then you must close your eyes—and keep them closed. [*pause*] Why say that again? [*pause*] I used to think ... [*pause*] ... I say I used to think there was no difference between one fraction of a second and the next. [*pause*] I used to say ... [*pause*] ... I say I used to say, Winnie, you are changeless, there is never any difference between one fraction of a second and the next. [*pause*] Why bring that up again? [*pause*] There is so little one can bring up, one brings up all. [*pause*] All one can. [*pause*] My neck is hurting me! [*pause*] Ah that's better. [*with mild irritation*] Everything within reason. [*long pause*] I can do no more. [*pause*] Say no more. [*pause*] But I must say more. [*pause*] Problem here. [*pause*] No, something must move, in the world, I can't any more. [*pause*] A zephyr. [*pause*] A breath. [*pause*] What are those immortal lines? [*pause*] It might be the eternal dark. [*pause*] Black night without end. [*pause*] Just chance, I take it, happy chance. [*pause*] Oh yes, abounding mercies. [*long pause*] And now? [*pause*] And now, Willie? [*long pause*] That day. [*pause*] The pink fizz. [*pause*] The flute glasses. [*pause*] The last guest gone. [*pause*] The last bumper with the bodies nearly touching. [*pause*] The look. [*long pause*] I hear cries. [*pause*] Sing. [*pause*] Sing your old song, Winnie.

> [*Long pause. Suddenly alert expression. Eyes switch right.* WILLIE's *head appears to her right round corner of mound. He is on all fours, dressed to kill—top hat, morning coat, striped trousers, etc., white gloves in hand. Very long bushy white Battle of Britain moustache. He halts, gazes front, smooths moustache. He emerges completely from behind mound, turns to his left, halts, looks up at* WINNIE. *He advances on all fours towards centre, halts, turns head front, gazes front, strokes moustache, straightens tie, adjusts hat, advances a little further, halts, takes off hat and looks up at* WINNIE. *He is now not far from centre and within her field of vision. Unable to sustain effort of looking up he sinks head to ground.*]

WINNIE: [*mondaine*] Well this is an unexpected pleasure! [*pause*] Reminds me of the day you came whining for my hand. [*pause*] I worship you, Winnie, be mine. [*He looks up.*] Life a mockery without Win. [*She goes off into a giggle.*] What a getup, you do look a sight! [*giggles*] Where are the flowers? [*pause*] That smile today. [WILLIE *sinks head.*] What's that on your neck, an anthrax? [*pause*] Want to watch that, Willie, before it gets a hold on you. [*pause*] Where were you all this time? [*pause*] What were you doing all this time? [*pause*] Changing? [*pause*] Did you not hear me screaming for you? [*pause*] Did you get stuck in your hole? [*Pause. He looks up.*] That's right, Willie, look at me. [*pause*] Feast your old eyes, Willie. [*pause*] Does anything remain? [*pause*] Any remains? [*pause*] No? [*pause*] I haven't been able to look after it, you know. [*He sinks his head.*] You are still recognizable, in a way. [*pause*] Are you thinking of coming to live this side now ... for a bit maybe? [*pause*] No? [*pause*] Just a brief call? [*pause*] Have you gone deaf, Willie? [*pause*] Dumb? [*pause*] Oh I know you were never one to talk, I worship you Winnie be mine and then nothing from that day forth only titbits from *Reynold's News*. [*Eyes front. Pause.*] Ah well, what matter, that's what I always say, it will have been a happy day, after all, another happy day.

[*pause*] Not long now, Winnie. [*pause*] I hear cries. [*pause*] Do you ever hear cries, Willie? [*pause*] No? [*Eyes back on* WILLIE.] [*pause*] Look at me again, Willie. [*pause*] Once more, Willie. [*He looks up. Happily.*] Ah! [*Pause. Shocked.*] What ails you, Willie, I never saw such an expression! [*pause*] Put on your hat, dear, it's the sun, don't stand on ceremony, I won't mind. [*He drops hat and gloves and starts to crawl up mound towards her. Gleeful.*] Oh I say, this is terrific! [*He halts, clinging to mound with one hand, reaching up with the other.*] Come on, dear, put a bit of jizz into it, I'll cheer you on. [*pause*] Is it me you're after, Willie . . . or is it something else? [*pause*] Do you want to touch my face . . . again? [*pause*] Is it a kiss you're after, Willie . . . or is it something else? [*pause*] There was a time when I could have given you a hand. [*pause*] And then a time before that when I did give you a hand. [*pause*] You were always in dire need of a hand, Willie. [*He slithers back to foot of mound and lies with face to ground.*] Brrum! [*Pause. He rises to hands and knees, raises his face towards her.*] Have another go, Willie, I'll cheer you on. [*pause*] Don't look at me like that! [*Pause. Vehement.*] Don't look at me like that! [*Pause. Low.*] Have you gone off your head, Willie? [*Pause. Do.*] Out of your poor old wits, Willie?

    [*pause*]

WILLIE: [*just audible*] Win.

    [*Pause.* WINNIE's *eyes front. Happy expression appears, grows.*]

WINNIE: Win! [*pause*] Oh this *is* a happy day, this will have been another happy day! [*pause*] After all. [*pause*] So far.

    [*Pause. She hums tentatively beginning of song, then sings softly, musical box tune.*]

> *Though I say not*
> *What I may not*
> *Let you hear,*
> *Yet the swaying*
> *Dance is saying,*
> *Love me dear!*
> *Every touch of fingers*
> *Tells me what I know,*
> *Says for you,*
> *It's true, it's true,*
> *You love me so!*

    [*Pause. Happy expression off. She closes her eyes. Bell rings loudly. She opens her eyes. She smiles, gazing front. She turns her eyes, smiling, to* WILLIE, *still on his hands and knees looking up at her. Smile off. They look at each other. Long pause.*]

CURTAIN

George C. Wolfe

The Colored Museum (1986)

The civil rights movement of the 1960s brought with it an increased concern for diversity in drama and theatrical production. One result was the greatly increased number of plays by and about African Americans. There are now a large number of skillful dramatists, as well as more than two hundred African American producing groups in the United States. Among the playwrights, George C. Wolfe has become one of the most influential, both through his writing and his work as a director and as head of the New York Shakespeare Festival.

Wolfe's *The Colored Museum* is conceived as a series of eleven exhibits of African American history and life. In this way, Wolfe confronts audiences with behavior and attitudes reflecting both the oppressions of the past and the compromises and hopes of the present. In doing so, he alternates between (and sometimes combines) comic exposure and fierce defense. Some audiences have been offended by the play because they have failed to recognize the serious purpose of the humor. Wolfe satirizes black stereotypes to force African Americans to recognize that, even as they seek to escape stereotyping, they are living according to labels forced on them not only by others but also by themselves. Wolfe says that he wrote *The Colored Museum* "in order to undefine myself in relation to all these labels." He does not ask African Americans to forget their past; rather, he suggests, they should face it and move beyond it. As one of the characters in the final exhibit says: "I can't live inside yesterday's pain, but I can't live without it." A major concern of the play, then, is how African Americans can both honor and escape the baggage of the past.

The most interesting scene for those interested in theatre is *The Last Mama-on-the-Couch Play,* a satirical look at the familiar stereotypes of black drama that ends in a production number using "a myriad of black-Broadwayesque dancing styles" undercut by projected images of "coon performers," who in earlier times had presented song-and-dance shows demeaning to blacks but favored by whites. The final exhibit, *The Party,* brings together all the characters of the play, acknowledging the great variety, good and bad, of black experience, past and present. It suggests that the power of African Americans lies in the contradictions of their past. Taken all together, these eleven exhibits ask us to look at attitudes and stereotypes that have shaped important aspects of African American sensibilities. It does so in a form both imaginative and entertaining.

George C. Wolfe

The Colored Museum

THE CAST————*An ensemble of five, two men and three women, all black, who per-form all the characters that inhabit the exhibits. (A little girl, seven to twelve years old, is needed for a walk-on part in* Lala's Opening.)

THE STAGE————*White walls and recessed lighting. A starkness befitting a museum where the myths and madness of black/Negro/colored Americans are stored. Built into the walls is a series of small panels, doors, revolving walls, and compartments from which actors can retrieve key props and make quick entrances. A revolve is used, which allows for quick transitions from one exhibit to the next.*

MUSIC————*All of the music for the show should be prerecorded. Only the drummer, who is used in* Git on Board, *and then later in* Permutations *and* The Party, *is live.*

There is no intermission.

THE EXHIBITS AND CHARACTERS

Git on Board
  MISS PAT
Cookin' with Aunt Ethel
  AUNT ETHEL
The Photo Session
  GIRL
  GUY
Soldier with a Secret
  JUNIE ROBINSON
The Gospel According to Miss Roj
  MISS ROJ
  WAITER
The Hairpiece
  THE WOMAN
  JANINE
  LAWANDA
The Last Mama-on-the-Couch Play
  NARRATOR
  MAMA
  WALTER-LEE-BEAU-WILLIE-JONES
  LADY IN PLAID

MEDEA JONES
Symbiosis
   THE MAN
   THE KID
Lala's Opening
   LALA LAMAZING GRACE
   ADMONIA
   FLO'RANCE
   THE LITTLE GIRL
Permutations
   NORMAL JEAN REYNOLDS
The Party
   TOPSY WASHINGTON
   MISS PAT
   MISS ROJ
   LALA LAMAZING GRACE
   THE MAN (*from* Symbiosis)

GIT ON BOARD

Blackness. Cut by drums pounding. Then slides, rapidly flashing before us. Images we've all seen before, of African slaves being captured, loaded onto ships, tortured. The images flash, flash, flash. The drums crescendo. Blackout. And then lights reveal MISS PAT, *frozen. She is black, pert, and cute. She has a flip to her hair and wears a hot pink miniskirt stewardess uniform.*

She stands in front of a curtain which separates her from an offstage cockpit.

An electronic bell goes "ding" and MISS PAT *comes to life, presenting herself in a friendly but rehearsed manner, smiling and speaking as she has done so many times before.*

MISS PAT: Welcome aboard Celebrity Slaveship departing the Gold Coast and making short stops at Bahia, Port au Prince, and Havana, before our final destination of Savannah.

Hi, I'm Miss Pat and I'll be serving you here in Cabin A. We will be crossing the Atlantic at an altitude that's pretty high, so you must wear your shackles at all times.

[*She removes a shackle from the overhead compartment and demonstrates.*] To put on your shackle, take the right hand and close the metal ring around your left hand like so. Repeat the action using your left hand to secure the right. If you have any trouble bonding yourself, I'd be more than glad to assist.

Once we reach the desired altitude, the Captain will turn off the "Fasten Your Shackle" sign . . . [*She efficiently points out the "Fasten Your Shackle" signs on either side of her, which light up.*] . . . allowing you a chance to stretch and dance in the aisles a bit. But otherwise, shackles must be worn at all times.

[*The "Fasten Your Shackle" signs go off.*]

MISS PAT: Also, we must ask that you please refrain from call-and-response singing between cabins as that sort of thing can lead to rebellion. And, of course, no drums are allowed on board. Can you repeat after me, "No drums." [*She gets the audience to repeat.*] With a little more enthusiasm, please. "No drums."

[*after the audience repeats it*] That was great!

Once we're airborne, I'll be by with magazines, and earphones can be purchased for the price of your first-born male.

    If there's anything I can do to make this middle passage more pleasant, press the little button overhead and I'll be with you faster than you can say, "Go down, Moses." [*She laughs at her "little joke."*] Thanks for flying Celebrity and here's hoping you have a pleasant takeoff.

    [*The engines surge, the "Fasten Your Shackle" signs go on, and over-articulate Muzak voices are heard singing as* MISS PAT *pulls down a bucket seat and "shackles up" for takeoff.*]

VOICES: GET ON BOARD CELEBRITY SLAVESHIP
GET ON BOARD CELEBRITY SLAVESHIP
GET ON BOARD CELEBRITY SLAVESHIP
THERE'S ROOM FOR MANY A MORE

    [*The engines reach an even, steady hum. Just as* MISS PAT *rises and replaces the shackles in the overhead compartment, the faint sound of African drumming is heard.*]

MISS PAT: Hi. Miss Pat again. I'm sorry to disturb you, but someone is playing drums. And what did we just say . . . "No drums." It must be someone in Coach. But we here in Cabin A are not going to respond to those drums. As a matter of fact, we don't even hear them. Repeat after me. "I don't hear any drums." [*The audience repeats.*] And "I will not rebel."

    [*The audience repeats. The drumming grows.*]

MISS PAT: [*placating*] OK, now I realize some of us are a bit edgy after hearing about the tragedy on board The Laughing Mary, but let me assure you Celebrity has no intention of throwing you overboard and collecting the insurance. We value you!

    [*She proceeds to single out individual passengers/audience members.*]

Why, the songs *you* are going to sing in the cotton fields, under the burning heat and stinging lash, will metamorphose and give birth to the likes of James Brown and the Fabulous Flames. And you, yes *you*, are going to come up with some of the best dances. The best dances! The Watusi! The Funky Chicken! And just think of what *you* are going to mean to William Faulkner.

    All right, so you're gonna have to suffer for a few hundred years, but from your pain will come a culture so complex. *And*, with this little item here . . . [*She removes a basketball from the overhead compartment.*] . . . you'll become millionaires!

    [*There is a roar of thunder. The lights quiver and the "Fasten Your Shackle" signs begin to flash.* MISS PAT *quickly replaces the basketball in the overhead compartment and speaks very reassuringly.*]

MISS PAT: No, don't panic. We're just caught in a little thunderstorm. Now the only way you're going to make it through is if you abandon your God and worship a new one. So, on the count of three, let's all sing. One, two, three . . .

NOBODY KNOWS DE TROUBLE I SEEN

Oh, I forgot to mention, when singing, omit the T-H sound. "The" becomes "de." "They" becomes "dey." Got it? Good!

NOBODY KNOWS . . .

NOBODY KNOWS . . .

Oh, so you don't like that one? Well then let's try another—

SUMMER TIME

AND DE LIVIN' IS EASY

Gershwin. He comes from another oppressed people so he understands.

FISH ARE JUMPIN' . . . come on.

AND DE COTTON IS HIGH.

AND DE COTTON IS . . . Sing, damnit!

[*Lights begin to flash, the engines surge, and there is wild drumming.* MISS PAT *sticks her head through the curtain and speaks with an offstage* CAPTAIN.]

MISS PAT: What?

VOICE OF CAPTAIN: [*offstage*] Time warp!

MISS PAT: Time warp! [*She turns to the audience and puts on a pleasant face.*] The Captain has assured me everything is fine. We're just caught in a little time warp. [*trying to fight her growing hysteria*] On your right you will see the American Revolution, which will give the U.S. of A. exclusive rights to your life. And on your left, the Civil War, which means you will vote Republican until F.D.R. comes along. And now we're passing over the Great Depression, which means everybody gets to live the way you've been living. [*There is a blinding flash of light, and an explosion. She screams.*] Ahhhhhhhhh! That was World War I, which is not to be confused with World War II . . . [*There is a larger flash of light, and another explosion.*] . . . Ahhhhh! Which is not to be confused with the Korean War or the Vietnam War, all of which you will play a major role in.

Oh, look, now we're passing over the sixties. Martha and the Vandellas . . . "Julia" with Miss Diahann Carroll . . . Malcolm X . . . those five little girls in Alabama . . . Martin Luther King . . . Oh no! The Supremes broke up! [*The drumming intensifies.*] Stop playing those drums! Those drums will be confiscated once we reach Savannah. You can't change history! You can't turn back the clock! [*to the audience*] Repeat after me, "I don't hear any drums! I will not rebel! I will not rebel! I will not re—"

[*The lights go out, she screams, and the sound of a plane landing and screeching to a halt is heard. After a beat, lights reveal a wasted, disheveled* MISS PAT, *but perky nonetheless.*]

MISS PAT: Hi. Miss Pat here. Things got a bit jumpy back there, but the Captain has just informed me we have safely landed in Savannah. Please check the overhead before exiting as any baggage you don't claim, we trash.

It's been fun, and we hope the next time you consider travel, it's with Celebrity.

[*Luggage begins to revolve onstage from offstage left, going past* MISS PAT *and revolving offstage right. Mixed in with the luggage are two male slaves and a woman slave, complete with luggage and I.D. tags around their necks.*]

MISS PAT: [*with routine, rehearsed pleasantness*]
    Have a nice day. Bye bye.
    Button up that coat, it's kind of chilly.
    Have a nice day. Bye bye.
    You take care now.
    See you.
    Have a nice day.
    Have a nice day.
    Have a nice day.

COOKIN' WITH AUNT ETHEL

As the slaves begin to revolve off, a low-down gut-bucket blues is heard. AUNT ETHEL, *a down-home black woman with a bandana on her head, revolves to center stage. She stands behind a big, black pot and wears a reassuring grin.*

AUNT ETHEL: Welcome to "Aunt Ethel's Down-Home Cookin' Show," where we explores the magic and mysteries of colored cuisine.
    Today, we gonna be servin' ourselves up some . . . [*She laughs.*] I'm not gonna tell you. That's right! I'm not gonna tell you what it is till after you done cooked it. Child, on "The Aunt Ethel Show" we loves to have ourselves some fun. Well, are you ready? Here goes.
    ' [*She belts out a hard-drivin' blues and throws invisible ingredients into the big, black pot.*]

FIRST YA ADD A PINCH OF STYLE
AND THEN A DASH OF FLAIR
NOW YA STIR IN SOME PREOCCUPATION
WITH THE TEXTURE OF YOUR HAIR

NEXT YA ADD ALL KINDS OF RHYTHMS
LOTS OF FEELING AND PIZAZZ
THEN HUNNY THROW IN SOME RAGE
TILL IT CONGEALS AND TURNS TO JAZZ

NOW YOU COOKIN'
COOKIN' WITH AUNT ETHEL
YOU REALLY COOKIN'
COOKIN' WITH AUNT ETHEL, OH YEAH

NOW YA ADD A HEAP OF SURVIVAL
AND HUMILITY, JUST A TOUCH
ADD SOME ATTITUDE
OOPS! I PUT TOO MUCH

AND NOW A WHOLE LOT OF HUMOR
SALTY LANGUAGE, MIXED WITH SADNESS

THEN THROW IN A BOX OF BLUES
AND SIMMER TO MADNESS

NOW YOU COOKIN'
COOKIN' WITH AUNT ETHEL, OH YEAH!

NOW YOU BEAT IT—REALLY WORK IT
DISCARD AND DISOWN
AND IN A FEW HUNDRED YEARS
ONCE IT'S AGED AND FULLY GROWN
YA PUT IT IN THE OVEN
TILL IT'S BLACK
AND HAS A SHEEN
OR TILL IT'S NICE AND YELLA
OR ANY SHADE IN BETWEEN

NEXT YA TAKE 'EM OUT AND COOL 'EM
'CAUSE THEY NO FUN WHEN THEY HOT
AND WON'T YOU BE SURPRISED
AT THE CONCOCTION YOU GOT

YOU HAVE BAKED
BAKED YOURSELF A BATCH OF NEGROES
YES YOU HAVE BAKED YOURSELF
BAKED YOURSELF A BATCH OF NEGROES
[*She pulls from the pot a handful of Negroes, black dolls.*]
But don't ask me what to do with 'em now that you got 'em, 'cause child,
that's your problem. [*She throws the dolls back into the pot.*] But in any case,
yaw be sure to join Aunt Ethel next week, when we gonna be servin' our-
selves up some chitlin quiche . . . some grits-under-glass,
AND A SWEET POTATO PIE
AND YOU'LL BE COOKIN'
COOKIN' WITH AUNT ETHEL
OH YEAH!
[*On* AUNT ETHEL's *final riff, lights reveal* . . .]

THE PHOTO SESSION

. . . *a very glamorous, gorgeous, black couple, wearing the best of everything and perfect
smiles. The stage is bathed in color and bright white light. Disco music with the chant:
"We're fabulous" plays in the background. As they pose, larger-than-life images of their
perfection are projected on the museum walls. The music quiets and the images fade
away as they begin to speak and pose.*

GIRL: The world was becoming too much for us.
GUY: We couldn't resolve the contradictions of our existence.
GIRL: And we couldn't resolve yesterday's pain.
GUY: So we gave away our life and we now live inside *Ebony Magazine*.

GIRL: Yes, we live inside a world where everyone is beautiful, and wears fabulous clothes.

GUY: And no one says anything profound.

GIRL: Or meaningful.

GUY: Or contradictory.

GIRL: Because no one talks. Everyone just smiles and shows off their cheekbones.
    [*They adopt a profile pose.*]

GUY: Last month I was black and fabulous while holding up a bottle of vodka.

GIRL: This month we get to be black and fabulous together.
    [*They dance/pose. The "We're fabulous" chant builds and then fades as they start to speak again.*]

GIRL: There are, of course, setbacks.

GUY: We have to smile like this for a whole month.

GIRL: And we have no social life.

GUY: And no sex.

GIRL: And at times it feels like we're suffocating, like we're not human anymore.

GUY: And everything is rehearsed, including this other kind of pain we're starting to feel.

GIRL: The kind of pain that comes from feeling no pain at all.
    [*They then speak and pose with a sudden burst of energy.*]

GUY: But one can't have everything.

GIRL: Can one?

GUY: So if the world is becoming too much for you, do like we did.

GIRL: Give away your life and come be beautiful with us.

GUY: We guarantee, no contradictions.

GIRL/GUY: Smile/click, smile/click, smile/click.

GIRL: And no pain.
    [*They adopt a final pose and revolve off as the "We're fabulous" chant plays and fades into the background.*]

A SOLDIER WITH A SECRET

Projected onto the museum walls are the faces of black soldiers—from the Spanish-American through to the Vietnam War. Lights slowly reveal JUNIE ROBINSON, *a black combat soldier, posed on an onyx plinth. He comes to life and smiles at the audience. Somewhat dim-witted, he has an easygoing charm about him.*

JUNIE: Pst. Pst. Guess what? I know the secret. The secret to your pain. 'Course, I didn't always know. First I had to die, then come back to life, 'fore I had the gift.

    Ya see the Cappin sent me off up ahead to scout for screamin' yella bastards. 'Course, for the life of me I couldn't understand why they'd be screamin', seein' as how we was tryin' to kill them and they us.

    But anyway, I'm off lookin', when all of a sudden I find myself caught smack dead in the middle of this explosion. This blindin', burnin', scaldin' explosion. Musta been a booby trap or something, 'cause all around me is fire. Hell, I'm on fire. Like a piece of chicken dropped in a skillet of cracklin' grease. Why, my flesh was justa peelin' off of my bones.

But then I says to myself, "Junie, if yo' flesh is on fire, how come you don't feel no pain!" And I didn't. I swear as I'm standin' here, I felt nuthin'. That's when I sort of put two and two together and realized I didn't feel no whole lot of hurtin' 'cause I done died.

Well I just picked myself up and walked right on out of that explosion. Hell, once you know you dead, why keep on dyin', ya know?

So, like I say, I walk right outta that explosion, fully expectin' to see white clouds, Jesus, and my Mama, only all I saw was more war. Shootin' goin' on way off in this direction and that direction. And there, standin' around, was all the guys. Hubert, J.F., the Cappin. I guess the sound of the explosion must of attracted 'em, and they all starin' at me like I'm some kind of ghost.

So I yells to 'em, "Hey there Hubert! Hey there Cappin!" But they just stare. So I tells 'em how I'd died and how I guess it wasn't my time 'cause here I am, "Fully in the flesh and not a scratch to my bones." And they still just stare. So I took to starin' back.

[*The expression on* JUNIE's *face slowly turns to horror and disbelief.*]
Only what I saw . . . well I can't exactly to this day describe it. But I swear, as sure as they was wearin' green and holdin' guns, they was each wearin' a piece of the future on their faces.

Yeah. All the hurt that was gonna get done to them and they was gonna do to folks was right there clear as day.

I saw how J.F., once he got back to Chicago, was gonna get shot dead by this po-lice, and I saw how Hubert was gonna start beatin' up on his old lady which I didn't understand, 'cause all he could do was talk on and on about how much he loved her. Each and every one of 'em had pain in his future and blood on his path. And God or the Devil one spoke to me and said, "Junie, these colored boys ain't gonna be the same after this war. They ain't gonna have no kind of happiness."

Well right then and there it come to me. The secret to their pain.

Late that night, after the medics done checked me over and found me fit for fightin', after everybody done settle down for the night, I sneaked over to where Hubert was sleepin', and with a needle I stole from the medics . . . pst, pst . . . I shot a little air into his veins. The second he died, all the hurtin'-to-come just left his face.

Two weeks later I got J.F. and after that Woodrow . . . Jimmy Joe . . . I even spent all night waitin' by the latrine 'cause I knew the Cappin always made a late night visit and pst . . . pst . . . I got him.

[*Smiling, quite proud of himself.*] That's how come I died and come back to life. 'Cause just like Jesus went around healin' the sick, I'm supposed to go around healin' the hurtin' all these colored boys wearin' from the war.

Pst, pst. I know the secret. The secret to your pain. The secret to yours, and yours. Pst. Pst. Pst. Pst.

[*The lights slowly fade.*]

THE GOSPEL ACCORDING TO MISS ROJ

The darkness is cut by electronic music. Cold, pounding, unrelenting. A neon sign that spells out "THE BOTTOMLESS PIT" clicks on. There is a lone bar stool. Lights flash on and off, pulsating to the beat. There is a blast of smoke and, from the haze, MISS ROJ appears. He is dressed in striped patio pants, white go-go boots, a halter, and cat-shaped sunglasses. What would seem ridiculous on anyone else, MISS ROJ wears as if it were high fashion. He carries himself with total elegance and absolute arrogance.

MISS ROJ: God created black people and black people created style. The name's
  Miss Roj . . . that's R.O.J. thank you and you can find me every Wednes-
  day, Friday, and Saturday nights at "The Bottomless Pit," the watering
  hole for the wild and weary which asks the question, "Is there life after
  Jherri-curl?"
  [*A* WAITER *enters, hands* MISS ROJ *a drink, and then exits.*]
  Thanks, doll. *Yes,* if they be black and swish, the B.P. has seen them, which
  is not to suggest the Pit is lacking in cultural diversity. Oh no. There are
  your dinge queens, white men who like their chicken legs dark. [*He
  winks/flirts with a man in the audience.*] And let's not forget, "Los Mucha-
  chos de la Neighborhood." But the specialty of the house is The Snap
  Queens. [*He snaps his fingers.*] We are a rare breed.
  For, you see, when something strikes our fancy, when the truth comes
  piercing through the dark, well you just can't let it pass unnoticed. No darling. You must pronounced it with a snap. [*He snaps.*]
  Snapping comes from another galaxy, as do all snap queens. That's
  right. I ain't just your regular oppressed American Negro. No-no-no! I am
  an extraterrestrial. And I ain't talkin' none of that shit you seen in the
  movies! I have real power.
  [*The* WAITER *enters.* MISS ROJ *stops him.*]
  Speaking of no power, will you please tell Miss Stingy-with-the-rum, that
  if Miss Roj had wanted to remain sober, she could have stayed home and
  drank Kool-aid. [*He snaps.*] Thank you.
  [*The* WAITER *exits.* MISS ROJ *crosses and sits on bar stool.*]
  Yes, I was placed here on Earth to study the life habits of a deteriorating
  society, and, child, when we talkin' New York City, we are discussing the
  Queen of Deterioration. Miss New York is doing a slow dance with death,
  and I am here to warn you all, but before I do, I must know . . . don't you
  just love my patio pants? Annette Funicello immortalized them in "Beach
  Blanket Bingo," and I have continued the legacy. And my go-gos? I realize
  white after Labor Day is very gauche, but as the saying goes, if you've got
  it, flaunt it, if you don't, front it and snap to death any bastard who dares to
  defy you. [*laughing*] Oh ho! My demons are showing. Yes, my demons live
  at the bottom of my Bacardi and Coke.
  Let's just hope for all concerned I dance my demons out before I
  drink them out 'cause, child, dancing demons take you on a ride, but those
  drinkin' demons just take you, and you find yourself doing the strangest
  things. Like the time I locked my father in the broom closet. Seems the
  liquor made his tongue real liberal and he decided he was gonna baptize me

with the word "faggot" over and over. Well, he's just going on and on with "faggot this" and "faggot that," all the while walking toward the broom closet to piss. So the demons just took hold of my wedgies and forced me to kick the drunk son of a bitch into the closet and lock the door. [*laughter*] Three days later I remembered he was there. [*He snaps.*]

[*The* WAITER *enters.* MISS ROJ *takes a drink and downs it.*]
Another!

[*The* WAITER *exits.*]

[*Dancing about.*] Oh yes-yes-yes! Miss Roj is quintessential style. I corn row the hairs on my legs so that they spell out M.I.S.S. R.O.J. And I dare any bastard to fuck with me because I will snap your ass into oblivion.

I have the power, you know. Everytime I snap, I steal one beat of your heart. So if you find yourself gasping for air in the middle of the night, chances are you fucked with Miss Roj and she didn't like it.

Like the time this asshole at Jones Beach decided to take issue with my coulotte-sailor ensemble. This child, this muscle-bound Brooklyn thug in a skin-tight bikini, very skin-tight so the whole world can see that instead of a brain, God gave him an extra thick piece of sausage. You know the kind who beat up on their wives for breakfast. Snap your fingers if you know what I'm talking about. . . . Come on and snap, child. [*He gets the audience to snap.*] Well, he decided to blurt out when I walked by, "Hey look at da monkey coon in da faggit suit." Well, I walked up to the poor dear, very calmly lifted my hand, and . . . [*He snaps in rapid succession.*] A heart attack, right there on the beach. [*He singles out someone in the audience.*] You don't believe it? Cross me! Come on! Come on!

[*The* WAITER *enters, hands* MISS ROJ *a drink.* MISS ROJ *downs it. The* WAITER *exits.*]

[*looking around*] If this place is the answer, we're asking all the wrong questions. The only reason I come here is to communicate with my origins. The flashing lights are signals from my planet way out there. Yes, girl, even further than Flatbush. We're talking another galaxy. The flashing lights tell me how much time is left before the end.

[*very drunk and loud by now*] I hate the people here. I hate the drinks. But most of all I hate this goddamn music. That ain't music. Give me Aretha Franklin any day. [*singing*] "Just a little respect. R.E.S.P.E.C.T." Yeah! Yeah!

Come on and dance your last dance with Miss Roj. Last call is but a drink away and each snap puts you one step closer to the end.

A high-rise goes up. You can't get no job. Come on everybody and dance. A whole race of people gets trashed and debased. Snap those fingers and dance. Some sick bitch throws her baby out the window 'cause she thinks it's the Devil. Everybody snap! *The New York Post.* Snap!

Snap for every time you walk past someone lying in the street, smelling like frozen piss and shit and you don't see it. Snap for every crazed bastard who kills himself so as to get the jump on being killed. And snap for every sick muthafucker who, bored with carrying around his fear, takes to shooting up other people.

Yeah, snap your fingers and dance with Miss Roj. But don't be fooled by the banners and balloons 'cause, child, this ain't no party going on. Hell no! It's a wake. And the casket's made out of stone, steel, and glass and the people are racing all over the pavement like maggots on a dead piece of meat.

Yeah, dance! But don't be surprised if there ain't no beat holding you together 'cause we traded in our drums for respectability. So now it's just words. Words rappin'. Words screechin'. Words flowin' instead of blood 'cause you know that don't work. Words cracklin' instead of fire 'cause by the time a match is struck on 125th Street and you run to midtown, the flame has been blown away.

So come on and dance with Miss Roj and her demons. We don't ask for acceptance. We don't ask for approval. We know who we are and we move on it!

I guarantee you will never hear two fingers put together in a snap and not think of Miss Roj. That's power, baby. Patio pants and all.

[*The lights begin to flash in rapid succession.*]
So let's dance! And snap! And dance! And snap!

[MISS ROJ *begins to dance as if driven by his demons. There is a blast of smoke and when the haze settles,* MISS ROJ *has revolved off and in place of him is a recording of Aretha Franklin singing "Respect."*]

THE HAIRPIECE

As "Respect" fades into the background, a vanity revolves to center stage. On this vanity are two wigs, an Afro wig, circa 1968, and a long, flowing wig, both resting on wig stands. A black WOMAN *enters, her head and body wrapped in towels. She picks up a framed picture and after a few moments of hesitation, throws it into a small trash can. She then removes one of her towels to reveal a totally bald head. Looking into a mirror on the "fourth wall," she begins applying makeup.*

The wig stand holding the Afro wig opens her eyes. Her name is JANINE. *She stares in disbelief at the bald woman.*

JANINE: [*calling to the other wig stand*] LaWanda. LaWanda girl, wake up.
    [*The other wig stand, the one with the long, flowing wig, opens her eyes. Her name is* LAWANDA.]
LAWANDA: What? What is it?
JANINE: Check out girlfriend.
LAWANDA: Oh, girl, I don't believe it.
JANINE: [*laughing*] Just look at the poor thing, trying to paint some life onto that face of hers. You'd think by now she'd realize it's the hair. It's all about the hair.
LAWANDA: What hair! She ain't go no hair! She done fried, dyed, de-chemicalized her shit to death.
JANINE: And all that's left is that buck-naked scalp of hers, sittin' up there apologizin' for being odd-shaped and ugly.
LAWANDA: [*laughing with* JANINE] Girl, stop!
JANINE: I ain't sayin' nuthin' but the truth.

LAWANDA/JANINE: The bitch is bald! [*They laugh.*]

JANINE: And all over some man.

LAWANDA: I tell ya, girl, I just don't understand it. I mean, look at her. She's got a right nice face, a good head on her shoulders. A good job, even. And she's got to go fall in love with that fool.

JANINE: That political quick-change artist. Everytime the nigga went and changed his ideology, she went and changed her hair to fit the occasion.

LAWANDA: Well at least she's breaking up with him.

JANINE: Hunny, no!

LAWANDA: Yes, child.

JANINE: Oh, girl, dish me the dirt!

LAWANDA: Well, you see, I heard her on the phone, talking to one of her girl-friends, and she's meeting him for lunch today to give him the ax.

JANINE: Well it's about time.

LAWANDA: I hear ya. But don't you worry 'bout a thing, girlfriend. I'm gonna tell you all about it.

JANINE: Hunny, you won't have to tell me a damn thing 'cause I'm gonna be there, front row, center.

LAWANDA: You?

JANINE: Yes, child, she's wearing me to lunch.

LAWANDA: [*outraged*] I don't think so!

JANINE: [*with an attitude*] What do you mean, you don't think so?

LAWANDA: Exactly what I said, "I don't think so." Damn, Janine, get real. How the hell she gonna wear both of us?

JANINE: She ain't wearing both of us. She's wearing me.

LAWANDA: Says who?

JANINE: Says me! Says her! Ain't that right, girlfriend?

[*The* WOMAN *stops putting on makeup, looks around, sees no one, and goes back to her makeup.*]

JANINE: I said, ain't that right!

[*The* WOMAN *picks up the phone.*]

WOMAN: Hello . . . hello . . .

JANINE: Did you hear the damn phone ring?

WOMAN: No.

JANINE: Then put the damn phone down and talk to me.

WOMAN: I ah . . . don't understand.

JANINE: It ain't deep so don't panic. Now, you're having lunch with your boy-friend, right?

WOMAN: [*breaking into tears*] I think I'm having a nervous breakdown.

JANINE: [*impatient*] I said you're having lunch with your boyfriend, right!

WOMAN: [*scared, pulling herself together*] Yes, right . . . right.

JANINE: To break up with him.

WOMAN: How did you know that?

LAWANDA: I told her.

WOMAN: [*stands and screams*] Help! Help!

JANINE: Sit down. I said sit your ass down!

[*The* WOMAN *does.*]

JANINE: Now set her straight and tell her you're wearing me.

LAWANDA: She's the one that needs to be set straight, so go on and tell her you're wearing me.

JANINE: No, tell her you're wearing me.

> [*There is a pause.*]

LAWANDA: Well?

JANINE: Well?

WOMAN: I ah . . . actually hadn't made up my mind.

JANINE: [*going off*] What do you mean you ain't made up you mind! After all that fool has put you through, you gonna need all the attitude you can get and there is nothing like attitude and a healthy head of kinks to make his shit shrivel like it should!

> That's right! When you wearin' me, you lettin' him know he ain't gonna get no sweet-talkin' comb through your love without some serious resistance. No-no! The kink of my head is like the kink of your heart and neither is about to be hot-pressed into surrender.

LAWANDA: That shit is so tired. The last time attitude worked on anybody was 1968. Janine girl, you need to get over it and get on with it. [*to the* WOMAN] And you need to give the nigga a goodbye he will never forget.

> I say give him hysteria! Give him emotion! Give him rage! And there is nothing like a toss of the tresses to make your emotional outburst shine with emotional flair.

> You can toss me back, shake me from side to side, all the while screaming, "I want you out of my life forever!!!" And not only will I come bouncing back for more, but you just might win an Academy Award for best performance by a head of hair in a dramatic role.

JANINE: Miss hunny, please! She don't need no Barbie doll dipped in chocolate telling her what to do. She needs a head of hair that's coming from a fo' real place.

LAWANDA: Don't you dare talk about nobody coming from a "fo' real place," Miss Made-in-Taiwan!

JANINE: Hey! I ain't ashamed of where I come from. Besides, it don't matter where you come from as long as you end up in the right place.

LAWANDA: And it don't matter the grade as long as the point gets made. So go on and tell her you're wearing me.

JANINE: No, tell her you're wearing me.

> [*The* WOMAN, *unable to take it, begins to bite off her fake nails, as* LAWANDA *and* JANINE *go at each other.*]

LAWANDA: Set the bitch straight. Let her know there is no way she could even begin to compete with me. I am quality. She is kink. I am exotic. She is common. I am class and she is trash. That's right. T.R.A.S.H. We're talking three strikes and you're out. So go on and tell her you're wearing me. Go on, tell her! Tell her! Tell her!	JANINE: Who you callin' a bitch? Why, if I had hands I'd knock you clear into next week. You think you cute. She thinks she's cute just 'cause that synthetic mop of hers blows in the wind. She looks like a fool and you look like an even bigger fool when you wear her, so go on and tell her you're wearing me. Go on, tell her! Tell her! Tell her!

[*The* WOMAN *screams and pulls the two wigs off the wig stands as the lights go to black on three bald heads.*]

THE LAST MAMA-ON-THE-COUCH PLAY

A NARRATOR, *dressed in a black tuxedo, enters through the audience and stands center stage. He is totally solemn.*

NARRATOR: We are pleased to bring you yet another Mama-on-the-Couch play. A searing domestic drama that tears at the very fabric of racist America. [*He crosses upstage center and sits on a stool and reads from a playscript.*] Act One. Scene One.
　　　　[MAMA *revolves on stage left, sitting on a couch reading a large, oversized Bible. A window is placed stage right.* MAMA's *dress, the couch, and drapes are made from the same material. A doormat lays down center.*]
NARRATOR: Lights up on a dreary, depressing, but with middle-class aspirations tenement slum. There is a couch, with a Mama on it. Both are well worn. There is a picture of Jesus on the wall . . . [*A picture of Jesus is instantly revealed.*] . . . and a window which looks onto an abandoned tenement. It is late spring.
　　　　Enter Walter-Lee-Beau-Willie-Jones [SON *enters through the audience.*] He is Mama's thirty-year-old son. His brow is heavy from three hundred years of oppression.
MAMA: [*looking up from her Bible, speaking in a slow manner*] Son, did you wipe your feet?
SON: [*an ever-erupting volcano*] No, Mama, I didn't wipe me feet! Out there, every day, Mama, is the Man. The Man, Mama. Mr. Charlie! Mr. Bossman! And he's wipin' his feet on me. On me, Mama, every damn day of my life. Ain't that enough for me to deal with? Ain't that enough?
MAMA: Son, wipe your feet.
SON: I wanna dream. I wanna be somebody. I wanna take charge of my life.
MAMA: You can do all of that, but first you got to wipe your feet.
SON: [*as he crosses to the mat, mumbling and wiping his feet*] Wipe my feet . . . wipe my feet . . . wipe my feet . . .
MAMA: That's a good boy.
SON: [*exploding*] Boy! Boy! I don't wanna be nobody's good boy, Mama. I wanna be my own man!
MAMA: I know, son, I know. God will show the way.
SON: God, Mama! Since when did your God ever do a damn thing for the black man. Huh, Mama, huh? You tell me. When did your God ever help me?
MAMA: [*removing her wire-rim glasses*] Son, come here.
　　　　[SON *crosses to* MAMA, *who slowly stands and in an exaggerated stage slap, backhands* SON *clear across the stage. The* NARRATOR *claps his hands to create the sound for the slap.* MAMA *then lifts her clenched fists to the heavens.*]
MAMA: Not in my house, my house, will you ever talk that way again!
　　　　[*The* NARRATOR, *so moved by her performance, erupts in applause and encourages the audience to do so.*]
NARRATOR: Beautiful. Just stunning.

[*He reaches into one of the secret compartments of the set and gets an award, which he ceremoniously gives to* MAMA *for her performance. She bows and then returns to the couch.*]

NARRATOR: Enter Walter-Lee-Beau-Willie's wife, the Lady in Plaid.

[*Music from nowhere is heard, a jazzy pseudo-abstract intro as the* LADY IN PLAID *dances in through the audience, wipes her feet, and then twirls about.*]

LADY: She was a creature of regal beauty
  who in ancient time graced the temple of the Nile
  with her womanliness
  But here she was, stuck being colored
  and a woman in a world that valued neither.

SON: You cooked my dinner?

LADY: [*oblivious to* SON]
  Feet flat, back broke,
  she looked at the man who, though he be thirty,
  still ain't got his own apartment.
  Yeah, he's still livin' with his Mama!
  And she asked herself, was this the life
  for a Princess Colored, who by the
  translucence of her skin, knew the
  universe was her sister.

    [*The* LADY IN PLAID *twirls and dances.*]

SON: [*becoming irate*] I've had a hard day of dealin' with the Man. Where's my damn dinner? Woman, stand still when I'm talkin' to you!

LADY: And she cried for her sisters in Detroit
  Who knew, as she, that their souls belonged
  in ancient temples on the Nile.
  And she cried for her sisters in Chicago
  who, like her, their life has become
  one colored hell.

SON: There's only one thing gonna get through to you.

LADY: And she cried for her sisters in New Orleans
  And her sisters in Trenton and Birmingham,
  and
  Poughkeepsie and Orlando and Miami Beach
  and
  Las Vegas, Palm Springs.

    [*As she continues to call out cities, he crosses offstage and returns with two black dolls and then crosses to the window.*]

SON: Now are you gonna cook me dinner?

LADY: Walter-Lee-Beau-Willie-Jones, no! Not my babies.

    [SON *throws them out the window. The* LADY IN PLAID *then lets out a primal scream.*]

LADY: He dropped them!!!!

    [*The* NARRATOR *breaks into applause.*]

NARRATOR: Just splendid. Shattering.

[*He then crosses and after an intense struggle with* MAMA, *he takes the award from her and gives it to the* LADY IN PLAID, *who is still suffering primal pain.*]

LADY: Not my babies . . . not my . . . [*Upon receiving the award, she instantly recovers.*] Help me up, sugar. [*She then bows and crosses and stands behind the couch.*]

NARRATOR: Enter Medea Jones, Walter-Lee-Beau-Willie's sister.

[MEDEA *moves very ceremoniously, wiping her feet and then speaking and gesturing as if she just escaped from a Greek tragedy.*]

MEDEA: Ah, see how the sun kneels to speak
her evening vespers, exalting all
in her vision, even lowly tenement
long abandoned.

Mother, wife of brother, I trust
the approaching darkness finds you
safe in Hestia's bosom.

Brother, why wear the face of a man
in anguish. Can the argument of thine
feelings cause the shape of your
countenance to disfigure so?

SON: [*at the end of his rope*] Leave me alone, Medea.

MEDEA: [*to* MAMA]
Is good brother still going on and on and on
about He and The Man.

MAMA/LADY: What else?

MEDEA: Ah brother, if with our thoughts and
words we could cast thine oppressors
into the lowest bowls of wretched
hell, would that make us more like the
gods or more like our oppressors?

No, brother, no, do not let thy rage
choke the blood which anoints thy
heart with love. Forgo thine darkened
humor and let love shine on your
soul, like a jewel on a young maiden's hand.
[*dropping to her knees*]
I beseech thee, forgo thine
anger and leave wrath to the gods!

SON: Girl, what has gotten into you.

MEDEA: Julliard, good brother. For I am no
longer bound by rhythms of race or
region. Oh, no. My speech, like my
pain and suffering, have become
classical and therefore universal.

LADY: I didn't understand a damn thing she said, but girl you usin' them words.

[LADY IN PLAID *crosses and gives* MEDEA *the award and everyone applauds.*]

SON: [*trying to stop the applause*] Wait one damn minute! This my play. It's about me and the Man. It ain't got nuthin' to do with no ancient temples on the Nile and it ain't got nuthin' to do with Hestia's bosom. And it ain't got nuthin' to do with you slappin' me across no room. [*his gut-wrenching best*] It's about me. Me and my pain! My pain!

THE VOICE OF THE MAN: Walter-Lee-Beau-Willie, this is the Man. You have been convicted of overacting. Come out with your hands up.

[SON *starts to cross to the window.*]

SON: Well now that does it.

MAMA: Son, no, don't go near that window. Son, no!

[*Gunshots ring out and* SON *falls dead.*]

MAMA: [*crossing to the body, too emotional for words*] My son, he was a good boy. Confused. Angry. Just like his father. And his father's father. And his father's father's father. And now he's dead.

[*Seeing she's about to drop to her knees, the* NARRATOR *rushes and places a pillow underneath her just in time.*]

If only he had been born into a world better than this. A world where there are no well-worn couches and no well-worn Mamas and nobody overemotes.

If only he had been born into an all-black musical.

[*A song intro begins.*]

Nobody ever dies in an all-black musical.

[MEDEA *and* LADY IN PLAID *pull out church fans and begin to fan themselves.*]

MAMA: [*singing a soul-stirring gospel*]
OH WHY COULDN'T HE
BE BORN
INTO A SHOW WITH LOTS OF SINGING
AND DANCING

I SAY WHY
COULDN'T HE
BE BORN

LADY: Go ahead, hunny. Take your time.

MAMA: INTO A SHOW WHERE EVERYBODY
IS HAPPY

NARRATOR/MEDEA: Preach! Preach!

MAMA: OH WHY COULDN'T HE BE BORN WITH THE CHANCE
TO SMILE A LOT AND SING AND DANCE
OH WHY
OH WHY

OH WHY
COULDN'T HE
BE BORN
INTO AN ALL-BLACK SHOW
WOAH-WOAH

[*The* CAST *joins in, singing do-wop gospel background to* MAMA's *lament.*]
OH WHY
COULDN'T HE
BE BORN
(HE BE BORN)
INTO A SHOW WHERE EVERYBODY
IS HAPPY

WHY COULDN'T HE BE BORN WITH THE CHANCE
TO SMILE A LOT AND SING AND DANCE
WANNA KNOW WHY
WANNA KNOW WHY

OH WHY
COULDN'T HE
BE BORN
INTO AN ALL-BLACK SHOW
A-MEN
      [*A singing/dancing, spirit-raising revival begins.*]
OH, SON, GET UP
GET UP AND DANCE
WE SAY GET UP
THIS IS YOUR SECOND CHANCE

DON'T SHAKE A FIST
JUST SHAKE A LEG
AND DO THE TWIST
DON'T SCREAM AND BEG
SON SON SON
GET UP AND DANCE

GET
GET UP
GET UP AND
GET UP AND DANCE—ALL RIGHT!
GET UP AND DANCE—ALL RIGHT!
GET UP AND DANCE!
      [WALTER-LEE-BEAU-WILLIE *springs to life and joins in the dancing. A foot-stomping, hand-clapping production number takes off, which encompasses a myriad of black-Broadwayesque dancing styles—shifting speeds and styles with exuberant abandonment.*]
MAMA: [*bluesy*]
    WHY COULDN'T HE BE BORN INTO AN ALL-BLACK SHOW
CAST: WITH SINGING AND DANCING
MAMA: BLACK SHOW
      [MAMA *scats and the dancing becomes manic and just a little too desperate to please.*]
CAST: WE GOTTA DANCE

WE GOTTA DANCE
GET UP GET UP GET UP AND DANCE
WE GOTTA DANCE
WE GOTTA DANCE
GOTTA DANCE!
>   [*Just at the point the dancing is about to become violent, the cast freezes and
>   pointedly, simply sings:*]

IF WE WANT TO LIVE
WE HAVE GOT TO
WE HAVE GOT TO
DANCE ... AND DANCE ... AND DANCE ...
>   [*As they continue to dance with zombie-like frozen smiles and faces, around
>   them images of coon performers flash as the lights slowly fade.*]

SYMBIOSIS

The Temptations singing "My Girl" are heard as lights reveal a BLACK MAN *in corporate dress standing before a large trash can throwing objects from a Saks Fifth Avenue bag into it. Circling around him with his every emotion on his face is* THE KID, *who is dressed in a late-sixties street style. His moves are slightly heightened. As the scene begins the music fades.*

MAN: [*with contained emotions*]
>   My first pair of Converse All-stars. Gone.
>   My first Afro-comb. Gone.
>   My first dashiki. Gone.
>   My autographed pictures of Stokley Carmichael,
>   Jomo Kenyatta, and Donna Summer. Gone.

KID: [*near tears, totally upset*] This shit's not fair, man. Damn! Hell! Shit! Shit! It's not fair!

MAN: My first jar of Murray's Pomade.
>   My first can of Afro-sheen.
>   My first box of curl relaxer. Gone! Gone! Gone!
>   Eldridge Cleaver's *Soul on Ice.*

KID: Not *Soul on Ice!*

MAN: It's been replaced on my bookshelf by *The Color Purple.*

KID: [*horrified*] No!

MAN: Gone!

KID: But—

MAN: Jimi Hendrix's "Purple Haze." Gone.
>   Sly Stone's "There's A Riot Goin' On." Gone.
>   The Jackson Five's "I Want You Back."

KID: Man, you can't throw that away. It's living proof Michael had a black nose.

MAN: It's all going. Anything and everything that connects me to you, to who I was, to what we were, is out of my life.

KID: You've got to give me another chance.

MAN: "Fingertips Part 2."

KID: Man, how can you do that? That's vintage Stevie Wonder.

MAN: You want to know how, Kid? You want to know how? Because my survival
depends on it. Whether you know it or not, the Ice Age is upon us.

KID: [*jokingly*] Man, what the hell you talkin' about. It's ninety-five damn degrees.

MAN: The climate is changing, Kid, and either you adjust or you end up extinct.
A sociological dinosaur. Do you understand what I'm trying to tell you?
King Kong would have made it to the top if only he had taken the elevator.
Instead he brought attention to his struggle and ended up dead.

KID: [*pleading*] I'll change. I swear I'll change. I'll maintain a low profile. You
won't even know I'm around.

MAN: If I'm to become what I'm to become, then you've got to go. . . . I have no
history. I have no past.

KID: Just like that?

MAN: [*throwing away a series of buttons*] Free Angela! Free Bobby! Free Huey,
Duey, and Louie! U.S. out of Vietnam. U.S. out of Cambodia. U.S. out of
Harlem, Detroit, and Newark. Gone! . . . "The Temptations Greatest Hits!"

KID: [*grabbing the album*] No!!!

MAN: Give it back, Kid.

KID: No.

MAN: I said give it back!

KID: No. I can't let you trash this. Johnny man, it contains fourteen classic cuts by
the tempting Temptations. We're talking, "Ain't Too Proud to Beg," "Papa
Was a Rolling Stone," "My Girl."

MAN: [*warning*] I don't have all day.

KID: For God's sake, Johnny man, "My Girl" is the jam to end all jams. It's what
we are. Who we are. It's a way of life. Come on, man, for old times sake.
[*singing*]
I GOT SUNSHINE ON A CLOUDY DAY
BUM-DA-DUM-DA-DUM-DA-BUM
AND WHEN IT'S COLD OUTSIDE
Come on, Johnny man, you ain't "bummin'," man.
I GOT THE MONTH OF MAY
Here comes your favorite part. Come on, Johnny man, sing.
I GUESS YOU SAY
WHAT CAN MAKE ME FEEL THIS WAY
MY GIRL, MY GIRL, MY GIRL
TALKIN' 'BOUT

MAN: [*exploding*] I said give it back!

KID: [*angry*] I ain't givin' you a muthafuckin' thing!

MAN: Now you listen to me!

KID: No, you listen to me. This is the kid you're dealin' with, so don't fuck with me!
[*He hits his fist into his hand, and* THE MAN *grabs for his heart.* THE KID
*repeats with two more hits, which causes the man to drop to the ground,
grabbing his heart.*]

KID: Jai! Jai! Jai!

MAN: Kid, please.

KID: Yeah. Yeah. Now who's begging who. . . . Well, well, well, look at Mr.
Cream-of-the-Crop, Mr. Colored-Man-on-Top. Now that he's making it,
he no longer wants anything to do with the Kid. Well, you may put all kinds

of silk ties 'round your neck and white lines up your nose, but the Kid is here to stay. You may change your women as often as you change your underwear, but the Kid is here to stay. And regardless of how much of your past that you trash, I ain't goin' no damn where. Is that clear? Is that clear?

MAN: [*regaining his strength, beginning to stand*] Yeah.

KID: Good. [*after a beat*] You all right, man? You all right? I don't want to hurt you, but when you start all that talk about getting rid of me, well, it gets me kind of crazy. We need each other. We are one. . . .

    [*Before* THE KID *can complete his sentence,* THE MAN *grabs him around his neck and starts to choke him violently.*]

MAN: [*as he strangles him*] The . . . Ice . . . Age . . . is . . . upon us . . . and either we adjust . . . or we end up . . . extinct.

    [THE KID *hangs limp in* THE MAN's *arms.*]

MAN: [*laughing*] Man kills his own rage. Film at eleven. [*He then dumps* THE KID *into the trash can, and closes the lid. He speaks in a contained voice.*] I have no history. I have no past. I can't. It's too much. It's much too much. I must be able to smile on cue. And watch the news with an impersonal eye. I have no stake in the madness.

    Being black is too emotionally taxing; therefore I will be black only on weekends and holidays.

    [*He then turns to go, but sees the Temptations album lying on the ground. He picks it up and sings quietly to himself.*]

I GUESS YOU SAY

WHAT CAN MAKE ME FEEL THIS WAY

    [*He pauses, but then crosses to the trash can, lifts the lid, and just as he is about to toss the album in, a hand reaches from inside the can and grabs hold of* THE MAN's *arm.* THE KID *then emerges from the can with a death grip on* THE MAN's *arm.*]

KID: [*smiling*] What's happenin'?

BLACKOUT

LALA'S OPENING

Roving follow spots. A timpani drum roll. As we hear the voice of the ANNOUNCER, *outrageously glamorous images of* LALA *are projected onto the museum walls.*

VOICE OF ANNOUNCER: From Rome to Rangoon! Paris to Prague! We are pleased to present the American debut of the one! The only! The breathtaking! The astounding! The stupendous! The incredible! The magnificent! Lala Lamazing Grace!

    [*Thunderous applause as* LALA *struts on, the definitive black diva. She has long, flowing hair, an outrageous lamé dress, and an affected French accent, which she loses when she's upset.*]

LALA: EVERYBODY LOVES LALA

EVERYBODY LOVES ME

PARIS! BERLIN! LONDON! ROME!

NO MATTER WHERE I GO

I ALWAYS FEEL AT HOME

OHHHH
EVERYBODY LOVES LALA
EVERYBODY LOVES ME
I'M TRES MAGNIFIQUE
AND OH SO UNIQUE
AND WHEN IT COMES TO GLAMOUR
I'M CHIC-ER THAN CHIC

[*She giggles.*]
THAT'S WHY EVERYBODY
EVERYBODY
EVERYBODY-EVERYBODY-EVERYBODY
LOVES ME
[*She begins to vocally reach for higher and higher notes, until she has to point to her final note. She ends the number with a grand flourish and bows to thunderous applause.*]

LALA: Yes, it's me! Lala Lamazing Grace and I have come home. Home to the home I never knew as home. Home to you, my people, my blood, my guts.

My story is a simple one, full of fire, passion, magique. You may ask how did I, a humble girl from the backwoods of Mississippi, come to be the ninth wonder of the modern world. Well, I can't take all of the credit. Part of it goes to him. [*She points toward the heavens.*]

No, not the light man, darling, but God. For, you see, Lala is a star. A very big star. Let us not mince words, I'm a fucking meteorite. [*She laughs.*] But He is the universe and just like my sister, Aretha la Franklin, Lala's roots are in the black church. [*She sings in a showy gospel style:*]
THAT'S WHY EVERYBODY LOVES
SWING LOW SWEET CHARIOT
THAT'S WHY EVERYBODY LOVES
GO DOWN MOSES WAY DOWN IN EGYPT LAND
THAT'S WHY EVERYBODY EVERYBODY LOVES
ME!!!
[*Once again she points to her final note and then basks in applause.*]
I love that note. I just can't hit it.

Now, before I dazzle you with more of my limitless talent, tell me something, America. [*musical underscoring*] Why has it taken you so long to recognize my artistry? Mother France opened her loving arms and Lala came running. All over the world Lala was embraced. But here, ha! You spat at Lala. Was I too exotic? Too much woman, or what?

Diana Ross you embrace. A two-bit nobody from Detroit, of all places. Now, I'm not knocking la Ross. She does the best she can with the little she has. [*She laughs.*] But the Paul la Robesons, the James la Baldwins, the Josephine la Bakers, who was my godmother you know. The Lala Lamazing Graces you kick out. You drive . . .
AWAY
I AM GOING AWAY
HOPING TO FIND A BETTER DAY
WHAT DO YOU SAY

HEY HEY
I AM GOING AWAY
AWAY
> [LALA, *caught up in the drama of the song, doesn't see* ADMONIA, *her maid, stick her head out from offstage.*]
> [*Once she is sure* LALA *isn't looking, she wheels onto stage right* FLO'RANCE, LALA's *lover, who wears a white mask/blonde hair. He is gagged and tied to a chair.* ADMONIA *places him on stage and then quickly exits.*]

LALA: AU REVOIR—JE VAIS PARTIR MAINTENANT
JE VEUX DIRE MAINTENANT
AU REVOIR
AU REVOIR
AU REVOIR
AU REVOIR
A-MA-VIE
> [*On her last note, she sees* FLO'RANCE *and, in total shock, crosses to him.*]

LALA: Flo'rance, what the hell are you doing our here looking like that. I haven't seen you for three days and you decide to show up now?
> [*He mumbles.*]

I don't want to hear it!
> [*He mumbles.*]

I said shut up!
> [ADMONIA *enters from stage right and has a letter opener on a silver tray.*]

ADMONIA: Pst!
> [LALA, *embarrassed by the presence of* ADMONIA *on stage, smiles apologetically at the audience.*]

LALA: Un momento.
> [*She then pulls* ADMONIA *to the side.*]

LALA: Darling, have you lost your mind coming onstage while I'm performing? And what have you done to Flo'rance? When I asked you to keep him tied up, I didn't mean to tie him up.
> [ADMONIA *gives her the letter opener.*]

LALA: Why are you giving me this? I have no letters to open. I'm in the middle of my American debut. Admonia, take Flo'rance off this stage with you! Admonia!
> [ADMONIA *is gone.* LALA *turns to the audience and tries to make the best of it.*]

LALA: That was Admonia, my slightly overweight black maid, and this is Flo'rance, my amour. I remember how we met, don't you, Flo'rance. I was sitting in a café on the Left Bank, when I looked up and saw the most beautiful man staring down at me.

"Who are you," he asked. I told him my name . . . whatever my name was back then. And he said, "No, that cannot be your name. Your name should fly, like Lala." And the rest is la history.

Flo'rance molded me into the woman I am today. He is my Svengali, my reality, my all. And I thought I was all to him, until we came here to America, and he fucked that bitch. Yeah, you fucked 'em all. Anything black and breathing. And all this time, I thought you loved me for being me. [*She holds the letter opener to his neck.*]

You may think you made me, but I'll have you know I was who I was, whoever that was, long before you made me what I am. So there! [*She stabs him and breaks into song.*]

OH, LOVE CAN DRIVE A WOMAN TO MADNESS
TO PAIN AND SADNESS
I KNOW
BELIEVE ME I KNOW
I KNOW
I KNOW

[LALA *sees what she's done and is about to scream but catches herself and tries to play it off.*]

LALA: Moving right along.

[ADMONIA *enters with a telegram on a tray.*]

ADMONIA: Pst.

LALA: [*anxious/hostile*] What is it now?

[ADMONIA *hands* LALA *a telegram.*]

LALA: [*excited*] Oh, la telegram from one of my fans and the concert isn't even over yet. Get me the letter opener. It's in Flo'rance.

[ADMONIA *hands* LALA *the letter opener.*]

LALA: Next I am going to do for you my immortal hit song, "The Girl Inside." But first we open the telegram. [*She quickly reads it and is outraged.*] What! Which pig in la audience wrote this trash? [*reading*] "Dear Sadie, I'm so proud. The show's wonderful, but talk less and sing more. Love, Mama."

First off, no one calls me Sadie. Sadie died the day Lala was born. And secondly, my mama's dead. Anyone who knows anything about Lala Lamazing Grace knows that my mother and Josephine Baker were French patriots together. They infiltrated a carnival rumored to be the center of Nazi intelligence, disguised as Hottentot Siamese twins. You may laugh but it's true. Mama died a heroine. It's all in my autobiography, *Voilà Lala!* So whoever sent this telegram is a liar!

[ADMONIA *promptly presents her with another telegram.*]

LALA: This had better be an apology. [*to* ADMONIA] Back up, darling. [*reading*] "Dear Sadie, I'm not dead. P.S. Your child misses you." What? [*She squares off at the audience.*] Well, now, that does it! If you are my mother, which you are not. And this alleged child is my child, then that would mean I am a mother and I have never given birth. I don't know nothin' 'bout birthin' no babies! [*She laughs.*] Lala made a funny.

So whoever sent this, show me the child! Show me!

[ADMONIA *offers another telegram.*]

LALA: [*to* ADMONIA] You know you're gonna get fired! [*She reluctantly opens it.*] "The child is in the closet." What closet?

ADMONIA: Pst.

[ADMONIA *pushes a button and the center wall unit revolves around to reveal a large black door.* ADMONIA *exits, taking* FLO'RANCE *with her, leaving* LALA *alone.*]

LALA: [*laughing*] I get it. It's a plot, isn't it. A nasty little CIA, FBI kind of plot. Well let me tell you muthafuckers one thing, there is nothing in that closet, real or manufactured, that will be a dimmer to the glimmer of Lamé the star. You may have gotten Billie and Bessie and a little piece of everyone else who's come along since, but you won't get Lala. My clothes are too fabulous! My hair is too long! My accent too French. That's why I came home to America. To prove you ain't got nothing on me!

[*The music for her next song starts, but* LALA *is caught up in her tirade, and talks/screams over the music.*]

My mother and Josephine Baker were French patriots together! I've had brunch with the pope! I've dined with the queen! Everywhere I go I cause riots! Hunny, I am a star! I have transcended pain! So there! [*yelling*] Stop the music! Stop that goddam music.

[*The music stops.* LALA *slowly walks downstage and singles out someone in the audience.*]

Darling, you're not looking at me. You're staring at that damn door. Did you pay to stare at some fucking door or be mesmerized by my talent?

[*to the whole audience:*]

Very well! I guess I am going to have to go to the closet door, fling it open, in order to dispel all the nasty little thoughts these nasty little telegrams have planted in your nasty little minds. [*speaking directly to someone in the audience*] Do you want me to open the closet door? Speak up, darling, this is live. [*once she gets the person to say "yes"*] I will open the door, but before I do, let me tell you bastards one last thing. To hell with coming home and to hell with lies and insinuations!

[LALA *goes into the closet and after a short pause comes running out, ready to scream, and slams the door. Traumatized to the point of no return, she tells the following story as if it were a jazz solo of rushing, shifting emotions.*]

LALA: I must tell you this dream I had last night. Simply magnifique. In this dream, I'm running naked in Sammy Davis Junior's hair. [*crazed laughter*]

Yes! I'm caught in this larger-than-life, deep, dark forest of savage, nappy-nappy hair. The kinky-kinks are choking me, wrapped around my naked arms, thighs, breast, face. I can't breathe. And there was nothing in that closet!

And I'm thinking if only I had a machete, I could cut away the kinks. Remove once and for all the roughness. But then I look up and it's coming toward me. Flowing like lava. It's pomade! Ohhh, Sammy!

Yes, cakes and cakes of pomade. Making everything nice and white and smooth and shiny, like my black/white/black/white/black behiney.

Mama no!

And then spikes start cutting through the pomade. Combing the coated kink. Cutting through the kink, into me. There are bloodlines on my back. On my thighs.

It's all over. All over . . . all over me. All over for me.

[LALA *accidentally pulls off her wig to reveal her real hair. Stripped of her "disguise" she recoils like a scared little girl and sings.*]

MOMMY AND DADDY
MEET AND MATE
THE CHILD THAT'S BORN
IS TORN WITH LOVE AND WITH HATE

SHE RUNS AWAY TO FIND HER OWN
AND TRIES TO DENY
WHAT SHE'S ALWAYS KNOWN
THE GIRL INSIDE
> [*The closet door opens.* LALA *runs away, and a* LITTLE BLACK GIRL *emerges from the closet. Standing behind her is* ADMONIA.]
> [*The* LITTLE GIRL *and* LALA *are in two isolated pools of light, and mirror each other's moves until* LALA *reaches past her reflection and the* LITTLE GIRL *comes to* LALA *and they hug.* ADMONIA *then joins them as* LALA *sings. Music underscored.*]

LALA: WHAT'S LEFT IS THE GIRL INSIDE
THE GIRL WHO DIED
SO A NEW GIRL COULD BE BORN
SLOW FADE TO BLACK

PERMUTATIONS

Lights up on NORMAL JEAN REYNOLDS. *She is very Southern/country and very young. She wears a simple faded print dress and her hair, slightly mussed, is in plaits. She sits, her dress covering a large oval object.*

NORMAL: My mama used to say, God made the exceptional, then God made the special, and when God got bored, he made me. 'Course she don't say too much of nuthin' no more, not since I lay me this egg.
> [*She lifts her dress to uncover a large, white egg lying between her legs.*]
Ya see it all got started when I had me sexual relations with the garbage man. Ooowee, did he smell.

No, not bad. No! He smelled of all the good things folks never shoulda thrown away. His sweat was like cantaloupe juice. His neck was like a ripe-red strawberry. And the water that fell from his eyes was like a deep, dark, juicy-juicy grape. I tell ya, it was like fuckin' a fruit salad, only I didn't spit out the seeds. I kept them here, deep inside. And three days later, my belly commence to swell, real big like.

Well my mama locked me off in some dark room, refusin' to let me see light of day 'cause, "What would the neighbors think." At first I cried a lot, but then I grew used to livin' my days in the dark, and my nights in the dark. . . . [*She hums.*] And then it wasn't but a week or so later, my mama off at church, that I got this hurtin' feelin' down here. Worse than anything I'd ever known. And then I started bleedin', real bad. I mean there was blood everywhere. And the pain had me howlin' like a near-dead dog. I tell ya, I was yellin' so loud, I couldn't even hear myself. Noooooooo! Nooooooo! Carrying on something like that.

And I guess it was just too much for the body to take, 'cause the next thing I remember . . . is me coming to and there's this big white egg layin' 'tween my legs. First I thought somebody musta put it there as some kind of joke. But then I noticed that all 'round this egg were thin lines of blood that I could trace to back between my legs.

[*laughing*] Well, when my mama come home from church she just about died. "Normal Jean, what's that thing 'tween your legs? Normal Jean, you answer me, girl!" It's not a thing, Mama. It's an egg. And I laid it.

She tried separatin' me from it, but I wasn't havin' it. I stayed in that dark room, huggin', holdin' onto it.

And then I heard it. It wasn't anything that coulda been heard 'round the world, or even in the next room. It was kinda like layin' back in the bath tub, ya know, the water just coverin' your ears . . . and if you lay real still and listen real close, you can hear the sound of your heart movin' the water. You ever done that? Well that's what it sounded like. A heart movin' water. And it was happenin' inside here.

Why, I'm the only person I know who ever lay themselves an egg before so that makes me special. You hear that, Mama? I'm special and so's my egg! And special things supposed to be treated like they matter. That's why every night I count to it, so it knows nuthin' never really ends. And I sing it every song I know so that when it comes out, it's full of all kinds of feelings. And I tell it secrets and laugh with it and . . .

[*She suddenly stops and puts her ear to the egg and listens intently.*]
Oh! I don't believe it! I thought I heard . . . yes! [*Excited.*] Can you hear it? Instead of one heart, there's two. Two little hearts just pattering away. Boom-boom-boom. Boom-boom-boom. Talkin' to each other like old friends. Racin' toward the beginnin' of their lives.

[*Listening.*] Oh, no, now there's three . . . four . . . five, six. More hearts than I can count. And they're all alive, beatin' out life inside my egg.

[*We begin to hear the heartbeats, drums, alive inside* NORMAL's *egg.*]
Any day now, this egg is gonna crack open and what's gonna come out a be the likes of which nobody has ever seen. My babies! And their skin is gonna turn all kinds of shades in the sun and their hair a be growin' every which-a-way. And it won't matter and they won't care 'cause they know they are so rare and so special 'cause it's not everyday a bunch of babies break outta a white egg and start to live.

And nobody better not try and hurt my babies 'cause if they do, they gonna have to deal with me.

Yes, any day now, this shell's gonna crack and my babies are gonna fly. Fly! Fly!

[*She laughs at the thought, but then stops and says the word as if it's the most natural thing in the world.*]

Fly.
BLACKOUT

THE PARTY

Before we know what's hit us, a hurricane of energy comes bounding into the space. It is TOPSY WASHINGTON. *Her hair and dress are a series of stylistic contradictions which are hip, black, and unencumbered.*

Music, spiritual and funky, underscores.

TOPSY: [*dancing about*] Yoho! Party! Party! Turn up the music! Turn up the music!

Have yaw ever been to a party where there was one fool in the middle of the room, dancing harder and yelling louder than everybody in the entire place? Well, hunny, that fool was me!

Yes, child! The name is Topsy Washington and I love to party. As a matter of fact, when God created the world, on the seventh day, he didn't rest. No child, he P-A-R-T-I-E-D. Partied!

But now let me tell you 'bout this function I went to the other night, way uptown. And baby when I say way uptown, I mean way-way-way-way-way-way-way-way uptown. Somewhere's between 125th Street and infinity.

Inside was the largest gathering of black/Negro/colored Americans you'd ever want to see. Over in one corner you got Nat Turner sippin' champagne out of Eartha Kitt's slipper. And over in another corner, Bert Williams and Malcolm X was discussing existentialism as it relates to the shuffle-ball-change. Girl, Aunt Jemima and Angela Davis was in the kitchen sharing a plate of greens and just goin' off about South Africa.

And then Fats sat down and started to work them eighty-eights. And then Stevie joined in. And then Miles and Duke and Ella and Jimi and Charlie and Sly and Lightin' and Count and Louie!

And then everybody joined in. I tell you all the children was just all up in there, dancing to the rhythm of one beat. Dancing to the rhythm of their own definition. Celebrating in their cultural madness.

And then the floor started to shake. And the walls started to move. And before anybody knew what was happening, the entire room lifted up off the ground. The whole place just took off and went flying through space—defying logic and limitations. Just a spinning and a spinning and a spinning until it disappeared inside of my head.

[TOPSY *stops dancing and regains her balance and begins to listen to the music in her head. Slowly we begin to hear it, too.*]

That's right, girl, there's a party goin' on inside of here. That's why when I walk down the street my hips just sashay all over the place. 'Cause I'm dancing to the music of the madness in me.

And whereas I used to jump into a rage anytime anybody tried to deny who I was, now all I got to do is give attitude, quicker than light, and then go on about the business of being me. 'Cause I'm dancing to the music of the madness in me.

[*As* TOPSY *continues to speak,* MISS ROJ, LALA, MISS PAT, *and* THE MAN *from Symbiosis revolve on, frozen like soft sculptures.*]

TOPSY: And here, all this time I been thinking we gave up our drums. But, naw, we still got 'em. I know I got mine. They're here, in my speech, my walk, my hair, my God, my style, my smile, and my eyes. And everything I need to get over in this world, is inside here, connecting me to everybody and everything that's ever been.

So, hunny, don't waste your time trying to label or define me.

[*The sculptures slowly begin to come to "life" and they mirror/echo* TOPSY's *words.*]

TOPSY/EVERYBODY: . . . 'cause I'm not what I was ten years ago or ten minutes ago. I'm all of that and then some. And whereas I can't live inside yesterday's pain, I can't live without it.

[*All of a sudden, madness erupts on the stage. The sculptures begin to speak all at once. Images of black/Negro/colored Americans begin to flash—images of them dancing past the madness, caught up in the madness, being lynched, rioting, partying, surviving. Mixed in with these images are all the characters from the exhibits. Through all of this* TOPSY *sings. It is a vocal and visual cacophony which builds and builds.*]

LALA: I must tell you about this dream I had last night. Simply magnifique. In this dream I'm running naked in Sammy Davis Junior's hair. Yes. I'm caught in this larger-than-life, deep, dark tangled forest of savage, nappy-nappy hair. Yes, the kinky kinks are choking me, are wrapped around my naked arms, my naked thighs, breast, and face, and I can't breathe and there was nothing in that closet.

MISS ROJ: Snap for every time you walk past someone lying in the street smelling like frozen piss and shit and you don't see it. Snap for every crazed bastard who kills himself so as to get the jump on being killed. And snap for every sick muthafucker who, bored with carrying about his fear, takes to shooting up other people.

THE MAN: I have no history. I have no past. I can't. It's too much. It's much too much. I must be able to smile on cue and watch the news with an impersonal eye. I have no stake in the madness. Being black is too emotionally taxing, therefore I will be black only on weekends and holidays.

MISS PAT: Stop playing those drums. I said stop playing those damn drums. You can't stop history. You can't stop time. Those drums will be confiscated once we reach Savannah, so give them up now. Repeat after me: I don't hear any drums and I will not rebel. I will not rebel!

TOPSY: [*singing*]
THERE'S MADNESS IN ME
AND THAT MADNESS SETS ME FREE
THERE'S MADNESS IN ME
AND THAT MADNESS SETS ME FREE
THERE'S MADNESS IN ME
AND THAT MADNESS SETS ME FREE
THERE'S MADNESS IN ME
AND THAT MADNESS SETS ME FREE
THERE'S MADNESS IN ME
AND THAT MADNESS SETS ME FREE

TOPSY: My power is in my . . .

EVERYBODY: *Madness!*

TOPSY: And my colored contradictions.

[*The sculptures freeze with a smile on their faces as we hear the voice of* MISS PAT.]

VOICE OF MISS PAT: Before exiting, check the overhead as any baggage you don't claim, we trash.

BLACKOUT

Milcha Sanchez-Scott (1955–)

Roosters (1987)

Like African American drama, Latino drama has become increasingly well known since the mid-1960s, when Luis Valdez achieved wide recognition with plays designed to help migrant farm workers gain better working conditions. Although the number of Latino playwrights thereafter grew significantly, few prior to the 1980s were female. Among recent Latina playwrights, Milcha Sanchez-Scott has been one of the most successful.

Sanchez-Scott's *Roosters*, first produced jointly by INTAR Hispanic Arts Center and the New York Shakespeare Festival in 1987, uses cockfighting as its central metaphor. Set in the desert Southwest, the major action focuses on a struggle between the father of a family, Gallo ("rooster," "macho"), whose life is given meaning by cockfighting (winning at which in his eyes justifies any behavior, including cheating, con games, and even murder) and his son Hector, who wishes to escape the kind of life his father has led. Their struggle is focused on their rival claims to Zapata, a fighting cock. Eventually Gallo (apparently willing to kill his own son in order to gain possession of the rooster), using a stiletto, forces Hector to fight him.

Caught in this struggle between males are the three women of the family: Juana, Gallo's worn-down wife who supports the family, always deferring to her adored husband; Chata, Gallo's promiscuous sister; and Angela, Gallo's adolescent daughter who wears angel wings and clings to childhood and religion as buffers against hurt. Angela's faith is shattered when her father, after cajoling her into revealing the whereabouts of Zapata, abandons her after he recovers the rooster. During a superhuman effort to regain her faith, she levitates. The atmosphere of the play moves easily between realism and fantasy in the manner of Latino "magic realism." Overall, *Roosters* is a powerful play that has much to say about machismo, women, love, and psychological need in a male-dominated Latino culture.

Developed and originally produced on the stage by INTAR Hispanic American Art Center in New York City in 1987.

Milcha Sanchez-Scott

Roosters

CHARACTERS

GALLO
ZAPATA
HECTOR
ANGELA
JUANA
CHATA
ADAN
SHADOW #1
SHADOW #2
SAN JUAN

TIME:———*The Present*
PLACE:———*The Southwest*

ACT ONE

SCENE I

Stage and house are dark. Slowly a narrow pinspot of light comes up. We hear footsteps. Enter GALLO, *a very, very handsome man in his forties. He is wearing a cheap dark suit, with a white open-neck shirt. He carries a suitcase. He puts the suitcase down. He faces the audience.*

GALLO: Lord Eagle, Lord Hawk, sainted ones, spirits and winds, Santa María Aurora of the Dawn . . . I want no resentment, I want no rancor. . . . I had an old red Cuban hen. She was squirrel-tailed and sort of slab-sided and you wouldn't have given her a second look. But she was a queen. She could be thrown with any cock and you would get a hard-kicking stag every time.

I had a vision, of a hard-kicking flyer, the ultimate bird. The Filipinos were the ones with the pedigree Bolinas, the high flyers, but they had no real kick. To see those birds fighting in the air like dark avenging angels . . . well like my father use to say, "Son nobles . . . finos. . . ." I figured to mate that old red Cuban. This particular Filipino had the best. A dark burgundy flyer named MacArthur. He wouldn't sell. I began borrowing MacArthur at night, bringing him back before dawn, no one the wiser, but one morning the Filipino's son caught me. He pulled out his blade. I pulled out mine. I was faster. I went up on manslaughter. . . . They never caught on . . . thought I was in the henhouse trying to steal their stags. . . . It took time—refining,

516

inbreeding, cross-breeding, brother to sister, mother to son, adding power, rapid attack . . . but I think we got him.

[GALLO *stands still for a beat, checks his watch, takes off his jacket and faces center stage. A slow, howling drumbeat begins. As it gradually goes higher in pitch and excitement mounts, we see narrow beams of light, the first light of dawn, filtering through chicken wire. The light reveals a heap of chicken feathers which turns out to be an actor/dancer who represents the rooster* ZAPATA. ZAPATA *stretches his wings, then his neck, to greet the light. He stands and struts proudly, puffs his chest and crows his salutation to the sun.* GALLO *stalks* ZAPATA, *as drums follow their movements.*]

Ya, ya, mi lindo . . . yeah, baby . . . you're a beauty, a real beauty. Now let's see whatcha got. [*He pulls out a switchblade stiletto. It gleams in the light as he tosses it from hand to hand.*] Come on baby boy. Show Daddy whatcha got.

[GALLO *lunges at* ZAPATA. *The rooster parries with his beak and wings. This becomes a slow, rhythmic fight-dance, which continues until* GALLO *grabs* ZAPATA *by his comb, bending his head backwards until he is forced to sit.* GALLO *stands behind* ZAPATA, *straddling him, one hand still holding the comb, the other holding the knife against the rooster's neck.*]

Oh yeah, you like to fight? Huh? You gonna kill for me baby boy? Huh?

[GALLO *sticks the tip of the knife into* ZAPATA. *The rooster squawks in pain.*]

Sssh! Baby boy, you gotta learn. Daddy's gotta teach you.

[GALLO *sticks it to* ZAPATA *again. This time the rooster snaps back in anger.*]

That's right beauty. . . . Now you got it. . . . Come on, come.

[GALLO *waves his knife and hand close to* ZAPATA's *face. The rooster's head and eyes follow.*]

Oh yeah . . . that's it baby, take it! Take it!

[*Suddenly* ZAPATA *attacks, drawing blood.* GALLO's *body contracts in orgasmic pleasure/pain.*]

Ay precioso! . . . Mi lindo. . . . You like that, eh? Taste good, huh? [*He waves the gleaming knife in a slow hypnotic movement which calms the rooster.*] Take my blood, honey. . . . I'm in you now. . . . Morales blood, the blood of kings . . . and you're my rooster . . . a Morales rooster. [*He slowly backs away from the rooster. He picks up his suitcase, still pointing the knife at* ZAPATA.] Kill. You're my son. Make me proud.

[GALLO *exits.* ZAPATA *puffs his chest and struts upstage. Lights go up a little on upstage left area as the rooster goes into the chicken-wire henhouse. He preens and scratches. Enter* HECTOR, *a young man of about twenty. He is very handsome. He wears gray sweatpants and no shirt. On his forehead is a sweatband. His hair and body are dripping wet. He has been running. Now he is panting as he leans on the henhouse looking at* ZAPATA.]

HECTOR: I saw what you did to those chicks. Don't look at me like you have a mind, or a soul, or feelings. You kill your young . . . and we are so proud of your horrible animal vigor. . . . But you are my inheritance . . . Abuelo's gift to me . . . to get me out. Oh, Abuelo, Grandfather . . . you should have left me your courage, your sweet pacific strength.

[*A ray of light hits downstage right. In a semi-shadow, we see a miniature cemetery, with small white headstones and white crosses. We see the profile of a young angel/girl with wings and a pale dress.* ANGELA *is kneeling next to a bare desert tree with low scratchy branches. She has a Buster Brown haircut and a low tough voice. She is fifteen, but looks twelve.*]

ANGELA: [*loudly*]
Angel of God
My Guardian Dear
To whom God's love
Commits me here
Ever this day be
At my side
To light and guard
To rule and guide
Amen.
[*Her paper wings get caught in a tree branch.*] Aw, shit! [*She exits.*]

SCENE II

As the light changes we hear the clapping of women making tortillas. Lights come up full. Center stage is a faded wood-frame house, with a porch that is bare except for a table and a few chairs. The house sits in the middle of a desert agricultural valley somewhere in the Southwest. Everything is sparse. There is a feeling of blue skies and space. One might see off on the horizon tall Nopales or Century cactus. JUANA, *a thin, worn-out–looking woman of thirty-five, comes out of the house. She is wearing a faded housedress. She goes to mid-yard, faces front and stares out.*

JUANA: It's dry. Bone dry. There's a fire in the mountains . . . up near Jacinto Pass.
[*The clapping stops for a beat, then continues. She starts to go back into the house, then stops. She sniffs the air, sniffs again, and again.*] Tres Rosas . . . I smell Tres Rosas. [*She hugs her body and rocks.*] Tres Rosas. . . . Ay, St. Anthony let him come home. . . . Let him be back.
[*The clapping stops.* CHATA *enters from the house. She is a fleshy woman of forty, who gives new meaning to the word "blowsy." She has the lumpy face of a hard boozer. She walks with a slight limp. She wears a black kimono, on the back of which is embroidered in red a dragon and the words "Korea, U.S.S. Perkins, 7th Fleet." A cigarette hangs from her lips. She carries a bowl containing balls of tortilla dough.*]
I smell Tres Rosas. . . . The brilliantine for his hair. . . . He musta been here. Why did he go?
CHATA: Men are shit.
JUANA: Where could he be?
CHATA: First day out of jail! My brother never comes home first day. You should know that. Gotta sniff around . . . gotta get use to things. See his friends.
JUANA: Sí, that's right. . . . He just gotta get used to things. I'll feel better when I see him. . . . I gotta keep busy.
CHATA: You been busy all morning.
JUANA: I want him to feel good, be proud of us. . . . You hear anything when you come in yesterday?

CHATA: Who's gonna know anything at the Trailways bus station?

JUANA: You ain't heard anything?

CHATA: Juanita, he knows what he's doing. If there was gonna be any trouble he'd know. Ay, mujer, he's just an old warrior coming home.

JUANA: Ain't that old.

CHATA: For a fighting man, he's getting up there.

[JUANA *slaps tortillas.* CHATA *watches her.*]

Who taught you to make tortillas?

JUANA: I don't remember. I never make 'em. Kids don't ask.

CHATA: Look at this. You call this a tortilla? Have some pride. Show him you're a woman.

JUANA: Chata, you've been here one day, and you already—

CHATA: Ah, you people don't know what it is to eat fresh handmade tortillas. My grandmother Hortensia, the one they used to call "La India Condenada" . . . she would start making them at five o'clock in the morning. So the men would have something to eat when they went into the fields. Hijo! She was tough. . . . Use to break her own horses . . . and her own men. Every day at five o'clock she would wake me up. "Buenos pinchi días," she would say. I was twelve or thirteen years old, still in braids. . . . "Press your hands into the dough," "Con fuerza," "Put your stamp on it." One day I woke up, tú sabes, con la sangre. "Ah! So you're a woman now. Got your own cycle like the moon. Soon you'll want a man, well this is what you do. When you see the one you want, you roll the tortilla on the inside of your thigh and then you give it to him nice and warm. Be sure you give it to him and nobody else." Well, I been rolling tortillas on my thighs, on my nalgas, and God only knows where else, but I've been giving my tortillas to the wrong men . . . and that's been the problem with my life. First there was Emilio. I gave him my first tortilla. Ay Mamacita, he use to say, these are delicious. Aye, he was handsome, a real lady-killer! After he did me the favor he didn't even have the cojones to stick around . . . took my TV set, too. They're all shit . . . the Samoan bartender, what was his name . . .

JUANA: Nicky, Big Nicky.

CHATA: The guy from Pep Boys—

JUANA: Chata, you really think he'll be back?

CHATA: His son's first time in the pit? With "the" rooster? A real Morales rooster? Honey, he'll be back. Stop worrying.

JUANA: Let's put these on the griddle. Angela, Hector . . . breakfast.

SCENE III

ANGELA *slides out from under the house, wearing her wings. She carries a white box which contains her cardboard tombstones, paper and crayons, a writing tablet, and a pen. She, too, sniffs the air. She runs to the little cemetery and looks up, as* HECTOR *appears at the window behind her.*

ANGELA: Tres Rosas. . . . Did you hear? Sweet Jesus, Abuelo, Queen of Heaven, all the Saints, all the Angels. It is true. It is certain. He is coming, coming to stay forever and ever. Amen.

HECTOR: Don't count on it!

ANGELA: [*to Heaven*] Protect me from those of little faith and substance.

HECTOR: I'm warning you. You're just going to be disappointed.

ANGELA: [*to Heaven*] Guard me against the enemies of my soul.

HECTOR: Your butt's getting bigger and bigger!

ANGELA: And keep me from falling in with low companions.

HECTOR: Listen, little hummingbird woman, you gotta be tough, and grown-up today.

[ANGELA *digs up her collection can and two dolls. Both dolls are dressed in nuns' habits. One, the St. Lucy doll, has round sunglasses. She turns a box over to make a little tea table on which she places a doll's teapot and cups.*]

ANGELA: As an act of faith and to celebrate her father's homecoming, Miss Angela Ester Morales will have a tea party.

HECTOR: No more tea parties.

ANGELA: Dancing in attendance will be that charming martyr St. Lucy.

HECTOR: He will not be impressed.

ANGELA: Due to the loss of her eyes and the sensitivity of her alabaster skin, St. Lucy will sit in the shade. [*She sits St. Lucy in the shade and picks up the other doll.*]

HECTOR: Who's that?

ANGELA: St. Teresa of Avignon, you will sit over here. [*She seats St. Teresa doll.*]

HECTOR: Just don't let him con you, Angela.

ANGELA: [*pouring pretend tea*] One lump or two, St. Lucy? St. Teresa has hyper-glycemia, and only takes cream in her tea. Isn't that right, St. Teresa?

HECTOR: He's not like Abuelo.

[ANGELA *animates the dolls like puppets and uses two different voices as St. Lucy and St. Teresa.*]

ANGELA: [*as St. Teresa*] Shouldn't we wait for St. Luke?

HECTOR: Stop hiding. You can't be a little girl forever.

ANGELA: [*as St. Lucy*] St. Luke! St. Luke! Indeed! How that man got into Heaven I'll never know. That story about putting peas in his boots and of-fering the discomfort up to God is pure bunk. I happen to know he boiled the peas first.

HECTOR: I don't want you hurt. It's time to grow up.

ANGELA: [*as St. Teresa*] St. Lucy! I can only think that it is the loss of your eyes that makes you so disagreeable. Kindly remember that we have all suffered to be saints.

HECTOR: Are you listening to me, Angie?

ANGELA: [*as St. Lucy*] Easy for you to say! They took my eyes because I wouldn't put out! They put them on a plate. A dirty, chipped one, thank you very much indeed! To this day no true effort has been made to find them.

HECTOR: Excuse me! . . . Excuse me, St. Teresa, St. Lucy, I just thought I should tell you . . . a little secret. . . . Your hostess, Miss Angela Ester Morales, lies in her little, white, chaste, narrow bed, underneath the crucifix, and mas-turbates.

ANGELA: Heretic! Liar!

HECTOR: Poor Jesus, up there on the cross, right over her bed, his head tilted down. He sees everything.

ANGELA: Lies! Horrible lies!

HECTOR: Poor saint of the month, watching from the night table.

ANGELA: I hate you! I hate you! Horrible, horrible Hector.

JUANA: [*from offstage*] Breakfast!
> [HECTOR *leaves the window.* ANGELA *sits on the ground writing on a tombstone.*]

ANGELA: [*lettering a tombstone*] Here lies Horrible Hector Morales. Died at age twenty, in great agony, for tormenting his little sister.

JUANA: [*offstage*] You kids . . . breakfast!

HECTOR: [*pops up at window*] Just be yourself. A normal sex-crazed fifteen-year-old girl with a big gigantic enormous butt. [*He exits.*]

ANGELA: [*to Heaven*]
> Send me to Alaska
> Let me be frozen
> Send me a contraction
> A shrinking antidote
> Make me little again
> Please make my legs
> Like tiny pink Vienna sausages
> Give me back my little butt.
> [JUANA *and* CHATA *bring breakfast out on the porch and set it on the table.*]

JUANA: Angie! Hector! We ain't got all day.
> [ANGELA *goes to the breakfast table with the St. Lucy doll and the collection can.*]

And take your wings off before you sit at the table. Ain't you kids got any manners?
> [ANGELA *removes her wings, sits down, bows her head in prayer.* CHATA *stares at St. Lucy. St. Lucy stares at* CHATA. JUANA *shoos flies and stares at the distant fire.*]

I hope he's on this side of the fire.

CHATA: That doll's staring at me.

ANGELA: She loves you.
> [*Lights fade on the women, come up on the henhouse,* ADAN, *a young man of twenty, is talking to* ZAPATA—*now a real rooster, not the actor/dancer—and preparing his feed.*]

ADAN: Hola Zapata . . . ya mi lindo . . . mi bonito En Inglés. Tengo que hablar en English . . . pinchi English . . . verdad Zapata? En Español más romántico pero Hector say I must learned di English. [ZAPATA *starts squawking.*] Qué te pasa? Orita vas a comer.
> [HECTOR *enters.*]

HECTOR: English, Adan . . . English.

ADAN: No English . . . pinchi English.

HECTOR: Good morning, Adan.

ADAN: A que la fregada! . . . Okay this morning in the fields, I talk English pero this afternoon for fight I talk puro Español.

HECTOR: Good morning, Adan.

ADAN: Sí, sí, good morning, muy fine. . . . Hector el Filipino he say . . . [*He moves away from* ZAPATA, *so bird will not hear him.*] He say to tell you que Zapata

no win. Porque Filipino bird fight more y your bird first fight y your first
fight y you got no ex . . . ex . . .

HECTOR: Experience.

ADAN: Sí eso, he say you sell bird to him y no fight. . . . He say is not true Morales
bird porque Gallo not here. El Filipino say if you fight bird . . . bird dead.
If bird still alive after Filipino bird beat him. . . . Bird still dead porque nobody pay money for bird that lose.

HECTOR: But if he wins, everybody wants him.

ADAN: I say, ay di poor, poor Hector. His abuelo leave him bird. He can no sell.
El Filipino say, "Good!" Inside, in my heart I am laughing so hard porque
he not know Gallo gonna be here. We win, we make much money.

HECTOR: It's my bird, I have to do it myself.

ADAN: You tonto! You stupido! You mulo! Like donkey. . . . He help you, he the
king . . . he you papa. For him all birds fight.

HECTOR: No!

ADAN: Why? Why for you do this? You no even like bird. Zapata he knows this,
he feel this thing in his heart. You just want money to go from the fields, to
go to the other side of the mountains . . . to go looking . . . to go looking
for what? On the other side is only more stupid people like us.

HECTOR: How could you think I just wanted money? I want him to see me.

ADAN: Sorry. . . . I am sorry my friend. . . . I know. . . . I stay with you y we win
vas a ver! Okay Zapata! We win y esta noche estamos tomando Coors, Rip-
ple, Lucky Lager, unas Buds, Johnnie Walkers, oh sí, y las beautiful señori-
tas. [*He gives* ZAPATA *his food.*] Eat Zapata! Be strong.

HECTOR: I almost forgot, look what I have for you . . . fresh, warm homemade
tortillas.

ADAN: Oh, how nice.

HECTOR: Yes, how nice. Aunt Chata made them.

ADAN: Oh, much nice.

HECTOR: Today she woke up at five o'clock, spit a green booger the size of a small
frog into a wad of Kleenex. She wrapped her soiled black "7th Fleet" kimono around her loose, flaccid, tortured, stretch-marked body and put her
fattooed, corned yellow hooves into a pair of pink satin slippers. She
slap-padded over to the sink, where she opened her two hippo lips and
looked into the mirror. She looked sad. I looked at those lips . . . those lips
that had wrapped themselves warmly and lovingly around the cocks of a
million campesinos, around thousands upon thousands of Mexicanos, Sal-
vadoreños, Guatemaltecos. For the tide of brown men that flooded the
fields of this country, she was there with her open hippo whore's lips, saying, "Bienvenidos," "Welcome," "Hola," "Howdy." Those are legendary lips,
Adan.

ADAN: Yes . . . muy yes.

HECTOR: What a woman, what a comfort. Up and down the state in her beat-up
station wagon. A '56 Chevy with wood panels on the sides, in the back a
sad, abused mattress. She followed the brown army of pickers through
tomatoes, green beans, zucchinis, summer squash, oranges, and finally Cas-
troville, the artichoke capital of the world, where her career was stopped by
the fists of a sun-crazed compañero. The ingratitude broke her heart.

ADAN: Oh my gooseness!

HECTOR: She was a river to her people, she should be rewarded, honored. No justice in the world.

ADAN: Pinchi world. [*He and* HECTOR *look to mountains.*] You look mountains. In my country I look mountains to come here. I am here and everybody still look mountains.

HECTOR: I want to fly right over them.

ADAN: No, my friend, we are here, we belong . . . la tierra.

JUANA: [*from offstage*] Hector, I ain't calling you again.

> [*Lights up on the porch.* JUANA *and* CHATA *are sitting at the table.* ANGELA *is sitting on the steps. She has her wings back on. St. Lucy and the collection can are by her side. She is writing on her tablet.*]

JUANA: Oh Gallo, what's keeping you?

CHATA: Men are shit! That's all. And it's Saturday. When do they get drunk? When do they lose their money? When do they shoot each other? Saturdays, that's when the shit hits the fan.

> [*Enter* HECTOR *and* ADAN *with* ZAPATA *in a traveling carrier.*]

JUANA: It's because I'm so plain.

HECTOR: We're better off without him.

CHATA: Buenos días Adan. Un cafecito?

ADAN: Ah. Good morning, Mrs. Chata, no gracias, ah good morning, Mrs. Morales y Miss Angelita.

> [ANGELA *sticks out her collection can.* ADAN *automatically drops coins in.*]

JUANA: Angela!

ADAN: No, is good, is for the poor. Miss Angela, she good lady . . . eh, girl. [*He pats* ANGELA *on the head.*]

JUANA: Why don't you leave the bird, so your father can see him when he gets home.

HECTOR: He's my bird. He can see it later.

JUANA: I can't believe you would do this to your own father. Birds are his life . . . and he's so proud of you.

HECTOR: This is news. How would he know, he hasn't seen me in years.

JUANA: It isn't his fault.

HECTOR: It never is.

JUANA: Your father is with us all the time, he got his eye on us, he knows everything we're doing.

ANGELA: Everything!?

JUANA: I brag about you kids in my letters. . . . His friends they tell him what a smart boy you are . . . that you're good-looking like him. . . . He's proud. . . . "A real Morales," that's what he says.

HECTOR: And did he call me a winner? A champ? A prince? And did you tell him I was in the fields?

ANGELA: What did he say about me, Mama?

HECTOR: Nothing, you're a girl and a retard. What possible use could he have for you? Grow up!

CHATA: No, you grow up.

> [ANGELA *buries herself in* CHATA'S *lap.*]

JUANA: Hector, please, Hector, for me.

HECTOR: No, Mother. Not even for you.

JUANA: You give him a chance.

HECTOR: What chance did he give us? Fighting his birds, in and out of trouble. He was never here for us, never a card, a little present for Angela. He forgot us.

JUANA: You don't understand him. He's different.

HECTOR: Just make it clear to him. Abuelo left the bird to me, not to him, to me.

JUANA: Me, me, me. You gonna choke on this me, me. Okay, okay, I'm not going to put my nose in the bird business. I just ask you for me, for Angie, be nice to him.

HECTOR: As long as we all understand the "bird business," I'll be nice to him even if it kills me, Mother.

JUANA: Now you're feeling sorry for yourself. Just eat. You can feel sorry for yourself later.

HECTOR: Why didn't I think of that. I'll eat now and feel sorry for myself later.

JUANA: Now, you kids gotta be nice and clean, you papa don't like dirty people.

CHATA: Me, too, I hate dirty people.

JUANA: Angie, you take a bath.

HECTOR: Oh, Angela, how . . . how long has it been since you and water came together? [ANGELA *hits him.*] Oww!

JUANA: You put on a nice clean dress, and I don't wanna see you wearing no dirty wings.

HECTOR: Right, Angie, put on the clean ones.

JUANA: You say "please" and "excuse me" . . . and you watch your table manners. . . . I don't want to see any pigs at my table.

HECTOR: [*making pig noises*] What a delicious breakfast! Cold eggs, sunny-side up. How cheery! How uplifting! Hmm, hmmm! [*He turns so* ANGELA *can see him. He picks up eggs with his hands and stuffs them in his mouth.*] Look, Angela, refried beans in a delicate pool of congealed fat. [*Still making pig noises, he picks up gobs of beans, stuffs them into his mouth.*]

CHATA: A que la fregada! Hector, stop playing with your food. You're making us sick.

JUANA: [*looking at watch*] 7:20, you got ten minutes before work.

[HECTOR *drums his fingers on the table.*]

HECTOR: Nine minutes. . . . I will now put on the same old smelly, shit-encrusted boots, I will walk to the fields. The scent of cow dung and rotting vegetation will fill the air. I will wait with the same group of beaten-down, pathetic men . . . taking their last piss against a tree, dropping hard warm turds in the bushes. All adding to this fertile whore of a valley. At 7:30 that yellow mechanical grasshopper, the Deerfield tractor, will belch and move. At this exact moment, our foreman, John Knipe, will open his pig-sucking mouth, exposing his yellow, pointy, plaque-infested teeth. He yells, "Start picking, boys." The daily war begins . . . the intimidation of violent growth . . . the expanding melons and squashes, the hardiness of potatoes, the waxy purple succulence of eggplant, the potency of ripening tomatoes. All so smug, so rich, so ready to burst with sheer generosity and exuberance. They mock me. . . . I hear them. . . . "Hey Hector," they say, "show us whatcha got," and "Yo Hector we got bacteria out here more productive than you." . . . I look

to the ground. Slugs, snails, worms slithering in the earth with such fero-
cious hunger they devour their own tails, flies oozing out larvae, aphids,
bees, gnats, caterpillars their prolification only slightly dampened by our
sprays. We still find eggsacks hiding, ready to burst forth. Their teeming
life, their lust, is shameful . . . a mockery of me and my slender spirit. . . .
Well it's time. . . . Bye Ma. [*He exits.*]

JUANA: [*yelling*] Hector! You gotta do something about your attitude. [*to herself.*]
Try to see the bright side.

> [JUANA *and* CHATA *exit into the house, leaving* ANGELA *on the porch steps.*
> ADAN *runs up to her.*]

ADAN: Pssst! Miss Angelita! . . . di . . . di cartas?

ANGELA: Oh, the letters . . . that will be one dollar.

ADAN: One dollar! Adan very poor man. . . .

> [ANGELA *sticks the collection can out and shakes it.* ADAN *reaches into his
> pockets and drops coins into the can.*]

Oh, sí, you are very good.

> [ANGELA *puts on glasses and pulls out a letter.*]

ANGELA [*reading letter*] Adored Señora Acosta: The impulses of my heart are
such that they encourage even the most cautious man to commit indiscretion. My soul is carried to the extreme with the love that only you could in-
spire. Please know that I feel a true passion for your incomparable beauty
and goodness. I tremulously send this declaration and anxiously await the
result. Your devoted slave, Adan.

ADAN: [*sighing*] Ay, que beautiful.

ANGELA: P.S. With due respect Señora, if your husband should be home, do not
turn on the porch light.

ADAN: Ah, thank you . . . thank you very much.

> [ADAN *hurriedly exits.* ANGELA *gathers her St. Lucy doll and her collection
> can, and exits quickly.* CHATA *enters from the house wearing "colorful" street
> clothes. She looks around, then swiftly exits.* HECTOR *enters, picks up
> ZAPATA, hurries off.*]
>
> [*The stage darkens, as if smoke from the distant fire has covered the sun.
> Drum howls are heard. In the distance we hear a rooster crow and sounds of
> excited chickens as the henhouse comes to life.* GALLO *appears.*]

GALLO: Easy hens, shshsh! My beauties. [*He puts his suitcase down, cups his hands
to his mouth, and yells to the house.*] Juana! Juana! Juana! [JUANA *opens the
door.*] How many times, in the fever of homesickness, have I written out
that name on prison walls, on bits of paper, on the skin of my arms. . . . Let
me look at you . . . my enduring rock, my anchor made from the hard parts
of the earth—minerals, rocks, bits of glass, ground shells, the brittle bones
of dead animals.

JUANA: I never seen you so pale, so thin. . . .

GALLO: I'm home to rest, to fatten up, to breathe, to mend, to you.

JUANA: How long? How long will you stay?

GALLO: Here. Here is where I'll put my chair. . . . I will sit here basking in the
sun, like a fat old iguana catching flies, and watching my grandchildren re-
plant the little cemetery with the bones of tiny sparrows. Here. Here I will
build the walks for my champions. Morales roosters. The brave and gallant

red Cubans, the hard and high-kicking Irish Warhorses, the spirited high-flying Bolinas.

JUANA: Don't say nothing you don't mean. . . . You really gonna stay?

GALLO: [*gently*] Here. Here is where I'll plant a garden of herbs. Blessed laurel to cure fright, wild marjoram for the agony of lovesickness, cempasuchie flowers for the grief of loneliness.

> [GALLO *gently kisses* JUANA, *picks her up and carries her into the house. The door slams shut.* ANGELA *enters, her wings drooping behind her. She trips over* GALLO'*s suitcase. She examines it. She smells it.*]

ANGELA: Tres Rosas!

> [ANGELA *looks at the house. She sits on the suitcase, crosses her arms over her chest as if she were ready to wait an eternity. The shadows of two strangers fall on her.*]

ANGELA: What do you want?

SHADOW #1: Where's Gallo?

ANGELA: Nobody's home to you, rancor.

SHADOW #2: Just go in, tell him we got something for him.

ANGELA: Nobody's home to you, resentment.

SHADOW #1: Who are you supposed to be?

ANGELA: [*holding St. Lucy doll*]
I am the angel of this yard
I am the angel of this door
I am the angel of light
I am the angel who shouts
I am the angel who thunders

SHADOW #1: She is pure crazy.

SHADOW #2: Don't play with it, it's serious.

ANGELA: You are the shadow of resentment
You are the shadow of rancor
I am the angel of acid saliva
I will spit on you.

SHADOW #1: There's time.

SHADOW #2: Yeah, later.

> [ANGELA *spits. The shadows leave.* ANGELA *crosses her hands over her chest and looks to Heaven.*]

ANGELA: Holy Father. . . . Listen, you don't want him, you want me. Please take me, claim me, launch me and I will be your shooting-star woman. I will be your comet woman. I will be your morning-star woman.

SCENE IV

Lights become brighter. ANGELA *exits under the house. The door opens.* GALLO *comes out in T-shirt and pants and goes to his suitcase.* JUANA *comes to the door in slip and tight robe.*

GALLO: I never sent him to the fields.

JUANA: I know.

GALLO: I never said for you to put him there.

JUANA: No, you never said. . . .

GALLO: Then why is my son in the fields? [*They look at each other. He looks away.*] Don't look at me. I see it in your eyes. You blame me. Just like the old man.

JUANA: Abuelo never said a word against you.

GALLO: I never let him down with the birds, nobody could match me. They were the best.

JUANA: He knew that. . . .

GALLO: So, he left the bird to Hector.

JUANA: He wanted him out of the fields. We didn't know when you would be out or maybe something would happen to you.

GALLO: He let the boy into the fields, that was his sin. He allowed a Morales into the fields.

JUANA: He was old, tired, heartbroken.

GALLO: Heartbroken, he wasn't a woman to be heartbroken.

JUANA: His only son was in jail.

GALLO: Yes, we know that, the whole valley knows that. You . . . what did you do? Didn't you lay out your hard, succulent, bitch's teat at the breakfast table? So he would have the strength to stand behind a hoe, with his back bent and his eyes on the mud for ten hours a day.

JUANA: Hard work never killed anybody.

GALLO: Ay, mujer! Can't you think what you've done, you bowed his head down.

JUANA: What was I suppose to do? There ain't no other work here. I can't see anything wrong with it for a little while.

GALLO: The difference between them and us, is we never put a foot into the fields. We stayed independent—we worked for nobody. They have to respect us, to respect our roosters.

> [HECTOR *and* ADAN *enter. They are both very dirty.* HECTOR *has* ZAPATA, *in his carrier.* ADAN *has a carrier containing a second rooster.* GALLO *and* HECTOR *stare at each other.*]

Well . . . you are taller. This offshoot . . . this little bud has grown.

HECTOR: Yeah, well . . . that must be why you seem . . . smaller.

GALLO: Un abrazo!

HECTOR: I'm dirty, I'm sweaty.

GALLO: I see that.

HECTOR: I'm afraid I smell of the fields.

GALLO: Yes.

HECTOR: Of cheap abundant peon labor . . . the scent would gag you.

GALLO: It's going to kill you.

HECTOR: Mama says hard work never killed anyone . . . isn't that right, Mother?

JUANA: It's only for a little while. Your papa thinks that—

GALLO: I'll tell him what I think. Now what about those tamales you promised me?

JUANA: Ah sí, con permiso . . . I got some work in the kitchen.

ADAN: Oh sí, Mrs. Juana, los tamales . . . que rico.

JUANA: [*smiling at* ADAN] I hope they're the kind you like. [*She exits into house.*]

GALLO: Hijo, you always take the bird with you into the fields?

HECTOR: No, not always.

GALLO: This bird has to look like he's got secrets . . . no one but us should be familiar with him.

HECTOR: This is Adan.

ADAN: Es un honor, Mr. El Gallo.

[ANGELA *sticks her head out from under the house.* ADAN *and* GALLO *shake hands and greet each other.*]

GALLO: [*referring to* ZAPATA] Let him out. . . . He needs a bigger carrier. . . . He's a flyer.

ADAN: Como Filipino birds?

GALLO: Yes, but this baby boy, he's got a surprise. He's got a kick.

ADAN: Like Cuban bird?

GALLO: He'll fight in the air, he'll fight on the ground. You can put spurs or razors on that kick and he'll cut any bird to ribbons. You can put money on that.

ADAN: Hijo! Señor . . . how you know? He never fight. Maybe he only kick in cage.

GALLO: I know because I'm his papa. . . . [*pointing to the other carrier*] That your bird?

ADAN: Sí, pero no good . . . no fight. San Juan, he run away.

GALLO: I'll make him fight. Just let him out.

ADAN: Mr. El Gallo, you give this pendejo bird too much honor. Gracias Señor, pero this poor bird, he no can fight.

GALLO: Is it the bird, or you who will not fight?

HECTOR: The bird is too young. He doesn't want him to fight.

GALLO: I've never seen a bird that won't fight, but there are men who are cowards.

HECTOR: He is not a coward.

ADAN: This is true, pero I am not El Gallo. In my country all men who love di rooster know Mr. El Gallo. They tell of di famoso día de los muertos fight in Jacinto Park.

GALLO: Ah, you heard about that fight. You remember that fight, Hector?

HECTOR: No.

GALLO: First time you saw a real cockfight. . . . Abuelo took you. . . . How could you forget your first cockfight? [*to* ADAN] Go on, take your bird out. I'll make him fight.

[GALLO *takes a drink from a bottle, then blows on* SAN JUAN. *As he does this, lights go down almost to black. Pinspot comes up center stage, as other lights come up to a dark red. During this process, we hear* GALLO's *voice—"Ready," then a few beats later "Pit!" On this cue two dancer/roosters jump into the pinspot. This rooster dance is savage. The dancers wear razors on their feet. The* ZAPATA *dancer jumps very high. The poor* SAN JUAN *dancer stays close to the ground. Throughout the dance, we hear drums and foot-stomping. At every hit, there is a big drum pound. During the fight,* HECTOR *appears on the porch.*]

HECTOR: [*to himself*] It was in Jacinto Park. . . . The crowd was a monster, made up of individual human beings stuck together by sweat and spittle. Their gaping mouths let out screams, curses, and foul gases, masticating, smacking eager for the kill. You stood up. The monster roared. Quasimoto, your bird, in one hand. You lifted him high, "Pit!" went the call. "Pit!" roared the monster. And you threw him into the ring . . . soaring with the blades on his heels flashing I heard the mighty rage of his wings and my heart soared with him. He was a whirlwind flashing and slashing like a dark avenging angel then like some distant rainbow star exploding he was hit. The monster crowd inhaled, sucking back their hopes. . . . In that vacuum he was pulled down. My heart went down the same dark shaft, my brains slammed against the earth's hard crust . . . my eyes clouded . . . my arteries gushed . . . my lungs collapsed. "Get up," said Abuelo, "up here with me, and you will see a miracle." You, Father, picked up Quasimoto, a lifeless pile of bloody feathers, holding his head oh so gently, you closed your eyes, and like a great wave receding, you drew a breath that came from deep within your ocean floor. I heard the stones rumble, the mountains shift, the topsoil move, and as your breath slammed on the beaches, Quasimoto sputtered back to life. Oh Papi, breathe on me.

> [ANGELA *appears and stands behind her brother. Her wings are spread very far out. Drums and stomping crescendo as* ZAPATA *brutally kills* SAN JUAN. *Blackout.*]

ACT TWO

SCENE I

Early afternoon. The table is set up in the middle of the yard in a festive way, with tablecloth, flowers, a bowl of peaches, and bottles of whiskey and wine. GALLO *is in the henhouse with* ADAN. HECTOR *is in the bathroom,* JUANA *and* CHATA *are in the kitchen.* ANGELA *is by the little cemetery writing on a tombstone.*

ANGELA: Here lies Angela Ester Morales died of acute neglect. Although she is mourned by many, she goes to a far, far, better place, where they have better food.

> [ANGELA *slides under the house as* JUANA *comes out wearing a fresh house-dress and carrying a steaming pot.*]

JUANA: [*yelling*] Hector! Angela! You kids wash up, it's time to eat.

> [JUANA *hurries back into the house, almost knocking* CHATA *down as she comes out with a tray of tortillas. She is heavily made up, wearing tight clothes, dangling earrings, high-heeled shoes. A cigarette dangles from her mouth.*]

CHATA: Why are you eating out here?

JUANA: He wants it. Says he don't wanta hide in the house.

CHATA: Begging for trouble.

JUANA: What can I do, he's the man. [*She goes into the house.*]

CHATA: Ah, they're all shit! Just want trouble. Soup's on!

> [CHATA *pours herself a quick shot of whiskey, shoots it down and makes a face.* JUANA *comes out with another pot.*]

JUANA: You better tell 'em that the food's ready. [CHATA *goes to henhouse.*] Hector!

HECTOR: [*coming out on porch*] What?

JUANA: It's time to eat. . . . You look real nice, honey. Makes me proud to have your papa see you all dressed up.

HECTOR: Okay. Okay. Don't make a big deal about it. I just don't want him to think—

JUANA: I just feel so happy—

HECTOR: I just don't want him to think—

JUANA: Hijito! You love your papa . . . don't you?

HECTOR: Mother!

JUANA: I know you a little mad at him . . . pero when he comes home it's like the
sun when it—

HECTOR: Shshshsh!

[CHATA, GALLO, *and* ADAN *come out of the henhouse.*]

GALLO: We have to sharpen and polish those spurs. I want them to flash.

JUANA: [*to* GALLO] The food's ready. . . . We fixed what you like . . . mole, rice,
frijolitos . . . tamales.

GALLO: Tamales estilo Jalisco!

CHATA: [*looking* HECTOR *over*] Ay Papi que rico estás! [HECTOR *quickly sits
down.*] Honey! You gonna have to beat all them women off with a stick,
when they see you and that rooster tonight.

ADAN: No worry, Hector, I be there . . . down you mujeres, women leave de Mr.
Hector and me alone. . . . Ay Mama! [*He has a giggling fit.*]

GALLO: [*kissing* JUANA] It's wonderful to be in love . . . to be touched by the noble fever.

CHATA: Ah, you're better off with a touch of typhoid.

JUANA: I . . . gracias al Señor que . . . my whole family is here. [*She looks around.
She yells.*] Angela! Angie!

HECTOR: Mom!

JUANA: Where is she? Where is your sister?

HECTOR: Talking to the saints! I don't know.

[JUANA *gets up, goes to the spot where* ANGELA *slides under the house, gets
down on her hands and knees and yells.*]

JUANA: Angela! Angela! You leave them saints alone. You hear me!

[*As everybody looks at* JUANA, ANGELA *comes from behind the house and
tiptoes toward the henhouse.* HECTOR *is the only one to see her. Using hand
signals, she pleads to him to be quiet.* JUANA *peers under the house.*]

Angie! Honey . . . your mama worked for days to fix this food and now it's
getting cold. [*to* GALLO] You should see how sweet she looks when she's all
dressed up. [*to under the house*] You ain't got no manners . . . ain't even said
hello to your father. [*to* GALLO] She prays a lot . . . and she's got real pretty
eyes.

CHATA: [*to* GALLO] She's sorta . . . the bashful type . . . you know.

JUANA: [*to* GALLO] And she ain't spoiled.

CHATA: [*taking a drink*] Nah, all them kids smell like that.

JUANA: [*to under the house*] Angie!

GALLO: Juana, leave her alone.

JUANA: Okay. Angie, I'm gonna ignore you, 'cause you spoiled my day, this day
that I been looking forward to for years and years and now you making me
look like a bad mama, what's your papa gonna think of us.

GALLO: Juana, she'll come out when she's ready.

[JUANA *goes back to the table.*]

CHATA: Maybe was them roosters fighting got her scared.

ADAN: Poor San Juan.

GALLO: Adan, drink up and I'll see you get one of our famous Champion Morales birds.

HECTOR: What famous Champion Morales birds?

GALLO: The ones I paid for dearly, the ones I came home to raise . . . isn't that right, mi amor?

JUANA: Yes . . . you see, honey, your papa's gonna stay home . . . raise birds. . . . I think Abuelo would want that.

GALLO: And after they see our bird tonight . . . See, first I want them to think it's just you and the bird up there. After the bets are down, I'll take over and they're gonna know we got roosters. A toast . . .

> [*As* GALLO *stands up, everybody raises a glass, except* HECTOR. ANGELA *tiptoes from the henhouse carrying* ZAPATA. *She goes behind and under the house. Only* HECTOR *sees her.*]

To the finest fighting cocks ever to be seen. [*He slides bottle to* HECTOR.]

HECTOR: [*sliding bottle back.*] No.

> [*pause*]

GALLO: Too good to drink with your old man.

HECTOR: I only drink with people I trust.

CHATA: Me . . . I drink with anybody. Maybe that's my problem.

GALLO: I am your father.

HECTOR: Yes. You are my father.

CHATA: I like it better when I drink alone. Ya meet a better class of people that way.

HECTOR: But it's my bird. Abuelo left it to me.

GALLO: Abuelo was my father, and you are my son. I see no problem. Now let's eat.

HECTOR: Mother!

JUANA: Let's eat, honey, and we can talk about it later.

ADAN: Ay the mole muy delicious . . . the mole muy rico . . . the mole muy beautiful y Mrs. Juana. Today, you look beautiful, like the mole.

GALLO: Hm, sabroso, exquisito.

JUANA: I bet you been in plenty of fancy places got better food than this.

GALLO: This is home cooking, I know that your hands made it. . . . These . . . these are the hands of a beautiful woman. . . .

HECTOR: Ha! Bullshit.

GALLO: We say your mother is beautiful and you call it bullshit! I find that very disrespectful.

JUANA: Hijo, you're right. . . . It's just the way people talk, I know I ain't beautiful.

GALLO: I say you are beautiful.

ADAN: Sí, muy beautiful.

GALLO: Ya ves! . . . If your son doesn't have the eyes, the soul, the imagination to see it . . . it's his loss.

HECTOR: That's right. I just can't seem to stretch my imagination that far.

GALLO: This is an insult to your mother.

HECTOR: It's the truth. That is a plain, tired, worn-out woman.

GALLO: Shut up.

HECTOR: The hands of a beautiful woman! Those aren't hands, they're claws because she has to scratch for her living.

JUANA: Please, Hector, let him say what he wants. . . . I know I ain't beautiful. It
    don't go to my head.

HECTOR: But it goes to your heart which is worse. Did he ever really take care of
    you? Did he ever go out and work to put food on the table, to buy you a
    dress? All he has is words, and he throws a few cheap words to you and you
    come to life. Don't you have any pride?

GALLO: Your mother has great courage to trust and believe in me.

HECTOR: Stupidity!

GALLO: You know nothing!

HECTOR: You don't seem to realize that it is my rooster. And that after the fight,
    depending on the outcome, I will sell him or eat him. I have made a deal
    with the Filipinos.

JUANA: Ay, Hector! You've spoiled everything. All this food . . . I worked so hard
    . . . for this day.

GALLO: You're not selling anything to anybody. This is nothing to joke about.

HECTOR: I don't want to spend my life training chickens to be better killers. And
    I don't want to spend my whole life in this valley. Mother, Aunt Chata, ex-
    cuse me.

CHATA: Ah? . . . O sí hijo pase . . . sometimes Hector can be a real gentleman.
    [HECTOR *starts to leave.*]

GALLO: Son! . . . You have no courage, no juice. . . . You are a disgrace to me.

JUANA: Ay, Gallo, don't say that to him.

HECTOR: Do you think I care what you think . . . Father.

JUANA: Hijo no . . . for me, just once for me. I don't wanna be alone no more.

HECTOR: What about me? You have me, you'll always have me, I'll work, I've al-
    ways worked, I can take care of you. I won't leave you.

JUANA: It ain't the same, honey.

HECTOR: Yeah. . . . He comes first for you, he will always come first.

GALLO: If you sell that bird, it will be over your dead body.

HECTOR: You can't stop me.
    [*Exit* HECTOR. CHATA *takes a plate of food and bowl of peaches to the
    under-the-house area and tries to tempt* ANGELA *out.*]

GALLO: He doesn't seem to realize . . . coward . . . too bad.
    [GALLO *goes to the henhouse.* JUANA *starts to follow him.*]

JUANA: Talk to him. . . . He's a good boy. . . . If you just talk . . . [*Seeing* ADAN *still
    eating.*] Is it good? You really like it?

ADAN: Hm! Sabroso!

CHATA: Come on, Angie. . . . It's real good.
    [GALLO *returns running.*]

GALLO: He's gone. . . . The bird is gone. . . .

ADAN: Yo no see nada, nada.

JUANA: He'll bring it back, he's a good boy. He's just a little upset . . . you know.

GALLO: Nobody fools with my roosters. Not even this over-petted, over-
    pampered viper you spawned. Go and pray to your Dark Virgin. You know
    what I'm capable of.
    [*Exit* GALLO. ADAN *stops eating and tries to comfort* JUANA *as she puts her
    head down on the table and cries.*]

ADAN: No cry, no cry, Mrs. Juana. Di women cry y Adan, he not know what to
do. [JUANA *cries louder.*] Ay, Mrs. Juana, for sure di flowers will die . . . di
trees will be torn from di ground, freshness will leave di morning, softness
will leave di night . . . [JUANA's *cries increase.*] Ay Dios! [*From his pocket,
he brings out the letter* ANGELA *wrote for him. He crosses himself.*] Mrs. di
Juana . . . [*reading with great difficulty*] Di . . . impulses . . . of my . . .
heart . . . are such . . . [*throwing letter aside*] A que la fregada! Mrs. Juana,
Adan have mucho amor for you. My heart break to see you cry. I will not
a breathe. When you no cry then I will breathe.

> [ADAN *takes a big breath and holds it. Slowly* JUANA *stops crying and lifts
> her head.* ADAN, *suffering some discomfort, continues to hold his breath.*]

JUANA: I been dreaming. Nothing's gonna change. I gotta face facts.

> [ADAN *lets his breath out in a great whoosh.* ANGELA *pops out from under
> the house and takes a peach from* CHATA's *hand. She stares at the peach with
> great intensity.*]

CHATA: Angie, ain't it nice to have the family all together again?
ANGELA: There is no pit in this peach. It is hollow. Instead of the pit, there is a
whole little world, a little blue-green crystal-clear ocean, with little schools
of tiny darting silver fish. On a tiny rock sits a mermaid with little teenie-
weenie kinky yellow hair. A tiny sun is being pulled across a little
china-blue sky by teenie-weenie white horses with itty-bitty wings. There
is an island with tiny palm trees and tiny thatched hut. Next to the hut
stand a tiny man and woman. She is wearing flowers and leaves. He is wearing one single leaf. On their heads are little bitty halos. In their arms is a
little bitsy baby. He isn't wearing anything.
CHATA: Let me see. . . . [*Looking at peach.*] I can't see dick!
BLACKOUT.

SCENE II

Later in the afternoon. CHATA *sits on the porch steps, her legs spread out, fanning herself.* JUANA *sits on a straight-back chair, her hands folded on her lap. She rocks herself
gently. She watches* ANGELA, *who is sitting on the ground drawing circles in the dirt
and humming softly. The circles get deeper and deeper.*

CHATA: It's hot. . . . I am waiting for a cool breeze. . . .
ANGELA: Uh ha uh ha uh ha uh haa.
CHATA: Aire fresco . . . come on, cool breeze, come right over here.
ANGELA: Uh ha uh ha uh haa.
CHATA: Women! We're always waiting.

> [ANGELA *hums for a beat, then there is silence for a beat.*]

JUANA: It's because I'm so plain.
CHATA: Ah, you just work too much.
JUANA: Plainness runs in my family. My mother was plain, my grandmother was
plain, my great-grandmother—
CHATA: It was the hard times . . . the hard work that did it.
JUANA: My Aunt Chona was the plainest.

CHATA: I don't remember her.

JUANA: The one with the crossed eyes and the little mustache.

CHATA: Ay, Juanita, that woman had a beautiful soul, sewing those little tiny out-fits for the statues of the saints. That woman was a saint.

JUANA: She's the one told on you that time you was drinking beer with them sailors at the cockfight.

CHATA: Disgusting old bitch!

[ANGELA *hums for a beat as she continues drawing circles.*]

JUANA: I get up at six, I brush my teeth, no creams, no lotions, what they gonna do for me? I work, that's all. I take care of people and I work. People look at me, they know that's all I do. I ain't got no secrets. No hidden gardens. I keep busy, that's what I do. Don't stop, that's what I say to myself. Don't stop, 'cause you're not pretty enough, exciting enough, smart enough to just stand there.

ANGELA: Mama, I don't wanna be plain.

CHATA: Honey, you're too colorful to be plain.

ANGELA: Yeah, that's what I thought.

CHATA: Your mama forgets . . . those years when her heart was filled with wild dreams when she use to weave white star jasmine vines in her hair and drive all the men crazy.

JUANA: It ain't true. . . . She was the one always getting me in trouble.

CHATA: I wasn't the one they called Juanita la Morenita Sabrosita.

JUANA: Oh, Chata. We was young girls together . . . in the summer, at Jacinto Park . . . cockfights, fistfights, the music. At night we would jump out of our bedroom windows in our party dresses. With our good shoes in one hand, our hearts in the other, we ran barefoot through the wet grass, above us all the stars twinkling go, go, go.

CHATA: Nothing could stop us. . . . We had a short time being girls.

JUANA: Now, all I am is an old hag.

CHATA: It ain't true.

JUANA: Sí, it's true enough. I carry burdens, I hang sheets, I scrub, I gather, I pick up, "Here sit down," "I'll wash it," "Here's fifty cents," "Have my chair," "Take my coat," "Here's a piece of my own live flesh"!

CHATA: Es la menopause, that's what it is. You getting it early. I knew this woman once, use to pull out her hair.

JUANA: I don't care, I don't want any stories, I don't care what happens to Fulano Mangano. . . . I just wanna stand still, I wanna be interesting, exciting enough to stand still.

CHATA: Ay, mujer!

JUANA: And I want to look like I got secrets.

CHATA: Juana!

JUANA: Don't call me Juana. Juana is a mule's name.

CHATA: Ah, you're crazy! That new gray hen, the kids named her Juana. See, they think of you.

JUANA: A gray hen! An old gray hen, that's all I am. An old gray hen in a family of roosters. No more! I want feathers, I wanna strut, too. I wanna crow.

ANGELA: Mama!

JUANA: Don't! Don't call me "Mama." I am not Mama. . . . I am . . . I am that movie star, that famous dancer and heartbreaker "Morenita Sabrosita" . . . and now if my fans will excuse me I'm gonna take a bath in champagne, eat cherry bonbons and paint my toenails. [*She goes into the house.*]

CHATA: [*to* JUANA] We got champagne?

[CHATA *goes into the house as* ANGELA *goes to the little cemetery and puts up a new tombstone.*]

ANGELA: [*printing on tombstone*] Here lies Juana Morales. Beloved Wife of El Gallo, Blessed Mother to Angela and Horrible Hector. Died of acute identity crisis sustained during la menopause.

SCENE III

Lights go down, as ANGELA *sits on her box/table at the little cemetery. The long shadows of men fall on* ANGELA *and the cemetery.*

SHADOW #1: There's that spooky kid. You go, brother.

SHADOW #2: Ah, it's just a weird kid. Hey! You! Kid!

[ANGELA *does not acknowledge them.*]

SHADOW #1: Call her "Angel."

SHADOW #2: Hey, Angel.

[ANGELA *looks up.*]

SHADOW #1: See what I mean.

SHADOW #2: Listen kid, tell your old man, we got business to discuss.

SHADOW #1: Yeah, and you make sure he gets the message.

ANGELA: My old man, my Holy Father, my all powerful Father, sees no problems. If there are problems, I am the angel of this yard. I am the comet. I am the whirlwind. I am the shooting stars. Feel my vibrance.

SHADOW #1: I feel it, right behind my ears, like . . . like . . .

ANGELA: Locust wings.

SHADOW #1: Let's get outta here.

SHADOW #2: Tell Gallo some pals dropped by to settle an old score.

SHADOW #1: Come on!

SHADOW #2: [*voice trailing off*] Hey! That kid don't scare me, see.

SHADOW #1: [*voice trailing off*] I'm telling ya, my ears hurt.

[*Exit shadows. Lights go back up.* ANGELA *folds her hands in prayer.*]

ANGELA: Holy Father, please help me, I feel the illumination, the fever of grace slipping away. I need to know that you are with me, that you take an interest in my concerns. Send me a little demonstration, a sign. Any sign . . . I don't care. Stigmata, visions, voices, send an angel, burn a bush. . . . I am attracted to levitation . . . but you choose. . . . I'll just lay here and wait.

[ANGELA *lies on the ground waiting. After a few beats* HECTOR *enters. He slowly walks up to* ANGELA *and looks down on her for a beat.*]

HECTOR: What are you doing?

ANGELA: [*sitting up*] Ohhh . . . you're no sign.

HECTOR: What is going on?

ANGELA: Weird, shady men came here looking for Gallo. Two of them. They were not polite.

HECTOR: I see. . . . So your reaction is to lay stretched out on the dirt instead of going into the house.

ANGELA: Hector, please, I am scared. . . . I wanted a sign.

[HECTOR *sits down next to* ANGELA.]

HECTOR: Hey, you're the shooting-star woman, you can't be scared.

ANGELA: I am scared. Really scared. If I grow up will I still be scared? Are grown-ups scared?

HECTOR: Always scared, trembling . . . cowering . . . this . . . this second, now . . . this planet that we are sitting on is wobbling precariously on its lightning path around the sun and every second the sun is exploding . . . stars are shooting at us from deep distant space, comets zoom around us, meteor rocks are being hurled through distances we measure in light. . . . This very earth which we call our home, our mother, has catastrophic moods, she keeps moving mountains, receding oceans, shifting poles, bucking and reeling like an overburdened beast trying to shake us off. . . . Life is violent.

ANGELA: You're scared about the fight . . . huh?

HECTOR: No. Whatever happens, Papi will still only care about the rooster. That's his son, that's who gets it all.

ANGELA: Maybe if we gave him the rooster he'd stay here and be happy.

HECTOR: He has to stay for us, not the rooster. . . . Angela . . . you . . . you were great taking the rooster.

ANGELA: He kept killing the little chicks. How could he do that, Hector? He's their papa.

HECTOR: Training. Look, Angela, you're the angel of this yard. You keep a close guard on that rooster. Don't let anyone near him . . . promise me.

ANGELA: Yes.

HECTOR: That's a real promise now. No crossed fingers behind your back.

ANGELA: I promise already. [*She spreads her hands out in front of her, then kisses the tip of her thumb.*] May God strike me dumb, make me a plain whiny person and take away my gift of faith. Forever and ever, throughout my mortal years on earth, and throughout the everlasting fires of hell. Amen. Satisfied?

HECTOR: Yes.

ANGELA: Gee, maybe I should have given myself a little leeway, a little room for error.

[CHATA *enters from the house with a bottle and glass.*]

HECTOR: Too late now. Can't take it back.

CHATA: Oh, oh, look who's here. Angie, your mama needs some cheering up, a nice hug, an angel's kiss, maybe a little song.

ANGELA: Litany to the Virgin. That's her favorite. [*She exits.*]

CHATA: Men are shit. Pure shit.

HECTOR: And you're still drinking.

CHATA: Stay outta my drinking. You hurt your mama, Hector.

HECTOR: Too bad.

CHATA: Ay Dios, what a man he is now.

HECTOR: Yeah, well, what about you? Didn't you break Abuelo's heart when you became a whore?

CHATA: They called me the encyclopedia of love. You want to turn a few pages? Your Aunt Chata could show you a few things.

HECTOR: You're disgusting.

CHATA: Is that what fascinates you, honey? Is that why I always find you peeping at me, mirrors at the keyhole, your eyeballs in the cracks, spying when I'm sleeping, smelling my kimono.

HECTOR: You're drunk.

CHATA: I ain't drunk, honey.

HECTOR: You drink too much. It's not . . . good for you . . . It makes you ugly.

CHATA: Ain't none of your business. Don't tell me what to do, Hector.

HECTOR: I have to, it's for your own good.

CHATA: You got nothing to say about it, you ain't my man, and you ain't your mama's man. The sooner you learn that the better. . . . Take your bird, leave it, eat or sell it, but get out of here. [HECTOR *stands alone in the yard, as she goes to the door. She turns. They look at each other.*] What are you hanging around here for? Go on! Get out! It ain't your home anymore. [*She takes a broom and shoos* HECTOR *from the yard.*] Shoo! Shoo! You don't belong here, it ain't your place anymore.

HECTOR: Stop it, stop it, stop it.

[HECTOR *goes to the outside boundary of the yard, where he falls to his knees and buries his face in his hands, as* CHATA *comes slowly up behind him.*]

CHATA: I feel like I'm tearing my own flesh from my bones. . . . He's back. Honey, we got too many roosters in this yard.

HECTOR: Did you sleep with my father? Did he yearn for you as you slept in your little white, chaste, narrow bed? Did he steal you when you were dreaming?

CHATA: [*embracing him*] Shshsh . . .

HECTOR: I'm not like him.

CHATA: You're just like him, so handsome you make my teeth ache.

HECTOR: Whore, mother, sister, saint-woman, moon-woman, give me the shelter of your darkness, fold me like a fan and take me into your stillness, submerge me beneath the water, beneath the sea, beneath the mysteries, baptize me, bear me up, give me life, breathe on me.

[CHATA *enfolds him as the lights fade. We hear* ANGELA *reciting the litany.*]

ANGELA: [*offstage*] She is the Gate of Heaven, the Mystical Rose, the Flower of Consolation, the Fire of Transcendence, and the Queen of Love.

SCENE IV

Lights come up to indicate that time has passed. ANGELA *is alone in the yard. She sniffs the air.*

ANGELA: Tres Rosas!

[ANGELA *slides under the house as* GALLO *enters. He sees a brief flash of* ANGELA *from the corner of his eye. He walks slowly into the yard. He stops by the little cemetery and reads the tombstones. Feeling the urge for a drink, he goes to the table and has a shot. He sits.*]

GALLO: Acute neglect? . . . uh-huh . . . I thought I felt a little spirit, slight, delicate . . . yes, I feel it. A little tenderness . . . a little greenness . . .

[*examining the ground*] What's this? Tracks . . . little tiny paws . . . there . . .
[*following tracks*] and there . . .

> [GALLO *pretends to be following tracks to the porch. Then with one great leap he jumps in the opposite direction, surprising the hell out of* ANGELA, *and pulls her from under the house by her heels.*]

Ah, ha!

ANGELA: Shit! Hey! You're ripping my wings! You shithead! Put me down! Don't touch me!

> [GALLO *puts* ANGELA *down, throws his hands up to indicate he won't touch her. They stand and stare at each other.* ANGELA *goes to the little cemetery, never taking her eyes off* GALLO. *They continue to stare for a beat, then* ANGELA *looks up to Heaven, slapping her hands together in prayer.*]

There is a person here trying to con me, but I don't con that easy.

GALLO: [*slapping his hands in prayer*] There is a person here who swallows saints but defecates devils.

ANGELA: [*to Heaven*] He comes here smelling of rosas using sweet oily words. . . . It's phony, it's obnoxious, it's obscene. . . . I wanna throw up.

GALLO: I came here to see my baby, my little angel, my little woman of the shooting stars, my light delicate splendorous daughter. But she is as light, as delicate, as splendid as an angel's fart.

ANGELA: Angels do not fart. They do not have a digestive system. That's why they can all scrunch together on the head of a pin.

GALLO: Oh . . . I only come with my love—

ANGELA: You only came with words. . . . Well, where were these words on my birthday, Christmas, my saint's day? Where's my Easter outfit, my trip to Disneyland, the orthodontist. . . . You owe me.

GALLO: Sweet Jesus. . . . What a monster! I owe you . . . but Angela! Angela! Angela! How many times have I written that name on prison walls. On bits of paper, on the skin of my arms.

ANGELA: [*to Heaven*] He's hopeless! You write everybody's name on your arms.

GALLO: Women like to know that they're on your flesh.

ANGELA: I am not a woman. I'm your baby daughter. You said so yourself.

GALLO: I'm afraid . . . fathers to daughters . . . that's so delicate. I don't know . . . what to do . . . help me, Angela. How do I know what to do?

ANGELA: Instinct! Ain't ya got no instinct? Don't you feel anything?

GALLO: [*moving closer to* ANGELA] When you were a little baby, you were a miracle of tiny fingers and toes and dimples and you had a soft spot on the top of your head.

ANGELA: I still have it, see.

GALLO: I wanted to take you into my arms and crush you against my chest so that I could keep you forever and nobody, and nothing, could ever, ever hurt you because you would be safe . . . my little offshoot, my little bud, my little flower growing inside my chest.

ANGELA: Papi . . .

GALLO: Sí, sí, hijita. Your papi's here.

ANGELA: And Papi, these men come all the—

GALLO: [*holding* ANGELA] Shshsh . . . it's nothing, nothing and you thought I forgot about you. . . . Well, it just hurt too much, do you understand?

ANGELA: You had to pull down some hard time and the only way to survive was to cut off all feelings and become an animal just like the rest of them.

GALLO: Well, something like that. Honey, you know what I wish—

ANGELA: Papa, did the lights really go down when they put the people in the electric chair?

GALLO: Angela, what a . . . Honey, you know what I wish—

ANGELA: Did they force you to make license plates? Hector and I would look real close at the ones that started with a G. We thought you made them. "What craftsmanship!" Hector used to say.

GALLO: Don't you have any normal interests?

ANGELA: Like what?

GALLO: Like swimming. . . . You know what I wish? That we could take a trip and see the ocean together.

ANGELA: I've never seen the ocean. When?

GALLO: Just you and me. Laying on our bellies, feeding the seagulls, riding the waves.

ANGELA: I can't swim.

GALLO: I will teach you, that's what fathers are for—

ANGELA: [*to Heaven*] Angels and saints, did you hear? My father's going to teach me to swim!

GALLO: Now Angela, I didn't promise.

ANGELA: But you said—

GALLO: I want to but I have to hurry and fix things. I have to find Hector, talk to him and find that rooster fast before Hector sells him. Honey, you pray to St. Anthony, your prayers are powerful . . . unless . . . St. Anthony, he listen to you?

ANGELA: [*crossing her fingers*] Hey, we're like that.

GALLO: Ask St. Anthony, Angela . . . then we can go to the ocean.

ANGELA: Truly, Papi? Just you and me? And will you stay with us forever and ever?

GALLO: Wild horses couldn't drag me away.

ANGELA: Close your eyes. Tony! Tony! Look around, Zapata's lost and can't be found. [*She goes under the house, gets* ZAPATA, *and gives him to* GALLO.] I found him, Papi, he was—

GALLO: Ya lindo, ya. [*to bird*] Papa's got you now. Angela, you keep quiet now, honey, this is our secret.

ANGELA: What about Hector?

GALLO: I'm going to talk to Hector now. You go inside and get all dressed up. So I can be proud of my girl. I'll pick you up after the fight. [*He exits.*]

ANGELA: Your girl! [*singing*] *We are going to the ocean, we are going to the sea, we are going to the ocean to see what we can see . . .*
  [ANGELA *goes into the house. We hear cha-cha music.*]

CHATA: [*offstage*] One, two . . . not like that . . . I'm getting tired. . . . What time's "Zorro" on?

JUANA: [*offstage*] No, no. . . . Just one more. [*singing*] *Cha, cha, cha, que rico . . . cha, cha, cha.* . . . Ay, I could do it all night.
  [*Enter* GALLO *running, breathing hard. He has* ZAPATA's *carrier. He goes to the door and yells.*]

GALLO: Juana! Juana!
> [JUANA *and* CHATA *come to the door.*]
> I need money . . . and my stuff. I gotta leave. . . . Something's come up. . . . Do you hear me? I need money now.

JUANA: I hear ya. . . . You ain't even been here a day and already you're gone. . . . Nothing's going to change with you . . . nothing. I was having fun, dancing, remembering old times, do you know how long—

GALLO: I don't have time for this, just give me the money.

JUANA: I ain't got any!

CHATA: I got some. [*She goes in the house.*]

GALLO: The Filipino, somebody told him about the bird. Oh, ya, ya my little hen, don't you ruffle those pretty feathers, I'll be back.

JUANA: No, you always gonna be running.

GALLO: If it was just me, I'd stay. You know that, Juana? You know I'd stay, but I got the bird to think of, gotta hide him, breed him good, soon as I get some good stags I'll come home. . . . This is just a little setback.
> [CHATA *returns with suitcase and money.*]

JUANA: You know how long it's been since I went dancing?

CHATA: Here, you're gonna need this. [*Gives him the suitcase.*] And this is all the cash I got.
> [ANGELA *enters as* GALLO *counts the money. She is dressed in a red strapless dress made tight by large visible safety pins, high heels, and a great deal of heavy makeup and jewelry. The effect is that of a young girl dressed like a tart for a costume party. She carries a suitcase, purse, and her collection can.*]

GALLO: Is this all you got?

ANGELA: [*shaking the can*] Don't worry, Papa, I got my donation-can money.
> [*They all stare at her for a beat.*]

JUANA and CHATA: Angela?!!

JUANA: Angie, you got on your mama's old party dress.

CHATA: Yeah, and all my jewelry. . . . Where you going?

ANGELA: Papa, didn't you hear me? I have money. [*She shakes the can.*]

GALLO: Oh honey, don't you look pretty. . . . Now you got a little bit too much lipstick on, let your mama wipe some off.

ANGELA: Are we leaving now?

JUANA: Gallo!

GALLO: Shshsh Juana . . . Angela, I gotta talk to your mama for a few minutes. You go in the house and I'll come and get you.

ANGELA: Are you sure?

GALLO: Don't you trust me, Angie?

CHATA: Come on, Angie, I'll show you how to draw eyebrows. First you draw a straight line across your forehead and then spit on your finger and rub out the middle. Let's go in and try it.

ANGELA: Really, Aunt Chata, I'm not a child, you don't have to patronize me.

CHATA: Okay, I'll give you the low-down on blow-jobs.
> [ANGELA *and* CHATA *go into the house.*]
> Now, don't tell your mama . . .

GALLO: Juana, keep her in the house until I leave.

JUANA: You promised to take her with you?

GALLO: I had to get the bird. I said I would take her to the ocean.

JUANA: Ay bruto! How could you do it?

GALLO: How was I to know this would happen . . . and Juanita, it hurts me to say this but that kid is crazy. . . .

JUANA: No, no, Señor, she is not crazy and I ain't gonna let you call her crazy. She got the spirit they broke in me. I ain't gonna let it happen to her.

GALLO: Shshsh! Don't get so excited. It isn't important.

JUANA: It's important. . . . It's her spirit, her soul and you ain't gonna stomp on it . . . you hear me.

[ADAN *enters running.*]

ADAN: Mr. El Gallo . . . bad men! Mucho bad, y mucho ugly. Looking for you y Zapata. All ober they look for you . . . Big Nicky's, Castro Fields, Don Pancho's. . . . You leave, Mr. El Gallo. You go far away. I take you. I go for my truck.

GALLO: You are a good friend, Adan, and my new partner.

ADAN: Oh, thank you, Mr. El Gallo. I am proud. But is better I come back here to Mrs. Juana y Hector.

JUANA: Thank you, Adan.

GALLO: We better hurry.

ADAN: Sí, sí, I come back with truck. [*He exits.*]

[JUANA *goes into the house.* HECTOR *enters as* GALLO *starts to pack his suitcase.*]

HECTOR: [*seeing* ZAPATA] You must have really sold her a bill of goods to get Zapata.

GALLO: Look, there's trouble. . . . The Filipino send you?

HECTOR: No, how could you think I would work for him, but I came to get Zapata.

GALLO: You're the one told him about the bird.

HECTOR: Yes. I made a deal with the Filipino. He'll leave you alone if I give him the rooster.

GALLO: That's a lie and you fell for it.

HECTOR: No, he is an honorable man, we were here unprotected for seven years and he never bothered us. It's his bird, Papi.

GALLO: No, I paid seven years of my life for this baby.

HECTOR: And he lost his son. It's the right thing to do.

[*A truck horn is heard.* ANGELA *comes out of the house with her suitcase,* JUANA *and* CHATA *follow after her.*]

ANGELA: Papa? Are we leaving now, Papa?

JUANA: Angie! No!

HECTOR: So that's it. . . . Angela, get back in the house.

ANGELA: I'm going with him, Hector.

HECTOR: Get back in the house, nobody's going anywhere.

ANGELA: No! I don't have to listen to you anymore. You're not my father.

JUANA: Angie . . . he's not going to the ocean. . . . He can't take you.

[*We hear the sound of* ADAN's *truck. The horn is heard as* GALLO *starts backing away, picking up* ZAPATA's *carrier.*]

ANGELA: Papi, wait for me! Papa, you promised.

GALLO: You're all grown up now, you don't need your old man.

CHATA: Hector!
> [GALLO *turns, tries to run out.* ANGELA *grabs him, knocking* ZAPATA's *carrier out of his hand.* HECTOR *picks up the carrier.*]

ANGELA: No, Papa, we need you and Mama needs you, we've been waiting, and waiting, you can't leave, you promised me.

JUANA: They'll kill you, Gallo.

GALLO: [*throwing* ANGELA *off*] Stop sucking off me. I got nothing for you.

ANGELA: [*beating her fists on the ground.*] No, no, Papa! You promised me! . . . Oh, Hector . . . . No, no, I promised Hector.
> [*Drums begin as punctuation of the pounding of* ANGELA's *fists on the ground. Lights change. A special on* ANGELA *and another on* GALLO *and* HECTOR *come up, as shadows appear.* ANGELA *sees them.*]

Ah . . . Holy Father, Abuelo.

GALLO: [*to* HECTOR] Give me that bird.

ANGELA: Saints, Angels, Mama.

JUANA: [*trying to pick up* ANGELA] Come on, Angie, get up.

GALLO: [*to* HECTOR] What do you want?

HECTOR: You, alive, Papi.

CHATA: Careful, Hector.

ANGELA: I've lost my faith. I am splintered.

GALLO: [*imitating* HECTOR] You Papi. . . . Give me life. . . . Make me a man. [*He whips out his stiletto.*] This is how you become a man. [*The drums get louder. We hear howling.*] Come on, baby boy, show Daddy whatcha got.

JUANA: Are you crazy! That's your son!

ANGELA: I am cast down! Exiled!
> [GALLO *stalks* HECTOR *as drums follow their movements.*]

JUANA: Oh Gallo, you're killing your own children.

CHATA: Move, Hector, don't think, move!

GALLO: Oh yeah, mi lindo, you like to fight . . . eh?

JUANA: No, stop them! Please, please stop this.

ANGELA: Fallen from the light, condemned to the mud, to the shadows.

GALLO: You gotta learn, baby boy.

CHATA: Look at him, Hector. He's getting old, his hand is shaking. . . . Take the knife! Stay down, old warrior. Stay down.

ANGELA: Alone and diminished. This loneliness is unendurable.

JUANA: Hector!

HECTOR: Do I have it? Is this what you want me to be . . .

ANGELA: [*looking to Heaven*]
> My brains are slammed against the earth's hard crust.
> My eyes are clouded.
> My arteries gush
> My lungs collapsed.

HECTOR: [*letting go of* GALLO] No! I am your son.
> [*Drums and cries stop.*]

ANGELA: Holy Father, Abuelo, Hector, breathe on me.
> [*Celestial sound as a white narrow shaft of light falls on* ANGELA. *She levitates, her wings spreading. Only* CHATA *and* JUANA *see this.*]

HECTOR: [*taking a deep breath*] Oh sweet air! [*He gets the rooster and sees* ANGELA.] Angela!

ADAN: [*rushing in*] I am here, I have truck. . . . [*Seeing* ANGELA, *he crosses himself.*] Ay Dios. [*He kneels.*]

JUANA: [*at* GALLO'*s side*] Gallo, look!

GALLO: Did you see the hands on that kid, just like steel, never seen finer hands . . . [*seeing* ANGELA] Sweet Jesus, my beautiful monster. [*He crosses himself.*]

CHATA: No, it ain't true.

HECTOR: [*standing before* ANGELA *holding the rooster*] Oh sweet hummingbird woman, shooting star, my comet, you are launched.

ANGELA: Abuelo, Queen of Heaven, All the Saints, All the Angels. It is true, I am back. I am restored. I am . . . Hector, take me with you.

HECTOR: Everywhere. . . . Over the mountains, up to the stars.

ANGELA: To the very edge.

ADAN: Hector! Angelita! You take Adan. [*He goes to* ANGELA.]

CHATA: [*looking at* ANGELA] Shit happens. . . . Been happening all my life, that's all I know.

JUANA: [*holding* GALLO *like the Pietà*] We seen it, Gallo, with our own eyes.

ANGELA: [*to* HECTOR *and* ADAN] And I want my doorstep heaped with floral offerings . . . and . . .

> [HECTOR, ADAN, *and* ANGELA *freeze.* CHATA *removes the flower from her hair and holds it in her hand, trying to decide what to do. She freezes.*]

GALLO: Ay, Juanita, I had a vision of a hard-kicking flyer . . . [*He yawns.*] the ultimate bird, noble, fino. [*He falls asleep.*]

> [JUANA *looks at* GALLO, *smiles, then looks out half-smiling.*]

END OF PLAY

Philip Kan Gotanda (1950-)

Yankee Dawg You Die (1991)

Although Asian characters have a long history in American drama and films, they have been reduced, for the most part, to a limited number of stereotypes: dutiful houseboy, inscrutable detective, wise Confucian patriarch, treacherous dragon lady, submissive doll bride, or sadistic military officer. Such oversimplifications are the subject of Gotanda's play.

Yankee Dawg You Die, as the title suggests, is a satire (sometimes comic, at others serious) on the stereotypical roles that Asian American actors are forced to accept if they wish to be employed in theatre or film. The cast is limited to two characters (both actors), although several other persons are referred to and are sometimes treated as being just out of sight offstage. One of the actors, Vincent Chang, is in his sixties and has decades of experience. Once confident that through the strength of his acting he would win acceptance as a star, he has come to realize that, though he is one of the most prominent and successful Asian American actors in Hollywood, he will always be relegated to subordinate and stereotypical roles. The other actor, Bradley Yamashita, is in his twenties. In the early scenes, he is brash, confident of his talent, and patronizing toward Vincent, who he thinks has failed adequately to resist stereotypes. The play shows how such stereotyping influences the lives and careers of these actors.

The action of the play traces the erratic relationship of the two men as they alternately reject and support each other and as they unwittingly learn from each other. Over time, Bradley's resistance to stereotypical roles is eroded as his desire to act overwhelms his objections. In turn, Vincent gradually accepts the responsibilities he has avoided, and eventually he refuses a role that he considers demeaning and instead accepts one in a play being produced by an unknown company that depicts Asian Americans truthfully. By the end of the play, both characters have changed, but though they have achieved a much fuller understanding of themselves, they seem no nearer to discrediting the stereotypes that have restricted their careers.

The play's treatment of Hollywood's stereotypes is almost always satirical, emphasizing their absurdity, but though one may laugh at or reject them, one also recognizes the tangible damage they have done to the two actors.

Philip Kan Gotanda

Yankee Dawg You Die

CHARACTERS

VINCENT CHANG, *Actor. Mid to late sixties. Former hoofer.*
BRADLEY YAMASHITA, *Actor. Mid to late twenties.*

SET———*Minimal with a hint of fragmentation and distortion of perspective to allow for a subtle dream-like quality. Upstage, high-tech shoji screens for title and visual projections. Set should allow for a certain fluidity of movement. Allow for lights to be integral in scene transitions. Suggested colors—black with red accents.*

LIGHTING———*Fluid. Interludes should use cross-fades. Dream sequences might experiment with color and shafts of light cutting at askew angles, film-noirish.*

MUSIC———*Minimal instrumentation. Classical in feel.*

INTRODUCTION

Darkness. Filmic music score enters. Then, on the projection screens upstage we see emblazoned the following titles:

"[*Name of Producing Theatre*] *PRESENTS* . . ."

"*VINCENT CHANG* . . ."

VINCENT *lit in pool of light, staring pensively into the darkness. The music dips and we hear the faint beating of a heart. A hint of bloodred washes over* VINCENT *as he lightly touches his breast near his heart area. Fade to black.*

"*AND INTRODUCING* . . ."

"*BRADLEY YAMASHITA*"

BRADLEY *lit in pool of light. Restless, shifting his weight back and forth on his feet. The music dips and we hear the light rustling of large wings. As he looks skyward, a large shadow passes over head. Fade to black.*

"*IN* . . ."

"*YANKEE DAWG YOU DIE* . . ."

The entire theater—stage as well as audience area—is gradually inundated in an ocean of stars. Hold for a moment, then a slow fade to black.

INTERLUDE 1

Lights come up. VINCENT *portraying a "Jap soldier." Lighting creates the mood of an old forties black-and-white movie. Thick Coke-bottle glasses, holding a gun. Acts in an exaggerated, stereotypic—almost cartoonish manner.*

Sergeant Moto pretends to be falling asleep while guarding American prisoners. The snakelike lids of his slanty eyes drooping into a feigned slumber. Suddenly Moto's eyes, spitting hates and bile, flash open, catching the American prisoners in the midst of their escape plans.

VINCENT: [*as Moto*] You stupid American G.I. I know you try and escape. You think you can pull my leg. I speakee your language. I graduate UCLA, Class of thirty-four. I drive big American car with big-chested American blond sitting next to . . . Heh? No, no, no, not "dirty floor." Floor clean. Class of thirty-four. No, no, not "dirty floor." Floor clean. Just clean this morning. Thirty-four. No, no, not "dirty floor." Listen carefully. Watch my lips. [*He moves his lips but the words are not synched with them ala poorly dubbed Japanese monster movie.*] Thirty-four. Thirty-four! Thirty-four!!! [*Pause. Return to synched speaking.*] What is wrong with you? You sickee in the head? What the hell is wrong with you? Why can't you hear what I'm saying? Why can't you see me as I really am? [VINCENT *as Sergeant Moto dims to darkness.*]

END OF INTERLUDE

ACT I

SCENE ONE

"YOU LOOKED LIKE A FUCKING CHIMPANZEE"

Night. Party. House in Hollywood Hills. VINCENT CHANG, *a youthful, silver-maned man in his late sixties stands on the back terrace balcony sipping on a glass of red wine. Stares into the night air.* BRADLEY YAMASHITA, *twenty-seven, pokes his head out from the party and notices* VINCENT. *Stops, losing his nerve. Changes his mind again and moves out on the terrace next to* VINCENT. BRADLEY *holds a cup of club soda.*

Silence. VINCENT *notices* BRADLEY, BRADLEY *smiles,* VINCENT *nods. Silence. They both sip on their drinks.*

BRADLEY: Hello. [VINCENT *nods.*] Nice Evening. [*silence*] God. *What a night.* Love it. [*Silence. Looking out.*] Stars. Wow, would you believe. Stars, stars, stars. [*pause*]

VINCENT: Orion's belt. [BRADLEY *doesn't follow his comment. Vincent points upwards.*] The constellation. Orion the Hunter. That line of stars there forms his belt. See?

BRADLEY: Uh-huh. [*Pause. Sips his drink.* VINCENT *points to another part of the night sky.*]

VINCENT: And of course, the Big Dipper.

BRADLEY: Of course.

VINCENT: And, using the two stars that form the front of the lip of the dipper as your guide, it leads to the . . .

BRADLEY: The North Star.

VINCENT: Yes. Good. Very good. You will never be lost. [*Both quietly laugh.*]

BRADLEY: Jeez, it's a bit stuffy in there. With all of them. It's nice to be with someone I can feel comfortable around. [VINCENT *doesn't understand.*] Well, I mean, like you and me. We're—I mean, we don't exactly look like . . . [*nods towards the people inside.*]

VINCENT: Ahhh. [BRADLEY *laughs nervously, relieved that* VINCENT *has understood.*] Actually, I had not noticed. I do not really notice, or quite frankly care, if someone is Caucasian or oriental or . . .

BRADLEY: [*Interrupts, correcting* Asian. VINCENT *doesn't understand.*] It's Asian, not oriental. [VINCENT *still doesn't follow.* BRADLEY, *embarrassed, tries to explain.*] Asian, oriental. Black, negro. Woman, girl. Gay, homosexual . . . Asian, oriental.

VINCENT: Ahhh. [*pause*] Orientals are rugs? [BRADLEY *nods sheepishly.*] I see. [VINCENT *studies him for a moment, then goes back to sipping his red wine.*] You don't look familiar.

BRADLEY: First time.

VINCENT: You haven't been to one of these parties before? [BRADLEY *shakes his head.*] Hah! You're in for a wonderful surprise. Everyone here is as obnoxious as hell.

BRADLEY: I noticed.

VINCENT: [*laughs, extends his hand*] Vincent Chang . . .

BRADLEY: [*overlapping*] Chang! [BRADLEY *grabs* VINCENT'S *hand and manipulates it through the classic "right-on" handshake.* VINCENT *watches it unfold.*] You don't have to tell me. Everybody knows who you are. Especially in the community. Not that you're not famous—I mean, walking down the street they'd notice you—but in the community, whew! Forget it.

VINCENT: Ahhh. And you?

BRADLEY: What?

VINCENT: Your name.

BRADLEY: Oh. Bradley Yamashita. [*Pronounced "Yamasheeta" by him.* BRADLEY *shakes his hand again.* VINCENT *repeats name to himself, trying to remember where he's heard it. He pronounces the name correctly.*] This is an amazing business. It really is. It's an amazing business. One moment I'm this snotty nose kid watching you on TV and the next thing you know I'm standing next to you and we're talking and stuff and you know . . . [*Silence. Sips drinks. Looks at stars.*] Mr. Chang? Mr. Chang? I think it's important that all of us know each other. Asian American actors. I think the two of us meeting is very important. The young and the old. We can learn from each other. We can. I mean, the way things are, the way they're going, Jesus. If we don't stick together who the hell is going—

VINCENT: [*interrupts, waving at someone*] Ah, Theodora. Hello!

BRADLEY: Wow . . .

VINCENT: Theodora Ando. The *Asian American* actress.

BRADLEY: God, she's gorgeous.

VINCENT: [*coldly*] Don't turn your back on her. [BRADLEY *doesn't follow.* VINCENT *mimes sticking a knife in and twisting it.*]

BRADLEY: [*staring after a disappearing Theodora*] Oh . . . [*Silence. They sip and stare out into the darkness.* BRADLEY *begins to turn and smile at* VINCENT *in hopes that* VINCENT *will recognize his face.* VINCENT *does not.*] New York. Jesus, what a town. Do you spend much time out there? [VINCENT *shrugs.*] Yeah. I've been out in New York. That's where they know me most. Out in New York. I come from San Francisco. That's where I was born and raised. Trained—ACT. But I've been out in New York. I just came back from there. A film of mine opened. New York Film Festival. Guillaume Bouchet, the French critic loved it.

VINCENT: [*impressed*] Guillaume Bouchet.

BRADLEY: Uh-huh. Called it one of the ten best films of the year.

VINCENT: It's your film? You . . . directed it? [BRADLEY *shakes his head.*] Wrote it?

BRADLEY: No, no, I'm in it. I'm the main actor in it.

VINCENT: [*mutters under his breath*] An actor . . .

BRADLEY: It's a Matthew Iwasaki film.

VINCENT: I have heard of him, yes. He does those low-budget . . .

BRADLEY: [*interrupts, correcting*] Independent.

VINCENT: Ahhh. *Independent movies* about . . .

BRADLEY: [*interrupts, correcting again*] Films. Independent films, they play in art houses.

VINCENT: Ahhhh. *Independent films* that play in *art houses* about people like . . . [*nods to* BRADLEY *and to himself*]

BRADLEY: Uh-huh

VINCENT: I see. Hmmm.

BRADLEY: I'm in it. I star in it. Eugene Bickle . . .

VINCENT: [*interrupts*] Who?

BRADLEY: Eugene Bickle, the film critic on TV. You know, everybody knows about him. He used to be on PBS and now he's on the networks with that other fat guy. He said I was one of the most "watchable" stars he's seen this year.

VINCENT: Really?

BRADLEY: He said he wouldn't mind watching me no matter what I was doing.

VINCENT: *Really?*

BRADLEY: Well, that's not exactly—I'm sort of paraphrasing, but that's what he meant. Not that he'd wanna watch me doing anything—you know, walking down the street. But on the screen. In another movie.

VINCENT: Film.

BRADLEY: What?

VINCENT: You said "another movie."

BRADLEY: Film.

VINCENT: Ahh.

BRADLEY: My agent at William Morris wanted me to come to L.A. I have an au- . dition on Monday. One of the big theatres.

VINCENT: [*impressed, but hiding it*] William Morris?

BRADLEY: [*notices that* VINCENT *is impressed*] Uh-huh. [*pause*] Who handles you?

VINCENT: Snow Kwong-Johnson.

BRADLEY: Oh. [*pause*] I hear they handle mainly . . .

VINCENT: [*interrupts*] She.

BRADLEY: Oh, yes. *She* handles mainly . . . [*motions to* VINCENT *and himself*]

VINCENT: Yes. Mainly . . . [*motions to* BRADLEY *and to himself*]

BRADLEY: Ahhh, I see. Well. [*silence*]

VINCENT: It's a bit warm tonight.

BRADLEY: I feel fine, just fine. [VINCENT *takes a cigarette out and is about to smoke.* BRADLEY *begins to steal glances at* VINCENT's *face.* VINCENT *remembers to offer one to* BRADLEY.] I don't smoke. [*The mood is ruined for* VINCENT. *He puts the cigarette away. About to take a sip of his red wine.* BRADLEY *notices* VINCENT's *drink.*] Tannins. Bad for the complexion. [*holds up his drink*] Club soda.

VINCENT: I imagine you exercise, too?

BRADLEY: I swim three times a week. Do you work out?

VINCENT: Yes. Watch. [*Lifts drink to his lips and gulps it down. Pause.* VINCENT *notices* BRADLEY *looking at his face.* BRADLEY *realizes he's been caught, feigns ignorance, and looks away.* VINCENT *touches his face to see if he has a piece of food on his cheek, or something worse on his nose.* VINCENT's *not sure of* BRADLEY's *intent. Perhaps he was admiring his good looks.* VINCENT's *not sure.*] Bradley? Was there something? You were . . . looking at me? [VINCENT *motions gracefully towards his face. Pause.* BRADLEY *decides to explain.*]

BRADLEY: This is kind of personal, I know. I don't know if I should ask you. [*pause*] Ok, is that your real nose?

VINCENT: What?

BRADLEY: I mean, your original one—you know, the one you were born with?

VINCENT: [*smile fading*] What?

BRADLEY: Someone once told me—and if it's not true just say so—someone once told me you hold the record for "noses." [*barely able to contain his giggling*] You've had all these different noses. Sinatra, Montgomery Clift, Troy Donahue—whatever was *in* at the time. Sort of like the "Seven Noses of Dr. Lao . . ." [*notices* VINCENT *is not laughing*] That's what they said. I just thought maybe I would ask you about . . .

VINCENT: [*interrupts*] Who told you this?

BRADLEY: No one.

VINCENT: You said someone told you.

BRADLEY: Yes, but . . .

VINCENT: [*interrupts*] Someone is usually a person. And if this person *told you* it means he probably has lips. Who is this person with *big, fat, moving* lips.

BRADLEY: I don't know, just someone. I forget—I'm not good at remembering lips.

VINCENT: No. [BRADLEY *doesn't follow.*] No, it is *not* true. This is my natural nose. As God is my witness. [*Silence.* VINCENT *sipping drink. Turns to look at* BRADLEY. *Repeating the name to himself.*] Yamashita . . . Ya-ma-shita . . . You worked with Chloe Fong in New York? [BRADLEY *nods.*] Ahhh.

BRADLEY: What? [VINCENT *ignores* BRADLEY's *query and goes back to staring out at the night sky. Occasionally, glances at* BRADLEY *knowingly.*] What? [*pause*]

VINCENT: Now this is kind of personal. And tell me if I am wrong. I heard you almost got fired in New York.

BRADLEY: Who said that—what?

VINCENT: You are the fellow who was out in that play in New York, correct? With Chloe?

BRADLEY: Yeah, so?

VINCENT: I heard—and tell me if I am wrong, rumors are such vicious things—I heard they were not too happy with you, your work.

BRADLEY: What do you mean, "not happy with me?"

VINCENT: Now, this is probably just a rumor—I do not know—But, that is what I . . .

BRADLEY: [*interrupts*] That's not true. That's not true at all. I was a little nervous, so was everybody. And I never, "almost got fired." Did Chloe say that?

VINCENT: No, no, no.

BRADLEY: Cause I was OK. Once I got comfortable I was good. You ask Chloe. The director came up afterwards and congratulated me he liked my work so much. White director.

VINCENT: Ah, rumors.

BRADLEY: [*mutters under his breath*] Bullshit . . . [*Silence.* VINCENT *takes a cigarette out, lights it and takes a deep, satisfying drag.*]

VINCENT: Ahhh. I needed that. [*pause*]

BRADLEY: Who said I almost got fired? Was it Chloe? She wouldn't say something like that. I know her. [*beat*] Was it her?

VINCENT: It is just a rumor. Take it easy. Just a rumor. Remember this? [*taps his nose*] Dr. Lao? It comes with the terrain. You must learn to live with it. It happens to everyone. Sooner or later. *Everyone.* You are walking along, minding your own business, your head filled with poems and paintings— when what do you see coming your way? Some ugly "rumor," dressed in your clothes, staggering down the street impersonating you. And it is not you but no one seems to care. They want this impersonator—who is drinking from a brown paper bag, whose pant zipper is down to here and flapping in the wind—to be you. Why? They like it. It gives them glee. They like the lie. And the more incensed you become, the more real it seems to grow. Like some monster in a nightmare. If you ignore it, you rob it of its strength. It will soon disappear. [*beat*] You will live. We all go to bed thinking, "The pain is so great, I will not last through the night." [*beat*] We wake up. Alive. C'est dommage. [*pause*] Have you seen my latest film? It has been out for several months.

BRADLEY: Was this the Ninja assassin one?

VINCENT: No, that was three years ago. This one deals with life after the atomic holocaust and dramatizes how postnuclear man must deal with what has become, basically, a very very hostile environ . . .

BRADLEY: [*interrupts*] Oh, the one with the mutant monsters—they moved all jerky, Ray Harryhausen stuff—and the hairy guys eating raw meat? You were in that film? I saw that film.

VINCENT: I got billing. I got . . .

BRADLEY: You were in it?

VINCENT: . . . the box.

BRADLEY: I'm sure I saw that film. [*looking at* VINCENT'*s face*]

VINCENT: I came in after everyone signed so my name is in the square box. My name . . .

BRADLEY: Nah, you weren't in it. I saw that film.

VINCENT: . . . is in all the ads. There is a big marquee as you drive down Sunset Boulevard with my name in that box.

BRADLEY: [*Staring at* VINCENT's *face, it's coming to him.*] Oh, oh . . . You were the husband of the woman who was eaten by the giant salamander? [BRADLEY *is having a hard time suppressing his laughter.*]

VINCENT: [*shrugging*] It was a little hard to tell, I know. The makeup was a little heavy. But it was important to create characters that in some way reflected the effects. . . .

BRADLEY: [*overlapping, can no longer contain himself and bursts out laughing*] Makeup a little heavy? Jesus Christ, you had so much hair on your face you looked like a fucking chimpanzee! [BRADLEY *stops laughing as he notices* VINCENT's *pained expression. Awkward silence.* VINCENT *smokes his cigarette.* BRADLEY *sips on his soda.* BRADLEY *occasionally steals a glance at* VINCENT. VINCENT *watches the North Star. Dim to darkness.*]

END OF SCENE

SCENE TWO

"WIN ONE FOR THE NIPPER"

Audition waiting room at a theater. VINCENT *seated, reading a magazine.* BRADLEY *enters, carrying script.*

BRADLEY: [*calls back*] Yeah, thanks, ten minutes. [BRADLEY *sees* VINCENT, *cautiously seats himself.* VINCENT *pretends not to notice* BRADLEY *and turns away from him, still buried in his magazine. They sit in silence. Breaking the ice.*] Mr. Chang, I'm sorry. I really didn't mean to laugh . . .

VINCENT: [*interrupts*] Excuse me young man, but do I know you?

BRADLEY: Well, yes . . . we met at that party over the weekend in the Hollywood Hills . . .

VINCENT: [*interrupts*] What did you say your name was?

BRADLEY: Bradley. Bradley Yamashita.

VINCENT: And we met at that party?

BRADLEY: Yeah. On the balcony. [VINCENT *stares intently at* BRADLEY, *who is becoming uncomfortable.*]

VINCENT: You look familiar. You must forgive me. I go to so many parties. Did I make a fool of myself? I do that sometimes, I drink too much and do not remember a thing. That makes me an angel. You see, angels have no memories. [VINCENT *smiles and goes back to reading.*]

BRADLEY: Look, whether you want to remember or not, that's your business. But I'm sorry, Mr. Chang. I sincerely apologize. I can't do more than that. I shouldn't have laughed at you. [*silence*]

VINCENT: You say your name is Bradley? Bradley Yamashita? [BRADLEY *nods*] Which part in the play are you reading for?

BRADLEY: The son.

VINCENT: They want me for the part of the father. I am meeting the director. We could end up father and son. It might prove to be interesting.

BRADLEY: Yeah.

VINCENT: Then again, it might not. [*Silence. Awkward moment.* VINCENT *studies* BRADLEY.] Maybe they will cast Theodora Ando. As your sister. Make it a *murder* mystery. [VINCENT *mimes stabbing with a knife and twisting the blade.* BRADLEY *recalls* VINCENT's *earlier reference to Theodora at the party and laughs.* VINCENT *laughs, also. Pause.*]

BRADLEY: You know, Mr. Chang, when I was growing up you were sort of my hero. No, really, you were. I mean, I'd be watching TV and suddenly you'd appear in some old film or an old Bonanza or something. And at first something would always jerk inside. Whoo, what's this? This is weird, like watching my own family on TV. It's like the first time I made it with an Asian girl—up to then only white girls. They seemed more outgoing—I don't know—more normal. With this Asian girl it was like doing it with my sister. It was weird. Everything about her was familiar. Her face, her skin, the sound of her voice, the way she smelled. It was like having sex with someone in my own family. That's how it was when you'd come on the TV. You were kind of an idol. [*pause*]

VINCENT: You know who I wanted to be like? You know who my hero was? Fred Astaire. [*noticing* BRADLEY's *look*] Yes, Fred Astaire.

BRADLEY: You danced?

VINCENT: [*nods*] Un-huh.

BRADLEY: I didn't know that.

VINCENT: Yes, well . . . [*Awkward pause. Both want to pursue conversation but unsure how to.* VINCENT *starts to go back to script.*]

BRADLEY: What kind of dancing did you do? I mean, Fred Astaire kind of dancing or Gene Kelly–like, or, or, like the Nicholas Brothers—flying off those risers, landing doing the splits—ouch!

VINCENT: [*laughs*] You know who the Nicholas Brothers are?

BRADLEY: Yeah, sure, of course. And Fred Astaire—Jesus, so smooth. I loved him in *Silk Stockings.* And Cyd Charisse was great.

VINCENT: No, no, *Ginger Rogers, Top Hat.* The two of them together, Ahhh. [*silence*]

BRADLEY: Would you show me something? [VINCENT *doesn't follow.*] Some dance moves.

VINCENT: Now? Right here?

BRADLEY: Yeah, come on, just a little.

VINCENT: No, no, I haven't danced in years.

BRADLEY: Come on, Vincent. I'd love to see you . . .

VINCENT: [*overlapping*] No, no, I can't.

BRADLEY: . . . dance. No one's around. Come on, Vincent, I'd love to see it.

VINCENT: Well. Alright. [*He gets up.*] A little soft-shoe routine . . . [VINCENT *does a small sampling of some dance moves ending with a small flourish.*]

BRADLEY: [*applauds*] Great! That was great!

VINCENT: Back then you did everything. Tell jokes, juggle, sing—The Kanazawa Trio, great jugglers. Oh, and Jade Wing, a wonderful, wonderful, dancer. The Wongettes—like the Andrews Sisters. On and on, all great performers. We all worked the Chop Suey Circuit.

BRADLEY: Chop Suey Circuit?

VINCENT: In San Francisco you had of course, Forbidden City, Kubla Kan, New York's China Doll—some of the greatest oriental acts ever to go down. That's my theater background. [VINCENT *tries to catch his breath.*] See, there was this one routine that Jade—Jade Wing, she was my partner—and I did that was special. We had developed it ourselves and at the end we did this spectacular move where I pull her up on my shoulders, she falls back, and as she's falling I reach under, grab her hands and pull her through my legs thrusting her into the air . . . And I catch her! Tadah! We were rather famous for it. This one night we performed it—we were in town here, I forget the name of the club—and as the audience began to clap, these two people at one of the front tables stood up, applauding enthusiastically. Everyone followed. It was an amazing feeling to have the whole house on their feet. And then we saw the two people leading the standing ovation. We couldn't believe our eyes—Anna Mae Wong, the "Chinese Flapper" herself, and Sessue Hayakawa. The two most famous oriental stars of the day. They invited us to their table, Hayakawa with his fancy French cigarettes and his thick accent. It was a good thing that I spoke Japanese.

BRADLEY: You speak Japanese?

VINCENT: A little, I speak a little. But Anna Mae Wong spoke impeccable English. In fact, she had an English accent, can you believe that? "Vincent, you danced like you were floating on air." We nearly died then and there. Jade and I sitting at the same table with Anna Mae and Sessue.

BRADLEY: God, wasn't Anna Mae gorgeous.

VINCENT: Yes. But not as pretty as Jade Wing. I think Anna Mae Wong was a little jealous of all the attention Sessue was paying to Jade. God, Jade was beautiful. She was twenty-three when I met her. I was just nineteen. She was a burlesque dancer at the Forbidden City.

BRADLEY: What? Did you two have a thing going on or something?

VINCENT: For a while. But things happen. You are on the road continuously. She wanted one thing, I wanted another. I was pretty wild in those days. There were things about me she just could not accept. That was a long, long time ago.

BRADLEY: What happened to her?

VINCENT: I do not know. I heard she ended up marrying someone up in San Francisco who owned a bar in Chinatown. I forget the name of the bar— "Gumbo's" or some such name. I always meant to go and see her.

BRADLEY: I've been there a couple of times. There's . . .

VINCENT: [*overlapping*] I think she may have passed away. She was . . .

BRADLEY: . . . this old woman who runs it, a grouchy old bitch . . .

VINCENT: . . . so beautiful. . . . [*Awkward pause.* VINCENT *had heard* BRADLEY *speak of the old woman.*] Remember this? [*Reenacting a scene from his most famous role.*] "A sleep that will take an eternity to wash away the weariness that I now feel."

BRADLEY: I know that, I know that. . . . *Tears of Winter,* opposite Peter O'Toole. You were nominated for best supporting actor! It's out on video, I have it. I know it by heart. [VINCENT *feels good. Decides to launch into the whole scene. Saki is mortally wounded.*]

VINCENT: [*as Saki*] Death is a funny thing Master Abrams. You spend your entire life running from its toothless grin. Yet, when you are face to face with it, death is friendly. It smiles and beckons to you like some long lost lover. And you find yourself wanting, more than anything in the world, to rest, to sleep in her open inviting arms. A sleep that will take an eternity to wash away the weariness that I now feel. [VINCENT *stumbles towards* BRADLEY.]

BRADLEY: Vincent? [VINCENT *collapses into* BRADLEY's *unexpecting arms. They tumble to the ground.* VINCENT, *cradled in* BRADLEY's *arms, looks up at him.*] You surprised me.

VINCENT: Don't speak.

BRADLEY: What?

VINCENT: Don't speak. That's your line, Peter O'Toole's line. *Don't speak.*

BRADLEY: Oh-oh. Don't speak, Saki. You must save your strength. We did the best we could. All is lost my little "nipper." The dream is dead. [*Saki is fading fast. Starts to close eyes. Then suddenly.*]

VINCENT: *No!* A dream does not die with one man's death, Master. Think of all the women, children, and babies who will suffer if we are defeated. You must smash the enemy! You must win! [*Pause. Coughs up blood. Continues with heroic efforts.*] Then I can sleep the final sleep with only one dream, the most important dream to keep me company on my journey through hell. [VINCENT *nudges* BRADLEY *to feed him his line.*]

BRADLEY: What dream is that Saki?

VINCENT: The dream of *victory!* [*Saki gasps for life.*] Master . . .

BRADLEY: Yes?

VINCENT: Win one for the . . . Nipper. [*Saki dies in his master's arms.*]

BRADLEY: Saki? Saki? [*He bows his grief-stricken head in Saki's breast. Then, recovering*] Oh, you were great in that film. Great.

VINCENT: You weren't so bad yourself. [BRADLEY *helps* VINCENT *to his feet.*] I'm ready for the director now.

BRADLEY: Can I run my audition piece for you? This is the first Asian American play I ever saw. Characters up there talking to me, something inside of me, not some white guy. I'd never experienced anything . . .

VINCENT: [*interrupts*] Just do it, do it. Don't explain it away. [BRADLEY *stands in silence. Closes eyes. Shrugs, fidgets, clears throat. Opens eyes, finally, and begins.*]

BRADLEY: It was night. It was one of those typical summer nights in the Valley. The hot dry heat of the day was gone. Just the night air filled with swarming mosquitoes, the sound of those irrigation pumps sloshing away. And that peculiar smell that comes from those empty fruit crates stacked in the sheds with their bits and pieces of mashed apricots still clinging to the sides and bottom. They've been sitting in the moist heat of the packing sheds all day long. And by evening they fill the night air with that unmistakable pungent odor of sour and sweet that only a summer night, a summer night in the San Joaquin Valley can give you. And that night, as with every night, I was lost. And that night, as with every night of my life, I was looking for somewhere, someplace that belonged to me. I took my Dad's car 'cause I just had to go for a drive. "Where you going son? We got more work to do in the sheds separating out the fruit." "Sorry, Dad. . . ." I'd drive out to the Yonemoto's and pick up my girl, Bess. Her mother'd say, "Drive carefully and take good care of my daughter—She's Pa and me's only girl." "Sure, Mrs. Yonemoto. . . ." And I'd drive. Long into the night. Windows down, my girl Bess beside me, the radio blasting away . . . But it continued to escape me—this thing, place, that belonged to me. . . . And then the DJ came on the radio, "Here's a new record by a hot new artist, 'Carol' by Neil Sedaka!" Neil who? Sedaka? Did you say, "Sedaka." [*Pronunciation gradually becomes Japanese.*] Sedaka. Sedaka. Sedaka. *Sedaakaa.* As in my father's cousin's brother-in-law's name, Hiroshi Sedaka? What's that you say—the first Japanese American rock 'n' roll star! Neil Sedaka. That name. I couldn't believe it. Suddenly everything was alright. I was there. Driving in my car, windows down, girl beside me—with a goddamned Buddhahead singing on the radio . . . Neil Sedaakaa! I knew. I just knew for once, where ever I drove to that night, the road belonged to me. [*silence*]

VINCENT: Bradley? Neil Sedaka is not Japanese.

BRADLEY: Yes, I know.

VINCENT: I have met him before. He's Jewish, or was it Lebanese. Very nice fellow. But definitely not Japanese.

BRADLEY: Yes, yes, I know. It's by Robinson Kan, the sansei playwright. It shows the need we have for legitimate heroes. And how when you don't have any, just how far you'll go to make them up.

VINCENT: Yes, yes. Well . . . [*awkward pause*] Say, do you sing?

BRADLEY: "Scoshi," a little.

VINCENT: Do you know the musical I was in, *Tea Cakes and Moon Songs?* Sure you do. Let's do Charlie Chop Suey's love song to Mei Ling. I'll play Charlie the Waiter and you play Mei Ling.

BRADLEY: Mei Ling?

VINCENT: [*dragging* BRADLEY *about*] Your part is easy. All you have to do is stand there and sing, "So Sorry, Charlie." You hit the gong. [*Standing side by side.* VINCENT *provides classic sing-songey intro.*] Da Da Da Da—Dah Dah Dah Dah Dah Da Da Da Dah Dah DAH! [VINCENT *looks expectantly at* BRADLEY *who doesn't have a clue and is feeling ridiculous.*] You hit the gong. You hit the gong. [VINCENT *demonstrates, then quickly hums intro and starts the song.* BRADLEY *feels awkward but is swept along by the enthusiasm of* VINCENT. VINCENT *singing.*]

> *Tea cakes and moon songs*
> *June bugs and love gongs*
> *I feel like dancing with you.*
> *Roast duck and dao fu*
> *Lop chong and char siu*
> *Strolling down Grant Avenue*
> Chorus: *Da Da Da Da—Dah Dah Dah Dah Dah*
> *So Solly Cholly.*

[*As they dance around,* BRADLEY *coquettishly hiding behind a fan,* VINCENT *urges him to make his voice more female sounding.*] Higher, make your voice higher! Da Da Da Da—Dah Dah Dah Dah Dah.

BRADLEY: [*struggling to go higher*] So Solly Cholly!

VINCENT: Higher! Higher!

BRADLEY: [*falsetto*] So Solly Cholly! [*They are whirling around the stage.* VINCENT *singing and tap dancing with* BRADLEY *in low singing in a high-pitched falsetto. Both are getting more and more involved, acting out more and more outrageous stereotypes.* BRADLEY *slowly starts to realize what he's doing.*] Wait, wait, wait, what is this—WAIT! What am I doing? What is this shit? [*Then accusingly to* VINCENT *who has gradually stopped.*] You're acting like a Chinese Steppin Fetchit. That's what you're acting like. Jesus, fucking Christ, Vincent. A *Chinese Steppin Fetchit.* [BRADLEY *exits.* VINCENT *glares in the direction of his exit.*]

END OF SCENE

INTERLUDE 2

VINCENT *lit in pool of light accepting an award.*

VINCENT: This is a great honor. A great honor, indeed. To be recognized by my fellow Asian American actors in the industry. I have been criticized. Yes, I am aware of that. But I am an actor. Not a writer. I can only speak the words that are written for me. I am an actor. Not a politician. I cannot change the world. I can only bring life, through truth and craft, to my characterizations. I have never turned down a role. Good or bad, the responsibility of an actor is to do that role well. That is all an actor should or has to be concerned about. Acting. Whatever is asked of you, do it. Yes. But do it with dignity. I am an actor. [VINCENT *dims to darkness. Flash!* BRADLEY *lit in pool of light. Holding a camera that has just flashed. Wearing stereotypic glasses. He is at an audition for a commercial.*]

BRADLEY: What? Take the picture, then put my hand like this—in front of my mouth and *giggle?* Yeah, but Japanese men don't giggle. How about if I shoot the picture and like this . . . Just laugh. [*listens*] I'm sorry but I can't do that. Look, it's not truthful to the character. Japanese men don't giggle. What? [*Listens. Turns to leave.*] Yeah, well the same to you Mr. Asshole director. [*Dim to darkness on* BRADLEY. *We hear a glitzy, Las Vegas version of* Tea Cakes and Moon Songs. VINCENT *lit in a pool of light. Wearing a big cowboy hat. He is the master of ceremonies at a huge Tupperware convention in Houston. Holding mike.*]

VINCENT: Howdy! Howdy! It is good to be here in Houston, Texas. In case you don't know me, I'm Vincent Chang. [*applause*] Thank you, thank you. And if you do not know who I am, shame on you! And, go out and buy a copy of *Tears of Winter.* It is out on video now I understand. Hey, you know what they call Chinese blindfolds? *Dental Floss!* [*laughter*] And I would especially like to thank Tupperware for inviting me to be your master-of-ceremonies at your annual national—no, I take that back—your *international* convention. [*applause, and more applause.*] Yeah! Yeah! What's the word? [*holds mike out to audience*] TUPPERWARE! Yeah! What's the word? [VINCENT *holds mike out to the audience. Blackout on* VINCENT. BRADLEY *lit talking to his Asian actor friends.*]

BRADLEY: I can't believe this business with the Asian American awards. I mean it's a joke—there aren't enough decent roles for us in a year. What? An award for the best Asian American actor in the role of Vietnamese killer. [*mimicking sarcastically*] And now in the category of "Best Actress with Five Lines or Less . . ." That's all we get. Who're we kidding. This business. This goddamned fucking business. And I can't believe they gave that award to

Vincent Chang. *Vincent Chang.* His speech—"I never turned down a role." Shi-it! [*dim to darkness*]

END OF INTERLUDE

SCENE THREE

"THEY EDITED IT OUT"

After an acting class. VINCENT *is upset.* BRADLEY *packing his duffle bag.*

VINCENT: You do not know a thing about the industry. Not a damn thing. Who the hell . . .

BRADLEY: [*interrupts, calling to someone across the room*] Yeah, Alice—I'll get my lines down for our scene, sorry.

VINCENT: [*attempts to lower his voice so as not to be heard*] Who the hell are you to talk to me that way. Been in the business a few . . .

BRADLEY: [*interrupts*] Look, if I offended you last time by something I said I'm sorry. I like your work, Mr. Chang. You know that. I like your . . .

VINCENT: [*interrupts*] A "Chinese Steppin Fetchit"—that is what you called me. A "Chinese Steppin Fetchit." Remember?

BRADLEY: I'm an angel, OK, I'm an angel. *No memory.*

VINCENT: And you do not belong in this class.

BRADLEY: My agent at William Morris arranged for me to join this class.

VINCENT: This is for *advanced* actors.

BRADLEY: I've been acting in the theatre for seven years, Mr. Chang.

VINCENT: Seven years? Seven years? Seven years is a wink of an eye. An itch on the ass. A fart in my sleep my fine, feathered friend.

BRADLEY: I've been acting at the Theatre Project of Asian America in San Francisco for seven years—acting, directing, writing . . .

VINCENT: Poppycock, Cockypoop, bullshit. Theatre Project of Asian America— "Amateur Hour."

BRADLEY: "Amateur hour?" Asian American theaters are where we do the real work, Mr. Chang.

VINCENT: The business, Bradley, I am talking about the business, the industry. That Matthew Iwasaki movie was a fluke, an accident . . .

BRADLEY: [*interrupts*] Film, Mr. Chang.

VINCENT: *Movie!* And stop calling me Mr. Chang. It's Shigeo Nakada. "Asian American consciousness." Hah. You can't even tell the difference between a Chinaman and a Jap. I'm Japanese, didn't you know that? I changed my name after the war. Hell, I wanted to work. . . .

BRADLEY: [*mutters*] You are so jive, Mr. Chang. . . .

VINCENT: You think you're better than I, don't you? Somehow special, above it all. The new generation. With all your fancy politics about this Asian American new-way-of-thinking and seven long years of paying your dues at Asian Project Theater or whatever it is. You don't know shit my friend. You don't know the meaning of paying your dues in this business.

BRADLEY: The business. You keep talking about the business. The industry. Hollywood. What's Hollywood? Cutting up your face to look more white? So my nose is a little flat. Fine! Flat is beautiful. So I don't have a double-fold in my eyelid. Great! No one in my entire racial family has had it in the last ten thousand years. My old girlfriend used to put scotch tape on her eyelids to get the double fold so she could look more "cau-ca-sian." My new girl-friend—she doesn't mess around, she got surgery. Where does it begin? Vincent? All that self hate, *where does it begin?* You and your Charley Chop Suey roles . . .

VINCENT: You want to know the truth? I'm glad I did it. Yes, you heard me right. I'm glad I did it and I'm not ashamed, I wanted to do it. And no one is ever going to get an apology out of me. And in some small way it is a victory. Yes, a victory. At least an oriental was on screen acting, being seen. We existed.

BRADLEY: But that's not existing—wearing some god-damn monkey suit and kissing up to some white man, that's not existing.

VINCENT: That's all there was, Bradley. That's all there was! But you don't think I wouldn't have wanted to play a better role than that bucktoothed, grovel-ing waiter? I would have killed for a better role where I could have played an honest-to-god human being with real emotions. I would have killed for it. You seem to assume "Asian Americans" always existed. That there were always roles for you. You didn't exist back then buster. Back then there was no Asian American consciousness, no Asian American actor, and no Asian American theaters. Just a handful of "orientals" who for some godforsaken reason wanted to perform. *Act.* And we did. At church bazaars, community talent night, and on the Chop Suey Circuit playing Chinatowns and Little Tokyos around the country as hoofers, jugglers, acrobats, strippers— anything we could for anyone who would watch. You, you with that holier than thou look, trying to make me feel ashamed. You wouldn't be here if it weren't for all the crap we had put up with. We built something. We built the mountain, as small as it may be, that you stand on so proudly looking down at me. Sure, it's a mountain of Charley Chop Suey's and slipper-toting geishas. But it is also filled with forgotten moments of extraordinary wonder, artistic achievement. A singer, Larry Ching, he could croon like Frank Sinatra and better looking, too. Ever heard of him? Toy Yet Mar—boy, she could belt it out with the best of them. "The Chinese So-phie Tucker." No one's ever heard of her. And Dorothy Takahashi, she could dance the high heels off of anyone, Ginger Rogers included. And, who in the hell has ever heard of Fred Astaire and Dorothy Takahashi? Dead dreams, my friend. Dead dreams, broken backs and long forgotten beauty. I swear sometimes when I'm taking my curtain call I can see this shadowy figure out of the corner of my eye taking the most glorious, dignified bow. Who remembers? *Who* appreciates?

BRADLEY: See, you think every time you do one of those demeaning roles, the only thing lost is *your* dignity. That the only person who has to pay is you. Don't you see that every time you do that millions of people in movie theaters will see it. Believe it. Every time you do any old stereotypic role just to pay the bills, someone has to pay for it—and it ain't you. *No.* It's some Asian kid in-nocently walking home. "Hey, it's a Chinaman gook!" "Rambo, Rambo, Rambo!" You older actors. You ask to be understood, forgiven, but you refuse to change. You have no sense of social responsibility. Only me . . .

VINCENT: [*overlapping*] No . . .

BRADLEY: . . . me, me. Shame on you. I'd never play a role like that stupid waiter in that musical. And . . .

VINCENT: You don't know . . .

BRADLEY: . . . I'd never let them put so much makeup on my face that I look like some goddamn chimpanzee on the screen.

VINCENT: [*overlapping*] You don't know . . .

BRADLEY: I don't care if they paid me a million dollars, what good is it to lose your dignity. I'm not going to prostitute my soul just to . . .

VINCENT: [*overlapping*] There's *that* word. I was wondering when we'd get around to that word. I hate that word! I HATE THAT WORD!

BRADLEY: . . . see myself on screen if I have to go grunting around like some slant-eyed animal. You probably wouldn't know a good role if it grabbed you by the balls!

VINCENT: I have played many good roles.

BRADLEY: Sure, waiters, Viet Cong killers, chimpanzees, drug dealers, hookers—

VINCENT: [*interrupts*] I was the first to be nominated for an Academy Award.

BRADLEY: Oh, it's pull-out-the-old-credits time. But what about some of the TV stuff you've been doing lately. Jesus, TV! At least in the movies we're still dangerous. But TV? They fucking cut off our balls and made us all house-boys on the evening soaps. [*calls out*] "Get your very own neutered, oriental houseboy!"

VINCENT: I got the woman once. [BRADLEY *doesn't understand.*] In the movie. I got the woman.

BRADLEY: Sure.

VINCENT: And she was *white.*

BRADLEY: You're so full of it.

VINCENT: And I kissed her!

BRADLEY: What, a peck on the cheek?

VINCENT: ON THE LIPS! ON THE LIPS! *I GOT THE WOMAN.*

BRADLEY: Nah.

VINCENT: Yes.

BRADLEY: Nah?

VINCENT: *YES.*

BRADLEY: [*pondering*] When was this? In the thirties. Before the war?

VINCENT: [*overlapping*] No.

BRADLEY: Because that happened back then. After the war forget it. Mr. Moto even disappeared and he was played by Peter Lorre.

VINCENT: No, no. This was the fifties.

BRADLEY: Come on, you're kidding.

VINCENT: Nineteen fifty-nine. A cop movie. [*correcting himself*] Film. *The Scarlet Kimono.* Directed by Sam Fuller. Set in L.A. Two police detectives, one Japanese American and one Caucasian. And a beautiful blond, they both love.

BRADLEY: Yeah . . . I remember. And there's this violent kendo fight between you two guys because you both want the woman. [*realizing*] And you get the woman.

VINCENT: See, I told you so. [*Pause.* BRADLEY *seated himself.*]

BRADLEY: Except when I saw it you didn't kiss her. I mean I would have remem-
    bered something like that. An Asian man and a white woman. You didn't
    kiss her.
VINCENT: TV?
BRADLEY: Late Night [BRADLEY *nods.* VINCENT *making the realization.*]
VINCENT: They edited it out. [*Silence.* VINCENT *is upset.* BRADLEY *watches him.*
    Dim to darkness.]
END OF SCENE

INTERLUDE 3

Darkness. BRADLEY *lit in pool of light. Silently practicing "tai chi," with dark glasses*
on. His movements are graceful, fluid. Stops. Poised in silence like a statue. Suddenly
breaks into savage kung-fu kicks with the accompanying Bruce Lee screams. Stops. Si-
lence. BRADLEY *shakes himself as if trying to release pent-up tension. Quietly begins the*
graceful "tai chi" movement. BRADLEY *dims to darkness and* VINCENT *lit in pool of*
light.

VINCENT: [*on the phone to Kenneth*] I can not. You know why. Someone might see
    us together. [*listens*] You do not know. People talk. Especially in this orien-
    tal community and then what happens to my career. I am a leading man.
    [*Kenneth hangs up on him.*] I am a leading man. [*dim to darkness.*]
END OF INTERLUDE

SCENE FOUR

"THE LOOK IN THEIR EYES"

After acting class, VINCENT *and* BRADLEY *in a crowded, noisy bar having a drink.*
They play a raucous verbal game.

BRADLEY: Mr. Chang, it's a . . .
VINCENT: [*interrupts, calls to a waitress*] Excuse me! Tanquery martini, straight up
    with a twist. Dry.
BRADLEY: [*pretending to be a casting agent making an offer*] Mr. Chang, it's a
    two-day contract.
VINCENT: [*no accent, straight, not much effort*] Yankee dog, you die.
BRADLEY: [*trying to suppress his laughter*] Mr. Chang, it's a "one-week" contract.
    And don't forget the residuals when this goes into syndication.
VINCENT: [*Big "oriental" accent. Barely able to contain his laughter.*] Yankee dawg,
    you die!
BRADLEY: Mr. Chang, it's a "three-month shoot" on location in the "Caribbean
    Islands." Vincent, we're talking a cool six figures here. You can get your
    condo in Malibu, your silver mercedes, you'll . . .
VINCENT: [*Overlapping. An outrageous caricature, all the while barely containing his*
    laughter.] YANKEE DAWG YOU DIE! YANKEE DAWG YOU DIE!
    YANKEE DAWG YOU DIE!
BRADLEY: . . . BE LYING ON SOME BEACH IN ST. TROPEZ, GETTING
    A TAN, HAVING A GOOD OLE TIME! . . .

VINCENT: My drink . . . [*Both calm down.*]

BRADLEY: I talked my agent into getting me an audition. It's that new lawyer series. He was very reluctant, the role wasn't written for an Asian. I said, "Jason, just get me in there." I showed up for the audition. I said, "I can do it, I can do it." They said, "No, the character's name is Jones." I said, "I can play a character named Jones." They said, "No." "I was adopted." "No." "I married a women and gave up my name." "No." Hell, if some white guy can play Chan, some yellow guy can play Jones. [*Pause. Sipping drinks.*]

VINCENT: Do you remember that film, *Bad Day At Black Rock?*

BRADLEY: [*remembering*] Yeah, yeah . . .

VINCENT: That role, that role that Spencer Tracy plays?

BRADLEY: Yeah, but it's about some Nisei 442 vet, right?

VINCENT: That's who the story revolves around but he does not appear. He's dead. Got killed saving Tracy's life in Italy. After the war Tracy goes to the dead soldier's home town to return a war medal to his Issei parents. Only they don't appear either. Their farm is burned down, they are missing, and therein lies the tale. I should have played that role.

BRADLEY: Whose role? Spencer Tracy's?

VINCENT: It's about a Nisei.

BRADLEY: Yeah, but none appear.

VINCENT: But he could have been a Nisei, Tracy's character. And I have always felt I should have played it.

BRADLEY: Me. Robert De Niro, Taxi Driver. "You talking to me? You talking to me?"

VINCENT: *Harvey.*

BRADLEY: Keitel?

VINCENT: No, no. The film with Jimmy Stewart.

BRADLEY: With the rabbit? The big fucking rabbit nobody can see?

VINCENT: God, Stewart's role is wonderful. Everyone thinks he is mad, but he is not. He is not. Original innocence.

BRADLEY: Mickey Rourke in Pope of Greenwich Village. "Hit me again—see if I change."

VINCENT: James Dean, East of Eden, Salinas, a farm boy just like me. [*As* VINCENT *enacts a scene from the movie,* BRADLEY *appears quiet and momentarily lost in thought.*]

BRADLEY: [*interrupts*] Forget what I said about Mickey Rourke. He's an asshole—he did that *Year of the Dragon.* I hated that film.

VINCENT: Not that film again. It is . . . just a "movie." [*calls after waitress who seems to be ignoring him*] My drink! [*They sip in silence.* BRADLEY *reaches into his bag and pulls out a script.*]

BRADLEY: Vincent? Want to work on something together?

VINCENT: We already are taking the same class. . . .

BRADLEY: [*interrupts*] No, no, over at the Asian American Theater. The one here in town.

VINCENT: No, no, all those orientals huddling together, scared of the outside world—it is stifling to an actor's need for freedom.

BRADLEY: It's a workshop production, a new play by Robinson Kan—a sci-fi, political drama about . . .

VINCENT: [*interrupts*] You should be out there doing the classics, Bradley. It is limiting, seeing yourself just as an Asian. And you must never limit yourself. Never. [BRADLEY *reaches into his bag and pulls out a small Godzilla toy.*]

BRADLEY: It's got Godzilla in it.

VINCENT: Godzilla? [*moving it playfully*] Godzilla. Aahk. [*calling to waitress*] My drink, *please.*

BRADLEY: You can do and say whatever you want there.

VINCENT: An actor must be free. You must understand that. *Free.*

BRADLEY: And they will never edit it out. [*Awkward silence. Sipping.*] I was in a theater in Westwood. I was there with a bunch of Asian friends. And then that "movie" starts. Rourke struts into this room of Chinatown elders like he's John Wayne and starts going on and on, "Fuck you, fuck you. I'm tired of all this Chinese this, Chinese that. This is America." And then these young teenagers sitting across from us start going, "Right on, kick their butts." I started to feel scared. Can you believe that? "Right on Mickey, kick *their* asses!" I looked over at my friends. They all knew what was happening in that theater. As we walked out I could feel people staring at us. And the look in their eyes. I'm an American. Three fucking generations, *I'm an American.* And this goddamn movie comes along and makes me feel like I don't belong here. Like I'm the enemy. *I belong here.* I wanted to rip the whole goddamn fucking place up. Tear it all down. [*silence.* VINCENT *picks up Godzilla.*]

VINCENT: Godzilla? Robinson Kan, a workshop production? [BRADLEY *nods.*] Well. "I never turn down a role." [*They both laugh.* VINCENT *picks up script.*] Let's see what we have here. [*Dim to darkness.*]

END OF SCENE

SCENE FIVE

"GODZILLA . . . AAHK!"

Darkness. Godzillalike theme music. High tension wires crackle across the projection screens.

VINCENT: [*voice-over*] I can't believe I let you talk me into this!

BRADLEY: [*voice-over*] Take it easy, take it easy.

VINCENT: [*voice-over*] I should have never let you talk me into this Asian American thing! And this costume . . .

BRADLEY: [*voice-over Interrupts*] We're on! [BRADLEY *lit in pool of light down right. He plays a reporter out of the fifties. He wears a hat and holds one of those old-style announcer microphones.*] Good evening Mr. and Mrs. America and all the ships at sea. Flash! Godzilla!

VINCENT: [*on tape*] AAHK!

REPORTER: A 1957 TOHO production. Filmed in Tokyo, to be distributed in Japan *AND* America. Starring Kehara Ken, the scientist who develops the anti-oxygen bomb that wipes out Godzilla . . .

GODZILLA: [*on tape*] AAHK!

REPORTER: . . . and Raymond Burr, an American actor who was so popular as Perry Mason that he just might be the drawing card needed to bring in those American audiences. Godzilla . . .

GODZILLA: [*on tape*] AAHK!

REPORTER: Rising, rising from the depths. In Japan it's released as *Gojira*. In America, it's Anglicized and marketed as *Godzilla!* . . . [VINCENT, *dressed up in a Godzilla outfit, bursts through the projected high-tension wires as the projection screens turn to allow him to enter. Smoke and flashing lights.*]

GODZILLA: AAHK! [*During the following, Godzilla acts out what the Reporter is describing.*]

REPORTER: It breaks through the surface just off the shores of San Francisco, SPPLAASSHH!!! It's swum the entire Pacific Ocean underwater and is about to hyperventilate. It staggers onto the beach and collapses. It looks like a giant zucchini gone to seed. A huge capsized pickle with legs.

VICTOR: [*struggling to get up*] Bradley! Bradley, I'm stuck! [BRADLEY *helps* VICTOR *up.*]

REPORTER: Five days later—refreshed and revived, it continues its trek inland. It takes the Great Highway up to Geary Boulevard, hangs a right on Gough and follows that sucker right onto the Bay Bridge. It pays no toll. Cars screech, children cry, mothers with babies scream. The men don't. They're "manly." Godzilla! . . .

GODZILLA: AAHK! [*Godzilla strolls over to the Reporter/*BRADLEY, *takes the hat and mike and now he becomes the Reporter.* BRADLEY, *in turn, now becomes the Little Boy acting out what is said by* VINCENT.]

REPORTER/GODZILLA/VINCENT: A little boy. A little boy watching TV. A little boy watching TV on Saturday night and it's "Creature Features" on Channel 2. Tonight the feature is "Godzilla . . ." [*Reporter momentarily becomes Godzilla.*] AAHK! [*back to reporting*] . . . And a little boy watching, watching, has a hunger, a craving for a hero, for a symbol, for a secret agent to carry out his secret deeds . . . Godzilla!

GODZILLA/LITTLE BOY: AAHK! [BRADLEY *grabs the hat and mike back and becomes the Reporter once again.* VINCENT *as Godzilla acts out the blow by blow account.*]

REPORTER: . . . In its anger it lashes out. It gouges out eyes of people who stare, rips out the tongues of people who taunt! Causes blackouts of old World War II movies! Godzilla. . . .

GODZILLA: AAHK!

REPORTER: It takes the 580 turn off and continues to head inland into the San Joaquin Valley. And there in the distance . . . STOCKTON! Stockton, a small aggie town just south of Sacramento, population 120,000 and the home of a little boy. A little boy who knows, understands, and needs Godzilla. . . .

GODZILLA: AAHK!

REPORTER: And who Godzilla . . .

GODZILLA: AAHK!

REPORTER: . . . with his pea-sized brain, regards with supreme affection and would do anything the little boy asked it to do. And this is what the little boy asked . . . [BRADLEY *puts hat and mike aside and becomes the Little Boy.*]

BRADLEY/LITTLE BOY: Godzilla, ya know Sammy Jones. She's this little fancy pants girl. She said she was watching this old war movie last night and that there was this female nurse—the *only* female in the whole entire army—and that a Japanese sniper shot her dead in the first ten minutes of the movie. Then she said I was the enemy. And *then* she called me a "dirty Jap." [*Godzilla looks appalled, then angry.*] You know what to do. [*Godzilla turns, picks up a 'Sammy Jones' doll, looks down, and then dramatically stomps his foot down as if he were crushing a bug.*] OH BOY! OH BOY! [*End of Scene.* BRADLEY *and* VINCENT *laughing. They had a good time together. They do a "right on" handshake. Godzillalike music swells. Dim to darkness.*]

END OF ACT I

ACT II

INTERLUDE 4

VINCENT *lit in a pool of light. Body microphone. Visual projections.*

VINCENT: I have this dream. In this dream there is a man. And though this man is rich, successful, famous—he is unhappy, so very unhappy. He is unhappy because the love around him, the love in the hearts of those he cared for most, was beginning to shrivel and wither away. And this, in turn, made his own heart begin to grow in order to make up for the love that was disappearing around him. And the more the love in the hearts of those around him shriveled up, the bigger his own heart grew in order to make up for the growing emptiness that he now began to feel. So the love kept withering away and his heart kept growing bigger. Until one day there was so little love around him and his own heart so big—it burst into a thousand red petals that filled the sky and fell slowly, so very slowly, to the earth. And the people, his friends, the ones who had withheld their love, began to swallow the petals, these remains of the man's glorious heart as they fell from the sky. Hungrily, they fed. Greedily they swallowed. They pushed and shoved each other, gorging themselves on these petals because they felt then, they too, would become like the man. Rich, famous, beautiful, lonely . . . [VINCENT *dims to darkness.*]

END OF INTERLUDE

SCENE ONE

"WE WENT TO SEE THE MOVIE"

BRADLEY *reading from a Shakespeare book. Rehearsing.* VINCENT *coaching.*

BRADLEY: Or art thou but
a dagger of the mind, a false creation,
Proceeding from the heat-oppressed—
[VINCENT *entering, correcting*]
VINCENT: Oppres-sed. Oppres-sed. [BRADLEY, *frustrated continues.*]
BRADLEY: . . . heat oppres-sed brain?

I see thee yet, in form as palpable
As this which I now draw.
[BRADLEY *draws a knife. Uncomfortable holding it.*]
VINCENT: [*overlapping towards end of* BRADLEY'*s speech*] . . . which now I draw.
BRADLEY: . . . now I draw, now I draw.
VINCENT: You should be elated you are doing Shakespeare. This is a great opportunity for you.
BRADLEY: [*holding up a script*] But this is Macbeth. I'm doing "Romeo and Juliet," Vincent—I'm doing Romeo.
VINCENT: [*holding his book up*] You must learn them all while you are still young. "Is this a dagger which I see before me, the handle toward my hand? Come, let me clutch thee." There is music to its language and you must know its rhythm so you can think clearly within its verse. I studied Shakespeare when I was younger. And I was—all modesty aside—the best Shakespearean actor in my class. But the only role I got was carrying a spear. And here you are with a gem of a role and you don't want to work. Come on, come on, let's hear it. [BRADLEY *puts his script aside and reads from his book.*]
BRADLEY: Is this a dagger which I see before me,
The handle toward my hand? Come, let me clutch thee.
I have thee not and yet I see thee still
Art thou not, fatal vision, sensible
To feeling as to sight, or art thou but
A dagger of the mind, a false creation,
Proceeding from the heat-oppres-sed brain?
I see thee yet, in form as palpable
As this which now I draw.
VINCENT: Thou marshal'st me the way that I was going—[BRADLEY *lowers his knife.* VINCENT *notices.*] Grip it. Hold it. You must be able to imagine it, feel it. Know the experience from the inside. Of course, you may not have wanted to kill someone. You must know the feeling.
BRADLEY: [*overlapping after "kill someone"*] I'm having trouble with this one, Vincent. I just can't. I can't. OK.
VINCENT: This is ridiculous. You're too tense, way too tense. Lie on the floor. [BRADLEY *resists.*] Lie on the floor. [*While speaking* VINCENT *lights up a cigarette. He needs a break and can do this role. Not paying attention to* BRADLEY *sprawled out on the ground, trying out different shapes.*] Become a . . . rock. You are a rock. Find your shape. Are you big, small, flat, oblong? Keep looking until you find your own particular shape. [BRADLEY *slowly gets up into an upright position.* VINCENT, *puffing, doesn't notice.*] Got it?
BRADLEY: Yeah.
VINCENT: What do you feel? [VINCENT *turns to see the standing* BRADLEY.]
BRADLEY: Alive. Conscious. But there is no hunger, no wanting. And no sense of time. It is now. Yes, that's it. Everything is *now*.
VINCENT: A rock that stands. With no appetite.
BRADLEY: No, no really I know. This is what a rock feels.
VINCENT: I have no reason not to believe.
BRADLEY: I have been a rock before.
VINCENT: Now I have a reason.

BRADLEY: I have. On acid. LSD. The first time I dropped acid I walked into a forest in the Santa Cruz mountains and became a rock.

VINCENT: Why did you do this?

BRADLEY: I was in college.

VINCENT: Alright. Let's work with it. Since we finally have something. [*putting out cigarette*] Go with it Bradley. Relive the experience. Relive it moment by moment. Pebble by pebble. [*suppressing giggle*] I'm sorry.

BRADLEY: I am walking. There is a tightness I feel in the back of my neck—I guess it's the acid coming on. With each step I go deeper into the forest. And with each step I can feel the civilized part of me peeling away like an old skin. Whoo, my mind is beginning to cast aside whole concepts. God, the earth is breathing. I can feel it. It's like standing on someone's tummy. And this rock. This big, beautiful rock. Our consciousnesses are very similar. I do a Vulcan mind-meld. [*touching the rock*] "I am waiting for nothing. I am expecting no one." [*releases Vulcan mind-meld*] It is beautiful in its own rockness.

VINCENT: Good. OK, let us work with . . .

BRADLEY: I began walking again.

VINCENT: OK.

BRADLEY: Thoughts of great insight float in and out of my mind like pretty butterflies. Skin holds the body together. And the head holds the brain together. But what holds the mind together? *What holds the mind together?* I panic! I feel my mind beginning to drift away. There in nothing to hold my mind together. Soon bits and pieces of my consciousness will be scattered across the universe. I'll NEVER GRADUATE! What? What's this? Cows. Ten, twenty, sixty, hundreds. Hundreds and hundreds of cows. Where did they come from? They spot me. They see that I am different. One cow steps forward. He is the leader. He wears a bell as a sign of his authority. He approaches me cautiously, studying me. This head cow nods in approval. He knows I am no longer a civilized human, but somehow different, like them. He turns and signals the others. They all begin to move towards me. Soon I am surrounded in a sea of friendly cows. Hello, hi—It's like old home week. Suddenly I hear a noise coming from far away. It tugs at something inside me. I turn to see where the noise is coming from. I see . . . I recognize . . . Jeffrey. My best friend. Calling my "name." I look at the cows. They are waiting to see what I will do. I look at Jeffrey, his voice ringing clearer and clearer, my name sounding more and more familiar. I look at the cows—They are beginning to turn away. Should I stay and run wild and free with the cows? Or, should I return to the dorms on campus? "HOWDY JEFFREY!" As I run back to see, the cows are once again pretending to be cows. They slowly lumber away, stupid and dumb. Moo, moo. [BRADLEY *notices* VINCENT *staring at him.*] It's a true story.

VINCENT: Cows?

BRADLEY: Yes.

VINCENT: Cows that have a double life? [BRADLEY *nods.*] The dumb facade they show to the outside world and their true cow selves that they show to one another when they are alone? Moo, moo? Well, back to the real world. Perhaps. Anyway, to the task at hand. The role you are playing. Let me rethink this. [*holding book*] "Is this a dagger which I see before me, the handle towards my hand? Come, let me clutch thee . . ."

BRADLEY: [*quietly*] I killed someone.

VINCENT: What?

BRADLEY: I think I killed someone.

VINCENT: Like in a person? A human being? [BRADLEY *nods.*] My God.

BRADLEY: I'm not sure. I may have. But I'm not sure. It was stupid. So stupid. I was about sixteen. I used to hang around a lot with some Chinatown boys, gangs and that sort of thing. I was walking down Jackson Street with my girlfriend, we were going to see the movies, when these two guys—they must have been college students come to gawk at all the Chinese people—turned the corner. Well, as they walked past, one of them looked at my girlfriend and said, "Hey, look at the yellow pussy." So I walked over to the one guy, "What did you say? What did you say?" He just laughed at me. So I pulled a knife and stabbed him. [*shocked silence*]

VINCENT: What happened then?

BRADLEY: We went to see the movie. [*pause*] I don't know. Sometimes it just builds up. The anger. [*pause*] That was over ten years ago. I hope he's OK. I hope with my heart he's OK. [*Dim to darkness.*]

END OF SCENE

INTERLUDE 5

Darkness. Over house speakers we hear: "Un Bel Di Vedremo" from Madame Butterfly. VINCENT *lit in pool of light. He relaxes at home, wearing a velvet bathrobe. He is seated, looking at himself in a mirror.*

VINCENT: [*repeated two times with different interpretations*] "You will cooperate or I will kill you." [*pause*] "You will cooperate or I will kill you." I will take my moment. They expect me to just read my lines and get the hell out of there, another dumb North Vietnamese general. "You will cooperate or I will kill you." Yes, I will take my moment. And I am not going to let the director know. I won't tell Robert. I am just going to do it. [*Pause. Smiling to himself.*] Yes, I will take my moment. Vincent Chang is an actor. [VINCENT *dims to darkness. Music lowers in volume.* BRADLEY *lit in a pool of light.*]

BRADLEY: [*on the phone*] But why? I don't understand, Jason. I thought we had an agreement, an understanding. I know the series fell through, but I'm going to get other roles. I'm a leading man. You told me so yourself. How many young Asian American leading men are there? [*beat*] I'm not *like* the rest of them. What? [*listening*] Yeah . . . I've heard of Snow Kwong Johnson. [BRADLEY *dims to darkness. Music up.* VINCENT *lit in a pool of light.*]

VINCENT: Why do you keep threatening to do it? I hate that. You know you won't do it. Besides I am not going to change my mind. [*pause*] We can still see each other. [*beat*] As friends. [*His eyes follow someone out of the room. Music fades.* VINCENT *dims. Music out.* BRADLEY *lit in a pool of light. He is talking to a friend.*]

BRADLEY: That's not true. Who said that about me? That's not true at all. What? I was an "ex-con?" I was a "hit man" for the *what?* [*Pause. Butterfly's suicide aria in.*] Who told you this? Huh? Who told you this? [*Music swells and peaks as lights go down on* BRADLEY.]

END OF INTERLUDE

SCENE TWO

"... HIT MAN FOR THE CHINESE MAFIA ..."

VINCENT'*s apartment.* BRADLEY *has stormed in.* VINCENT *is trying to put on his coat and pack a small duffle bag at the same time.*

VINCENT: [*putting things back into bag*] I cannot talk now. I cannot. Now, *please.*

BRADLEY: [*angry*] Who else could have told them, Vincent? You're the only one who knows.

VINCENT: [*in a great hurry*] Can't we talk about this later. I have to go some-where. [*pushing* BRADLEY *out of the way, continuing to pack*]

BRADLEY: I told you in confidence. Haven't you heard of "confidentiality?" What do they call it, what do they call it—"privilege." Doctor-patient privilege. Lawyer-client privilege. *Actor–acting teacher privilege.* [VINCENT *is all packed. Trying to get his coat on which has been dangling off his left shoulder.*]

VINCENT: I have to go Bradley. I have a very important appointment.

BRADLEY: [*interrupts*] Fuck your audition! What about *my* career? You told him, didn't you. Goddamn it. You told everybody I was an ex-con, a hit man for the *Chinese Mafia!* [*pause*] What if the casting agencies hear about it? Huh? Think they'll want to hire me?

VINCENT: [*quietly*] My friend is dying ...

BRADLEY: [*not hearing*] What happens to my ...

VINCENT: [*interrupts*] My friend is dying! [*silence*] He overdosed. Took a whole bottle of pills. I have to go to the hospital. Now, get out of my way, Bradley. [*pushing a stunned* BRADLEY *aside*] There are some things in this world more important than *your* career. .... What has happened to you Bradley? What the hell has happened to you?

BRADLEY: [*quietly*] I just wanted to know. That's all. If you told him. I haven't gotten a call lately and I thought you know ... [*Pause.* VINCENT *feels badly about his remarks.*]

VINCENT: Look. I am sorry. ....

BRADLEY: You better go Vincent, your friend ...

VINCENT: [*starts to leave, stops*] He always does this. My friend is just ... lonely. He wants me to come running.

BRADLEY: You said he took a whole bottle of sleeping pills?

VINCENT: Last time it was a whole bottle of laxatives. One week in the hospital. He was so happy. He lost fifteen pounds. [*pause*] Maybe I did. [BRADLEY *doesn't follow his comment.*] Mention it. About what happened in China-town. Just to a few people. I just never had someone tell me they killed ...

BRADLEY: [*overlapping*] He's probably OK, now. I'm sure the guy's fine.

VINCENT: ... someone before. I had to tell somebody. And I never said you were a hit man for the Chinese Mafia, or whatever. .... [*pause*] I am sorry, Bradley. Remember? [*taps his nose*] Dr. Lao? I have to go. The nurses may need some help with the bed pans. [*notices* BRADLEY] We all go through these periods when the phone does not ring. I, too, have had them. Of course, far and few between, but I, too. Try some *ochazuke* with some *umeboshi*—it's on the stove. My mother used to make me eat it when I was upset. Soothes the nerves. [VINCENT *turns to exit.*]

BRADLEY: Vincent? I was going to kick your ass. I was. [VINCENT *stops. Stares at* BRADLEY.] I just sit in my room, waiting for the phone to ring. Why won't the phone ring, Vincent? Huh? Why won't the goddamn phone ring? [*Dim to darkness.*]

END OF SCENE

INTERLUDE 6

Darkness. We hear BRADLEY's *voice. Gradually lights are brought up as he speaks. Up stage area, lit in a pool of light. Body microphone. Visual projections.*

BRADLEY: I have this dream. In this dream, I'm lying on a park bench. I wear only a very ragged black overcoat. Then, I fall asleep. My mouth wide open. It is a kind of perfect sleep. No hunger, no desire . . . no dreams. My heart stops beating. The blood comes to rest in my veins. [*noticing*] It's quite pleasureful. The whispering of warm breezes through my hair. Big, colorful maple leaves of red and orange that flutter down and cover my eyes like coins. Ahh . . . What's this? Two dark clouds circling high above. Now they swoop down, down, towards my sleeping corpse. I see what they are. Two magnificent vultures. I think of something to offer. "Here, here, take my fingers. Yes, yes . . . don't be afraid. Here, take the rest of my hand." That should be enough. No. They want more. . . . They've jumped on my chest. They're beginning to rip me open. It feels . . . so . . . so . . . [*Dim to darkness.*]

END OF INTERLUDE

SCENE THREE

"I SEE MYSELF 35 YEARS AGO"

Thunder. BRADLEY *seated on a bench in a small outdoor shelter. Raining. Umbrella on ground.* VINCENT *runs to the shelter holding two cups of hot coffee.*

VINCENT: [*hands coffee to* BRADLEY] Black, right? [BRADLEY *nods, takes coffee. Sips, watches rain.*]

BRADLEY: I finally got a call. I just came from an audition. It was for one of those evening soaps, everybody was there. Butler gig, glorified extra. I didn't get the role. I walked outside and I started crying. And I was crying, not because of the humiliation. But because, *I wanted the role.* I keep thinking, if I got it, the part, could I go through with it? I mean, actually show up and do that stuff?

VINCENT: When you walk on that set and there is all that expectation from everyone—the director, the writer, the other actors to be that way, it is so . . . I was watching TV last week. They had on this story about Martin Luther King. He was picked up by some night riders. Drove him to the outskirts of town, dragged him out of the car and surrounded him. And that night he felt something inside he never felt before—impotent, like the slave, willing to go along, almost wanting to comply. After that, he realized he had to fight not only the white man on the outside, but that feeling, the slave inside of him. It is so easy to slip into being the "ching-chong-china-man." [VINCENT *looks at* BRADLEY, *knowingly.*] Moo, moo.

BRADLEY: It's still raining pretty hard. I felt kind a bad about last time. That's why I called you up. Your friend OK? [VINCENT *nods. Pause.*]

VINCENT: I love the rain. It is like meditating. It seems to quiet all the distractions around you so you can better hear the voice of your own heart. The heart. A mysterious thing. Kind. Cruel. At times you would like to rip it out. It feels too much, gives you too much pain. And other times—aah, the ecstasy. You wish it were a huge golden peach so that everyone might taste of its sweetness. [*Pause. Thinks.*] It is also like a mirror. Yes, a mirror. And if one is brave enough to gaze into it, in it is reflected the truth of what we really are. Not as we would like to be, or as we would like the world to see us. But as we truly are. [VINCENT *looks at* BRADLEY *intently.*] Would you like to know what I see? [BRADLEY *motions to himself, questioningly.* VINCENT *nods.*]

BRADLEY: That's OK, I'd rather you didn't tell me. An egomaniac, right? A selfish, arrogant, insecure actor.

VINCENT: No, no, quite the contrary. I see a sensitive, shy and compassionate soul. [*pause*] And I see a driven, ambitious, self-centered asshole. In other words, I see myself thirty-five years ago. [*They laugh quietly.*]

BRADLEY: I know this sounds kind of silly. I've never told anyone. You know how everyone has these secret goals. You know what mine were? Obie, Oscar, Tony. OOT. [*They quietly laugh.*]

VINCENT: I was so cocky after my Oscar nomination. No more of those lousy chinaman's parts for me anymore. This was my ticket out of there. Hell, I might even call my own shots. My agent kept warning me though. "Vincent, you're an oriental actor. It's different for you." I said, "No way. Not anymore. From now on only good roles are coming my way."

BRADLEY: Did the offers for good roles come in?

VINCENT: No. I have this dream. I am standing in the* middle of a room with all these people staring at me. At first I think they are friendly towards me. Then I think, no, they are evil people out to get me. Then suddenly again, I think this is exactly where I want to be, it feels wonderful. Then I am seized with a strange fear and I feel I must get the hell out of there. A spotlight flashes on me. I am disoriented. Someone hands me a script. [VINCENT *glances at the lines.*] "Why do I have to do this?" Then this warm, soothing voice says, "Is there a problem Vincent? All we want you to do is fuck yourself. Take all the time you want. We'll get the most expensive lubricant if you need. Vincent, is there a problem? We hear Sly Stallone's doing it, so it must be OK. OK?" "Read the lines this way." [*pause*] I know what is going on, Bradley. I am not stupid. I know what I am doing. That is the problem. [*They sip their drinks in silence. Watch the rain.*]

---

*Dialogue based on a scene from the film, *Yuki Shimoda* by John Esaki and Amy Kato.

BRADLEY: Maybe you should call Gumbo's, that bar in San Francisco. Right now. Come on, let's be crazy!

VINCENT: What? And find out that my beautiful memory of Jade Wing has turned into—what did you say? A grouchy old bitch? No. I could not bear to kill any more of my dreams.

BRADLEY: That was probably just the bartender. Jade is probably rich, still beautiful, living in some expensive home in Pacific Heights, wondering this very instant, "What ever happened to Shig Nakada?" [VINCENT *sadly shakes his head.*]

VINCENT: We were married. Jade and I. No one ever knew that. Just us. We were so young. [*pause*] She left me one night. Never saw her again. I don't blame her. She caught me in bed with someone.

BRADLEY: Vincent.

VINCENT: Actually, she did not mind the idea of me playing around. Or rather she minded but she could live with it. What she could not stomach was who I was playing around with. [*pause*] Well. It is getting late. And the rain seems to have finally abated. [*Both get up.*] Bradley? Would you like to come over to my place? For a drink? [*awkward pause*]

BRADLEY: No, Vincent. No, I can't.

VINCENT: Right. Well. Good night. [*pause*]

BRADLEY: It's OK. [VINCENT *doesn't follow.*] It's OK, Vincent. It doesn't matter to me.

VINCENT: I do not know what you are talking about.

BRADLEY: It doesn't matter, Vincent. People don't care nowadays.

VINCENT: I do not know what you are talking about Bradley. I do not. It is late. Good-bye.

BRADLEY: Good night, Vincent. [BRADLEY *sadly watches* VINCENT *exit. Dim to darkness.*]

END OF SCENE

INTERLUDE 7

BRADLEY *lit in pool of light, sitting.*

BRADLEY: [*bragging*] They want me to play this Chinese waiter. I'll go, OK, take a look. I get there and look at the script. Jesus. I read the lines straight. No accent, no nothing. They say, "No, no, we need an accent." You know, THE accent. I told my agent—What? No, I quit them—if they pay me twice the amount of the offer, OK. I'll do it any way they want. Otherwise forget it. They paid it. The dumb shits. They paid it. [*laughing smugly*] On top of it, they liked me. Yeah, they liked me. [*Cross fade to an empty pool of light. The aria from* Madame Butterfly *softly underscoring this scene.* VINCENT *enters dancing. He is wearing headphones with a walkman and is practicing one of his old routines. Gradually the TV light and sound are brought up. We hear the Sergeant Moto monologue.* VINCENT *stops dancing, takes off headphones and watches the TV light. Upset. Reaches for the phone and dials for his agent.*]

VINCENT'S VOICE ON TV: You stupid American G.I. I know you try and escape. You think you can pull my leg. I speakee your language. I graduate UCLA,

Class of thirty-four. I drive big, American car with big chested American blond sitting next to—Heh? No, no, not "dirty floor." Floor clean. Class of thirty-four. No, no, not "dirty floor." Floor clean, just clean this morning. Thirty-four. No, no, not "dirty floor." Listen carefully. Watch my lips. Thirty-four. Thirty-four! Thirty-four!!! What is wrong with you? You sickee in the head? What the hell is wrong with you? Why can't you hear what I'm saying? Why can't you see me as I really am? [*Dim to darkness on* VINCENT *dialing the phone.*]

END OF INTERLUDE

SCENE FOUR

"AHHH . . . THE NORTH STAR"

Six months later. Party at the same home in the Hollywood Hills. Balcony. Night. VINCENT *sips on a drink and stares into the night sky.* BRADLEY *appears. Walks over and stands beside him. They watch stars in silence.*

VINCENT: [*Notices* BRADLEY's *drink.*] Tannins are bad for your complexion. [*They both laugh, clink glasses and sip.*] It's been a while. What, six months or so? I tried calling your service.
BRADLEY: It's been a little hectic. My girlfriend moved down from San Francisco.
VINCENT: Oh, I didn't know. I've been seeing more of my friend . . . Kenneth.
BRADLEY: Ahh, Kenneth. [*pause*]
VINCENT: You look good. Different. [*looking closer at* BRADLEY] What is it? Your hair? Your nose?
BRADLEY: Oh, yeah. I was having a sinus problem, so I thought, you know, while they were doing that they might as well . . .
VINCENT: Ahhh. It looks good.
BRADLEY: You look good.
VINCENT: Always.
BRADLEY: God. The night air. Ahhh. It was getting a bit stuffy in there.
VINCENT: I thought you liked being around Asians.
BRADLEY: Yeah, but not a whole room full of them. [*They both laugh.*] No way I can protect my back side. [*mimes jabbing a knife*]
VINCENT: Ahhh. [*Awkward pause.* BRADLEY *embarrassed that* VINCENT *didn't laugh at the knife joke.* VINCENT *looks up at the night sky. Pointing.*] The Big Dipper. Follow the two stars that form its lip and . . .
BRADLEY: The North Star.
VINCENT: Voila! You will never be lost, my dear friend. Never. [*Silence. They sip their drinks.*] Something interesting happened to me last week. I was offered a very well paying job in that new film everyone is talking about, *Angry Yellow Planet.*
BRADLEY: I read for that movie, too.
VINCENT: Playing "Yang, the Evil One."
BRADLEY: Yang! Hah! I read for the part of Yang's number one son. We could be father and son. Might be interesting.
VINCENT: Yes.

BRADLEY: Then again it might not. [*Both laugh at the old joke.*] You know what, Vincent? You won't believe this . . .

VINCENT: I turned it down. [*no response*] I just could not do it. Not this time. [*pause*] It feels . . . It feels good. Almost. I turned it down to be in Emily Sakoda's new film. It is about a Japanese American family living in Sacramento before the war. Just like my childhood. 16mm, everyone deferring pay. And my role, it's wonderful. I get to play my father. [*mimics father*] *Urusai, yo!* That. It's my father. And this . . . *So-ka?* I mean, it's so damn exciting, Bradley. I had forgotten what it feels like. What it is supposed to feel like. Do you know what I mean?

BRADLEY: I took it. [VINCENT *doesn't follow.*] I took *it.* The role.

VINCENT: Oh . . .

BRADLEY: I took the role of Yang's number one son. He's half Chinese and half rock.

VINCENT: I see.

BRADLEY: It's a science fiction movie.

VINCENT: Ahhh.

BRADLEY: I figure once I get there I can change it. I can sit down with the producers and writers and explain the situation. Look, if I don't take it then what happens? Some other jerk takes it and plays it like some goddamned geek.

VINCENT: Yes. Well.

BRADLEY: I'll sit down and convince them to change it. I will. Even if it's a bit. Just a small change, it's still something. And, even if they don't change it, they'll at least know how we feel and next time, maybe next time . . .

VINCENT: Yes.

BRADLEY: And in that sense. In a small way. It's a victory. Yes, a victory. [*pause*] Remember this? [*sings*]
Tea cakes and moon songs . . .
[*They both laugh. Pause.* BRADLEY *looks at* VINCENT.] Moo, moo. [*muttering to himself*] Fucking cows.

VINCENT: Remember this? [*Starts Sergeant Moto monologue with the same stereotypic reading as in the opening interlude, but quickly loses accent. And, ultimately, performs with great passion.*] You stupid American G.I. I know you try to escape. You think you can pull my leg. I speakee your language. [*accent fading*] I graduated from UCLA, the Class of 1934. I had this big car . . . [*accent gone*] What? No, no, not "dirty floor." The floor is clean. Class of thirty-four. No, no, not "dirty floor." I had it cleaned this morning. How many times do I have to tell you. Thirty-four. Class of thirty-four. No, no, not "dirty floor." Listen carefully and watch my lips. Thirty-four. Thirty-four! Thirty-four!! What is wrong with you? What the hell is wrong with you? I graduated from the University of California right here in Los Angeles. I was born and raised in the San Joaquin Valley and spent my entire life growing up in California. Why can't you hear what I'm saying? Why can't you see me as I really am? [VINCENT *stops.* BRADLEY *is truly moved.* BRADLEY *quietly applauds his performance. They smile at each other. They turn to look out at the night sky. They are now lit in a pool of light.* BRADLEY *points to the lip of the Big Dipper and moving his hand traces a path to the North Star.*] Ahhh. The North Star. [VINCENT *and* BRADLEY *begin a slow fade to black. At the same time, the theater is again filled with a vast array of stars. The music swells in volume. As* VINCENT *and* BRADLEY *fade to black, the stars hold for a beat. Then, surge in brightness for a moment. Then, blackout. Screen: "THE END." Screen darkens.*]

Wendy Wasserstein (1950-)

An American Daughter (1997)

Although women are not a minority in numbers, they have usually been relegated to a minority status in theatre. They were rarely allowed on stage prior to the six-teenth century (in England, not until 1661), and even after being accepted as ac-tresses, seldom were any encouraged as playwrights. In the twentieth century, women wrote plays more frequently, but it is only during the past few decades they have achieved wide acceptance.

One of the most successful contemporary female playwrights is Wendy Wasserstein, whose *The Heidi Chronicles* won the Pulitzer Prize in 1989. *An American Daughter* has as its title character Dr. Lyssa Dent Hughes, who has been nominated to serve as Surgeon General of the United States and is awaiting the Senate hearings that are necessary for her confirmation. The play looks at the spe-cial demands made on (and prejudices against) women who rise to prominence and power, especially in the politicized atmosphere of Washington D.C. Al-though Lyssa is exceptionally well-qualified both professionally and personally for the appointment, her nomination is eventually withdrawn after a media frenzy develops out of the revelation that years ago she mislaid (and as a result ignored) a summons to appear for jury duty and because of an off-hand remark about her mother's cooking. Out of these, a campaign against her is generated (because she has disobeyed the law and because she is said to have demeaned women who stay home to cook and look after their families). The play argues that these things would have been ignored if done by a man. The larger implication is that too of-ten people who desire to serve their country are discouraged or prevented from doing so because of a political hypocrisy that demonizes public figures and mag-nifies minor lapses in judgment.

The play also concerns Lyssa's involvement with several other characters, all of whom claim to be her friends and supporters but most of whom are even more concerned about enhancing or maintaining their own careers. The only character who seems to support Lyssa unconditionally, and without thought of personal consequences, is Judith Kaufman, an African American oncologist and Lyssa's oldest friend.

An American Daughter is a realistic play; its action takes place in a full-stage living-room set; the action, costumes, properties, and lighting seek to create the privileged environment of the empowered class from which the characters are drawn. It reflects a world with which we are confronted daily on news programs, and it uses humor and repartee reminiscent of television situation comedies. Throughout, an added serious (and often cynical) overtone prevails.

Wendy Wasserstein

An American Daughter

THE CHARACTERS

LYSSA DENT HUGHES
QUINCY QUINCE
JUDITH B. KAUFMAN
WALTER ABRAHMSON
MORROW MCCARTHY
TIMBER TUCKER
SENATOR ALAN HUGHES
CHARLOTTE "CHUBBY" HUGHES
JIMMY
BILLY ROBBINS
TELEVISION CREW
VOICES OF TELEVISION AND RADIO PERSONALITIES
VOICE OF BOY

TIME———
Act One: the present
Act Two: one week later

PLACE———
A Georgetown living room, Washington, D.C.

This play is for Michael Kinsley.

ACT ONE

SCENE 1

A Saturday in September. Around noon. A living room leading to a garden of a George-town house. LYSSA DENT HUGHES, *a forty-two-year-old woman in a cotton shirt and jeans, is watching herself on the television news.*

LYSSA: [*on television*] Good health care begins with education. For example, both women and men need to learn to recognize the symptoms of heart disease. Advancing health care is a matter of advancing scientific knowledge but just as important is advancing every individual's knowledge. As physician to the nation, I will be in a unique position to further this administration's goal that every American, male or female, adult or child, has access to the best heal . . . excuse me . . . the best health care information. The surgeon general has the opportunity to educate every American about their individual health. The greatest protection is prevention.

ANCHORMAN'S VOICE: Elsewhere in the news, a fire broke out this morning at a Bethesda florist . . .

>[LYSSA *turns off the television and starts picking up toys.*]

LYSSA: . . . the best health care information . . .

BOY'S VOICE: [*from upstairs*]: Mom, Mom . . . you made a mistake.

LYSSA: Tell me I was great.

BOY'S VOICE: Information . . .

LYSSA: Yeah, I know, but just tell me I was great.

BOY'S VOICE: You were great.

LYSSA: Thank you. I was great.

>[LYSSA *turns on the radio.* "*It's Washington, D.C., home of the oldies, and you're sixteen, you're beautiful, and you're you-know-who's on* WOLD 91.3." *Song begins:* "*You walked out of my dreams into my arms, now you're my angel divine.*" LYSSA *begins to dance along.* QUINCY QUINCE, *a very pretty woman of about twenty-seven in a mini-skirt and leather bomber jacket, enters the living room through the garden.*]

QUINCY: Classic rock. Very simple. Very pure. Very paternal.

>[LYSSA *turns off the radio.*]

QUINCY: Imagine wanting "to come on like a dream, peaches and cream, lips like strawberry wine." [*She outstretches her hand.*] I'm Quincy Quince. You left the garden gate open. I'm here for Walter.

LYSSA: I'm afraid Walter's not home. He's at the Air and Space Museum with one of our boys. Can I help you?

QUINCY: I love the Air and Space Museum. I'm an aviatrix nut. Women in the twenties and thirties were able to excel in show business, cosmetology, and aviation. There's a chapter in my new book about flight and sexuality.

LYSSA: Walter should be back in a little while. I'll tell him you dropped by.

QUINCY: I love that Dr. Lyssa Hughes does her own cleaning on the day of her nomination. I love that! [*She takes a bag of raisins from her purse.*] Raisin? I also have baby carrots. I always carry snacks and water.

LYSSA: How do you know my husband?

QUINCY: I'm sorry. I thought you recognized me. I'm Quincy Quince. I wrote *The Prisoner of Gender.*

LYSSA: Oh, of course! You're Walter's celebrity student. The rebirth of feminism.

QUINCY: "Sexism made simple."

LYSSA: We saw you on *The Conan O'Brien Show.* Most of Walter's students don't make it to late-night.

QUINCY: Walter is brilliant! He's the only academic who can reshape liberalism into an active stance instead of a do-gooder whine. Walter is the only man who "gets it."

LYSSA: You're much kinder to him than I am.

QUINCY: And you're much different than I expected.

LYSSA: I am?

QUINCY: You have more bite. I thought you'd be sweeter. Sweet women are really very angry people. They're trapped by their own repressed hostility.

LYSSA: Usually I am sweeter. I just didn't know you'd be coming. I hope Walter hasn't forgotten his appointment with you.

QUINCY: Actually Walter didn't know I'd be coming. I'm in Washington doing the usual round of book signing and talk shows. But we had a few cancellations due to the Jewish holidays. I can't wait to get back on the air and talk about meeting you.

LYSSA: Please say that I'm not so nice. Say I have bite.

QUINCY: I'll say that the future surgeon general is one of the truly empowered, self-actualized real women.

> [JUDITH B. KAUFMAN, *forty-two, an African American woman in a floral skirt and tweed jacket, enters. She is boisterous and energetic.*]

JUDITH: How many times have I told you if you insist on leaving your gate open it's an open invitation for any *schvartze* on the street. They could just waltz right into your garden and walk off with your children, your furniture, and your raisins. [*She picks up the raisins and kisses* LYSSA.] Happy New Year, honey.

LYSSA: Isn't it a little early?

JUDITH: Okay. Happy High Holidays. There were two African Americans at the Washington Hebrew Congregation today—the rabbi's chauffeur and me. And when that rabbi blew his chauffeur in front of the entire congregation, I said to myself, Judith, next year in Jerusalem.

LYSSA: Quincy, this is my oldest friend, Dr. Judith B. Kaufman. Quincy wrote *The Prisoner of Gender.*

JUDITH: Of course, Quincy Quince. The next generation of feminists.

QUINCY: Are you OB/GYN?

JUDITH: No, I'm the other kind of woman's doctor. Oncology. Breast cancer. But it's possible I could have specialized in something women don't have, like heads, necks, or throats.

> [*The phone rings.* LYSSA *picks up the phone.*]

LYSSA: Hello. Dad! You're back! Yeah. Just a sec, let me go to another phone. [*She puts him on hold and says to* JUDITH:] The senator's back from his honeymoon.

JUDITH: Did they get it annulled?

LYSSA: Quincy, just think of my friend Judith's hostility as her overtly repressed sweetness. [*She exits.*]

QUINCY: How does Lyssa's father feel about her nomination?

JUDITH: Senator Hughes has almost a quarter century unblemished record of robbing from the poor to give to the rich. How do you think he feels about his daughter the bleeding heart? It's a low blow to the memory of Lyssa's great-great-granddaddy.

QUINCY: You mean Ulysses S. Grant? Walter used to talk about that in class all the time.

JUDITH: Your Walter married well.

QUINCY: He's not my Walter. He's my mentor.

JUDITH: Shame on you, Quincy. You didn't have a female mentor.

QUINCY: I think we're at a place now where we can look beyond gender for mentors.

JUDITH: I think we can look beyond or around gender for anything except prostate and ovarian cancer. Does your "Quincy" mean there's a president lurking in your bloodline also?

QUINCY: Our real name was Quintopolous. We're Greek. My father changed it
to Quince when he noticed the jelly at a breakfast function. He's a party
consultant in Astoria, Queens.

JUDITH: You mean he owns a coffee shop and caters office platters.

QUINCY: And your father? My book after the next one will be about fathers and
daughters.

JUDITH: My father was a French teacher at Boys' High, Brooklyn. Boys were
pulling knives on each other in homeroom and my dad taught them to say
"pardonnez-moi." They shipped me off to Miss Porter's for boarding
school. That's where I met Lyssa.

QUINCY: Your mother didn't mind.

JUDITH: My mother believed only art and education made life tolerable. She was
a Baptist piano teacher from Tuscaloosa, Alabama. Her family never for-
gave her for moving north with a freedom rider Jew.

QUINCY: So you're not technically Jewish because you're mother isn't.

JUDITH: Yes. I am, technically. I was bat-mitzvahed at Garfield Temple, Garfield
Place, Brooklyn, New York. Today I am a woman. I thank God every day I
was born half a man.

QUINCY: I learned from my mother that a woman's life can have no boundaries.

JUDITH: Do you mind if I lie down?

QUINCY: Should I get Lyssa? Are you not feeling well?

JUDITH: Quincy, time will teach you that a woman's life is all about boundaries.
Would you mind passing me that pillow? Organized religion always gives
me a migraine.

QUINCY: I see life completely differently than you do.

JUDITH: Diversity is the succor of the nineties.

[LYSSA *reenters.*]

LYSSA: Daddy's bringing Charlotte to my televised brunch tomorrow. Have you
ever heard of a television reporter called Lumber Tucker?

QUINCY: You mean Timber Tucker. He's on that newsmagazine *Time Zone*. He
did a great piece on the women of Sarajevo. He's a hero from the Gulf War.

LYSSA: Well, apparently the president's press secretary has convinced Timber and
Time Zone to do a puff piece on me.

JUDITH: This is going to make really boring television.

LYSSA: Judith, if I have to explain to Timber Tucker over pancakes that gun control is really a health issue, it's worth it to me. And if he wants to watch me
pick up my kids from soccer practice so every woman in this country is assured reproductive freedom it's also worth it to me. And I happen to know
it's worth it to you too.

QUINCY: I was so proud when you mentioned reproductive rights at the White
House this morning.

JUDITH: Were you at that breakfast?

QUINCY: No. But women's issues are my priority.

JUDITH: Did you hear that, Lyssa? The rest of us can all relax now.

LYSSA: Judith, please!

JUDITH: I'm sorry.

LYSSA: Quincy was one of Walter's best students. I know my husband thinks your
work is very impressive.

JUDITH: I'm sorry. Lyssa knows I get a little nuts when things are too important to me.

QUINCY: It's important to all of us. I hope Timber Tucker knows that. I mean I'd love to talk to him about Dr. Hughes from a younger woman's perspective.

JUDITH: Maybe you should come back here for brunch tomorrow. You haven't had brunch in Georgetown till you've tried Lyssa's homemade scones. Lyssa?

LYSSA: Absolutely. Come to brunch. Walter will be happy to see you.

QUINCY: I can't believe you make your own scones!

LYSSA: Yes, and I built that fireplace from scratch.

QUINCY: Are you sure you want to share this important time with me?

LYSSA: Sure.

QUINCY: [*opens her appointment book*] What time are they all coming tomorrow? Because I may have to do a little juggling.

LYSSA: We generally do brunch at about one.

QUINCY: I'll work it out. It's been a real honor to meet you. I just want to thank you for all the amazing work you've been doing.

LYSSA: You're welcome.

QUINCY: No, really. You put women's health care issues on the map. I'll be having a wonderful life because of you. [*She shakes* JUDITH'*s hand.*] It's been a pleasure meeting you, too. I hope you feel better. [*She exits.*]

JUDITH: Why won't she have a wonderful life because of *me?* [*She hits* LYSSA *with a pillow.*] Why isn't she happy to have the opportunity to thank *me?* [*She hits her again.*] Why does it always have to be *you?*

LYSSA: Why did you have to invite her back here for brunch? [*She hits* JUDITH.]

JUDITH: It's New Year's. I felt guilty. I was awful to her. Why didn't you stop me?

LYSSA: Who could stop you?

JUDITH: I behaved like a cow. An old and bitter envious cow.

LYSSA: Let it go. You'll buy her a pony tomorrow.

JUDITH: Lyssa, do you know what Holy *Tashlich is?*

LYSSA: Something floating in a soup?

JUDITH: *Tashlich* is the festival of regrets. It happens a day after New Year's when good Jews send 365 days worth of their sins and sadness out to sea. The upper echelons toss baguette crumbs and rosemary croutons of sorrow into the Potomac, while those of us still toiling for the public good fling yesterday's fat-free muffins. I will now be adding to my list of sins Miss Quincy Quince. Do you have any regrets, Lyssa, that you'd like me to set sail for you tomorrow?

LYSSA: *Remembrance of Things Past.* I should have finished it.

JUDITH: I regret my life, Lyssa. I can't believe I let the time go by.

LYSSA: You didn't let the time go by. You're a remarkable doctor.

JUDITH: A patient with bones like Swiss cheese asked me the other day when we would next be changing courses. I said, for perhaps the thousandth time in my career, "Well, Mrs. Mandell, it's like playing a fish. We'll watch where it swims and take it from there." What I didn't tell Mrs. Mandell is that the one certainty we have is this particular fish will painfully and untimely stop swimming.

LYSSA: I wish you would allow someone to cherish you.

JUDITH: I'm in no state of mind to be cherished. Especially by me.

LYSSA: But maybe this will be a good year.

JUDITH: Yes, and maybe there'll be a pill that makes white chocolate mousse the same calories as raw fennel. Maybe even sperm catalogue specimen 1147 will scramble up a few eggs with a nice Jewish African American doctor.

LYSSA: You know that at some point very soon you really have to put an end to this.

JUDITH: Why? Abraham had a child at a hundred.

LYSSA: I'm serious. For five years you've endured every in vitro and hormone treatment known to modern medicine. You're a very good doctor. What do you think this has all done to your system? Never mind your mental health.

JUDITH: I really don't want to talk about this right now.

LYSSA: You brought it up.

JUDITH: In jest. Then in true Lyssa fashion you turned it into a public issue.

LYSSA: This is not a public issue! You're my oldest friend. You're much too valuable to continue doing this to yourself. All lives don't have to be about children.

JUDITH: How would you know?

[*pause*]

LYSSA: Oh Judy. I'm so sorry.

JUDITH: You're the only person I know who dares to call me Judy.

LYSSA: That's because when I met you your name was Judy.

JUDITH: I'll know in a week. And then I promise I'll be sending that particular five-year cycle of great expectations and regret out to sea. Don't you just love being around me these days. I know I do.

LYSSA: Yes, you're a lot of fun.

JUDITH: Maybe you're right. Maybe this could be a very good year.

LYSSA: Maybe, just maybe, this time one tiny spermatozoid will take a look at your highly desirable eggs and say, "Hi there, cutie!"

JUDITH: You're not sixteen. You're not beautiful. But you're mine.

LYSSA: I was just singing that. Isn't that odd! After all these years we're still on the same wavelength.

JUDITH: It was on the "I refuse to believe I'm middle-aged and the culture isn't about me anymore" radio station when I was pulling up. I hate to disappoint you.

LYSSA: You never disappoint me. [*begins to sing slowly*] *"You stepped out of my dreams and into my car, now you're my angel divine."*

[JUDITH *harmonizes as they both sing.*]

JUDITH AND LYSSA: *"You're sixteen, you're beautiful and you're mine."*

SCENE 2

Saturday night. Around 7:30. WALTER ABRAHMSON, *around forty-seven, is smoking and watching television.*

ANCHORMAN: The president reconfirmed his commitment to education yesterday by visiting the Chevy Chase School. The president attended assembly and enjoyed a school lunch. Also, confirming yesterday's rumors, Dr. Lyssa Dent Hughes . . .

WALTER: Lyssa!

ANCHORMAN: . . . accepted the nomination of surgeon general following a White House breakfast this morning.

WALTER: Lyssa! Lyssa! You bumped Rwanda.

ANCHORMAN: Dr. Hughes is the daughter of Republican Senator Alan Hughes of Indiana . . .

BOY'S VOICE: [*from upstairs*] But Mom . . .

LYSSA: [*coming down the stairs and into the living room*] I'll play Space Invaders with you later.

ANCHORMAN: . . . and a former college classmate of the First Lady. Following the death of Surgeon General Dr. David Burns in a plane crash and the defeated nomination of Dr. Charles McDermott, Dr. Hughes is expected to have a swift confirmation. According to Capitol Hill insiders she's a popular choice with both pro-choice soccer moms and more conservative fast-food dads.

[WALTER *suddenly yells at the television:*]

WALTER: The point is, doofus, she's a popular choice because she has a record as a brilliant health-care administrator. The point is she still believes public health is good government.

LYSSA: I'm warning you, you shouldn't smoke.

WALTER: You're not the surgeon general yet. I don't understand you. Why doesn't this make you crazy.

LYSSA: He didn't really say anything.

WALTER: Lyssa, don't fall into a trap. The problem is they want you for all the wrong reasons. You're just like that breath mint.

LYSSA: What breath mint?

WALTER: The one that's also a candy mint. The senator makes you okay with the right-wing Nazis and your politics make you a pinup for the do-gooder Commies. You're "two, two, two mints in one."

LYSSA: And if I could only soothe sore throats I could be three mints in one. Why not make the third-party cuckoos happy too.

WALTER: I'm making a valid point here. Lizard, no compromise candidate can get the important work done.

LYSSA: You sound like a right-to-lifer.

WALTER: Honey, don't be naive.

LYSSA: Walter, you're the dean of naive. You're the author of *Towards a Lesser Elite.*

WALTER: The question is, Lizard, what do you really want to do?

LYSSA: Walter, you know exactly what I want to do.

WALTER: What? Make the world a better place? Do good on a grand scale? Teach the world to sing in perfect harmony? They'll never let you get away with it. Look what happened to national health insurance.

LYSSA: All right. I want to make heaps of money, get our children into Harvard, and have upper arms that don't jiggle. What do you want to do, sweetie?

WALTER: I want to be invited to Winona Ryder's next dinner party and be mistaken for someone her age. I want to conduct *Il Trovatore* to a standing ovation and come home and have sex on the dashboard of a '68 Chevy. I want to be the focus of attention. I want to make you happy.

LYSSA: I am happy, Walter. I'm always happy.

WALTER: I thought you were brilliant at that breakfast this morning. If we weren't married I would have hustled you right into the Lincoln Bedroom.

LYSSA: Walter, we don't have that kind of money. Goddamn it! Why don't your sons ever bother to put their shoes away?

WALTER: Why don't you sit down, honey? I'll put the kids' damn shoes away.

LYSSA: Do you know where they go?

WALTER: Sure. In the dishwasher. Did Kip say he had a good time with me today?

LYSSA: Uh-huh. Great.

WALTER: It's amazing how much Kip is like me. He's very sensitive. Very imaginative. You should have heard the stories he made up about the space shuttle. He's hilarious. Nicholas is much more like you. He's perfectly happy home alone with his computer.

LYSSA: Are you saying he's pedantic just like his mother?

WALTER: Don't be so defensive, honey.

LYSSA: You just told me that one of our children is funny and imaginative like you and the other is humorless and academic like me.

WALTER: I think this job thing is making you a little nutso. Look, worst-case scenario, if it doesn't happen I won't be profiled as one of the most enlightened husbands in America. So what? Even in your present overworked and highly emotional condition, I'll still love you.

LYSSA: Shut up, Walter.

WALTER: I'm just trying to be supportive. I'm so proud of you.

LYSSA: Walter, have you ever regretted your life?

WALTER: Looking back, I would have tried to have sex with Joanie Tenzer in high school instead of being terrified of her.

LYSSA: At forty-seven, Joanie Tenzer is your one regret?

WALTER: [*sings*] *"Love me Tenzer, love me do."* What's there to regret? I love you, I love our kids, I love my books, I love how we live.

LYSSA: Judith regrets her life.

WALTER: Judith is on megadoses of insane fertility drugs. She's not just angry. She's an accident waiting to happen.

LYSSA: Your friend Quincy Quince says anger is healthy. She says sweetness is a camouflage for repressed hostility.

WALTER: Have you been reading *The Prisoner of Gender?*

LYSSA: No. She made a guest appearance in your garden today.

WALTER: Quincy was here? In our garden?

LYSSA: Yup.

WALTER: And you forgot to tell me? I deeply regret that.

LYSSA: Judith hated her.

WALTER: Judith has no right to pass judgment on someone as valuable as Quincy. Quincy's committed to making a tired ideology new. Did she say when she'll be back?

LYSSA: Tomorrow for brunch to meet Daddy and some reporter who's doing a piece on the family.

WALTER: He's doing a piece on this family? Why wasn't I told?

LYSSA: Oh, he just wants to meet the famous in the family.

WALTER: *Towards a Lesser Elite* is still a standard text in over three thousand colleges. Even if I was recently featured in a *Where Are They Now?* column. [*picks up the telephone*] Maybe this reporter doesn't even know we're married.

LYSSA: Of course he knows we're married. Who are you calling?

WALTER: Morrow. Maybe he'd like to come.

LYSSA: Walter . . .

WALTER: [*on the phone*] Morrow, Lyssa and I want to invite you over to meet a hunky television reporter. Call us. [*hangs up*]

LYSSA: Jesus . . .

WALTER: What's the matter?

LYSSA: Do you really want Morrow to be here with that reporter?

WALTER: Why not, because he's gay?

LYSSA: Walter, don't be ridiculous. I love Morrow, but his new anti-abortion stand is not exactly how I want to represent myself.

WALTER: It's not new. He's always had his faith.

LYSSA: I just wish he'd find a boyfriend and leave women's reproductive rights alone. Do you realize we've known him over ten years and he's never shown up here with a man?

WALTER: So he keeps his personal life separate from us.

LYSSA: Walter, as Morrow would say, "Hello," we are his personal life.

WALTER: I'll call him back and cancel.

LYSSA: Don't. He'll only get paranoid. I'm going upstairs. I promised the kids I would play Space Invaders with them.

WALTER: I don't hear them complaining.

LYSSA: That's because by now they're probably on the Internet with a transvestite in Bucharest.

        [WALTER *hugs her.*]

WALTER: What's this?

LYSSA: What do you mean "What's this?" A Gap cotton blend, $39.95.

WALTER: And what's under this?

LYSSA: Olga 34B, fifteen bucks on sale at Nordstrom's.

WALTER: Can I see?

LYSSA: Walter . . .

WALTER: I saw you give birth to twins. I think you can show me your Olga 34B, fifteen bucks on sale at Nordstrom's.

LYSSA: Honey, let's go upstairs.

WALTER: I don't want to go upstairs. There are Space Invaders and nannies and grown-up things up there. How 'bout the car?

LYSSA: The Volvo?

WALTER: I've got the latest Big Head Todd.

LYSSA: What's a Big Head Todd?

WALTER: Lyssa, there's actual music past Aretha Franklin and the Beatles.

LYSSA: But I don't like music past Aretha Franklin and the Beatles.

WALTER: You're not even curious anymore. You want to know why I'm so taken with Quincy and Morrow? They're looking directly at the future. You're as rooted as any ardent right-winger.

LYSSA: And you? Are you constantly renewing yourself?

WALTER: I don't know what the hell I'm doing. But I'll be damned before I get old and boring and fat.

LYSSA: How could you get fat, Walter? You run daily from here to Virginia.

WALTER: [*patting his stomach*] Feel that.

LYSSA: Flat.

WALTER: [*making a muscle*] Feel this.

LYSSA: Mmmm. Also flat. Walter, you have the strong virile arms of a twenty-eight-year-old male hustler. No, a Green Beret. Walter, you should have been a Green Beret instead of a conscientious objector. I'm sorry, honey. I'm sorry. [*She unbuttons her shirt.*] Hi, I don't know if you remember me. My name is Joanie Tenzer. Lyssa had to leave suddenly on sabbatical. Whatever that means.

WALTER: Hi, Joanie. Nice to see you. It's been a long time.

LYSSA: I hear you've got a Big Head Todd. Can we go to your car and listen to it?

WALTER: Joanie, what do you want to listen to that junk for? Have I ever told you that according to my college roommate, Dr. Martin Brody professor of harmony at Wellesley College, the Beach Boys are the most sophisticated American composers since Gershwin.

LYSSA: Gosh, Walter, you know everything. I didn't even know you had a college roommate. But maybe that's because I've been in high school for the past thirty years.

WALTER: Take for example "I Wish They All Could Be California Girls."

LYSSA: Okay.

WALTER: Listen to this. [*He puts on "California Girls." He looks at her.*] Joanie.

LYSSA: Yes, Walter.

WALTER: That Olga looks like it comes from a nunnery.

LYSSA: It's from Nordstrom's. It lifts and separates.

WALTER: Joanie.

LYSSA: Yes, Walter.

WALTER: Could you send Lyssa back in here. [*He kisses her.*] I love you Lyssa Dent Hughes. Of all the choices I've made, the one I'll never regret is marrying you.

    [*They kiss and* LYSSA *leads* WALTER *to the car.*]

SCENE 3

Sunday morning. JUDITH *enters through the front door.* MORROW MCCARTHY *enters from the kitchen carrying five Sunday papers.* MORROW *is thirty and looks even younger, in a casual but studied fashion. He wears retro-fifties clothes. As* JUDITH *and* MORROW *enter the room, we hear a public radio voiceover.*

PUBLIC RADIO VOICE: Perhaps the greatest debate in the country this week will not be welfare reform but whether the president should adopt a dog or a cat as his best friend in the White House. A nationwide telepoll is accepting 1-800-VOTE-C-A-T or D-O-G calls. Votes can be phoned in till nine P.M. Friday.

    [MORROW *puts down the paper he's been reading.*]

MORROW: He's such a policy wonk. A Harvard-educated policy wonk. He may
be the commander-in-chief, but he still needs a poll to pick his animal
companion. [*dials phone*] Hello, is this the White House? This is Morrow
McCarthy. I want to cast my vote for Fluffy. [*hangs up*]
   [WALTER *enters carrying a tray with tomato juice.*]
MORROW: [*to Walter*] Does Lyssa realize the extent to which this administration
is using her? That McDermott nomination was a total debacle. Their only
choice is to go with someone bland and unobjectionable.
JUDITH: Lyssa isn't bland and unobjectionable.
MORROW: In this town, as Senator Hughes would say, perception is everything.
Focus, Judy.
JUDITH: Judith.
MORROW: This president's greatest skill is keeping himself afloat. Why do you
think he announced the nomination on Saturday? Judith, hello, your friend
is worth a lot more than this.
JUDITH: And this opinion has nothing to do with your newfound commitment
to the unborn?
MORROW: Don't divert the argument. It's a question of character.
JUDITH: And who would you say still does have "character"?
MORROW: The Walt Disney Company.
WALTER: Morrow just sold his screenplay to Disney for seven figures. He started
a bidding frenzy.
JUDITH: That doesn't mean they have character. That means Morrow's mastered
the art of appealing to the lowest common denominator.
MORROW: Judith, your nonpracticing heterosexuality is putting a definite cramp
in your *joi de vivre.*
JUDITH: Has it ever occurred to you, Morrow, that you and many of the brightest minds in this country have been waylaid into a simplistic position that
sexual preference is the reason for all personal and societal happiness.
MORROW: You mean it isn't?
JUDITH: There won't be national health insurance or decent schools because of
where you choose to place your penis.
MORROW: Wrong, Judith. Gay culture is penetrating the media, theatre, health
and education, and we're working on a secret alliance with straight men for
a "world without women. Amen." Aren't I right, Walter?
WALTER: I dare either of you to say any of this outside of this room.
MORROW: Why are you so bitter, Judith? You're the jewel in the crown of the
great society. Walter, this is another perfect example of the inconsistency of
the left and the reason for my happy transition to the far right.
JUDITH: Morrow, I'm a civilian. I'm not interested in your sound bites.
MORROW: All right. If it was up to me, Judith, I'd secure both our rights to life,
liberty and the pursuit of happiness—in my case that means sleeping with
men and in your case, self-perpetuation.
JUDITH: And you don't care if you contribute to the future?
MORROW: It takes a village to contribute to the future. I'm concerned with the
here and now. Does that make sense to you, Walter? You're the house
intellectual.
WALTER: Absolutely.

MORROW: You're surprisingly silent this morning, Walter. No opinions on world or local news. No nominations for whose column you could have written better.

WALTER: Did you read about this Harvard professor who took hostages at The Legal Seafood Restaurant?

MORROW: Yeah, that must have been really bad clam chowder.

WALTER: I know him. We did draft counseling together. He's a brilliant guy. Very respected sociologist. Left-wing. Still listens to Ravi Shankar. Two kids. Wife's a Russian professor. He must have just totally lost it. God, that's depressing.

JUDITH: Won't happen to you, Walter. You take too many vitamins.
> [*Voices are heard offstage.*]

LYSSA: [*offstage*] Hello! We're home!
> [LYSSA *enters with* TIMBER TUCKER, *around forty-five, handsome, deliberately casual.*]

WALTER: Hi Lizard.

LYSSA: Hi, honey. Hi, Judith, I'm glad you're here!

MORROW: Aren't you glad I'm here?

LYSSA: Yes, but you're always here! Timber, this is my friend Dr. Judith Kaufman. Timber Tucker.

TIMBER: Dr. Hughes mentioned you during her interview this morning. She certainly admires your work.

LYSSA: And this is our friend Morrow McCarthy. Tim Tucker.

TIMBER: I miss reading your column in *The Post*.

MORROW: The president doesn't.

LYSSA: No, he's very relieved you've turned your attentions elsewhere.

MORROW: Lyssa, you're looking incandescent.

LYSSA: And you, Morrow, are looking very, very taut.

WALTER: I don't know if Lyssa mentioned me, I'm her husband, Walter Abrahmson.

LYSSA: I'm sorry.

WALTER: We were expecting you later.

LYSSA: Timber watched me shop for brunch at Dean and Deluca and followed me home. Did you get the kids to Donnie's?

WALTER: Yes, they're at Donnie's house surfing the net for messages from Iceland.

LYSSA: We're encouraging our children to become cyberspies.

MORROW: I've been having the best time going online as a woman. Timber, perhaps you've seen my ad? "Single available female seeks domineering male for emasculating intrigue."

LYSSA: Walter, keep an eye out for the senator.

TIMBER: Lyssa, is that the portrait of the general's wife that you mentioned?

LYSSA: Yes. Julia Dent Grant. Ulysses wrote her every day during the war.

WALTER: She's Lyssa's namesake. Upstairs, we have a letter from Ulysses to Julia before the Battle of Vicksburg.

LYSSA: "My family is American and has been for generations in all its branches, direct and collateral."

WALTER: First line of the great "Unconditional Surrender"'s memoir.

LYSSA: Walter is very proud of his civil war ancestors. [*She exits.*]

TIMBER: Did your ancestors fight in the civil war, Walter?

WALTER: Different civil war. The one in Minsk.

MORROW: Speaking of courage under fire, Timber, my friend Gerry got an enormous crush on you during the Gulf War. He says he'll sleep with you before Barbara Walters anytime.

TIMBER: Thank you.

> [LYSSA *returns.*]

LYSSA: Timber caused quite a stir at Dean and Deluca.

TIMBER: Your wife is burying the lead. She also gave me a great interview this morning. I'm looking forward to following it up at brunch.

MORROW: Tell the truth, Timber. You're here for the good stuff. The ex–Mrs. Abrahmson in the basement, the runaway Chilean nanny on the fourth floor, and the joint abortion/assisted suicide clinic in the garage. And the tawdriest of all, the real scoop on Professor Abrahmson's panel "Liberalism: Wanted Dead or Alive."

JUDITH: Walter, are you really doing something called that?

MORROW: Next Sunday night at Georgetown University.

LYSSA: Timber, let me show you where we'll be having brunch.

MORROW: I'm meeting Gerry at the gym. Timber, would you sign this copy of *The New England Journal of Medicine* for him?

TIMBER: I was hoping you'd stay for brunch. No interview, no policy talk, a sort of informal Georgetown salon with friends.

MORROW: I think you'd better ask the Abrahmsons if they'd like me to remain in their picture.

WALTER: Of course we do. Morrow's family.

MORROW: Good. 'Cause I've been waiting for a chance to tell America, "I had a threesome with Jesse and Strom in the Senate cloakroom. Hello."

TIMBER: I'd prefer you limit your insights to Dr. Hughes. I hope you'll stay too, Dr. Kaufman.

JUDITH: Sorry. I'm on call today.

LYSSA: Really? You didn't tell me that.

JUDITH: I did. Services. The higher calling.

WALTER: Lyssa, the senator just pulled up.

LYSSA: Timber, let me show you the dining room. This is actually the oldest part of the house.

> [TIMBER *and* LYSSA *exit.*]

WALTER: I've got to warn the senator our guest is here already. [*He exits.*]

MORROW: I'll stay here and filibuster. Tell me something, Dr. Kaufman. What's wrong with heterosexual men?

JUDITH: Excuse me?

MORROW: Ever since that telegenic hunk walked in here I've been asking myself why isn't Judith B. Kaufman married. For secure men, smart women are a real turn-on. I'd have a child with you anytime. We could co-parent an amazing creation. Tell me what bank you're using and I'll make a donation.

JUDITH: How old are you, Morrow?

MORROW: Thirty. And recently worth over seven figures.

JUDITH: I don't get intimate with thirty-year-old predominantly gay men. However, you might want to meet my former husband.

MORROW: Does he like men?

JUDITH: Lumbermen. He lives in Seattle. He's a shrink who started the gay and lesbian psychiatric clinic there. He does have a friend who's an opera singer. Well, a florist who says he's an opera singer. Basically, he's a doctor's wife. Rodney keeps in shape and wears a very nice engagement ring.

MORROW: So that's why you're bitter, Dr. Kaufman.

JUDITH: Do you know how many AIDS benefits I've been to? Do you know how many donations I've made? But I am still waiting for one gay man to voluntarily come to my hospital and say "I'm concerned about a disease that's decimating my mother, my aunts, and my sisters." My ex-husband was interviewed in *The Seattle Post* and mentioned that I was his best friend. I'm not his best friend, Morrow. I want my time back.

> [WALTER *reenters with* SENATOR ALAN HUGHES, *around sixty-five, and his wife* CHARLOTTE "CHUBBY" HUGHES, *an attractive, sporty-looking woman of around sixty.*]

WALTER: The boys are over at the Graham's.

ALAN: Well, bring them by the Senate office sometime this week. Charlotte, this is my favorite other daughter, Dr. Judy. Looking good too, sweetheart. This is my favorite wife, Charlotte Hughes.

CHARLOTTE: Please call me Chubby. Everyone else does.

JUDITH: I'd slug someone who called me Chubby.

CHARLOTTE: But I never was. So it's all just amusing.

MORROW: Chubby, that's one respectable Republican cloth coat.

CHARLOTTE: I have a hat, but I left it at home.

ALAN: Morrow, how do you always manage to look younger than when I last saw you?

JUDITH: He works very hard at that, Senator.

ALAN: Walter tells me that reporter got a head start on us. How do you think Lyssa's faring with him?

MORROW: She took him brunch-shopping. That seems to have made him very happy.

CHARLOTTE: I know exactly what you mean. Sometimes I enjoy driving into Georgetown, parking the car at Dean and Deluca, and just cruising the cheese department. How can anyone be depressed when there are so many wonderful cheeses in the world?

WALTER: Would you like a drink, Alan?

CHARLOTTE: A Bloody might be nice.

ALAN: Make it two Bloodies.

MORROW: Three.

ALAN: Judy?

JUDITH: Too early for blood. I'll stick with apple juice.

> [WALTER *goes to the bar.*]

MORROW: Senator Hughes, how do you feel about Lyssa's nomination?

ALAN: Do you know how goddamned great it feels to be asked about Lyssa's nomination instead of tax reform? My daughter was always a do-gooder.

When she was around eight, she'd go to a birthday party and make me drop her off a block away because she didn't want anyone to feel badly because we had a nicer car. She was a candy striper in the hospital, she was on the Indian reservation for her college vacations, she was always busy starting rape centers, birthing centers, and let's-get-together-and-help-women centers. My daughter Lyssa believes that every day it's time to smile on your sister. I hope that reporter realizes how lucky this administration is to get her.

MORROW: You know, everyone who's seen Tim Tucker on *Time Zone* says he's gay as a goose.

CHARLOTTE: Impossible. He's a war reporter.

MORROW: Chubby, there are gay men who have served with distinction in the military and there are straight men who avoided the draft by dabbling in Canadian pornography, like your new son-in-law the distinguished Matlock Professor of Sociology at Georgetown.

CHARLOTTE: Walter, you never told me about any pornography!

WALTER: I did a little screenwriting to pay for my tuition in Canada.

MORROW: Chubby, next time you're at the Pleasure Chest Late Licks video section, ask for *The Hot and Sour Strawberry Statement*—it's a counterculture classic.

    [*The doorbell rings.*]

ALAN: That must be our camera crew.

MORROW: Finish making the drinks, Walter, I'll get the door. [*He goes to door.*]

ALAN: That boy was my brightest summer intern.

    [MORROW *opens the front door, sees* QUINCY *and announces:*]

MORROW: The Prisoner of Gender!

    [QUINCY *enters the room.*]

WALTER: Quincy!

QUINCY: Hello Walter. I hope Lyssa didn't forget to tell you I'd be coming.

ALAN: I don't believe we've met.

WALTER: Senator, this is Quincy Quince, my former student.

MORROW: And already a best-selling author.

WALTER: You're looking at the future players here.

ALAN: This is my wife, Charlotte Hughes.

WALTER: Quincy, can I get you a drink?

QUINCY: Just water. It's nice to see you again, Dr. Kaufman. I had such fun with you and Lyssa yesterday.

JUDITH: Yes, I was hoping you'd get here a little earlier.

QUINCY: I was doing a call-in breakfast show in Maryland.

CHARLOTTE: Politics?

QUINCY: Well, politics, single parenting, divorce, dating. The entire human agenda.

JUDITH: I'm so sorry but I'm afraid I have to say good-bye or I'll be late for services.

CHARLOTTE: Do you go to one of those marvelous churches with a gospel choir?

WALTER: Judith is Jewish. Today is Holy *Tashlich* the festival of regrets. "And you will cast all their sins into the depths of the sea." I was Jewish until I was bar-mitzvahed. Today I am a man. I choose to be agnostic.

ALAN: Perhaps my Christian brothers in the Senate should practice *Tashlich*. It would be bumper-to-bumper all the way to the Potomac.

QUINCY: Someday I'd love to talk to you about being black and Jewish. You're a walking Crown Heights.

[JUDITH *exits.*]

MORROW: I think she's an incredibly sexy woman.

WALTER: You find cosmic anger sexy?

MORROW: Why shouldn't she be angry? As far as she's concerned, there's only one way to save the world and people like me are screwing it up. In fact, I'm the worst kind of offender: gay, conservative, and total media hype.

QUINCY: I enjoy the media. I always have a good time.

ALAN: There's a healthy attitude. Maybe Quincy here's the one who should run for office.

QUINCY: No, sir. I have two more books to write and I want to start my family before I focus on my public life. My generation wants to do it all, but we want to have some fun too. Don't you think sex is wildly important, Walter?

WALTER: Sex is important. Sure.

ALAN: Wildly.

QUINCY: My next book is about women restoring their sexual identity. It's called *Venus Raging*. Sex for Lyssa's generation became just something else to be good at. Like weight lifting. We, on the other hand, want to come home to a warm penis.

MORROW: Walter, this woman is a visionary.

[LYSSA *reenters with* TIMBER.]

LYSSA: Hello, Charlotte, you're looking very well. Marriage suits you.

CHARLOTTE: We had a wonderful time.

LYSSA: Hello, Dad.

ALAN: Hello, Mousey.

QUINCY: Mousey?

ALAN: She was a mouse in *The Nutcracker* when she was six.

TIMBER: I bet you never called your son Mouse.

ALAN: No. We would have called him Rat King. You must be Timber Tucker. A good reporter can't resist an obvious question.

LYSSA: Timber, doesn't my dad have a great handshake? When I was eight and he first ran for mayor of Fort Wayne, my dad taught me how to shake hands. "Firm, not like a lady, not like a man. Just shoot from the hip."

ALAN: Look 'em straight in the eye.

QUINCY: Timber, I'm Quincy Quince. I was very moved by your report on the women of Sarajevo. I thought it was really terrific.

MORROW: Lyssa, we've been having a heated debate over the role of religion and sex in a secular society.

QUINCY: Senator, how much do your religious beliefs account for your anti-choice position on abortion?

ALAN: Miss Quince, I love saying your name, Miss Quince, I like to think that my beliefs account for an open dialogue.

LYSSA: Dad, your beliefs on this subject are untenable. How can you be so adamant about individual rights, and deny the most personal right: when and if to have a child.

MORROW: All life, physical or intellectual, begins at conception.

LYSSA: Oh, how would you know?

MORROW: Lyssa, you want to treat religion as random prejudice. But, in fact, my morality is based on logic. There is increasing evidence that who we are as human beings is determined by genetic structure. We've even discovered that in sexual preference. Therefore, I draw the line at conception. Where do you draw the line, Senator?

ALAN: "But Mary kept all these things and pondered them in her heart." Luke 2:19.

LYSSA: In times of conflict, my father always quotes the Bible. Is anyone hungry? I'll see how Carmelita's doing with that brunch.

TIMBER: Is Carmelita your nanny, Dr. Hughes?

LYSSA: No. Carmelita is our housekeeper and her Social Security is fully paid.

QUINCY: Lyssa, don't you think that the entire Nannygate incident was an outgrowth of the seventies having-it-all mythology?

TIMBER: Dr. Hughes, are you home when your kids get in from school?

LYSSA: Timber, would you be home when your kids got in from school?

TIMBER: No, I'd be in Rwanda. But my wife would be home.

WALTER: Are you kidding? If she worked she'd be out with a client. If she didn't work she'd be out with her trainer or driving the kids to gymnastics. Most women I know are booked solid from morning till night. For instance . . .

LYSSA: Walter thinks I'm slightly hysterical because I am overcommitted and determined to do everything well.

WALTER: It used to be whenever Lyssa was called for jury duty, she inevitably had to be out of town lecturing that day or at a world conference for gonorrhea.

MORROW: Who's hosting?

WALTER: Although a phone call to postpone would have sufficed, she would drag herself to the court bearing the full range of excuses: plane ticket, lecture schedule, and a case study of the feasibility of HMOs for any interested bureaucrat.

LYSSA: Walter, you're exaggerating. I did that once.

CHARLOTTE: I didn't even know doctors had to serve on a jury.

WALTER: The final notice arrived on a day when both boys had the chicken pox, our nanny disappeared to elope with the neighborhood drug-dealing security guard, and there was a crisis at the hospital only Lyssa could solve. So I advised her not to even open it. No professional woman of her class does. They're all too goddamn busy!

LYSSA: Walter, I didn't deliberately not open it. I just misplaced it.

WALTER: And you know what's so great about the American justice system? I was right. She never heard from them again.

ALAN: My daughter has always been a hard worker, and believe me, I know what hard work is. I grew up on a farm in Indiana. Miss Quince, I'd like to hear more about *Venus Raging*. Sounds like a pretty good country-western song to me. [*begins singing*] "*Oh she's mashing her potatoes, but Venus is raging just for me!*"

LYSSA: Dad!

ALAN: Imagine the humiliation this poor girl has suffered having me as her father.

MORROW: This is gold, Timber. Pure gold. Call your segment on Lyssa, "An American Daughter." It's another Emmy in the bag for you.

ALAN: How 'bout that brunch, Lyssa?

CHARLOTTE: I like to call it *petit déjeuner.*

ALAN: Let's show our reporter how real Washingtonians eat. Come along, young Morrow. Tell Timber how gay culture will redefine the Midwest.

MORROW: Have you been to Cincinnati recently, sir? One out of ten Republicans there is gay.

ALAN: That explains why the Cincinnati airport is in Kentucky. Transport homophobia.

LYSSA: If anyone's interested, we're eating now.

ALAN: Walter, would you put some nice music into the dining room and bring in another pitcher of Bloodies?

LYSSA: Timber, has my father told you that just like our famous ancestor, we rely on stimulants.

CHARLOTTE: And bring in some fizzy water. We want fizzy water.

[*They all exit, except* WALTER *and* QUINCY.]

QUINCY: I'll help you carry it in.

WALTER: How do you like your Bloodies, Quincy? Mary, Virgin, Typhoid?

QUINCY: I don't think your wife likes me.

WALTER: I thought all women like you.

QUINCY: I'm too happy for all women to like me.

WALTER: Are you saying my wife isn't happy?

QUINCY: I can't find her soul.

WALTER: You've only just met her?

QUINCY: I've become very spiritual.

WALTER: I don't connect to this current craze for spirituality.

QUINCY: People are searching for meaning now.

WALTER: You mean they never have before? How, then, do you explain Chartres?

QUINCY: You're so brilliant, Walter.

WALTER: Easy assessment. You've been on too many human agenda call-in shows. I, on the other hand, have been biding my time.

QUINCY: Are you kidding? *Towards a Lesser Elite* is practically like a classic now. Everyone at the Renaissance Weekend said it's like the blueprint for deconstructing liberalism.

WALTER: You went to one of those weekends. Who was there?

QUINCY: Well, I mean, like everybody. Walter, aren't they waiting for their Bloody Marys?

WALTER: I want to know who was "like" at this Renaissance Weekend.

QUINCY: Well, some *New Republic* people, some academics, some policy wonks, and some up-and-coming Northwest info highway types.

WALTER: And who, like, was the most impressive "type"?

QUINCY: I don't know. Maybe Teddy Kenwright.

WALTER: Oh. Him.

QUINCY: Walter, while you guys saw never-ending opportunities for women, gays, and blacks, Teddy Kenwright called the opposite. He's a real player now.

WALTER: He's not a player like you. According to *Time* magazine, you're one of our fifty top leaders under thirty.

QUINCY: You saw that?

WALTER: According to *Time,* you're bringing feminism into the twenty-first century. Has it ever occurred to you that maybe it should cease and desist in the twentieth century like Soviet communism or the rotary dial.

QUINCY: You don't believe that.

WALTER: You just said my wife isn't happy, and according to *Time,* she's one of our fifty top leaders over forty. I was on the waiting list.

QUINCY: I said I couldn't find her soul.

WALTER: Do you mean she's not sexy?

QUINCY: Walter, I don't want to get into this with you. You are one of my all-time heroes.

WALTER: You think my wife is one of those seventies good girls who came to prominence in the nineties and schedules half an hour a day for spontaneity.

QUINCY: Do you want to kiss me, Walter? 'Cause I think you've wanted to kiss me all these years. Is that what this is about?

WALTER: Is it?

QUINCY: Walter, you spend too much time in your head. Just kiss me, 'cause it's no big deal.

WALTER: Did Teddy Kenwright kiss you at the Renaissance Weekend?

QUINCY: No. I let him goose me under the table during the "Ethics in Society" panel.

WALTER: You still haven't told me if you like your Bloody Virgin or Mary.

QUINCY: Have I shocked you?

WALTER: No. But Teddy Kenwright is minor league talent.

QUINCY: In all departments.

WALTER: And you're wrong about my wife. She's a very happy woman.

QUINCY: Are you happy, Walter?

WALTER: Me?

QUINCY: You.

WALTER: I live in one of the nicest homes in Georgetown. My wife is Ulysses S. Grant's fifth-generation granddaughter. My children are both at the Sidwell Friends School and floating through cyberspace, and my five-year-old book is a standard for deconstructing liberalism. Am I happy, Quincy Quince? I want a Bloody Mary. Okay with you?

QUINCY: Fine. Walter, I'm scared of going in there.

WALTER: Don't be ridiculous.

QUINCY: There's real beltway power in there. I can tell Morrow thinks I'm like virtual stupidity.

WALTER: So what? Morrow thinks I'm like actual stupidity. That's Morrow's job.

QUINCY: I love it when you laugh. You're such a kind man, Walter.

WALTER: Do you like The Beach Boys?

QUINCY: "Surf City, here we come."

WALTER: That's Jan and Dean. "I've got a thirty-four wagon and I call it a woody!" The Beach Boys are "Help me Rhonda. Help, help me Rhonda!"

QUINCY: All that California crap is so limited in positive body imagery for women.

WALTER: Fine. No Beach Boys. Wilson Pickett it is.

[WALTER *puts on the music. He begins dancing with* QUINCY. *He kisses her.* LYSSA *walks into the room and inadvertently sees them.*]

LYSSA: Walter, can you bring Chubby the fizzy water, and Daddy says he prefers Mozart to Wilson Pickett. [*She exits.*]

WALTER: Quincy, would you carry the fizzy water for Chubby. Chubby likes her water fizzy.

SCENE 4

Later that afternoon. TIMBER *is stage left with* JIMMY, *a cameraman.* SENATOR HUGHES, MORROW, CHARLOTTE, WALTER *and* QUINCY *are informally seated.* LYSSA *is serving coffee.*

ALAN: "Off to the west, in Memphis, where the sun's
    Mid-morning fire beat on a wider stream,
    His purpose headstrong as a river runs,
    Grant closed a smoky door on aides and guards
    And chewed through scheme on scheme
    For toppling Vicksburg like a house of cards."
    And the poet is? Can you take it, Harvard?

WALTER: Carl Sandburg.

ALAN: Sorry. For twenty points, can you take it, Princeton?

MORROW: Walt Whitman.

ALAN: No. Time's up. The answer is Richard Wilbur. Perhaps we still need to fund arts education, gentlemen. Quality of life. It's an issue of quality of life.

LYSSA: Coffee, Dad?

WALTER: That was a great brunch, Lizard. Unbelievably good!

LYSSA: Carmelita.

WALTER: Don't give all the credit to Carmelita, honey.

LYSSA: Why not? You were certainly occupied elsewhere.

CHARLOTTE: Lyssa, darling, these madeleines are scrumptious.

LYSSA: They're just "lite" vanilla wafers from a box. Our boys like them.

MORROW: All "lite" references are really euphemisms for gay. Therefore, the expression, "He's a little lite in the loafers."

QUINCY: I've never heard that.

MORROW: Then you also wouldn't know that "lite" potato chips and cream cheese are officially approved gay products.

LYSSA: Timber, maybe we should do this another time. My family is getting tired.

ALAN: Nonsense, Mousey, we're all here now and having a great time!

TIMBER: We'll only use a minute of this. You're all doing great.

CHARLOTTE: Lyssa, you have nothing to worry about. You are the epitome of good breeding. You're so calm and collected.

LYSSA: Actually, I'm a person who always feels compelled to make an effort. I've always envied grace under pressure.

CHARLOTTE: Oh, me too. Timber, I'm not a quote-unquote feminist. But I was the first female manager of the Southampton Golf Club and the first to host the Dinah Shore Classic.

ALAN: [*singing*] *"See the USA in your Chevrolet. America is asking you to call!"*

ALAN AND CHARLOTTE: "Mwah!!"

ALAN: You're probably all too young to remember that. Lyssa's mother was a great
fan of Dinah Shore's! She wanted to see the USA in a Chevrolet.

LYSSA: I don't remember my mother having any sense of adventure at all. She was
the kind of ordinary Indiana housewife who took pride in her icebox cakes
and cheese pimento canapés.

TIMBER: Icebox cakes? I'm sorry, what are icebox cakes?

LYSSA: They were a sort of Mount Saint Helens that erupted overnight in the re-
frigerator. You alternate layers of cookies and whipped cream and then chill.

ALAN: She was a terrific woman. Unfortunately Lyssa lost her when she was only
fourteen.

MORROW: That must have been very difficult.

LYSSA: As I get older I regret not knowing her better. But I wasn't particularly
close to her at the time. And Dad sent me East to boarding school that year
so I didn't really suffer.

ALAN: I think my daughter has tremendous reserves of strength and compassion.
Maybe it is because she lost her mother at such a young age. I believe Lyssa
is about as close to a female role model as we get.

MORROW: Hear, hear! If I had to vote for the person I thought had genuine confidence and class it would be Lyssa.

LYSSA: Okay, Morrow. You can stay for supper.

MORROW: No, it's true. With your nomination another political dynasty like the
Roosevelts or the Kennedys is being established. Americans always en-
shrine their elite.

WALTER: I have to disagree. The future vitality of this country is not coming from
traditional sources but a diverse multicultural wellspring.

MORROW: But who's still in charge, Walter? Hello! It's not a common story that
the Asian gay president of the United States turns to his African American
disabled lesbian vice president and says we have to be sure to have at least
one straight white guy in the cabinet. Let's give him transportation.

LYSSA: Morrow, I would say that anyone who dined through Princeton at the Ivy
Club, wrote a column for *The Washington Post,* and just sold a movie for a
million dollars is far more elitist than individuals from families with a tradition of public service.

MORROW: I am an elitist. I have to be. I represent a persecuted minority. That's
absolutely true. But what's far more insidious is the current left-wing rage
for selective privilege or self-righteous entitlement. Am I right, Senator?

ALAN: Morrow, I lost you at the gay cream cheese.

MORROW: I'm making a legitimate point here. There are liberal professionals
who believe they deserve special treatment because their heart is in the
right place. For example, your daughter and my best friend, Dr. Lyssa Dent
Hughes, surgeon general nominee, a woman of impeccable commitment, at
the forefront of women's health issues, pro-choice, pro-gay has never served
on a jury.

LYSSA: I . . .

CHARLOTTE: Well, she's a very busy woman.

ALAN: Have you ever served on a jury, Morrow?

MORROW: I'm not a registered voter. I'm still technically Canadian.

LYSSA: I've always had work and family conflicts when the invitations arrived. I mean summons.

ALAN: A person has two choices, Morrow. You can either shoot the cattle or run for Congress. Old family homily.

MORROW: I don't follow, sir.

ALAN: Well, it makes about as much sense as your theory about selective privilege.

MORROW: Well, wait . . . wait. Are you saying that the people who do answer their "invitations," who do serve on juries, are less crucial to their family and work than your daughter? Not everyone can believe that their innate goodness, their superior agenda, simply gives them the right to ignore the invitation.

LYSSA: I always presented my conflicts to the court.

MORROW: Except for the time when you didn't.

CHARLOTTE: I once didn't pay a parking ticket and nothing ever happened.

ALAN: My daughter has been a diligent and brilliant public health administrator. She will be a brilliant and diligent surgeon general. [*gets up and shakes* TIMBER's *hand*] Thank you, Timber. This has been terrific fun. I'm sorry, Chubby and I are expected at another brunch. That's the great thing about brunch. It goes on all day.

TIMBER: Thank you, sir. I appreciate your time. Dr. Hughes, I'm sorry, I have to ask you something, just for clarification. [*He signals for* JIMMY *to move in with the camera.*] Did you deliberately not answer the jury duty notification?

LYSSA: No. I believe I misplaced it.

TIMBER: Subsequently, did you contact the county clerk's office?

LYSSA: No.

TIMBER: Were you intending to bring this up at your confirmation hearing?

LYSSA: It didn't occur to me.

WALTER: Timber, my wife is a mother of two small children. She is a professor of public health at Georgetown and ran a major public hospital. Not to mention a nationally known lecturer. She is, in fact, a very busy woman.

ALAN: Lyssa, please walk us to the car.

TIMBER: Senator, do you believe your colleagues who share your anti-choice position on abortion will seize on this information to embarrass the president's second nominee?

ALAN: Timber, now let me ask you something. "Who's buried in Grant's tomb?" The answer is about as interesting as what my daughter did with a piece of paper. I think most Americans would rather know more about my beautiful fourth wife. I fell in love with her when I found out her name was Chubby. Good-bye.

[ALAN, CHARLOTTE, *and* LYSSA *exit.*]

QUINCY: There's another way to look at this "Lyssa Dent Hughes Problem." Dr. Hughes is a prisoner of her gender. She took on so many obligations that the basic necessities of life, like responding to a simple jury form, became overwhelming. The best intentions in females often become the seeds of their own destruction.

TIMBER: Okay. We have it. Thanks. Dr. Abrahmson, do you mind if I go upstairs and get some footage of the letter from Vicksburg?

WALTER: Help yourself.

QUINCY: May I join you? I'm fascinated by homes. This is a uniquely historical but lived-in one.

[QUINCY, TIMBER, *and* JIMMY *exit.*]

MORROW: That woman is a moron.

WALTER: Why the fuck did you do that?

MORROW: I didn't do anything. He's the one who's making a meal out of this. He's just the kind of heterosexual man I can't bear.

WALTER: But you brought up the jury duty notice.

MORROW: Then you should have protected Lyssa and not mentioned it to begin with. You put it out there, Walter. If I hadn't caught it, imagine where Miss Warm Penis would have run with it. I just saved you, Walter. You should be grateful to me.

WALTER: Do you hate us all because we're straight?

MORROW: Only a straight man would be insensitive enough to ask that question.

[LYSSA *comes back in.*]

LYSSA: Daddy says he'll call us later.

MORROW: I thought your father gave a vintage performance. And I've got a secret yen for Chubby.

LYSSA: Isn't Gerry waiting for you at the gym, Morrow?

MORROW: Don't waste your time being upset about this, Lyssa. The more Timber's show is talked about, the greater the buzz for you. Why can't you just see it all as a game? I love you Lyssa. You'll never know how important you are to me.

LYSSA: Good-bye, Morrow.

[MORROW *exits.*]

WALTER: Don't worry, Lizard, everything's going to be fine. Your father's right. No one's interested. There are survivalist Nazis overturning the government in Idaho.

LYSSA: They haven't been nominated for surgeon general.

WALTER: We can spin you right out of this. I'll call my old roommate Ted Kramer at *The Times.*

LYSSA: I'm very tired, Walter. Why don't you take Quincy home?

WALTER: I don't want to take Quincy home. She can take a taxi. I want to be with you.

LYSSA: I'd feel better if you took her home.

WALTER: So then you could not speak to me for a week and tell me two months later it was because I took fucking Quincy home.

LYSSA: Fucking Quincy. You know, that's what girls of her generation enjoy doing, as opposed to the frigid, overextended no-fun narcissists of my generation. Isn't that why you kissed her?

WALTER: It just happened. It didn't mean anything.

LYSSA: In our house, it happened in our house.

[QUINCY *and* TIMBER *reenter the room. Jimmy exits the house.*]

QUINCY: I loved the letter from Vicksburg. It's very poignant. For a soldier, he had great depth. I can't imagine what it is to literally fight for one's principles.

LYSSA: Quincy, Walter said he'd drive you home.

QUINCY: I'm just at the Four Seasons. I can take a cab.

LYSSA: Georgetown isn't as safe as it used to be. Thank you for coming. Walter has always been so proud of your achievements. Where we erred you will surely transcend.
> [WALTER *exits.*]

QUINCY: Good-bye, Timber. I'll send you the book.
> [QUINCY *exits.*]

TIMBER: I didn't think you'd be capable of it.

LYSSA: What?

TIMBER: Pettiness.

LYSSA: That wasn't petty. It was out-and-out bitterness combined with envy and competition. I'm baiting my husband. Give me a little credit here, Mr. Lawn.

TIMBER: Who's Mr. Lawn?

LYSSA: You. Forrest Lawn. Piney Tucker, Timbarton Oaks, Timber Canoe and Tyler too. Frankly, of all of us Chubby is my favorite. At least she's genuine.

TIMBER: I think you're pretty genuine. And I specialize in sizing up people in fifty-second segments.

LYSSA: Can you not use it?

TIMBER: Are you asking me if I can ignore information I wish I didn't have?

LYSSA: No.

TIMBER: It's my job. Sometimes I wish it wasn't. I'd rather be covering the fanatic at Legal Seafood. It's clearer. But they'll probably use this tonight.

LYSSA: Will it be bad for my father?

TIMBER: Yes, but he's a veteran, he can handle it. I'm sorry I had to ask you those questions. I assumed you'd be ready with the answer.

LYSSA: Maybe Quincy has all the answers. Are you attracted to her?

TIMBER: Way too old. I'm into twenty-year-old bimbos. You with me?

LYSSA: Girls in swimsuits on the cover of *Sports Illustrated.*

TIMBER: I should title your segment "An American Snob." Swimsuit girls are much too upscale. I'm talkin' Dunkin' Donuts twins in Eugene. The cashier at the Shreveport airport. That's America to me. Ba-da-bing, Ba-da-boom. She gets you a beer and turns into a sandwich.

LYSSA: What kind of a sandwich?

TIMBER: Are you really choosing to continue this conversation with me?

LYSSA: Right now, my husband probably has his hand up Quincy's Quince, I've probably just set back the case for every cause I believe in, not to mention cast a dark shadow on women in government, and put the final lid on national health insurance. So, yes, I really do want to know what kind of fucking sandwich.

TIMBER: Brie with pesto and sun-dried tomatoes.

LYSSA: What a pretentious sandwich! She couldn't turn into a tuna!
> [*The doorbell rings.*]

LYSSA: Maybe it's Quincy. She's finished another book.

TIMBER: You're much more tart than I expected.

LYSSA: You two think alike. She told me exactly the same thing.
> [JUDITH *enters, sopping wet.*]

JUDITH: It's Elijah. I'm wet and I'm early.

LYSSA: Is it raining? Why are you wet?

JUDITH: A puddle. I was walking on M Street. Al Gore's dog jumped into a puddle and splashed me.

TIMBER: How do you know it was Al Gore's dog?

JUDITH: All right. It was Colin Powell's dog. He was showering me with sisterly love.

LYSSA: Judith, there's a robe in the laundry room. Why don't you change?
     [JUDITH *exits*.]

TIMBER: Is she okay?

LYSSA: I don't know.

TIMBER: My, my, lady, you've had a day!

LYSSA: Yes. It's been "Fun, fun, fun, till Daddy took the T-bird away." Walter likes The Beach Boys. Good-bye, Timber.

TIMBER: Dr. Hughes, I can't stop what's coming down the pike. Thank God, I'm not that powerful. But, I'd like to try and guide you through this.

LYSSA: Like a boy scout?

TIMBER: Like a friend. It all depends on how you play it. I'd say don't shoot the cattle yet. Keep running for Congress.
     [JUDITH *reenters*.]

LYSSA: Better?

JUDITH: Better.

LYSSA: Good-bye, Timber.

TIMBER: You can reach me at this number. I'd like to help you. Remember, grace under pressure. [*He exits*.]

LYSSA: Do you want a cup of tea?

JUDITH: Why does he want to help you?

LYSSA: Our post-brunch show didn't go very well. Morrow was a real shit.

JUDITH: Sounds like business as usual.

LYSSA: No. This was worse. I may be in some trouble.

JUDITH: I tried to drown myself Lyssa.

LYSSA: What?

JUDITH: I went to the festival of regrets. I prayed by the banks of the Potomac. There were old men davening in prayer shawls, and young lawyers in Brooks Brothers suits. I watched while the men tossed in their breadcrumbs of secret sorrow. "Oh Lord, my god, I cheated on my income tax. Oh Lord King of the universe I lust for the Asian check-out girl at Hany Farms delicatessen. Oh Lord, I have sinned, I dreamt about a strip of bacon." At first I remained silent. I stood there feeling my familiar distance and disdain. And then, almost involuntarily, I began shredding my low-fat cranberry orange muffin. I wanted this God, this Yahveh, to know me. So I tossed my first crumb into the water. "Oh Lord, my God, King of the universe, I have failed to honor my mother and father," and that regret floats out to Maryland. "Oh Lord, my God, I distrust most people I know, I feel no comfort in their happiness, no sympathy for their sorrow." A tiny cranberry sits still upon the water. "Oh Lord, our God, who is like you in earth or in heaven, I regret the men I've been with, I regret the marriage I made, I regret never having children, I regret never having learned to be a woman." I pull off the entire top and a wad of muffin sails like a frigate towards the Washington

Monument. "Oh Lord, my God, Mighty of Mighty, Holy of Holy, I can't make life and I can't stop death. Oh Lord, my God, the Lord is one, I've wasted my life," and I jump in.

LYSSA: And then.

JUDITH: It seems I'm still a very good swimmer.

LYSSA: Yes, I remember. Freshman phys. ed.

JUDITH: The Potomac isn't very cold in September. It's still warm from the summer night.

LYSSA: So you were fine.

JUDITH: I was great. I was bobbing up and down in my pearls and Liz Claiborne suit, when I noticed a box of Dunkin' Donut holes floating along. And suddenly I remembered the slogan from my mother's favorite donut shop, "As you ramble on through life, brother, whatever be your goal, keep your eye upon the donut, and not upon the hole." And I began laughing and laughing. Now I had a purpose. Now I had a goal. I must rescue the donut holes and bring them here to you on N Street. Lyssa, these are the donut holes of my discontent!

LYSSA: Thank you.

JUDITH: Of course no taxi would stop for a drenched black woman who just crawled out of the Potomac. So I walked all the way.

LYSSA: Well, I'm glad you're feeling better. [*She starts upstairs.*]

JUDITH: Where are you going?

LYSSA: Upstairs. I need to call my children.

JUDITH: They're fine. Please. Lyssa, I'm so cold! And I'm so sad!

LYSSA: Do you ever think that other people might have their own fears, their own sorrow?

JUDITH: I spend my life trying to relieve other people's pain and sorrow. I want a home.

LYSSA: Goddamnit, Judith! Then just grow up and make one.

JUDITH: I can't. Not just for me.

LYSSA: I'm sorry. I can't help you tonight.

JUDITH: You don't know what it is to want, Lyssa.

LYSSA: What gives you the audacity to believe you've failed if you can't make life or stop death?

JUDITH: Because I was taught if I was a good girl and worked hard I could.

LYSSA: Good-bye, Judith.

[LYSSA *exits.* JUDITH *looks at the portrait of Julia Grant.*]

JUDITH: Happy New Year, Julia. *La Shana Tovah.*

[*After a moment,* LYSSA *reappears.*]

JUDITH: Happy New Year, Lyssa.

LYSSA: Happy New Year, Judith.

ACT TWO

SCENE 1

Saturday afternoon. A week later. WALTER *is smoking and reading the morning paper. At least six other newspapers and magazines are on the floor.* LYSSA *is looking through the closed blinds of the window.*

LYSSA: Another television van just pulled up! Don't they have an election or a revolution to cover?

WALTER: It's all about the goddamn pimentos!

LYSSA: What?

WALTER: The cheese pimento canapés. You have single-handedly proven that no one in this country really gives a fuck about the jury system but they care an awful lot about the ordinary Indiana housewives who take pride in their icebox cakes and cheese pimento canapés.

LYSSA: Oh God, it's that girl with the teeth from the five o'clock news team.

WALTER: Are you listening?

LYSSA: What.

WALTER: *USA Today* says the housewives of Indiana are picketing the radio stations. The icebox cake and pimento canapé moms are apparently furious with you for "minimizing their lives." Even the boys found a fuckin' "Ladies Chat Room" about you on the Net.

LYSSA: Jesus, another van.

WALTER: Of course. In a fucking week you've gone from being a compromise candidate to the fucking soccer mom's anti-Christ.

LYSSA: Walter, can you please try to talk to me without saying "fuck" or chain-smoking?

WALTER: You're so goddamn prissy.
        [*Telephone rings.*]

LYSSA: I'm not answering that.
        [*Telephone rings again. They wait.*]

WALTER: Maybe it's the president.
        [*Telephone rings again.*]

LYSSA: [*on the phone*] Hello. No. No, Martha, I didn't know. Thank you. [*She hangs up.*] I've made the cover of *The New York Post*. There's a picture of me at Safeway yesterday and a headline "DR. ICEBOX SHOPS."

WALTER: I told you, Lizard, you've created a female sound bite on a fuckin' par with "I am not a crook" and George Romney being brainwashed.

LYSSA: If you didn't read six newspapers every morning, you wouldn't have to know all of this.

WALTER: You're my wife. Of course I have to know all of this. You can't go back on *Time Zone* without knowing what's been said about you. Did you read Quincy's op-ed in *The Post* this morning?

LYSSA: Yes. And I saw her on *Nightline, Equal Time, Crossfire,* and weekend *Good Morning America*. My nomination is going to sell Quincy a hell of a lot of books. They'll be taking prisoners of gender across America.

WALTER: I thought her op-ed was very sympathetic.

LYSSA: Fuck off, Walter.

WALTER: No, really, Lizard. She was right. You're being repositioned by the media as a victim feminist, which absurdly undermines your legitimacy as a power one.

LYSSA: Please don't quote Quincy to me.
        [*The phone rings again.*]

LYSSA: It's probably *Penthouse!*
        [*The phone rings again.*]

WALTER: [*calls offstage*] Carmelita! Can you take the calls?
    [*The phone stops ringing.*]

WALTER: Honey, we can fix this. This is not the time to be stubborn.

LYSSA: I'm not being stubborn. I know what I'm doing. I'm going to tell the truth.

WALTER: Fine. Great. Then you have to be able to handle it.

LYSSA: I can handle it. I will drag myself in front of every congressperson, every newspaper reporter, and every talk show host in the country. I will appear daily before the Senate hearings. I will tell Timber Tucker that what's happening is wrong. Here's a person who can do some good, who has done a lot of good, and a goddamn misplaced slip of paper is being used to unravel all her possibilities. That's unacceptable.

WALTER: It isn't just a person, Lyssa. It's you.

LYSSA: I know that.

WALTER: No, you don't. This has nothing to do with the goddamned slip of paper. It doesn't even have anything to do with your politics. It's the women of America who are furious with you, Lizard. You're pretty, you have two great kids, you're successful, you're admired, you're thin, and you have a great soul. Face it, Lizard, in the heartland that means you're one prissy privileged ungrateful-to-her-mother, conniving bitch.

LYSSA: So now I have to ingratiate myself to the housewives of Indiana?

WALTER: Trust me on this. I'm still a pretty decent sociologist even if I haven't written anything good in five years.

LYSSA: Oh God, Walter, everyone knows you're brilliant.

WALTER: Please, Lyssa, stop being Miss M.D.-Ph.D., holier-than-thou, with God on my side, give me your tired your poor, I speak for all women fuckin' role models.
    [ALAN *and* CHARLOTTE *enter with a young man of around twenty-eight,* BILLY ROBBINS, *who wears a blue blazer, chinos and sparkling clear glasses.*]

ALAN: Is this the home of a woman who hates icebox cakes and her mother?

LYSSA: You left out children and polio victims. I hate them too. Hi, Dad. Hello, Charlotte.

CHARLOTTE: Hello, darling. Lyssa, you look tired. Call my Eva at Elizabeth Arden's. She'll take care of you.

ALAN: Have you heard from the president?

LYSSA: No.

ALAN: This is Billy Robbins from my office.

LYSSA: Hello.

BILLY: Hello.

ALAN: He's the best spin control man in the Senate. And he's only twelve.

BILLY: Your dad invited me along with him today. I hope you don't mind.

CHARLOTTE: How can you bear having all those reporters camping out on your doorstep?

BILLY: Call me before you say anything to them. Even hello.

LYSSA: I'll just change their water daily.

WALTER: I told Lyssa all she needs is a strategy. And she'll believe a stranger before she believes me.

BILLY: Professor, I wrote a paper on your book for poly-sci sophomore year at Berkeley. It's amazing how quickly popular opinions change. Your father told me Tim Tucker's doing a follow-up interview tomorrow. Word is Barbara and Diane can't believe he nabbed you from under them. The Lyssa Hughes interview is a real "get."

LYSSA: What's a "get"?

CHARLOTTE: Like shopping, dear. Something you're just dying to get.

ALAN: Lyssa's best friend has also asked to speak with Timber.

BILLY: Who's that?

WALTER: A crazy lady.

ALAN: Dr. Judith B. Kaufman. Lyssa's known her since Miss Porter's.

BILLY: I wouldn't play up the Miss Porter's bit. Too elitist. Doesn't that school have another name?

LYSSA: Farmington.

BILLY: Fine. Tell her to say you met at Farmington High.

LYSSA: Judith was the first African American on full scholarship.

BILLY: Affirmative action. Also dicey.

LYSSA: All right. She was the first Jew on full scholarship.

BILLY: I just want to present you in the best possible light. You may be a privileged person but you're also a working mom, you love your husband, you love your kids, you've got great family values, and on Sunday you go to church and enjoy hiking.

LYSSA: Do I also coach the gymnastics team?

BILLY: I wish you did.

WALTER: Lyssa's being sarcastic.

BILLY: No sarcasm admitted. Nothing East Coast, Ivy League, smarty-pants, no women's lib, no highfalutin charm. Remember, you're from Indiana.

LYSSA: I haven't lived in Indiana in thirty years.

BILLY: Your father's the senator from Indiana. He was the mayor of Fort Wayne.

LYSSA: I see.

CHARLOTTE: I thought I'd hate Indianapolis, but it's really rather charming. And there's that enchanting little speedway restaurant.

BILLY: Basically, Americans will forgive a wife who with the help of her loving family overcomes a personal deficiency.

ALAN: My daughter has no deficiencies.

BILLY: Simple people who aren't great granddaughters of presidents and Ph.D.s in public health serve on a jury when they receive an official notice.

WALTER: Mr. Robbins is right, Lizard.

BILLY: Sometimes it's just a question of knowing what the people want and giving it to them and then get on with it.

LYSSA: I can't pretend to be someone I'm not.

BILLY: I don't agree with your politics, Dr. Hughes, but I have the greatest respect for you and Professor Abrahmson. You've gotten yourself into a mess and I'd like to try to get you out of it. Now, can I see the room where Timber will be conducting the interview?

LYSSA: This is it.

BILLY: Maybe we should do it in the kitchen. It's a little more homey.

LYSSA: Or we could do it in the laundry. I could be folding.

WALTER: Let's look at the kitchen.

[ALAN *puts his arm around* BILLY.]

ALAN: C'mon, Mr. Robbins, remind me to show you the famous letter from Vicksburg.

BILLY: By the way, I'd focus on Grant the general and not Grant the president. Someone's likely to bring up whiskey fraud and corruption.

LYSSA: That was over a hundred years ago.

BILLY: We don't want them to be reminded. In the latest CNN/*Washington Post* ranking of the U.S. presidents, Grant came in forty-first just above last-place Warren Harding. Morrow McCarthy mentioned that on *Charlie Rose* last night. Charlie got a three-share when Morrow was on which is very impressive for Charlie.

LYSSA: Well, I'm glad I could help.

BILLY: Morrow's a real crossover talent. We're lucky he's been publicly very supportive of you.

[BILLY, ALAN, *and* WALTER *exit.*]

CHARLOTTE: Do you think that man ever has sex?

LYSSA: Excuse me?

CHARLOTTE: Do you think that immaculate little man ever takes off those preppie little clothes and gets down and dirty and a little nasty-sweaty? Scary perma-pressed creature. Do you mind if I smoke? Oh God, of course you do. I won't light it. [*She takes out a cigarette, a cigarette holder and a gold lighter.*] I only started up again last month to celebrate the twentieth anniversary of my quitting. So how are you with all of this?

LYSSA: I'm going to fight it, in my own way.

[*Phone rings twice.*]

CHARLOTTE: Isn't the president an old friend of yours?

LYSSA: I went to Bryn Mawr with his wife. And two of Walter's classmates are in the cabinet. But Walter isn't speaking to either of them.

CHARLOTTE: Whatever. My point is you're the president's nominee and you're his wife's personal friend. It's his responsibility to defend you. Especially as he is the same party as you and your father is not.

LYSSA: I never asked for my father to defend me.

CHARLOTTE: You're lucky you never had to. Your father's getting at least two thousand calls a day. He's torn. He's a very good father but he's also a very good senator. And he'll be up for reelection.

LYSSA: I know but what can I do?

CHARLOTTE: Let me give you some advice. I know what it is to be out there on a limb. I raised two boys alone before it was chic or even admirable. Protect your family, protect your marriage, and if you don't, I certainly will protect mine. There are plenty of not-nice people in the world, Lyssa. They'll tear you apart just because they're jealous or disappointed or even worse, because they have nothing better to do. Then after it's all over, after all the damage and the hurt is done, you come back to yourself. So you can ruin your life by being valiant and impressive or find the most idiotic means to gracefully move forward. Frankly, that's why until I married your father I took two Anacins every morning for thirty years. I never expected to be this happy, especially in the derriere of my life.

[BILLY, ALAN, *and* WALTER *come back into the room.*]

ALAN: Ready to go, dear?

CHARLOTTE: Just let me put my accoutrement away.

ALAN: Can you believe I married a woman who carries a cigarette holder? Do you know how this goes over in Indiana?

LYSSA: I'm sure much better than me.

ALAN: There's a nun in South Bend who prefers you to Chubby. But she's the only one. [*He kisses her.*] See you tomorrow, Mousey.

BILLY: I'd suggest you wear a feminine attire tomorrow. Maybe a bow or head-band in your hair. Talk about your mother. How much you miss her. You've had a tough time but you're a survivor. Women respond to that. And if he brings up choice, do your father a favor and just soft-pedal it. Wait till you get into office. Pleasure meeting you both.

WALTER: Mr. Robbins, don't worry. My wife is a rational woman. This job is very important to her.

BILLY: See you tomorrow.

[BILLY, ALAN, *and* CHARLOTTE *exit.*]

LYSSA: Charlotte says this is putting a terrible strain on Dad.

WALTER: Lyssa, this is not about your father.

LYSSA: Oh Walter, I'm a rational woman. I know what this is and isn't about. Goddamnit, Walter! Would you stop smoking, I don't want the housewives of Indiana hating me for that too.

WALTER: Take it easy. You're making this all much harder than it has to be.

LYSSA: I never meant for our life to become about me.

BOY'S VOICE: [*offstage*] Mom! Mom! C'mere. Someone in Alaska hates you. You gotta c'mere!

WALTER: Lizard, please, let me try to help you.

BOY'S VOICE: Mom.

WALTER: I promise. We can get through this.

BOY'S VOICE: Mom, they think you're what's wrong with America.

[LYSSA *and* WALTER *go upstairs.*]

SCENE 2

Sunday morning. Cameras, lights, and cable are beginning to be brought into LYSSA's *living room.* TIMBER *is directing their placement. We can hear* QUINCY *on television.*

WOMAN: Quincy Quince, why has the "Lyssa Dent Hughes Problem" sparked such a nationally heated debate?

QUINCY: Women are always reduced into categories and in this case, the icebox cake and pimento canapé moms are justifiably furious at having their life choices minimized. Now, I don't think for a minute that was Dr. Hughes' intention, but that's certainly where this story is going.

[*Equipment is still being moved.* JUDITH *enters from upstairs.*]

TIMBER: Thanks for letting me squeeze this in, Dr. Kaufman.

JUDITH: Lyssa Hughes is my oldest friend.

TIMBER: Chances are we'll do very well with her interview. Probably beat *60 Minutes.* There's a lot of interest in "Jurygate."

JUDITH: If Dr. Hughes were a man, this wouldn't beat Roadrunner cartoons. It'd be a non-issue, an oversight. They'd blame it on the maid or a wife.

TIMBER: You think wives are still willing to take the blame?

JUDITH: Have you ever been married, Timber?

TIMBER: No, ma'am. I have fear of intimacy and commitment. Double negative and lethal.

JUDITH: Don't go into therapy, Timber. Stay just the way you are.

TIMBER: Have you ever been married?

JUDITH: I've been married.

CREW PERSON: Where do you want her?

TIMBER: We're set up over here.

      [MORROW *enters.*]

MORROW: Are they shooting *Hollywood Squares* here today? I'll take center square.

JUDITH: Well, Good morrow, Morrow.

MORROW: Do you know how many times I had to hear that in high school? And of course To Morrow and To Morrow and To Morrow.

JUDITH: You must have gone to a good high school!

MORROW: Timber, are you back by invitation?

TIMBER: I'm interviewing Lyssa this afternoon.

JUDITH: Morrow, are you back by invitation?

MORROW: Where's Walter? I've got good news.

JUDITH: Walter and Lyssa are upstairs getting ready for the interview.

MORROW: How are they doing?

JUDITH: Why don't you go up and ask?

MORROW: I think we've got Harrison and Demi for the movie.

TIMBER: What movie?

MORROW: My movie.

JUDITH: Who are Harrison and Demi?

MORROW: Don't tell her if she doesn't know. God, I despise those Hollywood people. They're going to the White House for dinner tonight so they had me give them ten-minute summaries of Jefferson and de Tocqueville.

JUDITH: Do they think the president will give them a pop quiz?

MORROW: They don't like to talk about Hollywood in front of civilians. They prefer to talk about government or art. For instance they all have opinions about Lyssa.

TIMBER: Like what?

MORROW: She's boring. She should only wear Armani. She has no sex appeal. She's the reason movies about smart women don't get made.

JUDITH: Can we please do this now? I have appointments.

TIMBER: Are we ready, Jimmy?

MORROW: What are we doing?

TIMBER: Dr. Kaufman has consented to go one-on-one with me. A sort of taped prelude to my interview with Lyssa.

JUDITH: Sit down, Morrow.

JIMMY: Ready?

TIMBER: Hold the work.

JIMMY: Quiet!

CREW PERSON: Quiet!

MORROW: What about hair and makeup? I insist on hair and makeup for Dr. Kaufman.

JUDITH: I already have hair and makeup.

TIMBER: Please, sit down Morrow.

JIMMY: Ready?

MORROW: Ready.

TIMBER: [*to cameraperson*] Just stay tight on Dr. Kaufman.

CAMERA PERSON: We're rolling.

TIMBER: I'm talking to Dr. Judith B. Kaufman, professor of oncology at Georgetown Medical School and a senior physician at its breast cancer unit. Thank
you for joining us, Doctor.

JUDITH: My pleasure.

TIMBER: Dr. Kaufman, how long have you known the nominee?

JUDITH: We went to high school at Farmington. We met in a production of *Julius
Caesar.* I was Calpurnia and she was Portia.

TIMBER: Interesting foreshadowing of political betrayal.

JUDITH: We also had a girl group at dances called "The Lyssettes." We sang "And
Then He Kissed Me." Lyssa had a great stage presence. I did not. I'm more
of a behind-the-scenes person.

TIMBER: And how are you "behind the scenes" in Dr. Hughes' embattled nomination? You know that national opinion is running five-to-one against her.

JUDITH: Timber, when I was a girl in Brooklyn and I looked around for women
I wanted to grow up to be, the only noteworthies I could muster were
Mamie Eisenhower, and I knew chances were slim that I'd marry a president or grow bangs; Dorothy Kilgallen, she wore a rhinestone eye mask on
What's My Line?—and I liked that; and Lena Horne, and I liked to sing, my
mother was a pianist, but "And Then He Kissed Me" was as good as I got.
I was a smart girl and I knew I wanted to grow up to be a scientist but the
only woman who even came close to my aspirations was Marie Curie. So I
had to make up for myself who I was going to be.

TIMBER: Dr. Kaufman . . .

JUDITH: I believe by denying Lyssa Hughes this post we will be denying the
country the talents of a remarkably concerned and inventive public servant,
but also denying the girls of America someone who they could, with pride,
imagine themselves growing up to be.

TIMBER: Is failing to respond to a jury notice an action you would encourage in
young women?

JUDITH: Who does your taxes, Mr. Tucker?

TIMBER: My accountant.

JUDITH: Who does your mail?

TIMBER: My secretary.

JUDITH: Who does your housecleaning?

TIMBER: Dr. Kaufman, who is the interviewer here?

JUDITH: Stay with me on this, Timber. Who does your housekeeping?

TIMBER: My housekeeper.

JUDITH: Any of them ever misplace a piece of paper?

TIMBER: Then why this outburst, this outcry against Lyssa Dent Hughes? Is this
feminist backlash? Has she become, as Quincy Quince says, a "disempow-
ered victim"?

JUDITH: I think we've got more serious issues here than trumped-up trends created by a would-be best-selling author.

TIMBER: Last question. As her best friend what advice would you give Dr. Hughes right now?

JUDITH: "As you ramble on through life, brother, whatever be your goal, keep your eye upon the donut, and not upon the hole."

TIMBER: Advice that's good for all of us. Thank you, Dr. Judith B. Kaufman.

JUDITH: Thank you, Mr. Timber Tucker.

JIMMY: Let's set up for a reverse.

TIMBER: No, we don't need it.

SOUND MAN: I'm not sure we got that.

TIMBER: We'll be fine. Thanks, Dr. Kaufman. Very helpful. You obviously came well prepared. Jimmy . . .

JIMMY: Where's Frank? We're going to have to knock back that sunlight.
       [TIMBER *and* JIMMY *exit.*]

MORROW: Can I say something? Just one thing. The Mayflower Donut Shop, 59th Street and Fifth.

JUDITH: You weren't even born when they closed.

MORROW: I collect fifties retro. That motto is on my favorite set of mugs. I thought you were really terrific.

JUDITH: Can I say something?

MORROW: Sure.

JUDITH: Why the hell did you do this to Walter and Lyssa?

MORROW: I was just making a point. Like writing a column. I forgot they were people I know and like.

JUDITH: That must be hard to live with.

MORROW: All right. I had eaten Twinkies ten minutes before. My blood sugar was up. The camera made me do it. What do you want me to say, Judith? I didn't know this would happen.

JUDITH: I don't feel sorry for you.

MORROW: Me either. I don't respect guilt. It's much too common. But I did endorse a healthy portion of my Harrison and Demi signing-on bonus as a donation to the Judith B. Kaufman oncology unit. It's not a new wing but it's still a very nice plaque. And the first time my largesse has not been for my own cause.

JUDITH: Morrow, I think you're bright enough to know it all goes smoother with a little redemption. Well, I certainly won't be used as your easy way out.

MORROW: Judith!

JUDITH: What?

MORROW: Would you have dinner with me sometime?

JUDITH: Morrow, if you've got a serious mother hang-up, I can refer you to a few numbers.

MORROW: I'm just looking for dinner or a conversation between Christians and Jews now and then.

JUDITH: Why?

MORROW: Because I was a smart boy. I had to make up for myself who I was going to be.

JUDITH: You didn't want to be Marie Curie either.

MORROW: No, but Dorothy Kilgallen was a genuine possibility. Judith, think of the trips we could take together to avoid family gatherings and holidays.

JUDITH: Morrow, I have the career of a fifty-five-year-old man, the infertile reproductive cycle of a forty-two-year-old woman, and the emotional stability of a fifteen-year-old girl. I don't need any more stimulation. I hope you make that donation and I hope you get my name the fuck off of it.

> [TIMBER *reenters with* JIMMY.]

JUDITH: Thank you Timber. Good morrow, Morrow. [*She exits.*]

TIMBER: That's a very angry woman.

MORROW: That's a very good woman.

TIMBER: I heard you got *Charlie Rose* a three-share Friday night.

MORROW: This all could have been avoided. You didn't have to run that piece. Lyssa's an earnest public servant. And she'd be a fine surgeon general.

TIMBER: I think so. That's why if I was them I wouldn't let you back in my house.

MORROW: Lyssa and Walter are my best friends.

TIMBER: Maybe I'm just a non–Ivy League dummy in TV news, but what I saw here last week didn't look like friendship to me. I'm curious, is there anything people like you really believe in?

MORROW: Let's see, I have my faith, my seasonal venison sausage at London's Bibendum Restaurant, the films of Keanu Reeves, and my Glenn Gould recordings of the *Goldberg Variations.* Those are really the only things people "like me" believe in. And of course my three-share on *Charlie Rose.* But people like you don't care about that at all. People like you are in it for the truth.

> [WALTER *enters from upstairs.*]

MORROW: Hello, Walter. Good luck with the interview. [*He exits.*]

WALTER: What did he want?

TIMBER: I don't think he has any idea what he wants.

WALTER: Lyssa's almost ready.

> [QUINCY *enters.*]

TIMBER: You're here early.

QUINCY: Am I?

TIMBER: We're still setting up. Let's get going, Jimmy. [*He exits.*]

WALTER: Why are you here?

QUINCY: Didn't you know? I'll be commenting with Timber right after the taping.

WALTER: No, I didn't.

QUINCY: It's a real zoo in front of your house. Even Teddy Kenwright's here with a crew.

WALTER: The Nazi from the Renaissance Weekend.

QUINCY: He's doing the male perspective for *The Jim Lehrer NewsHour.*

WALTER: Why can't Jim Lehrer do the male perspective?

QUINCY: Walter, you might not understand how important this has become. The buzz is that the president will have to personally go to the wall to save Lyssa or he'll be forced to pull her down. This is a very big deal.

WALTER: Apparently now so are you.

QUINCY: Well, actually, I was wondering if you could arrange for me to spend some time alone with Lyssa before the taping. I mean, she'd be much better off talking to me than one of the TV hunks or beauty queens.

WALTER: Quincy, my wife won't talk to you.

QUINCY: Why not?

WALTER: Are you serious?

QUINCY: But, I'm the one who can advance her cause.

WALTER: About as much as my former roommate Ted Kramer, *The New York Times* columnist who called this morning for the immediate withdrawal of Lyssa's nomination.

QUINCY: I don't think you appreciate what I'm doing for Lyssa. Whether she gets this job or not, she's still gotten a lot of heat out of it. And there'll be lectures, books, she can do science commentary.

WALTER: You're a lot tougher than she is.

QUINCY: I hope that's not a negative.

WALTER: My wife is not a "get," Quincy. I won't help you.

QUINCY: Hey, Walter, I hope this isn't about the other night because . . .

WALTER: You've got your commitments now and I've got mine.

> [LYSSA *enters. She is transformed, wearing a soft pastel suit and a matching headband.*]

WALTER: You look great, Lizard.

QUINCY: You don't think the headband is a little much?

WALTER: It's perfect. Quincy's commenting after the interview.

LYSSA: Of course.

QUINCY: How are you holding up?

LYSSA: You seem to be the expert on me these days. How do you think I'm holding up?

WALTER: Honey, lets go outside and let them take some pictures.

> [WALTER *and* LYSSA *start towards the door.*]

QUINCY: Lyssa, can I have some time alone with you now?

WALTER: [*to* QUINCY] What did I just tell you . . .

LYSSA: No, Walter, I want to talk to Quincy.

WALTER: You don't have to do this.

LYSSA: I'm fine.

> [WALTER *exits.*]

QUINCY: It looks like you and Walter have come to some decisions. Maybe it's none of my business. . . .

LYSSA: I am your business. I'm sorry.

QUINCY: Listen, I can think of a lot of reasons why you wouldn't like me. But it's not good for any of us to watch an established icon being hung out to dry.

LYSSA: You know, the last time I wore a headband was at a Miss Porter's school dance in 1969. [*She takes off the headband.*] I had a crush on Tommy Talbott from Hotchkiss and Tommy liked the girls who played lacrosse, wore "ladybug" dresses and headbands. So the night he showed up at a Miss Porter's dance I put one on.

QUINCY: And did he like it?

LYSSA: Loved it. We went out for the next two years. And whenever I got back from a date I'd pull that headband right off my head. My best friends were not the lacrosse girls that Tommy Talbott preferred. My friends were much more sensitive. They lit incense and stayed up all night reading Rilke. But what was odd about me was that the headband girls thought I was one of them and the girls who wouldn't be caught dead wearing one would swear I was one of them too. Quincy, I'm a senator's daughter. So I can put it on and I can take it off. I haven't had to do it for a long time. I thought I had earned the right not to. But I won't be hung out to dry, Quincy, even if I have to wear a headband, bake cookies, or sing lullabies to do it.

[TIMBER *and* WALTER *come in.*]

TIMBER: We're almost set up, Quincy. [*to* LYSSA] You're looking tidy, Dr. Hughes.

LYSSA: I'm feeling tidy.

QUINCY: Maybe a little too tidy.

TIMBER: This will all be fairly straightforward. I'll ask you a mix of questions about this past week. How you're dealing with the pressure. A little bit about your family. A little bit more about your politics.

LYSSA: Do we have to talk about my family?

TIMBER: Yes, but you can divert me. Here's a tip: if you get emotional, go for it. Don't hold back the tears.

LYSSA: Yes sir. I'm doing double doses of estrogen in preparation. Oooooooooops. I'll be good. I promise. [*She gets up.*] Excuse me. I'm going to say hello to our friends on our doorstep.

[LYSSA *and* WALTER *exit.*]

QUINCY: You think she looks tidy? She bears no resemblance to who she is.

TIMBER: Relax, that's her business.

QUINCY: I need some advice, Timber.

TIMBER: Yes ma'am.

QUINCY: Actually, I was hoping we could talk about it later. We probably both could use some time to unwind.

TIMBER: I never unwind.

QUINCY: *Time Zone* has expressed an interest in me for a permanent position.

TIMBER: Really? Women's issues? Personal profiles? It helps to get started by spending time in the field.

QUINCY: Actually, they offered me an exclusive on that fanatic at Legal Seafood.

TIMBER: Really? When did they do that?

QUINCY: Today. But what are like the chances for your show to survive? The buzz is before Lyssa Hughes, *Time Zone* wasn't long for this world.

TIMBER: Don't go into television, Quincy. Stay pure.

QUINCY: No, I'm into it. I'm totally psyched.

SCENE 3

As final preparations for the interview are taking place and the crew is moving lights and cameras into place, we hear:

ANNOUNCER: *Time Zone* with Timber Tucker, Rachel Sullivan, Gabe Riehle, Madaline Smith and special correspondent Quincy Quince. Tonight: a *Time Zone* exclusive, "An American Daughter: The Lyssa Dent Hughes Interview" continues. Part 2: "Jurygate."

[WALTER, LYSSA, *and* ALAN *are being interviewed by* TIMBER. CHARLOTTE, QUINCY, *and* BILLY *are present along with the television crew.*]

CAMERA PERSON 1: And we're rolling. 1 . . . 2 . . . 3 . . .

CAMERA PERSONS 1 AND 2: 4 . . . 5 . . .

CAMERA PERSON 2: We have sync.

TIMBER: Tonight, a *Time Zone* exclusive, "An American Daughter" a family under siege. We are at the Georgetown home of Dr. Lyssa Dent Hughes with her husband, Dr. Walter Abrahmson, professor of sociology at Georgetown University and her father, Senator Alan Hughes of Indiana. Thank you for letting us into your home, Dr. Hughes.

LYSSA: My pleasure.

TIMBER: Walter, is your wife one of those remarkable young women who does everything right?

WALTER: I'm a very fortunate man. My wife insists on spending as much time as possible with me and our twin boys. I still don't know how she survives on five hours sleep a night. But she'll give up her own sleep before she'd ever give up our family time.

TIMBER: Do you sleep more than your wife?

WALTER: My wife gets up at five A.M. to exercise. I'm crazy, Timber, but I'm not that crazy. I like to run in the daylight. But last summer Lyssa and our sons and I went wilderness hiking in Montana. And I have to admit there was something incredibly inspiring about watching the sunrise with all the family together.

TIMBER: Senator, how has this past week been for you? There is mounting pressure from your colleagues in the Senate and from women's groups, both from the left and the right, for the president to withdraw your daughter's name from nomination.

ALAN: Timber, I've been a senator for twenty-four years and a congressman for eight years before that. But first of all, I am a father. Lyssa and I don't see eye to eye on most issues, except cole slaw, we both like it dry, but there is no one I believe in more.

TIMBER: But your daughter committed a crime.

ALAN: My daughter committed an oversight.

TIMBER: Senator, you and Lyssa are the fourth- and fifth-generation descendants of Ulysses Grant. Grant was a man whose public life was not always within legal limits.

ALAN: Grant was a great general. He was also a man. He made bad investments, he drank, and some say he even screwed up Reconstruction. There are people who believe the race situation in this country would be moved forward at least a hundred years if the Grant Administration had moved quicker. But, of course, the race situation would be intolerable if General Grant hadn't moved at all. We're human, Timber, that's what's so timeless about Grant: his foibles are our foibles. He was a great American hero, imperfect just like all of us.

TIMBER: Is that how you think your daughter Lyssa at this moment should be looked at?

ALAN: I can't speak for my daughter. I haven't since she was five.

TIMBER: Walter, how has the past week changed your life?

WALTER: This week we've done a lot of talking and a lot of holding hands and just being there like old married couples do. I'm not ordinarily a religious man, but I have to admit I joined my wife last week in praying. If anything, actually, the events of the past week have brought us even closer. So for that, in some way, I'm grateful.

TIMBER: Do you think your wife's embattled nomination is indicative of the conflict inherent in liberalism?

WALTER: Let's not get academic here, Timber. Lyssa and I are just two real people who happen to be in a little trouble.

LYSSA: I made a mistake. I should have answered the notice. It was an oversight. And I apologize. It was simply bad juggling of a working mother.

TIMBER: Have you heard from the president, Dr. Hughes?

LYSSA: No. But this has been a very busy week for him. As you know Helmut Kohl is in Washington. We enjoyed your interview with him last night. And of course as my father could tell you the battle to balance the budget is on-going.

ALAN: I believe the president knows he made the best possible choice when he nominated my daughter. The president is a man with good family values and just like me he knows what it means to be a father and be so deeply proud of your daughter. I look at this remarkable doctor and remember a little girl I drove to dancing class. We must honor all our talented American women.

TIMBER: So here you are, Lyssa Dent Hughes, descendant of a president, one of the leading professional women of your generation, a pioneer in health-care reform, truly an American daughter of the highest caliber, in the midst of one of the great democratic and feminist maelstroms of this year. Who are the good guys and who are the bad guys?

LYSSA: I don't look at things in black and white. It's not even really good medicine. If there's any fault it's mine. As I said, I made a mistake. I was wrong. I take full responsibility. Like my dad said, "We all have our foibles."

TIMBER: Female public opinion is running against you four-to-one. Why?

LYSSA: I don't know. I was honestly surprised by that. Most of my work in medicine has been in increasing awareness of women's health issues.

TIMBER: When you refer to women's health issues, are you referring to your position on choice?

LYSSA: Reproductive rights is one of many issues. For instance, primary care doctors are twice as likely to refer men to medical specialists while women of the same age and identical symptoms and health histories are referred to psychotherapists. The . . .

TIMBER: But you are pro-choice?

LYSSA: Yes.

TIMBER: And your father is not.

LYSSA: My father and I have differing opinions on many topics, except cole slaw.

TIMBER: Do you consider yourself close to your father and his fourth wife?

LYSSA: Yes. I'm very happy my father met Chubby. I mean Charlotte.

TIMBER: Were you close to all of your father's wives?

LYSSA: I was away at college when he married Fay Francine. And I was a resident when he married Ginger Eichenberger.

TIMBER: So you weren't close to them.

LYSSA: They seemed to be nice women. But I was beginning my own life.

TIMBER: You have been for the past ten years on *The Ladies' Home Journal* List of American Women Role Models. Is that what makes women envious of you? Are you too perfect?

LYSSA: I hope not.

TIMBER: But you are privileged?

LYSSA: My greatest privilege is my family.

TIMBER: Let's talk some more about your family. Your mother?

LYSSA: My mother died when I was fourteen.

TIMBER: When we last talked you referred to your mother as an ordinary Indiana housewife who made the now infamous "icebox" cakes.

LYSSA: Yes. My mother enjoyed baking.

TIMBER: Last time we spoke you said she didn't bake the cakes. You said she put them in the icebox.

LYSSA: Yes.

TIMBER: What else can you tell us about her?

LYSSA: She was an attractive woman. She went to church.

TIMBER: Did you resent her?

LYSSA: No.

TIMBER: Did you feel her horizons were limited?

LYSSA: How is this relevant to my confirmation?

TIMBER: Many women in America feel your attitude towards your mother is your attitude towards them.

LYSSA: I promise you. It's not.

TIMBER: Well, were you always closer to your father than your mother?

LYSSA: My father and I have both chosen to have careers in public life.

TIMBER: Did your father's career in public life cause your mother to suffer like so many political wives? Many famous political wives battled substance abuse.

LYSSA: Timber, I don't believe we can really judge who will make the best surgeon general based on their mother's marital happiness.

TIMBER: But you and your husband agree that family life is important.

LYSSA: Yes, of course it's important. But it's also private.

TIMBER: The surgeon general is considered the physician to the nation. Many American women feel that your private life disqualifies you from such an important humanitarian position.

LYSSA: How would they possibly know about my private life?

TIMBER: They are convinced, at least according to our latest *Time Zone* poll, that you are both condescending and elitist.

LYSSA: The women of America should concern themselves with the possibility of their reproductive rights being taken away from them. The women of America should concern themselves with the fact that breast cancer, ovarian cancer, and uterine cancer research are grossly underfunded compared to prostate cancer. The women of America should concern themselves that their children are increasingly smoking, falling prey to drug addiction and to the rapid growth of teenage pregnancy. The women of America should not concern themselves with my father's wives, my cooking, or my mother.

TIMBER: So you're emotional on this subject.

LYSSA: Yes, I'm emotional. I share that with the women of America.

WALTER: My wife is a very committed doctor.

LYSSA: Would you like to know, Timber, why I have avoided public life until this nomination? Because I know I can make a difference in the world without going through any of this. I know if I raise money for a walk-in clinic where there never has been one it'll make a difference. I know I can take a splinter out of my son's hand and make a difference. The people I work with look at life and death every day. Sometimes we manage to save life and sometimes we don't. But it has nothing to do with whether we did or didn't like our mothers. It has to do with service.

TIMBER: Dr. Hughes, are you saying you're not fit for public life?

LYSSA: I'm saying I don't know what public life has become.

TIMBER: You mean you're too good for it?

LYSSA: There's nothing quite so satisfying as erasing the professional competency of a woman, is there? Especially when there's such an attractive personal little hook to hang it on. Oh we all understand it now! She must have hated her mother! That's why she's such a good doctor! She must be a bad cold person. That's why she achieved so much! And anyway it would be all right if she were a man and cold. That man would be tough. No one would give a damn what he felt about his mother! But a woman! A woman from good schools and a good family. That kind of woman should be perfect! And if she manages to be perfect, then there is something distorted and condescending about her. That kind of hardworking woman deserves to be hung out to dry. That's a parable the Indiana housewives can tell their daughters with pride. They can say for those of you girls who thought the Lyssa Dent Hughes generation made any impact, you're wrong! Statistically they may have made an impact but they're still twisting in the wind just like the rest of us.

TIMBER: How do you think the president will feel about this?

LYSSA: I really wouldn't know. I went to college with the president's wife. She's an intelligent, sensible person. She even has a sense of humor. But I can't speak about her opinion right now since neither she nor her husband has been in touch with me. But I'd be happy to take their call.

TIMBER: How do you think they will react to tonight's interview?

LYSSA: How do you think they'll react, Timber?

TIMBER: Senator, would you call your daughter's challenge to the president "unconditional surrender"?

[LYSSA *takes off her headband and microphone.*]

LYSSA: I think I've completed this interview.

TIMBER: Tonight, Lyssa Dent Hughes defends her nomination to the women of America. From all of us here at *Time Zone* thanks for joining us.

[*The camera lights go off and the crew strikes cameras, lights, and cables. There is a long pause before anyone speaks.*]

TIMBER: I'm sorry it turned out this way. I tried to warn you.

LYSSA: I appreciate it.

QUINCY: You got it. You really heard me, didn't you. That was fantastic. Is there anything else you want to add before I comment on it outside?

LYSSA: No. I've said what I have to say.

QUINCY: Good-bye, Mrs. Hughes, Senator.

[QUINCY *exits.*]

ALAN: I think I might like to mention this to a few colleagues before they watch it tonight. Is that all right with you, Lyssa?

LYSSA: Sure.

ALAN: Just as a courtesy to our young friend Billy Robbins?

LYSSA: Are you all right, Dad?

ALAN: I'm fine, if you are.

LYSSA: Bye, Dad. Bye, Chubby.

CHARLOTTE: Good-bye, dear. I'm so proud of my husband.

[SENATOR *and* CHUBBY *exit.*]

TIMBER: I don't suppose you'd like to do a follow-up?

LYSSA: I don't think so, Timber.

TIMBER: Have I ever told you my chaos theory of broadcasting?

LYSSA: No.

TIMBER: Whatever is happening this moment won't be happening three minutes later. So, in the long run, how important is it?

LYSSA: To the person it happened to it's a lifetime. It's a memoir.

TIMBER: We're just going to do a wrap-up outside, and then we'll be out of your hair.

[TIMBER *exits, followed by the crew carrying the last of the television equipment.*]

WALTER: And that's the ball game.

LYSSA: Are you angry?

WALTER: No. I'm just waiting to hear from the president. Maybe we should go to a movie.

LYSSA: I'm tired, Walter.

WALTER: The boys were looking forward to seeing you on television. They'll be really disappointed. How will we explain this to them?

LYSSA: Oh I'll just say life's unfair. The good guy doesn't always win. Being good at school doesn't necessarily mean you're so good at life. Something encouraging like that.

WALTER: I'm sorry I couldn't help you.

LYSSA: You tried.

WALTER: I thought you were great. Really magnificent. Your finest hour.

LYSSA: Judith says I don't know what it is to want. Well, I really wanted that job, Walter. I would have been good.

WALTER: We're smart people, Lizard. We deserve to have gotten everything out of it that the really smart ones get.

LYSSA: I don't know what "really smart" means anymore. Maybe Quincy's really smart. Did you sleep with her?

WALTER: Why did you wait till now to ask me?

LYSSA: I was busy. Jury duty.

WALTER: I'm sorry.

LYSSA: Me too. I'm sorry we couldn't have broken this to Timber. The women of America might have become quite sympathetic.

WALTER: I feel like I'm disappearing, Lizard. I don't know who I'm supposed to want to be anymore.

LYSSA: Walter, this was my nomination. Can we please not make it your humiliation?
   [LYSSA *exits.*]

SCENE 4

Late Sunday afternoon, dusk. WALTER *is listening to The Beach Boys singing "Wouldn't It Be Nice." He opens the blinds and light pours in the windows.* JUDITH *enters from the garden.*

JUDITH: I told you not to leave the gate open. Any kind of manic-depressive *meshugana* could just waltz in here.
WALTER: Do you like The Beach Boys, Judith? I find them unbelievably moving. Maybe it's because I grew up in Woodmere, Long Island, so they bring back nothing from my childhood.
JUDITH: I prefer the early song cycles of Marvin Gaye and Tammi Terrell. I just heard on an instant radio poll that the women of America, four-to-one, want the president to have a dog instead of a cat. [*She turns off the music.*] Walter, you study the patterns of American life. Can you explain something to me?
WALTER: I don't know if I'm the one to explain this. "Good Vibrations," yes. The women of America, no.
JUDITH: Just tell me how come there still seems to be a club and once you're admitted there's practically no rules or limitations. But to gain admission, certain applicants have to meet requirements that would make the most honorable member fall flat on his face.
WALTER: I've been working here on another question, Judith. Do you think the man who nominated your best friend, a good, well-educated man who reminds us so much of ourselves, is in fact far more insidious than someone who hates every goddamn thing we believe in?
   [LYSSA *walks into the room.*]
LYSSA: Why don't you ask your panel tonight, Walter? I'm sure they'll have plenty of opinions.
JUDITH: Is tonight "Wanted Dead or Alive"?
WALTER: I was planning to skip it. Stay home with my wife.
LYSSA: Don't skip it, Walter. I could be the subject of the final debate instead of my father's position on choice. At least we'll keep it in the family. Walter, you're going to be late if you don't get changed.
WALTER: Judith, I hope you know how much we both appreciate your friendship.
   [*He exits upstairs.*]
JUDITH: He's in a generous mood.
LYSSA: Is the festival of regrets still going on? I've got a coffeecake I might want to toss into the Potomac. I surrendered, Judy. At 4:26 eastern standard time, I called the president and withdrew.
JUDITH: I know. I heard it on the radio, as I was driving back from my last farewell to 1147. Just about the same time you called the president, my final quest for fertility collapsed.
LYSSA: Oh God. I'm sorry.

JUDITH: Aren't you even a little impressed with our timing? I was. So, I began to count my blessings. My years of sitting in doctors' offices surrounded by snapshots of children I'll never bear were over, and so was your hideous ordeal.

LYSSA: So now what do we do?

JUDITH: Personally, if I can't make life or stop death I've got some time on my hands for friendship. This will pass, honey, I promise.

LYSSA: And ba-da-bing ba-da-boom I turn into a sandwich.

JUDITH: What?

LYSSA: Just another useless allegory I learned along the way.

[SENATOR HUGHES *comes in, dressed in black tie.*]

ALAN: The reporters' vans have all pulled away. We won't have to serve refreshments. And I was hoping to do a swift business in souvenirs.

JUDITH: See, I'm right. No one will remember.

ALAN: Yes they will. They'll remember it was bad. But they just won't be sure why.

JUDITH: I have to go. I'm on call. Lookin' good, Senator.

ALAN: Are you off to more services? They're certainly keeping you busy.

JUDITH: No. I'm on call at the hospital. I've already had the answers to my prayers. I prefer the reliable variables of science. I'm going back to work. [*She kisses* LYSSA.] Good night, honey. Take care of her, Senator. [*She exits.*]

ALAN: I thought I'd have supper with you and the boys tonight.

LYSSA: In black tie? No wonder Walter says I'm too attached to you!

ALAN: Actually I thought I'd offer, you'd decline, and I'd escort Chubby to a fundraiser for the Lab School, glad a few hands, allow Chubby to display her accoutrement, and, overall, put on a fairly good front. Mousey, why didn't you call me before you withdrew?

LYSSA: I don't know. Would Ulysses have called his father? I made a quick assessment. The commander in chief thanked me for moving so quickly.

ALAN: You know that I would have stood by you no matter what.

LYSSA: You tried, Dad. You're off the hook. I'm the one who didn't heed the ancient wisdom of Billy Robbins.

ALAN: I figured out why. You read too many of those girl books about Eleanor Roosevelt and Florence Nightingale when you were young. I should have found you heroines who were more sensible people like Arianna Huffington and Amy Fisher.

LYSSA: You withheld privy information. You never told me it was going to be this hard.

ALAN: You never asked.

LYSSA: Did I tell you I got a telegram from a leather-goods company asking me to do an ad on horseback? "Ulysses S. Grant's fifth-generation granddaughter charges into battle with a Doone and Burkey purse."

ALAN: Was it a nice purse?

LYSSA: It was a handbag. A little olive-green and horsey for my taste. But perhaps Chubby would like it.

ALAN: Perhaps. She's turned out to be a rather good sport. Fourth time around I think I've managed to find a partner who actually protects me.

LYSSA: Maybe you should train her to bite. Sorry, Dad.

ALAN: You weren't like this in high school. I remember you as very sweet.

LYSSA: You sent me away to high school.

ALAN: After this term, Chubby and I have decided to take off for six months to visit her born-again golf-pro son in Sydney while I begin my memoirs. And if no one's interested in the memoirs of an old coot, I was thinking we could open an enchanting little pharmacy in Fort Wayne. I'd whip up the home remedies and Chubby would pedal her darling Eva's face cream. Maybe I could even sing a little country-western on the weekends.

LYSSA: And did you come to this conclusion in the past week?

ALAN: Jesus, I can't put anything over on you.

LYSSA: No, my daddy taught me to pay attention.

ALAN: Before Ulysses Grant became president, he gave a speech before Congress confessing that he wasn't particularly prepared for the presidency. But he was perfectly happy to stay in the White House for two terms because he wasn't particularly prepared for anything else either. Do you think I should stick around just because there's nothing else this old man can particularly do?

LYSSA: What about your principles?

ALAN: There's some idea of America out there right now that I just can't grab onto. I know I'm supposed to have opinions based on the latest polls, and not personal convictions or civil debate. It doesn't intimidate me. But it's certainly not our most illuminating or honest hour. With time getting short, I'd rather shoot the cattle than run for Congress.

LYSSA: Dad, do you remember when I was in elementary school, every two years just in time for your next election, you'd buy me a red Chesterfield coat? It was the only time you and I ever went shopping together.

ALAN: That was a classy coat.

LYSSA: It was classy for a five-year-old, and I was twelve. That coat was a red badge of wool. I even hid it in a shopping bag at school and said I was holding it for my cousin Mamie.

ALAN: But you took it out from storage for campaigns.

LYSSA: Always. Lyssa in red. Shaking hands, passing out brochures.

ALAN: Until you began telling the electorate you didn't support your candidate.

LYSSA: I developed a conscience both about the content and the garment. But you know what's so stupid?

ALAN: You're anything but stupid.

LYSSA: No I promise this is stupid. I was sitting here before thinking I'd give anything for you to show up and say, "Everything's going to be fine. Here's an awful red coat."

ALAN: Mousey.

LYSSA: Did I ever tell you I hated that name even more than the red coat? I don't know. Other people . . .

ALAN: Other people what, Mousey?

LYSSA: Other people might just know better.

ALAN: You mean other people might know better than to put themselves in a situation where everything might not be fine. I looked at you this afternoon, and I wished your mother could have known even for one night what it's like to be as strong and courageous as you.

LYSSA: Dad, did you love her?

ALAN: Your mother was a very bright and complicated person. If she were an ordinary Indiana housewife, she might have been in a lot less pain. Yes, I loved her. Very much. I have something for you. An auctioneer from Chicago called me when you were first nominated. He said he had something that might interest you. It's a letter from Ulysses to his daughter Ellen Wrenshall Grant. It's dated Cold Harbor, Virginia, June 4, 1864. Shall I read it?

LYSSA: Please.

ALAN: "My dear little Nelly, I received your pretty well-written letter today in my camp. You do not know how happy it made me feel to see how well my little girl not yet nine years old could write."

LYSSA: Dad.

ALAN: Gets better. "Your mother wrote that you no longer wish to portray The Old Woman That Lived in a Shoe at the fair. Dear Nelly, there are times when I don't wish to go on either. We've been fighting now for thirty days and have every prospect of more fighting to do before we get into Richmond. It seems to me, for both of us, our task is to rise and continue. Look after your mother, study your lessons and you will be contented and happy. Love, Papa." [*He gives her the letter.*] Bye, Mousey. [*He walks to the door.*]

LYSSA: Dad, Nelly Grant's life was a disaster. Her parents married her off to a philandering British adventurer. She was divorced with four children by thirty-five.

ALAN: Our family is American and has been for generations. [*He exits.*]

BOY'S VOICE: Mom. Mom. There's a person in Portland who says that you're honorable and there's a person in Pittsburgh who says that you're not. What should we do?

　　　[WALTER *enters.*]

WALTER: [*to kids*] I'll tell her. [*to* LYSSA] The kids want you to answer questions upstairs. They say you've got a chat room exploding in Pittsburgh.

LYSSA: Yes. It sounds like Pittsburgh's a rebel stronghold.

WALTER: Lizard, I can still skip my panel. Stay home and answer them.

LYSSA: No, I'll get there. You better get going, or liberalism will live or die without you.

WALTER: I'm afraid you won't be here when I get back.

LYSSA: Where would I go tonight?

WALTER: I don't know. It makes no sense. I'm just afraid like one of our kids.

LYSSA: Don't be afraid, Walter, I'll be here when you get home.

[WALTER *exits through the garden.* LYSSA *looks at the letter.*]

BOY'S VOICE: [*from upstairs*] Mom, Pittsburgh wants to talk to you now! What should we tell them? Mom!

LYSSA: "Our task is to rise and continue." [*She stands and glances out the window, as she walks upstairs.*] Prepare, gentlemen, for toppling Pittsburgh like a house of cards!

Credits